Files on JFK

Interviews with Confessed Assassin
James E. Files,
and More New Evidence of
the Conspiracy that Killed JFK

Compiled & Edited by
Wim Dankbaar

JFKMurderSolved.com

Files on JFK
Interviews with Confessed Assassin James E. Files, and More New Evidence of the Conspiracy that Killed JFK

© 2007-2008, 2011 Wim Dankbaar. ALL RIGHTS RESERVED.

Inquiries:
www.JFKMurderSolved.com
info@JFKMurderSolved.com

Dankbaar, Wim
Files on JFK

Interviews with Confessed Assassin James E. Files, and More New Evidence of the Conspiracy that Killed JFK / Compiled & edited by Wim Dankbaar — 1st ed.
   p. cm.
ISBN-13: 978-0-9794063-1-7   ISBN-10: 0-9794063-1-5   (acid-free paper)
1. Political Corruption—United States. 2. United States—Politics and Government—1960- . 1. Title
 364.

First Edition
10 9 8 7 6 5 4 3 2

Printed in the USA

Distribution to the Trade By:
  Independent Publishers Group (IPG)
  814 North Franklin Street
  Chicago, Illinois 60610
  312.337.0747
  www.ipgbook.com

FILES ON JFK
— Table of Contents —

Preface by Lt. Col. Daniel Marvin (retired) 5
Introduction 7
Interview with Wim Dankbaar 9
Cast of Characters 28
The investigation 34
Interview with James E. Files, March 22, 1994 43
Robert "Tosh" Plumlee Interview 6/4/1992, Dallas 109
Robert "Tosh" Plumlee Declaration 11/21/2004 136
Interview with Chauncey Holt, April, 1992 142
Transcript of video-interview with James E. Files, 19 November 2003 166
Is James Files telling the truth? 236
The Warren (C)om(m)ission 247
The Headshots 250
The Autopsy Pictures 252
Gerald Ford's motto: Attack is Best Defense 254
Did the Bushes help to kill JFK? 259
Masters of Terror 274
Luis Posada Carriles 276
Posada Carriles' US asylum application connects to JFK assassination 282
Background on Posada Carriles 287
Bob Bennett 303
Why is James Files in prison? 307
Interview with Fabian Escalante 315
Internet Discussions 323
A little novel writing 347
Correspondence between Joe West and James Files 353
Letters from James Files to Bob Vernon 393
Correspondence with Pamela Ray 502

Update from Wim Dankbaar, 2011:

The throat wound, where's the bullet, and where is the exit wound? From a post:

I am saying – defying the ruling consensus in the JFK research community – that the throat wound was NOT an entry wound, but an EXIT wound caused by a fragment from the explosive bullet that hit JFK in the head from the grassy knoll.

I have always believed it was caused by a complete bullet from the front, until Thom Robinson freed me from that dream.

Here are some thoughts I posted a few months ago:

Question: You are doctor with experience on bullet wounds, you see a tiny neat little round hole in a throat. What would you think first?

1) This is an entry wound of a small caliber bullet
2) This is an exit wound from a fragment of an explosive bullet that hit in the head.

Mind you, the doctors didn't know about about an explosive bullet, let alone a mercury bullet.

No, I don't blame the doctors at all. If it looks like duck, if it walks like a duck, if it sounds like duck, you're going to say it's a duck.

JFK was NOT shot in the throat.

I too have believed for a long time that he was shot in the throat. But it didn't happen. The only time that JFK COULD have been shot in the throat, was very early in the game, at the beginning of the Zapruder film. Why? Because after that, he slumps forward and his throat is not exposed anymore. It doesn't make sense for ANY shooter, not even a trigger happy one, to shoot from the front that early, if the plan was to frame a patsy from BEHIND. Moreover, it would be an EXTREMELY risky shot right thru the windshield (glass breaks the line of vision, and could also deflect the bullet path). The bullet hole, crack or whatever it was in the windshield, was the result from a missed bullet from behind over JFK's head. Just as the nick in the chrome lining was.

Additionally, his head and throat would be exposed for only a very short time, with no time to follow and aim. And the other passengers were in the way, JFK was the most rear passenger in the limo, hence an additional risk to hit someone else in the car. Finally, there was no wound of exit, neither a bullet found, found for such a shot.

The throat wound was caused by an exiting fragment, maybe even a drop of mercury from JF's mercury explosive bullet. The tiny perforations in JFK's face, as observed by embalmer Thom Robinson, were also the result of mercury drops.

Lastly, what you don't know is that I have an interview with Thom Robinson, wherein he states that the gaping hole in JFK's skull was probed with a tiny probe and that one of those probes from INSIDE the skull came out at the throat wound ! That's why he told me that he has always been very quiet about this, but that he has chuckled for all those years at the conspiracy buffs who claim JFK was shot in the throat from the front. He knew better since 1963. And I know better since I spoke to him. I should have known better earlier by listening to Jimmy, instead of to the JFK research community, and what they have brainwashed themselves with. I too was a victim of what I wanted to believe, and looked so self-evident.

James Files was right all along. He was the ONLY shooter from the front, and even he was not supposed to shoot. But he did, because JFK had not been hit in the head. Failure was never an option in a operation that Jimmy took part in, not even at age 21. That's what made him such a valuable asset for the Chicago mob and the CIA.

****

ONeill in his official report said agent Kellerman, now deceased, told him that Kennedy cried out, "My God, Ive been hit, get me to a hospital!" The second bullet hit Texas Gov. John Connally, sitting in a jump seat behind Kellerman. The third was the fatal wound to Kennedy. ONeill said recently in an interview that Kellerman insisted, when pressed how he knew it was Kennedy's voice, "I was with the man for three years, and know his voice like I know my own. And he was the only man in the back seat of the car that day who spoke with a Boston accent."

Hence another clue showing JFK was NOT shot in the throat and Jimmy was correct in assuming the throat wound was an exiting fragment from his exploding bullet. .

Wim Dankbaar

Preface by Daniel Marvin

If you thirst for the truth of who killed President John F. Kennedy you have come to a literal fountain of facts, supporting testimony and documentation that lay the essential ground work and permits you to judge for yourself what happened that fateful day in Dallas. The intricate planning, coordination, execution and cover-up; the who, the how and the why of the finitely orchestrated murder of our sitting president, together with its cover-up is brought to you in a format unique to this very special book by Wim Dankbaar. What could well be considered a "collection" rather than a nonfiction narrative is indeed the long overdue bringing together of a potpourri of people and facts that combine to provide the reader with a definitive basis for his or her quest for final judgment in this heinous crime.

For some thirty eight years I waited for that one person who would surface with the finances, the wisdom, the courage and the desire to pull together strong and resolute people dedicated to bring the truth to the world. Perhaps the fact that I was trained in assassination techniques by the U.S. Army Special Forces in 1964 and was involved in a number of assassination plots, including that of U.S. Navy LCDR William Bruce Pitzer, triggered my desire to help bring the facts to light – once I was saved and no longer feared our government sending someone like me to kill me for telling the truth. LCDR Pitzer was murdered to keep him from making public the actual films of the JFK autopsy which proved the Warren Commission findings were rigged to keep the truth from being known.

My knowledge of CIA/Mafia/Special Forces interaction is based on personal experience: In addition to having this interrelationship taught in school where I earned the right to wear the coveted Green Beret, I met with the Don of the Boston area Mafia family in the Spring of 1964 and he told me of a call that had been made to him by the "company" (CIA) asking for his involvement in the Kennedy "hit." He said his response to the company man was "no"– because they "had no problems with the Kennedys in Massachusetts."

It was in March of 2002 that Kris Milligan, publisher of my book *Expendable Elite – One Soldier's Journey Into Covert Warfare,"* introduced me to this man from the Netherlands who "would some day pave the path of truth." He spoke of Wim Dankbaar, the man who financed and directed Zack Shelton, a 28 years veteran of the FBI, to investigate facts long buried in an inter-departmental and agency mire of deceit, intimidation and subterfuge so as to inspire a wide ranging array of persons with actual experience in and intimate knowledge of government sponsored illegal activities to come forward. Together they would focus a shining light of reality where only the murky shadows of manipulated facts, fantasies and outright lies had persisted.

I first called Wim Dankbaar to transmit my concern that our nation was heading down a path of self-destruction, a direction perpetrated by evil forces within and without our government. We discussed my book and I asked him point-blank why he would risk his wealth and his family's security by heading up an effort to investigate the very soul of evil and corruption within our government, and particularly the CIA. Driven by an innate desire to delve into the "system" that seemed to dominate many elements of our government and which included activities organized and actions taken to forestall any attempt to complete a full and unbiased investigation, he resolved to bring the truth to the world about JFK's brutal murder. He wanted to be a part of whatever it took to make America once more a world recognized Defender of Freedom that was known as a nation dedicated to help those in need. He assured me that he was not concerned about danger to himself or his family and that he would do whatever necessary to get to the truth.

Jimmy Files, the central character in this book, was introduced to me by a lady named Pamela Ray as a brother in Christ Jesus who was incarcerated in Joliet Penitentiary. Independent investigation on my part with regard to File's claims of being a part of the "White Star Mobile Team" proved him to be true and my subsequent direct contacts with Jimmy via the U.S. mail secured my trust in his integrity. He and I understand each other and can relate to the potential danger involved when pointing accusing fingers in the direction of the CIA or the White House. This is true as we shared professional attributes involving assassinations, use of terror and other illegal activities - with his being mob related and mine being covert action and duty related as an officer in the U.S. Army's Special Forces.

Judicious reading of each and every piece of the "collection" contained herein will leave no doubt in your mind as to the veracity of Wim Dankbaar and the truth of what is contained herein.

Lieutenant Colonel Daniel Marvin
U.S. Army Special Forces (Retired)

Author of *Expendable Elite – One Soldier's Journey Into Covert Warfare*

Introduction

Did you just pick up this book and had you never heard that a man named James Files has confessed to killing JFK? If you understand why that is, you are already halfway in understanding what happened in Dallas on November 22, 1963.

This is a strange book in many ways. First of all because for a long time I did not intend to write it. It was originally intended to be written by others, and to a high extent, this is still the case. My involvement started merely as the financer for a documentary, which is still in the works, but to write a book on this subject was originally planned for Jim Marrs, and later for Pamela Ray. Due to a string of circumstances, this never materialized, so eventually I decided to put it together myself.

Secondly, because it is not a book in the classic sense. It is not a novel with a beginning and an ending. It is basically a collection of webpages, correspondence and interview transcripts. This is why the title Files on JFK was chosen. It seems appropriate for its double meaning. Most of the book deals with James Files, the confessed assassin of JFK. But Files is by far not the only participant, whose story is presented here. In addition there are news articles and reprints from the website. Thus it is a collection of files on JFK, as in records on JFK.

The webpages are reprints from my website, some of which I authored myself. These reprints do not contain the many pictures that appear on the website. In that regard the book is an encouragement to visit the website. After all, a picture or a document can say more than a thousand words. Apart from the technological hurdles to print electronic pictures on paper without quality loss, the book would get much too long with pictures. But I left the text captions for the pictures in, so you'll know when there was a picture on the original webpage. If applicable, the Internet link for the webpage can be found at the end of each chapter. Also, the website contains many more pages than reprinted in this book.

However, this book in turn contains lots of information never published before. In that regard the website is an encouragement to read the book. They complement each other. The additional information is in particular the extensive correspondence that James Files has had with various people over the last 13 years. These letters will give the reader the story in detail from A to Z. They will show how events unfolded over the years and they will give an in-depth view into the character of James Files. As one reader put it, he is a very complicated, very simple man. There is even the risk of getting to like him.

A third reason that this is not an ordinary book is that it presents for the first time two actual participants in the conspiracy to kill JFK. A third relates that he was a participant to prevent the assassination. One of these participants claims to have been the gunman firing the fatal headshot from the grassy knoll. A typical reaction is that he is not the first ……. but he is. There has never been a man alive to confess that he was one of the shooters in Dealey Plaza. A man that is still alive to be questioned about it. A man whose story is extremely detailed and has remained consistent over the past 15 years.

Why this book? Because I have come to realize that the issue is no longer finding the truth, but rather put it in front of a larger audience. A website just doesn't do that. Although visitors are steadily growing, it is no way near the readership that a book can accomplish. Additionally, surfing the Internet is usually not an activity that takes your attention and time for hours. But those who visit the website, agree virtually without exception that it is very good, intriguing, persuasive, dynamite, mind blowing or whatever other favourable expression is used. Also, the corporate media in the US do not seem eager to cover the assassination of JFK, other than re-iterating the lone assassin myth. Hence, it is a matter of finding a platform to reach a larger public. That is what I hope this book will do. I am confident that the details in it, will provide a counterweight against the massive disinformation and discrediting efforts. If the words "Kennedy assassination" are typed on the Internet, the first website that comes up, is the homepage of John Mcadams, a persistent lone assassin theorist, who attempts to "debunk" and discredit all evidence for conspiracy.

Does this book solve the murder of JFK? That depends entirely on the definition of solve. If solve means knowing the truth, or at least a big part of it, I guess it will be solved for many. If it means knowing beyond any doubt the identities of all the participants in the conspiracy and the cover-up, I guess not. If it means that people will be convicted in a court of law, even less. I now believe this will never happen. You will learn why when you read the book.

I dedicate this book to the late Joe West, who started this investigation, Lee Harvey Oswald, who was innocent, and my wife Corine, who put up with my passion that took too much time away from her and the kids.

Either for their courage of telling the truth, or simply for helping me out and giving me moral support, I wish to thank James Files, the late Chauncey Holt and his daughter Karyn, Tosh Plumlee, Zack Shelton, Bruce Brychek, Daniel Marvin, J. Bartell, Jim Marrs, Gary Beebe, Lois Gibson, Robert Groden, Steve Yarbrough, Ed Bishop, Kris Millegan, Pamela Ray, Jack O' Rourke, Sydney Wilkinson, Judyth Baker, Lynda Bauer, John Geraghty, Joy Swain West, Denis Mueller, Cher Johnson, Bob & Adri in Holland, John Ritchson, Dawn Meredith, Nick Whalen, Jean Guy Allard, all the people on whose work I built, all the people we interviewed, all the people who have told the truth before, all the people who have paid for that, and all the people I shamelessly forget to mention, which is a long list.

Wim Dankbaar,

Overveen,

Netherlands,

June 2005

Copyright: Wim Dankbaar 2003

Kennedy murder solved?

An interview with Wim Dankbaar

Wim Dankbaar, a dutch entrepreneur (41), financed a private investigation into the murder of the 35 th president of the United States of America. The results will be shown in a TV documentary. The investigation was conducted by retired FBI agents, led by Zack Shelton, a 28 year career FBI agent. They have recently submitted their investigative report to Attorney General John Ashcroft with the request to reopen the case. What we wanted to learn from Mr. Dankbaar is how these conclusions differ from the many conspiracy theories circulating about this case.

How did you get involved in all of this?

I have an interest in this case since 1988. It started with a british documentary airing on dutch television, where I saw a film fragment of Jack Ruby saying to the press that powerful people were behind this murder, and that they would do anything not to let the truth come to the surface. He clearly hinted that he had been forced to kill Lee Harvey Oswald. I had never seen this footage and I found it remarkable to see one of the main players confirm on camera that there was much more to it. Do you know the fragment I'm talking about?

No, I never saw it.

I thought so. I was rather fascinated by it, because until then I had always assumed that America was the ultimate example of freedom and democracy and like many others, I would never have thought a coup d' etat could occur in that country. But that was exactly what Ruby tried to hint at. Then you start to read books and look in depth into the case. Over the years this went with waves of intensity. I think I went through a similar process as Jim Garrison and other researchers.

Please explain who Jim Garrison was.

Image: Jim Garrison

Oh yes, he was the district attorney of New Orleans. He is portrayed by Kevin Costner in the movie JFK. When you start to study the evidence you quickly find the official conclusion is a total fraud. The lies that have been told are insulting your intelligence. From one astonishment into the next. No one of course is going to read all 26 volumes of the Warren Report. That's exactly what Allen Dulles said. He was the former CIA director who was fired by Kennedy for the Bay of Pigs invasion. Then he is appointed by Johnson for the Warren Commission. I mean, how can you have a man who hated Kennedy, investigate his murder? That whole commission was full of Kennedy haters. Anyway, those who closely looked at the evidence would quickly find the Warren Report is all baloney. But in those days the words of these honorable men were sacred. The views of the government were hardly questioned.

Image: Allen Dulles

Ok, but how did you get in touch with the people who are now your partners?

Two years ago I accidently discovered their website. The core of the story was the confession of a man who claimed to have fired the fatal shot from the grassy knoll. I started to read with extreme skepsis, but I discovered that this man had many details, which by the way fitted exactly with what I had learned over the years and deemed plausible. His name is James Files and he is serving a jail term for attempted murder on a policeman.

I was rather amazed that I didn't know his name , the more so because he had made his confession as long ago as 1994, and I was told the website had been up since 1995. When I entered the name James Files on the Internet, I found that 9 out of 10 articles tried to make it clear his story was totally incredible. I then set out to closely investigate all these criticisms and I came to the conclusion they were all superficial and didn't hold water.

Can you name an example?

Yeah sure! For example they said that the weapon Files claimed to have used, was more a pistol than a rifle and would have an enormous recoil. They said it "kicks like a mule". Therefore Files could never have seen what he said he had witnessed through the scope of his weapon. The first thing I did was sending an email to one of the gunshops I found on the Internet. I just acted as a potential customer and asked whether the Remington Fireball was a pleasant weapon. That man started advertising the weapon immediately. One of the most sophisticated guns ever made etcetera. When I inquired about the recoil, he said it was nice and steady. Ultimately I told him why I asked. He was quite amused and said that the alleged murder weapon of Lee Harvey Oswald had a lot more recoil. He even added that whoever said that the Fireball had big recoil, had a lot to learn about firearms.

I see, so you checked a lot of all the criticism?

Yes, all of it and it just didn't hold ground. So I got intrigued more and more by the confession of James Files.

What else did you check?

Much more, there was more than enough skepsis. Another statement was that Files would never have had the time to do all the things he said he did.
He states that he has bitten the shell casing after the shot and left it there on the on the picket fence on the grassy knoll. Then he put the weapon back in his briefcase and turned his jacket inside, put it on and walked away. All the critics shout he would never had the time to do all that, because all the bystanders stormed to the knoll right after the shots, since that is where most bystanders had heard the shots coming from.

Yes, that's what I have always heard too.

It's because the conspiracy theorists are eager to point out that a shot came from the grassy knoll, in front of the president. They are right and that's why they say everyone ran towards the grassy knoll. That is true, but not immediately. Files says that everyone stood frozen and stunned and even the policemen looked as if they were waiting for someone to tell them what to do.

I was quickly able to determine that Files was right. In one of my photobooks there's a picture of the grassy knoll with the press bus in front of it. No soul on the knoll yet. This was the last vehicle in the motorcade, so it must have taken at least 30 seconds for the bus to reach that point. The president's limousine had almost come to a stop and the press bus still take a sharp turn of 120 degrees.

Image: The grassy knoll 27 seconds after the shots

What did you do next?

I called Bob Vernon, he is the man behind the website. In subsequent conversations he gave me more and more background information. I asked him why this information had not been published to the world yet. He told me that he had been dealing with major television networks on two separate occasions. On the last occasion, they were in full swing already for weeks, up to the editing in their studios. He showed me selections of all that footage. What I saw, was professionally made with typical American newscasters etcetera. It was obvious that money had not been an issue.

But both projects were suddenly cancelled from the very top. He explained to me it had everything to do with interference by the CIA. I won't bother you with the details, but it made me realize that the only way to get this done is to make a production with independent money. That's how I ended up being the investor for this project.

What are the conclusions of the film? What do we get to see?

I wish I could answer that in just one sentence. The first thing people want to know is: Who fired the shots and who were behind it? It can't be answered in two seconds. If you want to hear who did it as quickly as possible, my answer would be: A combination of CIA, Mafia, Texan oil-millionaires, anti Castro Cubans and high officials in the military and government. In effect, of all the different theories on who was behind it, our answer is: "All of the above", excluding the KGB and Castro. Those are disinfo stories, tossed in there by the CIA on purpose.

All those groups together? That does not sound very credible!

That I cannot help. It's not my fault that the public does not know that all these groups worked tightly together and were in fact sides of the same cube. But it is so clear. Everything roots back to the Bay of Pigs. All those groups worked in paramount on that and they all had a common interest to get Cuba back.

What about concrete persons?

Well, our investigation identifies 4 shooters, two of them are still alive. The other two have been murdered in the seventies. They are proven and documented hitmen who worked both for the CIA and the Chicago mafia family. Their names are James Files, Charles Nicoletti, John Roselli en Marshall Caifano. Their boss was the legendary Sam Giancana, the head of organised crime in Chicago. Moreover, we have two other participants on camera involved in the planning of the murder. They both support and corroborate the confession of James Files.

Image: Sam Giancana   Image: Johnny Roselli

Who are they?

The other participants are Chauncey Holt and Tosh Plumlee. Both CIA contract operatives. Tosh Plumlee was a pilot and one of Chauncey Holt's specialties was counterfeiting and forgery of documents. Tosh Plumlee is still alive, Chauncey died a few years ago, but we have their testimonies on film. Chauncey also worked for mafiabosses like Pete Licavoli, the boss of Cleveland, and Meyer Lansky. Holt was one of the so called "three tramps". Three shabby dressed men who were arrested on Dealey Plaza. Photographers have taken 7 pictures of them. These men have always been the subject of intense and wild speculation. We show convincingly who they were: Chauncey Holt, Charles Rogers and Charles Harrelson. Charles Harrelson is a well known contract killer as well as the father of Woody Harrelson.

Image: Chauncey Holt   Image: Charles Harrelson

The actor of Cheers?

Yes, he's now serving a life-time jail term for killing a judge.

Gee, that sounds interesting, but how do I know all this is the definite truth and not just a well planned fantasy story?

You're going too fast. I already said this is not a painting of a few strokes. First, this is not the final and full truth. The Kennedy Assassination is a big jigsaw puzzle. We have placed many pieces, but we don't claim to have all of them. For example, it is clear that there were more hitteams on Dealey Plaza, and we have only one. Possibly the three tramps were another hitteam, but we cannot determine whether Rogers and Harrelson were shooters. But even if so, there were also gunmen in the Texas Schoolbook Depository and we do not know who they were for sure. We have indications, but we will stay away from unsubstantiated or inconclusive evidence. Our motto is: We offer no conjecture or theory, only hard evidence.

How do you convince someone this is not a nice scam?

Yes, I'll get to that. What you have to look at first is the people who conduct this investigation. Zack Shelton is a name you won't know but he worked 28 years for the FBI. He spent most of his career on the Organised Crime Task Forces of Chicago and Kansas city. So he knows all these mob figures and put several of them behind bars. The movie Casino with Robert de Niro for example, is based on a true story and Zack has busted some of those characters. Do you remember the James Byrd dragging death, where three white guys dragged the colored guy to death behind a car?

Image: Zack Shelton

Yes, did they not get the death penalty?

Yes, Bush did that when he was still Governor of Texas, but that case was Zack's too. We are talking about someone with a sparkling background and impeccable career in law enforcement, who is unlikely to risk his good name with a "scam". But it gets better still: Zack has called upon and received help of over a dozen of his former FBI collegues and they

are certainly not rookies. Jim Wagner was head of the Organised Crime Task Force in Chicago, Art Pzifenmayer had the same job in San Diego, he is now CEO of a big casino. Michael Wacks was the undercover agent who busted Carlos Marcello. Much like they did John Gotti, with an undercover surveillance sting. Carlos Marcello was the mafiaboss of New Orleans, one of the most powerful ever. Michael's brother, Peter Wacks, led an investigation into the illegal activities of Jimmy Hoffa and his Teamster's pension fund. He was also awarded as the FBI's "best street agent". Well, I can go on like this, I am not yet halfway and the number of agents helping Zack is still growing. So everyone who wants to accuse us of a scam accuses these people also. Every single one of them worked 20 years or more for the FBI. O wait, I forgot to mention James W. Sibert. He was a World War II hero, a bomber pilot who did many raids over Germany. He received several awards for courage and spent 21 years in the FBI thereafter. As a special agent he was present at Kennedy's autopsy. Thank God he's still alive, he's 84 now, but he tells crystal clear, for the first time on camera, how Gerald Ford and Arlen Specter have tampered with the evidence. Arlen Specter is the artist who fabricated the infamous "single bullet theory". He is now a senator for Pennsylvania. Ford and Specter are two surviving men who sat on the Warren Commission. They both have written books in an attempt to confirm the lie about Lee Harvey Oswald.
Ford wrote "Portrait of an Assassin" and Specter "Passion for Truth". It's just disgusting!

Image: Gerald Ford   Image: Arlen Specter

Your talking about some important people here!

I don't care. Hitler was important too. Should I therefore deny he was bad? "If you do the crime, you do the time". And even that, they didn't do. I have befriended the ex-girl friend of Oswald and know exactly what kind of man he really was. He was a CIA spy, a patriot, who has been used and discarded like trash. They duped him by telling him to infiltrate the plot and prevent the assassination. Very clever actually, if you think about it. It's the only way to get your patsy at the right place at the right time. And Lee thought he could sabotage the hit, right till the end. That's when he fully realized he had been duped. The truth is he was a real hero. And those crooks keep pounding their lies until this very day. They know better of course. Yep, it makes me angry. If you repeat a lie over and over, the public will swallow it, especially if it's told by people of authority.

OK, so the investigators are men of professional background, but that's still no guarantee they found the truth!

No that is correct, but I had not finished yet. You asked if it could be a scam? Then you first have to know that the original lead on James Files came from the FBI. Not from a tabloid reporter or something. The tip was given to Joe West, a private investigator, who was working on a lawsuit to exhume JFK's body. He wanted to prove that Kennedy was hit from the front. That already indicates that Joe was sincere. A new and independent autopsy would prove sure as hell that the first was a total fraud.

But Joe West has never heard a full confession from James Files. Files didn't want to talk. Only if Joe could arrange immunity for him, he would think about it. During that time Joe had to go in hospital for heart surgery. The operation itself was a big success, right after he was straight up in bed again, drinking a coke and talking your ears off. Then out of nowhere a complication arose, he went into a coma and never came out of it. With his death, his exhumation suit also died. We all think Joe was murdered by an overdose of the wrong medication. I'll spare you the details, but the attending doctor is still to be found for example. Joe's death is one of three reasons why James Files decided to tell his story to Bob Vernon, who took over from Joe.

What were the other two reasons?

Save it for later, I first need to finish this. James Files finally confessed to Vernon. Files says he acted on orders of his mentor Charles Nicoletti. Nicoletti was one of Giancana's most trusted hitmen. Files was the driver and bodyguard for Nicoletti. Six months before the assassination Nicoletti informed Files about the contract on Kennedy and that he and Johnny Roselli were to take part in it. Originally Files was only ordered to drive the weapons to Dallas, test fire them and explore the area. All orders came from Sam Giancana and the CIA. Files had been recruited for the CIA by David Atlee Phillips. This man was a spider in the web on the part of the CIA for the planning of the hit. His name pops up in almost every covert CIA operation, including the coup in Chile that left Allende dead and brought Pinochet to power. Phillips was also the CIA handler of Lee Harvey Oswald. His star rose to CIA director of covert operations for the Western Hemisphere.

Image: David Atlee Phillips

I won't sum up all the details, you can find them all on the website, but Files drove to Dallas a week before. On the morning of the assassination he met with Roselli and Nicoletti. He did not know how they had arrived in Dallas, nor did he ask. The only thing Roselli told him is that he had arrived on a military airplane.

But our other participants, Chauncey Holt and Tosh Plumlee, explain exactly how Roselli and Nicoletti came to Dallas. Tosh Plumlee was the pilot who flew Roselli the night before and Chauncey Holt had driven with Nicoletti all the way from the Grace Ranch in Arizona. That ranch was owned by Pete Licavoli. It is a fact that Plumlee, Holt and Files did not know each other, yet they all say the same thing and corroborate each other. If you say this is a scam, you say that these three men put it together and subsequently fooled a team of experienced FBI agents.

And me too of course. I threw my good money in there without looking? Or you could argue that these FBI men are part of the scam and risk their reputation with a nonsense report to Ashcroft. I trust you see this is far more unlikely than this being the simple truth. A scam involving so many people would fall apart sooner or later. I challenge anyone to shoot holes in it. We'll shake hands with the first one who can catch us in a lie. We are not talking about just someone who writes a book about JFK's alleged cocaine usage, which cannot be substantiated by the way. We are talking about world class investigators here, who check and double check everything. It's actually amazing that cocaine story is front page news and ours is not yet.

But according to you, the JFK assassination was also a scam involving many people. Why then has that not fallen apart yet?

That HAS fallen apart! How many do still believe the Warren Report? A majority of 90 % believes it is a lie. That's why that movie JFK was such a blockbuster. But by lack of hard evidence the lie has never been disproven. That's why they can keep it up.

You've got a point I guess, but what about that fourth shooter? So far I count three.

Yes, good question, the fourth shooter is Marshall Caifano. We did not get his name from Files. Giancana, Nicoletti and Roselli have all been murdered in the seventies. Coincidentally just before they were called to testify for the Church Committee and the House Select Committee on Assassinations. That was a second investigation into the murders of JFK and his brother RFK.

Image: Marshall Caifano

Files, just like many other mafia men, has a code not to talk about people that are still alive. He also claims to know the killer of officer J.D. Tippit.

Who was Tippit?

He was a cop that was killed 45 minutes after Kennedy. Lee Harvey Oswald was also charged with that murder. According to Files the real killer is still alive.

Ok, but how did you find Caifano?

Zack was given a name by colleague Jack O' Rourke. The name was Joe Granata, a prisoner in Wyoming who used to run with Charles Nicoletti. Granata has been a credible witness for the government. His testimony has sent several criminals to prison. Joe Granata has never given unreliable information. He told Zack that Nicoletti had told him on two occasions that Nicoletti, Roselli, Marshall Caifano en Jimmy Sutton, were the "hitteam op Dealey Plaza"

Is that on camera?

No, on audiotape. It's a phone conversation, because no camera was allowed in that prison. Anyway, Granata confirms the exact story of James Files. The strong part is that James Files was James Sutton in the sixties, that is his real name. He changed it later to James Files. But Granata also adds a new name. Caifano is 92 and still alive. That's a good explanation that he was not mentioned by Files. I cannot help it, but I have respect for the man. He has his own codes. He killed a lot of people of course, but in a way he's also a hero. Without him we would never have known the truth. Compare him with Arlen Specter and I'm not sure who the bigger criminal is.

Ok, for Files, Nicoletti and Roselli you have more than one source, but for Caifano only one?

Hold on, Zack never walks on thin ice. We also have Michael Corbitt. He just wrote a bestseller with the nephew and godson of Sam Giancana of the same name. Double Deal, check it, I hear it's good. Corbitt was a courier for Giancana. He testifies on camera that Caifano has bragged to him that he was on Dealey Plaza "when history was made".

But not that he was a shooter?

No, unfortunately, you can't win them all. I rather would have seen we had done more trouble to approach Caifano. Zack has called him, but he soon turned aggressive. Caifano's wife said to talk to her son Richard Caifano, he is a lawyer in Chicago. I was very much in favour of making a deal with Caifano to tell us what he knew in exchange for publication after his death. After all, he is 92 and somehow these guys are proud of their hidden place in history. Maybe I was naïve, but no shot is always a miss. So I sent Richard Caifano an email with exactly that proposal. Didn't get an answer. His secretary had already said he had nothing to say to me.

Yeah, that's to be expected!

That chance was big of course, but now he is implicated while he's still alive and the chance he will say anything is as good as gone. Therefore I thought it worth to try it. Also because I belong to the school that finds the truth more important than justice. The public needs to know these things are actually happening in the so called democratic United Sates. Only then you will be able to prevent it in the future. If it could happen then, it can happen now. I blame the pawns that fired the shots much less than the ones that ordered it. And they have escaped their penalties anyway. They will always have the pawns. When these pawns, like James Files, open their books endangering their own lives, I would almost give them an award. Probably debatable, but that's my view.

So you are actually taking part in the investigation yourself?

O yes, I can't keep my fingers from the cookie jar. For some things I have more time and knowledge than Zack and his associates. Searching the Internet for example. Everything is now published on the web. The whole Warren Report, the hearings, articles, interviews, entire books even. Once you know how to search you have it at your fingertips. I have given Zack some leads that really led somewhere. Moreover, you can now communicate with everyone in the world at no cost. Doesn't matter if they are in Sydney or Los Angeles.

What about erasing those records?

O yeah, that's a good one. Real funny too. Files says he was in the 82 nd second airborne in Laos. He says he was part of a operation called "White Star". So there should be records of Files in the 82 nd airborne, or Sutton as his name was then. But there weren't any. Bob then hired the historian of de 82 nd airborne. John Grady was his name, he died last year. But he has ultimately proven that Files was telling the truth. Jim Marrs also discovered something.

Jim Marrs?

Yes, He is on our project too. He wrote Crossfire, the book that was the basis for the movie JFK. He was a soldier too in Vietnam and had never heard of White Star. But when he told Colonel Fletcher Prouty – The man portrayed by Donald Sutherland, or Mr. X in JFK – Prouty confirmed the existence of this operation

Image: Jim Marrs

What was so funny?

Well, when that man Grady was investigating in 1998, he received a telephone call from a Secret Service agent: Why are you communicating with James Files? Like he didn't know, ha ha. Of course Grady simply explained and that agent told him that "The President and his staff are very concerned about James Files. He is considered a threat to national security". The President was Clinton at the time. In 1995 the FBI has declared Files "not credible". But the

President and his staff are still worried about this "liar". That's what I found funny. You know what's funny too? The FBI has indeed interviewed Files. One of their smarter questions was how Files could prove his association with Charles Nicoletti. Files gave them a dozen people who could confirm that. Among others Marshall Caifano, mind you. That was in 1995, long before we discovered Caifano's role in Dallas. None of those men have ever been approached. Instead they proclaim Files is "non credible". The authorities are still covering this up. Some people ask me why we can do what the government has failed to do despite millions of tax dollars. There's your answer. The government has been trying to cover up, what we are trying to expose. Maybe difficult to accept, but if you make the switch, everything falls into place.

Why has Files made his confession? Isn't this very incriminating for him?

Yes, you would come back on that. The first reason is Joe West. He thinks to know for sure that Joe was murdered for his digging into this case. Mainly because of his suit to exhume JFK. Moreover, there was a good chemistry between Files and West, they liked each other, but Joe has never heard the full confession of Files.

Image: James Files and Joe West

The second reason is that Files has turned religious. Born again Christian they say over there. An element of clearing his conscience also plays a role.

The third reason is that both Files and Bob Vernon had received clear threats to stop with all of this. Those threats came from organised crime as well as the government. To name just a few examples: Vernon has been shot at from a car, while barbecuing in his garden and Files received a message from a mob lawyer to "keep quiet and lay down by your doggy bowl". Bob's proposal to Files was then: "If they want to take us out, let's leave them something for history!" Files has stared in silence thru the window for a minute, according to Bob the longest minute of his life. Finally Files turned around and said: Ok, bring in the cameras tomorrow!

There is a fourth reason and that is that James Files thinks he will never be tried for JFK. He knows the powers behind it and they have too much too loose. I'm afraid that Files is right again.

By the way, all three participants before our cameras have something of remorse. They have been recruited for these jobs under disguise of patriotism, but began to doubt whether it was all so correct what they did.

So if I listen to you, you don't expect much from Ashcroft either?

A diplomatic answer would be let's wait and see, but an honest answer is No. We won't get any reaction at all or a bullshit standard letter that the matter has been looked into extensively and this is insufficient to justify re-opening the case.

Image: John Ashcroft

Why so pessimistic?

I am not at all pessimistic. At least for getting the truth to the surface. After all we didn't need the justice department to uncover what we have so far. I don't expect much of Ashcroft, because I am convinced that every president since Kennedy, except Carter maybe, has known exactly that Dallas was one big coup and the Warren Report one big lie to fool the American public.

So Bush knows that too?

Don't open my mouth about Bush. His dad was up to his neck in this. That is my personal opinion. Don't connect that to our production. We don't mention him there.

Yes, but now it's getting interesting!

Ok, there are numerous indications that Bush senior has a lot to hide in this case, but no conclusive evidence. That's why I want to stick to the hard facts and confessions.

Nevertheless I would like to come back on that.

Alright, save it for another time and consider it my personal opinion. Ask yourself first why George W. has just postponed the declassification of files about past presidents. He turns back an earlier decision of Clinton with that. What were we talking about?

About Ashcroft!

Yes, the pressure to make something happen has to come from the public, mobilized by the media. Just like with the movie JFK. If you saw how that movie was attacked, even before it was released, you start to see the big picture. But it became a blockbuster, because it offered a more plausible alternative. This despite the fact that it was not presented as the definite truth, but rather as a mix of facts and fiction. That is the difference with our film. We come with names, evidence, facts and documents. But Oliver Stone's movie was instrumental in establishing the Assassinations Records Review Board, but they didn't produce anything significant either. It was shut down in 1998 and the CIA has never released all the files.

So according to you this was much bigger than commonly thought?

Sure, if you think about it, that's the only logical explanation we still don't have the truth. And that while 9 of 10 Americans do not believe the official government position. Johnson had locked all the files on this case until the year 2039. The reason is "national security". Every intelligent person can see there is no national security interest to keep this case closed for over 40 years. We are talking about the security of the ones who did it.

But who were those actually?

We have no complete answers, but you can at least include Johnson, Hoover, Nixon, Texan oilmen like Sid Richardson, Clint Murchison and H.L. Hunt. Those were the richest Americans of that time. The night before the murder, there was a party on Murchison's estate. All these gentlemen gathered in a private meeting room there. They are all mentioned in our program. The people who have helped with the cover up are of course complicit too. We already covered Ford and Specter. Insofar as Warren Commission members had no high positions, they got them later. Most of them have been rewarded with splendid careers. It's all so crystal clear if you think a few steps bigger.

Image: Nixon   Image: Hoover   Image: Johnson

Is that not a problem for acceptance? I mean, lots of people are scared to even think that!

Unfortunately you are probably right. The average citizen has maybe a problem to switch that button. Many Americans can hardly accept their own elected government is simply lying to them. But the evidence lies on the table. Likewise they don't believe the CIA and mafia are working together. They pay their taxes to fund the CIA in order to protect society against enemies and criminals. Then you don't expect them to go into business with organised crime. However, the proof is as hard as a diamond.

O yes? Could you explain?

The mafiabosses involved in this were Sam Giancana of Chicago, Santos Trafficante of Florida and Carlos Marcello of New Orleans. Those three have provided their gunmen in paramount with the CIA. All three hated both Kennedy brothers, actually their very existence was threatened by the Kennedy's. It has now been documented that they worked closely together with the CIA. They are exactly the men who assisted the CIA in the plots to assassinate Fidel Castro. That has all become public in the seventies during the investigations on intelligence and assassinations. You can only guess what we don't know yet. The brother of Giancana has written a bestseller biography on him. Giancana explains perfectly how his organization and the CIA were "two sides of the same coin". He says "I have done more deals with the CIA than I have time to tell you". By the way, in that book he also says that Marcello had sent Charles Harrelson to Dealey Plaza.

Image: Carlos Marcello   Image: Santo Trafficante

But it appears that your scenario is the mob did it.

That is a wrong impression. The mafia supplied their personnel. That personnel was already half mafia, half CIA. The planning was done by their bosses and the CIA, financed by the Texan oil tycoons. Where the plan originated or who proposed it first, is unclear, but what is clear is that high government officials and military people went along with it. All those generals were in General Cabell's house, watching JFK's funeral on television. With a beer and all that. They were not even present at his funeral. Cabell had also been fired by Kennedy and his brother Earle was the mayor of Dallas.

Image: General Charles P. Cabell

The mafia of course, doesn't have the power either to cover-up the murder of a president and rig the American public.

You were talking about the three tramps. One of them is the father Woody Harrelson? What is the evidence for that?

Oh, that's very simple. Chauncey Holt was another one of the three tramps, he tells his whole story and confirms Harrelson. The days before he drove with Charles Nicoletti to Dallas and delivered Nicoletti at the Cabana hotel. Those orders came from Pete Licavoli. But he also had instructions from the CIA to deliver handguns and fake ID's on the parking lot at the railroad yard behind the picket fence. He was told he would meet with Charles Harrelson and Charles Rogers there, as well as a radical Cuban exile, Homer Echevarria. These instructions came from an undercover CIA man in the Coca Cola Company. Philip Twombly, a totally unknown name in the JFK research community. Chauncey's tale is as beautiful as stunning No one knows it yet. It shows perfectly how the CIA operates in such jobs. They send several teams that know nothing of each other. "Need to know" is what they call it. Or "compartimentalized". That's why Files and Chauncey say it looked like "old boys home" on Dealey Plaza. All familiar faces, but they had no clue what their business was there. Among other people, Files mentions Orlando Bosch and Frank Sturgis,

Image: Frank Sturgis aka Frank Fiorini

one of the later Watergate burglars, Chauncey mentions Luis Posada Carriles. Posada is a notorious anti-Castro Cuban, who is currently in a Panama jail for the latest foiled attempt on Fidel Castro's life. That happened in 2000. He was caught with 3 accomplices with bags of explosives during a Latin summit where Castro would speak. I guess you never heard of that, did you?

No nothing!

I thought so, you know why? Because this is not news that the Bush administration can use. But if you discover who those guys are, it will drop your mouth wide open. In 1976 Posada was convicted in Venezuela together with Orlando Bosch, for blowing up a Cuban airline jet. It left all 73 passengers dead. But he "escapes" from his Caracas cell in 1985, to surface in El Salvador that same year under another name, Ramon Medina. He gets that identity from the CIA and he comes to assist his CIA classmate Felix Rodriguez in the Iran Contra operations. Rodriguez is another veteran of operation 40 and a personal friend of Bush senior. That is well documented.

Image: George Bush and Felix Rodriguez

It's amazing what you discover when investigating JFK. You start to understand why so many witness have been murdered. It's incredible. Or do you think it's fine when a convicted terrorist, killing 73 citizens, can run free to do more dirty tricks for the CIA?

That's sounds pretty disturbing, yes.

Image: Luis Posada Carriles

Yes, check it if you wish! You'll also find that they are still trying to kill Castro. This Orlando Bosch by the way – his nickname is "Dr. Death" – is released in 1987 under diplomatic pressure by Otto Reich, the then US ambassador for Venezuela.. Reich is an avid anti Castro Cuban and he has just been appointed assistant Secretary of State under Colin Powell.

Image: Otto Reich, U.S. Assistant Secretary of State for Western Hemisphere Affairs

Some of these Cubans were also arrested for Watergate. Watergate has never been investigated because Ford gave Nixon a presidential pardon. Nixon had made sure to replace

Spiro Agnew by Ford as his Vice President. And as you recall, Ford was also a Warren Commission member. The official story is that the Watergate burglars broke in to place some bugs. But that is not believed by everyone. You don't need 7 men to place a bug and those burglars were all CIA men tracing back to Dealey Plaza. E. Howard Hunt worked together with David Atlee Phillips and it has been proven he was in Dallas that day. Just like Frank Sturgis. His real name was Frank Fiorini and he was a lieutenant for Giancana. Martinez, Gonzalez and Barker were also operation 40 members, anti Castro Cuban exiles like Posada and Rodriguez. There seems to be a connection between Watergate and Dallas and lots of researchers think the Watergate break in had nothing to do with listening devices but was done to steal incriminating documents files exposing the conspiracy of the JFK assassination. Unfortunately this remains speculation since the case was closed by Ford and his pardon.

Image: Felix Rodriguez

It is the same bunch popping up again and again. They all go back to the Bay of Pigs. Think again about the "War on Terror", they have their own terrorists too, but you never hear about those. The art of surpression. They hold back so much about 9/11 too. Through the media you can control public opinion. David Atlee Phillips was a propaganda specialist and has said to James Files something he still recalls: I can kill more people with my typewriter, than you running around with your shotgun. I can go on like this forever. It's all connected. I now understand what Deep Throat meant when he said to Woodward : You have no idea how big this is!

Could you explain who Deep Throat was. Not everyone knows that.

Yes, he was the anonymous source that fed Woodward and Bernstein with information. They were the journalists that broke the Watergate scandal.

Ok, we were in Dealey Plaza?

Yes, we were talking about Chauncey. Chauncey didn't even know that Nicoletti would be a shooter, those are things you don't talk about on such assignments. Chauncey did not fire a shot, but he is actually our strongest witness, because he still has all the documents to backup his story. Including the letters of Pete Licavoli and Meyer Lansky. You can see immediately those handwritings match with known letters of those two But the records on Files' past have all been erased by the CIA. Initially we wanted to call the program "The man who was never born".

How do you know they have been erased?

Later, that's interesting too, but let me first finish Harrelson. Chauncey had delivered his stuff to Harrelson. This Twombly had told him that he was to take part in an anti Castro demonstration, but there was no such demonstration there. At any rate, when problems would arise, he was to report back to a boxcar with number 22. Well, when Chauncey heard the shots ring out, he saw that as a problem and he raced for the boxcar. It was a wagon that appeared to be sealed from the outside, but it could be opened if you knew better.

When he arrived, Rogers and Harrelson were already there. It didn't take long for them to hear police and other people searching on the outside, but it took very long before the boxcar was finally opened, since it looked closed from the outside. They then identified themselves as agents of the tobacco and liquor agency, say the forerunner of the DEA. They said they were undercover on a job to catch smugglers. The fake ID's were made by Chauncey himself. By the way he also made the Alek Hidell card for Oswald. The Dallas cops didn't really know what to make of it and they were therefore escorted to the police office for questioning. There they have been released through the backdoor. That is why they don't look arrested at all on those pictures. They were just escorted. For the cops, they were just "collegues"

Chauncey was pretty distressed with the situation as you can also see on those photographs. But Harrelson was pretty lame with it, he even seemed to find it somewhat funny. That can also be seen on the pictures, Chauncey suspected he may have been "coked up", as he put it.

Image: The three tramps: Rogers, Harrelson and Holt

They don't look like tramps either.

No, they are too nicely dressed and too well groomed for real bums. That's what triggered all that speculation. They have nice haircuts and are clean shaven. Actually they were told to dress like workmen, so they could blend in with railroad workers

There are no arrest photo's for these men in the police archives, nor were their fingerprints taken. Of course this should be custom with any arrest, and certainly in connection to the murder of a president. In 1992 the so called arrest records surface. They produce only written records of three men. Without mugshots and fingerprints of course. A child can see these men are not the three tramps. No pictures of these three men from around 1963 are available. Otherwise you could compare them with the three tramps. A friend of mine always says: It's staring you in the face.

Image: Under arrest?

So the police was also part of the plot?

Not all of them of course, but Sheriff Bill Decker and captain Will Fritz for sure. Corrupt like hell, which is also very clear if you read the autobiography of deputy sheriff Roger Craig. That's why Dallas was the perfect place. The lion's den for Kennedy, full of right wing and wealthy extremists. Jack Ruby worked for Giancana and was a welcome guest at the Dallas police, friendly with over half of the cops. Most of them were frequent visitors of his nightclub. They also let him in the basement to finish Oswald. Just look at how captain Fritz makes room for Ruby to shoot Oswald. He does not even look back if Ruby jumps out. "I know nothing".

Image: Ruby shoots Oswald (Captain Fritz not in picture)

So your only confirmation for Harrelson is the story of Holt?.

No, oh no, there's more. When Harrelson was arrested for the murder he is now in jail for, he has said that he could clarify the Kennedy murder, or 11/22/63 as he called it, and he had been involved in it himself. Shortly after, he retracted his statement with the excuse that he had been using cocaine.

Image: Charles Harrelson compared with the "tall tramp"

And then we have Lois Gibson's identification. Lois Gibson works for the Houston police and is probably the best forensic artist in the world. She has the highest percentage of solved crimes based on composition sketches She just has been awarded by the Guinness book of Records for that. She knows everything about facial recognition. If you see her full presentation in our program, you have no doubts anymore that the three tramps are indeed Rogers , Holt and Harrelson.

Who was Rogers?

Wait a second, I forgot to tell about Don Ervin. That's a famous criminal attorney from Houston and he is also appearing in our program. He has represented both Files and Harrelson. When he saw the picture of the tramps for the first time he said: O my God, it's him!

Mmm, and Rogers?

Rogers was CIA and a childhood friend of Harrelson. Nobody knows where he is. If he is still alive, he is still wanted for the murder of his parents. That happened in 1965. He killed them and then chopped them to pieces in the bath tub and put them in the freezer. Probably to buy time and arrange for his leaving the country. To prevent the smell of decomposing bodies, you know. When the police found the bodies, they first thought that a hog had been slaughtered. Until they saw the heads of course. So Rogers is by no means a nice man. It looks like he killed his parents because they found out about his role in Dallas, possibly through the tramp photos. Anyway, the case is still open and unsolved for the Houston Police.

Amazing!

Yes, but Harrelson is alive and everyone knows where he is. It would be nice if he would also open up like James Files. You see, enough can still be done to solve the case. Posada Carriles was on Dealey Plaza and is also alive. But the government does nothing. Strange not?

Yeah, by the way, that story about the shell casing, That sound rather weird to me.

You mean that Files has bitten it and left it there?

Image: John Rademacher found the casing near the picket fence

Yes, I mean, who does that as a professional killer?

To tell you the truth, I would almost have wanted he had not done that, because it sounds incredible indeed. It's the biggest target for the critics. But you have to keep in mind that Files was 21 years old. He had been killing enough people In Laos and Vietnam, so he was used to that. A guy like that can develop a cockiness, that normal people cannot readily imagine. Then again, he was young enough not to use his brains. Now that he's old and mature he says: It was stupid, but I did that! In addition he hated Kennedy. He held him responsible for the Bay of Pigs failure, where he lost a lot of friends. He took pride in his kill shot and already had a habit for leaving a trademark. He said he always bit his bullet and that the taste of gunpowder was better than coffee.

That casing was been found in 1987, at a depth in the ground consistent with a time since 1963. It has received very little attention in the media. Some small article in a local newspaper. James Files gave his confession in 1994. When Bob heard that story about his shell casing he vaguely recalled a shell had been found. Files then said: "If it is mine you will be able to recognize it for my teeth marks are on it. The end will be oval not round." It is practically impossible that Files could have known this from the media, because nothing was said about dent marks. Even John Rademacher who found that shell, did not know what the indents were. Until then he had guessed they were "ejection marks". Bob contacted Rademacher and had the casing examined by a professor in orthodontology. This professor has certified that they were indeed human teeth marks. James Files says that if they really want to solve the JFK murder they can simply compare the dent marks with his dental records. But they don't. He claims the FBI has those. Do you understand now why our investigators are RETIRED FBI agents?

Yes, but I think the casing story will be met with skepsis. .

Yes, that's why I said he better had not done it. It would be easier if he had only done things that are easy to believe, but I can't help that the facts are not always obvious and credible. You've got to know something else too. A dating test was done on that casing, which indicates the casing is indeed from the 1963 timeframe The headstamp is also consistent with a manufacturing date from that period. It is an important piece of physical evidence. Maybe we can even take some DNA from it, but that's along shot I would say. .

Yes, that would be a killer!.

The casing is just like the other so called implausibilities. All critics who attack James Files, at least agree that he is a "good liar". My question then is: Why does a good liar invent a story with implausibilities? A liar wants be believed, right? Why then make your story implausible? They also forget that if Files is a hoax, Tosh Plumlee, Joe Granata and Chauncey Holt are also hoaxes. But they have been used as credible witnesses for the government in several cases.

Image: Tosh Plumlee

Yes, Well, I think Nicoletti would never have left that bullet.

No, exactly. He would never have permitted Files either. Some people say that James Files knows an awful lot of details, they can't deny Files was indeed the bodyguard for Nicoletti. But, so they say, Files is agrandizing himself, he just heard the whole story from Nicoletti who actually took the shot form the knoll. Yeah, and then Nicoletti left that bullet? That casing is actually more proof that Files is not lying. He was the only one, immature enough to do that.

Was that casing found where Files said he left it?

No, Files said he left on the fence and it was found in the ground a few yards away. Maybe one of the backup people took it and threw it away when he realized it wasn't smart to walk around with evidence. Something like that.

Files also claims he was asked at the last moment to take part in the hit. That's criticized a lot too.

Yes, Nicoletti asked him that morning at 10:30. Until then, Files was not supposed to be a shooter. That decision came from Nicoletti and Nicoletti only. But he had a good reason. Roselli got cold feet. He was aware that part of the CIA wanted the hit cancelled at the eleventh hour. He was afraid that if they went through with it, they would take an enormous risk Giancana and Nicoletti wanted the hit executed, so with one shooter less, Nicoletti asked Files to serve as his backup. Files was only to shoot if it became extremely necessary. The shots were supposed to come from behind and hit Kennedy in the head, but if Nicoletti would miss, Files had to finish the job from behind the fence.

Image: Kennedy after the impact of the shot from James Files

But Harrelson was also in that area!

Yes, but Nicoletti probably didn't know that. I explained that before. They sent in more teams unaware of each other. When someone is caught they can't rat on each other. That's how it's done. "Need to know"

So there is room for improvisation?

Yes, you can't prevent that. You are dealing with people and people make mistakes. Everyone assumes this was a perfectly and meticulously planned hit, but in fact many things went wrong. Nicoletti and Holt arrived only that morning from Arizona. They had car trouble and a storm causing their delay. They could have been too late as well. And if it would have rained the whole party was off, the bubble top of the limousine would then have been on. The shot of Files was in fact one big screw-up. Nicoletti was actually angry with Files, he thought that Files had fired too soon. Because of that, the Zapruder film had to be put lock and barrel, because everyone would see clearly that Kennedy was hit from the front. Other films have been taken by the FBI. But that could not happen with the Zapruder film. That's why it was kept from the public for 14 years. It was bought by Time Life. You would expect the film would be big news and go all over the world. But no, they put it in the vault. It's so clear, looking back. If the film would have gone public, no one would have believed the Warren Commission. This also illustrates the power of the CIA with the media. When you have the media you can make the public believe what you want them to believe.

Image: The impact of the shot : "Back and to the left"

Image: JFK's press secretary Malcolm Kilduff describes impact of the bullet

What else went wrong?

Well, the fact that Oswald was captured alive. The original plan was to kill him as the "fleeing assassin". So something went wrong there. Oswald could have blown off the lids and spill the beans. Maybe he has done so, but the records of his interrogations disappeared. How much clearer do you want it? Thus Ruby was ordered to silence Oswald.

Image: Lee Harvey Oswald

Furthermore it was not intended Holt, Harrelson and Rogers to be captured. But when you have the highest authorities to cover up the mistakes, than you can get away with a lot.

Anything else?

Well, there were way too many shots. Entire fusillades and too many misses. Oswald could only have fired three shots in such a short time with that old rifle. That's why that whole magic bullet theory is such a joke. A child can see that's not true. And of course Arlen Specter saw it himself. He should be between four walls. He is, but the walls are of his senate office. When I see that I ask myself why I pay my parking fines.

And of course many people have been killed, who saw the wrong things or knew too much. When I have to list those examples we'll be still talking tomorrow. Actually it is a miracle, they got away with it.

It is almost incomprehensible what you say.

Maybe, but this was just a coup d'etat that was kept hidden with a stronghold on the media. And also with kill power. That day , democracy was hit hard and the connection with the present day is easy to make. That's why it is still important. Those people who say that it is long ago, history actually, do not realize how it has changed history and the democratic process. Right up to today. In addition, it is not only about the death of JFK, but also the dozens of innocent citizens that were murdered over the years, just because they knew something, Not to mention their heirs and families. Even now, people that present inside information are still being threatened. Is that history?

I will tell you something else, I forgot, but it illustrates what a theatre show this Warren Commission was. Chauncey Holt relates that two of his CIA superiors were Joseph Ball and Frank Belcher. They were business partners in California. Joseph Ball was a big shot lawyer, who also served on the Warren Commission. Check it, he has interviewed several witnesses. At some point Chauncey was told by his parents that FBI agents had come to their home, looking for Chauncey. That worried Chauncey, so he called Frank Belcher. Belcher then called Joe Ball, who was in Washington for the Warren Commission. He reported back to Chauncey "not to worry", but just to make sure, they moved him and some other people to a CIA safe house in Acapulco. Out of reach for the Commission. It was a splendour holiday mansion that Ball and Belcher owned there. I can assure this information is known to only very few people.

Are you never concerned yourself to publicize this information?

That's a question I have heard before. But No, I have only made much of it possible, but many more people are involved in this. You have to share the information, that way you are safer. The film is done and the website is there for the world to see. Jim Garrison said: If the CIA can't kill you anymore, they will resort to discreditation.

But I am curious to see how they will discredit their own FBI agents and manage to paint this story as a fairytale. The key to the truth is the media. They will have to break it.

It has never happened before that a group of impeccable FBI agents have presented their report to the attorney general, full of hard evidence and confessions of actual participants, that demolish the official version of this case. It has never happened before that four actual gunmen have been identified in the crime of the century. Please explain why that is not news.

Cast of Characters

The list below is not exhaustive, but shows the greater part of people we have on-camera interviews with.

James E. Files

CIA operative and mafia hitman. He claims he fired the fatal headshot at JFK from behind the picket fence on the grassy knoll. Identifies Chicago mobsters/CIA operatives Charles Nicoletti and Johnny Roselli as the other members of his "hitteam". Nicoletti was with Roselli and fired from the Daltex building opposite of the Texas School Book Depository. James Files was Nicoletti's protegé, driver and bodyguard. Files was asked to serve as the backup shooter, in case Nicoletti would not kill JFK. Originally he had only been ordered to drive weapons to Dallas, test fire them and check out escape routes from Dealey Plaza. Files states that Roselli was afraid to shoot as he had come to Dallas with last minute instructions from the CIA to abort the assassination.

Files claims the contract to kill JFK came from Chicago crime bosses Tony Accardo and Sam Giancana. Giancana was a prime target of Robert Kennedy's campaign against organized crime. He felt deeply double-crossed by the Kennedy's after he had rigged votes in Illinois, securing JFK's election to the presidency. Giancana had ample documented dealings with the CIA, and was one of the key figures in the foiled CIA/Mafia plots to assassinate Fidel Castro. Files says Giancana could not have engineered the assassination on his own, let alone the subsequent cover-up. He also implicates the CIA, particularly his CIA controller David Atlee Phillips, who sent Lee Harvey Oswald to Files' motel to show Files the area. Files spent time with Lee Harvey Oswald the week prior to the assassination. He says Lee Harvey Oswald did not fire a shot. Files met with Roselli and Nicoletti on the early morning of the assassination but does not know how they arrived in Dallas. Giancana, Roselli and Nicoletti were murdered in the 1970's shortly before they had had been scheduled to testify for a government committee investigating the assassination of JFK.

Files further claims he left the shell casing of the bullet he fired on Dealey Plaza after he had bitten down on it. This was a habit of him for he liked the feel of a warm bullet and the taste of gun powder. In 1987 a .222 caliber shell casing was found with a metal detector on the grassy knoll, buried 3 inches in the ground. When Files was informed of this, he said that if it was his shell, the open end would be oval for he had put his teeth in it. As the casing had indeed an indentation of which nobody had known the cause, the casing was then examined by noted orthodontologists who verified that the indent had been caused by human teeth.

Chauncey Marvin Holt

CIA operative and mafia associate. Deceased in 1997. Worked for mafia bosses Meyer Lansky and Peter Licavoli. He testifies that he drove with Charles Nicoletti to Dallas from the Grace Ranch in Arizona. The Grace Ranch was owned by Peter Licavoli, serving as a base for CIA operations, drugs and gun smuggling. Holt was also carrying forged secret service badges and lapel pins to Dallas, on orders of his CIA contact Philip Twombly. Holt delivered the lapel pins to Charles Harrelson on the parking lot of Dealey Plaza behind the grassy knoll. Harrelson is a convicted hitman, currently serving a life sentence for the murder of judge

Woods in 1979. He is also the father of actor Woody Harrelson. After the assassination Holt, Harrelson and Charles Rogers were apprehended from a boxcar in the railroad yard and detained by the Dallas Police. They were released the same afternoon. While they were escorted over Dealey Plaza, seven pictures were taken by press photographers. These pictures became known in history as "the three tramps". Holt relates that during the Warren Commission, he and other CIA operatives involved in the Kennedy assassination, stayed in a luxurious CIA safehouse in Acapulco, owned by attorneys Frank Belcher and Joseph Ball. Ball served as senior counsel on the Warren Commission. The family of Holt has ample documentation to prove his story up to the written instructions of his CIA superiors and correspondence with Lansky and Licavoli. Holt did not know James Files. (On an interesting note, Holt has reportedly told close friends he was the sniper who killed Bugsy Siegel with an M1 carbine. As Holt worked for Meyer Lansky who was Siegel's partner and was ordered by the Crime Commission to get rid of Siegel, this is entirely plausible)

Robert "Tosh" Plumlee

CIA contract pilot for covert operations. Claims he flew Johnny Roselli from Miami to Dallas on a CIA supported flight, on a mission to abort the assassination. Plumlee was with CIA operative "Sergio" on the south side of Dealey Plaza, looking for possible assassins, when JFK was killed. He and Sergio realized they had failed their mission and exited from the Plaza. Plumlee does not know James Files.

Joe West

Private investigator from Houston, Texas, who located James Files in Joliet prison in 1992, acting on a lead of FBI agent Zack Shelton. West was preparing a lawsuit to exhume the body of JFK in order to prove a conspiracy. West had already uncovered evidence that Johnny Roselli and Charles Nicoletti had been involved in the assassination. Initially Files denied any knowledge of the JFK assassination, but West slowly developed a relationship with Files through personal visits and correspondence. Files ultimately agreed to tell what he knew in court on the condition that he would get immunity. West made efforts to arrange this with the help of Houston criminal attorney Don Ervin, who agreed to represent Files. During this time West suffered a heart attack and needed surgery in February of 1993. He passed away after complications from the operation. With his death, the lawsuit also died. Files believes that West's death was not natural and claims to have been informed of this by a source he does not wish to identify. West died, not knowing that Files had been the gunman on the grassy knoll. As Files had started to like Joe West, he felt indebted to West and his memory, but it took 13 more months before associates of West succeeded to persuade Files to tell his story on videotape on March 22 1994.

Zack Shelton

Retired FBI agent from Beaumont, Texas. Worked 28 years for the FBI. Served on organized crime task forces of Kansas City and Chicago. As such he was familiar with the names of Nicoletti and Roselli. When Shelton read about West's investigation in a local newspaper, mentioning Nicoletti and Roselli, his curiosity was peaked as he himself had always suspected involvement of the Chicago mob in the JFK assassination. He contacted Joe West to arrange a meeting. During this meeting Shelton told West about James Files. In 1979 Shelton had worked a case on James Files, involving a chop shop operation of stolen cars from Illinois, being sold in Texas. Files was eventually sent to prison for this crime. While debriefing an

FBI informant, the informant made mention to Shelton of an odd remark Files had made while driving over Dealey Plaza. The remark had been to the effect that "if the people really knew what happened here, they wouldn't be able to handle it." As this information had nothing to do with the case, Shelton did not act on it, but it stuck in his mind for over a decade until he met with Joe West. Upon his retirement in 1998, Shelton agreed to pick up the investigation where Joe West had left it. With the financial backing of a dutch businessman, Shelton called upon and received the assistance of a number of his retired FBI colleagues.

Joe Granata

Former member of the Chicago crime family and close associate of Charles Nicoletti. Now a reliable FBI informant in the witness protection program. Located by investigator Zack Shelton after being tipped by a colleague FBI agent, Granata verified that Nicoletti confided to him that he (Nicoletti), Marshall Caifano, Johnny Roselli and James Files were the hitteam on Dealey Plaza. "We blew his brains out".

Michael Corbitt

Corrupted former Chicago police officer and courier for Sam Giancana. Deceased in 2004. Authored a recent book "Double deal" about his life. Testifies that Marshall Caifano bragged to him that he was in Dealey Plaza "when history was made".

John Rademacher

Lawn service man who found the shell casing on the grassy knoll in 1987.

James W. Sibert

World War II veteran and Retired FBI agent. Was present at the autopsy of JFK in Bethesda to take notes and make a report for the FBI. After being contacted by Zack Shelton, Sibert testifies, at age 84 and for the first time on camera, of shocking tampering with the medical evidence by the highest elected officials. Sibert states that the wounds that he saw are not consistent with JFK's wounds described in the Warren Report. He tells that Warren Commission member and former president Gerald Ford, authorized a change in his report, raising JFK 's back wound by 5 inches to make it consistent with Arlen Specter's infamous "single bullet theory". The case of the lone-assassin-scenario against Lee Harvey Oswald is based on this implausible theory. Sibert further states that Specter, now a senator of Pennsylvania, lied when he advised the Warren Commission that Sibert had not made notes or issued a report. Sibert's report is in the Warren Report and describes the wounds as he saw them. A large gaping exit wound, the size of an orange, was visible in the back of JFK's head, indicating a bullet from the front. This is grossly inconsistent with the official autopsy photographs, that show in intact back of the head, indicating retouching and fakery of these photographs.

David W. Mantik

Physician with two PhD's at the faculty of Loma Linda University Medical Center in the department of Radiation Medicine. Has made an extensive study of the medical evidence, the autopsy photographs and X-rays. Mantik tells of the evidence that he found for two simultaneous shots in JFK's head, one from behind and one from the front in the right temple. This opposes the official conclusion that JFK was only hit once in the head from behind and refutes the theory that Lee Harvey Oswald acted alone. He further details the evidence for doctoring the autopsy photographs and X rays, in order to hide the shot from the front. Mantik discusses the witnesses he interviewed, who have seen two sets of photographs, one set showing the real wounds, the other set altered to hide these wounds.

Lt. Colonel Daniel Marvin (retired)

Retired member of the Special Forces (the Green Berets). Served in Vietnam as commander of a Special Forces team. Received classified CIA training in 1964 at Fort Bragg in assassinations and counter-intelligence. Was asked by the CIA to terminate Navy Commander Bruce William Pitzer, on the grounds that Pitzer was about "to furnish state secrets to the enemy". Marvin refused the assignment on the grounds that it had to be done in Bethesda on American soil, while he was trained for operations overseas. Almost 30 years later, in 1993 while watching a Kennedy documentary, Marvin discovered that Pitzer had been a photograph technician, present at Kennedy's autopsy in Bethesda. Pitzer had been found dead in his navy office in 1965, his death being ruled a suicide. Marvin contacted Pitzer's widow and learned that his family never believed in suicide and that Pitzer's wife had been intimidated by Navy officials not to talk about the case, at the risk of losing her pension. Marvin also made contact with Dennis David, a friend of Pitzer who told him that Pitzer had shown him photographs and film of Kennedy's autopsy, depicting a small bullet hole in JFK's right temple and a large exit wound in the back of the head. In the conviction that the "state secrets" were the undoctored autopsy photographs and "the enemy " was the American public, Marvin has since fought a crusade to expose the real cause of Pitzer's death.

Lois Gibson

Renowned forensic artist and facial expert for the Houston Police Department. Was recently awarded with a 2004 entry in the Guinness Book of World Records for solving the most crimes from composite sketches. Is also skilled in rebuilding a face from a human skull. Lois Gibson has made a study of the photographs of "the three tramps" and concludes with certainty that the individuals are Chauncey Holt, Charles Rogers, and Charles Harrelson. In her own words, she "bets the farm on it". Her findings are presented in a narrative slide presentation.

Michael Wacks

Retired FBI agent. Worked on organized crime in New Orleans. Was one of two undercover agents in the Brilab surveillance sting that sent New Orleans mafia boss Carlos Marcello to jail. Marcello was a partner of Sam Giancana and has long been suspected in the conspiracy to kill JFK and setting up Lee Harvey Oswald as the patsy through Guy Banister, a retired FBI agent relocated from Chicago to New Orleans. Banister is the character played by Ed Asner in Oliver Stone's movie JFK. The address stamped on Oswald pro Castro pamphlets for the "Fair Play for Cuba Committee", was the same address as Banister's offices. Marcello is on record making death threats to the Kennedy's and informing confidants of his plans to kill JFK, in order to stop the heat from Robert Kennedy. Marcello had been deported to Guatemala as an undesired alien by Robert Kennedy. Wacks tells of Marcello's outbursts of hatred towards the Kennedy brothers. Banister was found dead in his office in 1964. His office was sealed off as a crime scene, but his death was quickly ruled a suicide.

Richard Stilling

Retired FBI Agent. Former supervisor of Zack Shelton. Vouches for Zack's impeccable record and integrity. Emphasizes the validity of the new evidence Shelton has uncovered, as well as the need to re-open the JFK investigation based on this evidence. Becomes emotional with the realisation that his former boss J. Edgar Hoover covered up the greatest crime of his time.

David Scheim

Author of the book "Contract on America". Investigated the role of Organized Crime in the murder of JFK or over ten years. Details the organized crime connections, denied by the Warren Commission, of Oswald's assassin Jack Ruby. Particularly his ties with Sam Giancana, Carlos Marcello and Santo Trafficante, who was the mafia boss of Florida and Cuban operations before the mob was ousted by Fidel Castro. All three mobsters are now known to have collaborated with the CIA to assassinate Fidel Castro, and all three mobsters were targeted with indictments of Robert Kennedy. Both the CIA and these mafia bosses had their own reasons to reconquer Cuba and hate JFK. Scheim also describes the cover-up by FBI director J. Edgar Hoover, the reasons for his hatred for the Kennedy brothers, and his compromising friendships with Lyndon Johnson and crime bosses such as Frank Costello from New York, whose protegé was Carlos Marcello.

J. Bartell

Former CIA contract agent and close associate of Chauncey Holt. Verifies he was recruited by Holt and worked with him on many CIA sanctioned assignments, mainly contract murders overseas, and that Holt had close ties with organized crime. Shows emotion when talking about the memory of his former friend.

Jim Marrs

Renowned investigative journalist, a.o. for the Dallas Morning News, and author of the book "Crossfire", on which Oliver Stone based his movie JFK. Marrs has studied the JFK assassination since the day it happened and is considered one the greatest experts on the case. Together with Zack Shelton, Jim Marrs is the host for the program and explains the many violations of a proper and truthful investigation by the Warren Commission, willfully neglected and altered evidence, as well as its predetermined conclusion to convict Oswald as the sole assassin.

John Craig

Author of the book "The man on the grassy knoll". Conducted an investigation into the life of CIA operative Charles Rogers, who was one of "the three tramps" detained in Dealey Plaza by the Dallas Police, together with Chauncey Holt en Charles Harrelson. Rogers vanished from the face of the earth in 1965 after murdering both his parents, disecting the bodies into pieces and putting them in the freezer. The shocking "ice box murders" were headline news in Houston. If Rogers is still alive, he would be 86 now. Rogers is still being sought as the prime suspect in this unsolved murder case. John Craig verifies that his investigation indicates that Chauncey Holt was also involved in the events of Dallas.

James Fetzer

Professor at University of Minnesota in Duluth. JFK researcher and author of "Assassination Science" and "Murder in Dealey Plaza". Explains the procedures and prejudice of the Warren Commission. Demolishes the single bullet theory at the hand of the Commission's own evidence.

Karyn Harcourt Holt

Daughter of Chauncey Holt. Tells that her father asked her to tape his story shortly before he died, because he felt the American public had a right to know the truth and to vindicate Lee Harvey Oswald. "This is not for me , this is not for you, this is for the American public and my little granddaughter out there".

Jack Rivell

Dallas Police lieutenant at the time of the assassination. Tells that after the assassination he escorted Dallas mayor Earle Cabell on a flight to Washington DC, where they gathered in the house of the mayor's brother, general Charles Cabell. Charles Cabell had been the second man in the CIA and was fired by JFK after the Bay of Pigs, along with CIA director Allen Dulles, who was later appointed to the Warren Commission by Lyndon Johnson. Charles Cabell had openly called JFK a traitor. As mayor of Dallas, his brother was in charge of the security for Kennedy's visit and the motorcade route. Rivell recalls that on the day of JFK's funeral, Cabell's house was filled with high profile people and three stripe generals who watched the funeral on television in an upbeat atmosphere.

Tony Godinez

Former warden of Stateville prison, Illinois, where James Files is incarcerated for attempted murder of a police officer. Godinez has interviewed James Files more than anyone else. He has found his story about JFK meticulously detailed and consistent over the years, and he has never been able to catch Files in a lie or fabrication, no matter how hard he tried. He tells that James Files never bragged about the JFK assassination, and that the only emotion that Files displayed about it, was frustration that he missed his target by a few inches as he was aiming for Kennedy's right eye. Godinez states that Files was well respected in prison, that he had no fear for other inmates, most of whom are black, but that he requested to be in protective custody. Asked for the reason, Files explained he felt safer that way from retaliation by a government agency.

Robert Tanenbaum

Chief counsel for the House Select Committee on Assassinations. Resigned when he found the Committee was not designed to find the truth. One of the reasons for his disgust was the Committee's refusal to recall David Atlee Phillips, as many staff members found he had committed perjury in his original testimony.

Reprint from http://jfkmurdersolved.com/cast.htm

The investigation

CONFIDENTIAL REPORT

JAMES E. FILES a/k/a JAMES E. SUTTON
a/k/a Sergio Castillo a/k/a John Felter a/k/a Henry Sanders

© 1998 JFKMURDERSOLVED.COM All Rights Reserved

This private, impartial investigation started in 1989 and was initiated by a Texas Private Investigator, the late Joe West of Houston, Texas, through a non-profit, educational Texas corporation known as Truth, Truth, Truth, Inc.

As of this writing, the investigation has cost over $1,000,000 and has taken 13 years. The investigation is ongoing and all new evidence will be posted here as it is gathered and verified.

The following information was gathered by Certified Legal Investigator Joe H. West (deceased), Houston criminal attorney Don Ervin, California television producer Robert G. Vernon, John C. Grady, official historian for the 82nd Airborne, a major USA detective agency, and from the files of the Federal Bureau of Investigation.

OVERVIEW

In 1992, a Beaumont, Texas FBI agent, Zack Shelton, informed Truth, Truth, Truth Inc. And Houston criminal attorney Don Ervin that there was a man in prison that he believed to have knowledge of the assassination of John F. Kennedy.

Agent Shelton, a former Chicago Organized Crime Strike Force member, stated that the prisoner is a "legitimate mobster" - had been the "driver-bodyguard" for Chicago Mafia hitman Charles Nicoletti - has a long history of violent crime - and had been tortured and left for dead shortly after the murder of Charles Nicoletti in 1977, prior to Nicoletti testifying before the House Select Committee on Assassinations.

Agent Shelton also stated that he has long suspected that the Chicago Mafia was involved in the murder of President Kennedy, however, he has never been able to gather sufficient evidence to prove it.

(NOTE: Following Agent Shelton's disclosure of the prisoner to Truth, Truth, Truth, Inc. And attorney Ervin, Agent Shelton informed Houston criminal attorney Don Ervin that his FBI superiors had threatened him with the loss of his job and his government pension should Agent Shelton's name ever surface again in association with the JFK assassination. Texas State Judge Charles Carver of Beaumont also verified this fact after speaking directly with Agent Shelton. The FBI has twice declined written requests for Agent Shelton to be interviewed, on camera, regarding James E. Files.)

After an exhaustive search, Truth, Truth, Truth, Inc. located the prisoner in Joliet, Illinois.

This report is contains pertinent evidence and data gathered regarding the life of the prisoner, James E. Files alias James E. Sutton.

James E. Files a/k/a James E. Sutton a/k/a John Mandel a/k/a James Felter a/k/a Sergio Castillo was born in a small country farmhouse just outside Oakman, Alabama on January 24, 1942. His older sister, Mary Pearl Files, was born at the same farmhouse in 1936. Files' mother Vera (nee Lollar) was married to Jasper Daltman "J.D." Files although Lesley Sutton was the biological father of James E. Files. When J. D. Files learned of his wife's affair with Sutton, they were divorced. Vera left Alabama, moving to California, where she married Lesley Sutton. James Files took the last name of Sutton. Shortly thereafter Lesley Sutton was killed at Boulder Dam.

James E. Files's mother is deceased (1970). His mother's first husband, J. D. Files, passed away in 1997. The elder Files's sister-in-law, Christine Shelton of Nashville (Vera's sister), stated that there were also some adopted kids, at least two boys, possibly three, by J. D. Files during a later marriage. One is Raymond Files, an Alabama minister.

James E. Files states that he used the name Sutton (although he was born as "Files") until 1963 and there are numerous records available to substantiate his claim. His first wife Eleanor recalls that Files asked her of she wanted to be married under the name Sutton or Files. His aunt Christine recalls that he used the name Sutton all throughout his early school years. When his mother moved to California, he attended Castle Rock Grammar School in Valley Springs, California. There are no school records available.

The Sutton/Files family moved to Melrose Park, Illinois in the late 1940s, where he grew up in a tough Italian neighbourhood. He was labeled as a juvenile delinquent by the local police chief (Chief Giles or Jiles), bought his first car at age fourteen, was known for riding motorcycles and he raced stock cars when he was in his early to mid-twenties. His first wife's family expressed strong disfavor of the marriage due to his history of juvenile delinquency.

Files killed his first man at the age of sixteen, avenging his sister's murder (Mary Pearl Johnson) in St. Louis, decapitating her killer at close range with a shotgun.

Files stated that he joined the U.S. Army in 1959, entered the 82nd Airborne, and was sent to Vietnam (Laos) as part of Operation White Star. Files did intelligence work and was among the first U.S. covert combat troops sent into Laos in 1959.

(NOTE: Historical records indicate that Presidents Eisenhower and Kennedy called these first troops "advisors" and that US military troops were present in Vietnam as early as 1953 - Col. Fletcher Prouty, former Head of Clandestine Services for the Joint Chiefs of Staff and the liaison between the Pentagon and the White House from 1956-1963 stated that U.S. troops had been in Vietnam since WW II. Prouty also confirmed operation "White Star.")

In early interviews, Files stated that the CIA has tried to erase all traces of his service record (S-1 record), his school records and his birth certificate. No records of his school history or birth have been located, however, an aunt by marriage recalls an Alabama lawyer once located his birth certificate which was stamped *"deceased at birth."* Three recent searches (1994-95-96) for Files's birth certificate have been to no avail. For all practical purposes, James E. Sutton alias James E. Files is "the man who was never born."

Despite the fact that the FBI issued a written report questioning Files's military background, and a major national private investigative agency has issued a written report which states that no trace of Files's purported military records could be located, John C. Grady, the official historian of the 82nd Airborne and the 505th Parachute Division RCT, located Files's U.S. Army serial number and a Veterans Administration claim number in an "inactive" file at a remote regional VA office and through the VA computer in St. Louis.

After an exhaustive 18 month search, historian Grady verified that Files had indeed entered the Army in 1959 and went into the 82nd Airborne before being sent to Laos on July 10, 1959. Files speaks in a distinct military manner with no remorse for anyone he has ever killed. One year later, in early 1996, historian Grady checked the service record of Files again. No records were found and all files under the name "James E. Files" were marked "no further information available."

Files stated that he spent approximately 14 months in the armed services and that he was in danger of a court martial at Ft. Mead, Maryland for certain events that happened regarding the Laotian Army. He allegedly killed two of his own men to "save face" with the Laotian Army. Files has also identified the U.S. Army JAG officer that handled his court martial as "Howell" or "Powell." Files states that he was placed into the Hines Veterans Hospital in Maywood, Illinois for 90 days of "evaluation" - however, there were no hospital records located by the FBI.

Files states that he was then recruited by David Atlee Phillips of the CIA. There are no public records that indicate this is true, however, in a letter sent to his aunt Christine from Vietnam, Files wrote "the government has turned me into a killing machine." Files also confessed that his government work became "over-extended."

Several known CIA operatives and CIA contract pilot Robert "Tosh" Plumlee recall a "young hitter from Chicago, who got into trouble down in Mexico and had to be bailed out by Frank Sturgis of the CIA." Incarcerated Mafia assassin Lenny Patrick has testified that James E. Files alias Jimmy Sutton was associated with the Chicago mob and Charles Nicoletti. A former CIA-US ARMY intelligence officer who was stationed in Florida in 1963 has also identified James E. Files as being involved with the JM/WAVE CIA covert headquarters in Miami during the early 1960s.

Files was "handpicked" to drive for mob hitman/"enforcer" Charles Nicoletti in late 1961 or early 1962 and became a "favorite" of Nicoletti. There are several witnesses who testified that Files knew Nicoletti extremely well including members of Files's second wife's family (Arnold/ Kay Marbry) and a Chicago service station/garage owner.

The garage owner (where Files was once employed) stated that Nicoletti would let only Files "touch" or work on Nicoletti's personal vehicles. Two of Files's Chicago "buddies" recall Files and Nicoletti as "being very close" and have agreed to grant television interviews to that effect. Both "buddies" and Files's aunt and uncle by marriage recall that they were introduced to Charles Nicoletti by Files.

Files stated that the FBI has pictures of Nicoletti and him together and he has clearly detailed the circumstances of how and when the pictures were taken by the FBI

In July of 1995, Michael Cain - brother of notorious Chicago gangster-turned-informant Richard Cain - made inquiries in Chicago about James E. Files at the request of Robert G. Vernon. Mr. Cain contacted active Mafia members and his late brother's FBI contacts both of which verified that Files was "Nicoletti's boy."

Despite requests of Files to sign a notarized statement giving permission to retrieve any and all records of the FBI and CIA that pertain to James E. Files under the Freedom of Information Act (FOIA), his former attorney, infamous Mafia lawyer Julius Echeles of Chicago, refused to allow Files to give the permission for the FOIA document retrieval. Of special interest is the fact that attorney Echeles received payment for representing Files via cashier's check with a footnote "From The Friends of James E. Files." The source of these payments is not known *(SOURCE: Chicago Sun-Times)*.

Files was an "assault weapons trainer" for anti-Cuban forces training for the Playa Giron operation (the Bay of Pigs) in 1961. He claims (with some corroboration) he was an associate of several "key players" including David Atlee Phillips, Antonio Veciana, Gerry Patrick Hemming, and Frank Sturgis. Files has also named key CIA-anti Cuban forces, code names, events and certain historical places that were verified by cross reference with data supplied by known CIA pilot Robert "Tosh" Plumlee. Files also correctly identified Plumlee by his CIA codename, William R. Pearson.

Plumlee also recalls that a young Alabama boy "dropped off" Charles Nicoletti for a "CIA/Mafia flight" that Plumlee was piloting prior to 1963.

Files has stated that he signed a secrecy agreement with the CIA and has refused to provide much information about his CIA activities other than stating that he worked for the CIA from early 1961 to 1979 when he was arrested and sentenced to prison for running a Mafia "chop shop" *(NOTE: The government's case included over 50 witnesses)*.

In addition, Files's personal memoirs, located in his private storage vault in Illinois, indicate that Files has first hand knowledge of numerous CIA activities dating from 1959 to 1979 including the death of Orlando Letelier and numerous other CIA operations in Florida, Louisiana, Texas, Cuba, and South America.

Further, his unpublished memoirs indicate that his CIA "associates" have included Michael Townley, Frank Terpil, the notorious terrorist - Orlando Bosch - the incarcerated arms dealer Ed Wilson and the deceased David Atlee Phillips, who was Files's CIA "controller." Files has stated that he worked directly for Phillips.

Files also stated that the CIA administered drugs to him in the early 1960s in an effort to extract the truth from him regarding a "certain situation."

Files's FBI "rap sheet" (FBI # 66 945 E) dates back to 1959 and includes several minor crimes as well as such major crimes as Armed Violence, Aggravated Assault, Attempted Murder of a Police Officer, Explosives, and numerous counts of Interstate Transportation of Stolen Motor Vehicles (Mafia chop shop). Files has served time in several locations including Wisconsin, North Carolina, and Illinois.

In addition, FBI and ATF documents obtained by Files through FOIA in the early 1980s (while he was incarcerated in Oxford, Wisconsin) indicate that Files has been investigated under the Racketeer Influenced and Corrupt Organizations statutes (RICO), and for Interstate Transportation of Stolen Property, Theft from Interstate Shipment, Extortionate Credit Transactions, Illegal Gambling Business, Police Corruption, and Possession of Illegal Firearms and Explosives.

James E. Files has confessed to acting in a conspiracy to murder John F. Kennedy in Dallas, Texas on November 22, 1963.

Files confessed that Sam Giancana, Johnny Roselli and Charles Nicoletti were the other "players" in the conspiracy. Files confessed that Charles Nicoletti and he killed John F. Kennedy with two separate "head shots" fired within a split second of each other. Files confessed to firing the fatal last shot to Kennedy's right front temple from behind the grassy knoll "stockade fence."

Files confessed that he used a Remington XP-100 Fireball in the JFK assassination. He stated that the powerful, deadly accurate varmint/target pistol was given to him by David Atlee Phillips of the CIA but "not specifically for Kennedy." He claims that the "Kennedy hit" was the third time that he used the Fireball and that the weapon has been used since.

Files claims that he left a .222 caliber shell behind in Dealey Plaza after the murder. Files states that he bit the .222 shell casing, leaving his "teeth marks" on it.

In 1987, a Dallas resident and his son found a .222 "dented" shell casing buried in Dealey Plaza near the wooden fence on the grassy knoll. The casing was determined to have been buried in Dealey Plaza since 1963 by UCLA anthropology graduate Gary Hughes using the Terminus Post Quem layering technique.

Dr. Paul Stimson, a forensic orthodontologist from the University of Texas at Houston, as well as four other prominent forensic orthodontologists, examined the .222 casing and determined that the *dents in the casing were indeed teeth marks*. No positive identification can be made for Files now has dental plates. Of special interest is that the FBI has declined to locate Files's early dental records for a forensic dental examination by FBI experts and Dr. Stimson despite several written requests by Vernon to FBI Director, Louis Freeh.

Files stated that the .222 bullet that he fired at President Kennedy was a "special round" i.e.; a "mercury load" and that six "special rounds" were prepared for the 1963 trip by his main "weapons man," a Chicago area resident named "Wolfman" (A nickname). After being asked to have "Wolfman" corroborate this claim, Files summoned "Wolfman" to the Joliet prison and told him that he was planning on "opening up" about the JFK murder and asked "Wolfman" to speak with an investigator for Truth, Truth, Truth, Inc.

(NOTE: Wolfman died approximately one week after his visit with Files and before he could be interviewed by the investigator. His cause of death is unknown). Files also stated that the "weapons stash" kept by Nicoletti and him was secured at the old Bally Warehouse in Chicago. He stated that they kept about 40 firearms "on hand" at all times and that they were constantly modifying these guns for various "jobs."

The investigative parties herein have been unable to find any hard evidence that proves that Files was not in Dallas on November 22, 1963. The motel in which Files said he stayed in Mesquite, Texas during the week of November 18-23, 1963 was verified as having been built in 1961. The pancake house to which Files says he took John Roselli on the morning of November 22, 1963 in Ft. Worth, Texas was verified to have been built in 1962. During the time period in question (November 18-23, 1963), no evidence has been found indicating that Sutton or Files was incarcerated or hospitalized. There are no speeding tickets issued to Sutton or Files during the time period in question. No credible witnesses have come forth to indicate that Sutton/Files was not in Dallas on 11/22/63.

Eric Buesing and Associates of Santa Ana, California, administered a Voice Stress Analysis test (VSA) of Files's videotaped confession and found a high 70% confirmation of his veracity. Buesing concluded that Files _was_ in Dallas on November 22, 1963. A second voice stress analysis, administered by television producer Robert G. Vernon, indicated a confirmation of Files's veracity - as high as 86%.

When questioned about the "torture incident" as per the information supplied by FBI Agent Zack Shelton, Files stated that he was "kidnapped" by unknown persons shortly after the murder of Charles Nicoletti in 1977. He was held against his will in a "warehouse" at an unknown location in or near Chicago. Files's Aunt Christine also verified that Files had been tortured.

Following various methods of excruciating torture, including the insertion of an electric cattle prod into his rectum, Files was thrown, completely nude, from a speeding car and was found by police from a Chicago suburb.

Files stated that his kidnappers demanded a "package" which Charles Nicoletti gave to him following the JFK assassination. Files said that Nicoletti instructed him to "hold on to the package" for it may save his life someday.

Following his recovery from the kidnapping and torture incident, Files says he dug up the "package" and that it contained a map of the presidential motorcade route through Dealey Plaza and several Secret Service identification cards. Files stated that he destroyed the contents of the "package." Files stated that he does not believe that his kidnappers were associated with the Chicago Mafia or they would have killed him. He believes his captors were "government related."

James E. Files is currently serving 50 years at Stateville Correctional Center, Joliet, Illinois for the attempted murder of two Illinois police officers. He is in Protective Custody at the prison. His 1994 appeal was denied by the Court. Files's 1995 appeal was granted and he was scheduled for re-sentencing until he was informed, in 1996, that the appeal had been overturned.

James E. Files has written songs under the name of "Jimmy South": In two of his songs - entitled "Six Seconds in Dallas" and "I Remember Jackie" - Files's lyrics and melody paint a haunting, chilling picture of what occurred in Dealey Plaza on November 22, 1963.

"A Soldier Past" - a poem written by Files (located in his storage area) - was given special consideration by the editor of a magazine known as the National Vietnam Veterans Review.

Files and his oldest daughter have both received threats due to Files's confession to Truth, Truth, Truth, Inc. and producer Robert G. Vernon. Files says he has been threatened by both organized crime and the U.S. Government and has declined to further elaborate on those threats.

Files's daughter received a visit from a "representative" of organized crime in 1994 and has since - twice - relocated to a new address.

On November 18, 1994, television producer Robert G. Vernon testified to the Assassination Records Review Board (five scholars appointed by President Bill Clinton) in a public hearing in Dallas, Texas. Vernon informed the Review Board of the confession of James E. Files as relates to Files's participation in the daylight assassination of President John F. Kennedy.

In 1996, Beaumont FBI agent Zack Shelton broke a "four year silence" and verified to Michael Hytha, a Knight-Ridder reporter, that he (Shelton) had given the lead on James E. Files to Certified Legal Investigator Joe West. In a separate interview with journalist Marcella Kretter of UPI, Agent Shelton informed the reporter that the FBI had received a lead on Files from an informant. Shelton also asked Kretter not to reveal his name in her news story.

In August of 1996, Files received a letter from his new attorney (name unknown) which informed Files that a "$50,000 contract" had been placed on Files's head. Files also received a warning from a "friend in NY" that Files was in danger.

The investigation has also brought forth the man who flew John Roselli into Dallas on 11/22/63 and the man who drove Charles Nicoletti into Dallas on the morning of 11/22/63.

Robert G. Vernon has turned all evidence on James E. Files's confession to the murder of John F. Kennedy over to President Bill Clinton, Vice-President Al Gore, U.S. Attorney General Janet Reno, and FBI Director Louis Freeh.

ADDENDUM

In August of 1993, Houston criminal attorney Don Ervin negotiated a deal with the US Department of Justice - through the FBI - that included (1) immunity for Files; (2) the FBI and Ervin would go to Joliet and interview Files in a non-official capacity; and (3) following the "non-official" interview the FBI would investigate and then the US Department of Justice would possibly call a special Grand Jury to hear Files's testimony.

On August 9, 1993 - without the knowledge of attorney Ervin - two Chicago FBI agents (Zydron and Pecoraro) paid a surprise visit to Files. On August 16, 1993, the two agents authored a report of their visit with Files.

Following the FBI visit with Files, Files notified attorney Don Ervin and producer Vernon that the agents had "asked him to agree that Oswald was the lone assassin of JFK" and that the agents had threatened Files's pending appeal telling him that they had already talked to the appellate court judges (NOTE: Files's appeal was granted then later overturned).

This report was placed in the National Archives and was faxed to Vernon by the Executive Director of the Assassination Records Review Board, David Marwell, in December of 1994 (NOTE: The issuance of an official FBI report to the National Archives is highly unorthodox and the reason for this action is unknown as of this writing).

In 1996, Vernon located retired FBI agent Pecoraro in Florida. Pecoraro initially informed Vernon that he "felt like he had been used" and denied any knowledge of the US Attorney's (Chicago) approval of immunity for Files (a fact verified by attorney Ervin on August 3, 1993).

Vernon then faxed Pecoraro a copy of the 8/16/93 FBI report, which Pecoraro says he had never seen. Vernon also informed Pecoraro that it was reported that agents Zydron and Pecoraro had "muscled their way into the prison through Internal Affairs."

In their second phone discussion in 1996, retired agent Pecoraro stated that he and agent Zydron had not "muscled their way in through Internal Affairs" but had contacted the warden personally and spoken with the warden and that the warden had full knowledge of the FBI visit on 8/9/93.

Immediately following his conversation with retired agent Pecoraro, Vernon contacted former Stateville warden Salvador Godinez (now Deputy Director of the Michigan Department of Corrections) and informed Godinez that Pecoraro had told Vernon that Zydron and Pecoraro had spoken directly with the warden prior to their visit with Files and that the warden had full knowledge of their visit with Files in 1993.

Godinez' response: "That's a lie."

SPECIAL ADDENDUM

In May of 1996, the unedited confession of James E. Files was released in home video form only by a Chicago video distributor. Following the video release, the distributor was "invited" to the White House by President Bill Clinton and later given a special "nomination" to the Democratic National Advisory Board. Marketing and distribution plans were mysteriously changed, altered and even not implemented as planned. Despite these strange actions, several major video chains carried the video, including Blockbuster which promoted the video over the Thanksgiving holidays of 1996. Blockbuster re-ordered twice after starting with three rental copies for each store.

In addition, the distributor has attempted to discredit Vernon, attorney Ervin and former Warden Godinez to James Files.

In addition, in September of 1996, the tabloid program "HARD COPY" did a special two day story (9/10/96 and 9/11/96) which is still in syndication as of April 18, 1997. The focus of the story was the fact that Malcolm Summers, a reputable mature Dallas businessman - who was an eyewitness to the 1963 murder of JFK - and who is cited in the Warren Commission report as a witness - *IDENTIFIED JAMES E. FILES AS THE MAN HE SAW ON THE GRASSY KNOLL IN 1963.* The Hard Copy story resulted from a FIVE DAY special news series produced by a San Antonio, Texas TV station.

Immediately following the Hard Copy exposure, John R. Stockwell, a former CIA case officer, and John McAdams, a known CIA disinformation specialist and asset, went on the Internet and attempted to debunk the confession of James Files. The CIA disinformation specialist even created a special website claiming Files is a hoax.

Further, the plans of the Chicago distributor to produce a second video featuring the entire evidence gathered by the extensive investigation were mysteriously altered and on April 16, 1997, Robert G. Vernon received information from a reputable source that the distributors were releasing a second JFK video WHICH DOES NOT INCLUDE ANY INFORMATION OR MENTION OF JAMES E. FILES. This information was confirmed as true by the distributor when confronted.

In the summer of 1998, one of our top researchers was contacted by the Secret Service and was asked why he was communicating with James Files. When the researcher told the agent about Files' confession of JFK, the agent informed the researcher that "the President and his staff" were very concerned for James Files is a "threat to National Security."

It is the belief of Robert G. Vernon that the United States government, through its highest elected officials, and the CIA, are working closely together to stop any publication of the certified legal evidence supporting the confession of James E. Files.

Reprint from http://jfkmurdersolved.com/frept97.htm

Interview with James E. Files

THE CONFESSED ASSASSIN

OF JOHN F. KENNEDY

View a fragment of the video confession, preceded by comments of Jim Garrison : Click here

ABOUT THIS TRANSCRIPT

On March 22, 1994, television producer Robert G. Vernon videotaped the confession of James E. Files during which Mr. Files confessed that he fired the fatal last shot into the right front temple of John F. Kennedy on November 22, 1963 in Dealey Plaza, Dallas Texas. A transcript of Mr. Files's confession follows. Included in the transcript is documentation and research *(in italic font)* based on existing evidence uncovered by leading JFK assassination researchers and authors. The purpose of this writing is to compare the confession of James E. Files to a majority of the evidence that has been uncovered in the last 34 years relative to the assassination. Readers are invited to review the following and to judge the veracity of Mr. Files's confession for themselves.

A NOTE ABOUT REFERENCES

References in the text are numerically keyed to the bibliography. Each reference is assigned a number and is listed by that number in the bibliography. When a reference is cited in the text, the references bibliographic number is given. Page numbers, if any, appear after the reference number. If the entire reference is being cited, then only its number is given. For example, Mark Lane's book Rush to Judgment is listed as reference number 4 in the bibliography. If the entire book is being cited, the citation will look like this: (4). If pages 221-224 are cited from the book, the citation will appear as follows: (4:221-224). The only exceptions to this method are when information is cited or quoted from the Warren Commission's report and from the appendices to the report of the House Select Committee on Assassinations. Citations from the Warren Commission's report will be given as WCR, followed by the page number(s). Thus, WCR 32 refers to page 32 of the WCR. For the HSCA volumes, the volume number will be given, followed by the abbreviation HSCA and the page number(s). Thus, for example, 6 HSCA 110-111 refers to pages 110-111 of volume 6 of the appendices to the Select Committee's report.

TRANSCRIPTION
VIDEO TAPED CONFESSION OF JAMES E. FILES

March 22, 1994

Present: James Earl Files - Inmate, Robert G. Vernon - Producer, Bob Baxter - Cameraman, Mike Krolikiewicz - Prison Clinical Services

Location: Stateville Correctional Center, Illinois State Penitentiary, Joliet, Illinois

Time: 10:30 AM CST

Q: Please tell me your name.

A: My name is James Files and I changed my name basically at the end of 1963 for purposes of ...let me rephrase that. I took the name Files in 1963, my real name is James Sutton.

Q: Say that again.

A: My real name is James Sutton but I changed my name in late 1963 due to the fact that at that time I wished to get married and raise a family.

Q: And what is your name now?

A: Today, I'm incarcerated and I'm under the name James E. Files. I raised a family under that name, James Files.

Q: Did you change your name for any particular reason or anything involved in your past?

A: I changed my name for a particular reason because I had been working with a radical Cuban group and what we wanted to do at that time was to protect my identity so they wouldn't know who I really was when I got married because of my family life. I didn't want anyone to retaliate on the things that we were doing so I took on a different name that was authorized to me through a government agency.

Q: Were you ever in the armed services?

A: I was in the 82nd Airborne. I went in '59...1959, date of entry...January and in July 10 of 1959, I believe it was July 10, we shipped out to Laos. I was 82nd Airborne.[1]

Q: What were some of your duties?

A: My duties at that time...we were working a special operations group to work with the Laotian Army in Laos at that time. I was there strictly as an advisor .. on training...with small automatic weapons...setting detonators, explosives, mechanical ambushes. There was just a handful of Americans working with the Laotians at that time.

Q: How long did you serve there?

A: I was there through...approximately 14 months I was in Laos.. before I came home.

Q: You mentioned to me at one time that you were in jeopardy of being court martialed could you elaborate on that a little bit?

A: I really don't wish to elaborate on that part of the court martial. It had to do in the field but not of cowardice, it was something that I did to hold face with the Laotian Army.

Q: Could you tell me how you first became involved in organized crime activities?

A: Well, I first became...it's a strange way to start out...but I was racing stock cars and driving at a local track and Mr. Nicoletti had taken a shine to my driving and he'd watched me on several occasions and he had asked me once if I would drive him one evening. I took him out and test drove his car that we'd just picked up a brand new Ford...and he was pretty well pleased with my driving and from then on I became more like an assigned driver to him and I did several drivings for him on different jobs that he did.

Q: Who was Charles Nicoletti?

A: Charles Nicoletti, at that time, he was an up and coming figure with organized crime and he was known as one of the local hitman. As far as I'm concerned he was the best that ever lived, as far as I'm concerned.[2]

Q: What Mafia family did he work for?

A: He was out of the Chicago family.

Q: Who would have been the boss of the Chicago family?

A: At that time, Tony Accardo.

Q: That's before Giancana or after Giancana?

A: Tony Accardo handed it up...headed it up....then Giancana came after that. Giancana at that time was one of the underlings, I guess you might say he was the...one of the top lieutenants at that point. Things were handed out in different branches in organized crime such as someone might handle the liquor license, someone would handle the loan sharking and booking, someone would handle the contracts for murder for hire and anything like that.[3]

Q: James, where were you on November 22, 1963?

A: On November 22, 1963, I was in Dealey Plaza. I arrived at Dealey Plaza shortly before 10 AM that morning.

Q: What was your reason for being there?

A: My reason for being there at that point was to look the area over. I had driven a vehicle down there and I had taken several weapons to Dallas, Texas.

Q: For what purpose did you do this?

A: I did this for the sole purpose for the assassination of John F. Kennedy.

Q: Who instructed you to do this, James? Tell me the story...in your words...

A: The story started back....oh, roughly six months prior to that when Mr. Nicoletti contacted me one evening and I had met with him and he instructed me that we was going to do a friend of mine. It was more like a personal joke because I had never liked John F. Kennedy since the Chianos Bay affair which was the Bay of Pigs.

Q: Were you at the Bay of Pigs, Jimmy?

A: No, I was not at the Bay of Pigs but I had helped train several of the operatives that were involved at the Bay of Pigs.

Q: When you say "helped train them" what do you mean?

A: I helped train them on what they call ..we called it "Gator Ridge" back then, some people refer to it as "No Name Key" some people call it "Assassin Ridge" it was in the Everglades down there in Florida.[5] We worked solely with the Cubans at that time...we had supplied them with weapons...the weapons had come basically from the government...from the CIA...they had been heavily involved in that. And at that time, David Atlee Phillips was my controller. So I had never liked Kennedy since he had backed out on us and we didn't get enough firepower and I felt that we had been betrayed.[6] But, I, at that point, I had never even considered killing anybody at all over the situation, but when Charles Nicoletti told me that we were going to do my friend, I thought that they were referring to a local party in town and I said why what the hell did he do. He laughed, he says no not him, we're going to do John F. Kennedy, the president. I was a little bit shocked at first but I said hey fine, great, don't matter to me. I was game for anything he wanted to do. And then we discussed it and then he asked me what I thought about Johnny Roselli[9] working with us and I told him hey fine I like Johnny .. got no problems there.

Q: So you knew John Roselli before that day?

A: I knew John Roselli before that day.

Q: How did you meet him?

A: I had met John Roselli in Miami and discussed a few things with him and he...I had met him through David Atlee Phillips...David Atlee Phillips was an operative for the CIA. Through time everybody got to be fairly well good friends but I grew up basically under Chuck's wing...Mr. Nicoletti's wing. Chuck had told me we were going to do it. We'd first originally planned to do the assassination in Chicago but a lot of people didn't like that idea so then it was moved to another location.

Q: When you say "we planned it" could you clarify "we"?

A: Well when I say we...I was just with Mr. Nicoletti. Whatever he said do, I would do. When I say we, I'm referring like...the only thing I did was just drive the car or whatever that they needed me for. Mr. Nicoletti had asked me then at that point when we'd decided not to do it in Chicago and it was going to be moved to Dallas...when John F. Kennedy had decided to go to Dallas...a week in advance, I took the '63 Chevrolet that we had at that time .. I left and I went down a week earlier. I picked up the weapons from the storage bin that we had and loaded them in the car with everything that I thought we might need..with a various assortment...and I left and I drove to Dallas. I stayed out at a place in Mesquite, Texas.[11] Once I got there, I called back and notified Mr. Nicoletti that I was thee and on the scene. The following day, Lee Harvey Oswald came by the motel where I was at...they had given him my location...and he took me out to a place somewhere southeast of Mesquite where I test fired the weapons and calibrated the scopes on anything that might be needed. Then he was with me for a few days in town there...we drove around...so I would know all the streets and not run into any dead ends streets if anything went wrong and we had to flee from the area.

Q: So Lee Oswald spent time with you...he knew why you were there, you knew why he was there...?

A: Lee Harvey Oswald knew that I was there but I never told him why I was there. He had just been come over and told to stay with me and to help me out and to assist in any way he could. Lee Harvey Oswald and I never discussed the assassination of John F. Kennedy. I discussed that with no one. Because my part of it...I had no part of the assassination at that time...all I did was go down, take the car down, take the weapons down, clean the weapons, calibrate the scopes, make sure everything was functioning properly and then know the immediate area surrounding Dealey Plaza back to the expressways and the other local highways that could be used as an extraction point to leave Dallas in case something should go wrong. At that point, I had no involvement at all in the assassination outside of that...just doing my little job that I had to do.

Q: Could you give me the exact chronology of what happened from the time you arrived in Dallas...? You've already said that you went out and test fired some guns and things...take me back to maybe November 21, the day before, and in your own words, tell me what happened from November 21, 1963 until the night of November 22, 1963...

A: We go back...November 21, I had everything pretty well set up on my end of it as far as knowing the area, knowing the streets, memorizing a lot of the major points there and intersections... crossing railroad tracks and trestles and things... I had the weapons prepared and ready to go, I had those installed in the car where I wanted them. Everything had been calibrated..all ammunition had been set and ready to use. I got a good nights sleep that night, the following morning I got up early and I went to the Dallas Cabana Hotel to pick up John Roselli...I'm going to say somewhere shortly around 7:00 that morning, maybe a few minutes past seven...and I picked up Johnny Roselli and we drove from the Dallas Cabana to Ft. Worth, Texas to a pancake house[12] they had there just off the major highway. We went there to meet someone...I did not know who we was meeting...But he had already told me...Johnny Roselli said we was going to meet a man by the name of Jack Ruby...that he had some things that we had to pick up. When we got there, Johnny Roselli told me he said...I'm going to go in and sit in a booth...he says you wait and come in later...he said sit somewhere else where you can keep an eye on me...in case something goes wrong, I want you to cover my backside. So I positioned myself..after Johnny Roselli went in...I sit at the counter...ordered a cup of coffee and sit there and waited. This real heavy set gentlemen came in and he went over and he knew Johnny Roselli I assume cause they shook hands, they talked for a minute and they sit down in the booth together. They passed over, I'm gonna say probably a 5 x 9 envelope...manilla envelope that had some material in it, at that point. After a couple of minutes, he got up, they shook hands, he left. I went out into the parking lot, made sure the air was clear, started the car up, pulled up by the door, Johnny Roselli come out and got in the car. I never met Jack Ruby, never said hello or anything. Johnny Roselli got in the car with me and we started back to Dallas. He opened the envelope up and there was identification in there for Secret Service people and we had a map in there of the exact motorcade route that would take it through Dealey Plaza. Johnny Roselli said well they only made one change.[13] That was when he informed me they was coming off of Main Street on to Elm or on to Houston there...they made the zig-zag, the little turn that they should have never made. But when they made that, it was the only change in it. I drove him back to the Dallas Cabana, he went upstairs and I waited for Mr. Nicoletti to come down. Mr. Nicoletti came down and got in the car with me and we drove to Dealey Plaza. We got to Dealey Plaza shortly before ten o'clock. From there we parked the car...it had been drizzling rain that morning...kind of a cool morning out...I had parked the car beside the Dal-Tex building, Mr. Nicoletti and I got out and we walked up and down the complete area of Dealey Plaza, we covered every corner, walked by the buildings, looked over several different things. We were just talking, having casual talk about the weather and everything. At about 10:30, Mr. Nicoletti asked me how would I feel in supporting him...in backing him up on this...and he told me I wouldn't fire unless it became extremely necessary. I told Mr. Nicoletti, Jesus, I'd be honored to do anything to back you up. He asked me if you was to be outside here, where would you position yourself at in Dealey Plaza? I told him, I said well, from looking everything over and from walking it in the week I've been down here, I think I would choose up there behind the tree behind the stockade fence on the high ridge by the knoll up there. He says why there? I says well I've got the railroad yard in back of me, we've got a parking lot there and I've got a place to where I could stash whatever I would need. I said I can pass myself off as a railroad worker in the railroad yard for the time being until that time comes and nobody would really pay any attention to me.[14] He asked me then where do you think would be the best place for me? I said well, I think the Dal-Tex building...with the new change in it...I say I think the Dal-Tex building over there...that building would give you the best advantage point there. He said I think so too. So we took a walk over, went through the parking lot over by the tracks, walked around through there and he seemed pretty well pleased with that. Then at that point, oh it was about 11:10, he asked me what weapon would I choose to use over there. I told him I would like to use the Fireball. He said why that one? He said you've only got one shot. I said one shot's all I'm gonna get anyway if I wait until the last moment of fire and I may not fire, I said, and it's easy to conceal and I carry it in a briefcase and nobody will pay any attention to me and it's easier to walk away from there. And that's exactly what we did at that point. Shortly before noon, we went back to the vehicle, I took the briefcase out and turned my jacket inside out, I went back into the yard...the railroad yard there...I secured the briefcase, then I hung out back there and I walked down on the grassy knoll, no one paid any attention...people were gathering. Shortly before the motorcade came, I went back up there and started securing myself in a better position so I'd be able to reach the attache case at that point ...the briefcase...I knew once that I opened the briefcase up and pulled the weapon out, nobody's gonna be looking at me, the motorcade would be coming...making its first time...and I wouldn't have to remove the Fireball from the briefcase until approximately... they made the first turn on Elm Street there and I would have plenty of time at that point.[15] At that point when they started proceeding down Elm Street, shots started being fired from behind. I assumed that it was Mr. Nicoletti because he was the one that was in the building and I knew that Johnny Roselli was there. I remember the shots ringing out and even though the President was being hit with the rounds, I was considering it a miss because I knew that we were going for a head shot on the President. I had known that he had been hit in the body but I didn't know what part at that time. I seen the body lurch and I saw the body lurch again, I heard another shot that missed. We were supposed to hit no one but Connally, I mean no one but Mr. Kennedy. I guess Gov. Connally got hit with one of the rounds at that point. I wasn't even sure of that because I was keeping Kennedy as best I could in the scope on the Fireball. When I got to the point where I thought it would be the last field of fire, I had zeroed in to the left side of the head there that I had because if I wait any longer then Jacqueline Kennedy would have been in the line of fire and I had been instructed for nothing to happen to her and at that moment I figured this is my last chance for a shot and he had still not been hit in the head. So, as I fired that round, Mr. Nicoletti and I fired approximately at the same time as the head started forward then it went backward. I would have to say that his shell struck approximately 1000th of a second ahead of mine maybe but that what's started pushing the head forward which caused me to miss from the left eye and I came in on the left side of the temple. At that point, through the scope, I witnessed everything, matter and skull bring blown out to the back on the limousine and everyone on television watching saw Jackie Kennedy crawl out there to get it. I watched her hold it in her hand, crawl back on to the car, I put the Fireball back into the briefcase, and closed it up, I pulled my jacket off, reversed my jacket so I would have, instead of the plaid side out, I would have the grey like a dress jacket more or less and I put a cap on my head, my hat, to walk away, carrying a briefcase.

Q: How did you exit the plaza?

A: When I exited the plaza, I walked to the edge of the stockade fence, I did not walk down the steps, I walked back over, crossed the grass to the dead end street that ends there by the parking lot and I proceeded to, I believe that's Houston, crossed Houston, went into the Dal-Tex parking lot. When I got into the car, Mr. Nicoletti was already in the car and so was Johnny Roselli. I got in the car and drove away.

Q: What happened to the shell casing that you fired at John Kennedy?

A: The shell casing that I fired at John Kennedy, when I took it out of the weapon, It's one of those moments when you feel like you're above everything else and I guess I was a little bit cocky with it all. I took the casing and I put it in my mouth while I put another casing - cartridge - into that one. Before putting it into the case and as I started to leave, I took the casing and I bit down on the casing to leave teethmarks on it and I set the casing, as a symbol, right on top of the stockade fence which I know I should have never done but I did that. Over the years, through other people, I have left certain trademarks along the way.[17] But the casing was mine and it had teethmarks on it and no one knew it was teethmarks here until recently in 1994. And they just had that examined to find out that it was teethmarks on there. But I left it more or less as a signature of my calling card.

Q: Your trait...?

A: You might say my trait...

Q: How did John Roselli and Charles Nicoletti get into the Dal-Tex building?[18]

A: That I could not say but I would believe they went through the front door...we had a side door they would be exiting from and I had parked this burgundy colored Chevrolet there, the '63 that I was driving, I'd parked that in the lot there. But when they entered the Dal-Tex building I was not there, I was on-site, back into the railroad yard at that point.

Q: Are you sure that they were in that Dal-Tex building?

A: I'm positive cause I had the car parked there, they were going to come out through the door and put their weapon...well, Johnny Roselli had no weapon...Charles Nicoletti was the one that carried the rifle in there. That had been secured and he put that back into the trunk of the vehicle. I knew that was in the trunk because it was still there when I got to the motel...I took it out....cause that was....the plan was for him to come back...put his in the trunk...I would have the briefcase, I would slide it under the steering wheel. Johnny Roselli was sitting in the back seat...Charles Nicoletti was sitting in the right front passenger's seat...I opened the door of the Chevrolet...got in...and drove out. As I come out of the parking lot, I made a right hand turn on to Houston street.[19]

Q: Where did you go after that?

A: After that...I went...I don't remember just how many blocks I proceeded ahead...but I went...maybe five, six blocks ahead to a major street. I took a left...went up a few more blocks by the expressway where there was an intersection there...an underpass...they had a gas station there. They had another car waiting there for them. They got out of the vehicle I was in...they walked across the parking lot. I never saw which way they went. I turned from there, made a right...and I headed back out to Mesquite....and I went back to the hotel...pulled into the parking lot...parked my vehicle there...secured it...went to the room that I already had rented...that I'd been in all week....at that point I went in to clean...stripped myself...to shower...I used a hot wax to remove any resin from the skin pores...and when I finished with the details I had to do there...I waited until it was dusk...dark time...then I went out...I removed all the gun cases that had been put back into the car, brought everything into the unit...cleaned those...secured everything.. and later when it was after midnight and there was no activity, I went back out...I pulled the back seat from the car and I put the weapons back in behind the seat where they belonged where we had a compartment for'em...I went back in, went to sleep, waited till daylight....then I drove from there back to the southern part of Illinois...old 66 there...stayed overnight there then drove the rest of the way the next day into Chicago....cause I had been instructed in the beginning, when I went to Texas...not to be driving at night time...not to be pulled over by any police officers, not to speed, and to only travel during daylight hours...that there would be no questions asked. And I had always been good at following orders...and I used the same procedure going home.

Q: How much money were you paid for your participation on November 22, 1963?

A: Well, the money that I received for that job in Dallas...I had never asked for a specified amount, I'd never even asked for any money. I was just honored to do it with Mr. Nicoletti, but I had received $30,000 a short period thereafter....I don't remember....there was two or three weeks went by maybe a month even before I met him one evening...he gave me an envelope. I asked him what's this for...he said this is for down in Texas...He said you did excellent...the only thing he did...he criticized me once, he asked me...when I had left Dealey Plaza that day and got in the car with them...he says don't you think you over reacted and I says what do you mean and he says maybe you shot too fast because I know they didn't want a shot coming from the front...they tried to put everything from the back side. I told them at that point....I said it was my last chance for the option. I said if I didn't fire at that point...I couldn't fire without endangering Jackie.

Q: Jimmy, in Joe West's notes and in Don Ervin's interview notes with you and in what you told me before you told me you received $15,000....

A: $15,000....

Q: You just said thirty...

A: I just said thirty.

Q: How much did you receive?

A: All total...it was thirty.

Q: Are you telling me the truth?

A: I'm telling you the truth...I got $30,000 on the first part. I cut it in half from the beginning at fifteen because it was an awful lot of money back then and I didn't really think it would matter that much and I didn't never really plan to tell what money I got until I talked to Joe on that but the total figure was thirty.

Q: O.K. I just wanted to clarify it.

A: I'm clarifying everything now. We've been playing straight ball ever since...

Q: That's the only difference you've ever told me, right there....

A: Well, in the beginning I said 15 because I didn't think it mattered that much what the amount was...but since we've been playing square ball with everything else and I've given you everything that I have...I'm not going to go back on that part...I'm just going to give you the actual figure and that's what it was and I never received no more and no less...The next money I received after that was for something else that we had done. But like I say, as far as I know, the money I received was for Dallas...when he gave me that envelope because I never took checks, he gave me cash, and I usually got money every other week from him...just for local work around town.

Q: When did you first meet Lee Harvey Oswald?

A: I first met Lee Harvey Oswald in...God...it was back in early '63...we were running weapons down to....I believe it was '63...we were running guns down there when I first met him and I met him through David Atlee Phillips. Lee Harvey Oswald and I had never been friends at that point or anything. We became more friends that week in Dallas together. But I had met him down there in New Orleans[20] and outside of New Orleans in a little town and I believe it was called Clinton[21] down there, cause I had been taking down some semi-automatic, .45 calibre burp guns they were made by...I believe Knoxville Arms at that time.

Q: Am I to understand that Lee Harvey Oswald was working for the CIA?

A: Lee Harvey Oswald had the same control agent...the same controller that I had, David Atlee Phillips...cause David Atlee Phillips introduced me to him.[22]

Q: And so that means that you have worked for the CIA also...?

A: I had involvement with the CIA...yes.

Q: Can you talk about any of that?

A: I don't wish to touch base with the CIA and I think that some of the people that you have dealt with...you have recently found...confirming proof of what I have told you through their knowledge and what they found out about the CIA but I don't want to touch base or get back into the state of operations because it doesn't pertain to a lot of this other stuff.

Q: Did the CIA have anything to do with what happened in Dallas in 1963?[23]

A: The CIA...someone in government organizations...had a heavy hand in it because they supplied Secret Service identification for different people...I don't know who used it but I saw the identification that day....that morning at the assassination. David Atlee Phillips had given me the Remington Fireball at that time back then...but not specifically for Kennedy. He had given me that weapon and it had been used prior to the assassination of John F. Kennedy when we had did some other work. I had used it...I believe that was the third time for Kennedy...would have been the third one...and whether it was used a few times since then. But at that point, I know a lot of people that see...knew Kennedy was going to be assassinated but whether they had planned it or ordered it or not, I have no idea who ordered his assassination.

Q: When you were in Dealey Plaza, did you see any other people there that you recognize that may have been involved with the mob or either with the CIA?

A: Yes, I did. I saw Frank Sturgis[24]

...and at one point I'm going to say he was probably no more than 40, 50 feet away. Again later when I looked at him I was farther from the yard I was about 40 yards from him...maybe 35 yards away. I scanned the crowd....I saw him...he was still there at the time of the assassination and I was looking at him through a 3X scope also. I scanned the crowd to see if he was still there and he was there.

Q: Did you see anybody else there you recognized?

A: Yes, I did. Eugene Brading, he was there...James Braden some people referred to him as but I knew him as Eugene Brading.

Q: Why was he there?

A: That I have no idea. I never talked to the man there...never discussed anything with the man. But I know that he had been there with Johnny Roselli and with Charles Nicoletti...because he was at the Dallas Cabana[25] that morning...and he had been out front talking to Johnny Roselli when I pulled up in the Chevrolet.

Q: Why was Sturgis there?

A: I have no idea. I never discussed anything with Sturgis but I knew him very well and I know it was him.

Q: Did you ever see Sturgis with Nicoletti or Roselli or was he involved in planning in any way or anything?

A: As far as I know Frank Sturgis had no involvement in the planning and I had never saw him speak with Mr. Nicoletti or Johnny Roselli that morning although Sturgis did know John Roselli but they wasn't together that morning to my knowledge.

Q: Did you know that Lee Harvey Oswald was on the 6th floor, Jimmy?

A: I did not know that Lee Harvey Oswald was on the 6th floor of the Book Depository that morning. I wasn't even sure he was in the building or anywhere around because I had not seen Lee Harvey Oswald that day.

Q: Did Nicoletti or Roselli ever tell you that Oswald was part of the hit?

A: Chuck told me that Lee Harvey Oswald was going to show me around the area down there and that's why he...someone[26] had got a hold of Lee Harvey Oswald and told him where I was at the Mesquite hotel over there in Mesquite and he had showed up the second day I was in town. But like I say, Lee Harvey Oswald and I had never discussed anything about the assassination...even though I assume we both knew what was happening but we never discussed it....

Q: Is there anything you can tell me about the death of Officer J.D. Tippit?

A: I do not wish to touch base on that. I have no comment on that.

Q: Do you know who killed him?

A: Yes, I do.[27]

Q: Is the man still alive?

A: The man that killed J.D. Tippit is still alive. He was alive as of three years ago. I haven't talked to him in the past three years. Lee Harvey Oswald did not kill J.D. Tippit.[28] Because the man that killed a police officer that afternoon had come by my motel and told me...he said that things got messed up today he said and I killed a cop...and my remarks to that was well you did what you had to do and he left shortly thereafter.

Q: So then there was one other person that was part of the team other than you, Nicoletti and Roselli?

A: The person that I am referring to now was not a part of the team to assassinate JFK...as far as I know his job would have been to kill Lee Harvey Oswald from what I understood without asking any direct questions because I did not want to know what anyone else was doing. All I wanted to know was what my assignment was, what I was to do, and the least I know about other people, the better off I am because I didn't want very many people knowing who I was or what I'm doing.

Q: Would you have known who would have given him orders to kill Officer Tippit?

A: No, I would not because that contract would have come from a different source.

Q: Did you see Jack Ruby[29] in that plaza that day?

A: Yes, Jack Ruby was in the plaza that day.

Q: Where was he?

A: At one point he was standing on the same side with his back to me from the grassy knoll, down close to the sidewalk. But I didn't watch other people in the plaza that day, I scanned the crowd, I just seen a few faces...but I solely concentrated...the few moments that I had the weapon out looking through the scope, I was concentrating on the primary target. When that was over with I wasn't looking behind me to see who was coming or who was running. I remember that when the shots were fired and it was all over....nobody...nobody responded immediately...I don't care how fast they say the police acted, people were stopped...they were stunned...including the police officers. The police officers on the motorcycles, it took them, I'm going to say maybe ten seconds before they even responded to what was happening.[30]

It was like everybody was waiting for someone to tell them what to do. And at that point I started to walk away. There had been a couple of people in the vicinity that I was in...I'm going to say probably 15 yards in front of me...close to the edge of the fence where I was at...and I was about 15 feet from the end of it...as I was walking away the police was running up the grassy knoll and other people and I know that these two men were turning people back. Who they were, I don't know...I didn't bother to turn and look back...I kept walking away.

Q: Did you notice a man dressed in a suit and tie, and I believe he had a hat on, with a camera standing up on the pergola?

A: No. I did not notice him.

Q: I'm talking about Abraham Zapruder.[31]

A: I did not notice him. I was still walking...but if I would have seen someone making my picture at that point I don't honestly know what my reaction would have been...I know that after I had put the Fireball away, I know I had a Colt 45 inside my pocket on the left side of me...my briefcase was in right hand and I was prepared to shoot my way out of there if it came down to that....

Q: There was a picture made of you behind the fence. It was taken by Mary Moorman from across the street, you probably couldn't see her....does that surprise you?

A: Yes, it surprises me because I really figured that everyone who would have cameras would have been pointed at the motorcade because when I pulled my weapon from the briefcase...at that point...there's nobody standing down there looking at me or looking up at the knoll...everybody is waiting for the motorcade to make the turn to come down through there...everyone's excited...and the uproar and the people murmuring, the noise is louder at this point...and like I say there is no one looking behind them. Even the security and the police officers that are situated through the crowd, there's nobody looking at areas, there is nobody looking at rooftops, there is nobody looking at windows that I could see, everybody is concentrating strictly on the motorcade.

Q: I have a picture of you standing behind the fence, will you autograph it for me someday?[32]

A: Someday...but not now.

Q: What type of shell was in that Fireball that you fired...and could you tell me about the Fireball?[33]

A: The Fireball was designed basically in early '61...manufactured and produced...a few production models came out in '61 and '62...but the barrel was too thin and they kept exploding on us...and finally they got the barrel re-done, rebored to heavier...the material...and originally it went from a .221 to a .222 calibre which is nothing but a .22 shell over exaggerated and expanded for higher velocity...what it fired was a .221 and its called the XP-100 Fireball but it took a .222 casing. Its a single shot, bolt action pistol...scope mounted on it. It's a pistol that was actually way ahead of its time. If you was to see one, I don't know if they're going to show you a picture of one or not, but it is a very beautiful handgun and one of the most elite pistols I believe ever manufactured...although a lot of your people like .44 magnums and everything else.....and 357s....at this point I prefer a smaller calibre for something like that because at 100 yards the gun is very effective. 'Cause most people take a pistol to be only good for 30-40 feet and something you would use in a room but a Remington Fireball is more of a modified cutdown rifle.

Q: It shoots a regular shell...?

A: .222, it's a lot longer than your average .22 round that you put into a .22 rifle...and it's a special casing and you can not fire this through a .22 rifle...through a .22 calibre.

Q: .Now correct me if I'm wrong...the Remington Fireball XP-100 will fire both .221s and .222s?

A: Yes, they will...

Q: It takes some sort of modification though to fire a .222, what exactly does it take?

A: The barrel had to be reinforced...if you didn't have the barrel reinforced the barrel would....could possibly blow up in your face...

Q: Did you shoot a regular shell in it or was it some sort of loaded or modified shell...?

A: I shot a .222 with a mercury load in it.[34] We used a mercury load...the .222 was designed to fragmentate...but what a lot of people didn't realize at that time because the gun was still an early production model and didn't go on sale to the public until 1963...but the .222 had a habit...it would ricochet if it didn't get a direct hit...and we couldn't afford for something to ricochet...so that was why I...a friend of mine had made special rounds for me at that time and I had taken six rounds with me down there...whoever you hit at...if you've got any type of bone structure, the round would fragmentate and explode and the round would be traveling at approximately about 3100 feet per second...which meant you would get penetration and explosion...but without the mercury load and I did not get a direct hit...there is a strong possibility it would ricochet and I would not have time to reload and fire a second shot.

Q: Who gave you the orders to shoot JFK?

A: Charles Nicoletti...that morning at 10:30...and we didn't know if I was going to shoot then or not...I was only in there as back up in case something went wrong or they missed.

Q: Do you know where Mr. Nicoletti got his orders?

A: He got his orders from Sam Giancana.

Q: Would you have any idea where Mr. Giancana got his orders or if he even got an order?

A: I would have no knowledge of that whatsoever...

Q: Would Tony Accardo have been involved?

A: If Sam Giancana handed something out...I would say yes that Mr. Tony Accardo had to be involved...

Q: Would any of the other families have been involved or do you have any way of knowing?

A: I have no way of knowing...but I don't believe this is something that Mr. Giancana would engineer on his own...word had to come from somebody...who approached those people....I have no knowledge...I can only go back to the point of Mr. Nicoletti, Johnny Roselli and myself at that point...and Lee Harvey Oswald and his part...showing me around the area...letting me know the major roads there and where I can go out and test fire a weapon...[35]

Q: Has anybody paid you any money for this interview, Jimmy?

A: Nobody has paid me any money for this interview and I have asked for nothing.

Q: Why are you telling all of this, why are you coming forth with this after 30 years?

A: In the beginning of this, Mr. Joe West had got a lead on me and came to me...first he wrote me a letter...I denied any knowledge of it...told him he had me mistaken with someone else...and they had been calling the institution..the councilor came one day while I was on visit and wanted me to call somebody on the phone...I told him I'm here 365 days a year, don't bother me while I am on my visit, they can talk to me some other time or you can talk to me anytime you want to because I'm locked up here. The following day they come got me out of my cell and said they wanted me to call Mr. West. At that point I called Mr. West and I told him at that time, I said Mr. West you have approximately three minutes to convince me why I should even talk to you.

Q: That's exactly what you said....

A: And those are my exact words...

Q: I heard the tape...

A: Mr. West started talking to me on the phone and he started touching personal points and the phone calls in the prison are all recorded and I told him whoa, stop Mr. West if you wish to see me or talk to me...come see me, I don't want to talk on the phone no more. Mr. West immediately therefore came to visit me. The first day him and I sit and we talked basically about weather...sports...about a lot of other things because I refused to discuss the Kennedy assassination with him. He came back the second day...I felt more comfortable with him and he explained to me that he was getting the case reopened and that he was taking it back to trial that he wanted JFK's body exhumed....he had the petition for exhuming the body[36]...he wanted to have me subpoenaed to testify in court if he could get the trial...the case reopened. At this point, I told him I said...if he could get me immunity...I said I can't talk about it for the simple reason I would be facing criminal charges. He told me that he had an excellent attorney and what they would do...they would try to proceed to get me immunity so that I could come forth and talk if I was subpoenaed. At that point we sit and we talked for awhile and finally I agreed that I would testify and come forward if they got me the immunity. Things didn't go accordingly as planned...I don't know how to say a lot of it...but the government went around the proper parties and they came to visit me and we had a situation that I don't want to touch base on at this time....my life has already been threatened over this whole mess...I'm giving this tape right now and I don't want to be identified at this time but I'm not coming forward for any patriotic causes but I'm coming forward only because of Mr. Joe West himself.

Q: Who has threatened you, Jimmy?

A: I have been threatened by both organized crime and by the government.

Q: Can you identify the people in the government who threatened you?

A: I wouldn't do that because I have never given up anyone in my life and I won't start now. If they wish to kill me then I have to accept the fate that comes with it. I will not finger point anyone or anything like that at this time.

Q: Has the FBI been here to visit you?

A: Yes, the FBI was here to visit me. The FBI has tried to discredit me on a lot of things but people that you have conversed with that has things...that I have given you information....not to put anybody in prison....I've given you information on special operations that was carried out by the government that no one could have possibly have known about...outside the agency itself and I believe that you have corroborated my story on several different aspects.[37]

Q: Do you know anything about the death of David Ferrie?

A: Yes, I do but at this time I do not wish to discuss that....when we start talking about people dying. we're talking about murder and we're talking about a crime that has no statute of limitations on it. And as long as I have no immunity, there is not much that I can say about David Ferrie or a couple of other parties that I have been asked about....

Q: Well then, obviously you know who killed David Ferrie?

A: Obviously, yes I do know who killed David Ferrie. He died of a severial brain hemorrhage but the severial brain hemorrhage was brought on in a specific way and if they was to examine they would find out...and I have already stated at one point....where the tear in the tissue became in the severial brain hemorrhage and I am waiting for someone to confirm that.

Q: What's your really inner feelings about all this, Jimmy...as a person...as a human being?

A: As a person...as a human being...I just want everybody to forget about me...put it all behind me...I'm sorry anybody ever caught up with me or find out who I was or that what my involvement was.

Q: Why did you open up to Joe West?

A: Joe West is the type of person...you have to meet him and talk with him to really understand the man....but he's somebody that...just somebody that you like and you respect and you're willing to do what you can to help him. I've given Mr. West more than I've ever given anyone else in my life...and why?...I don't really understand except he's just that type of person...he has a magnetism about him...Joe West is a great man. I knew him a short time but the time that I've known him I felt like I knew him all my life. There was only two other men in my life that I really treasured or valued.....one was Mr. Nicoletti and the other man is still alive and I can't use his name...he's in his eighties...but he's a wonderful man and I would do anything either one of those men ever asked me to do...and when I say anything, I mean anything and everything.

Q: Do you have any remorse about what happened in Dallas in November of '63?

A: It's hard to have remorse for something that has been done...for so long ago...and at that time everyone felt was right. And if I didn't like someone...how could I have remorse for someone I didn't like?

Q: So you felt personally that Mr. Kennedy should have been taken out?

A: Oh, I felt that all along. But my reasons was specifically because of the Bay of Pigs. Me and a lot of other Cubans felt that way....because we felt betrayed.

Q: By John Kennedy...?

A: By John F. Kennedy. We had airborne waiting to go in...we had battle wagons ready...and they go no support whatsoever....they got slaughtered....they went to prison...they were captured, they were killed, they were punished...tortured....that's because Mr. Kennedy wouldn't......the President..... wouldn't give his word to go. And all he had to do was give the authorization....the Cuban deal was all over with....it was ours...but he took it from us....he had the power to say yes or no and he said no....he vetoed it.

Q: Did you ever know a man named Richard Helms?[38]

A: Yes, I did....Deputy Director of the CIA.

Q: Did you ever know a man named Allen Dulles?

A: I know who he is but I never met him personally.

Q: Did you ever know a man named Antonio Veciana?

A: Yes, I did. I consider him to be a good friend of mine. And to my knowledge, Antonio Veciana was not involved in the assassination of JFK...whether he had knowledge or not, I do not know....but I know he was heavily involved with the CIA in many of their operations....certain groups....from the old Whitehand all the way through Alpha 66...to different groups we had.

Q: Was Mr. Helms involved?

A: Mr. Helms knew about the organizations but Mr. Helms gave me no directions direct from that. All my directives came from David Atlee Phillips because David Atlee Phillips was my controller.

Q: I understand that this is a serious question and I know you have already answered it once, but I just want to try and say it again...do you have any knowledge at all of the CIA participating in the hit on Kennedy?

A: The CIA never once told me that they were going to kill Kennedy...I never heard it from David Atlee Phillips or from anyone else.

Q: Do you know how Charles Nicoletti got to Dallas?

A: I do not know how Charles Nicoletti got there except for flying on commercial airlines. Johnny Roselli flew in I know...specifically...on a MATS airline because he told me.[39]

Q: On what kind of airline?

A: MATS....Military Air Service.....MATS is Military Air Transport Service is what it stands for...we call it MATS.

Q: Could you give me a full sentence on that?

A: Johnny Roselli...the morning we were going to Ft. Worth....he told me he was in Washington...said I was in Washington yesterday, I got lucky...I said what do you mean lucky...he said I caught a MATS flight out....for people who don't understand MATS...that's Military Air Transport Service....it was a military flight and allegedly...like I say...I don't know who flew the plane, Johnny told me he was on it, but he said he was being flown in by the CIA....he said they flew him there...basically that's all I know of...and whether they had a flight going there or not...I don't know what that flight was all about, I never had knowledge and I never ask people what they're doing or where they've been or any questions. I've always lived my life believing in silence, I have believed in not knowing what the other man is doing. If you're doing something wrong, don't come tell me what you're doing in case you have a problem later.....and I live that way here in prison...I have prisoners come up and tell me we've got this coming and we've got that coming I tell'em man I don't want no part of it, I don't want to know what you're doing, don't tell me cause if you get snitched off I don't want you thinking that's it's me.

Q: Tell me in your own words about the package that Mr. Nicoletti gave you after the assassination.

A: After many, many years...several years...we started having a small problem...things were arising...we had the Senate Intelligence Committee was calling people back....the Warren Commission...everybody had been involved in a lot of things....we were getting a lot of static...and at this point, I kept myself totally obsolete, local, out of the highlight, the spotlight...the only two people that knew I was in Dealey Plaza that day for sure was Johnny Roselli and Charles Nicoletti.

Q: Why do you think that is?

A: Well, we never went around telling people what we'd done....if we went out and we did something or we popped somebody or made a hit on them or whatever you want to call it...we didn't go sit around the tavern and brag about it or we didn't go down to the local restaurant and talk about what we had done...

Q: So, as far as Sam Giancana knew....Charles Nicoletti was the man who did the shooting?

A: That's all he knew. He knew that he was there and whether he knew that Johnny Roselli was there or not, I don't know but I would say yes that he knew Johnny Roselli was there....As far as I know the only thing that Sam Giancana knew for Dealey Plaza that day was the part of Charles Nicoletti and Johnny Roselli because Sam Giancana had never discussed it with me...only Charles Nicoletti and Johnny Roselli and I admit to that point...because we kept a very tight circle and we always thought that the less people know the better off we are...the safer we are....As the years went by, Sam got killed in June, I believe, in 1975, Sam Giancana...he was killed at his home in '75....Charles Nicoletti, excuse me....John Roselli was next....he was killed, I believe, I don't remember the exact date but I know it was September, I believe of '76...and Charles Nicoletti...I'd remember that date because him and I were very, very close and he wasn't supposed to go out that night unless I was with him.....but he was killed at a restaurant in the west suburbs of Chicago at a place called the Golden Horns....and he was executed there that night and that was on March 29th of 1977.

Q: Do you know anything about what happened to those three men or who might have done them in, Jimmy?

A: Well, on who killed those men, I do not know who the actual man was that killed Johnny Roselli or Charles Nicoletti but the night that Sam Giancana was killed, I know that Johnny Roselli was in town that night and I know that him and Sam Giancana was very close and I figure he was probably the only one that could get into his house that time of the morning...that Sam would let him in....but to say he specifically killed him, I can't say that because I don't really know...it was never admitted to me but I know that Johnny left and went back to Miami...but anyway after Sam was dead....Johnny was dead...I didn't know who killed Charles Nicoletti...if I had of known I would have went after them myself so that knowledge never became known to me. Right before Chuck was killed...we knew that there was a problem...and I had been riding constantly with him and staying in his companionship...more or less as his bodyguard...watching...on anyone that we went to meet....I would usually carry two 45s with me....I'd keep a windbreaker across my lap with each gun laying in my lap with a hand on each one. We had been very, very careful. Approximately, two weeks before his death, he had given me a package and told me put this away and keep it...someday you might need this...there may be people looking for it....he said do not let this fall into the wrong hands. Well, I took the package ...wrapped it in cheesecloth and put some plastic around it and put it in a little metal box and I went out and I had buried it...put it where no one would find it. I had left it there. After his execution and he was killed....on March 29 of '77...I'm gonna estimate that its probably between a week and a half to two and half weeks right there after...I don't know the exact date....that I was leaving one of our local clubs where we had card games going...and making book and everything...and it was shortly past midnight I guess one o'clock in the morning...as I walked out I was abducted...I was gassed...thrown into a vehicle and taken away....I had been interrogated for roughly...I dunno.... a day, a day and a half, whatever it was....two days even...I'm not even sure how long they had me at that point because when I come out of it, I was in pretty bad shape....but I had went through a very rough interrogation and I knew it wasn't the outfit that did it because if there was any doubt there they would have killed me so I figure that it had to be a government agency that picked me up...and they wanted the notes, and the books and the diary of Charles Nicoletti and I never gave it to them. I was thrown from a car, I was stripped, my legs and hands still bound behind me and I was picked up at one of the suburban towns just west of Chicago[40] and the police recovered me and took me in and my family was notified and they wanted to take me to the hospital and I didn't want to go to the hospital.....I went home and I had my right hand man come over at that point and stay like at the house with me cause I couldn't even get up and walk to the bathroom...he had to pick me up and carry me anywhere I went...that's how bad a shape I was in....at this point my wife had already thought that I was dead...so had everybody else in town when I had been picked up and carried away that way...as soon as I was able....I got up and made sure I wasn't followed or watched by anyone and I went and I dug the package up....In the package that was there...there was identification for Secret Service in that package...there was his personal diary that he had made a lot of notes on....things...that people had been killed over the years....and there was also the map that Johnny Roselli and I had received that morning in Ft. Worth from the man that was supposed to be Jack Ruby when we headed over there....and he had gotten that package...that map was there....and I destroyed that at that time because I knew then that somebody was really after it and wanted it.

Q: But you kept Nicoletti's diary?

A: Yes, I've still got that.

Q: Can you tell me anything about its contents at this point?

A: No, I won't get into that because we're getting involved in organized crime and I will not do anything to hurt anybody, anywhere in that branch. This way the only thing I'm saying here is Charles Nicoletti is now dead....so is Johnny Roselli and Sam Giancana. I can cause them no harm. But I will never, ever put a man in prison. I will not give anyone up right now for my own freedom....And that's how I stand and that is how I will live by it and I will die by that standard.

Q: Jimmy. you've lived around death and crime all your life...how do you feel about death?

A: How do I feel about death? To me....it's just another new adventure....Don't get me wrong, I'm in no hurry to die...when the time comes though...I will accept it. And I've looked at death several times in my life. I've had people from the outfit...the police officers....put guns to my head and threaten to kill me and I've looked them in the eye and told them...shoot...and a couple of them I've told them they didn't have the balls to shoot. A couple of the local cops, they come to my home one night and surrounded my house and took me out...after working me over severely in the front yard...took me down to the railroad tracks before they took me to the station house...took me to the railroad tracks...driven me out of the squad car, handcuffed, put a gun to my head...and told me you piece of shit...we're not taking you in we're gonna kill you and I told them you ain't got the balls to do it.

Q: Obviously they didn't....

A: And they didn't...they took me on in...my wife was waiting at the precinct station...the lawyers were there...and I was released approximately 45 minutes later

Q: Jimmy, is there anything else that you want to say from your heart about what has occurred in your life or particularly about November of 1963...is there anything you want to add or you want to say...personal?

A: No. I've lived a good life...did a lot of things...more then probably any hundred men has.....But I've lived my life and I can't look back and say well I would change this or I would change that because I wouldn't.

Q: When people see this interview on television, what do you think people will think?

A: Most of them...I don't think they'll believe me.

Q: How do we know it's true, Jimmy?

A: There's no way to really prove it except like I say some of the people you have corroborated a lot of the things I've told you...you've had people corroborate it...and everything I've told you so far it's been there and can be backed up and checked in the files from the CIA to the FBI...and I want to clarify one thing.....I've given you nothing on organized crime...on anything they've ever done....and I will never do that....and I am not a member of organized crime....I have never been a member...but I've had a lot of close associates with organized crime.

Q: Where were you born, Jimmy?

A: I was born January, 1942, Alabama....[41]

Q: You're a southern boy?

A: Southern boy....but I was taken from there at a very early age and I grew up as a child on the streets of Chicago.....and I love Chicago. I grew up in an all Italian community. When we first moved in, I was the only kid on the block that couldn't speak Italian...everybody spoke Italian...hardly anybody spoke English. But I ran with them....we finally started communicating...I would live in their homes with them eating stuff that I'd never even seen or heard of and they would come to my house and eat things that they'd never heard of...such things as black-eyed peas, cornbread, biscuits, red-eye gravy and things like that....I loved the pizza, I loved the pasta, the meatballs and everything...I thought it was great...so it was something that we shared and we all got along good...in the beginning we didn't get along but...after they beat up a few times and found out that I couldn't be discouraged and I kept running back to them.....we finally got to all be good friends and we grew up together. As a child, as a kid, I don't think I was probably anymore then 10 or 11 years old, I remember on Saturday mornings I would be sitting out in front of the deli and one of the all time gangsters used to come along....Guy Cerone...great man...come up in this big old black Cadillac....and me and my little Italian friend...we'd be out there...we'd be shining the hubcaps on his car and wiping it down with our big towels and he'd come out and he'd usually throw us a five dollar bill...back then that was a lot of money....and we thought we was really somebody just because we knew those people...and as we grew up then we started getting into more trouble our own self.

Q: Is that how you, more or less, got involved in working with them?

A: That's how more or less people knew that when I got caught I didn't tell on nobody...and I had a good name for being standup around town even early as a kid growing up as a teenager....wild...driving fast cars, riding motorcycles...had my first car when I think I was just turning fourteen.

Q: Did Charles Nicoletti know your background in warfare and in shooting and in murders?

A: Yes, he did. Charles Nicoletti knew of my background...he watched me around town....as time passed by...running around all the cars and stuff....he knew I'd been into the service...he knew I was familiar with weapons...And I came back from Laos, I did 90 days in the hospital being evaluated....and the day I walked out of there I was recruited...by....David Atlee Phillips showed up that day as I walked out of the hospital...my first assignment with the agency was after I had been shooting in Laos and made my mark there...they felt that I could be of use to the agency at that point....and I was training some Cubans at that time...that's when I first got involved with Chianos Bay, the Bay of Pigs....and after all that blew up and went down and everybody got their face dirty and the CIA got dirty in the Bay of Pigs and things...I was home for awhile and I started racing stock cars....Mr. Nicoletti took a shine to me and watched me race cars and he knew I was up and coming and he knew my involvement with weapons but he wasn't concerned about my weapons in the beginning...he was only concerned about with my driving ability. I admired him and to me he walked on water. I gotta tell you I loved the man...he was one of the two greatest men I ever knew.

Q: What kind of guy was he?

A: He was very well spoken, well mannered, quiet, he didn't swear...there was no profanity in the man....I probably only heard him swear maybe twice in my whole life and that was at the FBI when they had us under surveillance at a couple of different times....He was firm, he was very quiet but he was also very deadly...it's like a rattle snake you might say...without the rattlers...you never knew when he was going to strike....

Q: What kind of guy was Roselli?

A: Roselli was...he was flashy...did a lot of talking...he talked too much...that used to bother me....but he was one of those guys he liked to flash...he flashed some money.....he dressed nice. Mr. Nicoletti dressed nice also but Mr. Nicoletti did not flash in the same style that Johnny Roselli did. It was as much difference as night and day. Johnny was loud....boisterous with everything.

Q: What kind of guy was Sam Giancana?

A: Sam Giancana was a wonderful, loveable old man who was quiet...anybody's grandfather.....I mean he was great but boy if you got him riled up....he was like one of those little terrier bulldogs getting hold of you...he could just tear you up....He was good. I respected him a lot and everything else. Sam Giancana, I didn't work for him, he never gave me no orders, never told me to do anything. The only ones I took orders from was from two people....one was Charles Nicoletti...like I say the other man is still alive and I won't identify him.

Q: What kind of guy was David Atlee Phillips?

A: David Atlee Phillips was a cool character...very good natured...I guess I put him through a lot of paces...I couldn't understand his way of thinking in the beginning...but he used to tell me at that time that he could kill more people with a typewriter than I could kill with a machine gun running around trying to shoot everybody in the world. I couldn't believe that...I couldn't understand it. As time went by and me knowing David Phillips...and starting to listen after he grabbed me and shook me around a couple of times...he got me to pay attention to what he was saying and I got to thinking...I realized the man was right...that there is more to things then running around with a gun....there's your psychological warfare...and what you can do with a piece of paper.....writing a newspaper article confusing people in different countries...even here, I mean...it's just....people believe what they read more or less....especially when it comes down to the newspaper....now that they hear it on TV...they really get into it.

Q: What kind of guy was Lee Harvey Oswald?

A: Lee Harvey Oswald...everybody plays him up to be a nut job and everything else but the man was very intelligent...had a very high I.Q. He was very quiet...self centered...Lee Harvey Oswald was not a boaster, he was not a party man...he didn't run around drinking or ""cabareting" or none of those things....Lee Harvey Oswald led a very close and self secluded life....people lot of times...what they've said about him is totally untrue.

Q: What do you think his part was in that plaza that day, Jimmy?

A: I think his plot was to plant evidence to mislead everybody. I don't believe that Lee Harvey Oswald had any inkling that his life was in any danger whatsoever.

Q: How many shots do you think he fired?

A: Lee Harvey Oswald never fired a shot.[42]

Q: Somebody had to fire from that 6th floor according to the trajectory. Was there anybody else up there with him or do you know?

A: As far as I know there was nobody up there. I did not even know Lee Harvey Oswald was up there. Now when you're standing at a place like that...it's hard to tell where the noise is coming from...you've got echoes...you've got all these people...your sound is being muffled....but at this point, I don't even know Lee Harvey Oswald is in the Texas Book Depository Building there...I have no even knowledge of that at that point....the last time I saw him was the day before.

Q: How do you know he didn't fire a shot?

A: I just don't believe he would. Lee Harvey Oswald...as much as they proclaimed him to be an assassin and a killer...I don't believe he was....Even in the Marine Corp...he had a small scar up above his lip that he got hit with a rifle stock...he took a small scar in there....Lee Harvey Oswald wasn't the type of person to go running around and kill anybody.

Q: Did you ever notice if he was left handed or right handed?

A: I never paid that much attention to it...he never fired a weapon around me. We never sit down....we never wrote any letters together....when he drove....they say he couldn't drive but Lee Harvey Oswald could drive...he didn't have a driver's license maybe but the man could drive...hell, he drove military trucks even....and let's face it....anybody working...anybody that has been working at a...one of America's spy bases...especially like in Japan where he was at....there's no way this country is going to give them a visa to go anywhere near Russia...they photograph every man going in and out of the embassy in Mexico...all your embassies are watched....we watch them they watch us....back then...even today...they've never stopped watching each other. Nobody runs into another embassy without being spotted right away. They're under constant surveillance. And if you had a top secret clearance like Lee Harvey Oswald did, you just don't jump on a plane and fly off to a foreign country especially to a communist country unless somebody engineered it and set it up for you to go to give disinformation. Why Lee Harvey Oswald went to Russia, I'll never know and personally I never asked him when I knew him. They used to have an old saying curiosity killed the cat. All my life, I've never been curious. I've never asked people who they're dealing with or what they've done.

Q: What do you feel about your place in history?

A: I don't even want to be remembered in history.

Q: Why?

A: For what? I'm nobody. I'm nobody special...

Q: You're the man that killed John F. Kennedy....

A: Not necessarily...I hit him in the front...he was shot in the back also...I was just one of the two men....But other figures have been killed.....other political people in other countries have been killed....we've had gangsters killed here in this country...I never chose the people to be killed. Somebody else selected John F. Kennedy to be killed. Whether its a politician to be killed or whether it was a mob figure to be killed...I never chose the figures....somebody else said they was wrong said they did wrong....just followed the orders....to me.... it was like taking out the garbage.

Q: Did you think or have you ever thought about the fact that if you hadn't of fired that shot that Oswald may still be alive or Tippit, or does that matter to you

A: That doesn't matter to me....but I've...as far as that goes...If I hadn't of fired the shot...Kennedy would have been killed anyway....because the last shot from Nicoletti caught him in basically the left side of the skull from the back that pushed the head forward...so basically speaking he would have been killed either way...but I had waited until the last point for fields of fire for me before Jackie Kennedy would become in the line of fire....if I don't take it at this point I'm losing my last chance for field of fire...then I don't fire at all...and then if Nicoletti hadn't of fired and neither one of us fired.... he might have lived...then the job wouldn't have been done.

Q: Can you show me exactly using your finger where your shot hit President Kennedy?

A: Looking at the man would be to his left side for me but if you're sitting in his position then it would be on his right side....and it would have came in through on his head...it would have came in here (touches his right front temple right behind eye) and exited out the back side. And I would measure at that point that 60% of the skull in the back of his head had left upon the impact.[44]

Q: How can you measure that?

A: Well, if you've shot several people in the head....and I was known for head shots....not just on that...but I'm talking about prior to that and in the service....on things I have done....after while you get to know when the back of a skull is gone and approximately how much is missing.

Q: Jimmy, in all your years in the service and all the activities.....

A: My military service wasn't entirely that long but my involvement with government agencies became over extended after a while.

Q: In all of your years in organized crime in participating and around guns, death etc., do you have any idea of how many you have killed?

A: Yes, but I will not say. That has no bearing on it. The only party that we are discussing about death basically at this point is John F. Kennedy. The other people have no bearing on this case and I don't even wish to discuss that.

Q: I'm sorry I asked that....I just.....

A: Like I say...I don't even want to quote that figure. I only have one person to judge me and that's when I die.

Q: Do you believe in God, Jim?

A: Well, whether I say I believe or not, I don't know... I guess I do in a way because every time I've been in trouble, I've looked down and I've said Oh, God help me to get out of this or help me to get this done....so basically...I've caught myself praying to God on several occasions when I needed him. But like I say...I believe there's more to life than just here....I'm not saying I believe in heaven and hell, I'm just saying I believe there's another level of plane for us that we're going to all have to surface on someday.

Q: You told me one time on the phone that the two greatest lies in the world were religion and history...

A: Yep.

Q: Do you want to elaborate on that a second?

A: Well, history has been changed to fornicate to the way that the people have....how do you put it....if you look back and you investigate a lot of our history...you go into find that a lot of our great causes was instigated by the US itself and we covered it up and made it look like we were being infringed upon by our rights on humanitarian purposes and freedom and democracy...and so when you wave that banner...and all my life I've believed in mother, apple pie, the American way of life and freedom and democracy...but things over the years especially in the early 70s started changing my way of thinking a lot on things... because I seen how people were being abused and mistreated and being assassinated only because they knew something....not because they had the wrong politics...that they were trying to endanger this country....Religion has killed more people than all the wars we've ever had....people die every day in the name of religion...they started out that way in the beginning and nothing's ever changed...everybody wants to say that one person's religion is better than the other one...the Irish fighting each other over there and the Moslems, the Serbs, the Croations, you name it...there's always somebody wanting to kill somebody over their religion....over their God...yet they say there's only one God. I don't want to elaborate on the Bible or get into it because that only creates too many other things going and that leads from one product to another product. But I try to stay away from religion and I try to stay away from history as much as possible....the only interest to me of history is if I was going into another country or if I was going to do something...I want to read about them and know about their culture and I want to know what their beliefs were...and I wasn't interested in the beginning of their time...I only wanted to know about the last 10-15-20 years of how their government had been run and what their politics were....that's all I was interested in....and what religion was the strongest religion in that country and how I could deal with that situation...because I could learn more from knowing that country from what everybody thought about it...

Q: Jimmy, if today was November 22, 1963 and you were standing in Dealey Plaza right now, would you kill the President again?

A: If I was under orders or if I had been asked to assist, I would do exactly what I always did....I would follow orders...I never disobeyed an order. As far as John F. Kennedy goes...the President...even though he was the President.....today everybody tells us what a great man he was....back then, and I was there and I was seeing the things that was happening from the Cuban missile crisis to everything else...nobody really liked Kennedy back then that I could find...everybody I talked to didn't like him....like I say I had my own personal reasons for the Bay of Pigs...but yet other people....in the military to the secret service to the FBI...to everybody.....even the people around him...even his own staff...because he was....like I say...I won't get into all his bad habits but as far as I know nobody liked the man yet today they tell us what a great man he was but that's only history and only because he was President of the United States. And nobody likes to admit that we made a mistake....

Q: Did you or any of your friends, Nicoletti or Roselli or anyone know about Marilyn Monroe and John Kennedy?

A: I don't know if they knew or not....I never asked....and again as far as other people involved such as Marilyn Monroe and all those other stories that people have told...when we sit around or when we went somewhere once Mr. Nicoletti and I had done something....that was history...that was yesterday...we never talked about it thereafter....it was never brought up again....that was how he wanted it...with his training...his beliefs.....like I say...I wanted to follow in his foot steps because I believe in this man so much...I worshipped this man....at that time...you talk about God...he was my God back then....he walked on water.

Q: Did Mr. Nicoletti work for the mob and the CIA too on different occasions?

A: Mr. Nicoletti was strictly organized crime. As far as the CIA goes, Johnny Roselli was the liaison between the mob and the CIA and Nicoletti had talked with them a few times but this is what got Nicoletti killed I believe....was the involvement when he started talking with the CIA or the secret service or whoever had talked to him and he was being called back....because I think they killed him the day before he was to appear at the new intelligence committee hearing or whatever it was they had going....because somebody was afraid he was going to talk...and it broke my heart afterwards when somebody told me that Mr. Nicoletti had talked and that he was dirty because I found that hard to believe....and I always felt that if Mr. Nicoletti was dirty and that he had been giving people up...I felt he would have given the diary up...he could have made a deal for his own life and for security and protection but he didn't...he died...we knew that he was in great trouble at the time...I didn't really understand the depth of it because I did not believe that he would give anybody up....now I don't know who killed Mr. Nicoletti...I don't know whether the organized crime family did it or I don't know whether the government killed him...I have no knowledge of who killed him...like I say...if I had known...believe me...I would have been hunting them down and I would have died trying to get the people that got Mr. Nicoletti.

Q: So the US government will kill people?

A: Definitely...the US government will kill people....that's definite, there's no problems there.....there's no questions...he's not the only one they've killed...but like I say...if they killed Nicoletti I don't know for sure...I don't know who killed him....but if I did know, I would have put an all out effort and there's only one thing in my life I have ever feared and that was failure to complete an operation that I had started on...and like I say...when I say I loved Mr. Nicoletti...not as a man and a woman...I loved him as a protege, as a father as a brother or whatever...like I say...he was my God...he walked on water.

Q: When you were walking out of Dealey Plaza from behind that fence, did anybody try to stop you or anybody ask you anything did anybody see your gun, did anybody say anything to you?

A: As I was leaving Dealey Plaza nobody tried to stop me...there was two police officers within probably twenty - twenty-five feet of me that had been stopped by somebody posing as secret service agents...I could hear part of the conversation...I did not look back over my shoulder...I did not run...I did not stand around...I just carried a natural gait and proceeded to exit....just like a business man walking away from lunch.

Bibliography

1. Jacob Cohen, "Yes, Oswald Alone Killed Kennedy," Commentary, June 1992, pp. 32-40.

2. Robert Groden and Harrison Edward Livingstone, High Treason: The Assassination of President Kennedy and the New Evidence of Conspiracy, Berkley Edition, New York: Berkley Books, 1990.

3. Jim Moore, Conspiracy of One, Ft. Worth: The Summit Group, 1991.

4. Mark Lane, Rush to Judgment, Thunder's Mouth Press Edition, New York: Thunder's Mouth Press, 1992.

5. Jim Marrs, *Crossfire: The Plot That Killed Kennedy*, New York: Carroll & Graf Publishers, 1989.

6. Gerald Posner, *Case Closed: Lee Harvey Oswald and the Assassination of JFK*, New York: Random House, 1993.

7. Carl Oglesby, *The JFK Assassination: The Facts and the Theories*, New York: Signet, 1992.

8. Bonar Menninger, *Mortal Error: The Shot That Killed JFK*, New York: St. Martin's Press, 1992.

9. James DiEugenio, *Destiny Betrayed: JFK, Cuba, and the Garrison Case*, New York: Sheridan Square Press, Inc., 1992.

10. Harrison Edward Livingstone, *High Treason 2*, New York: Carroll & Graf Publishers, 1992.

11. Dick Russell, *The Man Who Knew Too Much*, New York: Carroll & Graf Publishers, 1992.

12. G. Robert Blakey and Richard Billings, *Fatal Hour: The Assassination Of President Kennedy by Organized Crime*, Berkley Books Edition, New York: Berkley Books, 1992. Although Blakey and Billings do posit a conspiracy in the assassination, they also provide a lot of misinformation, and they support a number of the WC's claims.

13. J. Gary Shaw, "Posner's Single Bullet Theory or How to Ignore the Facts When You Really Try," *Dateline: Dallas*, Special Edition, November 22, 1993, pp. 15-19.

14. Anthony Summers, *Conspiracy: The Definitive Book on the JFK Assassination*, Updated and Expanded Edition, New York: Paragon House, 1989.

15. Matthew Smith, *JFK: The Second Plot*, Edinburgh, England: Mainstream Publishing Ltd, 1992.

16. Alan J. Weberman and Michael Canfield. *Coup D' Etat in America: The CIA and the Assassination of John F. Kennedy*, Revised Edition, San Francisco, California: Quick American Archives, 1992.

17. Sylvia Meagher, *Accessories After the Fact: The Warren Commission, the Authorities, and the Report*, New York: Bobbs-Merrill, 1967; Vintage Press, 1976.

18. David S. Lifton, *Best Evidence*, Carroll & Graf Edition, New York: Carroll & Graf Publishers, 1988.

19. Jim Garrison, *On the Trail of the Assassins*, Warner Books Edition, New York: Warner Books, Inc., 1988.

20. Roger Craig, *When They Kill A President*, Dallas, Texas: JFK Assassination Information Center, 1971, reprint.

21. Craig Zirbel, *The Texas Connection*, New York: Warner Books, 1992.

22. Larry Ray Harris, "November 22, 1963: The Other Murder," *Dateline: Dallas*, Special Edition, November 22, 1993, pp. 31-34.

23. Bill Sloan, with Jean Hill, *JFK: The Last Dissenting Witness*, Gretna, Louisiana: Pelican Publishing Company, 1992.

24. Tip O'Neill, with William Novak, *Man Of The House: The Life and Political Memoirs of Speaker Tip O'Neill*, New York: St. Martin's Press, 1987.

25. David S. Scheim, *The Mafia Killed President Kennedy*, London, England: Virgin Publishing Ltd, 1992. First published under the title *Contract on America: The Mafia Murder of President John F. Kennedy*, New York: Shapolsky Publishers, 1988. The retitled 1992 edition is a revised and updated version of the 1988 original.

26. Carl Oglesby, *Who Killed JFK?*, Berkeley, California: Odonian Press, 1982.

27. Christopher Scally, *"So Near . . . And Yet So Far": The House Select Committee on Assassinations' Investigation into the Murder of President John F. Kennedy*, Dallas, Texas: JFK Assassination Information Center, April, 1980.

28. John Davis, *Mafia Kingfish: Carlos Marcello and the Assassination of John F. Kennedy*, Signet Edition, New York: Signet, 1989.

29. W. Anthony Marsh, "The Ramsey Report," *Dateline: Dallas*, volume 1, numbers 2 and 3, Summer/Fall 1992, pp. 14-16.

30. Letter to the editor, *Dateline: Dallas*, volume 1, numbers 2 and 3, Summer/Fall 1992. 6.

31. Joseph Forbes, Letter to the editor, *Commentary*, November 1992, pp. 15, 17.

32. Jay David, editor, *The Weight of the Evidence: The Warren Report and Its Critics*, New York: Meredith Press, 1968.

33. Charles Crenshaw, M.D., *JFK: Conspiracy of Silence*, New York: Signet, 1992.

34. Dennis L Breo, "JFK's Death: The Plain Truth From the MDs Who Did the Autopsy," *Journal of the American Medical Association*, Volume 267, May 27, pp. 2794-2803.

35. Harrison Edward Livingstone, "JAMA Article: A Travesty!," *Dateline: Dallas*, volume 1, numbers 2 and 3, Summer/Fall 1992, pp. 1, 29-35.

36. Victor Marchetti and John D. Marks, *The CIA and the Cult of Intelligence*, New York: Alfred A. Knopf, 1974.

37. Douglas Valentine, *The Phoenix Program*, New York: Avon Books, 1990. A disturbing history of a CIA covert action program in which thousands of Vietnamese civilians were killed, tortured, and imprisoned, all without even the semblance of due process of law.

38. Brian Freemantle, *CIA*, New York: Stein and Day, 1983.

39. Jonathan Vankin, *Conspiracies, Cover-ups and Crimes*, New York: Dell Publishing, 1992.

40. Leslie Cockburn, *Out of Control*, London: Bloomsbury Publishing LTD, 1987.

41. James DiEugenio, "Posner in New Orleans: Gerry in Wonderland," *Dateline: Dallas*, Special Edition, November 22, 1993, pp. 19-22. An excellent response to many of Posner's criticisms of Jim Garrison.

42. John M. Newman, *JFK and Vietnam: Deception, Intrigue, and the Struggle for Power*, New York: Warner Books, 1992.

43. Mark Lane, *Plausible Denial: Was the CIA Involved in the Assassination of JFK*, New York: Thunder's Mouth Press, 1991.

44. Thomas C. Reeves, *A Question of Character: A Life of John F. Kennedy*, New York: The Free Press, 1991.

45. Haynes Johnson, *The Bay of Pigs: The Leaders' Story of Brigade 2506*, New York: W. W. Norton & Company, Inc., 1964.

46. Ted C. Sorenson, *Kennedy*, New York: Harper & Row, Publishers, 1965.

47. Mario Lazo, *Dagger in the Heart: American Policy Failures in Cuba*, New York: Funk & Wagnells, 1968.

48. Arthur Schlesinger, Jr., *A Thousand Days: John F. Kennedy in the White House*, Boston: Houghton Mifflin Company, 1965.

49. William Manchester, *One Brief Shining Moment*, Boston, Massachusetts: Little, Brown and Company, 1983.

50. John F. Kennedy, *The Burden and the Glory: The Hopes and Purposes of President Kennedy's Second and Third Years in Office As Revealed in His Public Statements and Addresses*, edited by Allan Nevins, New York: Harper & Row, Publishers, 1964.

51. Edward J. Feulner, "Reading His Lips: How to Tell if Clinton Really Is a New Democrat," *Policy Review*, Winter 1993, pp. 4-8.

52. Jack Kemp, *An American Renaissance: A Strategy for the 1980's*, Falls Church, Virginia: Conservative Press, Inc., 1979.

53. Alicia Esslinger, "Assassination of One," *Dateline: Dallas*, volume 1, numbers 2 and 3, Summer/Fall 1992, pp. 24-25.

54. Daniel Oliver, "A 'Soak the Rich' Policy Is Just Bad Economics," *Human Events*, April 10, 1993, p. 11.

55. J. Gary Shaw, "'Case Closed' or Posner's Pompous and Presumptious Postulations," Dateline: Dallas, November 22, 1993, pp. 10-14.

56. Mark North, Act of Treason: The Role of J. Edgar Hoover in the Assassination of President Kennedy, New York: Carroll & Graf, 1991.

57. Anthony Frewin, Late-Breaking News on Clay Shaw's United Kingdom Contacts, Research Transcript, Dallas, Texas: JFK Assassination Information Center, 1992.

58. Jacob Cohen, Letter to the editor, Commentary, November 1992, pp. 18-21.

59. Josiah Thompson, Six Seconds in Dallas, New York: Bernard Geis Associates, 1967.

60. Michael Kurtz, Crime of the Century, Knoxville, Tennessee: University of Tennessee Press, 1982.

61. Gaeton Fonzi, The Last Investigation, New York: Thunder's Mouth Press, 1993.

62. W. Anthony Marsh, "Circumstantial Evidence of a Head Shot from the Grassy Knoll," June 1993. This paper was delivered at the Third Decade conference held on June 18-20, 1993, and was later posted on CompuServe's JFK Assassination Forum. It is now available in the JFK Debate Library in CompuServe's Politics Forum.

63. Harrison Edward Livingstone, Killing the Truth: Deceit and Deception in the JFK Case, New York: Carroll & Graf Publishers, 1993.

64. Anthony Summers, Official and Confidential: The Secret Life of J. Edgar Hoover, London: Victor Gollancz, 1993.

65. Linda Hunt, Secret Agenda: The United States Government, Nazi Scientists, and Project Paperclip, 1945-1990, New York: St. Martin's Press, 1991.

66. Wallace Milam, "Blakey's 'Linchpin': Dr. Guinn, Neutron Activation Analysis, and the Single-Bullet Theory," Unpublished paper, 1993, copy in my possession.

67. William Manchester, The Death of a President, New York: Harper & Row, Publishers, 1967.

68 Robert J. Groden, The Killing of a President: The Complete Photographic Record of the JFK Assassination, the Conspiracy, and the Cover-Up, New York: Viking Studio Books, 1993.

69. Walt Brown, "November 22, 1963: Origin of Media Apathy," Dateline: Dallas, April 12, 1994, p. 19.

70. Herbert S. Parmet, JFK: The Presidency of John F. Kennedy, New York: Penguin Books, 1984.

71. Henry Hurt, Reasonable Doubt: An Investigation Into the Assassination of John F. Kennedy, New York: Holt, Rinehart, and Winston, 1985.

72. Walt Brown, *The People v. Lee Harvey Oswald*, New York: Carroll & Graf Publishers, 1993.

73. Gerald Ford, with John Stiles, *Portrait of the Assassin*, New York: Simon and Shuster, 1965.

74. Gary Mack, "Review of Case Closed," *CompuServe JFK Assassination Forum file*, downloaded on 28 August 1993.

75. Cyril Wecht, with Mark Curriden and Benjamin Wecht, *Cause of Death*, New York: Dutton, 1993.

76. Harold Weisberg, *Selections from WHITEWASH*, New York, Carroll & Graf Publishers, 1994.

77. Paul Eddy, Hugo Sabogal, and Sara Walden, *The Cocaine Wars*, New York: W. W. Norton & Company, 1988.

78. John Prados, *Presidents' Secret Wars: CIA and Pentagon Covert Operations Since World War II*, New York: William Morrow and Company, Inc., 1986.

79. Alfred McCoy, with Cathleen Read and Leonard Adams, *The Politics of Herion in Southeast Asia*, New York: Harper & Row, 1972.

80. Craig Roberts, *Kill Zone: A Sniper Looks at Dealey Plaza*, Tulsa, Oklahoma: Consolidated Press International, 1994.

81. Connie Kritzberg, *Secrets from the Sixth Floor Window*, Tulsa, Oklahoma: Under Cover Press, 1994.

82. Stuart Kind and Michael Overman, *Science Against Crime*, London: Aldus Books, 1972.

83. Raymond Marcus, *The HSCA, the Zapruder Film, and the Single-Bullet Theory*, 1992.

84. Harold Weisberg, *Never Again: The Government Conspiracy in the JFK Assassination*, New York: Carroll & Graf Publishers/Richard Gallen, 1995.

85. Raymond Marcus, *The Bastard Bullet: A Search for Legitimacy for Commission Exhibit 399*, 1966.

86. Harold Weisberg, *Whitewash II: The FBI-Secret Service Cover-Up*, New York: Dell Publishing, 1967.

87 Richard Trask, *Pictures of the Pain: Photography and the Assassination of President Kennedy*, Danvers, Massachusetts: Yeoman Press, 1994.

APPENDIX A

On January 30, 1995, I interviewed James E. Files in person at Joliet, Illinois - for the fifth time in two years.

In an effort to take Mr. Files to a higher level of investigation in our quest for the truth regarding his knowledge and participation in the assassination of John F. Kennedy, I prepared 17 questions for Mr. Files.

My questions were based on points that remained unanswered by Mr. Files after our extensive research into letters, interviews, phone logs, and phone conversations with Files conducted by the late Joe West, Barry Adelman of dick clark productions, and me since August 17, 1992 and the discovery of Mr. Files by the late Joe West. I also received input on the preparation of these questions from John R. Stockwell, J. Gary Shaw, Frank Weimann, Gary Patrick Hemming, Tosh Plumlee, Peter Dale Scott, Fletcher Prouty and Josiah Thompson.

The questions (in regular type) and Mr. Files' answers and comments (in italics and quotation marks) appear below, verbatim, and are transcribed from my handwritten notes taken during the interview.

1- Jimmy, let me ask you about the "special rounds" that you used in Dallas on November 22, 1963. Did you start with hollow points or were they drilled from a solid bullet? Please describe the method used.

"Wolfman made the rounds. He is dead now. He died after Joe West asked me to bring forth a witness to corroborate my story. He drilled the rounds out of solid bullets. The top was then sealed with wax. I was not present when he made the rounds but I know they were filled with mercury.."

Do you know how Wolfman died, his cause of death?

"No. He died less than a week after I told him I was talking with Joe. I asked him to talk with Joe."

2- You said earlier that "it looked like old home week" in Dallas on November 22, 1963. Were any of the following people there?

Homer Echivarria, I don't know if that name is spelled right or pronounced correctly...

"No."

Aldo Vera Seraphine, also known as Aldo Vera?

"That is a Cuban name....it's difficult for me to talk about people that were there that are still alive..."

Jimmy, these questions are important for our final research while I'm preparing the final script for the TV program, please tell me the truth, I've shot straight with you, you've shot straight with me, I have to know the answers to these questions....Aldo Vera Seraphine...Did you see him there that day in the Plaza?

"Yes, I think he was there."

Lenny Patrick?

"No."

Richard Cain?

"Yes."

Milwaukee Phil Alderisio?

"Some of these people are still alive....yes, he was there."

Antonio Veciana?

"Yes, he was there but he had nothing to do with the assassination of John F. Kennedy. A lot of people were aware he was going to be hit...a lot of people knew..."

Edward Lansdale...of the CIA...?

"No, I didn't see him there."

Charles Harrelson?

"No."

Chauncey Holt?

"Who?"

Chauncey Holt. He says he drove Charles Nicoletti into Dallas during the early morning of 11/22/63. He also says he was one of the infamous "3 tramps."

"No, I don't know him."

Thomas Eli Davis?

"No."

Orlando Bosch?

"He is still alive, I can't talk about anyone who is still alive..."

"Jimmy, I must have these questions answered for my personal research. Please tell me the truth. It is very important. Was Orlando Bosch there?

"Yes."

Herminio Diaz?

"What was the first name?"

Herminio....

"There was a Diaz there. Could his first name have been Tony?"

I don't know. All I have is Herminio.

"Yes, there was a Diaz there."

"Bob, I told you earlier about seeing Eugene Brading there..."

Yes...

"Did I tell you what his purpose for being there was...?"

No.

"Brading had the contact that got Nicoletti and Roselli into the Dal-Tex building..."

Do you know the name of that contact?

"No."

"Bob, did I ever tell you why Chuckie put me behind the fence at the last moment..?"

No, why?

"Johnny Roselli was scared to be a shooter....he was to be a shooter...he was scared...he stayed on the second floor of the Dal-Tex...behind Nicoletti....he didn't shoot....the CIA had called the hit stopped.....Nicoletti said 'Fuck'em ..we go'...I hardly ever heard Mr. Nicoletti cuss but he said 'Fuck'em' that day..

Jimmy, that may explain why the CIA pilot, Tosh Plumlee. told me he was under the impression that their reason for flying in was to abort the hit on the president...and Roselli flew in on that CIA supported plane...

"He (Roselli) got there right on time, too."

Yeah.

"Did the CIA pilot ever admit that his name was Pearson?"

Yes, Jimmy. I knew that his name was Pearson when you identified him. He had already told me that his name was Pearson. That's when I first knew you were telling us the truth about picking up Roselli.

3- Did Nicoletti ever mention anything to you about the Grace Ranch in Arizona? Do you know about the Grace Ranch? Have you ever been there?

"Yes, I knew about the Grace Ranch but I never went there...wasn't that owned by James Licavoli's brother, Peter, the mob guy from Cleveland?"

Yes.

4- Did you ever meet J.D. Tippit, the Dallas police officer?

"No."

Did you know he (Tippit) first tried to join the 82nd Airborne but he was transferred to the 17th Division?

"No."

5- (I placed the picture of Jimmy at age 21 with a man in sunglasses on the table face up) Jimmy, you told me that this man with you was the man that killed J.D. Tippit. What is his name?

"I can't tell you that. You know that. You've asked me that before..."

He's still alive?

"Yes, he's still alive as of three or four years ago..."

6- The "solo" picture of you - at 21 - without your shirt on - where and when was that taken?

"It was taken by Lee Harvey Oswald at the hotel room in Mesquite in 1963."

How did you get the negative?

"I took the whole roll of film."

7- Who sent Oswald to meet you at the motel room in Dallas?

"David Atlee Phillips."

How do you know that?

"I only called two people when I got to Dallas. I had left Chicago the week before...the next day after I got there, I called Mr. Nicoletti and let him know where I was and I called David Atlee Phillips and told him I was in Dallas and where I was...the next day, Oswald showed up to take me around and show me the exit routes. I also went with him to test fire the weapons and aligned the scopes. Mr. Nicoletti did not know Lee Harvey Oswald. It could only have been David Atlee Phillips that sent Oswald to help me. He was Oswald's CIA controller and my controller, too."

8- Did Nicoletti tell you either before or after the assassination that he was headed to New Orleans after the hit?

"No. I dropped him and Roselli off at the car they had waiting and I don't know where they went...I didn't see Mr. Nicoletti until a week or two later when he paid me. The only thing he ever said to me after the assassination....we never talked about a job after it was over...was when I turned right out of the Dal-Tex parking lot...leaving the area...he asked me 'Don't you think that you overreacted by firing the shot when you did?'...I told him that was my only chance to fire or Jackie Kennedy would have been in my field of fire..."

9- Do you know Sgt. Gary Patrick Hemming and from where?

"I worked under him down in Florida...No Name Key...you know I told you about that place...Assassin's Ridge...in the Everglades..."

Sgt. Hemming said he remembered you as being a "young hitter from Chicago that got into trouble down in Mexico and that Frank Sturgis of the CIA had to go down and bail you out" of trouble...

"Yeah, and I'll tell you one thing....he didn't just bail me out of jail...he didn't pay any money.......if you know what I mean..."

10- What other aliases would you have used that would have the same initials...J.F.? You've already told me that you used John Felter or something like that...were there any more J.F. initials that you used?

"I don't recall. I used so many names. To one person I was Jimmy..to another Sam...to another Ted...I made up so many names I got confused sometimes..."

11- Did you know David Ferrie personally? Where did you meet him?

"Yes, I knew him but I wouldn't say he was my friend or anything like that. I met him in Louisiana and again in Florida."

In Louisiana...in Clinton...around Lake Ponchartrain?

"Yes."

Did you ever see a white haired man with him?

"No."

The man's name would have been Clay Shaw or Bertrand...

"No."

12- Did you know Antoinette Giancana was having an affair with Chuck Nicoletti?

"No. He wasn't the only one she was fucking...."

I imagine Sam wasn't too happy about the guys that messed with her..

"No, most died...he didn't mess with Mr. Nicoletti..."

Because he was Sam's right hand man...?

"Yes, he and Sam were close to each other. Chuckie and I used to go up to a pastry shop every Sunday morning and sometimes on Saturday and take pastries to the old man. He loved Mr. Nicoletti."

13- Where was your court martial hearing held?

"Ft. Mead."

You said that your JAG officer was named Howell. Do you recall the JAG officer's rank?

"It was either Howell or Powell. It's been so long ago. I think he was a major..."

14- Do you recall the license plate number of Nicoletti's '63 Chevy?

"No."

15- Did you ever meet or know Loran Hall?

"No."

Kerry Thornley?

"No."

James Jesus Angleton?

"I knew who he was but I never took any orders from him or did any work for him. I know he was respected by the Agency."

Sylvia Odio?

"No."

16- Did you ever drop Charles Nicoletti off at an airport to catch a private or a CIA flight to California or to Nevada?

"Yes, at a small airport named Palwaukee up 45 in Chicagoland and at Half Day, Illinois around Palantine Heights."

17- Did David Atlee Phillips ever use any other CIA codename other than Bishop?

"Yes, but I can't recall what it was...He used several..."

APPENDIX B

The investigation into the confession of James E. Files started on August 17, 1992 and is ongoing.

Since that date, hospital records, traffic court records, jail records, court records, newspapers, U.S. Government files and records have been searched and examined. Hundreds of personal interviews have been conducted.

There is no credible evidence that indicates that James E. Files was not in Dallas, Texas on November 22, 1963.

Several incidents have occurred:

1. A known Mafia lawyer from Chicago - Julius Echeles - was hired to represent James E. Files. Echeles received payment in the form of a cashier's check with a notation "From the Friends of James E. Files." Efforts to ascertain who issued the payments to attorney Echeles have been fruitless.

2. In late May of 1994, Files's lawyer and Files's first wife (and possibly Files's oldest daughter) conspired to create a false story in an effort to derail the investigative efforts of Robert G. Vernon and stop the publication of Files's confession on television. The false story was that Files had a twin brother and that Files allegedly told his first wife that the twin brother was with her during the week of November 22, 1963 and that Files was really in Dallas. Prior to the twin brother story, Vernon had promised Mr. Files that Files's family would not be bothered or questioned about Files's confession or his history. Due to the twin brother story, Vernon contacted Files's family members in Alabama, Illinois and Tennessee. Vernon spoke with Files's aunt - Christine. Files was born in her home in Alabama on January 24, 1942. She verified that Files did not have a twin brother. Vernon confronted Files's oldest daughter with the twin brother story. The daughter said that all she asked was that we leave her father alone for he is all she has. Vernon talked to Ray Files - a step-brother. Ray was aware that James had "fallen in with the wrong crowd." Ray, a minister, also verified that James did not have a twin brother. When confronted with the results of Vernon's investigation into his family and the twin brother story, James E. Files admitted that the twin brother story was concocted by Echeles and his first wife in an effort to derail Vernon's investigation and television program. Files said his first wife was only "doing what she has been told to do."

Files also informed Vernon that he had called his wife and told her to tell the truth to the Grand Jury for he did not want her to perjure herself and face jail.

3. In the summer of 1993, Vernon contacted an Arizona lawyer and told the lawyer that the man who confessed that he fired the fatal last shot into the right front temple of JFK has been located. File's name and location were not supplied to the lawyer. Approximately six weeks later, Vernon and attorney Don Ervin of Houston received a letter from James Files which stated that the Arizona lawyer had contacted the mob and that the mob had sent a visitor to see Files in prison. The purpose of the visit was that the mob was "surprised" that Files was talking. Files was told: "lay down beside your doggy bowl and go to sleep." In late 1994, Vernon learned that the Arizona lawyer had been hired by the Chicago mob and sent to the Joliet prison to visit Files. The Arizona lawyer questioned Files in depth, supposedly to

"verify" his confession on behalf of the mob. It is not known what the lawyer reported to the person(s) who hired him.

4. On May 3, 1993, during Vernon's first visit with Files, Files told Vernon that the CIA was desperately trying to erase all records on Files. A search for Files's birth certificate was negative. There is no trace of a birth certificate on Files or Sutton. Files's aunt told Vernon that Files has had a great degree of difficulty locating any of his past records. Files's aunt also informed Vernon that an Alabama lawyer had found James's birth certificate many years ago. According to the aunt, the birth certificate said "deceased at birth." As of this writing, the birth certificate has not been located despite the efforts of Vernon, Kroll Associates and two investigative journalists. The FBI and CIA have refused to release any records pertaining to Files unless Files gives his notarized permission for them to do so. Attorney Julius Echeles has instructed James Files not to give the notarized permission despite numerous requests by Vernon for Files to do so.

5. On October 11, 1995, Files informed Vernon, via phone, that the United States Marshall's office had placed a "hold" on him and that he may be transferred to the Federal maximum security prison in Golden, Colorado. Mr. Files is incarcerated under Illinois law in a state prison under state jurisdiction.

There is no known reasonable explanation why the Federal authorities would want to "hold" Files and transfer him to a Federal prison other than the fact that Files would be placed on maximum security lockdown 23 hours a day in the Colorado facility with no visitors allowed. At Golden, Files would not be allowed to make any collect phone calls or to send or receive any un-monitored mail.

6. On October 14, 1995, Vernon received a phone call from former CIA/DEA pilot Robert "Tosh" Plumlee. Vernon was able to tape record portions of Plumlee's call for the record. Plumlee told Vernon that he was "pulling no fucking punches..." Plumlee said "I'm getting all kinds of stuff from all kinds of places....IRS....everybody..." Plumlee said that in 1990 (two years before investigator Joe West first located Plumlee) that he and "author Jim Marrs ("CROSSFIRE"), Peter Lemkin and former CIA - Army Intelligence officer Bradley Ayers had a meeting in Solano Beach, California." During the course of the conversation they spoke about the "Mafia infiltration into the JMWAVE headquarters in Miami." Plumlee and Ayers recalled a "kid from Chicago who got into trouble down in Mexico" and that he was involved with the "boat people" and the "raider ship Rex." Plumlee also said they talked about Louisiana and the Hotel Dixie, Morgan City and Lamar (spelling?) Ranch and that the "kid from Chicago" was involved in those operations. Plumlee said that "the meeting was taped" and that Vernon should talk to Peter Lemkin or Jim Marrs about listening to the tape. Plumlee gave Vernon a contact fax number on Lemkin. Plumlee knew that the FBI is trying to discredit Files and that they "passed fake FBI names to him (Files). Plumlee said he has spoken to the FBI and that he is aware of from where the information came on Files. Plumlee told Vernon that the information the FBI had originally received on Files came from a CIA operative that was "in Louisiana" and "around the Hotel Dixie." Plumlee stated that he "thinks the operative's name was Reinaldo" and that Files "came (to Louisiana) on some gun running shit and that's how he (Files) got tied into JMWAVE." Plumlee said "I have told the truth about all of my operations with the U.S. Government to Congress and to the President of the United States and his alphabet people...the IRS, FBI, DEA, NSC, (etc)" and that "it has cost me dearly." Plumlee said that the truth was finally coming out soon about the Thunderbird Inn in Las Vegas and the Grace Ranch and the McCord Ranch. Plumlee expressed his dismay

with people who are "supposed to be researchers" and that they should "get off their ass and quit playing in the middle line....go for the truth and quit setting on the middle of the fence trying to please everybody."

7. On October 18, 1995, Vernon spoke with Tosh Plumlee and with JFK researcher Peter Dale Scott (Professor of English at the University of California) and Jim Marrs - in separate phone discussions. Plumlee stated that the last name of the man he calls "Reinaldo" could have been Martinez but he was not sure and again spoke of "raider ship Rex." Plumlee again stated that this man was the source of information to the FBI on the "prisoner" (James E. Files). According to Plumlee, "Reinaldo" was a CIA operative and involved in "Operation 40" which he described as a "counter-intelligence" operation.

Professor Scott verified that a "Rolando Martinez" was the Captain of the raider ship "Rex" and that Operation 40 was indeed a CIA counter-intelligence operation. Professor Scott informed Vernon that Operation 40 consisted of men who went ashore with the anti-Cuban forces and that they're job was to "take out" the men who gave them problems or could not be trusted. Let it be noted that Files has stated that he was court martialed for taking out "two of his own men" to "save face with the Laotian Army" after which he was "recruited by David Atlee Phillips" for work in the CIA, training anti-Cuban forces. Files is also on the record as saying his government service became "over-extended."

Jim Marrs stated that there were two men named "Reinaldo" involved in the Bay of Pigs, CIA covert operations. One man was Reinaldo Pico, who was a Bay of Pigs "soldier" and a CIA employee, and the other was Reinaldo Gonzales, who was a Cuban banker and avid Anti-Cuban operative who also worked with the CIA covert operatives. Both "Reinaldos" had contact with the JMWAVE operation and anti-Cuban - raider ship Rex - Operation 40 forces.

On October 19, 1995, Vernon spoke again with Professor Peter Dale Scott. Professor Scott informed Vernon that Reinaldo Pico was indeed involved in the Bay of Pigs, was a CIA employee, and was one of the infamous "Watergate Burglars" in association with Frank Sturgis, E. Howard Hunt and others. Professor Scott also informed Vernon that Pico was a former Narcotics Detective who only "made the busts he was told to do by the Mafia." Professor Scott believes Reinaldo was associated with JURE. Scott also informed Vernon that Reinaldo Gonzales was also not only a Cuban banker and anti-Castro supporter, but he was also involved in a 1962 assassination plot to kill Fidel Castro and referred Vernon to the October 29, 1962 issue of U.S. News and World Report.

Our conclusion is FBI agent Zack Shelton - when he informed investigator West about James E. Files and that the FBI had "run and informant in on Files years ago and that the FBI felt that Files knew something about the events in Dallas in 1963" - that agent Shelton was acting on the informant identified by CIA pilot Plumlee as "Reinaldo" and that informant was Reinaldo Pico. We are continuing our investigation on this matter.

Master researcher Michael T. Griffith of the United States Department of Defense has written one of the most compelling manuscripts on the JFK assassination evidence entitled "MORE THAN A REASONABLE DOUBT." The preface of his manuscript follows as an appropriate closing note for this report:

In September 1964, the Warren Commission released its report on the assassination of President John F. Kennedy. The Commission had been tasked by President Lyndon Johnson to investigate the tragic shooting. The Commission's report was met by nearly universal praise and acceptance. Its primary conclusions were that a lone gunman, Lee Harvey Oswald, shot the President, and that no conspiracy of any kind was involved in the murder. It was a freak occurrence of history, we were told, brought about by a supposedly disturbed loner using a cheap, war-surplus, mail-order rifle. There appeared to be little if any reason to doubt the Commission's conclusions, since the case against Oswald seemed indisputable.

However, in the months and years that followed, researchers found numerous errors and contradictions in the Commission's claims. It turned out that the case against Oswald was far from conclusive, and many questions were raised about how the Dallas police and the federal government had handled the evidence. Private researchers interviewed witnesses who had been ignored by the Commission, and in virtually every case their testimony indicated there had been a conspiracy. Then, in 1979 the public's growing doubts about the lone-gunman theory were strengthened when the House Select Committee on Assassinations formally concluded that President Kennedy was "probably assassinated as a result of a conspiracy."

Today, according to public opinion polls, approximately three out of every four Americans believe that Kennedy was killed by a conspiracy. The public's reaction to Oliver Stone's movie JFK, which argues that a high-level government plot killed Kennedy, caused the U.S. Congress to hold hearings on releasing the sealed assassination files. (Although some files have been released, many still remain sealed.)

Why is finding out the whole truth about the assassination of President Kennedy still important? Why does it matter? It matters for a number of reasons. Carl Oglesby has expressed the importance of the death of President Kennedy in three basic statements:

> One, an unknown group conspired to kill JFK.
>
> Two, we, as Americans, cannot feel good about our government again until we satisfy ourselves on this matter.
>
> Three, all of us should feel personally involved with this issue because it reflects so directly upon the quality of our citizenship. (7:13)

We have a right to expect the truth from our government. Yet, certain federal agencies continue to oppose releasing all the sealed assassination files. As a result of legislation passed in 1992, some of those files have been made public, but many are still inaccessible, and some of the documents that have been released have been heavily censored.

Our government still officially maintains the validity of the Warren Commission's infamous single-bullet theory. As Americans, we value the truth. We want to be told the truth. We don't want our government placing its (read: our) seal of approval on a falsehood. I believe it is painfully clear that the single-bullet theory was conceived for the sole purpose of deceiving the public about the true nature of the assassination. Without this theory, the Warren Commission would have had to admit that more than one gunman shot JFK. To this day, the official position of our government is that only Lee Harvey Oswald shot President Kennedy. It is time for this lie to end. It is also time for our government to acknowledge that there is considerable evidence that Oswald didn't fire a single shot during the assassination.

The assassination is important because it concerns the accuracy and credibility of what we teach and accept as history. When we accept false history, we are building on a foundation of sand. Without knowing the truth about the past, how can we learn from it? Only by understanding the whole shocking truth about the death of President Kennedy can we best be prepared to prevent such a tragedy from happening again.

And then there is the matter of justice. As Americans we have a strong sense of justice. We believe the innocent should go free and that the guilty should be punished. But those responsible for the death of President Kennedy have yet to face justice.

Although most of them are probably dead, it is likely that a few of them are still alive and could be brought to justice, if our government would pursue the case properly.

Moreover, we know the identities of several of the individuals who were involved in the cover-up. These persons could be subpoenaed and finally asked tough, probing questions about their disgraceful behaviour--and, if caught lying under oath, could be prosecuted for perjury. Who are these individuals? In my opinion, the list includes former WC counsels Arlen Specter and Wesley Liebeler, the three autopsy doctors, certain active and retired FBI agents and CIA officers, and former Dallas police lieutenant J. C. Day.

This case is by no means closed, and it certainly isn't dead either. In 1992, U.S. Marshal Clint Peoples was killed hours before he was scheduled to meet with an investigator for Oliver Stone. Before he died, Peoples reportedly stated that he had been run off the road (63:498).

A few days earlier, Peoples had told a researcher that he had information about a potential suspect in the case. Shortly before key assassination witness Jean Hill appeared on the nationally broadcast documentary The JFK Conspiracy in mid-1992, she received a threatening phone call. To this day, some witnesses are still afraid to talk for fear of being harmed or harassed.

Every person who lost a son, a daughter, a brother, or a sister in the Vietnam War ought to be intensely interested in learning the whole truth about the assassination. Why? Because if President Kennedy had not been shot, there would have been no Vietnam War. More than 50,000 Americans would still be alive. Many thousands more would not be crippled or emotionally troubled.

These considerations do not seem to have mattered to the defense industrialists and oil tycoons who wanted the war and who made millions of dollars from it. But defense and oil industry elitists were not the only ones who wanted to plunge America into war in Vietnam. The Central Intelligence Agency likewise favored greater U.S. involvement in the conflict. The agency's covert operations division knew that with an escalation of the war would come an increase in their budget and activities. So for these individuals the stakes were huge. By mid-1963, they knew they had a president who was not going to escalate our involvement in Vietnam, and who in fact wanted to disengage from the fighting after the '64 election. There is wide agreement among researchers that President Kennedy's refusal to escalate the conflict in Vietnam was one of the principal reasons he was murdered.

(As a staunch conservative Republican, for years I believed the Vietnam War was justified and necessary, and that we would have easily won it if weak-hearted liberals had not hindered our military. I am still a conservative Republican, but I now realize that the Vietnam War was neither just nor necessary, and that "turning loose" the military would not have guaranteed victory. Even if we had done so and had "won," the resulting "victory" would have been of questionable worth, since the government we were backing was almost as bad and corrupt as the one we were opposing.)

In the view of some researchers, another reason President Kennedy was killed was that he posed a serious threat to certain powerful international bankers who were making millions of dollars off the Federal Reserve System. The Federal Reserve prints our money and then loans it to the government at interest. In effect, we pay to use our own money. Kennedy wanted to end this arrangement. He reasoned that by having our currency issued directly through the U.S. Treasury, the national debt could be reduced by not paying interest to the bankers of the Federal Reserve System. During his final year in office, he took steps toward making this happen. On June 4, 1963, he signed an executive order that called for the issuance of over four billion dollars in U.S. Notes through the Treasury, and some of this money is still in circulation.

In conjunction with this order, he signed a bill changing the backing of one- and two-dollar bills from silver to gold, thus strengthening our weakened U.S. currency.

Even though JFK's executive order is still in effect, no subsequent President has had the courage to enforce it. Today, we continue to pay to use Federal Reserve notes as our currency. International bankers continue to make millions at our expense. And few of us can remember the last time our government had a balanced budget.

Kennedy's monetary reforms, had they been allowed to continue, would have given us a stronger, more stable currency and would have greatly reduced the influence of international bankers on the U.S. economy. These men stood to lose millions of dollars, if not more, if JFK remained in power. As veteran journalist and researcher Jim Marrs says, "Kennedy's . . . efforts to reform the money supply and curtail the Federal Reserve System may have cost him much more than just the enmity of the all-powerful international bankers" (5:275).

In 1963, a powerful, well-financed, and highly placed conspiracy killed President John F. Kennedy and then engaged in a massive cover-up to keep the American people from knowing the truth about the murder.

Many of the same groups and individuals suspected of being involved in President Kennedy's death later surfaced in other serious crimes, including the infamous Phoenix program, Watergate, the Iran-Contra affair, and the BCCI scandal. By all appearances, the forces that killed JFK still wield significant power in our government and media. Most of the names have changed, but the attitudes and goals remain the same.

Thankfully, despite the best efforts of the government and most segments of the media to close the case, interest in President Kennedy's death is strong and growing, as more and more citizens appear to be realizing its relevance and importance.

The question is sometimes asked, How much longer until it will be impossible to reinvestigate President Kennedy's murder? In my opinion, that point will not come for at least another ten to fifteen years. Many important witnesses are still alive. Although some of these people might die in the next few years, most of them should live for at least another decade. Moreover, there are important assassination-related films, photos, and documents that have yet to be properly studied. There could be many vital documents still locked away in government vaults. The films, photos, and documents will remain, but the witnesses will eventually pass away.

We have a right to demand that a new investigation occur soon enough that the remaining witnesses can be carefully and properly interviewed.

Even if our government refuses to reinvestigate the case, we the people can effectively overturn the false story that we have been given about it. This process is already well under way. Opinion polls show that most Americans reject the lone-gunman theory. Private researchers have presented significant evidence of conspiracy. They have picked up where government investigators left off, and have developed new evidence and leads that were previously missed or ignored.

Yet, we as Americans have every right to demand that our government reinvestigate the Kennedy assassination, and to ensure that inquiry, unlike the previous ones, is careful, honest, and thorough. We have every right to expect our government to once and for all renounce the national lie that President Kennedy was killed by an unstable loner using a cheap, war-surplus rifle.

The news industry handling has been almost as inadequate and disappointing as the government's.

For example, several important, ground-breaking books on the assassination were released from 1991 to 1993. These fine works went virtually unnoticed by the press. Yet, when Gerald Posner's severely flawed pro-Warren Commission book Case Closed was released in mid-1993, it received extensive, favorable publicity, and in some cases was even endorsed or recommended by major news outlets. Equally disturbing was the news industry's reaction to Oliver Stone's movie JFK. Although the film certainly has its faults, it is remarkably accurate on many important aspects of the assassination. Nevertheless, uninformed, highly critical stories about it appeared in the press even before it was released. Major newspapers and magazines, including The Washington Post, Time, and Newsweek, strongly condemned the film but ignored the valid and important information it contained. A free society depends on a tenacious press that is dedicated to reporting the facts and to keeping the American people informed. Sadly, however, the sad truth is that for the most part the press has chosen to blindly accept official leaks and pronouncements about the assassination, instead of examining the matter independently. If the press would begin to do its job on the case, a great deal of progress would be made and the government would face irresistible pressure to conduct a new investigation.

Much is already known about the murder of President Kennedy. I think we know the identities and motives of at least some of the main figures who were behind the assassination. Yet, there is still much to be learned--much that needs to be learned about the crime. A special prosecutor or a new Congressional investigation could uncover a great deal of important information about President Kennedy's death. If enough citizens become informed, get involved, and make it clear to their elected representatives that they will settle for nothing less than a new investigation, the case will be officially reopened.

It is my hope that this book will contribute to the growing call for a new federal inquiry into the death of President Kennedy.

MICHAEL T. GRIFFITH is a two-time graduate of the Defense Language Institute in Monterey, California, and of the U.S. Air Force Technical Training School in San Angelo, Texas. He is the author of three books on Mormonism and ancient religious texts. His articles on the JFK assassination have appeared in Dateline: Dallas and in Dallas '63.

Mr. Griffith lives and works in England and is an employee of the United States Department of Defense. He has a top secret security clearance. The views he expresses are his own personal views and are not the views of the United States Department of Defense.

APPENDIX C

John R. Stockwell is a former CIA case officer having served in the agency arena in Vietnam, the Congo and South America. In 1977, after having served as the Chief of the CIA's Angola Task Force, Stockwell left the CIA and was one of the first case officers ever to leave the agency and write about their innerworkings and clandestine operations. His book "IN SEARCH OF ENEMIES" was a Publisher's Weekly bestseller. The CIA sued Stockwell for breech of his secrecy agreement with them when his first book was published. The CIA won the suit and all royalties Stockwell earned from the book went to the CIA.

In 1991, Stockwell released "THE PRAETORIAN GUARD" (South End Press - Boston). On page 123, Stockwell writes:

"A team of CIA, Cuban exile and Mafia related renegades organized a simple military-style ambush in Dallas and successfully gunned him (JFK) down. The ambush and its cover-up were brazen and astonishingly open. In fact, several plots, in Chicago, Miami, and Houston, to kill Kennedy had misfired or been thwarted. The plot that succeeded in Dealey Plaza was so open that various people were reported prior to the event to have said that Kennedy would be killed with a rifle and a patsy would be blamed for the crime. Individuals like Joseph Milteer, the "umbrella man," and a CIA pilot Robert Plumlee went to Dealey Plaza on the 22nd of November to watch."

In the book "DOUBLE CROSS" - written by Sam & Chuck Giancana (Warner Books - 1992) - on Pages 356 & 357, the Giancana's state:

"Most of those who were involved in the 1963 assassination of President John F. Kennedy have been murdered. Some have committed "suicide" or spent their final days in prison, while others still linger behind bars."

There are some men, however, if we are to believe Mooney's (Sam Giancana's) tales of Mafia-CIA counterintelligence activities, who've prospered and remained free. Amassing incredible power from careers deeply rooted in the CIA, these men have reached America's loftiest positions of authority, from which they continue to influence world events."

Text of note found in the storage area of James E. Sutton alias James E. Files in Illinois:

THE MERCENARY

That....be not told of my death

Or made to grieve on account of me

And that I not be buried in consecrated ground

And that no sexton be asked to toll the bell

And that nobody is wished to see my dead body

And that no mourners walk behind me at my funeral

And that no flowers be planted on my grave

And that no man remember me

To this I put my name

Signed,

James E. Sutton/Files

1. Despite efforts by the FBI and Kroll Associates (a large detective agency made up mostly of former FBI and CIA agents) to discredit the military record of James E. Files, the official historian of the 82nd Airborne located the Army Serial Number and VA claim numbers of Mr. Files and verified that he was indeed a member of the 82nd Airborne who was shipped to Laos in 1959.

2. There is extensive evidence that James E. Files was the driver/bodyguard for Charles Nicoletti, as follows:

a. FBI agent Zack Shelton of the Beaumont, Texas FBI office (the man who gave Investigator Joe West the lead on Mr. Files) informed Mr. West that Files was Nicoletti's driver/bodyguard and close associate.

b. Files's aunt and uncle confirmed - on audio tape - that Files introduced them to Nicoletti in Chicago and that Files "did things" with Nicoletti.

c. Michael Cain, younger brother of the deceased known Mafioso Richard Cain, did a background check on Files at the request of Robert G. Vernon. Michael Cain informed Vernon that "Files was Nicoletti's boy."

d. Two of Files's friends from the Harlow Grill area in Chicago informed Vernon that Nicoletti was introduced to them by Files and that Files and Nicoletti were associates.

e. Former CIA and DEA pilot Robert "Tosh" Plumlee had flown Nicoletti on several occasions and gave Vernon information about flights with Nicoletti that only someone associated with Nicoletti could have known about. Vernon "cross-checked" the information with Files and was able to ascertain that Files had dropped Nicoletti off at various airports in the Chicago area to meet Plumlee for flights to Las Vegas and Santa Barbara, California.

3. A nightclub dancer and government informant named Rose Cheramie warned of the assassination before it occurred. She said she did so on the basis of information she had received from individuals in the Mafia. She also said she was told by Mafia men that it was common knowledge in the underworld that President Kennedy was about to be assassinated. Rose Cheramie was later killed in a suspicious car accident on a remote Texas highway.[4]

4. Posner rejects Cheramie's story as spurious (6:446 n). Marrs argues that it is essentially credible (5:401-402). J. Gary Shaw challenges Posner's claims about the Cheramie account point by point (55:12-14). For example, Posner claims there is no evidence that Cheramie worked for Jack Ruby, but Shaw points out that this was verified by the Louisiana State Police (55:13). Contrary to what Posner claims, Cheramie's death was not a cut-and-dried accident; rather, it was another suspicious death (5:402; 55:12-13).

5. Three known CIA operatives who were in Florida during the Bay of Pigs operation have identified James E. Sutton alias James E. Files as being a "young hitter from Chicago who got into trouble in Mexico and Frank Sturgis of the CIA had to go bail him out."

6. <u>The Bay of Pigs</u> (Research by Michael T. Griffith - U.S. Department of Defense)

President Kennedy's handling of the Bay of Pigs invasion continues to draw sharp criticism from conservatives. In their view, JFK simply lost his nerve and consequently caused the death of over 100 freedom fighters and the capture of hundreds more. This is how I used to view the Bay of Pigs debacle. I thought it was all Kennedy's fault, end of discussion. As I saw it, he had chickened out and had done great harm to the cause of freedom. Of course, those who have studied the Bay of Pigs incident know there was much more to it than Kennedy's supposed failure to follow through. Before going further, let us first examine the basic history of the event.

Shortly after taking office, President Kennedy approved a CIA plan to invade Cuba. The plan, which had been formulated toward the end of the Eisenhower administration, called for an invasion of Cuba by a force of Cuban refugees, Brigade 2506, covertly trained and backed by the CIA. The idea was to make it look like the Cuban exiles had carried out the invasion on their own with no outside assistance.

The invasion began on the morning of April 15, 1961, when eight American-supplied B-26 bombers flown by exile pilots departed from an airfield in Nicaragua and attacked Cuban air bases.[7]

7. 21. Some researchers say six planes were used for the first air strike, but such authors as strongly pro-Kennedy Arthur Schlesinger to anti-Kennedy Mario Lazo put the number at eight. [8]

8. 1. Says Haynes Johnson, "Why such a vast majority of all the supplies needed for any success whatsoever was committed to one ship is a question still unanswered by the CIA" (45:113). I agree wholeheartedly with Harrison Livingstone's comments on this matter:

No president is in a position to review an entire plan for each of many operations. He is the Commander in Chief and cannot micromanage every detail. He could not have known that the . . . CIA would be so stupid as to put all the ammunition on one ship which was easily blown up with a few bullets from one small trainer jet plane. (10:43)

9. "...FBI surveillance of Roselli loses his trail on the west coast between November 19 and November 27 (1963)" (ALL AMERICAN MAFIOSO by Charles Rappleye and Ed Becker - Doubleday Books 1991)

10. A key figure linking the Agency to the assassination was CIA man David Atlee Phillips, who was seen with Oswald a few months before the shooting (14:504-519; 61:128-171, 391-400, 408-409. Among many other things, Phillips was the propaganda chief for the Bay of Pigs operation and later rose to become the chief of the CIA's Western Hemisphere Division. In 1954 Phillips worked with E. Howard Hunt and others to overthrow the Arbenz government in Guatemala. Based on his extensive investigation of Phillips for the Church Committee and then for the Select Committee, Gaeton Fonzi believes that "David Atlee Phillips played a key role in the conspiracy to assassinate President Kennedy" (61:409). Phillips was in charge of the CIA's Cuban operations in Mexico City at the time of the assassination, so he was strategically positioned to frame Oswald, and it is very probable that he was involved in the phony Oswald visits to the Cuban embassy. Select Committee investigator Dan Hardway found that most of the individuals in Mexico City and Miami who were spreading post-assassination propaganda linking Oswald to Cuban or Soviet intelligence were "David Phillips's assets" (61:292).

11. Files stated that he stayed at the Lamplighter Motel in Mesquite in a telephone conversation with producer Robert G. Vernon. The Lamplighter Motel in Mesquite was opened in 1961. (Source: The Dallas Morning News - October 10, 1961)

12. Files told Vernon - in a telephone call - that the pancake house was on the corner of University and I-10 near a Holiday Inn in Ft. Worth. A check by Vernon revealed that the Old South Pancake house has been at that location since 1962. There is a Holiday Inn a block away. (Documentation: A letter from the owner stating that the business has been in that location since 1962)

13. Originally, the limousine would have proceeded straight down Main Street when it came to the end of the business district, and then gone directly onto Stemmons Freeway. Ordinarily, Secret Service regulations provide that the Presidential limousine is to proceed at a good speed and not take unnecessary or hazardous routes which would slow it down. The procedural manual requires the car to move at 44 miles an hour. But the route was changed so that the car made a right turn at Houston Street, at the end of the business district, and after a short block, made a left turn onto Elm Street, which led it towards and past the School Book Depository and down a small hill beneath the triple underpass. This was a perfect ambush site. (2:156)

14. The most striking find, however, was the exact location of the grassy knoll gunman. According to the acoustical calculations, this firing position was behind the picket fence, eight feet west of the corner. That was just two to seven feet from where S. M. Holland, a dozen years earlier, had placed the signs observed by himself and fellow railroad workers: the puff of smoke, muddy station wagon bumper, cigarette butts, and a cluster of footprints. (25:36)

15. (RESEARCH: Michael T. Griffith) Many of the Dealey Plaza witnesses who commented on the subject said shots were fired at the President from the front. They identified two possible sources for the frontal fire: the grassy knoll and the area immediately around the triple underpass next to the knoll. Most of the witnesses who heard shots from the knoll

believed the shots came from behind the wooden (picket) fence atop the knoll, while others believed the shots came from a point closer to the triple underpass.

A number of those who heard shots coming from the grassy knoll were actually standing on the knoll itself. One such witness is Gordon Arnold, who had just finished Army basic training and had fresh memories of the sound of live rounds. Arnold was standing near the wooden fence. He reports that two shots came from behind him, and that one of them was so close he heard "the whiz over my shoulder" (14:26).

Some have questioned Arnold's story because he does not appear in photos of the knoll at the relevant time (1:34). However, the nature of the photographs does not preclude Arnold's having been at the location he describes, especially since the area where Arnold was standing was in deep shadow. Moreover, Senator Ralph Yarborough, who rode in the motorcade, recalled seeing a man in Arnold's position. Yarborough recounted that when the first round was fired he saw a man in Arnold's spot throw himself to the ground, which is significant because Arnold says he "hit the dirt" as soon as he heard gunfire (14:26). WC defenders suggest that Yarborough was actually referring to Bill Newman. But Newman was accompanied by his wife and child, and all of the Newmans hit the ground. Yarborough, on the other hand, spoke of only one person hitting the ground.

In the A&E Network's documentary The Men Who Killed Kennedy, Texas graphics expert Jack White presents photographic evidence from the Mary Moorman photo that Arnold was where he says he was. No one who has seen Arnold's gripping testimony in that documentary can doubt his sincerity or the vividness of his memory.

Another witness, Jean Hill, was standing across the street from the grassy knoll when Kennedy was shot. On the day of the shooting, she indicated she heard more than three shots and said she heard shots fired from the grassy knoll. In recent years, she has reported that she saw a muzzle flash, a puff of smoke, and the shadowy figure of a man holding a rifle barely visible above the picket fence at the top of the knoll, and that she heard four to six shots (5:37-39; cf. 5:322-324; 23:22-24). There is reason to question most of these claims. However, her initial statements and testimony that she heard four to six shots and that at least some of them came from the knoll is highly credible. Certain WC defenders have suggested or implied that initially Mrs. Hill was unsure of the origin of the shots, and that only later did she mention gunfire from the knoll and hearing more than three shots. But statements she made to a newsman less than an hour after the shooting refute this claim:

At 1:20, before word came of the President's death, NBC cut away to a local affiliate, where Tom Whelan interviewed an eyewitness named Jean Hill. He asked her to tell what she knew of the events, and she told of seeing the President react to his wounds, although she did not mention the head shot, as she would not have seen it if, in fact, it originated from the right front. She did state unequivocally, however, that "shots came from hill" [i.e., the grassy knoll]. She said it twice, and then said the car [the presidential limousine] sped away. . . .

Anchors McGee, Huntley, and Ryan all heard her words, and they never heard her say "I think" or "perhaps". . . . She also indicated there were far more than three shots. (69:19)

For many years Mrs. Hill was criticized over her initial belief that she might have seen a small white dog in the limousine. Lone-gunman theorists have used this in an effort to discredit her account. However, at a JFK assassination conference held in 1994, a researcher displayed a photo showing Jackie Kennedy receiving a small white dog from an admirer at Love Field prior to the start of the motorcade (81:178-179).

I think it is significant that of the twenty sheriff's deputies who were watching the motorcade from in front of the sheriff's office, "sixteen placed the origin of the shots near the Triple Underpass" (5:435). The triple underpass, keep in mind, was right next to the grassy knoll. Dealey Plaza witnesses Abraham Zapruder and Cheryl McKinnon likewise said shots were fired from the grassy knoll (14:23-29; 12:97-101; 5:33-89; 71:111).

Indeed, when he was being questioned by Liebeler, Zapruder was prepared to reveal evidence that there was more than one gunman, but, incredibly, Liebeler refused to pursue the matter. Zapruder told the Secret Service on the day of the shooting that the shots had come from behind him. During his WC testimony, he stated that when the shots were fired his immediate impression was that they originated to his rear. Then, he said the following:

They claim it was proven it could be done by one man. You know there was an indication there were two?

And what was Liebeler's response to this tantalizing statement from a man who had been standing on the knoll itself? "Your films," he replied, "were extremely helpful to the work of the Commission, Mr. Zapruder."

In the 1990 View, Inc. documentary JFK: The Day the Nation Cried, a dismounted motorcycle patrolman can be seen, moments after the shots were fired, looking toward the knoll and giving every appearance of trying to spot an armed adversary. He seems to have his pistol drawn, and he is crouched down and weaving back and forth as if to present a difficult target. During this time he is intensely scanning the area of the knoll.

Two witnesses who provided particularly striking evidence of a shot from the front were Charles Brehm and Bill Newman. Brehm was standing on the grass between Elm Street and Main Street and therefore had an excellent view of the shooting. It should also be observed that Brehm was a former Army Ranger and a combat veteran who was wounded twice in World War II. Thus, he was no stranger to the sound of gunfire, nor to the effects of bullets on human bodies.

In a filmed interview with attorney Mark Lane, Brehm reported that when the bullet hit Kennedy's head, hair went flying from the head. To illustrate his account, Brehm briefly held his hand over the right rear part of his skull. Then, he told Lane that some type of fragment from the head blew out and traveled leftward and to the rear, landing beside a nearby curb. I quote from the interview:

LANE. Did you see the effects of the bullets upon the President?

BREHM. When the second bullet hit, there was . . . uh . . . [briefly puts his hand over the right rear part of his head] hair seemed to go flying. It was very definite, then, that he was struck in the head with the second bullet [i.e., the second bullet to hit JFK]. And, yes, I very definitely saw the effects of the second bullet.

LANE. Did you see any particles of the President's skull fly when the bullet struck him in the head.

BREHM. I saw a piece fly over in the area of the curb where I was standing.

LANE. And in which direction did that fly?

BREHM. It seemed to have come left and back.

LANE. In other words, the skull particle flew to the left and to the rear of the presidential limousine?

BREHM. Uh, Sir, whatever it was that I saw did fall both in that direction and over into the curb there.

LANE. Were you among the closest witnesses to the limousine when the shot struck the President?

BREHM. Yes, Sir, I would have to say that I was, if not the closest one, one of the closest to the unfortunate incident.

Not surprisingly, according to news reports, on the day of the shooting Brehm was convinced that at least one shot came from in front of the limousine. One must see the interview itself to really appreciate the full impact of Brehm's account.

Bill Newman was standing on the grassy knoll during the shooting, and was no more than twenty-five feet from the limousine when JFK was struck in the head. He told a newsman during a TV interview on the day of the assassination that the shots came from behind him, i.e., from the grassy knoll, and that he saw a bullet hit the President in the side of the head, in the right temple. As Newman was describing the bullet strike, he pointed to his right temple. I quote from the interview:

NEWMAN. As the car got directly in front of us, a gunshot apparently from behind us hit the President in the side, in the temple [points to his right temple].

Q. Do you think the first shot came from behind you too?

NEWMAN. I think it came from the same location, yeah. Apparently, back up on the knoll.

Q. So you think the shot came from up on top of the viaduct toward the President? Is that correct?

NEWMAN. No, not on the viaduct itself, but up on top of the hill--on the mound of ground.

So Newman saw a bullet hit JFK in the right temple, and Brehm saw hair and a piece of skull from the President's head fly backward and to the left. Moreover, it should be pointed out that Newman was not the only witness who saw a bullet strike President Kennedy in the area of the right temple. Secret Service agent Sam Kinney said he saw one shot "strike the President in the right side of the head. The President then fell to his left" (72:419). Another witness, Marilyn Sitzman, who was standing next to Abraham Zapruder, said she saw a shot hit JFK on the side of his face "above the ear and to the front . . . between the eye and the ear" (63:142).

This explains why brain matter and skull fragments were blown fiercely backward and to the left by the fatal head shot. Officer Bobby Hargis, who was riding to the left rear of the limousine, was struck so hard by a piece of skull flying toward him that he thought he himself had been hit. Hargis was also splattered by blood and brain. And Officer B. J. Martin, who was riding to Hargis's right, was likewise splattered by the spray from Kennedy's head. As none other than Dallas police chief Jesse Curry admitted, "by the direction of the blood and brains from the president from one of the shots [i.e., the head shot] it would just seem that it would have had to be fired from the front rather than behind" (25:37).

Bethesda mortician Tom Robinson, who reassembled Kennedy's skull after the autopsy, has stated that there was a small hole in one of the temples, and he believes it was in the right temple (10:579-580). On the day of the shooting, White House official Malcolm Kilduff, speaking at a news conference at Parkland Hospital, reported to the press that Kennedy was shot in the right temple, and he even pointed to his own right temple to illustrate what he was saying (18:330; 68:59). Furthermore, all but one of the Dallas doctors and nurses who treated the President said there was a large wound in the rear of his head, and they identified that wound as an exit wound. Clearly, the fatal head shot came from the front, exited the back of the head, and blew blood, brain, and skull fragments to the rear.

Moore points out that thirteen out of fifteen witnesses in the presidential motorcade who were asked about the origin of the shots said "that the shots came from above, not street level" (3:35).

Some conspiracy theorists suggest that the testimony of the people in the motorcade might be colored and should therefore be "cautiously assessed" (4:37). Moore strongly objects to this suggestion (3:35). "Colored?" Moore asks. "Just because the witnesses happened to be government employees or their spouses?" One indication that such might be the case came from Tip O'Neill, the former Speaker of the House of Representatives. O'Neill recounted a dinner conversation that he had five years after the assassination with two Kennedy aides who were riding in the motorcade, Kenneth O'Donnell and Dave Powers:

I was surprised to hear O'Donnell say that he was sure he had heard two shots that came from behind the fence [i.e., the wooden fence on the grassy knoll].

"That's not what you told the Warren Commission," I said.

"You're right," he replied. "I told the FBI what I had heard, but they said it couldn't have happened that way and that I must have been imagining things. So I testified the way they wanted me to...."

Dave Powers was with us at dinner that night, and his recollection of the shots was the same as O'Donnell's. Kenny O'Donnell is no longer alive, but during the writing of this book I checked with Dave Powers. As they say in the news business, he stands by his story. (24:211, emphasis added)

How many other persons did the FBI pressure into testifying "the way they wanted me to"? How many other witnesses really heard shots from the front but changed their story to satisfy federal agents?

Some people reported seeing individuals with rifles or rifle cases, and puffs of smoke, on or near the grassy knoll. And several people, including Senator Yarborough and two police officers, said they smelled gunpowder on or near the grassy knoll just after the President was shot.

16. Numerous witnesses reported that two of the shots came in very rapid succession, nearly simultaneously. These witnesses said the two shots came so closely together that they sounded like a single burst (see, for example, 8:249, 253, 278, 298; 72:92, 93, 99, 115, 407, 427)

17. In 1987, a Dallas man (John Rademacher) and his son dug up a .222 caliber shell casing in Dealey Plaza near the wooden stockade fence. The casing had dents in it. A lab examination by Dr. Paul G. Stimson, a noted forensic orthodontologist at the University of Texas in Houston, issued a written medical opinion that marks or dents in the casing were made by human teeth.

18. The HSCA's photographic panel found strong evidence in the Zapruder film that Kennedy was struck between frames 186 and 190. The panel concluded that "President Kennedy first showed a reaction to some severe external stimulus by Z207 as he is seen going behind a street sign that obstructed Zapruder's view" (6 HSCA 16). The panel believed the shot was fired a few frames before Z190, i.e., during the foliage break (cf. 12:119-120). When the panel did a blur analysis of the film, it detected a significant blur episode during frames 189-197, indicating that the shot that caused the jiggle was fired a few frames before frame 189. Numerous private researchers have studied the film and have likewise determined that this shot was fired a fraction of a second before frame 190. The most reasonable conclusion, therefore, is that this shot was fired from one of the buildings adjacent to the TSBD, quite possibly from the Dal-Tex Building.

19. Dallas businessman Malcolm Summers is on record in both the Dallas Sheriff's Department Report and The Warren Commission Report as stating that he saw a burgundy or maroon Chevrolet with three men in it drive out of the Dal-Tex parking lot and down the street away from the Plaza.

20. A check of Oswald's whereabouts in early and mid-1963 by Robert G. Vernon showed that Oswald was indeed in New Orleans during the period Files says he and Oswald met there.

21. Gerald Posner dismisses the testimony of the witnesses in Clinton and Jackson, Louisiana, who said they saw Oswald and Ferrie together in the summer of 1963 (6:141-148). These highly credible witnesses included a state representative, a deputy sheriff, and a town registrar of voters. Posner's reasons for rejecting their testimony are strained and unconvincing. He even suggests that the witnesses never actually saw Oswald. Jim Garrison and his staff found the Clinton and Jackson witnesses to be credible (19:122-126). Years later, the House Select Committee interviewed these witnesses in executive session and concluded they were honest, sincere, and believable (12:193-194).

22. Former Senator Richard Schweiker has declared,

I personally believe that he [Oswald] had a special relationship with one of the intelligence agencies, which one I'm not certain. But all the fingerprints I found during my eighteen months on the Senate Select Committee on Intelligence point to Oswald as being a product of, and interacting with, the intelligence community. (14:266)

In addition, three former U.S. intelligence agents maintain that Oswald was working for at least one U.S. intelligence agency.

After he was arrested on the day of the assassination, Oswald tried to call a man named "Hurt" in Raleigh, North Carolina, at two different numbers listed for that name. Oswald had no known contacts or friends in North Carolina. Former CIA officer Victor Marchetti points out that Oswald's call was made to a number in the same general area as a base where, according to Marchetti, Naval Intelligence once planned infiltration missions into the Soviet Union (14:146). One of the two Hurts in Raleigh at that time was a John D. Hurt, who had worked in military intelligence during World War II. Oswald was unable to contact Mr. Hurt because two Secret Service agents instructed the switchboard operator at the Dallas police station to unplug the connection before the call could go through (14:146). Marchetti believes Oswald worked for the Office of Naval Intelligence (ONI) and that it was the ONI which sent him to Russia as a phony defector.

Former HSCA investigator Gaeton Fonzi reports that he found strong evidence of an Oswald-CIA connection. Says Fonzi,

There is . . . a preponderance of evidence that indicates Lee Harvey Oswald had an association with a U.S. Government agency, perhaps more than one, but undoubtedly with the Central Intelligence Agency. (61:408)

Fonzi discusses this subject at length in his book The Last Investigation (New York: Thunder's Mouth Press, 1993).

23. JFK and the CIA were in a virtual state of war from the moment of the Bay of Pigs disaster until the day he died. JFK did not trust the CIA and he reportedly intended to dismantle it after the 1964 election. In Vietnam, the CIA refused to carry out instructions from the ranking American official in the country (4:ix). The CIA ignored President Kennedy's directive that it not initiate operations requiring greater firepower than a handgun (43:99-100). It also ignored JFK's orders to stop working with the Mafia. When Kennedy heard the news that South Vietnam's dictator Ngo Diem had been murdered by a CIA-backed coup, against his express wishes, he was outraged. Kennedy was no fan of Diem's, but he did not want to see him murdered. General Maxwell Taylor wrote that upon learning of Diem's death JFK "leaped to his feet and rushed from the room with a look of shock and dismay on his face" (70:334). George Smathers reported that Kennedy blamed the CIA for Diem's murder. According to Smathers, Kennedy said he had to "do something about" the CIA and that the Agency should be stripped of its exorbitant power (70:334-335).

One of the more troubling cases of CIA disobedience to presidential authority was its behaviour in relation to Cuba. In September 1963, long after President Kennedy had ordered a halt to the covert campaign against Castro, senior CIA staffers, including the deputy director, Richard Helms, and Desmond Fitzgerald, the head of the Agency's Cuba unit, approved plans to kill Castro, without seeking presidential authorization. They also continued other covert operations against Cuba in violation of the President's instructions. Needless to say, these CIA officers did not inform the President of their activities; nor did they inform Congress or the Attorney General, Robert Kennedy. They didn't even tell then-CIA director John McCone, probably because he was appointed by President Kennedy following the Bay of Pigs disaster. In short, as Anthony Summers has observed, "in September and October 1963--a crucial moment politically--CIA officers were acting in a way that gravely endangered White House policy" (14:322).

Livingstone rejects a CIA role in the assassination, reasoning that the Agency couldn't have been involved since Kennedy replaced Allen Dulles with a man of his own choosing, John McCone. But this argument ignores the fact that the Agency has a history of working around directors it doesn't like. As for McCone, he exercised very little control over the CIA and was kept in the dark about a number of its activities. For instance, Fonzi notes that "Richard Helms, who was McCone's Deputy Director and head of the dirty tricks department, admitted he never told McCone about any of the Agency's plans to kill Castro, or about the CIA's working relationship with the Mafia" (61:334; cf. 61:361).

A key figure linking the Agency to the assassination was CIA man David Atlee Phillips, who was seen with Oswald a few months before the shooting (14:504-519; 61:128-171, 391-400, 408-409. Among many other things, Phillips was the propaganda chief for the Bay of Pigs operation and later rose to become the chief of the CIA's Western Hemisphere Division. In 1954 Phillips worked with E. Howard Hunt and others to overthrow the Arbenz government in Guatemala. Based on his extensive investigation of Phillips for the Church Committee and then for the Select Committee, Gaeton Fonzi believes that "David Atlee Phillips played a key role in the conspiracy to assassinate President Kennedy" (61:409). Phillips was in charge of the CIA's Cuban operations in Mexico City at the time of the assassination, so he was strategically positioned to frame Oswald, and it is very probable that he was involved in the phony Oswald visits to the Cuban embassy. Select Committee investigator Dan Hardway found that most of the individuals in Mexico City and Miami who were spreading post-assassination propaganda linking Oswald to Cuban or Soviet intelligence were "David Phillips's assets" (61:292).

Another former CIA agent who has come under suspicion is E. Howard Hunt. Hunt, a former high-ranking covert operator and a propaganda specialist, was a key figure in the Bay of Pigs invasion. As mentioned, Hunt and David Atlee Phillips helped to overthrow the Arbenz government in Guatemala. According to former (and now deceased) CIA operative Frank Sturgis, who knew Hunt well, Hunt was involved in CIA assassination operations. Hunt has made no secret of his intense dislike for John Kennedy. To this day, Hunt blames JFK for the failure at the Bay of Pigs. When Watergate whistleblower John Dean opened Hunt's private safe, he found bogus telegrams that falsely linked JFK with the assassination of South Vietnam's corrupt dictator Ngo Dinh Diem (16:79).

Where was E. Howard Hunt on November 22, 1963? Hunt has given conflicting accounts of where he was at the time of the shooting. In his 1985 libel trial in Miami, Florida, the jury concluded Hunt was not being truthful about his whereabouts on the day of the assassination.

24. Another former CIA agent who has come under suspicion is E. Howard Hunt. Hunt, a former high-ranking covert operator and a propaganda specialist, was a key figure in the Bay of Pigs invasion. As mentioned, Hunt and David Atlee Phillips helped to overthrow the Arbenz government in Guatemala. According to former (and now deceased) CIA operative Frank Sturgis, who knew Hunt well, Hunt was involved in CIA assassination operations. Hunt has made no secret of his intense dislike for John Kennedy. To this day, Hunt blames JFK for the failure at the Bay of Pigs. When Watergate whistleblower John Dean opened Hunt's

private safe, he found bogus telegrams that falsely linked JFK with the assassination of South Vietnam's corrupt dictator Ngo Dinh Diem (16:79).

25. The day before the assassination, Eugene Hale Brading, a Mafia man with a long arrest record, visited Hunt's office building in Dallas. Brading was arrested in Dealey Plaza on the day of the shooting when he was found to have taken an elevator to the ground floor of the Dal-Tex Building shortly after the shots were fired. Brading was released, however, because he gave the police an alias. While in Dallas, Brading stayed at the Cabana Hotel.

On January 30, 1995, Files informed Vernon that Brading's "mission" was to get Nicoletti and Roselli into the Dal-Tex Building.

26. On January 30, 1995, Files informed Vernon that David Atlee Phillips was the person who had Oswald meet Files in Dallas.

27. Mr. Files has supplied Robert G. Vernon with a color photograph of the man who killed J.D. Tippit and a positive identification is under investigation as of this writing. Mr. Files will not name the alleged killer of Officer Tippit.

28. <u>The Murder of Officer Tippit</u> (Research by Michael T. Griffith)

Posner says that eyewitnesses, ballistics, and physical evidence prove that Oswald murdered Officer J. D. Tippit a little over forty minutes after he allegedly shot JFK (6:273-280). Posner ignores significant evidence of Oswald's innocence and merely repeats the WC's untenable version of the killing. The case against Oswald in Tippit's murder is so weak that I see no need to analyze all of Posner's assertions. For more information on the tenuous nature of the evidence against Oswald in the Tippit affair, I would invite the reader to compare Posner's treatment of the issue with that of such writers as Marrs, Lane, Summers, and Hurt (5:350-353; 4:190-208; 14:84-97; 71:139-169). However, I would like to examine some of the evidence that Posner ignores:

* The witness with the best view of the shooting, Domingo Benavides, at first said he could not identify Tippit's killer. Then, after his brother had been murdered, Benavides told the WC that a photo of Oswald "bore a resemblance" to the assailant. It was three years after the shooting until Benavides made a somewhat firm identification of Oswald.

* Two witnesses to the Tippit slaying described a killer who did not resemble Oswald.

* Two other witnesses said Oswald entered the Texas Theatre just a few minutes after 1:00 P.M., and that he remained in the theatre until he was arrested there about an hour later. But Tippit was killed at no later than 1:10.

* Officer J. M. Poe marked two of the empty shells found at the crime scene with his initials, a standard chain-of- evidence procedure, but none of the shells produced by the FBI and the WC as evidence of Oswald's guilt had Poe's markings on them.

* Helen Markham, Posner's star witness against Oswald in the Tippit shooting, gave such wildly conflicting and confused testimony that one WC staffer called her an "utter screwball." Mrs. Markham gave different descriptions of the assailant. Although by all accounts (including Posner's) Tippit died instantly, Mrs. Markham said she conversed with him after he

was shot, for an astounding twenty minutes. Some of the witnesses denied Mrs. Markham was even at the scene of the crime.

A Frantic 43 Minutes

A telling point for Oswald's innocence is the fact that he did not have enough time to go from the TSBD to the scene of the Tippit slaying. The WC said he left the Depository at 12:33 P.M. and killed Tippit 43 minutes later, at 1:15. But even a casual review of Oswald's alleged movements shows he could not have done what the Commission said he did.

Posner disagrees, saying,

Could Oswald have physically been at the Tippit scene by 1:15, the time of the shooting? A reconstruction of the time that elapsed since he left the Depository shows it is more than possible. (6:274 n)

But Posner's TSBD-to-Oak-Cliff scenario relies heavily on the WC's untenable version of Oswald's post-assassination movements. For example, Posner accepts the WC's claim that Tippit was shot at 1:15 P.M. However, eyewitness statements and Dallas police radio transcripts indicate the shooting occurred no later than 1:12. Posner departs from the Commission version by saying that Oswald left his rooming house just before 1:00. Posner does this in order to get Oswald to the Tippit scene by 1:15. Yet, according to Oswald's landlady, he did not leave the house until 1:03 or 1:04 (14:92). The plain fact of the matter is that any reconstruction which places Oswald at the Tippit scene by 1:12, or even by 1:15, is contrary to the evidence. Oswald simply could not have made it there in time to commit the crime.

Helen Markham said Tippit was shot at around 1:06. Other witnesses agreed that the shooting occurred just a few minutes after 1:00. T. F. Bowley, who radioed the police dispatcher from Tippit's car, reported that his watch said 1:10 when he drove up to the crime scene. Bowley contacted the police dispatcher at right around 1:16, according to the police radio transcripts. This was after Domingo Benavides waited in his truck for "a few minutes" (out of fear the killer would return), got out of his truck, attempted to help Tippit, climbed into the squad car, and then fumbled with the radio trying to figure out how it worked. It was at this point that Bowley appeared inside the car, took the radio from Benavides, and contacted the dispatcher.

In all probability, Tippit was shot between 1:08 and 1:10, and absolutely no later than 1:12. But Oswald did not leave his boarding house until around 1:03 or 1:04, and his landlady reported that he lingered in the immediate vicinity of the house for a little bit. Oswald did not drive, and an inquiry of residents in the area failed to produce anyone who had seen a man running at the time in question. Even assuming a good walking speed of four miles an hour, it would have taken Oswald no less than twelve minutes to reach the Tippit crime scene. Therefore, Oswald could not have been present to shoot Tippit at 1:15, much less three to seven minutes earlier.

A research team from the All American Television Company did a reconstruction of Oswald's movements from the TSBD to the Tippit scene for the 1992 documentary The JFK Conspiracy, which was hosted by world-famous actor James Earl Jones. The team confirmed that Oswald could not have arrived to the scene of the crime even by 1:15. I quote from James Earl Jones' narration:

At 12:33 the Warren Commission said Oswald left the Depository and walked seven blocks to catch a bus. . . . Meanwhile, after traveling a couple of blocks, the bus was caught in an immense traffic jam. They said he got off the bus.

At 12:48, they said Oswald climbed into a taxi. They gave him six minutes to reach his next stop [his neighbourhood in Oak Cliff]. It took us over eight [minutes], without traffic.

The Commission said Oswald entered his boarding house at one o'clock. At 1:03, his landlady said he [Oswald] left the house and went to the northbound bus stop. Yet, in order to kill Officer Tippit, he had to travel south. So, the Commission said he must have changed his mind.

The witnesses all said Tippit was killed no later than 1:10 [nearly all of them said this], and that was after the policeman and his killer had a conversation [according to the WC's star witness, Helen Markham]. Seven minutes [for Oswald to get from his house to the murder scene]. Oswald simply didn't have enough time.

In every case, the Commission failed the time test, and we had no congested traffic to deal with.

29. A witness named Julia Ann Mercer said she saw a man who looked like Jack Ruby driving a truck next to the grassy knoll prior to the assassination. Sources: Marrs, Crossfire, pp. 18-19, 324-325; Smith, JFK: The Second Plot 76-81; Garrison, On the Trail of the Assassins, pp. 16-17, 251-253. Jack Ruby was a Mafia man and an important Dallas mobster. Sources: Davis, Mafia Kingfish, pp. 156-160, 180-184, 282-297; Scheim, The Mafia Killed President Kennedy, pp. 112-305.

30. In the 1990 View, Inc. documentary JFK: The Day the Nation Cried, a dismounted motorcycle patrolman can be seen, moments after the shots were fired, looking toward the knoll and giving every appearance of trying to spot an armed adversary. He seems to have his pistol drawn, and he is crouched down and weaving back and forth as if to present a difficult target. During this time he is intensely scanning the area of the knoll.

31. Zapruder is on record as saying he heard a shot come from behind him, over his right shoulder.

32. In Josiah Thompson's book "SIX SECONDS IN DALLAS" - there is a blow-up of the Moorman photograph which clearly shows what appears to be a grey fedora (hat) sticking up above the top of the wooden stockade fence in the exact area where Mr. Files said he was standing. Files has confessed that he put on the grey fedora after he reversed his jacket from a plaid lining to grey to walk away. Lee Bowers, the railroad worker, testified that he saw a man behind the stockade fence wearing a plaid "jacket." (Warren Commission Report)

33. In a letter to Certified Legal Investigator Joe West in 1992, Mr. Files stated that he kept the Fireball after the assassination of JFK. Files further stated that while he was incarcerated in the early 1980's, that his cousin had taken the Fireball from his aunt's home where he had it stored and the cousin was arrested and the weapon confiscated by the police. Investigator West contacted the police department where Files said the weapon was located. West was informed that there was no record of the weapon. After West's death in 1993, producer Vernon contacted the Illinois police and they acknowledged that the weapon was indeed there

at one time and an old report (typed and handwritten) was finally located. The weapon was not in the police department locker and has disappeared. Vernon offered a $10,000 reward for the weapon in 1994, however no one has come forth with the weapon or with any information about the weapon.

34. THE JANUARY-FEBRUARY 1995 BLUE, TEXAS, BALLISTICS TESTS RELATING TO THE MOVEMENTS OF PRESIDENT JOHN F. KENNEDY'S HEAD IN FRAMES CIRCA 312-323 OF THE ABRAHAM ZAPRUDER FILM

The Blue, Texas, tests were conducted on a series of weekends in January and February 1995 by John Stockwell, Art Stockwell, and Jodi Peterson on private property near Blue, Texas.

For ten years, John Stockwell was a hunter in the Belgian Congo in Africa. Then he was trained and served for seven years as a Marine Corps infantry officer and "recon" officer. For thirteen years he was a CIA intelligence officer and paramilitary specialist with field experience in the "low intensity" conflicts in the Congo, Vietnam, and Angola.

Since 1978, Stockwell has been a writer, lecturer, and critic of the U.S. national security complex. Since 1981, he has studied and researched the John F. Kennedy assassination. He was a paid consultant (eventually a dissenting consultant) in Oliver Stone's JFK film project.

Art Stockwell is an expert shooter who can hit 8-inch targets with a pistol at ranges greater than 40 yards.

Jodi Peterson is also a shooter.

PURPOSE

To re-examine the Alvarez and Lattimer findings regarding the direction in which a target is propelled following impact by a high-velocity bullet.

(Alvarez and Lattimer found that the "jet effect" of an exiting bullet propels the target towards the rifle. They concluded that this was scientific proof that no shot fired into President Kennedy's head from the direction of the grassy knoll or the railroad overpass could explain the violent backward movement of Kennedy's head and shoulders that is clearly revealed in frames #313-323 of the Zapruder film, but that the shot into the back and top of Kennedy's head that blew away the right top side of his head could explain that backward movement.)

CONCLUSIONS

A clear pattern emerged in the Blue, Texas, tests. When a solid target roughly the size and density of a human head was struck dead center by a solid round, a hollow point or a special exploding round, the "jet effect" did seem to work, propelling the target in the direction of the rifle that fired the shot (hereafter "the rifle").

However, when the solid target was struck in the upper quadrant (where the autopsy X-rays and photographs definitively place the shot to Kennedy's head from behind) the target was propelled away from the rifle.

When a target that was not solid (for example, a melon in which the seed core had substantially dried) was struck dead center, there was no "jet-effect" and the target was propelled neither forward nor backward and instead remained balanced on the stand. However, when such melons were struck in the top quadrant, they rolled in the direction away from the rifle.

These findings, in the case of the Kennedy assassination, seem to confirm the Alvarez/Lattimer principle, but clearly demonstrate a contradictory phenomenon that seems to make it possible that, a) the shot that struck the back of President Kennedy's head from behind initially could in fact have made his head start forward and b) a shot from the grassy knoll (i.e., from the right front) could have provided the energy that drove his head and shoulders backward and to his left.

BACKGROUND

In 1964, the Warren Commission concluded in its report that, in his assassination in Dealey Plaza, President John Kennedy had been struck by one bullet high in his back and one in the back of his head. Although there were grumblings of doubt, there was no substantial challenge of these findings until researchers, beginning with Professor Josiah Thompson, viewed the Zapruder film of the assassination.

In the Zapruder film, it is clear that Kennedy is struck in the back of the head after frame 312, with the bullet exiting dramatically in the region above the right temple in frame 313. With the impact of this bullet, his head starts forward. However, a split second later his head and upper body lurch violently backwards and to his left. To both expert shooters and laymen alike, the movement backwards could only be explained by a second shot striking him from the right front (i.e., the area of the grassy knoll).

More than any one piece of evidence, this backward movement of Kennedy's head between frames #313-323, with the seemingly overpowering logic of the visible, "common sense" explanation, fueled a broad movement of skepticism of the Warren Commission Report and the "lone shooter" hypothesis, literally to the point of compelling the House Select Committee on Assassinations investigation of the assassination in 1976-1978.

However, a Nobel Prize-winning scientist, Dr. Luis Alvarez, demonstrated both theoretically and experimentally that, according to the Law of Conservation of Momentum and the Law of Conservation of Energy, the material exiting after the bullet in such a head wound will work like a small rocket engine, driving the target backwards and towards the rifle! To prove his theory, Alvarez (caused to be) fired rifle rounds into seven melons that had been reinforced with filament tape. Six of the melons recoiled towards the rifle.

Alvarez was criticized for the procedures and setup he used in his tests (for example, he used a rifle with a muzzle velocity of about 3200 feet per second and he used soft-nosed bullets in testing a hypothesis relating to Oswald's Mannlicher-Carcano which had a muzzle velocity of 2200 feet per second and fired a steel-jacketed bullet).

Thereafter, Dr. John K. Lattimer, a urologist with no forensic experience or training in head wounds, set up an experiment using human skulls that were packed with solid melon and white paint and then taped and sewn tightly together. He used an Oswald-type rifle and steel jacketed rounds. In each of his twelve experimental test-firings, the skull fell towards the rifle.

The Alvarez and Lattimer tests seemed to deal a serious blow to the hypothesis of a shooter on the grassy knoll. Clearly, a shot coming from the right front would be expected to cause the president's head to lurch towards the grassy knoll, rather than violently back into the seat of the limousine. At the same time, they seemed to offer a plausible explanation of how a shot from behind could in fact, contrary to "common knowledge" perceptions, account for the backward movement of Kennedy's head and shoulders.

It is also noted that, in early 1964, Dr. Alfred Olivier of the U.S. Army's Edgemont Arsenal in Maryland had fired rounds into twelve empty human skulls. The skulls were propelled neither forward nor backward from the stand on which they were sitting.

THE BLUE, TEXAS, BALLISTICS TESTS

In the Blue, Texas, ballistics tests, 14 targets similar in weight and density to those used by Drs. Alvarez and Lattimer were balanced on a saw horse in such a way that it would be clear whether they jumped frontwards or backwards when struck by rifle bullets.

Rifles with comparable ballistics characteristics to Oswald's 6.5 Mannlicher-Carcano and James E. Files's Remington Fireball were used. These were an Enfield .303 with a muzzle velocity of 2400 feet per second and an AR-15 .223 with a muzzle velocity of 3200 fps. (The AR-15 round is virtually identical to the Remington Fireball .222-.223. The Enfield .303 fires a 16% larger round about 10% faster than the Mannlicher-Carcano.)

With the AR-15, hollow point and special rounds were used to duplicate James E. Files's exploding rounds.

RESULTS

3 targets that were struck in the center did not fall either towards or away from the rifle (apparently because of insufficient density in the melons.)

4 targets that were struck in the center were propelled towards the rifle.

6 targets that were struck in the upper quadrant were propelled away from the rifle.

There were no exceptions. i.e., no target that was struck in the center was propelled away from the rifle, and no target that was struck in the upper quadrant was propelled towards the rifle.

THE MELONS:

2 melons struck in the center by bullets from the Enfield did not jump either forwards or backwards.

2 melons struck in the upper right hand quadrant by rounds from the Enfield rolled away from and to the left from the rifle.

1 melon struck in the center by a bullet from the AR-15 did not jump forwards or backwards.

1 melon struck in its center by a bullet from the AR-15 rolled off the saw horse in the direction of the rifle.

1 melon struck in its center by a bullet from the AR-15 jumped about 3-4 inches towards the rifle.

In these tests a pattern seemed to be indicated, that when the melons were struck in the center by an exploding round, they either did not move or they recoiled towards the rifle. However, when they were struck in the upper quadrant, they moved away from the rifle. We surmised that our melons did not have sufficient density to provide a satisfactory test of the "jet effect."

THE 1-GALLON SEALED CANS OF HOMINY, WEIGHING 6 LBS.:

1 can, struck in the center by an exploding hollow point round from the AR-15 jumped about 2 feet towards the rifle.

2 cans, struck in the upper quadrant by special exploding rounds (comparable to the ones used by Files) jumped over one foot away from the rifle.

1 can, struck in the upper quadrant by an exploding hollow point jumped away from the rifle.

1 can, struck dead center by a jacketed, 175-grain bullet from the Enfield (Oswald's rounds were about 160 grains) jumped 6 feet towards the rifle.

1 can, struck in the upper quadrant by a 175-grain bullet from the Enfield jumped 2 feet away from the rifle.

35. On page 588 of Volume 25 of the Warren Commission Report, there is evidence not pursued by the Warren Commission of Oswald being seen with a "teenager" firing weapons in a field. A picture of James E. Files at age 21 was given to investigator West by Files. Robert G. Vernon had the picture examined by police sketch artist Lois Gibson of the Houston Police Department. Ns. Gibson is one of the leading photo identification experts in the USA and handles work of this nature for the FBI, DEA, State of Texas, State of New Mexico and the State of Arkansas. Ms. Gibson verified that the picture of the 21 year old man is indeed James E. Files. In the picture, Files appears to be a "teenager."

36. In 1992, Investigator Joe West filed a suit to exhume the body of JFK in both Federal Court in Houston and in the 160th Judicial District of Dallas. While the Federal action was thrown out of court for lack of standing, the Dallas action was deemed valid. In late 1992, Mr. West had a series of heart attacks and died in early 1993. The legal case died with him.

37. On August 9, 1993, the FBI - after making a deal with Files's attorney, Don Ervin of Houston to talk to Files with Ervin present - went around Ervin and visited Files at Joliet. Former Joliet Warden Salvador Godinez (now the Deputy Director of the Michigan Department of Corrections) informed Vernon that the FBI "muscled" their way into the prison to see Files through Internal Affairs and that there is no record of their visit. The FBI did release a report on their visit with Files and gave the Assassination Archives Review Board a copy of the report. The report indicates that the FBI attempted to discredit Files by doubting his military record and trying to trick him into identifying FBI agents with Italian names as

Mafia members. Mr. Files's confession to the FBI regarding his part in the JFK assassination is consistent with the transcription herein.

38. Richard Helms committed perjury when he appeared before a Congressional Committee in the 1970's and has since retired from the CIA and lives abroad.

39. Former CIA - DEA pilot Robert "Tosh" Plumlee has confessed that he was the co-pilot on a CIA supported flight that flew Johnny Roselli into Dallas on the morning of 11/22/63. Mr. Plumlee also related that Roselli had come from Washington before catching the flight to Dallas in Tampa.

40. When FBI agent Zack Shelton first gave investigator West the lead on James E. Files, Shelton verified that Files had been stripped and tortured and left for dead. Shelton also told West that the FBI had been unable to "break" Files into talking about any crimes in which he was involved.

41. Files's birthdate, place of birth and various aspects of his younger years were confirmed by his mother's sister to Vernon. His aunt also told Vernon that Files had sent her and her husband letters from Vietnam in the early 60's telling them that the "Government has turned me into a killer."

42. According to lone-gunman theorists, Oswald used the alleged murder weapon to shoot and kill President Kennedy on November 22, 1963. However, when a paraffin test was performed on Oswald's cheek to detect the presence of gunpowder residue, it came back negative. Lone-gunman theorists reply that the paraffin test performed on the cheek of an FBI man who test-fired the Mannlicher-Carcano for the WC was also negative. This supposedly proves the paraffin test is irrelevant. However, for the FBI's test-firing to have been valid, the rifle would have had to be in direct contact with the agent's cheek when fired. The WC did not specify that this requirement was met, and the Commission refused to allow a lawyer acting in Oswald's behalf to observe the test conducted by the FBI agent.

Perhaps the negative results of the November 22 paraffin test explain why the Dallas police declined to test the Mannlicher-Carcano to see if it had been fired in the last several hours.[43]

43. This is staggering to consider. Here you had the alleged murder weapon in the most important murder case of the century, but the Dallas police department failed to test it to see if it had been fired that day!

44. According to author Gerald Posner, the fatal head shot came from behind and exploded out of the "right side" of Kennedy's head (6:307-316). There is massive eyewitness testimony against this view and for the fact that the fatal head shot came from the front and exited the right rear portion of the President's skull. Virtually all lone-gunman theorists deny there was a large defect in the rear of JFK's head, but the wound was closely observed by numerous witnesses, including Parkland and Bethesda medical personnel. Harrison Livingstone has superbly documented this eyewitness evidence in his books High Treason 2 and Killing the Truth.

Posner attacks two of the Dallas doctors who continue to maintain that the large wound was in the back of the head, Dr. Robert McClelland and Dr. Charles Crenshaw, who recently wrote a book rejecting the autopsy findings.

Posner engages in a scurrilous attack on Dr. Crenshaw, questioning his sanity and veracity. As part of his attack, Posner quotes some disparaging comments about Crenshaw made by an anonymous "close Crenshaw friend" (6:313-314). Posner does not inform his readers that Dr. Crenshaw, a man of impeccable reputation, is Clinical Professor of Surgery at the University of Texas Southwestern Medical School and is on the staff of John Peter Smith Hospital and St. Joseph Hospital in Fort Worth, Texas. In addition, Dr. Crenshaw has been honored with inclusion in several medical and professional societies and has published extensively.

Dr. Crenshaw was present during the efforts to save JFK's life. He noted "much of what was going on, and his recollections are extensive" (10:110). Dr. Crenshaw says the large defect was in the back of the President's head, and he is certain the wound could only have been caused by a shot from the front. After the President had been pronounced dead, Dr. Crenshaw stood right behind Aubrey Rike as Rike helped to put Kennedy's body in the coffin. He remembers Rike commenting that he could feel the edges of bone around the hole in the back of the President's head (10:112). Rike has confirmed this in numerous interviews (e.g., 10:118).

Apparently Posner couldn't find an anonymous "close friend" of Dr. McClelland's to assail his sanity and character, so he questions the doctor's judgment and memory. Three of the other Dallas doctors, along with Dr. Michael Baden, a long-time defender of the single-assassin theory, are enlisted to assist in the attack (6:312-313). However, Dr. McClelland, a deeply religious man, has been consistent in his descriptions of JFK's head wound. He told the WC that the large defect was in the back of the head, and, unlike some of the other Dallas doctors, he has never had a convenient change of memory. Moreover, it is strange that when Dr. McClelland testified before the WC, not one of the other Parkland doctors questioned or contradicted his testimony on this issue. In fact, all but one of the Dallas doctors who testified before the Commission on the subject placed the head wound in the right rear part of the skull, just as Dr. McClelland did (18:308-337). And, the one Dallas doctor who seemed to differ with his colleagues on the head wound later placed it more toward the right rear part of the head in a filmed interview (68:87).

Dr. Peters' change of memory seems to be especially pronounced. According to Posner, Dr. Peters now accepts the WC's placement of the head wound. However, when asked about the wound for the documentary The Men Who Killed Kennedy, he said,

I could see that he had a large, about seven-centimeter, opening in the right occipital-parietal area [i.e., the right rear part of the head]. A considerable portion of the brain was missing there, and the occipital cortex, the back portion of the brain, was lying down near the opening of the wound, and blood was trickling out.

As Dr. Peters gave this description of the head wound, he repeatedly illustrated his explanation by placing his right hand on the right rear part of the head, exactly where Crenshaw and McClelland locate the wound.

Just what is the evidence that there was a large wound in the back of President Kennedy's head? The following individuals got a good look at, and in many cases also handled, the President's head and are on record that the large wound was in the rear of the skull:

* Audrey Bell, a nursing supervisor at Parkland Hospital.

* Diana Bowron, Parkland Hospital nurse. Nurse Bowron actually cleaned the large defect and packed it with gauze squares in preparing the body for the casket. She vividly remembers that the large head wound was in the right rear part of the skull.

* Dr. Kemp Clark, Parkland Hospital.

* Dr. Charles Crenshaw, Parkland Hospital.

* Jerrol Custer, the x-ray technician at Bethesda Hospital who took the President's autopsy x-rays.

* Dr. Richard Dulaney, Parkland Hospital.

* Dr. John Ebersole, Bethesda Hospital radiologist. In an extensive interview with his hometown newspaper in 1978, Dr. Ebersole said, "When the body was removed from the casket there was a very obvious horrible gaping wound in the back of the head"

(18:543).

* William Greer, Secret Service agent, who drove the presidential limousine.

* Clint Hill, a Secret Service agent who was taken to the morgue for the express purpose of viewing the President's wounds and who was also in the Parkland trauma room when the President was being treated. It was Agent Hill who climbed onto the back of the limousine to get Jackie Kennedy to return to her seat. Hill testified that as he was lying over the top of the back seat "I noticed a portion of the President's head on the right rear side was missing and he was bleeding profusely" (8:285, emphasis added).

* Patricia Hutton (now Patricia Gustaffson), a nurse at Parkland Hospital who placed a bandage against the wound in the back of the head.

* James Curtis Jenkins, a Navy lab technician at Bethesda Hospital who was present at the autopsy.

* Dr. Robert Karnei, Bethesda Hospital, who was present at the autopsy.

* Roy Kellerman, a Secret Service agent who was present at the autopsy.

* Dr. Robert McClelland, Parkland Hospital.

* Doris Nelson, a chief nurse at Parkland Hospital.

* Floyd Riebe, a photographic technician who took pictures of the President's body at Bethesda Hospital.

* Aubrey Rike, an ambulance driver and funeral home worker in Dallas. Rike was called to Parkland Hospital soon after the shooting and assisted in placing the President's body in the casket. Rike could actually feel the edges of the large wound in the back of the head.

* Tom Robinson, the mortician who had the job of putting the President back together after the autopsy in case the family wanted to take one last look at him. Robinson, of course, had to spend a good part of his time handling the President's head. He saw and felt the large wound in the back.

* Jan Gail Rudnicki, a lab assistant at Bethesda Hospital who was present at the autopsy.

* Roy Stamps, a Fort Worth newsman who saw Kennedy lying in the limousine before he was moved into Parkland Hospital. Said Stamps, "I rushed up and saw Kennedy lying in the car.... The back of his head was gone" (5:362, emphasis added).

* Dr. David Stewart, Parkland Hospital.

Reprint from http://jfkmurdersolved.com/confession2.htm

Robert "Tosh" Plumlee Interview 6/4/92 Dallas

Q: Tosh, how do you make your living, what kind of occupation are you in?

A: I'm a pilot, commercial pilot.

Q: When did you first become a pilot?

A: I started in 1956. I was an aircraft mechanic prior to going in and getting my license.

Q: And, you've been flying for a living ever since?

A: Off and on and also doing other jobs in those lean, lean years so to speak.

Q: In your times as a pilot, have you ever been associated with or worked with the CIA?

A: Yes I have.

Q: What was the first time?

A: The first time was 1956 and the first time I became involved, connected with the CIA, through out of military intelligence, was the M-267 and that was a gun running supply operation to supply guns and ammunition to the students at the University of Havana inside Cuba. This was pro-Castro days. This was before Castro came into power. And, that was the beginning.

Q: Have you worked with the CIA since that time?

A: Yes, I've worked with the CIA.

Q: On just another occasion or many occasions?

A: On many occasions.

Q: Over a period of how many years?

A: Off and on, over a period of 30 years.

Q: Have you ever met, in your lifetime, a person named John Roselli?

A: Yes, I knew John Roselli rather well.

Q: When did you first meet him?

A: I met Roselli in about 1960, last part of '60, first part of '61. And, this was at Biscayne Park, we'd just came from a meeting place called Sloppy Joe's on Flagler Street in Miami. And, Johnny, John Farentello was there, the person that introduced me to John Roselli.

Q: Have you ever had an occasion to fly in an airplane or to fly John Roselli?

A: I've flown John Roselli, I would say, perhaps more than 6 or 7 different occasions. These were to islands, well not islands, but to the Marathon Key in Florida, Bimini, once to Havana, one other time from Houston to Galveston to see about getting a raider ship which was going to O'Rourke's operation, and another time from Salt Lake City to Thunderbird Inn in Las Vegas, and then from Las Vegas to Santa Barbara, California. And, that particular transition of flights was 1963.

Q: On those occasions, did you get to know John Roselli personally?

A: Yes, I knew John Roselli personally.

Q: Where were you on November 22, 1963?

A: I was observing the attempt on Kennedy's life. I was at Dealey Plaza on the South Knoll.

Q: Did you have occasion on that day to see John Roselli?

A: Yes, I did. I saw John Roselli. John Roselli was on board the flight coming out of Houston. We had taken a flight out of Tampa, Florida and went through New Orleans, New Orleans to Houston and Roselli had boarded the flight at Tampa, Florida, and he was staying at the Congress Inn the night before he boarded the flight. Our team flew out of West Palm Beach, a place called Lantana, and to Tampa and then Roselli and a couple of other people got on board in Tampa. We flew to New Orleans where two people got off, three other people got on, Roselli stayed on board. We flew to Houston and then the next morning, we had some weather, and we left for Dallas, and we had to...we were heading for Thunderbird, I mean for Redbird Airport, and we had to make a stop a Dallas/Garland because of weather. We did not have an IFR flight plan filed at that point. We did not want to file a flight plan. The impression I was under at that time is we were flying a team into Dallas to abort the assassination and John Roselli was on board that flight as well as a couple of other Cubans and people that were connected with organized crime in New Orleans.

Q: Did this flight have any association with the CIA or do you know?

A: No, well, the CIA acted as support. Our flight was a military intelligence flight. How this flight originated was a few months prior to the Kennedy matter, there was a couple of Cubans that was CIA operations (Jim Wade) was to fire a bazooka on Castro in the Palace. That was aborted and then these same Cubans came back into Southern Florida, this was around the 15th/16th of November, and they were going to attempt to fire the bazooka on Air Force One which was parked at West Palm Beach at that particular time, November 17th, and as a result of that information coming out, that team, those Cubans, were picked up and from the interrogation of those Cubans that was the beginning of finding out about an attempt on Kennedy's life.

Q: On the morning of November 22, 1963, did the flight that arrived in Garland, Texas, just outside of Dallas, have anything to do with the CIA?

A: The CIA was....yes it did, the CIA was our support people. We were military intelligence. The CIA was running support and coordinating certain flights, making different arrangements, or necessary arrangements, for us.

Q: What happened when the flight arrived in Garland, did anyone get off or did anyone get on?

A: There was 3 people got off in Garland and they were picked up about 30 minutes after we arrived there, by car. Then we took the aircraft and jumped over to Redbird Airport after the weather had cleared for us to be able to get in there VFR.

Q: Then what happened at Redbird Airport in Dallas, Texas?

A: We went to the "safe" house over by Oak Cliff Country Club on Bar Harbor Drive, and that was just prior to going down to the Plaza.

Q: Who got off of the airplane at Redbird?

A: Everybody else got off at Redbird. John Roselli got off a t Redbird and everybody went their own way. Where they went, I have no idea, at that point and time I have no idea where they went.

Q: Do you know a person named Charles Nicoletti?

A: I've heard of Charles Nicoletti and I've seen Charles Nicoletti. Yes, I know of him. But, I don't know him personally.

Q: Was Charles Nicoletti on the flight?

A: Charles Nicoletti was not on that flight but Charles Nicoletti was in Dallas.

Q: Did you see Charles Nicoletti in Dallas or how do you know that he was in Dallas?

A: From back from the Church committee years ago. The picture of Nicoletti was shown to me by a member, by investigators of Senator Church, and prior to that I had already pulled Nicoletti's picture out of a line-up of 10 pictures. I did not know his name at that point. On another occasion I saw him at Sloppy Joe's with John Roselli, in Biscayne Park, when they were going over some maps.

Q: How do you know that Charles Nicoletti was in Dallas?

A: Well it's been....well, O.K.. It's been told to me, by Federal Investigators and private investigators, pictures and everything else, that he was there. In fact, it's been alleged that I actually flew him in with John Roselli. Roselli was on board the aircraft Nicoletti was not on board that aircraft. I'd already known pictures of Nicoletti, but I did not know him personally.

Q: After Nicoletti got off the aircraft do you know where he went?

A: I have no....he was not on the aircraft. After John Roselli got off the aircraft, I have no idea where John Roselli went.

Q: Where did you go after you got off the aircraft at Redbird?

A: I went...I was taken over to the "safe house" that was located in Oak Cliff right next to the Country Club on Bar Harbor Drive and that's where we congregated and then from there we went directly, in a car, down to the Plaza and was dropped off. Our objective there on the Plaza was to go in and be spotters, to try to stop cross-triangulation gunfire on an ambush. We had people that filtrated out into the Plaza and the object there was to get next to anyone that possibly could have been a shooter and take'em out. Now that doesn't mean go shoot'em and take'em out that means get next to'em, stop the timing, do anything you can to eliminate the actual assassination or impending assassination by creating a diversion, bumping shoulders, anything that you could do, if you thought that that was a shooter team. We were under the impression that on a shooter team there would be 3, there would be a spotter, a shooter, and a breakdown man.....So we were looking for 9 people on cross triangulation. We were looking for 3 on the South Knoll, 3 on the upper knoll, and some in the buildings.

The objective was to stop the ambush. We had prior knowledge that the attempt was going to be made. The information that came down earlier that the attempt was going to be made outside the Adolphus Hotel. And for whatever reasons, it was changed at the last minute to the Dealey Plaza. The Dealey Plaza would have been the most logical place to make an ambush style hit on cross-triangulation.

Q: Where you there just as a pilot or were you there as a participant in this operation?

A: I've said I was there as a pilot. I was there as a participant. I was a spotter. We were finding to find out if this was a legit operation, if it was going to be a "hit" and then we would take'em out.

Q: Where were you standing in Dealey Plaza when the shots were fired?

A: I was over on the South side, directly in line with the light posts. Sergio and I were attempting to evaluate where the most logical place to be to make the "hit". We had just got there to the Plaza and everything was all messed up, timing was off, people were not in....where they were supposed to be, the limited radio contacts that we had were not working. Whether the team that I flew in was a combination of the abort team or the shooter team, I have no way of knowing. It could have been a combination of both or it could have been a complete 100% abort team, I don't know.

Q: Tell me exactly where you were standing in Dealey Plaza.

A: I was standing on the South Knoll up from about 150 feet from, well, wait a minute, about a hundred yards from the triple underpass, somewhere along in there, up on the shoulder of the hill that goes up to the other side.

Q: Tell me exactly where you were standing in Dealey Plaza.

A: I was standing about 150 yards, which would have been east, I guess, of the triple underpass up on the south grassy knoll about 5 feet up on the side of the hill, in line with the light posts that were at the Plaza.

BQ: Excuse me Joe. Could you just have Tosh say that same thing again just including the question you answered? I was standing...

A: I was standing about 150 yards, I think its east of the triple underpass, on the south knoll, about 5 feet up the hill, in line with the light posts.

Q: Can you tell me exactly where you were standing in Dealey Plaza?

A: Yes, I can. We were standing approximately 150 feet east of the triple underpass on the south knoll up on the hill about 5 feet in line with the light posts.

Q: Could you tell how many shots were fired that day?

A: I recall myself, I'd say 4 or 5. That's what I recall. I've heard that there were more, I've heard that there were less.

Q: Could you tell the direction of those shots?

A: I couldn't tell the direction of the shots, but however, but my memory is that I feel a shot went over or head to the left of us. I'm familiar with gunfire. Also, when we left the area, we got a taste of gunpowder when we went over the railroad tracks which would have been south of the north grassy knoll.

Q: After the shots were fired, where did you go?

A: We went over the railroad tracks, slid down the hill, went down the hill, now I'm talking about the south knoll. We had transportation waiting for us which was a, I think it was, a '51 Ford, black '51 Ford. We got in that and we went back to...toward Oak Cliff to the "safe" house but we stopped off at Ed McLemore's Sportatorium and Sergio changed clothes because he'd gotten muddy when he slid down the railroad tracks.

Q: When was the next time...?

A: Let me interject something here. The reason that we left...if we were spotted in the Plaza that particular day, or our whole team was....it would have been a real problem for us because we had prior knowledge that an attempt was going to be made. It was imperative that we get out of the area.

Q: Did you then go back to Redbird Airport?

A: Went back to the "safe" house and then eventually to Redbird and we waited for two other people for about an hour maybe an hour and a half and then we left. And I was under the impression that another aircraft was to take two people to Sheppard Air Force Base just north of Dallas.

Q: Did John Roselli return to Redbird?

A: John Roselli did not return. In fact, he was one of the people that I thought we were waiting for.

Q: What kind of plane were you flying that day?

A: We were flying a DC-3.

Q: Do you remember what runway you landed on at the airport?

A: Well, no. The main runway which was the longest one. I think that is a north/south runway.

Q: Did you land that day to the North or to the South?

A: That day we landed to the North. We'd just...a front had just came through the night before and we had to come in on the backside of that front and wait for weather to clear otherwise if we tried to come in...we'd had to come into Dallas/Love Field if we were doing an IFR approach so we waited at Garland until the weather had broke out and hopped over to Redbird and landed Redbird BFR. I'm pretty sure we landed to the North because of the front that just came through.

Q: What part of the airport at Redbird did you park on?

A: I think there was two hangers there and we parked between those two hangers not far from the fuel dump that was located. There was two other aircraft there and we had to move one aircraft in order to get our DC-3 into this particular parking area. And, one of the ramp people helped us move that aircraft.

Q: Did you take on fuel at Redbird?

A: No, we did not take on fuel.

Q: What time of the day on November 22, 1963 did you land at Redbird?

A: About 9:30, 10:00, maybe right around 11:00 it could have been.

Q: What time did you leave Redbird that day?

A: We left there about...pretty close to 2 o'clock.

Q: And how many passengers were on the plane when you left Redbird?

A: There was Rojas, myself, Sergio, a person by the name of Gator, and two other individuals that I didn't know. I don't know who they were.

Q: Did you ever see John Roselli after that?

A: Ah, sometime..no, as a matter of fact I didn't see Roselli after that. Right after that flight I got back to West Palm Beach and then shortly after that I ended up in Denver, Colorado.

Q: Did you ever have an occasion after that to provide any information to the FBI about John Roselli?

A: Yes, through the Farentello Brothers and through a person by the name of Nick Nicholas. I was told that a hit was going, this was in 1976 a few months, that a friend of mine was gonna be...that a hit was made out on him because of his testimony. I immediately, because the FBI had asked me to do this, I immediately informed the FBI of the information that I had about a pending "hit" being made on John Roselli. Two weeks later John Roselli was found in Biscayne Bay and I immediately contacted the FBI and said "hey this is the individual that we were talking about" and "why wasn't something done"?

Q: Are you aware of any FBI records that give this account of you informing them of the death of John Roselli?

A: Yes, I am. There are numerous...there's over 342 files...ah, pages, pertaining to John Roselli. The FBI 105 file from Phoenix Organized Crime Detail, which I think you have copies of, is one of the files...one of the pages, that I am making reference to.

Q: Who was the one to make the "hit" on John Roselli?

A: I have no idea who "hit" Roselli?

Q: Do you have any idea about any organization that might have been behind it?

A: Well, there's no doubt in my mind that the organized crime...let me put it this way...elements within the organized crimes, I think was responsible for the "hit" on Roselli. The organized crime, quote, quote, per se, I don't think had anything to do at all with killing Roselli.

Q: What kind of elements?

A: Well, as we say in CIA. "There's many, many rouges out there". You have just as many rouges in Mafia. In fact, Roselli himself was very, very keen on Kennedy, he loved that man. That's why I find it difficult to say Roselli was an actual hitter or a shooter. Roselli's liaison...contacts was with CIA, but mostly with military people, some here in the Dallas area...4th Army Reserve out of Love Field, 49th Armored Division, Capt. Edward G. Siwells outfit at 4th Army Reserve. He had known these people. As far as Roselli being connected with the CIA, he had a lot of friends in CIA, military intelligence, and also within the government. Mainly, when they had the party at the Fountainbleu Hotel, the opening of the Fountainbleu Hotel, Sam Giancana, John Roselli, and many, many military intelligence personnel was at that opening so that's the reason that I say these things. Roselli was connected with military intelligence.

Q: Do you remember what airport you landed in Houston before you went to Dallas on that day?

A: Houston International which was the main airport there. And, I think it was a Hilton Hotel was were the people had stayed. We'd used that airport and the Hilton had just been built and the parking area where we used was on the Trans-Texas side and it was a National Guard. The National Guard was located right next to the Trans-Texas Airlines and they had just received a couple of AT6-Texans which we were training Cubans to fly in the back seat to make transitions to P-51's. That was the earlier stages, around the '60-'61 area.

BQ: This first question is a little strange. You're a very young looking man but you say you've been working since 1956. Do you mind saying how old you are to the camera?

A: I'm 55 years old. I joined the Army underage at 16 years old, or 15 actually. The Army found out about my age and then I was honorably discharged providing I would assign myself to the Texas 49th Armored Division until I turned 17 at which time I would go back into the active service, that did happen, and then I was immediately attached to the 4th Army Reserve Military Intelligence out of Dallas, Texas.

BQ: On these various flights that you mention taking, are there flight logs that exist?

A: There has been a report of a flight plan that was uncovered in 1976 by Thomas Downing and Rick Feeney, I believe, where they allege that they had found the actual flight plan of the Dallas flight. I take exception to this because there was no flight plan filled out or filed on the Dallas flight, from Houston to Dallas. There was no flight plan filed from Tampa to New Orleans. We went open water across ADIZ zone. Then from New Orleans to Houston there was no flight plan. The flight plan that they're making reference to was the flight plan for 6393 Echo out of Thompson Flying Service, Salt Lake City, which was a 172 Cessna which had Roselli's name on it, and also had some other player's names on it, some of them military intelligence, some coded operations that were written. But, this was random writing on the back of a flight plan at that particular time. It was just making notes. I saw that. One investigator tried to tell me that that was the actual flight plan and I said absolutely not.

BQ: You said that you were familiar with gunfire.

A: Yes.

BQ: Why would that be?

A: Well, I've been in a lot of operations. I was in Cuba. I worked with Column 9, Frank Perez's outfit. I worked as a "military advisor" in the early stages of anti-Castro movements with operations like, well, independent operations like Alpha 66 and Omega 7 and others and then I was in Southeast Asia. I'm extremely familiar with gunfire. Lot's of it.

BQ: The people who were on the flight grouping and the people you were on the flight that you left Dallas with, what was the difference in the grouping there?

A: The time that we left Dallas, I felt something was drastically wrong. My pilot, I felt, and still feel all these years, had known more about that operation than what I had known. The flight out of Dallas was one of the strangest flights I've ever been on in my life. It was not a.....it was a team that was in total dejection. I mean we were...we'd...we'd actually, by our own disorganization, we had fouled...we had fouled up. Whether the information and intelligence that we'd got had been tampered with prior to that flight, or on that day, I have no way of knowing. The people that were on flight was very quiet. It was, for everybody that was on board, it seemed to be an extremely sad day. That's why I take issue, if these had been shooters or assassins themselves, I think they would have been very excited because they had carried it off. That's why I take issue with the fact that I....CIA had anything to do with flying an attack team in.

BQ: So, why do you think Roselli didn't go back on the plane with you?

A: I have no idea why he didn't come back. It may have been already plan, everybody had their own agenda. I wouldn't be at that level to know what the actual planning was if it was a military style abort team.

BQ: So, Tosh, you were not the pilot of this plane?

A: I was the co-pilot. Rojas was my pilot and Rojas, Emmanuel Rojas had been active in the Cuban, he'd worked for Cugana Airlines and also Rejana Airlines earlier back in the late 50's and early 60's. He was the son of the Rojas that was with Batista's Secret Police that was executed two days after Castro came into power.

BQ: Who was Sergio?

A: Sergio was a friend of mind. We had been on many missions together. We were on the William Pawley raid to remove Eddie Bayou out of Cuba and also Huesto Carillio and Barkeen, ransom release prisoners that were a friend of Sylvia Odio's grandfather or father. We were sent into Cuba on two separate occasions, one, to remove missile technicians, the defectors out of Cuba, the other one to remove a Cuban prisoner that had been released from the Isles of Pine; on the second occasion an aircraft was supposed to be inside Cuba to fly these people out and it wasn't available or it was pretty well shot up so we were taken out by rubber raft to a boat then eventually back to Marathon key.

BQ: You mentioned the spotter, the shooter, and a breakdown man. Could you explain to us what those functions are?

A: O.K. In Locksahatchie, where we were being briefed and after we had received the information on what we were going to do, we discussed where to go, how to abort, and what to look for. In doing that, that's where we came up with we would probably be looking for a minimum of 19 or 20 people that would be in that Plaza. This was military operation and if we had reacted to abort this with violence, there would have the damnest massacre you ever saw in Dealey Plaza. Some it was our instructions to take them out quietly.

BQ: The shooter is obvious, what is the spotter and the breakdown man?

A: The spotter is to make sure the perimeter is secure so the shooter can do his job. The breakdown man is, the shooter will leave immediately, the spotter will make sure the perimeter is secure so that he can get out without being seen, and the breakdown man will immediately break the rifle down and stash it and take it to wherever he was going to take it. This was supposition on our part at that particular time. Crossfire Triangulation is the mark of an ambush. The light poles that I make reference to would be the most logical place to do your sighting and lineup. If anybody knows any Vietnam people here or Vet guys know that a sniper does not move his scope with a moving target. He waits until something comes into the field of view. That was the reason for the lineup of the light posts. If you look at all the shots, exactly where Kennedy was "hit" is directly in triangulation with those light posts. So my feelings at that point, and Sergio's also, was that they needed a reference point to make the "hit". And, the most logical place would be in line with those light posts that go down the Plaza both ways.

BQ: You were standing in line with those light posts?

A: Yeah, just maybe a little bit to the left.

BQ: Tosh, if you could, I'd like for you to take us back to the sequence of events that occurred from the time you arrived in Dealey Plaza until the time you got into the car, everything you can remember, seeing anyone in particular that you know was there, if you could just tell us that story.

A: After we left the "safe" house on Bar Harbor drive near the Oak Cliff Country Club, we proceeded down to the Plaza area and, I think its Industrial and where the triple underpass, anyway that's where we were let out and we walked from there underneath the triple underpass to the South grassy knoll. We had other people in the area that were supposed to be securing the South knoll and the other buildings up behind, what's that, the Del-Tex building or something like that. Sergio and I went to the South knoll and Sergio was looking for the most logical place for a shooter to be which would have been behind the South grassy knoll fence. There was absolutely nothing in that parking lot other than a couple of cars parked. We came on and angled across and down to the area where I make reference to the light posts and that's where we stood, and that's where I personally saw Kennedy's head shatter. I mean, just went. At that point, Sergio turns to me and he says "We f---ed up, let's get the hell out of here", and then so we turned and started up, a little bit on an angle, up that hill toward the fence on the South grassy, yeah, South grassy knoll, stayed along the fence perimeter and went across the railroad tracks, slipped down in the backside of the hill there near the railroad tracks, and our man was out in that, at that point I think there was a vacant field like a parking lot out there which was right next to Industrial Blvd., is that the name, I can't remember the name of the street, and that's where we were picked up and then we made a, I think we made a U-turn 'cause there was traffic backed up there, and we went back out Katy's or toward Ed McLemore's Sportatorium where we stopped in the parking lot at Ed McLemore's and the driver had an extra change of clothes for both of us. I did not change clothes but Sergio did change clothes 'cause he was pretty muddy; in other words he hit the railroad tracks, tripped over the railroad tracks, fell down the backside of the hill and rolled a little bit and he was pretty much of a muddy mess. So then we got out that way. Went back to the Bar Harbor "safe" house and then was transported over to Redbird for the flight out.

BQ: Thank you. Did you see Roselli in Dealey Plaza that day?

A: No, I did not.

BQ: Did you see anything from the 6th floor window?

A: Nothing that would look suspicious to me, however, the most significant thing that I remember, we were looking for a diversion. It would be logical for a team to set up a diversion to focus in that direction while something was going on in this direction. I remember an incident where people congregated right out in front of the Texas School Book Depository and I'd heard the sound of ambulances and this so we thought that that could be the first sign of a diversion so instead of going toward the sound and going toward the people, Sergio and I went back up to the knoll there to check the parking lot. We thought at that point if a shooter was getting in place, he would be getting in place now because we were probably, at that point, 5-10 minutes before the motorcade would be coming down.

BQ: Did you see any smoke or anything coming from the grassy knoll?

A: No, I didn't see any smoke or anything like that. I smelt smoke as we went over the railroads, just prior to the railroad tracks.

BQ: How many people were in that car that picked you up?

A: There were just one driver.

BQ: Just you and Sergio got in?

A: Sergio, myself, and the driver.

BQ: Why do you think they picked a '51 Ford?

A: I don't know if they picked a '51 Ford or if it was a car that was available. There was an older car but we've used a lot of older cars,. you know. My feeling is that it was someone local around there and that it was their automobile.

BQ: Do you have any feeling that Roselli was involved in the shooting?

A: Well, I've got mixed feelings on that. Personally, from my background, going back to the '60's with Roselli, the things we were involved with in Cuba and gun running operations out of LaBar Ranch in Louisiana and Bayou Boeuf and Morgan City, the times we went into Havana and the people he knew in Havana, my feelings is that Roselli was gathering intelligence for military operations. I do not feel that Roselli was the assassin.

BQ: Why do think he was killed?

A: Mainly, because he was getting ready to testify and we have to understand that the Kennedy assassination was one of many, many black-op operations that was going on at that particular time and Roselli was up to his neck in making liaison with the members of organized crime for, not necessarily, well for elements within CIA and military Intelligence. The whole Castro assassination plot, from JM/Wave, and Mongoose, and all that, Roselli was aware of what was going on those particular things because in some cases the shooters and people that were involved in those things, particularly Trujillo, came out of organized crime. I don't say that families of organized crime conspired and sent these people in. These people had tremendous contacts with military intelligence even to the point to where, in some cases, that operatives would be referring to some people as "Colonels" and things like that, that were actually organized crime. Charlie, "the blade", had good liaison, in the early days of Cuba, of setting up a gun operation, the LaBar training camp, the Morgan City operation, the West Coast Thunderbird Inn operation, the Farentello Brothers. All these people were not military intelligence but they had tremendous contact with CIA personnel and military intelligence people. It would be, at that point and time, to our benefit to have these people feeding us information about what organized crime members were doing. In the early stages of the Kennedy assassination, there were many, many, many reports that Kennedy was going to be "hit" and many, many reports that Kennedy was going to be "hit" by organized crime so this was all investigated. That's why I don't feel that any direct involvement on a high level from our government was involved in the Kennedy assassination but I certainly believe that there were certainly rouges within CIA, rouges within military intelligence, rouges within Mafia, and rouges within high-ups in the National Security Council that was certainly aware that an attempt was gonna be made. The mechanics of the attempt, I don't think that they were aware and I think that they launched an extensive intelligence gathering investigation to find out if the rumors that were circulating around Southern Florida were true, that Kennedy was going to be "hit", first in Austin, Texas, later in some other area, no, West Palm Beach and then Austin, Texas then it turned out to be Dallas.

BQ: Just gonna ask you two or three more questions. Could you explain to the layman, like myself, how the CIA would go about hiring a team like yours in this kind of situation?

A: Well, they would never do it direct for one thing. It would be done through intermediaries. And then it would be like what I call the "good ol' boy" network. One guy knows this guy, this guy knows this guy, eventually this guy's tied in with this guy and then he comes up and gets busted and then immediately hollers "I work for the CIA". Does that answer your question?

BQ: Ah, yeah, I guess what I'm saying is that I think it would be surprising to a layman that the CIA would, how can I put this, that the CIA would hire a group like yours knowing that there was an assassination attempt coming and that they would use a team like yours to thwart the assassination, can you explain the thinking behind that?

A: Well, number one, the CIA would have absolutely nothing to do with the actual planning because their position at that point was to gather intelligence and assimilate that to the proper people. In our particular case, that intelligence would be passed back to military intelligence operatives so CIA would be acting as a support level for our particular operations. As far as the CIA being involved in the planning stages as a upper level agency, I find that very difficult to believe because the method of operation on recruiting agents and operatives or recruiting operatives doesn't work that way., The CIA would gather this information, assimilate it, decipher it, and then pass it back to appropriate authorities, in this case, I would say it would be military intelligence even though some of the information had came from operatives in military ranks which were involved in Mafia.

BQ: Has it ever crossed your mind that there could have been, I don't know how to put this, let me rephrase it, has it crossed your mind that they could have told you were there for one purpose but actually you might have been there for the opposite purpose?

A: Yes, that's crossed my mind many times, that when we say the anonymous "they", they could have told us anything, but the people that would be "they" would be special interest groups within the agency, in my opinion.

BQ: So, could you just take that scenario of what that might have been, you know, what you might have been thinking over the years as you look back on this for a possibility?

A: The possibility would be, I'd go back all the way back to William Bill Harvey, old Wild Bill, and his operations and coming out of the OSS and the beginning of the "good ol' boy" network and the formation of the CIA. The CIA at that point was pretty well closely related. Everybody sort of knew everybody. Everybody knew what teams that other members had been on, even back in Germany's days when Colby was with the OSS, so we had a family. And then when the Cuban matter came, because of intelligence gathering in the vast network of the Cuban community, it was imperative that the CIA recruit those people that knew something and knew how to make the contacts and the roadways into the Cuban community in order to, which these people could be used to implement a form of foreign policy. Am I answering your question or am I rambling?

BQ: No, but that's all right. This is difficult, but what I'm saying is that somewhere in this last 29 years, if it's crossed your mind maybe if they told you were going in to thwart the assassination, but actually you were there to be part of the assassination, if you could articulate that....

A: Yes, this question has come up a lot. Maybe a part of the team could have been an actual "hit" team. But, if we go back to "they", when we say "they", CIA implemented that "hit" team, I say CIA as an agency did not implement that "hit" team but perhaps as we call them now, rouges, or special interest groups within the agency because of the "good ol' boy" network could have certainly been involved in an operation to assassinate the President. Maybe I'm not making myself clear on this. For instance, like we all work for a particular company. Some of us are loyal and some of us aren't. It takes time to spot those people. If a guy's got a particular tremendous asset, then he'll be utilized.

As soon as he breaches that asset he'll be eliminated. I mean as soon as he no longer becomes an asset, he'll be eliminated. I guess what I'm saying in answer to your question that I believe that within the agency itself and the vast Cuban network that was recruited for covert operations at that time, that became the nuclei that led up to the Kennedy assassination and not from the White House, even though they may have had prior knowledge and may have had motives, and not from the CIA, and definitely not from the military intelligence community as a whole. But, people within that operation and those operations could certainly have conspired, aligned themselves, because of all the gun running that was going on, because of all the "dirty tricks" that were being pulled in many, many hot spots of the World, including the Dominican Republic at that time, I definitely believe that rouge operatives within the agency orchestrated the whole events that we are now getting into, in my opinion.

BQ: Is there anybody on your team that you think may have been shooters?

A: Perhaps the 3 people that I couldn't ever get a handle on exactly where they come from. When you're in an operation like that and you have a little bit of discussion, usually you can get a pretty good feeling from where individuals on a team come from. I mean you've either run across'em some place or you know of their particular operation even though you won't know the specifics of that operation. In this particular case there were three people on board that I could not get a handle on.

BQ: You said that you once saw Nicoletti and Roselli together looking over maps. Can you tell us what those maps where?

A: Those maps were pertaining to a gun running operation that was gonna be set up in the Bahamas on a place called Cat Cay, I believe it was, it was known as a staging area. The gentleman that Roselli was talking with had connections with the maritime arm of operations in Cuba which the old raider ship Rex, O'Rourke, some of these operations, Sullivan, I think it was Danny Sullivan, Jim Buchanan and all these. These were the ships, the raider ship known as the Rex, the Violent 3, the Windjammer and the Thor were all raider ships that were sent to carry out sabotage missions through the Florida Straits into Cuba and into other areas including the Dominican Republic.

BQ: The general "they" that we've been talking about, can you be specific as to who gave you your instructions for November 22, 1963?

A: Yes, my handler at that point was a person by the name of Bob Bennett. The people that would be CIA direct liaison aliases names, Bill Rogers, Rex Beardsley, Bob Bennett, and Larry Allen. And a guy by the name of Johnny Smith, which was actually John Roselli, those are found in the 105 files.

BQ: You said Roselli was one of the people you got your instructions from, correct?

A: Not on that particular day, not Roselli. That particular day my instructions came through Locksahatchie through Robert Bennett and also Rex Beardsley, I believe it was.

BQ: But Roselli was a key figure and someone you did get instructions from?

A: Well, Roselli's name was mentioned that day that he would be picked up at Tampa airport and he was staying at the Congress Inn so I guess as far as that particular mission the first time I heard Roselli's name was through Bob Bennett who instructed me and Sergio and Rojas. Rojas came from Miami to Lantana and we came from Locksahatchie to Lantana but I was already instructed through Bennett that we were to pick up John Roselli, and he was referred to as the Colonel, and I knew who that was because I had already had previous contact on many, many occasions with Johnny Roselli.

BQ: Did you find it odd at all that you had many, many contacts with him prior to November 22 and none after?

A: Well, after then we get into my personal story of what happened to me on the aftermath. As the record shows, I was in lockup shortly after that, two weeks before the Warren Commission convened, and I was released from lockup one month after the Warren Commission was over.

BQ: Can you say why you were in lockup?

A: Yes, I was extradited from Florida on a $50 no-account check in Denver, Colorado which had been dismissed. But that was agreed to. In other words, I was instructed to write it out. A lot of people say I was taken away for my own protection, some people say I was double crossed. I have no firm opinion on that.

VQ: Tosh, did any of your team which you flew in fire any questions at JFK?

A: Not to my knowledge. I doubt that very seriously. My team that I flew in, and I'm gonna stand behind the abort theory. Right now, I'm fully aware that it is a story but I do know that in time, a very short time, it will be confirmed.

VQ: Did they fire any shots at anybody?

A: They fired absolutely...well, I can't speak for the whole team. I can only speak for Sergio and myself and a couple of others that were there that I know did not fire any shots. Now, the people that left New Orleans and came up, the people that left Garland and went out, I'm not sure, they could have been getting set up, They could have fired. There was no doubt in my mind that it was an abort mission but the people that got off at Garland, the 3 people, could have been, I have to be fair with myself, they could have been shooters because I did not have a handle on those people.

BQ: Do you know the names of those people?

A: No...well, I know some operative names but that wouldn't, you know, these names have been batted around so much over the years since the Church Committee and the JM/Wave Amlash operations that I'm extremely confused on who's on first, and who's on second and who's on third. Names mean absolutely nothing and when you get into the research community, we could not seem to get this through to the research community, that if you're gonna go on a military operation the first objective is to protect that operation so you're not going in with I.D. Even the tatoos that I have on that operation, I got myself in tremendous amount of trouble because I tattooed my arm so we go to great pains to make sure that we protect those operations.

Q: Tosh, did you know Lee Harvey Oswald?

A: Yes, I knew Lee Harvey Oswald.

Q: Where did you first meet him?

A: I first meet Lee Harvey Oswald at a secret base called Illusionary Warfare Training at Nagshead, North Carolina in 1959 prior to him going to language school and going to Russia.

Q; Did you just meet him or did you get to know him?

A: I got to...well, I just met him and remembered him....At the time that I met him in '59 he was a Marine, we were all in Illusionary Warfare Training, or something...propaganda stuff, and he was there and he was doing language study at that particular point. I didn't recognize him as anybody them other than just another black operative.

Q: Did you ever see him after that?

A: Yes, one time in Honolulu with another guy at a radar installation and that was about....oh I guess shortly after that...shortly after Nagshead... my dates may be wrong. It could have been '58 or '59 right around that area.

Q: Were there other occasions when you saw him?

A: Well, the one at the radar complex there on either Ohau or...I can't remember exactly where it was. But he was there at that time and I saw him briefly at Wheeler Air Force Base there at there at Oahu outside Honolulu and he was getting ready to leave an go to Dal...the whole group was getting ready to leave and we had been just completing jungle warfare training.

Q: Did you ever see him again after that?

A: Yes, in '62 when I came back into Dallas area, that, through the Dallas Cubans over on, not Harlendale Street, but there was a "safe" house here in Dallas, Oak Cliff, two of'em. There was a small two bedroom frame type house that was located in Oak Cliff not far from the zoo where the old inner urban track used to go through, I mean there's a highline down through there now, at that place and then I think it was Zang's Blvd. there used to be "safe" house there that was run by Hernandez out of Miami that had connections with Alpha 66 at one point that se up a "safe" house for Dallas Cubans that were filtrating out of the Miami area. Oswald, from those two "safe" houses, I went to another "safe" house and that "safe" house was directly behind where Oswald had rented a room, in the alley, and I carved my initials on the draining board up there at that time and that was a gun running operation and Oswald was renting the front house. I saw him there briefly but did not talk to him.

Q: Is that the house he lived in when the assassination occurred?

A: I'm not sure of the dates. Researchers would have to get the dates but this was just prior.. I had just came in from flying Roselli and John Martino from Houston to Galveston and my next trip was from Houston back to Dallas so that would have been around June of '63, or no...before June...it would have been around April or May of '63.

Q: Did you know Roscoe White?

A: Roscoe White was at the radar complex and jungle warfare training in Honolulu and that's where I first met him. When I say met him...I would have never, never have picked Roscoe White and my feelings, it's a tragedy of what happened to Roscoe White's life. He was an operative. He was military intelligence. Basically, I think he was a good man. This other investigation a few years ago that came out...that however that went...the sensationalism of that was done very poorly because what it has done nowadays has totally discredited Roscoe White as being a military operative. The fact that Oswald and Roscoe White, the radar complex, and jungle warfare training, and Nagshead, North Carolina and all these things......

Q: When was the last time you saw Roscoe White?

A: The last time I saw Roscoe White was over in Honolulu and that was about '59. I had no liaison with White, you know, after that. I wasn't even aware that he was possibly in the Plaza until some researchers indicated that to me by pictures and I identified him as working at the radar complex from pictures that researchers had shown me stating he was in Dallas.

Q: Are you saying that you saw Roscoe White and Lee Harvey Oswald together?

A: Not together, at the same place and the same time. There was a ship that went over with White and a bunch of Marines and I can't remember the name of that particular ship, and I think that Oswald was on board that ship.

Q: Do you think or do you know?

A: Well, I've been told that he was and it confirmed a rumor that I had heard from Bernard Fensterwald some years later.

Q: Have you ever in your life time found out that a person was a desperate criminal when you thought maybe they would have been a deacon maybe in a Baptist Church? You were not correct in what you believed about them?

A: Yes, including myself. I'm a Mormon Elder in the Mormon Church, extremely active in the '70's. So the illusions that we set up on ourself, especially in view of the Kennedy assassination, I wouldn't be surprised... you could have been there, Joe, for all I know.

Q: Even though you believe that Roselli might not have been involved, is it possible that he could have been involved in the assassination?

A: Oh, it's possible. My feelings are I just don't believe that he was. But, the documents that are being accumulated in the last few years are starting to point in that direction, that he was more involved in the actual attempt then what's been reported. But documents are only as good as what someone...what you want someone to believe and there have been a tremendous amount of planted documents over the years.

BQ: Did you ever see Roselli and Oswald together?

A: No I never saw Roselli and Oswald together.

BQ: Did you ever see Roselli and White together?

A: Not, not, no...not together.

BQ: Sam Giancana?

A: Sam Giancana, Roselli, yes, I saw them together many times in fact one of them was when they opened the Fountainbleu Hotel in Miami. They had a big bash there and I think Frank Sinatra and portions of what they refer to in the circle as the "rat pack" was there. And then a tremendous amount of military were there, retired people, and a lot of CIA people were there for the opening.

ROBERT "TOSH" PLUMLEE 6/4/92 DEALEY PLAZA INTERVIEW

VQ: Tosh, In your own words, without me asking you any questions, where were you standing, what did you see, and what happened on November 22, 1963?

A: When we first got here, we were dropped off on the other side of the triple underpass here. We walked through this portal right here and we cut up this area here. The objective here was to check this parking lot, make sure it was secure, make sure that no team could be lingering back there around the cars and stuff and come up to the fence later. Sergio and I felt that this area was secure. We knew that we had other team members over here in this other area and we assumed that that area was also secure. We also had a team or team members that was supposed to be securing the Records Building rooftops and the County Jail rooftops. At that point and time, it didn't dawn on me or it didn't dawn on Sergio to even consider the Texas School Book Depository. Our objective was to try to find a military style type ambush which would have been cross triangulation for a shot. We, at this point, came down and at that time the motorcade was about turning or maybe halfway between the City Jail...or the County Jail...and the turnoff, right through there. Sergio and I came over here, looked at these light posts here and decided, o.k. if we had a shooter, more than likely he would be right along in here using the left or the right side of these posts as a reference point for timing or whatever. We felt this area was really secure. We walked down about right along in here and then we observed the rest of the motorcade as it came around. At this point, we noticed, I think I was standing about like this or maybe back a little bit, and we noticed a lot of commotion as it started coming into view and then the shots came out and that's when all hell broke loose. At this point right here, I remember seeing Kennedy's head going way back like that. Sergio turned to me and he said "Oh my gosh, we f---ed up, Let's get the hell out of here". So, at this point, I turned like this and then made a step to come up and around. Sergio was about right along here. We went up here. There was a gentleman down here in a parked car...a truck...as we got to about this area, he hollered something to Sergio...Sergio was maybe a little bit down ..he says "It looks real bad". Then we continued to proceed up through this way just casually walking like we were going to go back over where the crowd... The crowd was congregating going to that section right there. There was a few congregation up there at the deal. I looked back once or twice in time to see the limousine go under the triple underpass which we were about, at that point, probably right along here. We continued on over here. This picket fence was up. There was a little opening right through here. We went through this area, across the railroad tracks, slid down the hill to our waiting automobile, which was in this lower parking lot at that particular time. We got in the car. This new freeway wasn't there at that point like that. And then went a u-turn, went up to that red light, went left down here to Ed McLemore's Sportatorium where Sergio changed clothes. I didn't change clothes and then from the Sportatorium we went to the "safe house" over by Redbird Airport in Oak Cliff, next to the Country Club and that's how we got out of the Plaza that day. We did not continue to even look back over this way. At that point and time we both felt that it was imperative that we get out of the area due to the fact that if we were picked up there we had absolutely no cover story of why we were in the area, and the fact that we had military and CIA contacts and liaison, coordination with them. It would have been a very hard one to explain why two operatives were caught on the south knoll if there was more than one shot fired. At that point, we thought there was a battery of shots coming from up here and on out. Now later, when we got back to Redbird, Sergio and I sort of debriefed ourself and we both felt....that back here in this area right through here, approximately right along in here...that a shooter probably shot through here because we were about 25-30 feet to the right and we both felt that a shot went to our left and up above our head. When we got to this point right here we did smell gunsmoke. We felt that maybe that gunsmoke had drifted, because of the North wind, across here from the time span it took us to get from the light post to this intersection right here, we definitely picked up a good solid smell of gunpowder. Now it could either have been a shooter standing here that we had missed that may have been in the parking lot concealed in a car, I don't rule out John Roselli could have been involved as a spotter...the theory of the "abort" end of it could have been a mixed jumble of communication or information to us so that we would happily go on this particular mission thinking we were aborting an attempt on the assassination. At that point, we decided that the best thing to do was to just stay quite about it and let the investigators do their work. Also in any operation, military or otherwise...CIA, the first thing to do is to protect the operation at all cost. At that point and time that was exactly what we felt that we were doing. We felt that we went in, Sergio and I at least felt, that we went in to abort or with a team to abort. However, with a view of the fact of the people that was on that aircraft, and the contact that I'd had with organized crime in Miami and Nevada, and the people that were on board that aircraft at that time, I don't rule out the possibility that we could have possibly flown the attack team in. Over the years, I've tried to sidestep that issue or haven't came forward and came out too public about that, and I thought I'd let the investigators which, obviously, nowadays they have done some fantastic work.

BQ: Again, I'd like to ask you, who was on the plane that you were a co-pilot on, that landed in Dallas?

A: O.K., the personnel on the plane was Sergio, who I'd been in other operations with back in the early 60's and late 50's; Rojas, Emmanuel Rojas, who was my pilot, I was acting as co-pilot; John Roselli, and we all had code names that we had assigned to ourself like eagle, raven, hawk, and this type thing. These were the people who were on the aircraft.

BQ: You're aware that there is one school of thought that placed Charles Nicoletti on that airplane?

A: Yes, I am aware that it's said that Charles Nicoletti was on board the aircraft. In the early stages of the investigation that I came in with, I had picked out a picture of Nicoletti when I was shown 10 pictures by a Senate investigator. Then later, the story came back to me that Nicoletti was in town because he picked up John Roselli at Redbird Airport and then at that point I lost contact with all of them.

BQ: Did you see Nicoletti pick up Roselli?

A: No, I didn't see Nicoletti pick up Roselli, but because of the liaison that we had had and the discussion that was on board the aircraft, there was no doubt in my mind that Nicoletti was the person that John Roselli was referring to meet in Dallas on that particular morning.

BQ: Could you give us a little glimpse of that conversation, the propensity of that?

A: Well, it goes back to about April of '63, when Nicoletti, and the Thunderbird Inn in Vegas, and a money transaction to purchase aircraft.....

BQ: Let me ask you that question again. What did you hear on the airplane that convinced you that Nicoletti would be meeting Roselli in Dallas?

A: It was the things that John Roselli had said about people that he was going to be meeting in this town which immediately made me think of the individual that I had in mind which later turned out to be identified as Nicoletti. The pickup, the transportation mode, the fact that I knew of the liaison contact between John Roselli and Nicoletti because of the previous flights that we had made back in April with John Martino and it was my opinion that the party that John Roselli would be meeting in Dallas that day was Charles Nicoletti.

BQ: Was there a code that you had heard in the past that you heard that day?

A: There was a code name by the name of "Raven" which other investigators later tried to tell me was Lee Harvey Oswald, but I don't buy that. I'd buy that the code name given out as "Raven" was Nicoletti.

BQ: You knew in the past that Roselli had referred to Nicoletti as "Raven"?

A: Yes, in the past John Roselli had referred to Nicoletti as "Raven". One specific incident was a gun running operation out of Cat Cay, at Biscayne Bay, at Sloppy Joe's when maps were exchanged and Nicoletti was responsible for getting.....I'm sorry.....John Roselli was responsible for getting the maps to the place in Bimini which was a "safe haven" to Nicoletti. At that point in time, I was under the impression that there was a hit coming up someplace but I did not know, I was not at the level, to know that intimate planning. The meetings and the fact that Johnny Roselli had tremendous liaison with Charles Nicoletti dating all the way back to Arizona at the Caravan Inn, the Thunderbird Inn in Nevada, Burbank, California and Santa Barbara. These were people I had flown earlier. Roselli was one of them. Like I said, Nicoletti's picture was shown to me but I did not identify him as Nicoletti. I identified him under an operative name with the code name "Raven" at that point. It was only some years later that one of the investigators on the Senate staff come back and said "Nicoletti was on board your aircraft" and I made the statement to him at that point and time that "No, Nicoletti was in Dallas and picked Roselli up. I think you have your names transposed of Roselli and Nicoletti on who was on that flight."

BQ: So the modus operandi on the flight into Dallas matched the same modus operandi every time that Roselli was to meet Nicoletti?

A: The M.O., the method of operation, was the same each time that John Roselli and Nicoletti met whether it be at Biscayne Bay, or whether Marathon Key, or whether it be at LeBar Ranch in New Orleans or whether it be with the old gun running operation out of Midland...Menilothan, Texas, I think it was. So these were the areas where John Roselli and Charles Nicoletti had previous contact. At that time, my point of view, there was no doubt in my mind that Nicoletti was here to pick up Roselli and the others with the cartons that came on board the aircraft to go out to wherever they were going to go and then we came over to Redbird.

BQ: You were present all those other times that you just named?

A: Yes, the times that I just referred to, I was present because I was the pilot that had flown these people in to these particular meetings at Caravan Inn which the 105 documents make reference to.

BQ: So you would have no reason in the world to suspect that there would be a new "Raven" or that Roselli was not meeting Nicoletti based on the five or six separate times.

A: No, I would have no reason. In fact, with Charles...Roselli, the liaison that Roselli had with Nicoletti and other...like Charlie "The Blade" or Farentino, which was maybe Frank Sturgis or whoever, I would have no reason to doubt that Nicoletti was the pickup man. Now maybe, I'm getting into opinions now, I think that Roselli was carrying the instructions for Nicoletti. Now, whether Nicoletti was the shooter or a member of the abort team, I don't know. Over the years, it's hard for me to accept the fact that I was told "abort" and might have played a major, major role in actually bringing the team into Dallas on that day.

BQ: How would you feel about that personally if that turns out to be the case?

A: I would feel I've been double-crossed. If that was the case. All the evidence is pointing to the fact that, or pointing, not necessarily a fact, or pointing to that we flew the attack team in. The documents that are being uncovered nowadays is indicating more in that direction then the documents that we had 10 years ago that would indicate more into a military abort team.

BQ: How did you feel about JFK personally?

A: I loved the man. I never had any qualms with the administration. Back in those particular days when we were doing those "ops" it was a very honorable thing to be part of a "black" crew and a military intelligence because I guess we were young and impressionable, if you want to call it that.

BQ: So can you give me your thoughts when you do reflect on this and you figure the possibility that it was a double cross that you might have been, unwittingly, responsible for the assassination of JFK.

A: Unwittingly, yes, I would say that. It's beginning to appear to me that in the very early stages of the coming together of this team that we had infiltration into our intelligence network and I think that that's where the pickup and the transition and it would appear that higher-ups in the CIA and military intelligence out of the Pentagon planned the operation. I don't believe that's the case. I believe that our information had been intercepted and as a result of that it was definitely used a cover because of the contacts that these Mafioso's had with military intelligence and the CIA.

BQ: Do you think Sam Giancana enters into this?

A: I think Sam Giancana is a major, major player in this and in fact a bigger player than John Roselli. I think, In fact, I know Sam Giancana knew Charlie Nicoletti extremely well and I think Nicoletti was a hitman for Sam Giancana and others in the Mafia and others in the Mafia at that time, mainly located out of New Orleans, Louisiana, and the old gun running operations that dated back to the '50's.

BQ: What was the "Cuban Peso" operation you mentioned earlier?

A: That was another operation just prior to...we were transporting money for the purchase of...buying military hardware and aircraft and I was given $8,000 to transfer to John Martino in West Palm Beach, which was put into a Greyhound Bus locker. The Cuban Peso deal was s deal where we flew in a PBY, which belonged to Texaco, or registered to Texaco at that time, and we flew boxes of pesos into Cuba to be distributed inside Cuba to undermine the economy. This was not one of my operations, I was only a recruited pilot to fly that operations because the C-46 that they had could not get down into the mountains so we went to a Catalina PBY that was available through Texaco and we dropped the money off in rubber rafts and it was floated to shore.

BQ: Can you just tell me from your own personal experience why you've come to this conclusion why Nicoletti may have been the hitman for Giancana?

A: Well, I have to go back into some real touchy, touchy stuff. Let me see if I can explain it to you in this way. The operations that we were involved with were many, many operations. Assassination attempts, going all the way back to Arbenz in '54, Pinochet in Argentine, the Che Guevara situation, the prior Cubans. All these things were operating without knowledge of any Federal entity. For instance, we can go into the Kennedy thing and the files are opened, that's not going to prove anything about Kennedy at all. What it will prove is that there were maybe 50-75 "black-ops" going on that involved assassinations all the way from Trujillo down to Arbenz, dissension in the Caribbean, propaganda, dropping leaflets, everything we could do, dirty tricks, as a unit, for the sake of fighting Communism in the Cold War was what we did. So, when we get into the Kennedy documents everybody is looking for a document that is going to be a "smoking gun". The "smoking guns" are going to be the various operations that I played in, Charles Nicoletti played in, John Roselli played in, Sam

Giancana played in, and some of the other people that was involved in the Cuban cause in the early days going back to Carlos Peral, Sicarrez, and Myron Coley, I think it is. So, its a continuation of the early-late 50's with Wild Bill Harvey's group that continued to function all the way up to the '60's with many, many operations. The reason that I could circulate within those compartmentalized operations was, in some cases, that other pilots that could not fly those missions, or the plan would be down, or the plane was destroyed by snipers or whatever happened, well, they would go out on the block, recruit another aircraft which would be a completely independent crew of that operation, so therefore I could bounce around and see these people operating in their own environment for a particular mission. Then as a result of that, I began to have a good rapport with members of organized crime, that in return led to me knowing Nicoletti, John Roselli and Sam Giancana, the Fountainbleu Hotel and the military intelligence that operated out of the Fountainbleu and Sloppy Joe's and this type stuff with Roselli. Roselli was refereed to as the "Colonel" by more than one CIA, not operative, but agent. He did have carte blanche to Jim Wave headquarters out of Miami. It was not surprising to me know that we either sanctioned or otherwise was using Mafioso hitmen to carry out foreign policy. But in those days, it did not surprise me because that was the way you fought the cold war and communism. Nowadays it's a little bit different. You can't take today's standards and apply them back then and say why didn't you stop this because it was impossible. The other side of the coin is that I was in my mid-20's in those days and it was a great honor to be selected to go into a military operation to uphold the integrity and this constitution of the United States. Most of the gentlemen that I was connected with were about my age, in the operative level, and we were extremely patriotic. If that's a good word to use nowadays, I'm not sure if that's a good word to use. We felt that is was a tremendous honor to be selected. Just like Ollie North felt like it was tremendous to come out of the Pentagon and connected with the National Security Council. You have to remember that operative's first responsibility, at all costs, is to protect that operation. Now if that is an illegal operation, that doesn't matter, it's not our job to question. Even to the point of an assassination. Even to the point of an assassination of a sitting President. It's not our policy to question those things. Now that might seem hard and callous and unreal but if a particular operation was launched and then you balked that operation, blew that operation, because of your personal preference politically or morally then you're not going to be around very much longer to carry off another operation. And besides that, people and investigators have to remember that tremendous effort went into code names, aliases and covering up any type of paperwork that would elude to those operations. Now when I'm talking about "those operations", I'm talking about Kennedy, I'm talking about all those "black" operations that were implemented during that time span. It's not for us to question at that point. It's only came in the last five to ten years when I really began, with inside myself, to doubt what I really did. It's a very hard adjustment for me to come through to find out, when I mention double-cross earlier, to find out that maybe, inadvertently, people within my own military intelligence were perhaps on the take with Mafia, and used the intelligence that was gathered by good solid agents and manipulated that intelligence to plan a hit right here in this Plaza.

BQ: So you think it's quite possible that Roselli and Nicoletti could have been shooters?

A: Not Roselli. Roselli would not have been a shooter. Roselli would not even have been a spotter. But, Roselli, I believe, was the coordinator and I think his liaison was directly with Nicoletti and I think Nicoletti was probably your "finger man". Now whether Nicoletti was the shooter or was associating with the three shooters that was in this Plaza, one here, one over there, and one up there, which turned out to be the School Book Depository, which we did not even take into consideration because the most logical place to shot would be up on the City Record's Building, or up on this building, and right over there or right here.

BQ: Did Giancana always give the orders to Roselli and Nicoletti? Was that the M.O.?

A: That was the M.O. and that came from New Orleans, not from Chicago. I've heard a lot of researchers say that his liaison contact was Chicago, that's crap. That is New Orleans and Jacksonville, Florida. I also flew Sam Giancana's girlfriends from New Jersey to Miami two or three different times so I mean my liaison with Roselli and Sam Giancana, and I understand exactly what this could cause, going on open camera, but it's time to clear the air and it's time to get the truth out.

BQ: What do you think about at night?

A: Well, that's a tough question. Over the years it's like one of those things that, you see a good buddy get massacred or killed, you don't want to think about it. You don't pick up a book and study. You don't go read these books that come out over the last 10-15 years cause it tears your guts out. It's like living with a monkey on your back. You want to talk. You want to tell your story. There was a time when it was extremely derogatory to be even connected with the Kennedy assassination and immediately if you said anything "Oh, I know something about the Kennedy assassination", they say "Yeah, it's time for you to go to Bellevue and we're gonna lock you up" Just now, it's coming around that the new generation is demanding some answers and I think the new generation deserves those answers and I think the truth should come out and I think it's my responsibility, whether anybody believes this story or not, or wherever the confirmation has come and does come, it's immaterial to me what people think. If they're really sincere, let them do their own investigation and there's enough documentation out there to support this story as well as other stories about black-op operations. Our military was extremely active, pro and con.

BQ: Why did they go to the Mafioso in the first place to carry out this operation?

A: Because they're available and because they have the know how and they have the technique and there's not an operative or an agent that can actually work in the bureaucracy of government and keep those type of secrets so if a hitman was selected from the CIA or military and something went sour, that's a direct connection to the United States Government as a whole. It would only be feasible that the planners, which were not high level CIA planners, but it was mid-level and rouges. During that time, you got to remember, we come out of the Eisenhower administration with military operatives that was very loyal to the OSS back in the 40's and then we come into a new Kennedy breed that is gonna change all that up. As a result of that, information was gathered and we were actually fighting each other. We became similar to what DEA and people are doing now in the drug war, where agencies begin to fight with themselves. That's what we were facing in those days. And not to mention the propaganda that was being perpetrated and played by special interests within agencies that would throw our intelligence gathering off. We could go around the Caribbean for weeks. In fact, in one case with the Raider ship and O'Rourke, it was reported that we were landing commandos in Cuba, and were down in Port Everglades and we were cleaning the boat and painting it and going fishing for two weeks. But then we would read in the paper about the raids we were carrying out inside Cuba. So, there's a lot of propaganda out there about what we did and in some cases we used to laugh about it and think it was very cute.

BQ: What motivated you to come forward at this time?

A: My motivation to come forward at this time, I guess you would say because of the work that Oliver Stone did do. I think that's it's important that the younger generation know the truth behind the Kennedy assassination. I'm under the impression for myself, after all these years, it's time, if for no other reason, than to cleans my soul and to tell the public the truth about what role I played that day in the Kennedy assassination and put all this behind me and live a life and go into my autumn years and be done with it.

BQ: Do you have any personal regrets about that day?

A: The only personal regrets I have about that day that Sergio and I did not take the initiative to do more observation from other areas in this. We should have been a little more diligent in our approach to this particular operations than what we were.

Reprint from http://jfkmurdersolved.com/TOSHTRANS1.htm

Clarifying emails from Tosh:

From: Robert Morgan

To: Wim Dankbaar

Sent: Sunday, October 10, 2004 1:10 AM

Subject: Re:

Yes I thought about that at the time. But she lived on Northwest Highway near the end of the runway of Dallas Love Field. Some of the people who left Garland were going over to Love Field (as I have stated before that is where we were going to land, but because of weather we went into Garland. I decided to go over to Love Field and see my step mother because I had not seen her for a number of years.. I had time while at Garland waiting for weather to clear at Red Bird) I was only gone from Garland for a short while about one and half hours. As I have said we got to Redbird about " 9:30 or 10 A.M. or perhaps even close to 11 A.M. We were at Garland (landed) about 6:30 about daylight, (note: for years one of the instructors at Garland a pilot by the name of "Farris" remembered the early morning sunrise landing of the DC3 and the airport logging of that flight) Never wanted to have any of my family involved in any of what I was associated with. I was not close to any of my family for a lot of years from 1957 until the Dallas visit. My Dad had died in Sept 1961 and I had not seen "Effie" Mrs. Plumlee, Charles's mother since my father had died. Charles went into Law enforcement about 1971. None the less about my reasons this only proves I was in Dallas on the early AM on the day Kennedy was killed. The FBI and the Senate knows my whereabouts during the time frame and that has been and still is "Classified". I did mention this to Jim Marrs and Peter Lemkin when I told them about my brother being with the Dallas PD and too I told him I did not want Charles or his mother involved in any of this. The reason it now comes out is because I asked Charles Edward if he remembered what his mother had told him about that day. He told me a few months ago that he did and did not think it would make any difference today if he confirmed what "Effie" his mother, my step-mother told him. He gave me the OK to tell the story.

Point Two: I said in the interview that Roselli got off at Redbird.. I corrected that with John Stockwell and Joe West and clarified that Roselli got off at Garland. BUT later after it was typed up that part was left in the "confession" and was a mistake. I was told on transcribing and would be corrected... It never was and I complained many times to all of them and too to Jim Marrs and I re stated "Roselli got off at Garland"... Now you can see what has happened over the years. As you can tell Joe West tried to lead me many times into saying Nicoletti was on that flight as well as other things. Vernon was in on that also. Later I asked him to change it and the wording as to "The Confession".. I do not care at this point. Point being I was in Dallas that morning and that's about it. There has been a lot of twisting of facts but not by me. Later Tosh

From: Robert Morgan
To: WIM Dankbaar
Sent: Monday, November 29, 2004 3:11 PM
Subject: Vernon's Testimony to Texas Com.

Wim: I never said Roselli got off at Redbird. Yet Vernon says I changed my story? Then, he lied to a committee, under oath, in Texas. If he had thought I was lying, then how could he even testify to this committee. This needs to be exposed. It's more documentation. "...Roselli got off at Garland at 6:30 a.m....". His own words in 1994. Call me if you like I will be here most of the day.... In and out. Tosh

Note: forwarded message attached.

From: Robert Morgan
To: Wim Dankbaar
Sent: Monday, November 29, 2004 6:05 PM
Subject: Re: Vernon's Testimony to Texas Com.

The point. It was corrected at the time 1992. He said I said Garland in 1994. He knew it had been corrected. He also said just last week He KNEW I was LYING at the time of the interview... You don't think that says something about his credibility... This is bullshit... I have to prove but he can say anything... I done with it...

Explanation:

In the spring of 2003, Bob Vernon came in financial troubles and asked Dankbaar to buy him out of the JFK project. In July of 2003, this resulted in a purchase agreement for all rights and properties of the project. Payment was agreed to occur in two installments, one half up front, and the other half upon making a sale for the TV Program. Approaching the 40st anniversary of the JKF assassination in november 2003, Vernon began to make claims that "the spirit of the agreement" was to accomplish a sale before that time. This was not only possible, but also no such time limit was defined in the agreement. Nevertheless Vernon demanded payment of the second installment, despite the fact that the condition for that payment had not been met.

Upon learning that Dankbaar was not going to comply with Vernon's demands for payment, Vernon launched a public campaign on the Internet to devalue and discredit the properties sold under the purchase agreement. Vernon has also outdone himself in maligning Dankbaar and his associates, many of whom were Vernon's former partners and associates in this project. Vernon has further qualified the main three witnesses in the evidence, (James Files, Tosh Plumlee and Chauncey Holt) as hoaxes, liars and or/questionable, after promoting them as the absolute and irrefutable truth for a decade before selling the properties to Dankbaar. This conduct was in direct violation of paragraph 8 of the agreement, which reads as follows:

Seller agrees that he shall not take any action or make any statement that may be reasonably considered detrimental to the exploitation of the Project by Purchaser.
Specifically, Seller agrees that if he is asked any question whatsoever by anyone with regard to the project after sale to the buyer that he will say only "No Comment" and nothing more for a period of three (3) years from the date hereof. Seller reserves the right to publish his personal memoirs of his life should Seller ever deem to do so, however, Seller agrees not to publish his personal memoirs of his life for three (3) years from the date of the purchase

hereof. In the event, seller chooses to make any comments whatsoever regarding his experiences in investigating the murder of JFK while preparing his personal memoirs after three (3) years as stated above, seller may make any comments he so desires.

Dankbaar was urged by associates who knew Vernon longer, to include this clause in the agreement.

As Vernon also has discredited the persons interviewed as listed in the properties of the agreement, and has published video footage of these persons, as sold to Dankbaar, Dankbaar was permitted to issue statements from the persons involved, as the one below:

Statement of Lois Gibson - Cease and Desist

It has come to my attention that my recorded statements, likeness, images and/or video footage of me, have been published on a website operated by one Robert G. Vernon.

It is my opinion that Mr. Vernon has made public, footage in which I appear, and has used my likeness and/or my name through fraudulent means. I do not want my name associated with Mr. Vernon. Therefore, I hereby demand that Mr. Vernon cease and desist by immediately removing any and all footage in which I appear and that he remove any still images of me and/or my name.

If he refuses to do at once, I will seek legal counsel in order to stop these publications on the website of Mr. Vernon.

Signed,

Lois Gibson

Robert "Tosh" Plumlee Declaration 11/21/2004

For a collection of documents on Tosh Plumlee click here

The following statements contained within this paper, are my personal story. Anything in previous publications is subject to question and is or has not been, reviewed, approved, or authorized, by me. My purpose in producing this unadulterated information and statement is to clarify previous errors of fact, which have been attributed to me. Therefore, this statement supersedes all previous versions of what others have claimed, speculated, or produced in media and print form, as being my true testimony and story.

Any reproduction of this article, in whole or in part, without written permission from the author is prohibited, and will be considered as a copyright violation and subject to the penalties provided by law.

I hereby declare the following to be true and correct to the best of my knowledge.

Dated this 21st day of November 2004.

Part 1: Background Information

My name is William Robert Plumlee, also known as 'Tosh" I am a retired commercial pilot and have worked for and with the United States Government for many years. My background follows:

I was enlisted and assigned to military specialized operations at Fort Bliss, Texas in April of 1954. (RA18389060; Recon Training Command, RTC-D8) I was associated with various Military Intelligence units of the Fourth Army based at Fort Bliss, Texas, and also the Fourth Army Reserve, located at Dallas Love Field, Dallas Texas. This service period was in the early to mid fifties and into the early sixties.

Approximately 1962 through 1963, I was assigned to Task Force W Section- C-7 tab B and D during the Cuban Project which operated at the time from the JM/WAVE station attached to Miami, Florida's 'Cuba Desk' of the Central Intelligence Agency (CIA). I operated as a contract "Undercover pilot" and also, at times, I was assigned to specialized Cuban operations of the CIA's "Covert Action Group" (CAG) I was engaged in many secret operations through out the early sixties.

Some years later, after brief retirement, known as 'The Farm'. I reactivated myself and became attached as an undercover operative and contract pilot for the federal government during President Reagan's "Drug War". I was attached to a secret team known as 'America-Mexico Special Operations Group' ("AMSOG"), HQ'ed Panama Southern Command. I was also a pilot and associated with the Contra Resupply Network.

I have testified four times in close door session, to various Senate and congressional investigative committees (Director FBI 1964; J Hoover; Senator Church, 1976-75; closed-door testimony, classified TS; to Congressmen Tom Downing's investigators, before the HSCA was formed; to Senator John Kerry's Committee of 1988-91 also classified " "TS Committee Sensitive" and the "Tri-State Drug Task Force", (Arizona, Colorado, New Mexico) chaired by Arizona Governor, Bruce Babbit. The cover operation contact cut out was the Phoenix Organized Crime Div. Phoenix AZ,1975-86. I worked with Senator Gary Hart and his security adviser Bill Holden, on previous intelligence matters with the NSC and the drug war with Colombia and Costa Rica. I worked UC operations with KiKi Camarena and his pilot, before they were murdered and I was a Military/DEA contract pilot, attached to Panama and Colombia, Costa Rica Investigative Task Force on Narcotics.

I have a secret classified file as defined within the National Security statutes under the name of William Robert (Tosh) Plumlee aka William H "Buck" Pearson code named "Zapata", Miami Cuba Desk, 1960-63 MI/CIA OMC-TFW7; Section C (locate Tab B & D) classified information; portions declassified Aug 1998. Associated with Operation 40 connected to the NSC and the "White House Situations Rooms briefings. I was a contract operative for the CIA, associated with Tracy Barns, Wild Bill Harvey, Frank Bender, John Martino and many others.

I have limited this paper to one particular mission that I was assigned to on November 20, 1963. I was a covert 'contract' military Intel pilot on civilian status for this secret operation. I have titled this work as: "The Flight To Dallas; A Pilots Memoirs". I have certified this copy as a declaration and personal testimony; a true account of my activities between November 20 through November 22, 1963

***

Part 2: Flight to Dallas - November 20-22, 1963

Beginning November 20, 1963, I was assigned to be a co-pilot on a top secret flight, which was attached to a Military Intelligence unit and supported by the CIA. Our mission, we were told, was to 'Abort' a pending attempt on the President's life which was to take place in Dallas. We were contracted as "cut-outs" a system used to shield a secret operation from public exposure. Our team was based out of South Florida. My pilot for this operation was Emanuel Rojas. We had flown together before. I was the co-pilot for this operation. The first leg of the flight would be from Lantana, Florida (about five miles south of West Palm Beach) to Tampa Florida. The aircraft used for the first phase of this trip was a D-18 Twin Beach aircraft. We took-off before day break on November 21, 1963 expecting to arrive in Tampa about sunup. We were to pick up other personal at Tampa. One of these people was John Roselli, whom I knew.

I had known John Roselli before this flight. I had flown Roselli and others to places like Cuba, Bimini, Galveston Texas, Las Vegas and California. He was also known to me as"Colonel Rawlston" or just "the Colonel". We (Rojas and I) were to pick up 'the Colonel' at Tampa's Congress Inn that morning. We changed aircraft at Tampa to a waiting DC-3 that was registered to 'Atlantic Richfield', and continued our trip to New Orleans, where a couple of people, who I did not know, got off and a few others got on. The Colonel stayed on board the DC-3. We continued our trip leaving New Orleans and continuing to Houston International Airport where we spent the night at the Shamrock Hilton, not far from the airport. We parked the aircraft on the Trans Texas side of the airport not far from the Texas Air National Guard and their AT6 type aircraft.

The next morning, November 22,1963, about 4:30-5 a.m., our weather briefing was not favorable for a VFR flight into Dallas's Red Bird airport. We selected Garland as an alternate in case the weather had not improved by the time we arrived near Dallas air space. We did not file a flight plan nor intended to file IFR. This would have left a record of our flight with air traffic control. We continued to Garland, in northeast Dallas instead of Redbird Airport in Oak Cliff, a suburb of Dallas. We made this decision because of possible bad weather southwest of Dallas that had not cleared as yet.

We arrived in Garland near daybreak. There had been so many threats against the President's life that we didn't have a great sense of urgency about this particular one. While waiting out the bad weather in Garland, and about thirty minutes after landing three of the passengers were picked up by car, including Roselli. (There are three documented corroborations of my presence at Garland airport that morning). After the weather had cleared sufficiently for the plane to continue via VFR flight rules to Redbird Airport in Dallas, we left Garland for the ten minute flight to Red Bird. We landed at Redbird around 9:30 or 10:30 a.m., perhaps as late as 11 a.m. where everybody got off and went their own way.

It was my impression at that time that I was flying an abort team into Dallas, comprised of John Roselli, a couple of Cubans and some people that I surmised were connected with organized crime in New Orleans. The CIA's specific information about the assassination, which their field personnel had obtained from Texas informants and international sources, was past to Military Intel units attached to the Pentagon. Some of this information, I had been told, came from the interrogations of Two Cubans who had plotted to fire on Air Force One with a bazooka on November 17 in West Palm Beach, Florida.

The pre-mission briefing was held at Loxahatchee, Florida on the evening of November 20th, but since I was not "field operational" at that time, except as a 'contract pilot', I was not directly addressed at the briefing, other than routing and weather reports pertaining to flying the team into position. There would be no formal flight plans filed and the routing would be conducted under VFR (Visual Flight Rules) I only began to learn the full scope of the operation from my pilot Rojas and a field operative friend of mine named Sergio. Most of the details of this operation were told to me only after we had become airborne. I would learn more operational details upon reaching Redbird Airport.

I learned that it had been discussed by the abort team where to go, how to abort, and what to look for. I had not at first paid much attention to any of these details as bits and pieces unfolded. I was told that the abort team, for whom I was only the pilot at that time, would probably be looking for a minimum of 19 or 20 people that would be in the Plaza. Most of the team members felt that this was another false alarm, there had been many during the past few weeks. The detailed instructions to the team had come from Robert Bennett and Rex Beardsley, as well as another case office whose name I can not recall.

Although my specific assigned function was only a pilot. Upon arriving at Redbird Airport, Sergio asked me if I wanted to come along and see the President. I could also act as a spotter for him and his team, which, he said, were assigned to the south side of the plaza. I was told other members of the team would be patrolling the north side and the overpass. I understood we would be looking for a type of triangulation ambush. I gladly accepted Sergio's offer. It seemed like an adventure I didn't want to miss. We were driven from Red Bird Airport to a place not far from the Oak Cliff Country Club, then driven to Dealey Plaza, where we (Sergio and I) checked various areas and attempted to spot potential members of an attack team from the position on the South Knoll. The original information the team had received from sources in Texas and the CIA was an attempt was going to be made outside the Adolphus Hotel, but for reasons unknown to them, I was told ,the routing of the motorcade had been changed at the last minute to Dealey Plaza.

While on the south knoll, Sergio and I were attempting to evaluate the most logical places where shooters might be located, but everything was confused, the timing was off, team members were late getting into position. They were not where they were supposed to be and the limited radio contacts that we had with them were not working, or spotty at best. It was soon after our arrival that the motorcade arrived. When the shots rang out, I had the impression of 4 or 5 shots, with one being fired from behind and to my left on the South Knoll, near the underpass and south parking lot. While leaving via the south side of the underpass near the train tracks, Sergio and I smelled gunpowder. I never saw Roselli in Dealey Plaza that day.

We were picked up on the back side of the underpass, southwest side, by a person who had previously been at the Country Club. After driving away, and on the way back to Red Bird we stopped in the parking lot of Ed McLemore's Sportatorium, where Sergio changed out of the clothes he had muddied when he fell down the slippery west side of the railroad tracks. We stopped by the place in Oak Cliff, then returned to Redbird Airport. We waited for a few of the operatives who had been on our flight into Dallas to return. We waited as long as we could before departing without Roselli and some of the others. At approximately 2 o'clock in the afternoon, we took off from Red Bird without filing a flight plan. Our original flight out of Dallas called for us to fly to Shepard Air Force Base in Wichita Falls, Texas. But because of the assassination that routing was changed at the last minute by Rojas. We would head for Houston and back to south Florida.

On the plane, besides myself, were Rojas, Sergio, a person who I knew as Gator from the Loxahatchee camp, and two other individuals that I didn't know. Gator had identifying characteristics of an unusually large Adam's Apple and a missing finger, which had supposedly been bitten off at an alligator farm.

The people on the flight out of Dallas were very quiet. I interpreted their silence as dejection at the mission's failure to abort the assassination of the President. I believed that if these men had been the shooters or assassins themselves, they would have been very excited because they had carried it off. That's why to this day I take issue with the idea, which I have been asked to speculate on many times, that the attack on the President was in behalf of the CIA, Mafia, or Military Intelligence, and I had unknowingly flown an attack team in which had assassinated the President.

Part 3 - Conclusion

When I later learned that Oswald had been arrested as the lone assassin, I remembered having met him on a number of previous occasions which were connected with intelligence training matters, first at Illusionary Warfare Training in Nagshead, North Carolina, then in Honolulu at a radar installation and at Oahu's Wheeler Air Force Base, then in Dallas at an Oak Cliff safe house on North Beckley Street run by Alpha 66's Hernandez group, who had worked out of Miami prior to the assassination.

The post-mission debriefing was held on November 25th, my birthday, in West Palm Beach by Rex Beardsley, Bob Bennett and, I believe, Tracy Barnes. There was some discomfort or unhappiness about my having been present in the Plaza without authorization. Sergio was reprimanded for taking me along as a 'spotter'. The report was transmitted to field headquarters Miami to JM/WAVE Headquarters, and the CIA's Miami Cuban Desk.

I regret that prior to the production of this narrative, the context and substance of my story has been changed and/or misstated by others to suit their own purposes. When I have spoken on tape, I have been asked to speculate on certain facts which were inaccurately produced as my own factual assertions. One of the most significant problems has been that my story has been tailored and changed to support the claims of others, about whom I knew nothing.

I certify this declaration to be true and correct to the best of my knowledge.

Dated this 21st day of November, 2004

William Robert "Tosh" Plumlee, aka William H."Buck" Pearson.

***

Notes Regarding References:

Certified military Records can be found on William R. Plumlee at the Texas Adjutant General, State of Texas, Headquarters,Texas National Guard; also at the archived files of the Fourth Army Reserve and Fifth Army, located at Camp Mabry, Austin Texas.

The following is a brief summary of these records:

Enlistment Record of William Robert Plumlee:

Texas National Guard 49th, Armored Division; United States Army, Fourth Army HDQ, Fort Bliss Texas; Fourth Army Reserve, Dallas Love Field, Dallas, Texas.

Recap of documents found at the Texas Adjutant General, Camp Mabry, Austin Texas:

William Robert Plumlee S/N RA- 18389060; 9th of Feb 1955; grade CPL; Auth for grade 25-1; enlisted under authority of (NGR25-1) For service in NGS Texas; Company C 156Tk Bn. Fourth Army Reserve; DoB 11 25 37; Civil Trade or Occupation: Aircraft Mechanic, Southwest Airmotive, Dallas Love Field, Dallas, Texas.

Enlistment Records:

22Oct52 thu 8th Feb53 NG Enl s/n25926077 Pvt disc. HonMin; Disc. 8Feb53; re enl.

28th Sept53 thu 2Mar54USAR 4th Army; 18389060 Grade at disc.USAR, CPL.

3Mar54 thu 2Jul USA s/n18389060 rank CPL; United States Army (USA) Ft Bliss Texas assn. temp dty (unknown).

6Jul54-No Record of Disc. tnsf. Texas 4th Army Res, Dallas Love Field, Dallas Texas. Co C156Tk Bn.CO Capt. assn 'Specialized operations, Intel: Commanding officers; Capt. Gilbert B Cook; Texas National Guard: 2ndLt. Charles R Brannon, Arty; Ft. Bliss, Texas, (RTC); Capt. Edward G Seiwell, Fourth Army Reserves, Dallas, Texas; MOS: WR Plumlee 1795,

3795 Tank Crew man Tk Commander, Sherman Tank. Cpl. Plumlee USA MOS 'Unknown'; Unknown sta. Ft. Bliss, Texas; Fort Hood,Texas, National Guard; Unknown.

Office of Origin (OO) Records at Office of Adjutant General State of Texas Camp Mabry, Texas.

Texas National Guard; Texas Fourth Army Reserve; Certified Copy of Available Documents By; XXX referenced doc loc. "on file".

Medical reports: Personnel Records Center, St Louis, MO.

NOTE: For anyone interesting in taking the time to open up the following links I think you will find the information more that interesting in reference as to how J. Edgar Hoover obstructed Justice in withholding important files from investigative committees:

There are two different sets of FBI files on William Robert Plumlee. One set was released to the HSCA; 1978, while the other (Plumlee/Roselli; 62-2116 file) was not declassified until 1997. A careful review of these pages will show how J Hoover withheld information contained within FBI files from the HSCA as well as other investigative committees:

NOTE: THE FOLLOWING REFERENCED FBI FILES HAVE BEEN REMOVED. (DECEMBER 1, 2004) AFTER I WAS ADVISED THAT WITHIN THOSE RELEASED FOIA FBI PAGES CONTAINED MATTERS WHICH ARE STILL CLASSIFIED "TOP SECRET COMMITTEE SENSITIVE", AS RECLASSIFIED ON AUGUST 12, 1991. I WAS NOT AWARE OF THIS AT THE TIME SOME OF THESE PAGES WERE POSTED BY ME ON THIS FORUM. I WILL REVIEW THESE PAGES AND REPOST THE REFERENCES THAT ARE CONSIDERED NOT TO "COMPROMISE" PROCEDURES AND METHODS

Reprint from http://jfkmurdersolved.com/toshfiles.htm

Interview with Chauncey Holt

THE MAN THAT DROVE CHARLES NICOLETTI INTO DALLAS

Image: Chauncey Holt is pictured above.

He was the tramp in the hat in the

infamous Three Tramps pictures.

He drove Charles Nicoletti into Dallas

on the morning of 11/22/63.

To read one of the first articles on Chauncey Holt click here

TRANSCRIPT OF VIDEOTAPED INTERVIEW WITH CHAUNCEY MARVIN HOLT.

HOUSTON, TEXAS, OCTOBER 19, 1991.

INTERVIEWERS PRESENT- JOHN CRAIG, PHILLIP ROGERS, GARY SHAW.

TRANSCRIBED BY WILLIAM E. KELLY, APRIL, 1992.

Names followed by question mark are spelled phonetically.

- The gentleman we are interviewing is Chauncey Marvin Holt.

Holt: My true name is Chauncey Marvin Holt. Throughout the years I have used many, as many as 25, perhaps 30 aliases, I don't remember them all. Starting with the first ones that I do remember, that were prominent in operations, there was Robert Ralston, Jack Hall, Jack Moon, Kearney Sigler, William Dean Rutz...John Moon...

Those were the main alias that we used throughout the years. We did use other aliases, which are called, "floating identities", one time things, that you just sign your name on, which was used not only by me, but others as well. The best known one, I suppose, was Edward Joe Hamilton, which was used by a number of people. And I used that also, from time to time.

-When were you born?

Holt: I was born on October 23, 1921, in a little hamlet called Pine Knoll, Kentucky. My date of birth is October 23, 1921 although on some records it is referred to I was born in January of 1921, for the simple reason that I entered the (military) service before I was 18 years old and I moved my date of birth back. But I was born on October 23, 1921.

I have three social security numbers, at least three. My legitimate social security number is 402-32-1339. I am presently drawing social security under three different numbers because I worked under those names and I paid under those names.

-Can you give us some background on your military career?

Holt: On October 11, 1939 I joined what was then the Army Air Corps. It was part of the Army at that time. It was known as the Brown Shoe Air Force in those days. While in flight training I was very rebellious. I didn't take very well to hazing that we came under. The Army at that time was full of misfits. You had guys in there that couldn't do anything else and made a career of it. And do they delighted in hazing people. It was part of the game as far as the Air Force was concerned, but I didn't take too well with it. There was on guy who picked on me. He always picked on me. His name was Lada (?) He was a disgrace to the uniform.

So one day he came out and he picked on me on the wrong day, and he made some serious remarks and I hit him with a Springfield and chased him across the quadrangle. Hit him at every jump. I would have killed him if it wasn't for the MP's. Of course I got a general court martial. They gave me five years and sent me out to the U.S. penitentiary barracks at Fort Leavenworth, Kansas, where you really do hard time. Of course general court marshals are always subject to review by reviewing authorities. So after 7 months they decided to review my case and reduce my sentence to that 7 months that I had served up to that point and turned me back to duty, although they didn't put me back in the Air Corps. I went into the newly formed Armor Force that was formed in January of 1940. After I was turned back to duty, this is in June, 1940, I found it very difficult to adjust to the Army life. I had a bad reputation. I got all the worst assignments. I am not making excuses for what happened. But it really wasn't any picnic. We continued on. I would be in and out of trouble until 1941. Of course in December,...After I was turned back to duty, I had bad luck in getting bad commanding officers and that sort of thing. And being a rebellious teenager in the first place, I mean I didn't take to well to it. Actually I didn't adjust to Army life too well. It was a bad time. I struggled through it until 1941...until, you know, Pearl Harbor.

You know, I think that Pearl Harbor,...another guy and I went AWOL on Pearl Harbor day. We went back and continued our duty until the early part of 1942. This friend of mine said he had an automobile from his cousin, and we decided to go from Fort Knox to Louisville.

-This is early 1941 or 1942?

Holt: This is early 1942. In any case we got caught joy riding in this automobile, and the FBI frankly, tried to make a (federal) case against us. They didn't identify themselves and asked us questions and so forth and did lots and lots of work trying to prove we had taken this car, which the cousin said "No, he didn't do it." So we wouldn't plead guilty and went to trial and they did a great deal of work trying to prove we took this car across state lines, which we didn't. But they finally ended up charging us with 4 or 5 counts of violations of the Dyer Act. One charge going over, one charge coming back, one charge going here. Although the FBI claimed we pleaded guilty, I got the original FBI report. It indicates they had done considerable work on this. The Commonwealth of Kentucky refused to indict us, the FBI office in Louisville.

Through the Freedom of Information Act we got our FBI file. Hoover himself sent a wire from Washington D.C. to the Special Agent In Charge in Louisville wanting to know why we hadn't been convicted.

Now here we are, in the middle of a war, and he's taking his time out. They actually perjured themselves and we were convicted. And we were given just two years, and gave us time served so that reduced it to 18 months. Chillicotte, Ohio. The U.S. Industrial Reformatory at

Chillicotte, where I met some very interesting individuals, including Bob Swick, who was an enforcer for the Licavoli's.

And it was through Swick...I was paroled in December of 1942. He (Swick) said "Hey, if you ever need too, I'll give you an introduction to Licavoli." So I went to the draft board and talked to them about re-entering the service, and a parole officer said to me, "No, you need special permission from the Secretary of War to do this. Why don't you just sit out the war and work in a defense plant?" So for the rest of the war I worked for the Bethelem-Fairfield Shipyard Company. I worked in the design department, time and motion department. I designed, primarily, bulkheads. So I stayed there until the end of the war. And at the end of the war, I contacted Peter Licavoli. I gave him my background. And we went to Florida.

-Would you identify Licavoli for us.

Holt: Licavoli was a high ranking member of the Mafia who was involved in three of the most sensational murders in American history. The killing of Jerry Buckly, a crusading reporter, a supposedly crusading reporter in 1935, the killing of Jackie Kennedy, the beer baron of Toledo, not the president, and of course he was one of the principles in the St. Valentine's Day massacre, because it was their trucks. But Bugs Moran was highjacking to Capone.

But he didn't talk very much about that until many, many years later. But years later he'd reminiscence about those things.

Licavoli, he was originally from St. Louis, but at the time he was in Detroit. He was one of the five ruling Dons of Detroit, along with John Prisoli?, Angelo Mali?, Black Billdetoko? and Anthony Zerilli. Those five ran Detroit. Their activities ranged all the way from St. Louis to Youngstown. They controlled race tracks...they owned Hoyel (?) Track in Detroit, River Downs in Louisville, and James Licavoli, who was notorious in his own right, actually ran Youngstown, Ohio. They were, of course, into Florida. Most of the casinos in Florida at that time were owned 1/3 New York, 1/3 Trafficante-Lansky, 1/3 Detroit. They were into everything.

-Who were your major associates during that time?

Holt: When we went to Florida, the person we answered to in Florida was an individual by the name of Mert Whorhammer (?).

First I was in Jacksonville Beach, Florida, where they put me in there as a book keeper at a place called Kite's Bar & Grill. Now it looked like an innocent sort of place, but it was the center for all numbers rackets in the Jacksonville area.

The reason I went down there was Kite was coming up short in his proceeds. Their business was dropping off about $15,000 a week and they figured that Mr. Kite probably had his hand in the till. So we went down there and I stayed there about a month as a book keeper, numbers writer, that sort of thing. And as soon as we found out that, yeah, he was stealing, I moved on. Then I went on....

-What happened to him? To Kite?

Holt: He ended up with a pea in his head, as they say. They found him floating in the surf off Jacksonville Beach.

Then I went down to the casino area. The Miami area. Broward County at that time was in full swing. I immediately went to work for an accounting firm, a very respectable accounting firm. But they handled all of Meyer Lansky's accounting work. All the companies that worked for Lansky. Many of them were noted philanthropists. Max Horowitz, Dan Ruskin, Barry Berheishyer?, Sam Becker...

The firm that I worked for at the time was a firm called Albis?, Aldimus?, Morgan and Weinberg. They handled all of Lansky's accounting work, among other things. They were very, very respectable. We did accounting work during the day and we handled gambling proceeds at night.... The principle that I worked for more than any other,...at the Colonial Inn, which is next door to the Gulton? Park Race Track. It was the plushiest of the carpet joints at that time. That and La Boheme. They were both in Broward County. They referred to Broward County as 'Lansky County'. He owned the sheriff, he owned everything.

-What was your knowledge of Lansky at that time?

Holt: Well, I knew that he had been a long time,...he wasn't a Mafia member, of course, but he was a Mafia associate and he went back a long way, to the Bugsy Siegel days when they were actual enforcers for the Mafia. They were executing contracts for them. Lansky was always a real money maker for them. That's why they associated with him, although he was Jewish. Just as Licavoli cooperated with the Cleveland branch, who also was all Jews, or like New Jersey, ones like Longie Zwillman, were Jews. The Jews and Italians collaborated and cooperated with one another although those guys, the Jews, were actually never members of the Mafia.

-Were you hired by Lansky or by an associate?

Holt: I was hired by him personally.

-So you knew him well?

Holt: I knew him well after I went to work for the firm - Adison-Costa...Then Mr. Costa did, he was Italian. Then it became Adison, Morgan, Aldis, Weinberg. Then Adison left and formed a bank for Lansky, actually the Industrial Bank, which they owned.

Even when working for the accounting firm we had offices, ...I had an office in Miami Beach at one of Lansky's companies, which was called the Gator Corporation, which he used as a vehicle for practically all the other work that he did, including at the time, the main thing at that time, he was working with Louis Wolfson and they were trying to make a raid on American Motors. They didn't take it over, but they bought a lot of stock. Max Orbitson, Dan Ruskin were planning for Lansky at the time, and both of them ultimately got convicted for their association with Lansky.

-Were you ever in and out of Cuba at this time?

Holt: Many times. They were involved in setting up the casinos with Trafficante and others. Norman Rothman for instance. In Cuba...we went to Cuba many times. At that point in time

Carlos Prio was President of Cuba and Batista was in exile. It was Lanksy who was instrumental in getting Prio to allow Batista back into the country. He came back into the country and one day he just walked into the Presidential Palace apparently, and made Prio an offer he couldn't refuse. This is how Batista,...Batista was always in Lansky's pocket. So we were back and forth there in regards to the casinos.

Later on, when Castro started kicking up a force, and of course after he had landed there in the Escambray Mountains, Lansky, to hedge his bet, began offering assistance to Castro in the form of money and arms that were flying in. So although he was a very close friend of Batista, he was still assisting Castro. Around that time flying arms to Castro was no problem. The State Department didn't bother you at all. They just tolerated it. So that was the experience in Havana.

-Was it at this period in time that you got involved with the CIA?

Holt: That came later. We went into Cuba many times before, without having anything to do with the CIA. How I came to be connected to the CIA in the beginning was the formation, in May 1950, of the Kefauver Committee. The Kefauver committee was scheduled to begin hearings in May 1950. At that time I was working for an accounting firm, the Eisner Firm, Dan and Seymour Eisner. They were scheduled to be the first witnesses subpoenaed before the Kefauver committee and we knew we wouldn't be far behind. And Lansky, of course, they tried to subpoena him but they were never able to get him before the committee. He was probably the only organized crime figure that evaded the Kefauver Committee. Every other one they got, but him. So I started looking around for another job. I had to leave there and Lanksy said, "I'll put you into the International Rescue Committee - the IRC- as Controller."

-What was the IRC ?

Holt: At the time I thought it was a philanthropic organization like the Red Cross or something. But when I went over there, Lansky didn't explain anything about the position, he just said to go over there and your job description will be forthcoming. So I went over there and sat around for a couple of weeks reading the Racing Form when a guy by the name of Sluder? came down from Washington, I suppose, and informed me that this IRC was a propriety interest of the CIA. That its main function was dispensing funds for the agency. At that time I didn't know what a propriety interest was. Didn't even known what the CIA was.

-He said you would be working for him?

Holt: Yes, well, that I would be working for the agency. At that time of course, I was a pilot. I had been a pilot since 1937. I was an accomplished artist. I was one of the best shots around. I was probably in....?? too.

Richard Sluder, I assumed that he came from Washington D.C. He did not show me any credentials.

- Your impression was that the CIA was working in conjunction with organized crime in carrying out its activities, with propriety interests and so forth?

Holt: Yes. I was sure of it. Actually I talked with Meyer Lansky about it as soon as I was informed about what kind of operation it was. I went to him and asked him. And he said they had been in bed, ...his exact words were, "We've been in bed together since 1944." He elaborated a little bit on how they were able to get Lucky Luciano deported and the deals they made and how they made the deals with the Anastasia brothers, Tony and Albert, who were in control of the docks. So they wouldn't have any more acts of sabotage like the Normandy, and that sort of thing. And so we knew they scratched each other's backs.

-What about the IRC?

Holt: The IRC was concerned with two things. First was the situation in Cuba, and secondly, their primary concern at that time was in Guatemala.

It looked like Arbenz, who was a left leaning individual, had a good chance of winning an election. In 1948, (Jorge) Ubico had been the dictator of Guatemala at that point. They overthrew him in 1948 and they were concerned that Arbenz would win the election and consequently the communists would have a foothold in Latin America. So we turned our full attention to Guatemala, both from a fiscal standpoint in trying to send money down there to try to effect the election, and to even to interfere with the election that was coming up, to the extent of knocking off (Franscisco) Arana and blaming it on Arbenz. And he won the election....

As far as organized crime went, Meyer Lansky, we were loyal to Meyer Lansky and to Peter Licavoli even though I was working for the IRC. We were involved in handling various accounting functions for both Licavoli and Lansky. Even after the closing of the casinos.

In Miami, in 1948, in Broward County, they closed them all up in 1948. All of them. But Lansky had for....really interesting. Once you had his loyalty and respect. Then we did a number of things that concerned us at the time. You had to remember that casino operators were just beginning in Las Vegas. They were building the Flamingo. It was rumored that Bugsy Siegel was squirreling away some money that he and Virginia Hill were going to take off with. They got the word, and organized crime had some $6 million invested in the Flamingo at the time. I went out with Lansky, simply because I was an accountant. We went out in December 1946, I guess it was. Of course that predated when I was with the IRC. But that was one of the things we were doing. We went out to check on Bugsy Siegel. He was killed in 1947. But we did the same sort of thing all though the 50s and 54 and all the way up to 1958. Never deviated from that, as far as doing the work for Licavoli and Meyer Lansky. It had very little to do with Trafficante. He of course, was the number one guy in Florida. But he was in Tampa. We had very little to do with him.

-When did you start to forge documents and run proprietaries for the CIA?

Holt: We started almost at once, in 1950, to try to figure out ways to establish identities. The first one we did was the name of Robert Ralston, which was the name I used when we went down to Guatemala. They had suggested that I use,... at the time I was using the name Holt, and they suggested that I create some kind of an identity. And I started at once, creating the Moon identity, which went back to that time. But we were doing documentation in a small way, even then. It didn't really come to full fruitation until we went to California, in which they really wanted various documentation mills.

-Was it a proprietary interest?

Holt: A proprietary interest is what you call a wholly owned subsidiary. It is owned by the CIA. I mean they own it lock, stock and barrel, as opposed to,...they also have assets. They are someone who does something else and are called on, like newspaper men,...a lot of things. They have agents of influence - they are agents who are used form time to time to do the CIA's bidding. They have, of course, the full blown contract agents, who usually work for some propriety interests, or they are freelance, that they call on. They have contract agents so they can have plausible deniability. That's the number one thing.

During the Bay of Pigs it was reputed that they owned 56 companies in the Miami area. They had detective agencies, they had insurance companies, they had printing companies, airlines, they had their own little fleet, and of course they had the Lykes Line, which was out of New Orleans. But the Lykes Line was always at their beck and call, although it wasn't really owned by them.

-What is a documentation mill?

Holt: I am talking about providing full sets of ID identity, either floating ones, that anyone can use, or deep cover ones. Usually on a deep cover ones would be partially...You would use the IDs that are produced to actually generate something that is actually genuine. In other words, if you needed a driver's license you would use something like a birth certificate to get the documents that were real. We use to produce credit cards and so forth, functional, but not usable, used for ID identification. But you didn't charge anything on them.

-How did you create the identify of John R. Moon?

Holt: As far as Moon went, I knew a John R. Moon. I knew enough about him. And this is the same technique used in establishing all of these things. I know enough about John R. Moon. I knew where he was born, I knew where he went to school, I knew everything about him. We acquired this information in a very simple way. We simply advertised (for a job) and he sent in his resume. In which I just picked it up. Now the resume that was sent in, this man's name was actually Jack Ralph Moon. Now everybody knows that Jack is the nickname for John. His name was actually Jack, but I decided to....(break in tape).

-Please repeat the answer.

Holt: We used the standard procedure that we used in practically all of the long standing ones that we were going to use. You found out as much as you could about this individual, where he was born, parents, school, everything about him. In the case of Moon, we got the information from the resume he sent us. He put everything on there.

You have to remember that back in that period, establishing identification was much easier than it is today. For instance, I could go into the Department of Motor Vehicles and get a drivers license without any problem. You could go to a bank and open an account by just putting money in there. You could go to the Post Office and get a P.O. box. They didn't ask you for anything at all. No problem. You didn't need to verify anything. Later, throughout the years, it became more difficult. They wanted authenticated verification. So we had to develop some information that would get us a genuine driver's license or something like that. An authentic drivers license is a must because you can not run around using a forged driver's license.

-What is the advantage of using the name of a real person, as opposed to making up a fictitious alias?

Holt: So long as you don't have interference from the real person, because this person actually exists. In the case, as in most of them, you had people running around actually with 2 names. In some cases, of course, you would pick a person that had to be dead. Unless someone actually knew they were dead, they would have an advantage. It is very hard to build up an identity that is completely false that will absolutely stand up. You have got to have some kind of a background.

-How did you develop your skills as a forger? How did you learn your craft?

Holt: Well, I was interested in art from the time I was six, seven years old. I sold my first painting in 1927 and I had been painting continually. During the war, when I worked at the Bethelem-Fairfield Shipyard Company, I was very interested in art and thought I'd like to make a career of it. I went to the Baltimore Art Institute. I also did anatomical drawings for some well known scientists at the John Hopkins University, actually the School of Medicine. Mostly there were physical anthropologists, so I was always interested in increasing my skills as a draftsman, and I was noted as being one of the better ones around. It just naturally followed that you could forge.

-What about the CIA operations against Castro you were involved in?

Holt: Operation Mongoose was the yoke and seed, almost idiotic plan to assassinate Castro, in which they decided, of the plans that they had, the one that ended up as Mongoose was the most ridiculous of all, in which they decided to use organized crime. The idea, I guess, was that organized crime was as skillful at that sort of thing.

There may be certain types of assassination that they're good at, but other types they're not. So they enlisted the better known names, Giancana, Roselli, in Operation Mongoose. And you had Edward Lansdale, and William King Harvey, all the guys who became legends. And there is no use in expounding on their careers and how they got involved in this.

Also, one of the lesser known people involved in this was Peter Licavoli. Licavoli was a confidant, close to both Giancana and Roselli. And he had a ranch in Tucson, Arizona. It was very nicely placed and had a landing strip on it. So he was involved in Mongoose because of the location (of his ranch), and it was a nice place to have meetings and they had meetings there. His involvement in Mongoose was a marginal type thing.

I really don't think that Roselli or Giancana or Maheu ever were all that serious about knocking off Castro. They wanted to get some leverage against the government. They were trying to deport Roselli, they were chasing Giancana all over the landscape and they were willing to use anything they could to actually give them an edge.

-You were involved in this operation. What were your duties?

Holt: We provided some assistance to them in the form of identification. We did very little actually as far as the operational end of it. As for as they were trying to poison Castro, they had some plan that we understood to be a viable plan that had been hatched by (Rafael) Trujillo. Of course you forget that Trujillo hated Castro with a passion and was an old hand at assassination. He was the one they could turn to if they,....I thought that was the best plan. Though they had a pretty good plan in place at one time where they were going to knock off Castro during one of those harranges at the television studio where he walks back and forth. But before they had a chance to implement it, the CIA and the State Department decided they were going to rid the country of Trujillo, so they concluded this thing.

But I am not as knowledgeable about Mongoose as some other operations. We (I) knew what was going on, we talked to William King Harvey. We discussed, we had seen Lansdale one time. We met down at Ray Ryan's place in Palm Springs. Ray Ryan was a big gambler, an oil man. He was friends with Licavoli and Giancana. He had a propriety interest in Palm Springs - the Bermuda Dunes Airport, which is owned by the CIA. We had a meeting down there in which time, it was the only time I participated when all those groups got together. Which was in December, 1961, when they discussed project ZR/RIFLE. How they intended to proceed, they also indicated that James J. Angleton knew about it. And that they were going to insert things into what was called, we referred to as the Central Registry. They referred to them as the 201 Files. We were referring to them as the Central Registry. Frankly I don't know the difference between the 201 File and the Central Registry. Now the Central Registry was...I don't know the difference.

-What other operations were you more involved in than Mongoose?

Holt: Well after Castro came to power in January, 1959, there was a very, very short honeymoon, and the CIA began at once, or certain elements of the CIA was involved. The official stance from Langley was that they wanted no part in it. But other operatives from the CIA, together with organized crime, together with some anti-Castro Cubans, some of them were from Batista, some of them were from the Carlos Prio regime and so forth, were very anxious to get rid of Castro.

At that time Castro's grip on Cuba was actually not that great. I mean that he was very heavily opposed, not only by Cubans in Miami, but by Cubans who were in Cuba at the time. They had a second front organization, which was critical. The second front organization which we were flying material, providing money and buying boats for them, and that was what led to the operation that William Alexander Morgan, that I knew very well, whose career paralleled my own. I knew him. He was down there. He came to Miami, he and a guy named Talaha?, who had been an official in the Batista government. They were trying to develop funds for this operation. It turns out that Morgan was a double crosser and Castro knew all about the entire matter. And they actually had a bunch of Globemasters that were outfit by a company that Jimmie Hoffa owned, and they were actually scheduled to fly troops. One group actually went into Trinidad. They were putting up a big demonstration for them. Guns fired, and they saw signs all over the place saying, "Viva Americans", "Down With Castro." It was all really hyped.

Actually they were trying to get the principle down there to execute him. It turned out that only a handful went down there, 10-12 guys, in a C-54, and Castro grabbed them.

-What about the Bay of Pigs?

Holt: Well our involvement, I was still with the IRC - the International Rescue Committee. Our involvement as far as the IRC went, was strictly from a fiscal point of view.

Initially the Bay of Pigs was to be a very small, secret operation. It depended upon the uprising of the Cuban people. It wasn't going to be an over the beach amphibious assault that it finally turned into. But after it got transformed, a guy from the Marine Corps, Jack Hawkins came over, then it got to be a, like a Terra-type of assault. It became a great logistical problem. The thing to do was to look around and get, especially the ships and other equipment, this was simply, principally what the IRC did at that time. It was a conduit for all of those funds,...but the logistical problems.

....Like some of the others like Rip Robertson and Grayston Lynch, who as far as I know were the only two Americans that were actually on board ship at the time. We had very little involvement in that.

-Where were you?

Holt: I was in Miami. I left in t he latter part of April, almost immediately after the Bay of Pigs. I went to California. It w as partly because a purging from the company and partly at the insistence of Licavoli and Lansky. I just wanted a change of scenery and they said, "Why don't you go to California? We need a documentation mill out there. We have a lot of friends out there,..." And that's when I went out there, before the assassination of Trujillo. I went to California in May, 1961.

-Would you characterize your activity at this time as criminal, but authorized?

Holt: It was all very criminal and involved,...was authorized by the CIA, and some was not. Every contract agent that I knew had some little thing going on the side. And the CIA never objected, so long as it did not interfere with their operations. When we had a documentation mill and we were forging documents and disinformation for them, and if we wanted to do something else on our own, we got no interference from them at all.

-What about the Bay of Pigs fiasco. It was a disaster for this country, and much of the blame was laid at the feet of John Kennedy. Do you recall the scuttlebutt? What was going through the grapevine of your group at this time?

Holt: It ran very strongly against him, not only with the Americans, but with the Cubans, to the point where his conduct was characterized as cowardly, as treasonous and they felt they had been led into something and they were simply deserted. And this would not have happened if there was another president.

-How did Licavoli and Lansky feel about it?

Holt: Both of them held great resentment...although both of these individuals, as they knew it, thought the plan was too hard. They didn't think that was the way to retake Cuba. They were as interested as anyone else in getting back because it cost millions in casino receipts and they were very interested in it, but both of these individuals thought, their viewpoint was that this couldn't have happened under a president like Eisenhower, and Eisenhower, of course, was president during the Guatemala operation, and he gave full responsibility to the commanders there to do what they would, and if they needed military backup, they would have it.

-In California you worked for both the CIA and organized crime. Would you describe that?

Holt: When I first went to California I had a long list of friends of either Lansky, organized crime and the Company, and of course, I was looking for employment and the company was looking for businesses there. Perhaps one that I could run. Something within my capabilities. So one of the long-time assistants of Meyer Lansky was Doc Stacher. He finally ended up, ...he was a titan of organized crime, like Lansky. The only time they ever got Lansky was on some gun wrap in upstate New York. And Stacher was arrested with him. So he had a lot of influence in California and we went out there and were given a lot of very prominent names of people who we could count on for employment or for assistance. Among those were Goodwin Knight, a former governor of California. There was Alfred Gitelson, who was a Superior Court Judge, and a whole group of individuals who worked with him, known as the KG Group. They had a company called KGO, and maybe a dozen companies they operated.

Among the individuals that was with him was Morris Kawin, Sid Colby?, Isadore Reinhard?, these were guys who Lansky said, "If you want a job, you go to these guys. They are always looking for someone whose talented, yet not to scrupulous to do these things."

On the other hand, we also had some democrats. These guys were all dyed in the water republicans, but we also had some democrats. Principally among these was Frank Belcher, who was one of the most prominent attorneys in California, president of bar association, he was very rich, his wife was a Penitz?, and he could be counted on to provide service. His grand daughter was with the Bank of America. So we were given these people, and they said, "We're also looking for some other interests. We're looking for a documentation mill. We'd like to have an on going firm. So we started looking into an old line company - the Los Angeles Stamp and Stationary Company, LASCO, which was owned by Philip Shore. He was the board director, and he was in dire financial straits. So the Company came in and bailed him out. He had a real nice building in downtown Los Angeles. They did all types of badges, banners, that sort of thing. They had police badges actually, from every municipality in the United States. They had drawers of them. So it was the type of operation the CIA was looking for.

-When you say "the Company" you mean the CIA.

Holt: Yes.

-They actually gave you instructions to look for a specific propriety company that they could acquire in LA to produce documents that we have described here as illegal, illicit forms that could pass for real documents?

Holt: Yes. LASCO, we referred to it, we bailed them out and brought in a man by the name of Tony Materna?, who had been very high up in the Hughes organization, to run the company. 95% of their business was legitimate, and they continued to do their legitimate business. Probably 5%, not more, would be for the Company. But if you needed something, then they had a wonderful facility. Four stories, the lower three stories were devoted to their, what you would call legal activities. The top floor had all this specialized graphics equipment, photograph studio....we used that from 1961 till 1972.

They were also interested in a fixed base operation where they had hangers, airport repair facilities and that sort of thing. We found that at Bermuda Dunes, which is between Palm Springs and Indio, California. It was isolated. It was a nice area, and the Company put up the money to buy Bermuda Dunes Airport, which was fronted by Ray Ryan, a big developer in that area, and Ernie Dunlevy, who had been an Air Force pilot and had connections with the OSS.

We also located at the Van Nuys Airport, where we had a facility that was operated by an individual by the name of Roger Clarke. His last name had an 'e' on the end. He had a number of very qualified flight instructors, all of whom had flown for Paragon Air Service in Miami and Inter-Mountain, which was another propriety interest of the Company which was not as well known as Air America or CAT, but was the same type of operation. Ray Lafferty was a full time flight instructor who had flown for Paragon Air.

James J. Canty was a high level official of the Veterans Administration. He was able to, this gave him plenty of opportunity to fly all over the country. He had no problem at all going anywhere he wanted to. At the same time Frank Belcher Jr. had a company, Belcher Aircraft. Although his father and mother were worth millions, they sort of looked down the nose at him because he married the wrong girl. So they weren't giving him too much in the way of financial assistance. So he went into Belcher Aircraft, and we also used him from time to time because he was an ATR? rated pilot and he was a very close personal friend. He was the type of person who would not shrink from asking you to do anything and you wouldn't shrink from asking him to do anything. There are very few individuals in that business that fit into that category.

-At this time you did some printing that ended up with Lee Harvey Oswald?

Holt: Among the assignments we got, and I guess I should elaborate. I should point out of course, one name I haven't mentioned and probably the most important on the West Coast was Phillip A. Twombly. Twombly had been at one time an Executive Vice President of Coca Cola for their Caribbean operations. And along with Donald Kendall (Pepsi Cola), was considered by the CIA to be the eyes and ears of the CIA down there. So he came to California and bought a bank in Fullerton, which was strictly for the use as a conduit of finances.

All of the instructions that came to the West Coast came through Twombly. Twombly in turn, we would, we rarely met face to face. He had two assistants, one, a man by the name of David L. Palmer, and he had a gentleman by the name of Marlin Mahab?, who used to pass on all the information to us in the way of instructions as to what we were to provide.

All of the requests that came for the stuff that we were to produce for Oswald, whom we had never heard of, didn't even know, came from, through Twombly. These were pamphlets we were supposed to do, false identifications, a number of false identifications that ended up in the hands of authorities. We did ID's for Oswald in both his name and Hidell. Some of which I know never ended up with anybody. What happened to them? I don't know.

-You prepared these ID's and leaflets for Oswald. What were you ordered to do with them?

Holt: Sometime between April and June of 1963 was when we first delivered the first documents and leaflets to Oswald. We were given instructions, Dave Palmer gave us instructions. He gave us the copy for them, and we printed them up. And we delivered the documents to George Reynolds. His aide delivered them to New Orleans. Also at that time, we had two kinds of ID's. We had one ID that had Oswald's name and Oswald's picture and another with Oswald's name, but obviously not Oswald's picture.

All of these went to George Reynolds. George Reynolds ran the Atchafalaya labor camp among other interests, in Morgan City, Louisiana. The order to produce them and where to deliver them came from Phillip Twombly's office in Fullerton, California. George Reynolds operated a number of companies in the Morgan City area, as far away as Lafayette, but most of his main interests was the Atchafalaya labor camp, which had a P.O. box in Morgan City, although the camp itself was further down in the swamp.

We came to know George Reynolds first, through an individual by the name of Guy Main, a close associate of Doctor Park, a Korean. It was our understanding that Park was on MacArthur's staff at the end of WWll and had close ties to the KCIA. And he came to California. Guy Main had an office in his building, which was located at 2600 Wilshire Blvd. in Beverly Hills.

George Reynolds accepted them I think that probably Leroy Young delivered them to Oswald. The first time they were used we were not present there in New Orleans because he was distributing them outside some naval base and got shooed away, or something happened. We did not get involved until some months later, in August of 1963. We were advised that Oswald needed some moral support to give out these leaflets. So we went over to create a presence there.

Phillip Twombly asked us if we would be willing to fly to New Orleans and give some support to Oswald, who was a stranger to us. The only thing we knew about Oswald at the time was we had detected the address on there as being 544 Camp Street. Although we were not familiar with Oswald we certainly knew what was at 544 Camp Street because we had gone there before. It was the HQ of Sergio A. Smith's organization, the CRC. There was a restaurant in the first floor and Guy Bannister had an office in the building, although he used an address around the corner, it was in the same building. And George Reynolds knew the man who owned the building, a guy by the name of Sam Newman, and he knew him.

So we knew the connection that way, but as far as who Oswald was, we got to see that there was some kind of a disinformation program because Oswald's name was on documentation and it wasn't his picture. And others had his picture and his name, although at the time we had never seen Oswald and we didn't know which one was the real guy.

I mean it could have been one of the others. Frank Belcher Jr., "Bud". He was called Bud to differentiate him from his father. We flew one of his airplanes down to Morgan City, stopped there and went up to New Orleans. We didn't fly into New Orleans International. We tried to avoid those airports if we could, not only because the traffic is heavy, but the controls and so forth. But we went up to some field near Lake Ponchartrain. I don't remember exactly which one we used.

One of George Reynolds' associates, who we had never seen before, although he was driving a station wagon with the firm's name on the door, George Reynolds' chemical company, who drove us down to New Orleans. That was the first time we saw Oswald. This was down on Canal Street when he was handing out pamphlets.

We stayed in New Orleans at that Hotel that was ....it had tropical in its name, not on the airport highway, and not the Town and Country, although I know George Reynolds stopped there.

We were there and Oswald started handing out the leaflets and we were right in anti-Castro country you know. Bud Belcher went down with me, and he actually handed out some of the leaflets. He was dressed almost like Oswald, but I wasn't. Leroy Young was there. I don't think he gave out any. There were some other people there I had never seen before. I didn't know who they were. People were coming and going, some seemed to be passers by, some seemed to have an unusual interest in it as if they were part of the group without actually taking part in it.

Image: Still frame of Lee Harvey Oswald handing out pamphlets. Handwriting is of Chauncey Holt. Chauncey is the man with sunglasses on the far right.

This was on Canal Street, on August 9th, I believe. They were one week apart. The other (incident of Oswald's leafleting was) in front of the Trade Mart was on the 16th of August, 1963. The first was when they had a little disturbance which didn't really amount to much, although it looked like it was going to evolve into something serious, and I didn't want to get involved. I wasn't about to defend Oswald or anybody else.

But when Carlos Bringuier came down there he didn't seem to be very serious about whipping Oswald real bad. It seemed like a joke to him. I thought it was maybe contrived.

Then I went back to California. Even before that incident, around April, the word came out that something was in the wind that was going to come down in the later part of that year. It was one of the few times we met directly with Phil Twombly. Because of the fact we met with him, suddenly, before that our funds had dried up to a trickle. Not that we were hurting for money. Because we still had the normal side of the business, but we weren't getting any assignments until April of 1963. Then they said something was in the wind and would happen that year.

After the incident with Oswald in August of 1963, there was a frenzy of activity, especially in September, for providing unusual orders for documents. Not the Secret Service documents, but a lot of documents being produced could be used for any type of operation you could think of. However, as it wore on, we began getting inquiries as to whether we could do the Secret Service documents, which is very different than doing other types because its in book form and it includes little recognitions like the lapel pins they wore every day.

In an emergency, in their coming and going, they are recognized by those pins. LASCO was set up nicely to do this kind of thing because they provide badges for police departments. They do all kinds of badges. So action really picked up and we were asked, in November, to produce a whole range, not all the Secret Service documents, just certain ones. We produced about, between November 15th,...we received orders on November 15th, on the type of pins that were going to be worn in Dallas that day. The pins themselves, it wasn't the background, that never changed, it was the markings on the pins that determined what was going to be used that day.

We were under a time constraint for when we received the order November 15th, and were told that we had to be in Dallas on the night of the 21st. George Reynolds had a plane that he had already bought that we were going to take back to California.

The plane that we had to use, a Cessna 175....was a poor airplane, it was really underpowered for a cross country flight. So since we were going to be leaving from Arizona, we felt we could drive it in about 20 hours.

-Who were we?

Holt: John J. Canty was the pilot coming along simply to fly the plane back with me. I could have flown the plane back myself. I had never flown a Comanche 260 before but it would have been no problem. You look at the handbook and that's it. But Canty wanted to come along and we said, "Yeah, Okay." At the last minute however, when we left Licavoli Grace Ranch, Charles Nicoletti and Leo Moceri indicated they wanted to make the drive with us. And we would all alternate driving so we could drive straight through.

They were going to Louisiana. I thought they were going to New Orleans, maybe not, maybe they were going to Lafayette, maybe they were meeting Marcello, I don't know.

So we left California by plane to Grace Ranch, simply to break it up. It's 1400 miles and 1000 more miles to Dallas. So we stopped there and Nicoletti and Moceri were at Pete Licavoli ranch outside of Tucson. We stopped to break up the trip and picked them up because they wanted to drive with us as far as Dallas.

So in the car there was James 'Joe' Canty, called Joe, Charlie Nicoletti, Leo Moceri and myself.

-What's the Grace Ranch. Where does the name come from? Holt: The Grace Ranch was named after Pete Licavoli's wife, whose name was Grace. It was a very, very nice setup. It was isolated at the time, not anymore. It was surrounded by a lot of acreage. It had a very nice landing strip on it. It was ideal. Organized crime used it all the time for meetings. It was set up like a motel style so there were eight or ten units there. Two swimming pools. It was a very nice place. When they had problems to solve in Las Vegas, for instance, they had the dispute with Gus Greenbaum at the Riviera. They met there and decided what to do about Mister Greenbaum. The Grace Ranch was probably the most popular meeting place for the Mafia. I would say it was the western counterpart to Marcello's Churchill Farm. It was like a fortification. You couldn't get in or out. It was fenced in, it had a landing strip. It was set up as a motel and had another advantage. It was near Marana, which was a main CIA base for the Company. They had a huge, huge facility at Marana, which was right outside Tucson. So it was a nice place to fly in.

The Italian wetbacks came by that route. They came to Point Marana's ranch in Vera Cruz, and came up and stopped often at Licavoli's. But mainly it was a meeting place.

-How many sets of documents were you delivering to Dallas?

Holt: I'd say we had at least ten sets of documents. Some I can remember who they were, some I can't. But we had some I don't have any idea whether they were there or not. I never saw them. We're talking about individuals like Rolando Otero. We had documents for Rolando Masferrer. We had some for other Miami based Cubans. I didn't know if they were produced for this operation or not. I'm confidant the Secret Service ID's were involved in this operation . Of course we gave them to Harrelson, Charles Harrelson. We gave them to an individual we knew by the name of Richard Montoya.

-Did you know Harrelson and Montoya personally?

Holt: I had seen a lot of pictures of him, because we provided the documents. I knew him by reputation because according to what was told to us, he was supposedly involved in the gunshop operated by John Masen, and we were told that and we had furnished a lot of ammunition for them. We were told by a guy, a gunrunner who probably ended up at Leavenworth,....Harrelson was associated with Masen's Dallas gunshop.

We had shipped, and by we I mean our operation we had at the Goleta Airport at Santa Barbara, which was known as the GMB Machine Tool Company. Our interest in that particular operation, which again the CIA rescued when they had money problems, was the fact that it was a weapons modification plant. We produced silencers by the hundreds, we hired an excellent re-loader, to reload ammunition to special specifications, including ammunition shipped or delivered to Masen's. Sometimes we shipped it, sometimes we delivered it by someone else.

-What was the purpose of this ammunition?

Holt: Most of the ammunition was specially loaded ammunition. Sometimes it would exceed factory specifications in some instances. We also loaded ammunition that was furnished to us. In other words they furnished the bullets and even the casings. There was nothing unusual about the primers, so we fired the primers. We loaded it with the amount of powder, according to the specifications, that included underpowered ammunition that would practically dribble out of the barrel of the gun. Almost like a co-shot when you used the primer only. The little bit of powder was to ensure that it didn't get stuck in the barrel.

-You were not an ammunition manufacturer, nor knew the purpose of the ammunition?

Holt: No. The only ammunition was,...we surmised it (the underpowered ammunition) was going to be shot without sufficient velocity to hurt anyone. It was not designed to actually shoot anyone, or hurt anyone.

We're talking about maybe 300 to 400 rounds of 6.5 and 7.5,... the hotloads of course, we wanted those to exceed the factory ammunition up to the very extent we could without blowing up the gun, in order to give it a lot of velocity.

What I want to point out was, we received from Masen's, we received what looked like pristine ammunition. Unfired ammunition. Upon first examination it looked like it was absolutely unfired and hadn't passed through anything. It was to be reloaded to their specifications, and we reloaded it. But upon closer examination, you could see it had been fired at least once. We had no idea what the purpose of it, except obviously we came into possession of some bullets that perhaps had been fired probably into water. It hadn't been damaged and had some markings on them that could be identified as having been fired from a rifle. They had been shipped to Masen's. We had been instructed to finish the documents and to deliver them to Dallas, with some other guns, all handguns. We didn't have a rifle in the bunch. We had some handguns that were silencer equipped and fit into aluminum cases, a regular photographer's case. Which we were going to deliver to Masen's.

-What caliber were these weapons?

Holt: These were all 9 mm with the exception of probably, maybe two that were .22, either .22 high standards or 22 lugers. We used them a lot, so there were .22s and the others were 9 mm Browning highpowers.

-Do you remember when you left Grace Ranch?

Holt: We left Grace Ranch on the evening of the 20th of November, planning to drive straight through and sharing the driving so that we could come straight through and expecting to arrive in Dallas sometime on the evening of the 21st. We were instructed to go directly to the Cabana.

-The Cabana?

Holt: The Cabana Hotel or Motel, not too far from Dealey Plaza. It was a motel built with Teamster money.

-Who was in the car again?

Holt: There was James J. Canty, whom I had known for a long time. He was a pilot. His activities were strictly limited to flying operations...ferrying...any type of operation like that. He had worked, at one time, for Inter-Mountain, which was located out of Tucson, Arizona. And he had also flown for Paragon Air Service in Miami. Both of these were proprieties of the Central Intelligence Agency. He (Canty) really was not a shooter. He was first an excellent pilot and flight instructor who worked for the Veterans Administration. He had plenty of opportunities to go anywhere he wanted to, cause he could coordinate it with his other business without any problem. The other individuals were Leo Moceri and Charlie Nicoletti, along with Canty.

-He was to fly back with you?

Holt: He, (Canty), was to fly the Comanche, which had already been purchased and was at Redbird Airport, which was a little bit south of Dallas. That place belonged to Southwest Aircraft Corp., another propriety interest of the CIA that had been incorporated many years ago. Licavoli had taken it over long before we ever got involved with the CIA, but at that time it was used time to time by the CIA. They paid all the tiedown fees for all the aircraft. We had at least 6 aircraft at the time, and they paid the tiedown fees, they paid the insurance, they paid all the expenses.

-Where did the funds to make that trip come from?

Holt: We had probably $4,000-$5,000 between us, because we always had lost of money, lots of cash, and we never, ever used any credit cards, never. An examination of all the bank accounts that we had, which we still have records of, would indicate the amounts of money that went through these bank accounts, thousands of dollars would go through them in a weeks time.

-What bank?

Holt: The Bank of America was the bank that their bank accounts were with. The bank from which their funds came to us was the bank at Fullerton, California, which is the Interstate

Bank. But at the time it was known as the Bank of Fullerton, California. The stock was 100% owned by Phillip A. Twombly. He was the president of the bank.

They would send money to the Bank of America, where we had five separate accounts in the names of John R. Moon and somebody else. The reason for having so many bank accounts was they were able to circumvent the restrictions of taking a lot of cash, we could take as much as $25,000 out in one day without it ever being recorded.

I'm not sure whether the recording requirements at that time, if anything in excess of $10,000 had to be recorded or not, I don't know, but we just didn't want to draw a lot of attention to ourselves. It was the same money, we were just switching it around. We'd rotate a check on one bank account for say about $1500, then the other $1500. So we could get large amounts of cash without being too obvious.

-Who were the other two men in the car with you and Canty?

Holt: The other two men, Nicoletti and Moceri were longtime associates of Peter Licavoli. Both of whom had been involved in Cuban politics and had been involved with Jimmy Hoffa. Although it wasn't common knowledge was that Hoffa was involved in Cuban politics up to his neck. He owned a company called ACROS?, and they produced airplanes. Huge transport planes. They were longtime associates of not only Licavoli, Moceri had known Licavoli longer than I had. He had known him for 40 years, and had been involved as one of the suspects in the Jackie Kennedy killing...(the bootlegger, not the President). He was a U.S. citizen, as was Charlie Nicoletti.

Nicoletti was also a hit man of some note. He was an enforcer and a contract killer. I don't know if he was on the payroll of the CIA or not. Or whether he was working independently or not. The same with Moceri. I have no idea who paid them, but we didn't give them any money.

They were going on to Louisiana, we assumed they were going to New Orleans,...to see Marcello. They had known him for a long time. Marcello and Licavoli were close, although they didn't associate too well because in the Mafia you can't afford to associate with each other. But they worked though intermediaries and they knew each other. Of course the ones who worked for Carlos Marcello and Civello and these guys, they knew and were close to the old timers in Dallas, like Benny Binion, Ernie "the Cap" Nobel and those guys. They knew all of those guys very well.

-When did you arrive in Dallas?

Holt: We didn't arrive in Dallas until early the following morning, on the morning of the 22nd, for the simple reason that we had some car trouble, some bad weather, and it took longer to drive than we thought. We were scheduled to go to the Motel, the Cabana, and get there that evening. We were told that Morgan Brown,...I knew who he was although I didn't know him that well... I knew his brother. But I understood that Morgan and Eugene "Jim" Brading, I knew him, and Dave Yaras, was suppose to be at the Cabana.

We were supposed to deliver all the documents and put them in a pickup truck. We already identified the pickup, with a camper shell and Texas license plates on it. It was supposed to be at the Cabana. If that didn't work out, if there was a delay for any reason, then we were all to...the pickup truck was to be in the parking lot at Dealey Plaza, and that's where we found it. They told us it was near the railroad yards behind the picket fence by the Texas Book Depository, near the tower by the railroad yards. We were suppose to put it in there, the truck, and we were supposed to wait around. And that ended our responsibility.

-You had communications equipment?

Holt: I had a state of the art, hand-held transceiver, which was made by ICOM, top of the line. We had been provided with the frequencies of the Dallas Police Department and were able to monitor the motorcade on the 2 channels they were operating on. To make sure there wasn't any mix-up, they were crystal controlled, although normally they aren't crystal controlled, but this was, just like an aircraft transceiver. So we could monitor what was going on. That was provided by Twombly at the very beginning, or from David Palmer. We had a lot of equipment. When I say it was provided by him, all of this equipment came from Twombly, purchased by them, and provided by others....It was fair to assume this was a strange trip.

-What was out of the ordinary, unusual about this trip?

Holt: The safety precautions. Eating at out of the way places. Not being up front about where we were going to go. Not being told the full extent of what was happening or what was going to happen. Not being told what personnel was going to be there, or whether we could trust these individuals, some of which we knew. Some of whom we knew as notorious double crossers and triple crossers, like ...Seraphin...we knew. Aldo Vera Seraphin was a premier assassin often used by the CIA. He was also suspected of being a double agent for Castro. He was also suspected of being an FBI informant. And reputed to be very untrustworthy. We had dealt with him for many years. Same way with...he was in the same category as Carlos Morales. The guy would double cross anybody, but he was useful and would be used from time to time. He was Cuban and we were to provide documentation for him. I didn't see Seraphin, nor did I see Orlando Bosch. The documents were left in the truck. These items were to be distributed by Homer Echevarria, who was as anti-Kennedy as you could absolutely get.

-At what point did you know JFK was going to be in Dallas?

Holt: We knew before we left, sometime probably after November 18th. We were advised that he was going to be in San Antonio, Houston and Dallas, although we were not privy to the route. We did not known what the route was going to be. We had been told an incident was going to be created which could be laid at the door of pro-Castro Cubans. The word attempted assassination was never used. We assumed that from all this light loaded ammunition that maybe somebody was going to try to take a shot from somewhere, probably the Dal-Tex building, or one of the buildings around there. But at no time was it ever intimidated to us that an assassination or attempted assassination on Kennedy, Connally,...there were other targets there as well. Somebody might have wanted to knock off Gonzalez. We had (been operating on) a need to know basis. It may sound stupid but, if they had (told us), I'd have been back at Grace Ranch, relaxing.

It was such an elaborate set up. When you think back, I couldn't possibly have been so duped. When we saw him on TV and he said, "I'm just a patsy!" I tell you the word really rang home.

-What is a "need to know" basis?

Holt: A need to know operation are central, not only to the CIA, but for organized crime or anything else. The information is imparted to individuals on a need to know basis. If you try to inquire, just one time, if you show some curiosity, just one time, as to what is going on, then you won't be around. You'll either be dead, or you'll be ostracized. Not only is it isolation from top to bottom, but latterly as well. It operates not only at the higher ups, naturally they are interested in protecting themselves more than anyone else. These guys down here are protecting themselves, too. It's just another example of plausible deniability. I say, "Hey, give me a lie detector test!" If they ask, "Did you, were you there for the purpose of assassinating Kennedy or engaging in an attempted assassination of Kennedy," and in all honesty, we could say, "No, I wasn't."

-Is it a fair assumption to say that on most operations you worked in the blind?

Holt: More often than not it is rare that you see the Big Picture, a broad stroke picture. Most of the time you are engaged in one little, small...(part)...with very generalized instructions, and in retrospect, they were rather bizarre. We had been assured that the whole incident would be over by 12:25 and that if anything went untowed or happened, that created any activity as far as law enforcement or any government agency or anything like that occurred in that area, that sitting on the siding would be this train. It could be identified as a Rock Island Train.

They said that the train would be locked on one side, but not the other side. It would be unlocked, and it would not be searched and we could go on the train and we would be concealed, and the train would be moved out almost immediately, and we could jump off very quickly and that's how we were to exit the situation.

No one suggested that we get back to the Oldsmobile and drive out of the parking lot. They should have given us that option I suppose. But when you receive those types of instructions, you don't really inquire as to the rational or even inquire. That's how you operate.

-Where were you when the motorcade went past?

Holt: At the time I was in the parking lot back near the railroad tracks, behind the grassy knoll. I couldn't even see the motorcade. I saw the lead cars come buy, but we never got a glimpse. I was the only individual back there at the time. Others were wandering around. There were a lot of people in the area, some were dressed in suits, others were dressed in work clothes, they had construction workers wandering around there. There were lots and lots of people around there, but as far as my colleagues went, I was the only one there at the time.

-You encountered Harrelson and Montoya there, who you knew ?

Holt: Harrelson came up and actually introduced himself to me as though we had just had a business meeting. He said to me, in his typical Texas accent, "I'm Harrelson." And we shook hands. But at the time this happened (the assassination), I hadn't seen him. He had been there for awhile I didn't see him at that particular...(moment).

When I encountered him was when I had went back and scooted to the railroad car. I thought probably I would be the only one there. Then I see Harrelson and the individual I knew as "Montoya", that I had seen three or four times over a three or four year period.

I met Montoya the first time in 1959. When we were trying to elicit funds from Orlando Peatra, who was Batista's paymaster. He lived on Pine Tree drive in Miami. And when I went over there, there were a number of individuals, bodyguards and such. And this individual introduced himself as "Richard Montoya", although I must admit he didn't look like the rest of the Cubans.

He looked like he might be Latin. He was dark, but he didn't look like....He was a cut away from the other Cubans, although he spoke excellent Spanish.

At the time of the shooting, the moment the shots were fired, we (I) knew something went awry. We didn't know why, but from the screaming and carrying on we knew that there had been one hell of a bad incident. At the time, what went through our minds was, "Hey, we had gotten ourselves into something that is way over our heads." So I scooted under the train, went under to the other side, encountered Harrelson and Montoya, we searched out the car, which was not too far from the engine, climbed in it, closed the door and sat there in silence, while I monitored the radio and listened to what was going on.

We were in the railroad car by 12:31-12:32, almost immediately,...as soon as the shooting started, and there was pandemonium and people were running all over the place. When actually, we look back on it, we could of easily have lost ourselves in all of this stuff. We could have gotten right up to the grassy knoll and thrown ourselves on the ground, like everybody else was, and started screaming, and that would have been the end of it.

We were in the box car a long time. Actually we heard a lot of transmissions. I estimated that it was almost 2 O'clock, although my watch was still on Arizona time. I had a bad habit of not changing my watch. So I think we stayed in there till practically 2 O'clock. We were still in there during the time when we heard the transmissions involving Tippit and back and forth. We heard a lot of other communications. We heard the call that an officer had been dying. I am told and I believe it was somewhere around 1:15 when we heard about the incident at the Texas theatre, although we didn't know what happened.

So I thought it was possibly 2 O'clock before the train actually started to move. We started to move, backing down the tracks a little ways. We thought it was going to move. I thought they were going to switch us onto another track.

Then suddenly the thing stopped. They opened the door and there was a whole bunch of police officers with shotguns and everything else. We saw, the box car was not a fully loaded box car, but in this box car was ammunition, unusual ammunition. Defcord?, crates that looked like they were possibly claymore mines, drums marked : MUD, which seemed like drilling mud, which was unusual to be with the rest of this material. Which I assumed to be C-4 or some plastic explosives.

The officers took us out, we tried to identify ourselves. We said, "Hey, we're federal agents working on this thing," and they said, "Come with us." So we strolled along and actually we went back, we came out of the yard, we went by the Texas Depository building, across the street. I would say Harrelson and I were sort of dragging along, but Montoya, he was really digging out. He was actually right up behind the lead officer. He turned us over to two officers, the officer in charge, we later learned was Harkness.

In the photos, the individual in front is the individual I knew as Richard Montoya. The individual behind him I knew as Charles Harrelson. I had reason to believe that's who he actually was, even though I didn't know him that well. I'm confident that's who it was. And I'm the gentleman in the back, carrying the bag with the radio in it.

We were not placed under arrest. We were taken across, and someone interviewed us momentarily, and turned us over to someone else. A person I later learned was Captain Fritz, he said not two or three words to us. He said he was turning us over to the FBI. His name was Gordon Shanklin.

He asked us who were, what we were doing there. Just about this time, while we were doing this, there was a lot of confusion, a lot of pandemonium, and actually a lot of, I would term jubilation on the part of all of the police officers in there, especially Gordon Shanklin, which led us to believe that our release was because of something that happened. Although they had said it on a number of occasions, someone else was arrested. They had caught someone in the Dal Tex building. I heard someone say, "We got one of them." But then when the matter came in that they had indicated they had got the individual that had killed the cop in Oakland (sic: Oak Cliff), all at once it seemed to me, even what I considered prematurely, they indicated they had the guy that shot the president too. And at that time the level of attention on us,...they had some other people they had detained and looked like they were going to arrest, including Braden.

Jim Braden was there. I didn't recognize him at first, because he had a hat on with some kind of Texas style hat band on it, and I didn't know him all that well, if you know what I mean. But I knew that I recognized him like I recognize you.

But once we got in there, and these events come off because they happened almost at the time we arrived there. Then the attention shifted a lot at once, from us to Oswald, who turned out to be Oswald. I assumed that it was their normal enthusiasm about having captured a cop killer, is what I thought. Because they treat cop killers a hell of a lot different than they treat killers of anyone else. Not the president of course. But at that point, Gordon Shanklin,...we hadn't been in there too long. We were there a little while. And all this time, ...then who we are came up, then they were very careless. We were strolling around, people were coming around. They didn't treat us like dangerous suspects. They didn't handcuff us. Plus they didn't search us, and we were heavily armed.

-What building were you taken to?

Holt: We were taken to the Sheriff's Department, right there on Dealey Plaza. Didn't walk far. We didn't make a statement. Weren't fingerprinted. Weren't taken to the jail (where) I assume we would have been taken. Then Gordon Shanklin said, "You're free to go."

We left together. They split and I split too. I didn't know what they were going to do. I was going to try to get back to California. Morgan H. Brown was going to take us to the airport. We (I) called (the Cabana) and they said that he had checked out at 2 O'clock. So we went down to try to find somebody to drive us out there. Looking back, I don't know why we just didn't get a cab and get ourselves as far away as we could.

They left Braden. Braden didn't get out until probably 3 O'clock. Braden had a car he was driving. Canty was ready at the airport. Reviewed the engines. Checked everything for us to go and he expected us to be at the airport before 1 O'clock. When we went out there he had already preflighted the airplane...He asked us if we wanted to file a flight plan and we said no, we'll file it en route to Wichita Falls, just get out of town.

-When did you know the president was shot?

Holt: We heard, within five months after the shooting, that somebody had been shot. The airwaves were very congested at the time. We heard sheriff Decker...We heard someone was being taken to Parkland hospital. Possibly within five minutes we knew both Kennedy and Connally had been shot and that a little after 1 O'clock that the president was dead.

-Describe the airplane you flew out of Redbird Airport in?

Holt: The airplane was a Comanche 250. But it was specially modified for short take off, with 3 bladed...I still have the end number, because I still have it somewhere, because Frank Belcher ended up selling the airplane for me. I don't remember the precise color, but I do remember that on the tail of the airplane it had a monstrous picture of a gear, because at one time it had belonged to someone in the business of making gears. That's all I can remember about the plane.

-What did you learn from monitoring the police radio?

Holt: We learned, we already knew that the president was dead. The news reports were constant. That Connally was going to survive and that the assassin had been captured. At that time of course, we realized we were involved to some extent. Although Canty wasn't privy to as much information as I was, and we simply dismissed the thing, I was sure that Oswald was set up.

-From 1942 till 1977 it appears you avoided arrest?

Holt: Well, it wasn't because I wasn't engaged in criminal activities. I would assume it was because most of the time we were under the protection of the U.S. government. That some of those activities we were engaged in, not for any government agency, but aside from it, they turned a deaf ear to it simply because of the fact they didn't want to interfere with other types of operations.

-What happened in 1977 that you weren't offered that protection?

Holt: It actually started in 1975 when Schlesinger and Turner came into the CIA. They proceeded to purge all the cowboys in the field and they sent a lot to prison. I was one of those at the time. I was indicted in 1975 and a fugitive till 1977, when I went to prison. At which time I had a whole series of charges against me, and pleaded guilty to one charge of mail fraud.

-Is it fair to say you are a career criminal?

Holt: Yes.

-Why have you come forward now?

Holt: Several individuals have been wrongly accused of having been the tramps. Possibly some of them deserve having been accused of that, or something else, and I specifically refer to someone like Frank Sturgis, who incidentally ran afoul of the law on something else and ended up in prison. Howard Hunt, who was falsely identified as the person I claim to be.

There's a lot of mystery surrounding the assassination. I felt that my information is from a point of view that probably, if I am believed, would lay to rest these ideas that Jack Ruby and Lee Harvey Oswald were just nuts that passed in the night.

And I always felt a sympathy for Oswald. I just didn't feel it's right, or his children should be stuck with that stigma, that's all.

-Do you feel harm could come to you?

Holt: Of course, but I'm certainly not going to shrink from it.

END.

Reprint from http://jfkmurdersolved.com/holt1.htm

Transcript of video-interview with James E. Files.

Location: Stateville Correctional Center, Joliet, Illinois.

Date: 19 november 2003

Interviewers: Jim Marrs (J) and Wim Dankbaar (W)

Camera: Gary L. Beebe

(The DVD of this interview can be purchased on the website www.jfkmurdersolved.com)

J – What is your recollection of how Joe West contacted you and what did you think of Joe West?

(Wim: Joe West was the private investigator who located James Files based on a tip from FBI agent Zack Shelton.)

JF – When Joe West first contacted me here at Stateville prison I was on a visit. The counselor came in the visiting room where I was at and stated that she wanted me to come out and make a phonecall. I told her : No way, I'm here 365 days a year. I'm not leaving my visit to make a phonecall. I said : Who's calling? Someone from Texas named Joe West. I do not know the party. Tell 'm I call them on my time, not their time. I'm on a visit. Don't bother me while I am on a visit. The next day they come and got me out of my cell, they took me downstairs, they got a phonecall hooked up. I call Joe West to talk to him. I told him: You have 3 minutes to convince me why I should talk to you. As Joe started talking to me, I told him: Woo, stop! You go through a lot of touchy spots, these phonecalls are all recorded. Every phonecall going in and coming out is recorded. If you want to talk to me that bad, then I suggest you come and visit me. Joe West had me put him on the visiting list. He came up to visit me. He spent two days of talking with me. The first day I wouldn't even talk to him about the Kennedy situation. We got into sports, weather, generally about prison, local things till I got comfortable with him. The next day, after I had thought it over all night, Joe West seemed like a pretty nice guy, I really liked Joe. He had a magnetism about him. The next day we sit down and got serious and then we started talking. I sit in the visiting room with Joe. They gave us a pencil and paper. I sketched the entire Dealey Plaza out for him, without any maps, without pictures, nothing present, and I explained to Joe at that time …. because Joe wanted to know where was I at. And I said: I'm going to put an X on the paper, to signify me, but this X is not in the correct spot. I said: When the time comes, then I'll put the X where it is supposed to be.

W - What had you told him that Joe knew you were in Dealey Plaza?

JF – Oh, I asked him. He said that someone had informed him that I was there He said he had a reliable source. And I didn't know for quite a while who that source was. It was quite some time later before I learned the fact that the FBI was aware of my presence as early as 1964. Because I never knew that anyone ever knew about me. But Zack Shelton, from what I understand, and I'm only quoting this from hearsay, that Zack was the one that stated and gave to Joe West the information on me: that I was in Dealey Plaza.

J - That's my understanding. Did you ever actually confess to taking the shot to Joe West?

JF – No, I never did.

J – Make a statement

JF – well, the whole thing is, like with Joe West …. Joe West died. He passed away, never knowing that I was one of two shooters there in Dealey Plaza that day. Joe West never knew I was on the grassy knoll.

J – do you have any thoughts on his death? Do you think that was natural?

JF – Joe West went in for heart surgery. And from what I was told and from what I understood, that he had come through it very well and he was on the road to recovery. But then I was informed there was complications with his medicine, he was allergic to it or had an allergy or something. But it killed him, the medication killed him. A couple of years ago, maybe a year and a half ago, I heard through the grapevine, and I won't go into the party that brought this information to me, they said that someone had tampered with Joe's medication and he had received the wrong medication. Because they wanted to silence him.

J – That's (also) according to his wife …

W – And why would they want to silence him?

JF – We had …. I shouldn't say we, Joe West had the case in court, he wanted to exhume John F. Kennedy's body. And that's what he was fighting for. And at this point when I talked to Joe West, I explained to him that John F. Kennedy had been hit in the head with a mercury round, a special load. At this point I explained to him he can use this in the court to have the body exhumed because there would still be traces of mercury because the traces of mercury do not disappear. That will always be there. So this is what Joe West wanted to go back with, more evidence, and use this to get Kennedy's body exhumed. To look for traces of mercury.

(It should be noted that James Files believes that Kennedy's body is not buried in Arlington. He overheard a conversation of CIA deputy director Theodore Shackley telling that the body had been "dumped into the sea". The day before this interview James Files pointed out to me that if the exhumed body would not contain traces of mercury, then it would not be Kennedy's body.)

J – And the court had accepted his case?

JF – The court had accepted his case. But with his death, the case died.

J – Uh, Do you feel like your memory is as good as it was 10 years ago?

JF – No, I do not, It's not that good. My memory as of 10 years ago was a lot more alert than what it is now. It's not that I'm just getting old and senile, but it's the conditions of prison, the conditions we live under. Our water here, when people come in and I'm sure you was advised not to drink the water from here and to buy a bottle of water. I've been drinking this water for the past 12 years with radium in it, so has every prisoner here. We wasn't aware of the water situation until Oliver Stone comes along tom make a movie here. And when he made his movie here, we see all these people from the movie company running around carrying bottles of water. Even the officers that worked here, they got suspicious and that's when we started finding out: this water is unhealthy.

J – Just at the side, you know: Sodiumfluoride is what they put in some city's watersupplies. That's what the Nazi's put in the watersupplies of those concentration camps to keep everybody pacified.

JF – Yeah, well, they keep us pretty well pacified and they really kept us pacified since we went on about a ten month lockdown and they took the prison back and run it under their order now. And I mean this place is really maximum control now. There is no movement here at all to speak of.

W – Did you actually meet Oliver Stone?

JF – I met Oliver Stone three times. As a matter of fact I have a paper that Joe West … no excuse me, not Joe West but Bob Vernon, had Oliver Stone sign. Now Bob Vernon had come in after the Joe West deal. Bob Vernon took over for Joe West. Bob Vernon met with Oliver Stone and he had him sign an agreement where they wanted to get me on film, but I refused to do that. I met with Oliver Stone three times.

J – And you never told him your story?

JF – No, I did not tell Oliver Stone my story. I refused to discuss it with him and uh …like I say, I 've got a copy, It's got Oliver Stone's signature on it, Bob Vernon's, the only signature that states what it's all about, the only thing missing is my signature because I would never sign that paper for the agreement.

J - Why was that?

JF – I didn't like the man!

J – Case closed!

JF – Case closed! And if you'd like I would be more than happy to send you a copy of the document. And it has got Oliver Stone's original signature on it. And it has Bob Vernon's signature on it.

(Wim: Well, I guess that answers the critics who say that Files is just a convict trying to get attention.) I mean, if you want attention, you want to talk to Oliver Stone, who was the director of the blockbuster movie JFK.

J – Well , I 've got a raft of questions, but it takes a while, let's just go back to.. let's go into chronology, just tell me your own account again. Go back to when you first learned there was a plot to kill Kennedy and then just bring us forward and how it all came about.

JF – Okay, the first time that I knew about anything being planned on Kennedy… Oh, I heard a lot of rumours, nobody liked Kennedy, they wanted to kill Kennedy, they wanted to assassinate him. They wanted to do everything to the man.

J- Were you kind of upset with him yourself?

JF – Oh I was upset with him over the Bay of Pigs, but I never paid any attention to any of this at first, because you know, everybody talks, somebody gets mad at somebody and right away: I'm gonna take this guy out, I'm gonna get that person out, woo, woo, woo, woo! You know, a lot of barking, junkyard dogs barking you know. But I was sitting in the Harlo Grill that evening, playing the pinball machine. Not the flipper kind, the kind with numbers where you gamble on, you put about 10 dollars in to play a game. And Charles Nicoletti walked in. The man that I did a lot of work with, a man that I respected. And he walked in the back room where I was at, he says: Jimmy let's go! I said: I'll be with you in a minute! He reached over the machine to me and he said: Let's go now! My reply was: Yes sir, Mr. Nicoletti! I knew he was in no mood to wait and hang around. He said: I wanna talk to you. I went out and we got into his car and went for a ride, and we made it a basic habit not to sit around in restaurants, talk, discussing things like that with a lot of people hearing. And we went for a ride and he told me: We are going to do a friend of yours! And I said: Jesus, what the hell did he do now? Because I thought he was referring to one of my friends in town, he had been robbing the pinball machines and the cigarette machines, he had a 1000-dollar-a–day-heroin habit. He was an all out junky, you know. They had beaten him up several times and everything else and threatened him, but so far they had never gone as far as to kill him. Chuck laughs at me and he says: No, not him, I'm talking about president Kennedy, JFK! And I looked at him and said: What? He says: JFK, …your buddy! I think he's just busting, giving me a hard time you know, he knew JFK and he knew how much I disliked the man. So I looked at him and I laughed. I said: Okay, fine! Fine with me! You get no arguments there! And at this point I still kind of thought, you know, he was just joking with me. But then he got real serious about it. And we started talking and he says: What I want you to do, is look around, search the areas around the town here, he says : you know everything pretty good. See where we are going to do it at, what kind of weapons we are going to need and other things like that. And he says: (inaudible) is going to bring Johnny Roselli in on it. Fine with me, I don't care who we work with. I like Johnny, I have no problems with him. And uh… originally we had planned to do it in the Chicago area, but certain people didn't like that idea. So then we put it off and this like 6 months before the assassination ever really took place.

(Wim: Charles Nicoletti was a trusted lieutenant of Chicago mafiaboss Sam Giancana. He was known as one of the local hitman. Johnny Roselli was another mobster working for Sam Giancana. In the 1970's it became known that in the early sixties, Roselli and Giancana had been recruited by the CIA for assassination plots to kill Fidel Castro.)

W- But you were not supposed to be a shooter?

JF- Oh no, never, I was not a shooter, I was …. Let's put it this way: I was to go for this, go for that, pick this up, pick that up, run around, driving around. When Chuck went somewhere, I was always with him.

J – did you ever get wind that the Secret Service might have found out about the plot in Chicago?

JF – No, I did get no wind on that at all. I just knew that certain people high up in organised crime, they weren't too happy about the idea of having something like that happen of that magnitude in their backyard. Because they figured Bobby would really be down there and they already had their own little private wars going. So we decided where to take the move, I had no idea it was going to Texas at that point. This had come to me down the road.

J – About when was that?

JF – Well, I wanna say .. probably two and half, three months, maybe four, before I ever made the trip to Texas, that they were talking about it. Because they didn't know where he was gonna go. They were looking for an area to go. But then they had heard that he possibly may take this trip to Texas, but there was nothing definite. And I didn't go to Texas until that had been confirmed. And …. they had several different locations, there was New Orleans and I don't know, there was other places he was going to. But when it came down to it, I had been told there was places that they had planned to do it, other people had been authorized and stuff like that, you know, just different rumours you hear. How much credibility there is to it, I cannot say. But when the time had come and we knew it was going to be serious and Chuck was sending me to Texas, that's when I went down on Belmont Avenue, the old (inaudible) place where they made the pinball machines. I had a shed down there, a place, a backroom, that was all owned by the Outfit too, the pinball machines. I kept a catch of weapons down there, we used to do a lot of work on them there. When I say we, I refer to a party named Wolfman, who is now deceased, but at that time he was excellent, remodifying weapons, manufacturing loads, whatever coming down to handguns, rifles. This guy was professionalized. He could manufacture things in his basement, like you wouldn't believe, from silencers all down the line, he did it all for them. So I went down there, got the stuff we needed. And we had the one car that he just bought, I had already secured everything in there, we had secret compartments in it. And every car that we had, even before the '63 Chevy, even in the '61 Ford that we had prior to that in '62, we had compartments in the dash where you could reach up under it and open things up, put grenades in there, handguns, whatever we might need. Behind the backseat we had gunracks in the cars. We had pull-off door panels that could snap off, we could put them back on, we had handguns and stuff in there. Whatever you might need, but we always had a work-car ready.

J – So what did Wolfman do for you?

JF – Wolfman, when I contacted him after all this went down, and this is several years later, this is when I first met Joe West and Joe West had come here and visited me, we talked and he asked me: Do you think this party called Wolfman would talk to me? And Joe asked me what his real name was and I told him: I won't divulge that but I will call him and talk to him. So I called him on the phone and I told him I was talking to Joe West from Texas, and he wanted to know who Joe was and I explained all this to him and I said: Joe would very much like to interview you. I did not give Joe West your name but told him that you was the one that manufactured the special rounds. He made six rounds for me to take to Texas, all mercury loaded. I said: He wants to talk to you very much. Will you talk with him? And he said: Get back to me! I'll let you know. He said: I wanna check a few things. The following week Wolfman was dead.

J – How did he die?

JF – I believe he had a heart attack. I have been in contact with nobody that was affiliated with Wolfman since that day.

J – Tell me about these mercury loads. Can you describe them ?

JF – Well, it was a 22 round and he took the tips off, he drilled them out and he inserted with an eyedrop, he put mercury into the end of the round and he restilled them with wax. This is to make them explode on impact.

J – Okay, so now you got …. Describe the car!

JF – The car was a '63 Chevy two door Burgundy. Chevy Impala.

J – With the special compartment?

JF- Oh yeah, we had a special compartment in the dash, we had the backseat, you could take that off, pull the bottom part up, raise the back up, snap it up little clams and take that out. We had the springs removed behind the seat there by it and we had little racks welded in there so we could mount weapons in there.

(Wim: A fragment from an article by organised crime expert Andy :

"By the late 1950's, Nicoletti had a feared reputation as a hitman and was one of the usual suspects brought in for questioning whenever cops thought they had a gangland-style-slaying on their hands. In 1962, he was arrested while driving a so-called "work" car, specially equipped with hidden compartments for guns, rear lights that turned off, a souped up engine, special reinforcement on both sides, bullet proof glass and a rotating rear license plate. It was no surprise the next day when a mob associate was found slain near where Nicoletti had been detained."

Source: http://www.ganglandnews.com/column80.htm)

J – Okay, so now you've got your weapons, you got your loads and you got your car. How did it come together after that?

JF – Well, just before I left, the final instructions Chuck told me: I want you to leave first thing in the morning. He said: I don't want you driving at night. I want you on the highway with a lot traffic during daytime where nobody pays any attention to you.

J – Go back and give me a date or approximately …

JF – I don't remember the date but I went down like week before the assassination. I wanna say I was in the Dallas area five days before the assassination took place.

W- And what was the purpose of that?

JF – The purpose of that was for me to go to Dallas, look over the area, learn dead-end streets, railroad crossings, times of train crossings. They already knew the regular motorcade route that he would be taking, and they had already looked that over and they wanted to see if there were any better places. A lot of people had already decided on, I'm not the one that chose Dealey Plaza, but I was told to look it over very closely and see if I thought there was any place better. And I did the whole area from the route they had. All the way through I had Lee Harvey Oswald with me.

W – What was the (motorcade)route at that time?

JF – That was the old route 66 (misunderstands the question).

W – No, I mean in Dealey Plaza.

J – He's telling about coming from Chicago. We'll get to that. All right, go back, about a week ahead of time, I think it was on Monday as I recall?

JF – I'm not sure…..

J – Okay, but you left Chicago. Let's start …You left Chicago and you went to….
JF – No, I didn't leave on a Monday. I left on uuh…I left either on a Thursday or a Friday morning, I don't remember which, I know I was in Mesquite, Texas Saturday morning. Because that was when Lee Harvey Oswald showed up at the motel where I was at. I arrived there on a Friday. I'm pretty sure it was Friday when I arrived there.

J – Did you call anybody when you got to Dallas?

JF – I made two telephone calls when I got there. I called Charles Nicoletti, I told him I was on the scene and where I was at in case he had to reach me. I turned around and made another phonecall, I called David Atlee Phillips. I had a number to call, the call was put through to David Phillips and he was notified where I was at. Because I had not told him in advance that I was going to Dallas, Texas.

(Wim: David Atlee Phillips is a man whose name is well known to assassination researchers. He was called to testify for the House Select Committee on Assassinations in the 1970's. Several members of the committee wanted to call him again for they believed he had not told the truth and committed perjury.

Phillips was traced as a suspect as a result of the testimony of Cuban exile leader Antonio Veciana, who claimed he knew his CIA case officer only under the alias of "Maurice Bishop" (personally I believe Veciana knew his real name too, but did not dare to disclose that). A composite sketch, based on the recollections of Veciana prompted a US senator Schweiker to recognize David Atlee Phillips. A confrontation between Veciana and Phillips was arranged but Veciana, apparently fearing for his safety, refused to identify Phillips as his former case officer, but later acknowledged privately that Phillips was indeed his CIA controller.

The following is known of David Atlee Phillips by now: He was one of the masterminds for the CIA staged coup by Pinochet in 1973, as well as the overthrow in 1954 of the Guatemala regime headed by Jacobo Arbenz. He was working closely with CIA officer E. Howard Hunt, another suspect in the plot to kill JFK and the leader of the infamous Watergate burglar team. In the 1950's and 1960's, Phillips was the CIA case officer for the anti Castro Cubans in Havana and Mexico City. The star of David Atlee Phillips rose to CIA director of Special Operations for the Western Hemisphere.)

J – And why did you call David Atlee Phillips?

JF – Because he always had to know where I was at because he was my controller?

J – For?

JF – CIA purposes, special operations or something that might be needed done.

J – Were you supposed to stay in contact with him?

JF – We always stayed in contact. We had numbers to call.

J – What happened after that?

JF – He said "thank you" and let it go with that. We didn't have any great discussion on the phone, I told him where I was at, the location. And … through David Atlee Phillips is the only way that Lee Harvey Oswald could have known where I was at. Because I called no one else. I made two phonecalls.

J – where were you staying?

JF - I was staying at the Lamplighter Inn, right there in Mesquite. Texas.

J - And then the next thing you knew, Lee Harvey Oswald shows up.

JF – The following morning Lee Harvey Oswald was there. When he knocked on the door, I opened the door and I was shocked to see him, because I didn't think that anybody knew where I was at except for these other two people.

W – Why is Phillips the only one who could have sent Lee Harvey Oswald?

JF – Because Charles Nicoletti had never met Lee Harvey Oswald.

W – He didn't know him?

JF – He did not know him.

J – You say you were shocked to see him, but did you know Lee Harvey Oswald?

JF – I had known Lee Harvey Oswald prior to that, yes.

J – How did you know him?

JF – I knew him from earlier operations that we were on with David Phillips when I was running semi automatic 45 caliber submachine guns down to Clinton, Louisiana. They were, I think they were manufactured by Knoxville Arms. They were not the old Thompson, they looked like a Thompson submachine gun, but they were not Thompson. They were only semi automatic and they were very cheaply made.

W – And how did you meet Lee Harvey Oswald? Who introduced you?

JF – I met Lee Harvey Oswald through David Atlee Phillips. When I got down there, he introduced me to Lee.

J – Was it your understanding that Phillips was also Oswald's CIA contact?

JF – I learned that when I was down there. That is the first time he introduced me to Lee Harvey Oswald and he also instructed me that Lee could be trusted and that he was Lee's controller.

J – I need that as a statement

JF – He made it a statement. Because I wanted to know who I was dealing with and who I was giving weapons to.

J – No, I need you to make a statement that "I was introduced by Phillips, who was my CIA handler and I was told that he was Oswald's handler."

JF – We didn't call them handlers back then, we called them controllers.

J – Okay.

JF - Okay, David Atlee Phillips, he introduced me to Lee Harvey Oswald. And upon doing this, he also explained to me that he was Lee Harvey Oswald's controller, the same as he was mine. That he was always in contact with Lee, with Lee Harvey Oswald.

J – So that's how you know…. That's where the word came from for Oswald to come meet you in Dallas?

JF – So that's how common sense told me the only one that could have sent Lee Harvey Oswald, was David Atlee Phillips. And when I opened the door and Oswald was there, I was kind of shocked to see him, because I didn't know that he knew I was there. And so I asked: Lee, what the hell are you doing here? Because I was shocked, you know. He said: I was advised to drop by and spend some time with you and see if I could help you out. "Help me out?" He said: Yes, somebody wants me to show you the area. And I said: Okay, come on in. So he came in and we sat down and we talked and I said: I'll be with you in a few minutes. And I was young and cocky at that time and had just come out of the shower and everything and I was combing my hair and actually I had a camera there, so I told Lee: Hey, make a couple of pictures of me while I'm here in Texas! And so Oswald made a couple of pictures of me and then he said: Let me have the film, I can have it developed! No, no, I said, I'll get the whole roll of film. So that's how I got a couple of pictures made, that people have recently asked me about.

J – Which camera was it? Yours or ..?

JF - My camera. But was gonna take the film, turn it in and get it developed. But I said: No, no!

J – You wouldn't let that film go!

JF – I do my own work! (smiling)

J – How did he arrive at the motel?

JF – He arrived driving a blue Falcon. Ford Falcon.

J – Do you remember what year model?

JF – No, I don't. It wasn't brand new, it was a couple of years old.

J – Mmm, so he could drive?

(Wim: Although Lee Harvey Oswald did not have a driver's license, many other witnesses have made statements that he could indeed drive very well. Several of these witnesses saw Oswald driving a car and have signed affidavits to that effect. Recently a woman by the name of Judyth Vary Baker, has come forward and she claims to have been Oswald's girl friend in the summer of 1963. She says she has made long distance trips by car, with Lee behind the wheel.)

JF – Yes, he could drive. When he met me in Clinton, Louisiana, he drove up in aah…. I wanna say a Chevrolet truck, it could have been a Ford, it was a pick-up truck, let me put it that way, it was an old pick-up truck. And we put the weapons into the back end of it and pulled the tarp down over the weapons.

J – What color? Do you remember what color pick-up?

JF – I believe it was green. It was a real…I don't know, dirty, yakkie, green, whatever you gonna call it. Darker green, you know, it hadn't been washed in a long time and there was a lot of rust on it. That's about the best way to describe it.

J – So did you and Lee Oswald drive around in Dallas?

JF – We drove around Dallas, Lee Harvey Oswald and I, we drove around Dallas for five days right up to before the assassination. I did not see Lee Harvey Oswald on the morning of the assassination. But prior to that Lee Harvey Oswald had been with me every day. We drove around, he showed me different streets, different areas. He was the one that took me out to the place southeast of Mesquite there, next to a big junkyard. We went out in a field, he said: Nobody is going to bother you out here. Because I wanted to calibrate the scopes, you know, not only for the Fireball but for the other weapons as well. And while I was out there firing weapons and ejecting shell casings, Lee was picking them up and holding them in his hand. Because I didn't want to leave no casings or nothing behind and I'm busy firing, so I looked at Lee and said: Lee, grab them casings. And that's what he did. He picked them and held on to them. I calibrated my scopes, set things up, put the stuff back in to the car and we got back in. We were driving around and I wanted to know the railroad crossings, I wanted to wait and see at what times trains come through, I wanted to know if they were passengers or freight trains. Whether they stopped, intersection is gonna be blocked . Dead-end streets, construction work, where every intersection was at, where all the lights were at, how long the lights were staying red,. I wanted to know all these little details.

J – Did anybody show up or give you any static while you were out there sighting the weapons?

JF – No, nobody. When I was test firing the weapons, nobody at all leaving or coming out, looked at me, and there wasn't any house or anybody close by, we were off the main highway there. Like I say, nobody came around, nobody even cared.

W – How much time were you two together during the day?

JF – We were test firing weapons for I would say approximately 20, 30 minutes. But during the day we probably spent no more than 5 hours, 6 hours together.

W – So all that time he could not have been working in the Texas school book depository?

JF – No, he worked in the book depository store, is what he told me. I was never in that place, but he had time off to come out and spend time with me and then I would drop him off in the area and he would go somewhere and I guess that's where he went. I never asked where he went, what he had done and who he saw.

W – So that must have been a cover job.

JF – Yeah.

J – Okay, it gets to be let's say Thursday before the assassination, how did it all come down?

JF – That Thursday I went on back to the motel, I dropped him off that afternoon, I went on back to the motel to get some rest. And the following morning, I had gotten a message that I was supposed to call Leo at the Dallas Cabana, and I called over there and answer the phone to Leo, because Mr. Nicoletti didn't want his name used. I knew he had come in late, I didn't know when he had come in, I didn't even know how he got there. But when I came in, I was told to come over there and park and Johnny Roselli was to come down. He wanted me to drive Johnny Roselli to Fort Worth. I pull out up front and waited, he came down a few minutes after I pulled up. I never went into the hotel and never asked for anybody. He came down and went outside because he knew I was in route. And I drove from there to Fort Worth, Texas with Johnny Roselli in the car.

(Wim: The "Leo" that James Files talks about is Leo Moceri. We now know from the testimony of CIA operative Chauncey Holt, that he drove Charles Nicoletti and Leo Moceri into Dallas. They came from the Grace Ranch in Arizona, that was owned by mafia boss Peter Licavoli of Cleveland. Leo Moceri was his underboss and was later murdered while under subpoena of the FBI.)

J – So Mr. Nicoletti went with you?

JF – No, Mr. Nicoletti did not go.

J – Just Roselli?

JF – Just Johnny Roselli went with me to fort Worth.

J – Did you know Roselli prior to that?

JF – I had met Johnny Roselli before. I met him in Florida, Miami.

J – Did you do any jobs with him?

JF – Never any jobs, but I talked with him and we went around. We were probably involved in some of the same operations and things, with the same people, but we never went out and did anything together.

J – Were you aware that Roselli was working together with the government in anti-Castro activities.

JF – Yes, I was well aware of that …

J – Make a statement.

JF – I was well aware that Johnny Roselli was involved in the government actions. He was like the liaison between CIA and organized crime. And he was heavily involved in the invasion of Cuba, the Bay of Pigs, Chianos Bay, whichever you prefer to call it. But he was also very tight with Frank Sturgis. Frank Sturgis headed up the S.A.O., which is the Secret Army Organization, what this is all about. And they had so many different codenames for wanting to kill Castro, I wouldn't even, I couldn't even name half of them. But every time you turned around, somebody had a new operation going.

J – Did you ever hear Mr. Roselli being called Colonel or did he have any military credentials.

JF - Aah, I don't remember what the total name was, I know he was called Colonel once in a while, I can't remember the name of it but I know he was called Colonel. But that was uh … as far as I know Johnny Roselli never held any rank of any kind. But like I say, he was involved heavily with the CIA, he was a liaison between them, what his actual part was I don't know, but I know he was heavily involved with them. And all through that.

W – I think it was Ralston, Colonel Ralston.

JF - Yeah, Ralston! That's it! Colonel Ralston! That's what they called him: Colonel Ralston.

J – Okay. So tell us about the trip over to Fort worth.

JF – The trip over to Fort Worth. Well, I didn't know we were going to Fort Worth. He told me he had directions and I don't know if he had ever been there before or not, but we went to Fort Worth, I remember the exit was like University Avenue or University Boulevard, it was named University, that's all I know. I know it was on the south side and then sitting on the west side of that street. Just a couple of blocks off there, the pancake house. Fairly new one.

J – It's still there!

JF – Well, I didn't know it's still there, but they make good pancakes, I know that. That's where I had my first Belgian waffle.

(Fort Worth is quite some distance from downtown Dallas and James Files has no clue why the meeting with Jack Ruby had to take place there, but it is quite understandable that Johnny

Roselli did not want to be seen with Jack Ruby in Dallas where Ruby was a well known figure.)

W – Why did you go all the way to Fort Worth?

JF – Excuse me, I've got to clarify one thing: I didn't have a Belgian waffle that morning. I had the Belgian waffle there a few years later. But that morning when I got there, Johnny Roselli went there to meet somebody by the name of Jack Ruby. I had never known Jack Ruby, nothing about him. When I got there and pulled in the parking lot, Johnny Roselli told me: Let me go in first, see where I'm going to sit, come in and position yourself. And he asked me: Are you carrying? And I said: Yeah, I'm carrying. He said: Good! When I sit down, where I am sitting at, I don't know what may transpire. He said: Something could go wrong. Be very alert! Keep my backside covered! I won't be in your line of fire. And I said: Okay, I pick an open field of fire. Where ever I figure I can handle it. I said: Go sit down and I'll come in position myself. Johnny Roselli went in and they had like, you can call it a booth, a table, there wasn't anything before it or nothing, but he sat down in that. And I went (inaudible) right behind him. I positioned myself at the counter, ordered a cup of coffee, I was served and sat there. And then I sit there and I watch and saw a short stocky built man come in, walked over, Johnny got up, they shook hands, they sit down, they talked for a couple of minutes. I see him take like a half-size, like a legal envelope, but only half that size, out of his jacket and he laid it and pushed it across the table to Johnny Roselli. He got up, they shook hands, this man left, Johnny waited maybe two minutes. Johnny looked at me, I got up, I walked out the restaurant, made sure the area was clear, nobody outside in the parking lot, I went over and got in the car, started up and pulled up by the door, Johnny Roselli walked out, got in the car and we drove away.

J – Did you ask him or did you find out in some way what was in the envelope?

JF- On the way back to Dallas, Johnny and me was driving down the road, he didn't open the envelope right away. We got almost up to, I think it's Arlington, it's about halfway there. I'm saying halfway, could be less one way or the other, it 's been a long time for me. But we were right about Arlington and Johnny opened the envelope, takes the stuff out and is looking at it. While he is looking at it, he noticed I am watching over while I am driving, and he 's got them little black wallets, like half-size, like identification wallets. And he opened them up and there is identification plates in them and there's badges on them. At that point I didn't know what the identification on it was. Because he is sitting there and looking at it, and I'm not going to lean over and I'm not going to say: Give me one of those!, or anything like that. I wait, when he wants me to know, he will tell me. And then he opened up a piece of paper and he unfolded it. And there has been a lot of discrepancy over this part now. But Johnny Roselli said: They only made one change in the route.

W – That was the motorcade?

JF – It was a map of Dealey Plaza, the motorcade route. When he looked at it, for Dealey Plaza, he said they have only made one alter, one change in it. He said: That's all. And I said: What's that? And he said: They are going to go down Elm Street. They're going to stop and make a detour, coming around this little street here. And he held it up and I kinda glanced over but I didn't get a chance to look at it real good at that point. But I had already reconned the area so I knew what he was talking about. And I know that everybody says: They had the motorcade in the newspaper, weeks and months ahead of time. Sure they did. But they didn't have that one change. And if anybody wants to show somebody a newspaper clip, anybody check real close, because the original route they were not coming down Elm Street there. On that little detour, where they had the slowdown.

(Wim: The little detour that James Files talks about is a zig-zag turn over Houston Street and then onto Elm Street. Such a sharp turn where the presidential limousine has to slow down considerably, is in violation with Secret Service regulations. This detour was in fact published in newspapers on Tuesday 19 November, but it is possible that the original plan for the motorcade route was to go straight over Main Street. The change over Elm Street appears to have been made prior to that tuesday.)

J – Had you heard prior to that, when they got to Dealey Plaza, that they would just continue straight on Main Street? Was that the idea?

JF – The original plan was that we would be shooting at a fast moving target. And Nicoletti had no military experience and I already had advised him that he would have to shoot high and the target would be running away from him. That he would have to shoot above the head. And we were going for a headshot, I told him "it's going to be hard for you to hit him from there". We're getting a little bit ahead though. Before we got into this part ..

J – Yeah, let's go back ..

JF – Because Chuck hadn't got to Dallas that week. He only came in, I hadn't seen him that morning. I had not seen Chuck in person until I went with Johnny Roselli to Fort Worth and come back. Johnny Roselli got out of the car and went upstairs, Charles Nicoletti came down. Mr. Nicoletti got into the car with me and we drove to Dealey Plaza.

J – Okay, backup for just a second: How did Roselli get to Dallas?

JF – At that point Roselli, he mentioned to me… Johnny Roselli… we were on the way to Fort Worth and I asked him: When did you get in? He said: I got in this morning. I got in early this morning. I haven't been here but for a couple of hours. And I said: How did you get in? And he said he got lucky. He caught a ride on a plane that is sponsored by the Central Intelligence Agency, the CIA. I said: How the hell did you manage that one? He said: I got lucky. He had somebody there. I didn't ask no more. He didn't elaborate any more than that, I didn't dig any deeper than that.

(Wim: We now know that a CIA contract pilot Tosh Plumlee has verified that Johnny Roselli was on board of his flight from Florida to Dallas. Tosh Plumlee has further testified that the mission of his flight was to abort a possible assassination attempt on the president in Dealey Plaza. Apparently some people of the CIA had intercepted information to that effect and it seems that there was a faction in the CIA who wanted to prevent the assassination.)

J – He didn't mention an abort team at that time?

JF – Not at that point. So we got all that. Now then, when we got back I still don't know that he was there on an abort mission. I have no knowledge of that at this point of the game. Johnny Roselli got out of the car, went back into the hotel. I waited maybe 5 or 7 minutes for Charles Nicoletti to come down. When he got down, Mr. Nicoletti got into the car with me and said: Let's go! We took off and I say : Whereto? He says: Take me over by the Plaza. We went over, we parked, it's drizzling rain, we get out and we're walking around. This is the first time that Charles Nicoletti has even mentioned to me about an abort team. And he asked me …

J – When was that?

JF – Well, when we were walking around, Charles Nicoletti asked me: How do you feel about being backup? I say: What do you mean backup? He says: How would you feel about being backup as a shooter for me? I said: What happened to Johnny? What's with Johnny? And he said: Johnny is a little bit paranoid on this. He says the CIA called the hit off. He said: They don't want the hit to go down. And I said: What do you say? Chuck's exact words were: Fuck 'm. It's going anyway! And I told him: What about Johnny? Well, he says, Johnny will be with me, but he is not gonna be a shooter. He doesn't want to go against the orders. He's been told… he flew in here specifically to abort this assassination.

W- Could you say he got cold feet?

JF – No….when we were talking when I asked him about Johnny Roselli and I said: How come Johnny is not going to be a shooter? , he said: Well, he doesn't want to go against the orders of the CIA. What he wants, he wants to call it off. He flew in here as an abort team. They flew a plane in here especially with him on it, to tell us to call it off. And so I asked him at that point, I said: what do you say? He said: Fuck 'm! It's a go! We're gonna do it. He says: Jimmy, you know we can't call this off. Only one man can stop it. He said: He's here and if he wants us to stop it, he'll notify me. I'm not going on somebody else's word. He says: As far as it is right now, I have a go from the boss. We're going!

J – Now who was the one man who could have stopped it?

JF – There was only one man. Charles Nicoletti did not say his name at that point. He just said "the boss" , I knew who he was referring to, he was referring to Sam Giancana.

W – Who was he?

JF – Sam Giancana, he was the number 2 man at that time. A lot of people is gonna tell you it was number 1. But it's not true. Tony Accardo was still running things. He turned things over, he had Sam Giancana running all his operations and everything, but Tony Accardo was still the man and he was still calling the shots on whatever went down, whatever was done.

J – The only thing Giancana said, had to have at least the okay of Accardo?

JF – It had to be sanctioned and it had to come through Tony Accardo.

W – We're talking about the Chicago crime family !?

JF – We're talking about only the Chicago area alone.

(Wim: Sam Giancana has widely been acknowledged by historians as the absolute leader of the Chicago crime family. However, the FBI and insiders know that Giancana had been put forward by crime boss Tony Accardo as his front man, running the daily operations. Accardo was still pulling the strings behind the scenes.)

J – I have a question right there. To your knowledge was there involvement of any other crime families? Marcello, Trafficante …?

JF – I knew of no other crime family being involved, I heard rumours, but do I know if anybody else was involved? No, I do not know if anybody else was involved. That would have been out of character for them to even notify me about that, or anybody else. That only stays up in the higher ranks of the family, or the people or the crime family, however you wish to describe it. And when things were handed out, like different departments, like different people get different things. Somebody might be into bookmaking, somebody handles the bookmaking, they passed that out to one party. This party, he distributed it amongst the people in the area, but everybody had a little what we call territory at that time. And somebody else might be in the loansharking. And you might have somebody running (inaudible). You might have somebody that was running chop shops, which eventually I got into, which led to my federal prison sentence. But when it comes down to murder contracts, that was a whole new thing. Then we had somebody else that handled the liquor licenses. But everything was distributed amongst different people. And whatever moved, including the garbage at that time, even the garbage was controlled by the Outfit. And one party, and this can all be confirmed, I believe he is still alive, he is very old now, but his name was Zucchero, he had the garbage pick-up at that time there. And he was strictly informed that if he picked up another can of garbage, he would be in his next garbage truck going out to the dump. They took over his business and then he went into the junkyard business. And later on down the road, he became involved in a place out in Elk Grove Village, a very big place called Globe auto wreckers. His sons now run it.

J – So once Mr. Nicoletti said: We're going anyway!, what happened then? Start with about what time that was!

JF – This would be approximately 10:30. This here would be approximately 10:30 AM Johnny Roselli, excuse me, about 10:30 AM Mr. Nicoletti told me, he asked me to be the backup shooter. And that was the first inkling of anything that I would be involved in the assassination itself. Prior to that I was to only know the area and transport weapons.

J – Was the weather clearing by that time?

JF - It had started to clear at about 10:45 I believe, the best I can remember, I could be off a few minutes. I know it had been drizzling rain, it was cold, it was damp, the sun didn't come out until after 11 AM I believe. But like I say again I could be off a few minutes on it. It's a long time ago.

J – Okay, the weather is clearing, it's about 10:00 and let's see, what happened?

JF – I told Mr. Nicoletti: Yes, I would be honored to back you on it. Anything you ask, you know, I'll do! And so, most of this had already been pre-arranged, beyond my knowledge, this Plaza had been selected, I did not select it, someone else had already selected it, and he asked me where I thought would be the best place for him. And I told him the Daltex building. Because the Daltex building gave him a better shot with them taking a straight run-through at a high rate of speed. And evidently, I'm quite certain that they had all that pre-arranged on that part of it, because that place was his location, for him and Johnny, as far as that goes, because they already had made an arrangement to be admitted into the building.

W – Why do you think he checked that with you then? Why did he ask you?

JF – Oh, he didn't check it, he just asked my opinion. He had always questioned me about different things. He used me like a sounding-board. Like maybe, you know, you're in a business or in an office, you might ask one of the people around you: What do you think about this? You don't really care what he thinks, you're just asking for an opinion to see what he thinks. Maybe you overlooked something, or maybe somebody has a better idea than you do at this time of the game.

J – Could it also be that you had military training and experience, when Nicoletti had…..

JF – Oh, that's possible. He respected me for my knowledge of weapons, my knowledge of knowing terrain, because I had been in combat and the first thing when you walk into an area, to you it's a landscape, to me it's terrain. Because if I walk in and I walk into an ambush, I want to know where the low spots are, where the high spots are, where all the coverage is. I gotta know where I can get my rear end down so I don't get it shot off. You've got to have a place to go to the ground in a hurry. You can not afford to stand around and be looking around and wondering: Geez, where can I go from here? If you do, you're dead! You've got to think, that's why you take all the training in the military. You are trained not to think, but to react.

J – And Mr. Nicoletti had never been in the military or had he?

JF – Not to my knowledge, he never served a day in the army. Or any military service as far as that goes.

W - Where did you serve?

JF – I was in the army, 82nd Airborne. I took my basic at Fort Leonard Wood, Missouri, I took my AIT at Fort Polk, they screwed up my orders and I went to Fort Seals and laid there for week, maybe ten days, from there I went to Fort Bragg to go airborne. I went into the service in January of 1959.

J – Where were you assigned?

JF – When I left, we left I think it was July, the tenth, we went from there to Laos. We were on an operation called operation called White Star. A handful of military advisors were going over to train people in Laos there, to do certain operations, at that time we really weren't supposed to do any black bag stuff and things, we were just going in to train and equip people, and I found a lot of it pretty hilarious: We armed a lot of them and gave them weapons and they all took the stuff and they ran up north and we had to fight them later. But that's how we basically had down all the way through the years in history …

J – Did they call it counter insurgency at that time?

JF – Oh yeah, they called it counter insurgency. What I found the most amazing of all was this place called Vientiane (inaudible), just outside of Vietnam…. Not Vietnam, don't get it confused, this is Laos, up in the central part of a place called the Plane of Jars, there is a large, well, a pretty good sized town up there, called Vientiane. On the runways, most of them were dirt, they had steel matting down on it for planes to land on. The Russians used the same runways that we did. We drank in the same taverns that the Russians drank in. We shopped at the same stores. We knew the Russians, they knew us. But we didn't bother each other. They trained their people, we trained other people. It was just a close operation.

J – Was there more than one of these White Star teams?

JF – There were several White Star teams but they all worked in individual groups and one group would never know what the other group was doing for a specific reason: Each group was on its own to a certain extent, but they did not know what the next group was doing in case they were captured, tortured, killed or whatever, they could give nobody up.

J - Did you ever hear the name Colonel Fletcher Prouty?

JF – Yes I did. Colonel Fletcher Prouty, he was the man in charge. Excellent man, excellent warrior, soldier. Good leader.

W – You knew him?

JF – I knew Colonel Fletcher Prouty personally, yes.

W – This vacuum cleaner is making a lot of noise.

G – I hear him very well, but ..
JF – They've got a buffer running out there. We can ask them to move it. You want it moved?

G – How long do they keep doing that?

JF – Probably an hour. If we want we can ask them to move it. (James Files goes out and asks the cleaners to stop)

- cut in tape -

J – Nicoletti, he decides the Daltex building is the place to go …. and what made you choose the grassy knoll?

JF – Well, When Chuck … he asked me first where would I think his place was and we have been through this I believe ….. Wanna start over? … Okay, Ask me the question again.

W- (talking to Jim Marrs) What I didn't like is that you said the Daltex had been decided as the place to go, like it was last minute like that it was not pre-decided long ago…

J – Oh no, he just got through saying that they had decided that was the place to shoot from. We got that on tape.

JF – Mmm, okay, so we don't have to talk about the Daltex building? That's over with, right?

J – Yeah.

JF – Okay, you got that part. Mr. Nicoletti asked me: So if you back me up, Jimmy, what do you think would be the best spot for you? And I said: Well, the spot I like best is up on the grassy knoll behind that stockade fence. He says: Why there? I said: I've got the railroad yard for cover. I said: With my clothes I can turn my jacket inside out, it's plaid on the inside, it looks like railroad workers. Somebody out there wearing a flanel shirt, nobody is going to pay attention to me. I said: I can go over there, walk around a piece of (inaudible), walk up and down those boxcars, cross the railroad tracks, look at things, I 'll just be another worker, nobody will even look at me. And he said, Okay, what weapon are you going to use over there? And I told him …. and I said: Well, what's the situation? Chuck said: We're going for a head shot now. I said: This I understand, I realize this. He said: You are not going to fire unless it becomes a necessity. He says: If I miss, then it's gonna be up to you. He says: But you don't fire, unless I miss. It's gonna be your call at that point. So you got to be very alert on this. And I told him: Don't worry about me. I got it, boss! And he said: What are you gonna use? I said: I'm gonna use the Fireball. And he looked at me and he says: Why? Why the Fireball? Now, the Fireball, for people who don't know what a Fireball is, it's like a cutdown rifle. It's actually basically this long. It's a weapon that was well ahead of its time, this was one of the prototypes, the agency had gotten a hold of it, it had been manufactured by Remington. Now, a lot of people are gonna tell you that this particular weapon was not available at that time. But this weapon was available. It didn't go on sale until a few years later. But this weapon had been manufactured as early as in 1961. We had a lot of trouble with the barrel blowing up when we used too big a round on it or something, overloads in it. A lot of problems with it, but they finally reinforced the barrel, we got it where it worked pretty good. And Chuck asked me: "Why the Fireball? Because you've only got one shot!" Because the Remington Fireball 2.22 is a single shot bolt action pistol and you can mount a scope on it. "Well, if I'm gonna wait until you are through, I said, I'm gonna get one shot anyway, so it doesn't really matter! Because I'll never get a chance for a second shot. Because I will wait till the last possible moment." He said: Okay, it's your call!

J – Where did you get hold of a prototype weapon like the XP-100?

JF – It was given to me by David Phillips. I had received this maybe a year prior or 8 months. A year prior to the assassination. The gun had been used twice before on assassinations, but nobody like a president or nothing. It was good for using … if you want to get into a close place area or somewhere …. somebody might say why use a pistol? Well, anybody that knows their weapons, this particular piece is very accurate. Very accurate up to a 100 yards. At a 100 feet I'm talking about , we're shooting now from the grassy knoll down to the highway, to the street there, we're talking roughly 30, 35 yards. We're only talking a 100 feet, this is like shooting fish in a barrel. And especially with a 3 power scope on it. But the weapon had been used before, you could put it in a briefcase, you could walk anywhere with it, nobody would pay any attention to it. The case I had set up, I had a little loading press inside for it, in case I had to manufacture anything, I had a little holder for all the special rounds that were in it. Everything was packed, foam rubber inside, the case was watertight, waterproof.

(Wim: Indeed, the XP-100 Fireball was introduced to the market in 1963, but prototypes were available well before that. It is not difficult to understand that the CIA would be highly interested in such a compact, yet such an accurate weapon. Interestingly, the weapon was originally chambered for a .222 caliber cartridge, which is the caliber that James Files used. That caliber was later changed to a .221 cartridge.

http://www.reloadbench.com/cartridges/p221rf.html

Introduced in 1963, the .221 Fire Ball and its Experimental Pistol Number 100 were the brainchild of Remington's Wayne Leek. An abbreviated single shot version of Leek's Remington Model 600 Carbine, the pistol was introduced to the shooting world as the XP-100. During it development stages, the XP-100 was first chambered for the .222 Remington cartridge, but Leek eventually decided it burned a bit more powder then was necessary in a 10-3/4 inch barrel. Consequently, the .222 case was shortened to 1.40 inches and the new cartridge became known as the .221 Fire Ball. Muzzle velocity with a 50 grain bullet was advertised as 2650 fps.)

J – What did the case look like?

JF – The case was black. It was like an oversized briefcase basically speaking.

J – Leather on the outside?

JF – Leather on the outside. It had some little metal flaps on it, you know, for locking it up, you could lock the case. But I wasn't concerned about locking it. But the thing is you could take it, you could go anywhere, you looked like a businessman with it. And I felt that was the best weapon to go with. And so … Mr. Nicoletti agreed with me on it and said: Okay, it's your call, Jimmy. And that's what we agreed on. So then … like I say, the Daltex building, that had to have been previously arranged with them, because they already had made arrangements to get the people in there. So the Daltex could not have been a last minute decision, as far as that goes. Like me saying: Okay, yeah, I think the Daltex building. He just used me as sounding board.

J – When you say "had arranged to get you in the Daltex", I mean that was an office building anybody could walk in and out. You are talking about getting into a specific office?

JF – Getting into a specific office, into a specific area somebody

J – Make a statement

JF – Okay. The reason they needed somebody there to get 'm inside: Anybody can walk in and out. But the sole purpose of having a connection there, somebody that could get you into a place, into an office where you could open the door and you could have a window to shoot from. If you don't have an opening, it don't do you any good to get in that building. You've got to be able to get into somebody's office, offices not being used, nobody around, otherwise the doors are just being locked, you have no way in.

J – Do you happen to know which office that was?

JF – No, I do not know which office it was.

J – So what did you do?

JF – What did I do? We walked around the plaza for a little bit. I took him back over, I dropped Mr. Nicoletti back off at the Dallas Cabana. And he got with Johnny, they therefore went back over there, I told them where the car would be pulled up alongside the building there and parked. He told me that they would come out of the building and they would get in that car. Now, I did not drop Charles Nicoletti or Johnny Roselli off at the Dal-tex building. They got into the building, they were there on their own. I told them where the car would be, it's his car, he knows this car. He knows what my job is, they will be in the car. He will be in front seat, Johnny will be in the backseat, I'll get under the driver's wheel, I'll set my briefcase between the front and the backseat and we'll drive away.

J – Where did you drop them off?

JF – When we pulled out from the side of the building, I made a right-hand turn onto Houston, I believe that would be going north, I'm not sure on my directions, but I made a right on Houston and I went up Houston to a major intersection, about four or five blocks, maybe six blocks, whatever it was. Then I took a left-hand turn. I went down close to the freeway there. There is a gas station there. I wanna say Texaco but it could have been something else, it might even have been a Mobil, I'm not sure now. But they had a car there. This is where they had told me to stop, this is where he told me he would be getting out at. You know: "Go down here, we've got a car there waiting for us" And I go down there, they open the door and they get out. They start walking across the parking lot.

J – Now this is before …?

JF – This is after the assassination.

J – After? Okay, I thought it was before, You said you didn't let them off at the Daltex building …

JF – No, I took Charles Nicoletti back to the Dallas Cabana to meet with Johnny Roselli. Okay?

J – After you were walking around Dealey Plaza?

JF – After we walked around Dealey Plaza. There is still another hour to go probably before the assassination is gonna go down.

J – Go back and make that statement: After we walked around for about an hour….

JF – Okay. After we walked around Dealey Plaza I took Mr. Nicoletti back to the hotel, let him out of the vehicle, he went up and got with Johnny Roselli. I took the car back to where it was supposed to be, made arrangements … because he had asked me: What if you can't get a parking space? I said: Don't worry, I'll have a parking space. If I have to, I steal a car and move it out of there. I said: We'll be parked there, just look for the car. And at this point he told me: If we come out, I want the car close so I can get into it right away. Because he would be carrying a rifle underneath this topcoat, his jacket, his topcoat. And would come out of there and secure that in the trunk. He would put it in the trunk, he had a key to the trunk. He put that in the trunk, close the trunk, Johnny Roselli would get in the backseat, he would get in the passenger side, I would come walking up, I would get in at the driver's side. I entered my attaché, briefcase, whatever you wanna call it, gun case in between the front and the backseat. I'd get in, start the car, we drive away. I'd make a right on Houston, I'd go down several blocks there, I forget the intersection, make a left-hand turn, go down by the gas station, just before you can get by that freeway there, and that would be the Stemmons freeway at that area, and they got out of the car. They had a car waiting there. Which car it was, I don't know. I never watched them walk across the parking lot to it. As soon as they got out, the door closed, I drove away. I went back to Mesquite, Texas.

J – Okay, again now, that was after all the shooting …

JF – That was after all the shooting

G – Hold it right there, let us change tapes, we've got an hour ….

W – Did we cover Jim Braden?

J – No .

- cut to change tapes -

J – So with Nicoletti you had walked around, you had determined the shooting positions, you take him back to the Cabana and he went up and met with Roselli. Did you stay at the hotel or did you go back to the plaza?

JF – After I took Charles Nicoletti back to the hotel, I went back to the plaza, secured the car, got my briefcase out with the gun, with the Fireball in it. I went into the railroad yard. I secured that over there, put it away, so nobody would see it. I reversed my jacket inside out, I had taken my hat, grey fedora, ….. and my jacket was a grey poplin , we had these car jackets back then, they were like waistelength, not a short jacket, they kind of come down a little bit, no car jacket like … made out of a material that they no longer use, it was called poplin. You might even remember that material, the poplin material? Grey color, had a shine to it. That's what the jacket was like that I was wearing. A pair of grey pants with it. And I reversed the jacket, it had the all-set plaids in it, kind-a-like checkers on the inside. When I turned it over it looked like one of the old grey flanel shirts we used to wear out, you know, when you're doing work in the yard or something out there. And I walked around the railroad yard and was waiting for the time to pass. The time was coming on. And then I go to the crowd, I went over there by the fence, I got there a little bit, a few minutes early, I reached down and I had taken the scope off the weapon. And I look up, I look over the fence and I was looking for people (thru the scope). What I was looking for, was not to see who I knew, but I was looking for people that would be carrying a bulge, like a butt under the arm, I am looking for somebody with a weapon. This way I have an idea …

J – Security people?

JF – I'm looking for security people, cops, undercover, security, off-duty, whoever might be carrying a weapon. Bulge along their hip, behind their back, like under the arm in a shoulderholster. I'm looking for these little bulges, most people don't pay no attention to that, but this is what I'm looking for. But then I was amazed when I recognized several people out of the past that were in Dealey Plaza. Did I go talk to them? No, but I recognized them and see them there.

J – Who was that?

JF – I remember Aldo Vera, remember seeing him there. Aah, a lot of people say Jack Ruby was never there, but he was there before the motorcade got there, I know that for a fact, and even though I never knew Jack Ruby, but I was as close to him as I was to you in the coffeeshop but I never spoke to him, I was never introduced to him. Never said a word to Jack Ruby. But I was that close, I'm looking at the backside of him and I'm pretty sure that was him. Aah …. Diaz was there, I believe his name was Tony, Tony Diaz is what I knew him as, ….aah … Richard Cain, he was on scene, he was in the crowd, he had been there, he was leaving, he was like walking away, …aah … Felix Alderisio, I know he was there that day, where he went I have no idea. But there is several people that I saw.

J – How about Frank Sturgis?

JF – Frank Sturgis, he was there.

J – How did you know Frank Sturgis?

JF - I knew Frank Sturgis from the Bay of Pigs and from the SAO. I also knew Orlando Bosch. He was on scene. Orlando Bosch, I don't know if you are familiar with his name or not, but he was also present. Ah … there was a few other faces I recognized, I just don't remember the names for them, because it's so long ago.

J – How do you figure all those people were in Dealey Plaza?

JF – You know, I couldn't figure that one out when I was there myself, but it's like anything else, it's like everybody … they know something is going to happen. Maybe they know a building is going on fire or something. You know, you 've got a building burning and it may collapse, everybody runs to see the fire, they should be going the other way. About the only time I have ever seen a lot of confusion was where people where trying to get away, it was a racetrack or some crowded place and somebody yelled "gun", everybody broke and stampeded. We had a few people out of the racetrack that got hurt that way, they were out of Maywood Park, they got hurt in a stampede like that. But basically speaking, if somebody knows something is going to happen, they have a tendency to go see it. Most people are curious. You know when you ever drive down the highway and you see a wreck, you're probably guilty of it. You slow the car down and look out the window. Everybody does it. So a lot of people had come there for that reason, probably because they had heard these rumors and stuff that he was going to be assassinated in Dallas. That was no secret. Even the National Security Agency knew that.

J – What about Eugene Brading?

JF – Eugene Braden? He was there that day. He was the …. Eugene Braden was there for a specific reason: He had the contacts inside the Daltex building. And he was the one that Charles Nicoletti and Johnny Roselli needed to get them into the private office, some way or another, I have no idea where that office was, I was never in the Daltex building myself, I can't even describe anything in there.

J – So you probably stood behind that fence there for some little time?

JF – Oh, only for a few …., I stayed away from the fence, I stayed basically in the yard, walk over to the fence, look over, stand a minute, then walk back away again. But I was observing the area.

J – Were you a smoker at the time?

JF – Oh yes, I did smoke.

J – Were you smoking cigarettes that morning?

JF – I had smoked that day. Careless! I probably stepped on several cigarette butts and left them there. Most of them Pall Mall.

J – Was it muddy back there?

JF – It was very muddy. Let me put it this way: A couple of times I even took my shoes, put them above up the little country ledger and scraped the mud off the bottom of them. I hated getting mud on them.

W- What clothes was Frank Sturgis wearing?

JF – I don't remember exactly the clothes, I remember he had on, like a bomber jacket. Remember the World War II bomber jackets that pilots used to wear? He was wearing one like that. (Jim Marrs is pointing at his jacket) Like that, like the one you got right there. He had the brass buttons on it, I remember that. You see that flashing you know.

W – Which location in Dealey Plaza was he standing? Approximately?

JF – I was …. where you got the country steps down there by the pergola and between the pergola and the stockade fence, you 've got a set of country steps to go down. I was to the right of those …

J – Draw me a map!

JF – I've got to put my glasses on for that! (laughing) But I don't wanna sit here drawing, it's going to take too much time. But he was to the left and just standing off the sidewalk, he was standing in the grass itself.

W – And this was shortly before the assassination or ….

JF – This was just a few minutes before the motorcade got there. Like I say, before the motorcade ever arrived on scene and I took the scope off – I didn't hold the gun up over the fence, I didn't want nobody to panic at that point – but I had the little scope up in my hand and I look over the fence so I could check to see what there was, I was looking like I said for security people, you know, somebody carrying, somebody packing, because I wanted to know who has got weapons when I go to leave there.

J – That fence is kind of an L-shape. You know there's a short area and a long area ..

JF – Yeah, it's on and off, there is a long area and a short area, but it is not exactly an L, it's on a slant, like 45 degrees.

J – So where were you?

JF – I was an eight or ten feet down there, there was a tree branch that hung right over me, I was behind that, kind of gave me a little camouflage.

J – Okay, uh… did you ever see an ambulance come by?

JF – No, I never paid no attention. I wasn't watching the vehicles that passed by, I 'm looking at people. I never noticed the ambulance.

J – You didn't see an ambulance with red lights?

JF – No, I might have heard a siren, I don't remember, I had all that tuned down, I am in another complete mode: Sirens, lights flashing, ambulances, that doesn't bother me. I'm not there to look for those things, I am there looking for other details, for other things.

J – Okay. So then what happened? The motorcade came?

JF – Aah, I'm checking everything , most everybody, basically where a lot of different people are standing at. And I want to make sure that there, like I say, I don't have any cops standing right next to me. Because you know, something happens and I have to shoot, you know, I don't want to have to shoot anybody else unless it becomes a necessity. So I had walked away from the fence and I come back over, secured everything, got it ready, I could hear the rumble, the people murmuring, so you know the motorcade is approaching. So I got ready and opened it up. I'm holding the Remington Fireball down below the fence at this point. The motorcade comes down I believe that's Main street there, come down at Houston, turn back around onto Elm and come down that little sidedrive there. And when it came down and made its first right, that's when I brought the weapon up. And then I'm over the fence and as they come down , made the turn onto Elm there, that's when I started focusing through the scope and following the car. As shots started ringing out, I started counting the shots, but I'm not counting like 1, 2, 3, and 4, I am counting them as: miss, miss, miss, because I know we are going for the headshot. So I don't care how many rounds are being fired as long as we get a headshot. So as I'm hearing the shots being fired, I'm counting them as a miss, as a miss, miss. And that's the only thing I am concerned about. I've got the sign there, for the Stemmons freeway, that is fixing to come into my field of fire. As far as I could see at this point, the president has not been hit in the head at this time. I've seen the body lurch, I know he has been hit, how serious I don't know. But my last instructions were: We're going for a headshot. If you have to take a shot, take it, but don't fire unless it's a necessity, unless you really have to. He said: Jimmy, don't fire unless you have to, we want everything from the backside. I am not asking why. Okay, whatever you say. At this point, as he starts to approach and come behind that freeway sign … and I've already been instructed not his anybody but Kennedy, because they didn't want Jackie to get hurt or anybody else, I'm fixing to lose my field of fire. And at this point …. either I shoot or I put it in the suitcase and leave. One or the other. I took the shot. I fired one shot, one shot only.

J – where were you aiming.?

JF – Oh, I was aiming for his right eye, which to me is the left side of his head looking head on. But for him it would be his right eye, and when I pulled the trigger, and I'm right in on it, and it's almost like looking 6 feet away through the scope. As I squeezed, take off my round, his head moved forward, I missed and I come in right along the temple. Just right behind the eye.

J – Here or in the hairline?

JF – Well, I'm not sure, you know I can't see the penetration, I know I hit him right here (pointing at temple). I know I hit behind the eye. Somewhere within a half inch diameter right there (pointing again).

W – So there were actually two shots almost simultaneously?

J – You think he got hit as you squeezed?

JF – What I believe is this : ….. And I got my readings as a marksman, I'm a good shooter, always was, I'm not bragging on my stuff, don't get me wrong, but that's what got me my start with David Phillips. Because of something that I did in the service, and I made a mark there and it's on record and it's recorded, for headshots, for what I did, and the things that I did. But anyway, to make a long story short, as I am preparing to squeeze off my round, Kennedy's head moved forward, just as I squeezed. It was already in process, the head started forward. To me … what I believe is, … and I did not see, let me clear the fact now, I never saw Mr. Nicoletti shoot Kennedy, but I know he was the man in the Daltex building, the man supposed to be doing the shooting. Therefore the head started forward and as far as I am concerned Mr Nicoletti hit him at that point. As I squeezed off my round, the head started forward, I hit it and blew the head backwards.

J – So the exit went where in the rear?

JF – I didn't hit the rear, but the exit blew out and you could see Jackie …

J – Yeah, but where was the exit? On the right side or on the left side?

JF – Aah, partially, most of it on the right side I guess, back there where this section came right out. Part of the back of the skull, you know, I didn't go look at it, I didn't examine it, and a lot of people may find this hard to believe, but I have never read anything on the Kennedy assassination, because I was never interested in it. I did not like John F. Kennedy …

W – Did you ever see autopsy pictures?

JF – They sent me a book and I looked at a few of them, but I didn't read the book. I wanna say the book they sent me was probably called High Treason. I never read it, I looked at a few other pictures, I just wasn't interested.

W – Can I show you a picture and ask you for your comments?

JF – You are gonna make me put my glasses on (smiling)

W – (handing over a picture) That's one! What do you think of that picture? That's the back of Kennedy's head.

JF – (Looking at picture) From what I'm looking at here, look like part of the flap on the side is missing. But I don't see very much on this picture here of the back of the head missing. What I'm looking at here is a lot of hair.

W – So what's your conclusion?

JF – What is my conclusion? That ain't the right picture!

W- Okay! (everyone smiles)

JF –That is my conclusion! You want my opinion on it, that's not the right picture!

J – Hold on! Take your glasses off !

JF – Okay.

W- It's a fake picture!

J – Yeah, go on and say "that's a fake picture" and then keep going …

JF – Okay. The photo that I just looked at is, in my opinion that's a fake picture, that is not the real picture. Because I had seen …. a lot of people might say you can't see nothing through a scope, but I'm gonna tell you something: When you see something burst, let's say like a watermelon, you 're gonna see pieces and stuff flying in different directions and people are gonna be splattered by it. And at this point …….. (loss of sound)

At this point, I got to figure what she was picking up was a piece of the skull … a lot of people will say you can't see nothing through a scope like this, but what you're going to see is like, and I saw it, the head explode. I saw the back side come out and I have seen blood, brains, whatever you're gonna call it, tissue, hair, the whole thing, going everywhere, just a spray. And if anybody disbelieves this, go and shoot somebody and look through a scope while you're doing it and watch.

J – Did you see anybody splattered with blood and matter?

JF – Oh, I don't know who was splattered I think one of the agents, probably one of the Secret Service agents riding on the back of the car. I am only assuming, I will say they probably got splattered because there was stuff everywhere. But one other thing I want to point out about the Remington .222 Fireball. It's a high velocity pistol, the round travels approximately 3180 feet per second. Now then, for this type of weapon there is very little recoil. Now a lot of people say there is a lot of recoil, it's gonna jump and you can see nothing. And I have had a lot of criticism over the years over this here. So I'd like for somebody to go out to a firing range somewhere, a gunstore and take one of these particular types of weapons that carry a .222 round. You're gonna find very little recoil. Especially when you are using an extended barrel weapon with a scope on it. You have the weight to hold it down, it's not jumping and bouncing, you're not shooting a 44 or 45.

W- We have verified all that.

JF – Okay, but ah …

J – Okay! So did the motorcade ever come to a stop?

JF – The motorcade to the best of my recollection to me and in my mind and everything had slowed down at this point, when the first shot went off, it's like it stopped, it's just like it slowed down almost to a crawl or barely moving, maybe it even stopped, I'm not really sure on that point. I know I was waiting, It kept moving, it had to be moving but very slow. Because I was waiting for it to get up behind the sign, I am waiting for something to happen so I don't have to shoot. Not that I'm afraid to, but if I don't have to, I don't want to. But like I say, when the car got even almost up to that Stemmons freeway sign there, and that was one of them old ones, not like these new ones they got today with a nice little skinny metal post and a little sign, these had these wooden legs on or what are you gonna call it. The posts that held it were wood. Anyway, I had my shot. It's either I shoot now or don't. I took my shot.

J – Did you ever notice if any of those rounds hit that sign?

JF - No. I don't know if anybody else's did or not, but as far as I know their rounds never hit it. I know my round didn't hit it. Like I say, I fired one shot, I was on target, I'm watching one thing, though that scope I'm watching one thing, I'm watching president John F. Kennedy.

J- So if a bullet hit that sign you probably didn't even see it anyway.

JF – No. I didn't even know Connally was hit at that point in the game.

W – Were you nervous in any way?

JF – Was I nervous? No. If I had been nervous, I would have been shaking, I couldn't have taken the shot. A lot of people may find this hard to believe, but you have got to understand something: The first time you go into the field of fire, when you go into a firefight in combat, you might be nervous or skimmish. But after you have been initiated into the field of fire or whatever you gonna call it, combat, firefight, a lot of people got different names for it, skirmishes, you get used to it, you get over it. You know, and to me .. a lot of people are going to think I am probably sick, but when you get into a firefight, that was the ultimate high. I 've never used drugs in my life. A firefight to me, being in the service, that was one of the greatest things there was. It was the ultimate high. And at this point, when you're stalking down somebody, and this particular thing … it stopped me from hunting animals all together. When I was young I used to love to go shoot deer, rabbit, squirrels, whatever I could get, pheasants. But after you went into the jungles and you have hunted men and you stalked a man down and you have hunted a man down on equal terms where he can kill you, you loose interest to go shoot a defenseless animal. I have come to where I loved animals much more than that. I couldn't kill animals. When my dog had to be put to sleep, my wife and one of my top right-hand men had to take the dog to the vet because I didn't have the heart to do it.

J – Were there any, while you were behind the fence, mostly before the shooting started, was there anyone in your vicinity?

JF – Aah, there was nobody behind that stockade fence but me at that point. Nobody. All the time I was there, I was alone. But in front of the fence the two people that I was mostly concerned about, they were a couple of guys wearing suits, roughly on top of the grassy knoll there, and they were a little away in front of me, 15 maybe 20 feet away, whatever, you know, I did not know who they were …

W – In front of the fence would be at the side of the railroad yard?

JF – No. The stockade fence. They are between the fence and the sidewalk. Between me and the motorcade. They are on top of the knoll there. They are kindalike looking over everybody and watching people. And this had me a little bit concerned, because I don't know who they are. At this stage of the game, well, I wanna take my shot, I've got the 45 ready if I've got to, like I say, I don't wanna shoot nobody unless I have to. At this point, and I 've checked them, shoulderholsters, the backsides, I saw no bulges. So as far as I knew they wasn't packing. So I figured maybe they were just a couple of businessmen. People that wanted to see the president go by. A lot of people are strange, everybody wants to see celebrities go by. But I took the shot and as I was walking away, and like I say I had seen Jackie crawl out there, a motorcycle cop, he threw his bike down, he jumped off and as he came running in a little zigzag or what you want to call it, like he's really into combat or something, it's still a wide open target, anybody can shoot him, he has got his pistol out. And uh … he's running up the knoll there, the two men at the fence, the guys in the suits, they go over and they open up identifications, so I have to figure: These were probably my cover that I've never been informed about, but I was told not to worry. They stopped him and he never came no farther. He went back down off the knoll.

Wim: The two businessmen that Files mentions were between him and the motorcade and he was somewhat concerned about them. The photographical evidence that is available at the time of the assassination, does not show men in business suits on the grassy knoll. But it is of course possible likely that these men were there before the assassination took place and that they sought a better place to stay out of sight at the time of the shots. As the motorcade was arriving, James Files was not paying attention to what happened around him as he was keeping Kennedy in the scope of his rifle. Several witnesses have testified they were turned back by men in suits on the grassy knoll, showing Secret Service credentials. Official Secret Service records show that no agents were assigned on Dealey Plaza or the grassy knoll.

W – You were told not to worry?

JF – I was told, Charles Nicoletti told me "when you take the shot, just walk away, don't run" He said "Just walk away naturally, Jimmy, don't draw attention!" I told him "Don't worry!" And I had no intention to break out of there running, but like I say, if somebody comes at me I'm willing to do whatever I have to do to leave the area. If I have to shoot somebody else, that's what I'll do at this point of the game.

J – Okay, so you are 10-15 feet or so down from the corner towards the railroad yard …

JF – Eight or ten feet, some like that, yeah, from the end where …

J – Were you halfway in between … at the halfway mark of the fence?

JF – No, I wasn't in the middle of the fence. You've got the left angle, you've got the 45 degree angle for the short part of the fence. Then I'm down maybe 10 feet from there. There's a treebranch, one branch comes right down the tree there, covered it real good. Halfway is a little more down to my right. That would have been halfway down.

J – Okay. Did you ever notice a GI? A guy in a cap and uniform?

JF – No, I did not.

J – Okay. Did you notice people on the railroad bridge?

JF – I knew there were people up there, but I didn't pay any attention to them.

J – They didn't have a good view of you, because you were under that tree under cover?

JF – I am pretty well under cover. The only time that people could have seen me from the viaduct or from the railroad yard, was when I walking down the tracks next to some of the boxcars.

W – So you recall that nobody was with you behind the fence?

JF – I said before, there was nobody behind the stockade fence with me. I am the only person back there. Anybody else back there is over at the railroad yard by the trains.

J – How about down by the corner there. Did you have a clear view? There's a lot of cars back there, right? Did you have a clear view? Could somebody have been down by that corner that you might not have seen?

JF – They could have been down there. A couple of cars drove through while I was there. But who they were and what kind, I don't even remember because I just wrote it off. As long as nobody got out and nobody come by me, they were of no concern.

W- But shortly before there was no one …

JF – Right before the assassination, there was nobody standing next to me.

W – How about three minutes before the assassination?

JF – Not by me. I was alone back there. I had no other party standing by me. Somebody was there in the yard or down at the other end, you know, 30 or 40 feet away, that has no bearing to me because I paid them no attention.

W – Well, there is this eyewitness report of the guy in the railroad tower, Lee Bowers.

JF – Well, he might have been in the tower, but I'm talking about people on the ground walking up by me or passing me.

W - No, but he's describing two persons behind the fence. One of them fits the description of you.

JF – Mmm, well, maybe he has figured two people when he see me change my jacket and walk away somebody different, I don't know. But I was alone and there was nobody with me.

J – All right, so as you walk away and these two guys cover for you, describe your actions then.

JF – Oh, as I'm walking away, I 've got my briefcase, guncase, in my right hand, I've got my left hand over by my coat pocket, I've got a 45 there, I've got it fully loaded with 6 rounds in it, it's ready to go if I need it …

J – You have already reversed your jacket?

JF – I've already reversed my jacket. When I picked up the guncase, I reversed my jacket, no plaid side, I 've got the poplin grey material on the outside, I took the fedora hat under the sleeve of it, snapped it out and put it back on my head and I walked away, carrying the briefcase and my 45 inside my coat pocket.

W – How long did it take to do all this?

JF – Just a few seconds. It don't take long.

J – Put your glasses back on. Is there any chance that is you off the wall back there?

W – I have a blowup here! This would be probably 50 seconds after …

JF – (looking at pictures) Looking at that, I couldn't say it's me, but I'm saying you can see somebody there, basically speaking. It could have been.

J – Is that the direction you took? Did you walk back towards the depository?

JF – Yeah, right! I went in that direction.

J – And there was nobody around you even at that point?

JF – At that point there's nobody around me. I'm not letting anybody get close to me at that point. Because like I say, somebody might try to grab me, they might want to pull a gun on me, I'm looking at people , aah.. somebody turns around, if they make the wrong move, if I see somebody pulling a weapon, they are going to be shot. If I see somebody aah …

J – This is … there's a little retaining wall, and right on the other side there is a sidewalk and on there is a little I don't know, like a garden patch, a little flower garden in that road, that little road that runs in front of the depository …

JF – Right! That's the one that comes into the dead end down here? Yeah, that's the one.

J – And that's right were you were walking?

JF – That's right where I was walking!

J – Were you on the south side or the north side of the street?

JF – I don't remember. All I remember is I'm walking and I'm watching over my shoulder. I'm trying to see if anybody is coming at me.

W - You've got the Moorman picture there? Or do you want to get that later?

J – No. Let's look at this right here (putting Moorman picture before James Files). Is that the tree you were talking about?

JF - Yep, you can see the branches from back over here coming right down over the wall.

W – And that's the vicinity where you were standing?

JF – Right there!

W – In this picture there is a uuh .. an object visible if you blow it up. Right here next to that tree. And if you blow it up it looks … it may look like a hat, or a fedora.

J – Do you remember which side of the tree you were on? Was it to your left or your right?

JF – (Thinking) I could be mistaken, I believe … no, the tree was to my right. It had to be to my right. The tree was to my right because I didn't want to have the tree in the way to my left. ….. And you can't see the sign here, but the sign is right on down here.

W – Yes, the sign is here … This is the blowup. This is sky and this is sky and this is the shape. Yeah …. Do you see a hat in there?

JF – Do I see what?

W – A hat.
JF – Not to me! You're asking the wrong man. I've got a hard time seeing with these glasses, believe me.

W – Okay, but this spot is right next to the tree

J – Did you ever notice those people?

JF – Aah, there was people out there ….. (looking at another picture) I remember more people than that being around. I don't know where they all disappeared to. But aah… I remember people falling down, laying down, jumping down, whatever you wanna call it. People moving to get out of the way, going in other directions, some standing around pointing, and who they were, what they were wearing, I couldn't even start to tell you.

J – What about these two guys right here (pointing at umbrella man and his accomplice)? Did you notice them? Or did any of those look familiar or did any of those look like some of the guys that you saw, that you recognized?

JF – Aah … They could have been. It's hard to tell from this here. But like I say, when the motorcade comes, I wasn't looking at nobody else. I don't know where everybody went, I didn't really care.

J – By the time the motorcade got there, the sun was out, pretty bright. It was warm right?

JF – Yep. Yep, it was nice out. It broke to be a nice day.

J – It was nice. Did you see anybody with an umbrella?

JF – Aah … I remember somebody down past me to the right towards the viaduct, they had an umbrella, but what they were doing I don't know. I've heard the theories of the umbrella man shooting somebody with an umbrella but ah …

W – You don't believe that?

JF – I don't believe that, not for one minute.

W – Why not?

JF – Why not? It would be kind of silly for somebody to take one an umbrella when you can't even aim it. All you can do is point it. And you're still gonna be shooting at a moving target, and it had to be a very small caliber, because they didn't come in big calibers and they were used basically for in-house operations when you are right on the target when you use it.

W – Ah … so it was a weapon that you knew of .. at that time?

JF – Oh yeah. The agency, they had those, yeah. Not only did they use them …

J – In 1963 it was the CIA, right? In 1963 the CIA had an umbrella weapon and then tell us what you just said.

JF – In 1963 the Agency, which I'm referring to as the CIA, they had weapons, basically based on an umbrella, like you can use it, walking canes, some of them carried a small caliber round. You couldn't put a big caliber in there. To me the weapon was strictly an in-house weapon where you had to be right on top of the target. There is no way you can stand out on a sidewalk and take an umbrella and point it at a moving target without aiming. I mean this is a lot of fantasy here. I thought the umbrellas, and they come out with them and they had the little darts in them, they had the poison on the end of them where you could jab a guy going downstairs or in a house or in a room, any place where there is a lot of people moving, molling around together. You can walk up to somebody and you can shoot a fairly small 22 caliber round in him. But as far as somebody using an umbrella on a sidewalk and firing a round, no, that's a lot of fantasy.

J – (Showing picture of umbrella man and accomplice) That guy is packing, isn't he?

JF – Yeah, he's packing! (smiles). Well, I gotta tell you: I don't know if it is or not for sure, but the one on the other side at the left of that pole that I'm looking at. On my right, this one right here, that sure favours Frank Sturgis.

W- It favours Frank Sturgis?

JF – Yeah, right here. Look at the hairline. It's a blurry picture, but look at that hairline.

W – The hairline? Well, it's too blurry too tell,

JF –Yeah.

J – Okay. Uuh ….All right, so you walk away … Oh, by the way, where did you park the Chevrolet? You parked the Chevrolet on Houston Street?

JF – I'm not sure if it's Houston. Right next to the Daltex building. No, Houston, Houston Street is the one that's going up and down.

J – The School Book Depository is over here and the Daltex building is over here!

JF – Yeah, right!

J – Ah .. Did you park on that street?

JF – I parked on the street right next to it, yeah.

J – Was it head-in parking, or was it a parking lot, or was it straight

JF – Well, what you want to call it. A parking space, parking lot. Aah .. parking aisle, whatever you want to call it. Cars were parked there.

W – A row of cars?

JF – Rail of cars, row of cars. I backed it in there and parked it so he (Nicoletti) could have access to the trunk.

J – So the back end to your … the front end to the road ?

JF – Yeah, Well, front end pointing forward.

J – Yeah, forward towards the road. I'm getting ahead here, but when you left you turned right?

JF – When I came out of there, I made a right hand turn.

J – Onto Houston?

JF – Onto Houston, yeah, going north.

J – All right. So that's where you parked it?

JF – That's where I parked the car.

J – So as you walked past, did you just walk straight to the car?

JF - I went straight to the car. I didn't bother and paid no attention to nobody. I went right to the car. What was going on around me, I don't know, I can't tell you what passed me, I can't tell you who was looking at me and I can't tell you how many people were around. I had one thing on my mind. Anybody approaching me with the determination to stop me, to question me, detain me, whatever you wanna call it, or anything else, all I wanna do now is to reach my destination, which is the car, put the case in the backseat there, on the floor, like Chuck and me had already figured out, I want to get in the car, start it up and drive away.

J – Was the car empty when you got there?

JF – No sir. When I got to the car, Charles Nicoletti was in the front seat, Johnny Roselli was in the backseat. There's only two seats in the front (inaudible) the seatcenter.

J – As soon as you got in the car, you could start up …

JF – As soon as I got to the car I opened the door, set the case in the back behind the front seat, got right in the car, lit the ignition and gone.

J – Did anybody say anything at that point?

JF – Nobody said nothing to me. At that point we pull out and as we went down the street heading for the intersection, the only thing that was said to me was … Mr. Nicoletti asked me "Jimmy, don't you think you overreacted?" I said "What do you mean?" He said: "Don't you think you fired too fast?" And I told him I was fixing to lose my field of fire, either I shoot then or I put it in my guncase and I leave! I said I had one choice. I said at this point, you told me we were going for a headshot, there had been no headshot. I said I was just following my orders. "I didn't want to explain to you why I didn't shoot!"

J – Did he say anything to that?

JF – That was the end of it. He told me at the intersection to make a left and pull over at the gas station. We get down there, he said "We're getting out, we are getting into another car there." And I said OK, I pulled out and parked, they get out of the car. He said: "I'll see you in Chicago!" And that was the only thing that was said.

J – Did you take that as criticism?

JF – I took it as criticism. Naturally!

J – Did he criticize you very often?

JF- No. The only thing he asked me if I thought I overreacted.

J – You told him no and he accepted?

JF – He accepted it.

W – The shell casing …

J – Oh yeah … Go back there to the point after you fired the round and tell us about ejecting the shell. Start with ' After the headshot'.

JF – Okay. The motorcade is coming down, I've got my target in the scope, my primary target is lined up and I am waiting. And like I said, we're going for a headshot. I don't want to fire unless I have to. At this point I am fixing to lose my field of fire. I took my shot. When I took my shot and I knelt back down at the briefcase, I injected the point casing in there, I picked up another live round, put it in and closed the bolt on it. I took this shell casing as it had come out into the briefcase, I put it in my mouth, tasted the sulphur from it (I loved the taste of sulphur by the way) closed the briefcase up and as I stood up, I did something that I shouldn't have done, but I did do it. I took the shell casing and I bit down on it. I took it out and I looked at it and I set it on the stockade fence. And there was an indentation from my teeth on the shell casing, on the ridge by the orphase? and I let it sitting on the stockade fence there. And I walked away.

W - Why did you do that?

JF- Well, you gotta understand: when you're young and you're cocky, everything is indestructable to you, you know. Nothing can go wrong. And you gotta be a strong believer in all that, I mean, you know, you're infallible. And I did that because …. We did a few other jobs and we did some … I might put a quarter on the forehead and we put him in the ground, you know, we might bury him somewhere ….lay a quarter on the head. Two bit gambler. Aah… I might put a nickel and a dime in each eyesocket, a nickel in one eye, a dime in the other one. You know … a nickel and dime thief.

J – You would leave that as a kind of your calling card?

JF- Aah, more or less, you might say that. Chuck .., Mr. Nicoletti had laughed at me when I do things like that. (Smiling) I said: "Hey .. We gotta let 'm know what they got hit for!" To me it was a symbol. You can say calling card, trait, whatever you wanna do. He used to laugh at me over it and he told me: Jimmy, just do the job, you do it and forget about it!

W- Would Mr. Nicoletti have been okay with you doing this in Dealey Plaza?

JF- (Smiling) Oh, if he would have known I did that in Dealey Plaza, right now he is probably turning over in his grave for me doing something that stupid. But uh .. Mr Nicoletti criticized me one other time … As a matter of fact, one other time, I won't get into the details, but we had somebody in the trunk and I stopped an bought a canary, cause this guy was a real snitch. And I come out of the dime store, the canary I broke its neck, because I wanted to leave the canary in the guy's mouth. And he gave me firm instructions: Don't you ever do anything like that again when we've got something in the trunk! (Laughing). You know, it's highly uncalled for in reality.

J – Jimmy. I'm pretty sure that you are aware they found two .222 shell casings

JF – I've heard that!

J – Have you got any speculation, any idea for a second .222 shell casing?

JF – I have no idea whatsoever! I fired one shot, one shot only. I ejected the shell casing. Mine was a Remington cartridge, manufactured prior to 1963, I bit it, I set it on the stockade fence. I had no empty shell casings for a 222 with me at all.

W - The shell casing by the way, was found not in the exact spot where you left it, but a little bit further at the other side of the fence.

JF – Well, I look at it this way: Whoever was searching, somebody looking, anybody could have looked at it, they could have thrown it over there, somebody could have stepped on it. Maybe somebody didn't want it found! Who knows? They didn't want to carry anything away from there in case they got stopped. Maybe they just stepped on it and buried it in the ground, I don't really know. I know where I put it! That's all I know!

J - The guns that you brought to Dallas, was the Fireball the only Fireball?

JF – No Sir, it wasn't!

J – You had another Fireball?

JF – No, I only had one Fireball! But I had a couple of rifles in the car. I had a shotgun in the car, I had a couple of other handguns. I brought down probably half a dozen of different weapons.

J – My impression though is: That was the only .222?

JF – That was the .222 round! Like I said, I has a total of six rounds, okay? I got six rounds for the Remington Fireball. I had no empty casings there. The other casings that I brought down with that, I had had six special loads, but the round that I fired were standard rounds and I had no empty casings with me. Those were disposed when I was out there in Mesquite. I didn't leave them where I test fired them, I picked them up and got rid of them later, make sure they couldn't be found, because I didn't want anybody to match anything up to the weapon. But with the Fireball there is no way they're going to match the ballistics, for the simple reason that the shell fragmentates, but you still got the firing pin that's going to strike the primer on the end of the shell casing. So … and a lot of times, if you got a weapon where you can match ballistics on, you want to melt the barrel down if you used it on some kind of job like that or whatever, in a local hit or something, also you want to take out the firing pin, because you don't want that to be discovered either to match up with the primer.

J - Because they can match?

JF – Yes they can.

W - Do you have any idea about the possibility of other hit-teams in Dealey Plaza that day?

JF - I've heard different stories about different teams there, different people shooting and this and that. To my knowledge, and to my knowledge only, I never knew of another hitteam that was in the area for Kennedy that day. If there was another team there, I have no knowledge of it whatsoever.

W – But it could be?

JF – Anything is possible. Anything is possible, there could have been another team, but what I am stating is this: As far as I know, from what I was involved in: Charles Nicoletti, Johnny Roselli was with him, cause Johnny Roselli was like his look-out, whatever, pick up any shell casings that eject from the rifle, we don't wanna leave shell casings on the floor, Mr. Nicoletti didn't want run around behind here "where's the casing, where's the casing?" You've got somebody picking them up as they come out. And like I say, I never saw Charles Nicoletti pull the trigger. But he was the shooter from what I understand with him.

W – You saw Richard Cain there. Could he have been a shooter?

JF – Richard Cain. He was on location and so was a guy by the name of Milwaukee Phil. His name is Philip Alderisio. But if they was another hitteam, cause they faded from the scene, I don't honestly know. I can't say yes, I can't say no.

J – You think Lee Harvey Oswald fired any shots that day?

JF – Lee Harvey Oswald never fired a shot. And if anybody knows what a paraffin test is, and we have actual court documents on where Lee Harvey Oswald was given a paraffin test by the Dallas Police Department, and on this document it plainly states: Deceased: J.D. Tippit. Deceased John F. Kennedy. Suspect: Lee Harvey Oswald. And they took a paraffin test. His face, his hand , his arm, I guess the side of his neck, …. the only trace of any nitrates, from powder burns or powder submissions, was in the palm of his hand. And anybody that goes to a firing range or fire a weapon, knows that if you fire a 38 revolver or any type of revolver, the blow-back is coming by this part of your hand (pointing at top of hand) and your wrist. The only reason he had those nitrates in the palm of his hand is because he was holding spent shell casings when I calibrated the scope. There were still traces of that. But Lee Harvey Oswald, like I said, that's a court document. And I don't believe anybody rigged that one up.

J – Okay, so you left Mr. Nicoletti and Roselli off this gas station where they had a car. Do you remember what type of car it was?

JF – I don't know. I'm not even sure which one it was. There was a car there. I mean, they said they had a car there, but there were several cars there parked up on the side. I did not wait, I did not watch them walk across the lot. They exited the car. When Mr. Nicoletti closed up the door…

- Break in tape because of sound problems –

JF – Okay, when I pulled out from the intersection, I made a left-hand turn there at the intersection, I went down by the gas station. When I pulled over at the gas station to let them out of the car, I left them out of the Chevy I am in. I'm in a 63 Chevy, burgundy Chevy, we'll get that fact straight, not a red one or anything, just burgundy, that's the color of the car. They opened the door as they exited it. As Mr. Nicoletti exited the car, just as he closed the door he said : Jimmy, I'll see you in Chicago! I told him: Okay Boss! He closed the door, they walked across to go into the parking of the gas station there. There were several cars parked over there. I have no idea, no knowledge which particular car they went to. I did not wait to see, I pulled out, made a right one to get back on the highway. I went back to Mesquite. I went back to my motel. I don't want to be riding around with a carload of weapons and somebody has just been hit. It would be highly unpractical. I went back to the hotel, pulled in, I parked my car right in front of my room where I could watch it. I get out of the car, I went into my room. When I got into the room, I sat down and relax, got a drink of water, stripped all my clothes off, went in and took me a shower. When I came out of the shower, I took some wax that I brought along for this particular purpose. And if anyone, you have to try it, it can be pretty painful. But I knew I would have residue here and on the side of face, from firing the weapon and across my hand and wrist. I took hot wax and I poured it on myself and let it cool, let I cut into the pores, on the side of my face and after a few minutes I peeled it off, which would remove all the nitrates from any gunpowder. I went back into the shower, I showered again, the shower I finished up with a good cold one because I felt like I was kind of on fire and burning. When I got out of the shower and dried up, I put a lotion on everything to cool the burning sensation and then I got dressed. I waited for dusk to come. Once it got dark, I went out to the car, nobody was around, I made sure everybody was inside whatever they were doing in their motelrooms, I open the trunk up, I took the weapon out of the trunk and when I had gotten out of the car earlier, I had taken the briefcase, the guncase with my Fireball in it, I had already taken that into the hotel. I went inside, I had one weapon I took in, cleaned it, (inaudible) to put it back in the car. I waited until midnight, I went back out to the vehicle, got in and pulled the backseat out, took the top part of the back, put the gun back into the rack, the rifle. I secured my Fireball, put the guncase in there, closed everything back up and went back into the hotel. I went to sleep and got up the next morning at first light. Went down the road, there is a restaurant down the road on the right hand side as you are coming back east. A breakfast and coffee shop, not too far, maybe a mile, a mile and a half down the road, something like that anyway, best I remember. I stopped there, had me some coffee, breakfast, got in the car and I left. I drove back to the southern part of Illinois. When I arrived at the southern part of Illinois, it was starting to get dusk, getting late, I pulled off in a motel there. Aah, as I got back in Illinois, I can't remember the name of it, I remember it was like a blue and white one. I wanna say "Southern something" or another. Like a truck stop, a lot of trucks there. I got in, got a room and I stayed overnight there. The next morning I went out, got in the car, proceeded to Chicago.

J – Are you a drinking man?

JF – At that time I was.

J- Did you have any drinks while you were in Dallas?

JF – No, I drank no alcohol, I am working. Mr. Nicoletti would frown at that very very much. When I was down there running around drinking.

J – what can you tell me about the death of J.D. Tippit?

JF – When it comes to J.D. Tippit, they say that Lee Harvey Oswald was the one that shot him. It's not true. The party that shot J.D. Tippit was someone else that had been brought in. I'm not sure where he was coming from, I didn't even know this party was on location. But after that, I am already back at the hotel, when the party comes up, somebody knocks on my door, I picked up my 45, walked to the door, pulled the little curtain back and I kind of looked out the door to see who is there, and I see this party standing there that I recognized, that I know. And I opened the door and I say "What the hell are you doing here?" He says: "I had to stop by, I got a problem." And I say: "You've got a problem?" And I am looking at him, you know, I am still trying to register: How does he even know I'm here? Nobody knows I'm here, you know, this is getting to be a habit, like everybody knows Jimmy is in town. And he said: "I had to burn a cop." And I said: "Well, you have done what you had to do." He said: "I missed Oswald". And I said: "Well, what are you doing here? You've burned a cop! "He says: "Here, you wanna take this and get rid of it (the weapon)?" "Hell no! That's yours!

You take it and get rid of it! You just shot a cop! I don't want this weapon. So you get rid of it. That's yours! Get out of here! Go!"

W – What are you talking about? The gun?

JF – I'm talking about the gun that he had. It was a revolver. And he said "I had to burn a cop". I told him: "You did what you had got to do! I don't want that thing! Get away from here, get out of here! Go where you got to go!

J – Kind of dangerous isn't it? You are kind of laying low and then this guy comes….

JF – Yeah, somebody knocks on my door at this point. I'm ready to start shooting again, you know. And he said Okay and some other things, I don't remember exactly what it was and he went out into his vehicle and he took off. I don't even know what he was driving because as soon as he walked out that door I closed the door and pulled the curtain back. I don't wanna know anybody, I don't wanna know anything whatsoever at this stage of the game.

W – You are not naming this party?

JF – No, I am not naming this party.

W – What is the reason for it?

JF – What is the reason for it? Well, I don't know if he is still alive or not, but late in 1991, when I got this case, I know for a fact the party was still alive and in good health, okay? But you know, he didn't shoot Kennedy, he shot a cop. You know everybody wants a cop killer, okay, but this guy, I don't know who he is, I mean I know who he is but I'm not going to tell anybody who he is. He is gone! That's out of there. I have no idea where he is at, I don't wanna know where he is at.

J – Give us a statement to the fact, I know that you told Bob Vernon this, and I understand this, that you don't mind talking about things that happened and people that are dead but that you never give up anybody that might still be alive.

JF – Well, when it comes to giving somebody up, I have never given up anybody in my life. I am not gonna put anybody in prison. And as a matter of fact, you probably couldn't get the FBI to admit to it, but when a couple of their people forced their way into Stateville, I was offered all kinds of deals and all kinds of agreements, if I would not give an interview on John F. Kennedy before. You know, I told them to do what they gotta do. They did, sorry to my regret, but the thing is this: I'm not gonna give anybody up, I'm not gonna put nobody in prison. I have never went to court and testified against anybody. And I have got a lot of deals offered in my time, I have told them to put me in jail. I went to jail, I've had cops tell me this and that. You know, we're gonna lock you up, we've got you dead bang! I've had prosecutors come in and tell me: You're dead coal! Plead guilty!

W – If you would hear that this party that killed officer Tippit is dead, would you have no problem revealing his identity?

JF – You're asking me a question right now I can't answer, cause I'm not really sure. Not that it would make any difference probably, if he is dead they couldn't put him on trial. But what

I'm saying is this: I really don't know how I feel about that, because you know, to me it's not that relevant, it's not that important. And as far as I am concerned, I'm not gonna help the FBI or anybody else close their records on a murder case. You know, this is Kennedy we are talking about. You know, to me, I never liked Kennedy, I don't even know why I ever did it, I don't even know why the FBI gave Joe West the lead on me. I have never understood that one.

W – But the Tippit killing is related to the murder of Kennedy!

JF – No, the Tippit killing is not related to the murder of Kennedy. If you want to get right down to it. The Tippit killing is related to Oswald. Because Oswald is the one that was supposed to die. Not Tippit. Tippit was just one of those people that stopped the wrong person, that got called into the wrong place. And when he got to ask the wrong party something, and you've got an officer in Round Lake Beach by the name of David Ostertag, when he goes out and gives his story, as he talks, he tells people how careful they have to be, these young recruits, cause you never know who you're stopping. Somebody should have given that talk to J.D. Tippit. Because he stopped the wrong party that got him killed.

J – So the party that killed Tippit though, was actually after ...

JF – He was after Lee Harvey Oswald.

J – Okay, make a statement.

JF – Okay. The party that killed J.D. Tippit, he wasn't there to kill J.D. Tippit. He had parked a little ways from Oswald's boarding house. They went down there to kill Oswald. They wanted to kill Oswald. They didn't want to make a big spectacle out of it. They wanted to silence him at that point of the game. Before anybody could get to him. But I guess ... I don't know if Lee got spooked or whatever it was, but then he went to theatre. And he knew who he was going to when he left there, because he was supposed to meet the controller there. Which is David Atlee Phillips. He was the one that was supposed to be at the theatre as far as I understand.

W – How do you know?

JF – Because I knew that's where he was supposed to be. I knew that Lee Harvey Oswald was going to go meet him ...aah ..

J – Start over! It was my understanding that he was meeting his handler ...

JF – It was my understanding that Lee Harvey Oswald when this was over with, that he was going to be in contact with David Atlee Phillips. I did not know that David Phillips was going to be at the theatre, but I knew Oswald was going to go meet him. …….. Let me start over again, I'm lost now!

W- It was my understanding ….

JF - My understanding was that Lee, that he was gonna meet his controller, which is David Phillips, who was my controller. He was gonna meet him. I didn't know it was gonna be at the theatre. I have no knowledge of that at that point. But if Lee Harvey Oswald ran to a theatre, that had to be where the meeting was going to take place. Lee must have left his house earlier or for whatever reason, I don't really know, but the party that went there, didn't find Lee there. And when he started to leave, he was stopped by the police. This is when he shot Tippit. What transpired there I can't tell you, who saw this guy there, I can't tell you whether he ran, I can't tell you whether he walked, I don't know. All I understand is this: A party that I know, that had come by my motelroom, told me he had to burn a cop. The cop he burned was J.D. Tippit. That was the only cop killed in Dallas that day, it had to be the one that he burned. At this point he says: "Here, do you want to get rid of that? " I said: " Hell no, you take care and get rid of your own weapon! I've got my own problems, Get out of here. Go! "

J – What kind of weapon was it?

JF – It was a … I didn't … I think it was a 38 revolver. I'm not sure, I couldn't swear that, I didn't handle it, I didn't touch it. He just had it in his hand, he pulled it out and handed to me. I said: I don't want it, take it out of here!.

J – Well, you know the difference between a revolver and an automatic …

JF – Yeah, he had a revolver he was gonna hand me.

W – How did you know that Lee was supposed to meet his contact?

JF – When it comes down to the part that this guy was going for Lee Harvey Oswald, the connection is this: Lee Harvey Oswald had just spent five days with me, Lee Harvey Oswald knew who I was, he knew I was in town, he knew what just happened, he was tied to me basically drastically. When I talked to Charles Nicoletti that morning, I told him this: I said: We 've got a slight problem. And he asked me: What's that, Jimmy? I said: Lee Harvey Oswald. At that time Mr. Nicoletti said: "Jimmy, who is Lee Oswald? I never heard of this guy!" I said he works with the Agency, that he is one of David Atlee Phillips' people. Chuck didn't know who David Phillips was. And I told him he is a tie back to me. I am a tie back to you! I said: This makes me nervous. I'm concerned about it! Mr Nicoletti told me: "Jimmy, don't worry about it. I'll talk to the boss." The only one he could have talked to is Sam. If he talked to Sam, Sam evidently told him: Don't worry, I'll take care of it! The only party that Sam could have called, and that's Sam Giancana, that would have been David Phillips. David Phillips was in the area that day. I know that for a fact. I didn't see him, I didn't talk to him, but I know he was there. Anyway, this party that was there, that killed J.D. Tippit, he was brought in at a last minute notice. He had to be on standby. And where-ever Phillips went, he usually kept several people around that he could use, people that he needed. Whether he needs them or not, they are gonna be available. They always had, what are you gonna call them, contract agents, operatives, co-operatives or whatever, he's got people that he can use. If he needs something done he can pick up a phone and have it initiated in a moments' notice. This party was evidently there on standby cause he did not live in that area. That's why I was shocked to see him at my motelroom. So evidently they took care of it that way.

J – Okay, so this party that shot Tippit, he was more connected to the Agency than the mob?

JF – To the agency. He wasn't tied to the mob. He might have done some work for them along the way, but he was strictly one of David Phillips' people. Because he did not even know Charles Nicoletti.

J – Were you aware of anybody using radiocommunication in the Plaza?

JF – No I was not.

J – Did you ever hear of man named James Hicks, or Jim Hicks?

JF – I've heard the name but I don't know him.

W – Have you ever heard of Chauncey Holt?

JF – I have heard of Chauncey Holt.

W - Did you know him?

JF – Aah, when you say know, it's like knowing somebody, seeing somebody, saying hello or how are you doing? But was we friends? No, we wasn't friends. I don't know him that well, I knew who Chauncey was. He was with the same people who I was with, when you get down to the crime family. But to say he was a friend, no. How well did I know him? Slightly. I knew who Chauncey Holt was, I know where he lived at.

J – You already said you saw Richard Cain in the Plaza.

JF – Yes, Richard Cain was in the Plaza.

J – Is there any chance he was a shooter?

JF – There's all kinds of chances. But like I say, do I know that? No! I can't say he was or he wasn't.

J – Do you think Mr. Nicoletti was aware of the identities of any other shooters, other than you and himself?

JF – If Mr. Nicoletti had been aware, he would have been made aware of it by Sam Giancana. And if he was aware of it, he wouldn't tell me. And if there was other shooters there, I can't see why anybody would tell Nicoletti.

J – Sounds to me like you had some from the mob and some from the Agency and they weren't necessarily talking to each other, but maybe Sam and Phillips would ...

JF – It very well could be. It's very possible that Sam Giancana and David Phillips could have been talking. But like I say, again: If I know everybody in that area and I get stopped, I can name every shooter there if there is other shooters there. I'm not saying there is other shooters, what I am saying is this: I have no need to know of everybody that is involved in an operation. What purpose would that serve? That's like me going into a communist country on a covert operation and me knowing everybody, all the other agents that are there in that field working. And if I get captured, they all get executed! So the same thing goes when it comes down to crime. You try to keep your people the least bit to know as possible. Because too many times, maybe partners, and that's like … I can use one deal, one party back east out of Philadelphia, I did time with him in the federal prison. His own brother gave him up. His brother knew that he was a big time cocaine dealer, he was a dentist. They called him Dr. Snow. I don't remember his real name, but they called him Dr. Snow. His brother got busted on a nickel bag of weed in New York. He gave his own brother up because he couldn't do a year in the jail. His brother told him: I'll give you a million dollars a year. For every year they keep you in jail, I give you a million dollars cash. Don't testify against me! He put his brother in jail.

- Change of tape -

W- (speaking to Jim) I wanna ask him "Why was Antonio Veciana a friend of yours?"

J – Okay, do you know Antonio Veciana?

JF – Yes I do, I did know Antonio Veciana, yes.

J – And how did you know him?

JF – I met him in Miami. And he was tied up with the JM/Wave and he was also tied up with the Alpha group. He knew all different people. He was I might say a little higher up in the ranks, but I met him. Did you ever meet someone you just like? Well, I liked him and he liked me, we had a good report, he had a good sense of humor, he could talk to you and you know, he didn't talk down to you.

J – Tell us about JM/Wave!

JF – JM/Wave was a special operation, set up with a lot of broadcasting and we had a lot of people running a lot of covert operations out of there, basically a radio station there, doing a lot of propaganda stuff there. That was all under David Phillips.

J - And where was that located?

JF – That was in Miami.

J – Where in Miami?

JF – Oh God …… Out of Port Homestead there.

J – Okay, tell us about David Ferrie.

JF – David Ferrie. I won't get into his personal lifestyle. David Ferrie, I did not like David Ferrie. I had only seen him on one or two occasions. Me, I wanna say he looked like a creep more or less. He was stock, heavy set, he had real heavy eyebrows and uh, me, I just don't like a guy who is a homosexual, okay? Child molestor as far as I'm concerned. I knew about a lot of things that he was doing and I didn't approve of it. But I'd like to say one thing about David Ferrie. He was a solid agent for the CIA. He was on their payroll. I don't care what anybody says.

W- Can we ask James if he can tell us anything about his death?

J – What, about Ferrie's death?

W – Yeah!

J – Do you know anything about David Ferrie's death?

JF – Yes I do. He had a cerebreal brain hemorrhage. But the cerebreal brain hemorrhage that David Ferrie had, that was brought on. And uh.. I explained to the coroner, and I had this checked out , he went and talked to them, I don't know who else they talked to and anything else. But I also know that when warden Godinez was the warden here at Stateville prison , it was on a Sunday morning, they made a call up here and wanted to come here and talk to me, some people, I'm not sure as to who it was that wanted to come here and talk to me. They said they had a Lear-jet on standby. And my reply was "Save your fuel, I got nothing to say to you!"

But the tissue tear and the brain itself is just above the palate of the mouth …. The hemorrhage was inflicted!

J – Icepick?

JF – No sir. Nailfile! A nailfile gives you the simulation of tear. You could use a stiletto, thin blade knife, icepick, but then you would see what it is. You get a clean cut. With a finger-nailfile you got a smooth edge, you've got a preparated edge. And when it goes through the tissue, it's like a tear, it's like something ripping apart.

J – Do you know who did that?

JF – Yes I do.

J – Was it you?

JF – Was it me? Of course not . Not me, I wouldn't do that! (smiling) I'm not admitting to a murder on there! JFK is bad enough , but nobody is going to prosecute me for JFK.

J – (looking at Wim) aah …

W – I'm fine.

JF – Who killed David Ferrie, I'm not saying.

J – But you know ….?

JF - I know who it was , yeah.

J – Okay, all right. Here's a question I want to tell you. John Roselli was actually pretty well known, and he was well internetted in Hollywood, he was kind of flashy dressing …

JF – VERY flashy! Very flashy, very loud. Liked to spend money. And liked for everybody to know basically what he was doing when he was in town. He wanted everybody to know he was there.

J – Why would the mob put somebody like that in such an important hit as JFK.

JF – Johnny Roselli had all the right connections. The reason that Johnny Roselli was brought into all this: He had the right connections, he was the liaison I can say between the government and the crime .... you know the crime people, mafia, what are you gonna call them, Outfit, the organization, crime family, they've got different names for it. They brought him on, not for what he was, and I think Chuck wanted to use him more or less, specifically because of the connections and the cooperation and the help that we would receive. This is only what I say. This is not fact, I got no document and proof on it. Nobody never sat me down and told me that, this is where I draw my own conclusions.

J- So he could kind of provide you with some high level contacts?

JF- Right, high level cover from Johnny Roselli's side. And at this point of the game, when I went down there, I did not know at that time that the CIA was heavily involved in this. After I talked to David Phillips, and let him know where I am at, and then when Lee Harvey Oswald shows up on the scene, I have at this point become aware. Only two people knew where I was: Charles Nicoletti and David Ferrie .. uh David Phillips, excuse me.

J – Start over!

JF- Okay, at this point of the game only two people know where I am at: Charles Nicoletti and David Phillips. Lee Harvey Oswald showed up at my hotel. This tells me automatically: David Phillips is in on it, David Phillips knows what's going down. Otherwise Oswald would never be there.

J – So Oswald was working for the agency is what you are saying?

JF- Oswald was CIA, oh, Oswald was CIA before I ever knew any of these people. Oswald was recruited when he was in the Marine Corps.

W- Was it obvious to you that Lee Harvey Oswald knew David Atlee Phillips under his real name? Or could it have been one of his aliases?

JF- Lee Harvey Oswald knew David Phillips by several names. He knew his real name, he knew him by different aliases, he knew him by different codenames. Lee Harvey Oswald had known David Phillips a lot longer than I had.

J - Phillips had several aliases?

David Phillips, he uses a lot of aliases. One of his most famous one, one of them that I can remember is Maurice Bishop. And Maurice Bishop had a lot of controversy whether it was him or whether it wasn't him, he's had other names but I can't even remember all the different names, I can't even remember all the names I've had on my different passports with my picture on it or different pictures and everything, you know.

J – What is your real name?

JF – My real name is James Sutton.

J – And you were born when?

JF - I was born January 24th, 1942, in Alabama. And if you find my birth certificate, it will plainly state "deceased at birth".

J - How then was that arranged?

JF – I have no idea. But when I was trying to get a birth certificate for my own records, they could not locate one at first. And the logger in Alabama went to do everything, went to the capital and when he got through, he found it 3 months later. I had a birth certificate in there, that says "deceased at birth".

J – Now can the mob do something like that or is that the government?

JF- That is only the government! The mob knows a lot of things, they've got ways to get things done, but when it comes to this kind of stuff, that's out of their category. I wanna tell that when it comes to the government and underhanded work, the mob, they are kindergarten. They are kindergarten! I might upset a lot of people in the family saying that, but they are kindergarten when it comes to working with the government. They are the goldfish in the shark's pond.

W- What kind of a man was David Atlee Phillips?

JF – David Atlee Phillips was a very secure man, lot of class, quiet. He was dominating, he demanded like attention when he was with you. When he was around he had a presence around him on his own. He was like he was in command. He was somebody like when he says something, you listen.

W- And what kind of a man was Charles Nicoletti?

JF – Charles Nicoletti, very quiet, well defined, I only heard Mr. Nicoletti swear on a few occasions, he did not use a lot of profanity like they portrayed him in Double Cross. Charles Nicoletti mostly got upset when there was FBI involved. And there were several other times that that happened, but like I say, Nicoletti was a quiet type of person. He didn't go out and talk about anything that he had done. He didn't go out and get drunk, I never saw the man drunk. He might take a sociable drink here and there, but he was not a man that used profanity.

W - You just told us: Fuck 'm, we go!

J – Yes, he said that, that was one of the times!

JF – Huh?

J- That was one of the times, when he said: Oh Fuck 'm, we 're going!

JF – Oh, that was one of the times. Definitely! When they called it off! Another time that I remember, was in Melrose Park. We had the car on the grease rack of the Shell station there. It used to be on Broadway and Division. And uh, there was a car parked out front. I told him:

Chuck, I said "Mr. Nicoletti, I don't know who it is over there, but it looks we might have a problem!" And he said "Ah, I don't know, we'll watch them for a few minutes!" So they went in and they serviced this car. And they kept sitting out there and they peeked a little way down from the station's lane. That would be on the east side of the street cause Broadway runs north and south, Division runs east and west. And at that time,…. The shell station sits on the northwest corner, yeah, on the northwest corner, … on the northeast corner was the Gulf Gas station. And they were parked just beyond that in front of a two-flat down there. They kept staring and they kept watching us. So Chuck says: I gotta see who they are! Jimmy, he says, cover me! So I told the kid doing the grease job on the car: "Lower the car a minute!." And they lowered it, I walked around back and the overhead door, I had them pull that down so they couldn't see what we were doing in there, I opened the trunk and I took a rifle out. I got that out, they raised the car back up in the air and I went over by one of the … (inaudible) … and I went out the back way. Then I crawled up on the roof and I get up behind the Shell sign. And I had told Chuck: Give me two minutes and then go! He walked out, he walked across the parking lot, he was well guested, he had kindalike his right hand down into his little watch pocket where he carried a small caliber weapon there. And I got the guy, the driver, zeroed up. Anybody who picks up a gun, he's gonna get it. He got to the middle of Broadway and the car pulled out and took off. So we don't know who it was. But the only thing he said inside when we had started to go, when I had started getting the gun out, he said: It's gotta be the fucking Feds! And that was just one of those times he was very upset, because they used to really paranoid him.

W – Okay, these are stories we wanna hear but, uh …

JF – Yeah, I understand , yeah …

W- But we need to focus on the Kennedy assassination a little bit, this is burning tape!

JF – Mmm, Yeah ..

J – Did Wolfman… the mercury loads he made, did he have any idea what they were going to be used for?

JF – On Wolfman, when I asked him to make the special rounds, the only thing he ever asked me was: Do you need any help? He never asked me what I was doing, because he would never breach that borderline, whatever you wanna call it there. In the trade you just don't ask people what they are going out to do. But when I told him what I wanted done and what I needed made, he told me he would do it, and the only thing he would say, he kinda grinned at me and said : Need any help? And I said: No, this is straight! And he said okay.

J- So he really didn't know?

JF – He said: See me in a couple of days.

J – You ever heard… Have you ever heard the story of Ed Hoffman?

JF – Yes, I've heard of him. I don't know who he is, but I've heard of him.

J – He is the deaf guy who was up on Stemmons and he says he saw a guy essentially in your position, but he saw him toss a rifle to somebody else. Have you got any idea …

JF – I never tossed anything to anybody! Never!

J – Okay …

W- How did you guys know the bubble top was off?

JF – Well, when Kennedy would come down to Dallas, we had one concern. We feared the limo might have a bubble top, because it never went anywhere without it. And if it was raining, the only thing is, if we would be told in advance that the top is on, it's a walk-away. You know, you abort it, you leave it. We would pick another place, we would try it again. And that would have probably fallen to someone else. But this question had been asked us: How you're gonna get through the top? Me, my answer was using some pretty heavy artillery like using uh … one of the old uh …what do you call these things, I've got the name on the tip of my tongue …

J - Armored piercing?

JF – No not armored piercing! One of the rounds knocking out tanks …. Bazooka's ! Today we got a lot of those rockets. But we didn't have those rockets to run around with back then, that's something new that has come down the pike. But anyway, they said: No, we do it sensible. But the thing was, they had been instructed they would go and work on his ego. They tried to make Kennedy believe he shouldn't go to Texas. That he should be afraid of Texas! And they worked on his ego: You've got to use the bubble top, you have to have the top on, you can't sit in an open car! You've got to, uh , whatever they think you've got to let them think, you're afraid of whatever, but there's a high risk here. Gotta have the top on! The more they worked on Kennedy about this, the more he wanted the top off. Kennedy wanted to prove: I'm not scared of anything, I want the top off, I want to wave the people, I want to see the people, I want to touch the people. So they played on his ego. The top was off.

J – Were you aware that David Ferrie was involved, among many other things, in cancer research?

JF – I did not know David Ferrie was involved in cancer research, no, I did not.

J – Okay, so have you got any thoughts about Jack Ruby's cancer? Do you think that was natural or unnatural?

JF- No, I'm going to say it was injected. There's one thing I'd want to say, when you talk about David Ferrie, as far as cancer research, I have no knowledge of that at all, but I do know he liked to play around with hypnosis. I think he used it on a lot of young kids. Because he was in charge of the Civil Air Patrol.

W- Yes, for a second back to that bubble top: What would you have done if it would be on?

JF – Well, back to the bubble top on the car, if they would have had the top on, it was a walk-away. But we would have known that before he ever got to the Plaza, because we would have been informed. If they had come out and had picked him up with the top on, they are not going to remove the top during the motorcade. Nobody would have been there, none of us would have been on hand to watch John F Kennedy come down theatre, but I couldn't care less about seeing the man. But if the top would have been on, I would already be on my way back to Mesquite and I am quite certain that Mr. Nicoletti and Roselli would have been on their way somewhere else.

W – So if it would have rained, it was a no go?

JF – If it would still have been raining, it was a no go. But if you plan something, all you can do, is hope for the best. It's like a football, you know, you gotta make the play, seconds are running out, you go for the long one. If it works, it works. If it don't, it don't, you walk away.

W - So there was no plan B?

JF- Pardon me?

J – No backup?

JF – There was no backup plan for that. The only backup plan that we had for when the top was on, is it's a no go!

J – Here's some question Pam had for you. What has changed in your life in recent years?

JF – Uh … I think probably the biggest change in my life is .. and let me go back just a little bit farther … before this change took place, I had no emotions, no feelings, basically speaking for anyone at all. My family never came first . The agency came first, crime family came first. Everybody was always ahead of my wife and my kids. Wrong ! I know that …. I know that know. I've got probably a lot of regrets, maybe some remorse for a lot of the things that I did do. I'm sorry at times I wasn't there, to see my kids go to their little schoolplays and do their dances, recitals or whatever. I'm sorry I wasn't there at their birthdays and a lot of their Christmases. But those things were part of my life and things that I accepted. Because to me other things were more important. My family, my wife, my kids, they were way down the list of priorities. Wrong, I know! After I got here… and when I got here, this place was pretty well wide open. This place was very violent, wild, and you know we've had recently several lockdowns due to deaths here, that weren't natural. But a few years ago, what happened to me was: I went to sleep one night. I had a lot of hate in me , I had a lot of anger in me. I had a list of names, I wanted to start writing names, why I wanted this person, and I wanted that person. A lot of hate in me. But I woke up there in the night, I find Jesus sitting by my bunk. A lot of people will say that was just a dream. Maybe it was a dream ! It's a dream to you, a dream to him. To me it's real! And I asked him: What are you doing here? And he said: I've come to take you! There's only one way. The Father sent me to tell you. He said that I'm for real , God is for real and that I am for real. The only way to the Father is through me. So we talked for a little while and I went back to sleep. The next morning I woke up: All the hate was gone. I used to wake up and come out of my cell every morning. It's not: "What am I gonna do today?" It's "Who am I going to kill today?" or "Who am I going to have to stab today?" Or "Who is going to try and stab me? Who am I going to fight?" You know, because there are a lot fights here, a lot of stabbings. But I had a new feeling in me. It was really like, you know, I felt I loved everybody! You know "Hey, how are you doing?" Boom! I talked to people I never talked to. I even talked to the guards. Hey, how 're you doing? What's going on? Hey, Hey, nice day! Well, after a little while I started slipping back again. I got back to being the old Jimmy again. I started getting these other, these angry feelings back. I wanted to fight, you know you look every wrong way, I'm gonna grab you, slam you against the wall, you know. Whatever you do! Ah … I got a second visit. And when I got this second visit, Jesus really got, really got my attention. And at this point, I had already heard from this one girl, this one lady, I don't know whether I should name her on tape or not, but I had become romantically involved with her. I fell in love with her. And I love her with all my heart. I love her more than I have ever loved anything in my life. And we were talking and writing, she was a good Christian lady, and she had told me a few different things, and on the second visit I got, Jesus told me to get my life in order, and that the Father was going to call me home. And I thought: Well, Jesus, I'm gonna die! And I'm gonna die right away! And so I told her that on the phone, and she was crying a little bit, you know, she was a little sad over this and that. But then I was reading in the Bible and I was reading In Matthew, chapter 24, about the earth giving the birthpain and all this. What he was telling me , Jesus was telling me: God is not calling me home at this stage of the game, but be prepared : You're ready for heaven, so I can have a life hereafter. And I'm reading all about this in Matthew. And then it struck on me what it was. But like I say, since then I have lived a whole different life here. I used a few words profanity in this interview, strictly for the purpose of what was said, they were actual words used verbatim. But when I am not, like not in this interview, I try not to use vulgar language, I try not to hate people, I try to maintain good thoughts. But in here it's hard to maintain good thoughts. Very hard in here, but I work at it very hard. And I pray every night, every day. I don't run around with my bible, I don't run around trying to tell you all about the word of God. That's not my job. You want to hear about it, I 'll be more than happy to sit down and talk to you about it. But I don't try to push it on anybody. We have a lot of different kinds of religions here.

J – Why don't you briefly tell why you are in prison right now?

JF – I am in prison for a specific reason. When I came out of the federal prison, I did a federal stretch and I was out for a little while and people started trying to kill me. When they started trying to kill me, the first time I was at Quentin road and Rilings, at Rilings Lake Beach, shortly past midnight, driving a little Chevy Chevette. And the cops had been harrassing me , they knew who I was. Every time they see me, they handcuffed me, get me out of the car, my papers, blew out my stuff all down the street. Well, in this particular night, I had pulled up the stoplight there, I am on Quentin road, fixed to make a right hand turn on Rilings road. I'm staying on my end (inaudible) this time about two blocks down from there. I looked up in the rearview mirror and I see this car pulling up behind me with no lights, next lane. And I thought: Shit, cops again! You know, I 'm going to get hassled again. It's not a squad car, but I figured it's just detectives, you know. As it pulls up alongside of me, I'm looking in the mirror sitting by the door, the little door there on my side, and I see an SMG coming up. For anybody who doesn't know what that is, it's a small machine gun, an automatic weapon, and as I see it coming out of the window, I roll across the seat, hit the door , hit the ground, roll back up against the (inaudible) of the car. They put 30 holes in my car! Four clips they put into it. As they were pulling away, I come up off the ground on my feet , so I got off about four rounds. I'm on federal parole at that point, I'm not supposed to be carrying a weapon, but you never find me without a weapon. I got off four rounds, took the back window out, they kept going. I jumped back in my car, took a right onto Rilings road, went down to Grove Avenue, pulled into the house at (inaudible) 1620 Grove, went in there and got the tarp from my uncle out of the garage and put it over the car, so they couldn't see the bullet holes. That was the first attempt on my life.

J - When was that?

JF – Aah… I got out of federal prison in '88 …This year was late '89 or early 90 I guess.

J – Has there been any attempt on your life in prison?

JF – Not in prison. I had a lot of fights, but that's not attempts on my life. I mean the things that happen here is just day-to-day living . I got a few scars from knives here and there, but that's irrelevant there.

J - You don't think it was people trying to take you out?

JF – Oh no, definitely not.

J – Well then, it doesn't have anything to do with the JFK job?

JF – No, definitely not. And when they started trying to kill me on the street, after the first attempt on my life in the free world, as I call it: Next day I went to see somebody down in the city and I wanted to ask him a specific question: If we had a problem? I said I did my federal time. I got busted on the chop shops. I didn't take nobody down with me. I said I went and kept my mouth shut, I didn't testify, I didn't give nobody up. I took the conviction, I have done my time. What is the problem? We got a problem? Let me know! And he told me: Jimmy - he always called me Jimmy - Jimmy boy, he says: Calm down, calm down! He says: Listen to me, he said: You got no problem with us! You did your things. He says: Hey, you didn't have no problems when you got down, you got money, we looked after certain people for you, took care of your family, you had no problems! When you came out , you went to the restaurant, everybody parked, everybody came by to see you. We dropped a lot of envelopes. He said: You have money when you come out. Everybody looked after you when you came out! That's respect! Don't think we are after you! Whatever you 've done, that's with your previous employers, not us! That's only the other side of the fence with people you worked for before. He said: No, not us, Jimmy, I'll give you my word on that!

The second attempt I was on my motorcycle and it's a long story and I won't go with you all through that …..

J – Hold a minute, so you are saying that attempt was not the mob, that was the Agency?

JF – That was the Agency, that was the government, somebody in the government!

J – So the government has tried to take you out ?

JF – That's what I honestly believe!

J – Okay, make a statement.

JF – Now then, the second time on my attempt … or are you talking about making a statement on the government?

J – Yeah

JF – After I talked to a certain party in Chicago down there in the city, about them trying to kill me, he was telling me that was my previous employers. What we're talking about here, is we're talking about a government agency. I won't say which agency it was trying to take me out, but at the time I had people with the DOD on me… because I had taken certain material off the computer at Oxford, from the arsenals that I worked, I had an access to classified materials there for building new tanks, new helicopters, everything (inaudible) with black hawk helicopters. I had the keys for everything, I had the range of firing, everything was classified because we made a lot of the stuff there. We made the nitrene? cable to fire the sidewinder missile, inside the federal prison.

Anyway, the second attempt, was .. - now I realize this is not the crime family that is after me, it has to be a government agency – the second attempt on my life was late at night, they ran me over on my motorcycle. They hit me so hard, they bent the frame on it. They towed the motorcycle out. That's all on record.

Next time that comes around, the third time, were these two off-duty officers. One of them is David Ostertag. They will never admit they had a contract on my life … and I want to state here: I have no hard feelings against either one of these officers, even though they tried to kill me. I don't take this as anything personal. I think that they were doing a job. They were doing what they were paid to do. They just blew it! But the thing is this: I'm here because somebody opened up on my partner and me, they tried to kill us in broad daylight on May 7th, 1991, 3:15 PM, maybe 3:30, at the middle of route 12 in a little place called Buffalo Grove. We were between Quentin road and Long Grove road on route 12. They forced us off the road, when they forced us off the road - they say it was a high speed chase, it really wasn't a high speed chase – they spotted me at a gas station, I didn't even see them, I paid for the gas, got in the car with my partner David Morley, he was driving. And we pulled out from there, they got in behind us. As they got up alongside, he started hitting the gas to go and I told him: No hold on! Pull over, we don't run from nobody! My exact words were: Fuck 'm, we don't run! Pull it over! We'll deal with it! As they cut us off, it's like he pulled into what was part of a driveway, it was gravel, a little fast, he hit the brakes and he littered a low tree. The tree we hit, wasn't any bigger than my arm. I threw the door open on my right hand side, to exit the car, this was a leased car, and after I opened the door to exit, they drove their car, which is a white unmarked car, into the side of our car. While I see the front of their car coming at the door, I jerked my leg back above the ground so I wouldn't get it cut off there and broken, and duck my head. And then they hit the door, the door hit me and knocked me back into the car and I bounced off the dash. And at that point, they opened fire. My partner David Morley, very good man, he saved my life on several occasions in the free world, his left hand is paralyzed, he has been shot a couple of times in shootouts. He can't use his left hand. At this point he's leaning down, fumbling under the seat of the car looking for his gun. Looking for a 9 mm. And I'm yelling: Get out! Get out! Get out! And to me it seems like it's taking forever. When he got the 9, he put it up under his arm, he's gotta close that arm, he reached across, to open the door to exit. Well, this is only a few seconds, but it seems like a lifetime to me. And we come out of the car and when he comes out, he took the first shot: David Ostertag went down. At this point I come out, there's no need for me to even shoot. The other officer, Bitler - and I didn't know they were cops at that time, neither did my partner, we had no idea they were police officers - he crawled up under the car. And he was screaming I guess: They're gonna kill us both! They're gonna kill us both! David Ostertag was already down. I grabbed the AK-47 out of the car, had it in the backseat. I had one picked out from the storage shed for a simple reason: I had a meeting prior to those people and somebody had poked me in the chest, and I just knocked him down and stumped on him a couple of times, and told him: Don't ever threaten me to tell me you're gonna trunk me! If you do, do it first and then come and tell me that you've done it! I went to tell David: We 've got problems, I want to get the

AK-47 out, got the ammo-can out., I had a 30-round clip in the AK-47, this is all in the logbooks, the ammo-can had 500 rounds of ammo in it. David Ostertag can tell you how many rounds we had for the 9 mm, the clips and all the loose rounds.

I went into a little swamp, it took them several hours to get me out. The AK-47, the tracker spring broke, it wouldn't fire.

W – Any witnesses to all this?

JF – A lot of people around. A lot of people. We had traffic backed up from the shooting incident there all the way to Wisconsin and all the way to the city of Chicago.

J – So who opened fire first?

JF – They opened fire first!

J – And they were in an unmarked car?

JF Unmarked car!

J – Plain clothes?

JF – Plain clothes. They had a windbreaker on, they were wearing a badge under their gunbelt underneath the windbreaker jackets, sitting in the car. They were shooting from inside the car. David Ostertag had exited and was coming around and shooting when David Morley dropped him.

W – Did they ever say you were under arrest or..?

JF – No.

J – Did they identify themselves, did they yell: Police officer ?

JF- Nobody identified nothing. I mean: The shooting started.

W- How many shots were fired before your partner took the shot?

JF – Well I'm gonna say they got off probably the first 14 shots. They say they fired 3 and 11 out of 52. They said we fired the rest of them. But there's not that many shell casings on hand. And if the only weapons that were fired, were 9 mm's that day, and my weapon hadn't been fired, that leaves 3 clips. It's only 45 rounds. There's 15 rounds to a 9 mm in a staggered clip. And they didn't fire that many, they still had rounds in theirs. So there's no way that 52 rounds were fired that day.

W – Are there witness reports on record?

JF – Oh, there's all kinds witnesses that have seen what went down. There's witnesses that plainly state as to who got out, who shot who, and who shot first. That's all in the court documents.

J – So how did they get a conviction if there are witnesses to say they fired first?

JF - That was very simple: We were tried in Lake County, Illinois. It didn't take them long to convict us. Everybody on the jury was related to a cop. You don't shoot a cop and walk away. If you shoot a cop, it don't matter whether it was self-defense or not.

W – Were these witness reports allowed …. as evidence?

JF – Some of those were denied. I had witnesses that had come here to testify on my behalf and that was irrelevant and they were not permitted to testify. My own aunt was not permitted to testify at my trial.

W – So this was a frame-up?

JF – As far as I'm concerned, it was a frame-up. It was self-defense. Over and out. And I didn't even shoot nobody.

J – All right, let's go back and tell us a little bit about your military background and when and how you were recruited into the CIA.

JF – I went into the military in January 1959. Regular army. I went into Fort Leonard Wood, Missouri, took my basic there. From there I went to Fort Polk. AIT training there, went to Bragg, Airborne, ….and Laos. And Laos, I got in trouble over there, well - not really trouble, we had some problems, I executed two of my own men. I was court martialled, I wrote my own court martial, I wrote the report, they got me court martialled, I didn't write the court martial itself, but the report I wrote was a result of it. And they knew that I was right, every JCS knew that I was right and I went for a ninety-days evaluation and I was recruited out of the Veteran's hospital. And there have been claim numbers located on that. Some say they are not mine, but they were. But anyway, to make long story short, David Phillips recruited me, due to a word of William Shackley. William Theodore Shackley. Ted Shackley, as he is known as.

J - So, did Phillips recruit you or did Shackley recruit you?

JF – Shackley recommended me. Phillips is the one that recruited me. He had come to see me and told me he had a job waiting for me. I walked out of the Veteran's hospital.

J – Where was that?

JF – That was there in Maywood, Illinois.

J – Who was the director at that time?

JF – I don't even remember that far back. I don't remember if Dulles was still there or if he was already out or not. I am not … I don't remember. At that time I knew virtually nothing about the CIA to speak of. I only knew it existed.

J – Did you go through any training?

JF – What they wanted me for, I had already been through all my training, advanced training to go to Laos. I had already been to Laos and back again, and he wanted me to work and train some of the Cubans.

J – Are you a pilot?

JF – I can fly, yes.

J – Did you ever get a pilot license?

JF – I had a pilot's license at one time, yes.

J – Who did you fly for?

JF – I flew basically for myself. Now if you want to ask me who was paying me, the agency was paying me. I did a lot of things, I flew a lot of planes but we uh, I didn't have no company name or nothing, I just had a plane and went up, a lot of that was considered to go back through Southern Air Transport , what we call SAT.

J – CIA front?

JF – Yeah, CIA priority company, yeah.

J - What about the DEA? Ever worked for them?

JF – Never worked for DEA.. I had a chance at one time and I turned it down. That's when … what they call the Halloween Massacre. I believe it was … and I'm going to say it was Bobby Ray Edmund that fired like 3000 contract agents at one time.

J – That was back in the seventies?

JF – Yeah, and at that time they were forming the DEA and they wanted a lot of people to go work for the DEA, because they had operations in that parts of the country down there, Central America and around. And they needed people that knew the area and I was approached and I was asked if I would be willing to join that force and I told them: No, I will not! I'm not going to work for anybody where you (inaudible) arrest people.

J – How long do you figure the government, CIA, FBI, as official agencies, has known about your participation in the JFK   ….

JF- Well, I didn't know it at the time, but I've learned and I've seen that, I've even been given the name of it, that the party that was the informant, and he was the tie-in between both the CIA and the FBI, and he was the one …- and how he knew I was in Dealey Plaza, I don't know – but he told the FBI that I was in Dealey Plaza and that I was one of the shooters.

J – When did that happen?

JF – He told them that as early as in 1964.

J – And nothing was done about it?

JF – I never even knew that anybody knew about it. Until I've seen some of the documents here, a couple of years back

J – Is it true that during the Clinton administration that you were presented as a threat to national security?

JF – That was in 1998. The historian of the 82nd Airborne, he was doing a lot of research on me, his name was John Grady. He recently passed away, which I'm sorry to say, he was a very nice man. He also was a good veteran, he served in World War II. He did a lot of research on me and checked through a lot of people, found out for me to be credible, he verified a lot of things that him and I discussed. He had come here to visit me and when him and I were corresponding, he was approached by the Secret Service. And they warned him that I was a threat to national security. And in 1998, I don't remember what month it was, but Janet Reno and President Bill Clinton at that time, declared me as a threat to national security. And it was basically for training manuals and formulas and information they had retrieved out of one of my storage sheds, when they raided it.

J – Today with Homeland Security they probably had declared you as a terrorist threat, because you know how to make bombs!

JF – That could be. I know there is a US Marshall detainer on me at this time.

J – US Marshall for what?

JF – There is a US Marshall detainer on me at this time.

J – What does that mean?

JF – That means the day I walk out here, the US Marshalls will be here to pick me up. They want to talk to me. There is no outstanding charges, there is no charges against me. What they have against me is a detainer. All they want to do is talk to me. What they want to know is they want to be notified when I leave here, in other words.

W – Why did this John Grady have to research your past?

JF – He was hired by …. I believe it was either Joe West or Bob Vernon, I'm not sure which one recruited him or who hired him or who paid him. All I know is that he was a historian for the 82nd Airborne and he had been hired to do a research on me. And he started researching me and after he did a lot research, he contacted me for more information and he came here to Stateville prison to visit me from Florida. We visited, we talked, I gave him dates, information and things and he verified a lot of it.

W- Why was this necessary? Were your records missing or….

JF – When It gets down to my records: Nobody had ever heard of me. It took Mr. Grady, I believe it was, don't hold me to this, but I wanna say roughly 18 months, to find any military trace of me and he found them in the archives in St. Louis, Missouri. Once those records had been discovered and he found them, he got down claim numbers, serial numbers, etcetera, etcetera. A few months later they went back to retrieve some more information from those records, and the records were missing and there was a thing there that said: "No more information is available".

J – Do you know the term sheepdipping?

JF – Yes I do.

J – Explain that and make a statement whether it is a very common practice.

JF – Sheepdipping is a very common practice. What sheepdipping is, that's the old term for it, back when I was first in. Like when we went to Laos. There was no Americans going over there. I mean, let's face it, no Americans went to South East Asia until like '62 or '63. But what a lot of people don't realize, South East Asia is the old Indo China. We were there during World War II. We never came out of there. And as the old saying goes: India, Alpha, Charlie, …. no, Charlie, India, Alpha went up into the northern part of Indo China and never came out. They went up there for the drugtrade. The opium trade, the heroine, because that's the Golden Triangle. That's where, going way ahead in years, that's where the golden … the body bags, the stuff coming out of Vietnam was all that, stashed onto human bodies coming out of the Corpses.

J – So you have personal knowledge about the drugsmuggling by the Agency?

JF- Oh I've got a lot of knowledge on that, but the thing is, back to the sheepdipping, you go in and you are sterile. You aren't wearing no dog tags, you are not registered to any country, to anybody. If you are caught or retrieved, you are sterile. What sterile means, is there are no ties back to anybody. You've got no trading validity. So what they do to a mercenary, they stand him up and they shoot him, he is executed. And you can't say you work for anybody, because they are not going to believe you anyway, because you can't prove it. So when you go sheepdip, when you go sterile, you're on your own. In other words your ass is hanging out there on a limb. Be careful that it doesn't get chopped off.

J – And that's a common practice?

JF – Common practice. Still practiced, still used today.

J – Aah… What level do you think the decision was made to hit Kennedy?

JF – I would say that that decision was made higher up. Way high up.

J – Higher than Sam Giancana?

JF – Oh, way higher!

J – Higher than LBJ?

JF – I would say much higher than LBJ. LBJ was fixing to go to prison. A lot of people may not realize that. But he was in a lot of trouble. J. Edgar Hoover, he was in a lot of trouble. That's a different ballgame right there, but they relished by his death. But J. Edgar Hoover had knowledge of Kennedy's assassination six months in advance. And that's documented records from the National Security Agency, because they forwarded the information to him. Because they picked it up on their link out of Scotland.

J – Are you aware of JFK's attempt to issue interest-free money?

JF – Ah, I didn't know that until very recently. Very recently I just read book "Rule by Secrecy" by Jim Marrs, and that's the first time I ever heard that John F. Kennedy had authorized money to be printed. I always thought it was by the Federal Reserve. But I have to say that I have never read much in that field. I have never cared for J.F. Kennedy, I have never read about him, I know very little about John F. Kennedy.

J – Are you remorseful? About shooting Kennedy?

JF – For many years, no, I wasn't. But as the time goes by, I'm not saying remorseful for shooting Kennedy, maybe I am more remorseful for how it has effected this country and for the things that have been done. Maybe John F. Kennedy DID do some good things for this country. I'm not really sure, but I've got a lot of remorse for a lot of things I have done, but that's for the simple reason I got my life turned around a little bit. So I can't be as hard as I used to be. I try to have a lot of compassion for my fellow man. But with John F. Kennedy? I've gotta be honest: …. Yeah , let's say I have a little remorse for him, not specificly for him, but for the family and the kids and all. But at the time when we acted, I felt that I was right in what we were doing.

W – Why? …. Why did you dislike the man?

JF – I disliked Kennedy .., for a reason you gotta understand. I didn't like Kennedy for one reason. I didn't know the man personally, never met the man, never seen him in person as far as I know. The whole thing was: I was heavily involved in training for the Bay of Pigs. I didn't go with them, I wasn't on their shoulder, I wasn't a soldier, I didn't go there and fight, I never fired a shot. I trained them, setting up. Demolitions, making bombs, weapons ambushes, we call 'm MA's mechanical ambushes, firing weapons, train them in weapon's trade, and some hand-to-hand combat. What I did was not all that important, but you get to know guys. You work with them all day. You're out there at the fire at night. You sleep out there in the (inaudible). You know, you live together for a while. They get trained, they go away. If I had my choice I would have gone with them. Luckily I didn't. But when they went there and they got slaughtered, got arrested and put in prison all their lives, tortured … , it was a mess. All because Kennedy – and we had all kinds of firing power sitting out there waiting – we (inaudible), they (inaudible) them bad. Kennedy wouldn't do it, he got scared, he wouldn't go for it. When I say Kennedy got scared, he was scared of Chroetsjov, Russia then. But the whole thing was this: That's one of those things: They called it off, it was a no-go. They had no support, they went in, they got their ass shot off.

J – So you felt like Kennedy had betrayed?

JF- Oh, Kennedy betrayed, I felt like he really betrayed me. He didn't know who I was, but he betrayed the operation itself. And this was a government sanctioned operation without a doubt. And then later I found out that a lot of people that we trained that were supposed to have been there, they were put on… ah, I wanna call it banana boat, like a freighter. And these people, they were trucked around several hundred miles on this freighter. And they are giving them like a five-eight joy ride around the Gulf of Mexico instead of taking them over to the fight. And these guys, these Cubans, I mean they were dedicated, they were dedicated, these were …… Well, when you get down to what's a patriot?, what's a terrorist? The Cubans may have been terrorists, that's for them being patriots, okay? A patriot and a terrorist, the only difference is what side of the fence you are on. Everybody is fighting for what they believe in. But these Cubans, they were fighters. They wanted to go! And they were very upset with the Agency and a lot of other people, because they didn't make the scene.

J – During that time, during the time of the Bay of Pigs, while you were training and moving around in the Caribean, No Name Key and all that, did you ever hear the name George Herbert Walker Bush?

JF – Oh Yeah!

J – What was his role?

JF – George Herbert Walker Bush. I don't know if … I think a lot of people are not going to believe this, but he worked for the CIA back as early as 1961 that I know of.

J – How did he work? What did he do?

JF – I don't know all he did, but he did a lot of recruiting work. I know he was there at the beginning for what we called Group 40, a special operations group, Group 40. If you wonder what Group 40 was, an assassination group.

- Cut to change tapes –

(None of us are aware the camera is running again, we're still thinking the tape is being changed)

W - We missed the torture so far.

J – Right!

W – The torture is important. And maybe a character impression of Lee Harvey Oswald?

J – O, thank you! Yeah, we'll get that.

W – You wanna talk about Marilyn Monroe here?

JF – No! No, that's irrelevant there.

J – Just to inject me, was it the Kennedy's or the mob that hit Marilyn?

JF – The mob hit her, but they had done, they did it on the request of the Kennedys

J - Yah, okay.

W – (looking at camera man) Okay, are you ready?

G – I'm rolling!

J – Okay, the lead into this: Ah, do you have any proof of what you told us in regard to the Kennedy Assassination?

JF – When it gets down to this part about where a lot of people ask a lot of different questions about things, the one thing that I could verify, right now, which cannot be made public, is the ledger. Diary, ledger, whichever you prefer to call it. Focus on papers and things that Charles Nicoletti gave to me before he was killed. Things got pretty active here. Ah, Sam Giancana was the first one to be killed and that was in uh…'75 and I'm not sure, maybe September, it was '75, go there. He was killed, and the night he was killed, Johnny Roselli was in town. Because I saw Johnny Roselli at the airport. And when Johnny Roselli came in – we didn't talk or anything – I was there to pick somebody else up that had come in on that flight, just by coincidence. And I'm picking up a party that I had done a lot of work for, collecting money and things. But anyway, I see Johnny and we nodded at each other, he had another man with him. When they left, we were right behind them. They got in their vehicle alongside, we got ours, we took off, we went down the road. We went down River Road proceeding South. Niki (inaudible) said the only place Johnny could be going is going over to see Sam. On fifth avenue and River Road in Belmont there, they had a place called the Blue Horizon. Johnny pulled in there momentarily and the guy with him went out. Whoever this guy was, he wasn't going to Sam's house, because Sam didn't like a lot of people coming to his house and if he didn't know them, they were not going to get in anyway. And Johnny went on. I went my way, Johnny Roselli went his. Johnny Roselli …….The next morning, I woke up: Sam Giancana had been executed, gangland style. When he was killed, bells rang off to me, Johnny Roselli had to be the one to do it. Because he was there, I know he went to Sam's house that night. The following year Johnny Roselli was killed. When Johnny Roselli was killed, the party I figure was the same guy that he dropped off ….. There was two people killed down there in Tampa, St. Peter in that area. They got rid of them at the same time. One was Johnny Roselli. The other one, another party unknown, whoever it was, I don't remember the name of him now, but evidently it was a friend of his that he traveled to Chicago with. I figured he knew something and somebody took him out too, because they knew that Johnny Roselli, what he had done, okay? This guy, he might have told this guy, this guy knew, so they got rid of him.

And when it comes down to it, the crime family did not have Sam Giancana killed. I don't know who killed him except for Johnny Roselli, but I believe that the government ordered it. A contract killing on Sam Giancana. I believe the government is the one that killed Johnny Roselli, to shut him up so he couldn't talk.

J – All of this was at about the time of the House Select Committee on Assassinations?

JF – All of it, yes. But anybody that knew Sam Giancana, would have known that Sam Giancana would never have talked. He would have gone to jail. He would have kept his mouth shut. He would NOT talk. The following year, Johnny Roselli, he got killed, and they silenced him. And then, in April, it was April 19th or … no march, march 29. This is the night that Charles Nicoletti was killed. And he was supposed to go testify before some committee. And he was killed at the Golden Horns, right there in Melrose Park, there on North Avenue and Mannheim Road, the Golden Horns restaurant. And I thought at first that maybe someone in the family had hit him, because we knew there was trouble, and right before his dead, he had given me this package and told me : this is my life insurance. He said: If I need someone to have it, you can always get to it. He said: And if anything happens to me, you might need it some day. So what he gave me was … I took it and I went out, got me some cheesecloth and I wrapped up the little package and put it in a little box. I went out, dug a hole and I buried it. Put it away and covered it all up. So … about a week, a week and a half later, you know, Chuck was killed. After he was killed, right after that, maybe another week or 10 days later…… I had two places on Lake Street there in Melrose Park. One was a restaurant called the Coffee Cup, it's no longer there, it has been closed down , they put a parking lot there for the Westlake hospital. And right down below it, going East on the following block down, it must have been the 1100 block, I had a club there, a social club. And what that was, we did bookmaking there, we had cardgames there, we had a couple of pooltables in there. And that's where a lot of the guys came and hang out there. We didn't have any booze there and we didn't have any women there. What we did: You wanted to gamble, you come in and you gamble and you come and you hang out to be with the guys. And when people came around, come to the club there to gamble and play, I didn't charge them for nothing. I wanted something I call it for resting out.

Well, it's about 11 o' clock, 11:30, I call up to the restaurant and I told my grillman, a guy called Gorilla, and I said: Fix me up a couple of dozen hamburgers, fries, a dozen of black coffees and get it ready! He said: Hey boss, let me bring it down to the club! I say: Stay where you are, you don't belong here, stay up there! Because Gorilla, he loved to come down there and hanging out and gamble and everything else. And I had him working behind the grill. I said: When you get it fixed, give me a buzz! When it's ready to be picked up! He said: Okay boss! He always called me boss. He got it ready, called back to the club: Hey boss, it's ready! Wanna pick it up? I'll run it down if you want to stay there! No, don't worry! I'll come and get it! So put it in a box!

He had a cardboard box and he put it in. It was ready to go, like always, we had done this many times. Time after time after time, there was nothing unusual about it, you know. Well, I walk out of the club. It's a nice night out, you know. So I walk down at the corner and a car is coming down off the side street onto Lake Street. When it comes up, it's like them rocking for a Hollywood stop, it comes up the stopsign and stop , hits the brakes and kind of rocks back. I step back on to the curb so I don't get run over. I'm thinking nothing about it, this is not shocking at all. And they said Hello, somebody sticks something out of the window and I got sprayed in the face. And I hit the ground, not even remembering falling down.

When I came to, I was strapped up, tied up, blindfolded. And uh ….. I went through a pretty severe torture test. And all this here has been verified also.
What they wanted, they wanted the ledger ……... They never got it. When they got through with me, my legs were still taped together and my arms and wrists were still taped behind my back. They threw me out of a car, up there in Elmhurst. People found me, they called the cops up. Police came out there, some of them recognized me. Everybody in town had known that I had gone missing. Everybody figured I was dead.

J – When they threw you out of the car, do you think they thought you were dead?

JF – Oh, they thought I was dead, definitely! Otherwise they had never left me alive. That's why I have always blamed the FBI for it. Because the family or the CIA, they would have put a couple of holes in the back of my head and four or five inside the mouth through the palate, gangland execution style. These people, they didn't know that. When I lost consciousness and couldn't be brought back, evidently they figured I was dead. They didn't bother to untape or nothing, I was still naked, they threw me out of the car, in the nude, ankles still taped, hands behind my back, everything still taped up. And so …. the Elmhurst police, they knew who I was. They picked me up, they took me in their place, wanted to put me in the hospital, they took me over to the emergency room as a matter of fact, and they made a couple of phonecalls and notified my wife. My wife had a heart attack. As soon as she answered the phone: "This is Elmhurst Police. Mrs. Files, we have found your husband", she didn't knew I wasn't dead, you know. So she broke down, she got all hysterical. Her mother was there and they got a hold of Gorilla and they all came out there to get me. They took me home, but they wanted to put me in the hospital. I said: "No, I'm not going to the hospital. Take me home!" I couldn't even talk, I'm writing notes: I wanna go home! I wanna go home! I'm scrapping it out on paper. My throat, I had screamed so much, I had no voice left.

So Gorilla, he is sitting in the house with me, and if I had to go to the bathroom, he picked me up to carry me to the bathroom. And he is sitting there, I got a Remington model 870, on the side of it stamped "law enforcement only", folding stock, 8 rounds in it. I had a gun (inaudible) each end of the block. Some of the (inaudible) police said: Man, you need (inaudible), we'll cover you, we'll park our cars there! I said: No, I got my own guys here, don't worry about it! Just tell 'm that nobody mess with them. We got you covered. You guys are okay, don't worry about it!

So over the next few days, like four days, until I could talk again, Gorilla stayed right there in the house with me, he didn't even go home.

And they never got the ledger. That's still missing. Not missing, I know where it is. And let me clarify one thing: Nobody in the world knows where that is but me! It's right here! (pointing to head). Nobody else can ever take them to it.

J – Still your insurance policy?

JF – It still is. And if I die, all those secrets in that book go to my grave with me.

J – And what's all in that package? It a little box, isn't it?

JF – It's a little box. A little package inside cheesecloth, inside a metal box.

J – What's in there?

JF – What is in there? Inside this ledger what they wanted … I 've got a few other things in there, but what they wanted is this ledger, because it's got just about everything in there , basically every murder that was carried out in the Chicago-land area. It has got dates, it has got names, figures of money, different things, reasons why, ….. people who ordered it.

J – Anything in there about the JFK hit?

JF – You've got a couple of little lines in there. It has got JFK down, it has got the date on it. Basically that's it.

J – Anything else in there that concerns the assassination?

JF – No, just that. Just the date, the name and everything, but it's all in Chuck's own handwriting.

W – Okay, what he originally gave you, was it only the diary? The ledger?

JF – No, what he gave me, he gave me…. what was in the package, I disposed of a lot of it, like Secret Service identification, I didn't need that, I disposed of (inaudible) map, the last minute change, that was irrelevant, I burned all that stuff, I got rid of that, the only thing that I kept, was the ledger. The ledger retains basically to the contract around town, local people, people that was paid, people that was hit, the dates, when it happened and sometimes the reason why.

J – And why would the FBI care about all that?

JF – Oh, they would have loved that, because they could have put a lot of people in jail.

J – and they could clear a lot of cases?

JF- Oh, they could have cleared a lot of cases. They could close the door on a lot of murdercases. I am going to say probably maybe sixty, sixty contract killings in Chicago over the years there.

W- Why did you burn the motorcade route?

JF – I didn't need it. It wasn't important to me. What's that good for? That was only an admission to part of a murder.

J – Evidence?

JF – Charles Nicoletti is dead. At this point the only thing that I am going to hold is the ledger. Like he said, the ledger is everything. Diary, ledger, whatever you 're gonna call it, but everything else I disposed of. I had no need for it.

J – Yeah. Tell us a little bit about Lee Harvey Oswald and your impression of him.

JF – My impression of Lee Harvey Oswald? Lee Harvey Oswald was a very quiet type of person, secluded, very private. Mind-own mannered, you might say, there wasn't one day, he didn't do a lot of boasting or bragging, he didn't do a lot of cavalrying, what he did he kept for himself. Lee Harvey Oswald as far as I'm concerned, I liked the guy. Very intelligent, very intelligent! When we got into certain subjects … I mean he could make me look like a dummy. Let's face it!

J – So he was a lot better educated than uh….

JF – Oh, he was a lot better educated than what people say. Lee Harvey Oswald, he had very good self-control, because …. he had a little scar upon his lip and I asked him one time how he got it and he told me it was in the Marine Corps. Somebody hit him with the butt of a rifle up here … and I thought … I said "You must have ripped their guts out, or ripped their ass off!" " No", he said. "I didn't do that." I said "What do you mean?" "No, it was an accident. I didn't even get upset about it," But that's the type of person he was. He was calm, he was collect.

W- Capable of killing someone?

JF No ! ... Lee Harvey Oswald ... well, everybody is capable of killing somebody, let's face it. If you've got your back to the wall. But as far as Lee Harvey Oswald a killer? No, he wasn't an assassin, no!

J – Do you think the American public really wants to know the truth of the Kennedy Assassination?

JF – Oh, I don't think they really do. I don't think they really care. But one more thing about Lee Harvey Oswald. Lee Harvey Oswald, and I say he wasn't a killer and anything like that, Lee Harvey Oswald, he had it all up here (pointing at head). Very very intelligent. I want to say: He had a good IQ. And he held a top secret security clearance. And there is another thing I'd like to state to get on record. They talk about Lee Harvey Oswald and this and that, and him running off to the Russians. The only way that Lee Harvey Oswald could have gone to Moscow, he held a top secret security clearance when he was on the base in Japan, he held a top secret security clearance and people can go check this anyway, and the days of the Cold War, you did not jump on a plane and fly to a communist country and I don't care who you was, you had to be cleared for it. The only people who could have engineered that for him to go to Moscow, was the CIA. And the Russians were so scared of Lee Harvey Oswald over there, not fearful of what he would do to them, they knew what was going down. They gave him a place to stay and he wound up marrying Marina over there. And they were so happy to put him back on a plane and send him back to the US.

W – What was going down then? What was the mission for Lee Harvey Oswald?

JF – I have no idea what the mission was, but he went over there for some reason. I never asked him, he never told me, I never asked him why he went to Russia, but you cannot tell me that he was disgruntled with this country and he wanted to go there and be a member of the communist party. There's no way. He took a cover and he went and they just wouldn't buy the story.

J – Would you describe him as patriotic?

JF – Ah, I would say Lee ..., he did a lot of work for his country, everything he did was basically on his country. He was not a traitor. I don't care what anybody says. All those research places, everybody can say all they want. I knew Lee Harvey Oswald, he wasn't that type of person, he wasn't a traitor.

J – Has any other journalist other than myself come and talk to you?

JF – As a journalist, outside of Joe West and Bob Vernon, no. I 've never given any other interviews to nobody.

J – Did you talk to Mike Cochran?

JF- Mike Cochran. Who is Mike Cochran?

J – He was with the Associated Press.

JF – Ah, No, I did not talk to Mike Cochran. I talked to a guy by the name of David Fulsom from there, but he never came here to visit me, we only wrote two letters.

J – Oh, okay! Why do you suppose the news media don't take an interest in your story?

JF – Nobody wants to admit it. Everybody thinks I am a nut job. But like I say, I've had enough things that I have said, it has been clarified, it has been verified, there's documents…….. But nobody really wants to solve the Kennedy case. The American people, I don't really think they care. The news media, they need something that they can go with every year. You've got a lot of people that make a lot of money writing books. I don't know how many books, how many books have been written about it?

J – A couple of thousand?

JF – Yeah. Why put all them people out of work?

G – Down to three minutes (before tape ends)

J – All right, if you consider that you were talking to the American people, what would you tell them about the Kennedy Assassination?

JF – At the time I believed the Kennedy Assassination was a necessity. The reason it was carried out, the reason it was ordered, and my own belief is the money people, the power people, they wanted to stay in South East Asia. It's not about "Who did what to who" over here, it's about the money that was to be made. John F. Kennedy wanted to bring all the boys home from South East Asia that were over there. Certain people wanted to keep those guys over there. We needed it, because there was going to be deep sea ports built, there was going to the biggest runways in the world built, for bombers in different places, in Guam, Okinawa, South East Asia is gonna be flooded with airbases. We're not talking millions or, we're talking maybe a trillion of dollars or more. You've got your chemical companies that's going to come in. This is the greatest ground there ever was for chemical warfare testing. And to have a war you need deep sea ports, you need runways, air planes, manufacturers, tanks, weaponry, ammunition, munitions to be made, bombs to be made. We're talking, we're talking an all time economics deal here. Big money! Sad to say: The rich get rich, the poor get poor. The poor died, the rich got richer.

J – All right, you are an explosive expert …

- Cut in tape -

Off camera, Jim asks an opinion about the WTC towers collapsing on 9/11.
James Files says it looked like a controlled demolition to him.

Camera comes back on, but participants are not aware of it.

J – So the one that got hit second, fell first!

JF – Right, they pushed the wrong button. Otherwise they would have waited another half hour, 45 minutes, for the other one going down. But those buildings ….

J – Was that a tip-off for you?

JF - That was a big tip-off for me when I see them come down. And I tell you were my knowledge is, and you can check this out with the FBI. They had me for the bombing in Chicago over there, on the North side, Ralston Motors. This place cover like a whole block. When this building came down, and I went to trial on it, 1983, right there in Chicago, they held me for 13 months in the MCC correctional center there. I hadn't put a brick across the sidewalk, I put everything inside the building. That's how good it was. They knew I had done it, everybody else knew I had done it.

J – Everything just plunged, right there?

JF – Yeah, I was already doing 20 years for the chop shop operation, and they wanted me to plead guilty and they would give me another twenty and run it concurrent, they told me. My words was: Fuck you! Put me on trial! I went to trial. Jimmy Gaudio, my partner, he wound up pleading guilty. First he was going to beef against me. There is another party, Lou Cavalaro, better known as Blind Louie, when he was young and we rubbed together, his name was Bad Boy Louie. And when I say bad, he was bad. But as we got older and went into crime-life and everything else, we separated for a long time and we got back together, but they called him Blind Louie. Blind Louie, we moved him out there to Arizona, from the Chicago area, he lived there in Elmhurst. As a matter of fact they did a thing on him on ABC one night. They were interviewing him about him living and this and that, (and that it) must be hard (inaudible). He said: It's really hard for me to get by. I have to struggle!" He didn't know they got cameras out back, showing the swimming pool in the backyard, all the Cadillacs in the driveway, he has got a beautiful home, 300 , 400.000 dollar home.

J –And he is struggling?

JF – And he is struggling, yeah! And we moved him out there anyway. But while we are out there and I'm on trial, he got a call from Louie. They got him hooked up to talk to Louie at the MCC in Chicago where he is being held on bond. And they told him: If you testify against Jimmy, you don't have to worry about going to prison. He (Louie) said : You don't ever testify against him! And so Jimmy Gaudio refused to testify against me. I was acquitted of the case.

J – Okay. Have you ever heard of operation Mongoose?

JF – Oh yeah! Who hasn't?

J – That was the nexus, wasn't it? That's where it all came together.

JF – Yeah, they had a whole bunch of them there, they had a bunch of different programs there, I can remember the names of all of them, but they had several of them.

J – Did you ever meet Lansdale?

JF - Lansdale, no.

W – The picture of you with the guy that did Tippit, where was that taken?

JF – New Orleans.

W – New Orleans?

JF – Yeah, New Orleans.

W – In 1961?

JF – No, that was in 1962, late '62.

W- Were you 21 at that time?

JF – No, 20.

J – How old are you now?

JF – I was born in '42. I am 61, fixed to go 62.

W – January, right?

JF – Yeah, January.

J – You're just a year older than I am.

W – Oh yeah, you said you think the American people don't really care about solving and knowing the truth about the JFK assassination.

JF – I don't, no. That's like with Bob ….

W – Well, I think they do, but their government is covering it up and they don't know …

JF- I think people are tired of hearing about it, I really do. That's why I tried to convince Bob to go with something else. I told Bob: Man, you gotta go listen to a couple of stories of South America. I said: Man I've got some good stuff about down there, but Bob did want no part of it.

W – But they are NOT tired of hearing about it. It's the 40 st anniversary now and all these TV shows are on!

J – Yeah, it's all the same old rehash.

JF – I watched another two hours last night on the American Experience. Monday night I watched 3 hours and I watched 2 more hours last night. And what I had told Pamela before, it was along time ago about JFK when he met with Chroetsjov, we talked about it yesterday (with Wim). And they had it on TV, how Chroetsjov talked down to him and he walked out of there, they showed the actual footage of him coming out the meeting and get in the car. They had to help him (JFK) in the car. He was stunned.

J – Mmm

JF - And like I told: He wasn't as big a war hero like everybody says. They finally put it on TV. They said Monday night that John F. Kennedy was not the big war hero that everybody made him out to be.

J – He had lost his ship!

JF - Yeah I know (inaudible)

W – Jimmy, tell him about the Bay of Pigs, I mean the Cuban missile crisis. That it was not really necessary, that blockade.

JF – Okay. Everybody was so concerned about going to nuclear war. All right. You know about Edwin P. Wilson, right" You've heard of him?

J – Yeah.

JF- He was with ONI back then. Office of Naval Intelligence. All right, he was pretty tight at that time with Frank Sturgis. But he knew about it, the Naval Intelligence people knew about this, when Kennedy had met Chroetsjov, okay? He made an agreement and nobody knew, this whole country never knew it. And they didn't want the country to know about it. He made an agreement to take our missiles out of Turkey that time. Chroetsjov would take his missiles out of Cuba, okay? They agreed to do this. They put the blockade up to hold face. He panicked the whole country to think we were going to nuclear war.

J – So the agreement was made before…..?

JF – Yeah, the agreement was made before the blockade. Once the blockade was up and the ships in route, it's too late to do anything (make an agreement). Because they had the one ship I guess coming with more missiles, and it pulled up to the blockade and then they backed off, they turned around and they went away.

J - So that was just to save face and …?

JF – Save face! That was another farce, just like the Maddox. Remember the Maddox?

J - Oh yeah!

JF – Okay. Another one of this deals there.

J – A phoney deal?

JF – Another phoney deal!

W – How do we know this is true what you're telling?

JF – Well, what I heard, was , like …. I was told that …, Wilson he heard it , he got it through the Office of Naval Intelligence and he had talked with Frank Sturgis about it and I was there when they were talking to Frank and he said: Hey, there ain't gonna be nuclear war! (I said) What do you mean? What do you know? Because I was concerned at this point too.

And Frank told me. And I say: Nah, you're shitting me! No, he said. I 'm serious. I'm telling you how it is. There ain't gonna be nuclear war. We're relaxed. Forget about it!

J – So that's how you knew it was a phoney deal?

JF – I told my mother: Don't worry about it, mash! (She said:) What do you know? You're a kid! What do you know? When she heard me swearing on the street or something (happened) when a woman was around the house, she run out of the house with a broom , chasing me down the street, beating me with the broom, up and down 22nd Avenue.

W – There goes my Kennedy legacy!

J – O man, Well, are they going to come when it's time? How does this work?

JF – Whenever you're ready to go, we can go out there and tell 'm.

J – Are you getting tired?

JF – Not me.

J – Well, I was just gonna say: Drink some more water ! But I noticed you have not been drinking any of that stuff.

JF – I 'm gonna tell you something: I have wanted to meet you for a long time, okay? Honestly, I wanted to meet you for a long time. When Pamela told me that Wim had got you and you were the one that was going to do the interview, I was totally excited about it.

- End -

(The DVD of this interview can be purchased on the website www.jfkmurdersolved.com)

Is James Files telling the truth?

Why do I believe James Files is telling the truth? Here is a non-exhaustive list of reasons in random order:

When I first learned about James Files some three years ago, I was rather amazed that I didn't know his name. After all, I had been studying the Kennedy assassination for over 12 years. I was more astonished because Files had made his confession in 1994 and I was told the website had been up since 1995. When I searched for the name "James Files" on the Internet, I found that 9 out of 10 articles attempted to completely discredit Files' story. I then set out to closely investigate these criticisms and came to the conclusion they were all superficial and didn't hold water.

For example, critics said that the weapon Files claimed to have used was more a pistol than a rifle and would have had an enormous recoil. They said it "kicks like a mule". Therefore, Files could never have seen what he claimed he had witnessed through the scope of his weapon. I sent an email to one of the gun shops I found on the Internet. I acted as a potential customer and asked whether the Remington Fireball was a pleasant weapon to fire. That man stated the weapon was one of the most sophisticated guns ever made, etc. When I inquired about the recoil he said it was nice and steady. Ultimately, I told him why I asked. He was quite amused and said that the alleged murder weapon of Lee Harvey Oswald had a lot more recoil than the Fireball. He added that whoever said that the XP-100 had substantial recoil had a lot to learn about firearms.

Files was also criticized with the allegation that the XP-100 was not available in 1963 and that the rounds used for this weapon were not a .222 caliber but rather .221. I found both accusations to be untrue. The weapon was introduced in 1963 and prototypes were available as early as 1962. The weapon was originally chambered for .222 rounds. To learn more about the Remington XP-100 Fireball click here.

Another statement was that Files would not have had the time to do all the things he claimed to have done. He states that he bit the shell casing after firing the shot and left it on the on the picket fence on the grassy knoll. He then put the weapon back in his briefcase, turned his jacket inside out, put it on and walked away. Critics shout he would never had the time to do all of that because numerous bystanders rushed to the knoll right after the shots, since that is where most bystanders had heard the shots coming from.

It is true that many bystanders ran towards the grassy knoll, but not immediately. Files says that everyone stood frozen and stunned and that even the policemen acted uncertain, as if they were waiting for someone to tell them what to do.

I was quickly able to determine that Files was right. One of the photos of the knoll shows the press bus in front of it. There is not a soul on the knoll yet. This was the last vehicle in the motorcade, so it must have taken, at the minimum, 30 seconds for the bus to reach that point. The president's limousine had almost come to a stop and the press bus had to make the sharp turn of 120 degrees from Houston street onto Elm, forcing it to a near-stop also. To see that Files was right click here.

The lead on James Files came from the FBI. Agent Zack Shelton (now retired) served 28 years with the FBI. He has an impeccable record and spent much of his career on organized crime task forces of Chicago and Kansas City. He is the man who gave the information on James Files to private investigator Joe West, because Zack Shelton had reason to believe that James Files knew more about the Kennedy assassination. This was based on a remark that James Files had made to an FBI informant. Joe West subsequently located James Files in Stateville penitentiary, which ultimately led to his confession of being the gunman on the grassy knoll.

It is important to note that James Files had never volunteered to give information on his role in the assassination. The tip from Zack was given to Joe West, who was working on a lawsuit to exhume JFK's body. He wanted to prove that Kennedy was hit from the front and by multiple gunmen and a new and independent autopsy would prove sure as hell that the first was a total fraud.

But Joe West never heard a full confession from James Files. Files didn't want to talk. Only if Joe could arrange immunity for him, would Files consider it. During that time Joe had to go into a hospital for heart surgery. The operation itself was a success, but then out of nowhere he went into a coma and never came out of it. With his death, his exhumation suit also died. Files, and others, thinks Joe was murdered by an overdose of wrong medication in order to silence him. He was informed as such by one of his sources. Indeed there are some strange details; the attending doctor is still to be found for example. And just before he went into coma and could not talk anymore, he scribbled a note for his family "Get me out of here, they are trying to kill me!" The official cause of death was Acute Deficiency Respiratory Syndrome. Bob Vernon was later told by a surgeon that this is more or less a standard method to cover-up medical errors, such as an overdose of drugs. Joe's death is one of the main reasons why James Files decided to tell his story to Bob Vernon, who took over from Joe.

A second reason is that Files has turned religious. An element of clearing his conscience also plays a role. In addition, he feels it was not his idea to put his name before the public. He says it was the FBI (Zack Shelton) and he was convinced the FBI would want the truth kept covered-up. Indeed J. Edgar Hoover had done his best. To James Files, the FBI is one big bad organization. What he does not understand, is that mostly honorable people work for the FBI and the cover-up was controlled from the top. Zack Shelton and his colleagues feel betrayed their own former boss covered-up such a big crime, while they were thinking they were doing the greatest thing in the world.

Another reason is that both Files and Bob Vernon had received clear threats to stop with all of this. Those threats came from organized crime as well as the government. To name just a few examples: Vernon claims he was shot at from a car and Files received a message from a mob lawyer to "keep quiet and lay down by your doggy bowl." Vernon's proposal to Files was then: "If they want to take us out, let's leave them something for history!" Files stared in silence through the window for a minute, according to Vernon the longest minute of his life. Finally Files turned around and said: "Ok, bring in the cameras tomorrow!"

A final reason is that James Files is convinced he will never be tried for the assassination of JFK. A trial would expose the government's involvement. He knows the powers behind it and they have too much to lose. To learn more about how it all evolved, read or hear the interview with Zack Shelton click here.

Image: Zack before losing his innocence

James Files implicates two accomplices in the murder: Johnny Roselli and Charles Nicoletti, both known dual operatives for the CIA and Mafia boss Sam Giancana of Chicago. Although James Files does not know how Roselli and Nicoletti arrived in Dallas, two other independent witnesses have furnished first-hand information as to how they transported Roselli and Nicoletti into Dallas on the morning of November 22, 1963. Tosh Plumlee, a CIA contract pilot, flew Roselli to Dallas on a CIA-supported flight originating in Florida. Chauncey Marvin Holt, deceased in 1997, was a CIA operative and a mob asset for crime-bosses Meyer Lansky and Peter Licavoli. Chauncey Holt has testified that he was one of the infamous three tramps, but also that he drove with Charles Nicoletti to Dallas from the Grace Ranch in Arizona, which was owned by Peter Licavoli, the Mafia boss of Cleveland. Moreover, when the Chauncey Holt story was published there was NO mention about Charles Nicoletti. The reporter who wrote it didn't think it was important enough to print it, although Chauncey Holt had told her. When Bob Vernon contacted Chauncey Holt, he learned that Nicoletti had been one of his passengers. This was AFTER Files had made his confession. This means that Files could not have learned from the Chauncey Holt publication that Nicoletti was in Dallas on november 22, 1963. It is clear that his source is his own memory. And Chauncey Holt corroborates that, as does Tosh Plumlee for Johnny Roselli. Chauncey Holt, Tosh Plumlee and James Files did not know each other, yet they give the same and independent information about the same people. This cannot be coincidence nor can it be a scam.

James Files also claims to know the man who killed officer J.D. Tippit, some 45 minutes after JFK was killed. A picture of this man is available on this website. To view it click here. Files has refused to disclose the identity of this man as the man is still alive. However, it seems unlikely that the man or his friends and family have not been made aware of the confession of James Files and have completely missed the picture. Up to this date, they have not come forward to deny the allegation, which would seem logical if the story were not true. It should be noted that it was never Files' intention that this picture would be publicized.

Some sceptics claim that if Files is telling the truth, he would have been killed. This is baloney. First of all, three failed attempts have been made on his life. They just weren't successful. Read about it here. But furthermore it is simply a myth that all those involved are dead or have been killed. In fact, enough persons with involvement or knowledge of the assassination are alive and could still be questioned. They are just not being looked at by the authorities. Examples include Charles Harrelson (another "tramp"), Orlando Bosch, Luis Posada Carriles, Guillermo Novo Sampol (Operation 40 members/CIA assets placed by witnesses in Dallas on 11/22/1963), Gerald Ford (altered crucial medical evidence), E. Howard Hunt and more. The lack of effort to question these people is illustrative for the willingness to solve the case.

All critics who attack James Files, at least agree that he is a "good liar". But it is claimed there are too many implausibilities in his account, for example the last-minute request to be the backup shooter for Nicoletti, as well as biting the shell casing. My question is: Why does a good liar invent a story with implausibilities? A liar inventing a hoax story, wants to be believed. Why then make your story implausible? And how did Files manage to have the shell casing found, seven years before his involuntary confession? These critics also ignore that if Files is a hoax, Tosh Plumlee, Joe Granata and Chauncey Holt are all endorsing the hoax.

James Files says he left the shell casing from the bullet that he fired at John F. Kennedy in Dealey Plaza. He put it on top of the picket fence on the grassy knoll, after he had bitten down on the shell casing, because he liked the taste of gun powder. This shell casing was found in

1987 by garden service man John Rademacher at some distance from the spot where Files said he left it. The casing was in the ground some 5 inches deep, consistent with a deposit of 24 years ago. The .222 casing was manufactured before 1971, as could be determined from the headstamp. The local press gave only very scant coverage on Rademacher's discovery and NO mention was made of any marks on the shell casing. It is very unlikely that James Files could have known of this discovery, but there is certainly no way he could have known about the indents on the shell casing. Even Rademacher was guessing what they could be, he thought they were "ejection marks". No one had thought about dentmarks until James Files came forward with this information. He said: "If the casing is mine, you can recognize it for my teethmarks are on it. The end will be oval, not round." It was then verified by a number of independent dentists (among others, a professor in orthodontology Paul Stimpson) that the marks were indeed made by human teeth. When Mr. Stimpson was asked to examine the casing he was not aware of a connection with the Kennedy assassination. All he was told was that is was used in a murder. James Files could not have known these marks were dentmarks, unless he put them there himself or heard it from someone that put them in the casing. However, it is simply unlikely that any other assassin would have been so unprofessional to leave this incriminating evidence on the scene of the crime. James Files, at that time only 21 years of age, said he felt "cocky" about his deed. He now recognizes that he should never have done that. The shell casing is therefore a crucial piece of physical evidence for his credibility. To learn more about the shell casing click here.

Recently another person was found who corroborates James Files. Zack Shelton was given a name by fellow FBI agent Jack O' Rourke. The name was Joe Granata, a Mafia member, who used to run with Charles Nicoletti. Granata has been a credible witness for the government. Apparently he is so valuable that he was put in the witness protection program. His testimony has helped send several people to prison. Joe Granata has never given unreliable information. He told Zack that Nicoletti had told him on two occasions that Nicoletti, Roselli, Marshall Caifano and Jimmy Sutton, were the "hit team on Dealey Plaza." Although James Files says he knows nothing about Marshall Caifano being on Dealey Plaza, his name was James Sutton at the time. To learn more about Granata and his reliability as a source click here.

James Files said that he was aiming for Kennedy's eye but missed and "came in on the left side of the temple." He says this was because Kennedy was hit in the back of his head by another bullet from behind at almost the same time, and that bullet pushed the head forward. Even the best Kennedy researchers have not noticed such a movement, yet this is EXACTLY what we see on the Zapruder film. To learn more about the simultaneous headshots click here.

Image: Three frames of the Zapruder film show the head going forward first

How does the available evidence coincide with James Files? Well, there is the testimony of Lee Bowers, who was the operator of the railroad tower with a clear view behind the picket fence. James Files says he wore a plaid poplin jacket. Lee Bowers described a young man with such a coat:

Mr. BOWERS. Directly in line, towards the mouth of the underpass, there were two men. One man, middle-aged, or slightly older, fairly heavy-set, in a white shirt, fairly dark trousers. Another younger man, about midtwenties, in either a plaid shirt or plaid coat or jacket.

Mr. BALL.. Were they standing together or standing separately?

Mr. BOWERS. They were standing within 10 or 15 feet of each other, and gave no appearance of being together, as far as I knew.

Lee Bowers also described three cars that drove into the parking lot behind the picket fence. One of these cars fits the description of the Oldsmobile stationwagon that Chauncey Holt and Charles Nicoletti had driven from Arizona:

Mr. BALL. What was the description of that car?

Mr. BOWERS. The first car was a 1959 Oldsmobile, blue and white station wagon with out-of-State license.

Mr. BALL. Do you know what State?

Mr. BOWERS. No; I do not. I would know it, I could identify it, I think, if I looked at a list.

Mr. BALL. And, it had something else, some bumper stickers?

Mr. BOWERS. Had a bumper sticker, one of which was a Goldwater sticker, and the other of which was of some scenic location, I think.

Note that Chauncey Holt and Charles Nicoletti had driven the car from Arizona and that Barry Goldwater, a senator from that state, was running for President. By the way, it is remarkable that Mr. Ball asks that question about the bumper sticker since Mr. Ball was one of Holt's CIA handlers.

Lee Bowers was also one of many witnesses that heard the last two shots very close together or almost simultaneously. As did Seymour Weitzman:

Joe Ball: How many shots did you hear?

Seymour Weitzman: Three distinct shots.

Joe Ball: How were they spaced?

Seymour Weitzman: First one, then the second two seemed to be simultaneously.

This is exactly what Files said: His shot hit JFK in the head at the same time as a shot from the back.

James Files also said there were two men in business suits in his vicinity, who later stopped bystanders by posing as Secret Service agents.

The two businessmen that Files mentions were between him and the motorcade and he was somewhat concerned about them. The photographical evidence that is available at the time of the assassination, does not show men in business suits on the grassy knoll. But it is of course very likely that these men were there before the assassination took place and that they sought a better place to stay out of sight at the time of the shots. As the motorcade was arriving James Files was not paying attention anymore to what happened around him as he was keeping Kennedy in the scope of his weapon. Several witnesses, for example Gordon Arnold and police officers Joe Smith and Seymour Weitzman, have testified they were turned back by men on the grassy knoll, showing Secret Service credentials. Official Secret Service records show that no agents were assigned on Dealey Plaza or the grassy knoll.

A very unknown witness who did not appear for the Warren Commission, was Charles Blankenship. His story was recently uncovered by researcher Michael Parks:

Michael Parks recently came across evidence of even another witness to the knoll agent. He relayed this to from Mrs. Charles Blankenship: Her husband, Charles "Charlie" Blankenship was with the DPS office from another county other than Dallas. She recalled him working out of the Fort Worth office but was not sure. He was off duty on 11/22/63 but had come to Dallas to see the president with other officers stationed in Dallas. He was standing on the east side of Houston Street in front of the Records Building. He heard the shooting and, like many other lawmen, ran to where he felt the shots had originated, this being the knoll area. He supposedly encountered *two men in suits that stated they were Secret Service agents.* They told him he could go no further and he turned and left Dealey Plaza. He was not interviewed by any agency and kept this story to his immediate family until his death. It was known that he had a relative on the Dallas Police force. Source:
http://www.jfklancer.com/knollagent/knollagent.html

There is also evidence that seems to conflict with the account of James Files. This is the story of Ed Hoffman, a deaf mute man, who was ignored by the FBI, but claims to have seen a man in a suit firing a gun from behind the picket fence. This man then tossed the gun to another man, who disassembled the rifle and put it in a briefcase. This other man was dressed as railroad worker and walked away with the briefcase in the direction of the railroad yard. James Files says that he was alone behind the picket fence. However, I tend to see Ed Hoffman as credible, although he is a single and thus uncorroborated source. If we assume Hoffman's account is true, and since there is evidence of more than one shot from the front, for example the wound in Kennedy's throat, it is not inconceivable that Files, concentrated as he was on the target, may have missed another shooter behind the fence and closer to the underpass. This man could have appeared at the last moment. He could have been hiding behind or in one of the cars behind the picket fence. It could well have been one of the men in suits, posing as Secret Service agents.

The critics of James Files claim that he is just a convict with "too much time on his hands" and that he must have read many books on the assassination to invent his story, which would be designed to get fame and attention. This claim can be discounted for many reasons:

1) Files has given his video confession only once in 1994. He had vouched he would never do it again. Indeed, I have worked for almost a year to get him to agree to a second and final interview. I had already given up until he finally consented for a specific reason that has nothing to do with getting attention.

2) Files has met with Oliver Stone three times and he told us (Jim Marrs and me) this:

JF - We wasn't aware of the water situation until Oliver Stone comes along to make a movie here. And when he made his movie here, we see all these people from the movie company running around carrying bottles of water. Even the officers that worked here, they got suspicious and that's when we started finding out: this water is unhealthy.

Wim - Did you actually meet Oliver Stone?

JF - I met Oliver Stone three times. As a matter of fact I have a paper that Joe West ... no excuse me, not Joe West but Bob Vernon, had Oliver Stone sign. Now Bob Vernon had come in after the Joe West deal. Bob Vernon took over for Joe West. Bob Vernon met with Oliver Stone and he had him sign an agreement where they wanted to get me on film, but I refused to do that. I met with Oliver Stone three times.

Jim - And you never told him your story?

JF - No, I did not tell Oliver Stone my story. I refused to discuss it with him and uh ...like I say, I 've got a copy, It's got Oliver Stone's signature on it, Bob Vernon's, the only signature that states what it's all about, the only thing missing is my signature because I would never sign that paper for the agreement.

Jim - Why was that?

JF - I didn't like the man!

Jim - Case closed!

JF - Case closed! And if you'd like I would be more than happy to send you a copy of the document. And it has got Oliver Stone's original signature on it. And it has Bob Vernon's signature on it.

Well, I guess that answers the critics who say that Files is just a convict trying to get attention. I mean, if you want attention, you want to talk to Oliver Stone, who was the director of the blockbuster movie JFK.

3) Tony Godinez is the former warden of Stateville Correctional Center. He has interviewed James Files more often than anyone else. He has testified that he never saw a book about JFK in the cell of James Files.

4) I found out first hand that James Files is not well read on the JFK assassination, just like he says. The day before the camera interview., I talked with him on an extended visit for four hours. We covered many subjects, one of them was Chauncey Holt and the three tramps. James Files started telling me that in his view the three men were not professionals. I asked him why? He then said that they did not know "how to improvise", and that they were stupid to get themselves arrested by the cops, because in a situation like that "you just have to shoot the cops". I explained to him that this would have been difficult since they were found in a closed boxcar and that they had been instructed by their superiors to hide in that boxcar, which would make their exit. I also told him that they were not arrested, because they identified themselves as undercover agents, and they were escorted to the Sheriff's office for a short hearing. Files then conceded and he said he did not know that, adding that I knew a lot more about the assassination than he did.

It is clear to me that the short and sweet "investigation" of James Files by the FBI was designed to discredit his information, rather than to get to the bottom of it. James Files was interviewed by two FBI agents eight months BEFORE his videotaped confession. The transcript of this interview can be found by clicking here.

Note how the interview starts out:

Agents further told FILES that IRVIN had provided information to the FBI that indicated he (FILES) had personal knowledge concerning the assassination of JOHN F. KENNEDY (JFK). Agents then told FILES that a review of his (FILES') information as provided by IRVIN determined that his (FILES') recollections were in significant contradiction to the WARREN COMMISSION report. Agents told FILES That the findings of the WARREN COMMISSION report had been accepted by the government as an accurate factual account of the JFK assassination.

Agents then told FILES that Agents further understood from IRVIN that he (FILES) was cognizant of his contradictions with the WARREN COMMISSION findings and that he (FILES) wanted to make available the "true story" of the JFK assassination out of respect to the deceased JOE WEST. Agents told FILES that in view of his obvious conflicts with the WARREN COMMISSION findings, he would unlikely be afforded subsequent opportunities for interview by the FBI or the U.S. Attorney in regard to the JFK assassination unless he established his credibility with the government. FILES was told that credibility could sometimes be established through corroboration of facts furnished by an individual during an interview. Agents told FILES that the purpose of the interview was to obtain additional information from him in an effort to establish him as a credible person rather than to build a murder case on him. FILES was told that the JFK assassination took place almost 30 years ago and it would take extraordinary corroboration to make recollections credible in view of the WARREN COMMISSION findings.

Basically, what the FBI agents say here to James Files: "We have a problem with your story because it contradicts the Warren Commission" !! This is before they even begin discussing any substance of the information ! Only an uninformed 10 % of the American people still accept the clearly ludicrous and demonstrably false conclusions of the Warren Report. Its conclusions were also easily refuted in a less publicized government investigation in 1977/78. The House Select Committee on Assassinations, DID conclude that JFK was killed as a result of a conspiracy which included more than one gunman.

Further on in the transcript we read this:

Agents asked FILES to name persons who could verify his relationship with NICOLETTI. FILES named JERRY ESPOSITO, COSMO IASCO, DOMINICK CIMINO, RONNIE BELL, RUPI REGO, KENNY LARRY, STEVE ANSELMO, JOE BUA and MARSHAL CAIFANO as some of the individuals who could verify his relationship with NICOLETTI.

Please let us make sure we understand this: The agents ask Files for corroboration of his association with Nicoletti. Files gives them a flurry of names, almost a dozen. He could have named many more, like Zack Shelton for one. Moreover, what the average reader does not know is that at least half of these individuals were POLICE OFFICERS! In addition, all of these people would confirm that Files was a mafia hitman.

Why did the FBI not check with ANY of these persons named by James Files? Some of them are still alive even now! Instead the FBI declared him "non-credible".

As for the willingness to check evidence not pointing to Oswald, it appears that little has changed within the FBI since Mr. Hoover "solved" the case on the day of the assassination, when he wrote "Not necessary to cover as true subject located". To see the document click here.

Everything that James Files has said and was checkable, proved to be true. Even the smallest details that have nothing to do with JFK. I'll give an example here. In the last interview on 11/19/2003 James Files told me this:

"I'm not saying there is other shooters, what I am saying is this: I have no need to know of everybody that is involved in an operation. What purpose would that serve? That's like me going into a communist country on a covert operation and me knowing everybody, all the other agents that are there in that field working. And if I get captured, they all get executed! So the same thing goes when it comes down to crime. You try to keep your people the least bit to know as possible. Because too many times, maybe partners, and that's like ... I can use one deal, one party back east out of Philadelphia, I did time with him in the federal prison. His own brother gave him up. His brother knew that he was a big time cocaine dealer, he was a dentist. They called him Dr. Snow. I don't remember his real name, but they called him Dr. Snow. His brother got busted on a nickel bag of weed in New York. He gave his own brother up because he couldn't do a year in the jail. His brother told him:! I'll give you a million dollars a year. For every year they keep you in jail, I give you a million dollars cash. Don't testify against me! He put his brother in jail."

Since James Files did not remember the name of "Dr Snow", I did a check on Google for "dentist" and "Dr. Snow" and I quickly saw that Dr. Snow is Larry Lavin. Two books have been written about the case. So I emailed one of the authors Carol Saline with the following results:

From: info@jfkmurdersolved.com

Sent: Wednesday, February 25, 2004 7:47 AM

To: csaline@ ....

Subject: Larry Lavin aka Dr. Snow

Hello,

Do you know if Larry Lavin is still alive? If so, can you contact him? Is he in prison? Is it true that he was given up by his own brother?

Thanks for getting back,

Wim Dankbaar

(Netherlands)

From: "Carol Saline"

To: info@jfkmurdersolved.com

Sent: Monday, March 01, 2004 9:37 PM

Subject: RE: Larry Lavin aka Dr. Snow

Larry is very much alive. We speak and write regularly. He is still in prison and will be released next January. Yes it's true that his brother was instrumental in his capture. Have you read my book Dr. Snow. It's all in there. You can buy it, including a update with larry's parole hearing which I covered, from buybooksontheweb.com.

****

Another detail described by Files is Nicoletti's car:

Jim Marrs – Okay, so now you got .... Describe the car!

James Files – The car was a '63 Chevy two door Burgundy. Chevy Impala.

Jim Marrs – With the special compartment?

James Files - Oh yeah, we had a special compartment in the dash, we had the backseat, you could take that off, pull the bottom part up, raise the back up, snap it up little clams and take that out. We had the springs removed behind the seat there by it and we had little racks welded in there so we could mount weapons in there.

I found this fragment here from an article written by an organised crime expert:

"By the late 1950's, Nicoletti had a feared reputation as a hitman and was one of the usual suspects brought in for questioning whenever cops thought they had a gangland-style-slaying on their hands. In 1962, he was arrested while driving a so-called "work" car, *specially equipped with hidden compartments for guns,* rear lights that turned off, a souped up engine, special reinforcement on both sides, bullet proof glass and a rotating rear license plate. It was no surprise the next day when a mob associate was found slain near where Nicoletti had been detained." Source: http://www.ganglandnews.com/column80.htm

James Files says that his CIA supervisor, who also recruited him, was David Atlee Phillips. David Atlee Phillips is a man whose name is well known to assassination researchers. He was called to testify for the House Select Committee on Assassinations in the 1970's. Several members of the committee wanted to call him again for they believed he had not told the truth and committed perjury.

Phillips was traced as a suspect as a result of the testimony of Cuban exile leader Antonio Veciana, a friend of Files, who knew his CIA case officer only under the alias of "Maurice Bishop". A composite sketch, based on the recollections of Veciana prompted US senator Schweiker to recognize David Atlee Phillips. A confrontation between Veciana and Phillips was arranged but Veciana, apparently fearing for his safety, refused to identify Phillips as his former case officer, but later acknowledged privately that Phillips was indeed his CIA controller.

The following is known of David Atlee Phillips by now: He was one of the masterminds for the CIA staged coup by Pinochet in 1973, as well as the overthrow in 1954 of the Guatemala regime headed by Jacobo Arbenz. He was working closely with CIA officer E. Howard Hunt, another suspect in the plot to kill JFK and the leader of the infamous Watergate burglar team. In the 1950's and 1960's, Phillips was the CIA case officer for the anti Castro Cubans in Havana and Mexico City. The star of David Atlee Phillips rose to CIA director of Special Operations for the Western Hemisphere.

David Atlee Phillips died of cancer on 7th July, 1988. He left behind an unpublished manuscript. The novel is about a CIA officer who lived in Mexico City. In the novel the character states: "I was one of those officers who handled Lee Harvey Oswald... We gave him the mission of killing Fidel Castro in Cuba... I don't know why he killed Kennedy. But I do know he used precisely the plan we had devised against Castro. Thus the CIA did not anticipate the president's assassination, but it was responsible for it. I share that guilt."

According to his nephew Shawn Phillips, who is quite a famous musician, David Atlee Phillips confirmed to his brother James Atlee Phillips that he was in Dallas the day Kennedy died. To read Shawn's email: click here.

Last but not least, in 1995 a nationwide NBC program on the confession of James Files, was cancelled after obvious CIA interference and this was done with PROVABLE lies. To read the details on that story click here.

Reprint from http://jfkmurdersolved.com/filestruth.htm

The Warren (C)om(m)ission

On these pages we will show beyond any doubt that the Warren Commission was a fraud designed to cover up the crime by the people that had most to gain from hiding the truth from the American public and the rest of the world.

The Warren Commission can be exposed as a fraud on many accounts, and in no way do we aim to be exhaustive here, but let us start with the excellent analysis of Professor James Fetzer as outlined in his book "Murder on Dealey Plaza", which can also be found here

The official account of the crime , known as *The Warren Report* after Earl Warren, Chief Justice of the United States, held that JFK was killed by a lone, demented assassin named Lee Harvey Oswald, who fired three shots with a high-velocity rifle from a sixth floor window of the nearby Texas School Book Depository, scoring two hits and one miss, which struck a distant concrete curb, and slightly injured by-stander James Tague.

Image: The Warren Commission

The presumptive shots that hit , however, wreaked considerable damage. The first is alleged to have entered the President's back at the base of his neck, traversed his neck without impacting any bony structure, exited his throat at the level of his tie, entered the back of Texas Governor John Connally (riding in a jump seat in front of him), shattering a rib, exiting his chest, impacting his right wrist, and deflecting into his left thigh.

The bullet supposed to have performed these remarkable feats is alleged to have been recovered virtually undamaged from a stretcher at Parkland Hospital, where both men were rushed for treatment, and has come to be known as "the magic bullet". The other struck JFK in the back of his head and killed him.

For the official government account of the death of JFK to be true, the following three hypotheses have to be true:

H1 - JFK was hit at the base of the back of his neck by a bullet that traversed his neck without hitting any bony structures and exited his throat at the level of his tie.

H2 - JFK was hit in the back of his head by a bullet fired from the sixth floor of the Texas School Book Depository, as its diagrams display, causing his death.

H3 - These bullets were fired by a sole assassin, Lee Harvey Oswald, using a high-powered rifle, which was identified as a 6.5 mm Italian Mannlicher Carcano.

As a point of deductive logic, if any of these hypotheses is false, then any account that entails from them cannot be true. Yet it is surprisingly easy to show that all three are false.

H1 is an anatomical impossibility, because the bullet would have had to impact bony structures. David W. Mantik, M.D., Ph.D., who holds a Ph.D. in physics and is also board-certified in radio oncology, has studied X-Rays of the President's chest. He has used the cross-section of a body whose upper chest and neck dimensions were the same of those of JFK and performed a simple experiment. Taking the specific locations specified by the HSCA for the point of entry at the base of the back of the neck and the point of exit at the throat, he has drawn a straight line to represent the trajectory that the bullet would have to have taken from that point of entry to that point of exit. Any such trajectory would intersect cervical vertebrae. Here is a visual CAT scan of such a trajectory:

In addition, the backwound was probed by Dr. Humes during the autopsy in Bethesda. It was determined it was only a shallow wound with no exit. This is all in the evidence of the Warren Report. Hence it is simply a lie that the bullet traversed the neck and exited at the throat. This is from the notes of FBI agent James W. Sibert, who was present at the autopsy:

"During the last stages of this autopsy Dr. Humes located an opening which appeared to be a bullet hole, which was below the shoulders and two inches to the right of the middle line of the spinal column."

(That happens to be five and a half inches below the neck line, not the location the Warren Report indicated)

"This opening was probed by Dr Humes with a finger, at which time it was determined that the trajectory of the missile entered at this point and entered in a downward position of 55 to 60 degrees. Further probing determined that the distance traveled by this missile was a SHORT distance, in as much that the end of the opening could be felt with a finger. In as much that no complete bullet of any size could be located in the brain area, and likewise no bullet could be located in the back or any other area of the body, as determined by total-body X-rays and inspection revealing that there was no point of exit. The individuals performing the autopsy were at a loss to explaining why they could not find no bullets."

H2 is the hypothesis that a bullet fired from the sixth floor of Texas School Book Depository entered the back of JFK's head and killed him. The building in question was horizontally located to the President's rear, while the sixth floor of that building was considerably above the President. Therefore, any such bullet must have entered the President's head from above and behind. That much is indisputable. No photographs of the President's injuries were published at the time, but *The Warren Report* did provide drawings. The drawings of the head wound therefore show a trajectory from above and behind, as the official account requires. Stewart Galanor, author of Cover-Up, however, has juxtaposed the official drawing with frame 312 of the Zapruder film, which the Warren Commission itself regarded as the moment before the fatal headshot occurring at frame 313:

When the President's head is properly positioned, the Commission's own drawing displays an upward rather than a downward trajectory. If the official drawing of the injury is correct, then the conjecture that the President was hit from above and behind cannot be true. And if the President was hit from above and behind, the official drawing must be false. Hypothesis H2 cannot possibly true. To learn more about the head wounds click here or here

Hypothesis H3 finally, maintains that three bullets were fired by Lee Harvey Oswald using a high-powered rifle, which the Warren Commission also identified as a 6.5 mm Mannlicher-Carcano. As many other authors have also observed, the Mannlicher-Carcano that Oswald is supposed to have used, is a 6.5 mm weapon, but it is NOT high velocity. Its muzzle velocity of approximately 2000 feet per second means that it qualifies as a medium-to-low velocity weapon.

The death certificates, The Warren Report, articles in the Journal of the AMA, and other sources state that the President was killed by wounds inflicted by high-velocity missiles. But the Mannlicher-Carcano is not a high-velocity weapon. Consequently, Lee Harvey Oswald could not have fired the bullets that killed the President. Thus hypothesis H3 cannot be true. This discovery is especially important, because the extensive damage sustained by JFK's skull and brain could not possibly have been inflicted by a weapon of this kind. The major trauma the President endured had to have been inflicted by one or more high velocity weapons.

The hypotheses H1, H2 and H3, therefore, are not only false but are provably false. If any or all of these hypotheses are false, then the Warren Report cannot be salvaged, even in spite of the best efforts of the Gerald Posners and ABC's of the world. Among the central findings of the Warren Commission therefore, the only one that appears to be true is the least important, namely that bystander James Tague was hit by debris from a bullet that missed its target, struck a distant curb instead and caused him minor injury. Visit the website of James Tague here

Now let us add a fourth hypothesis H4 which HAS to be true to accept the official account:

H4 - Lee Harvey Oswald fired a total of THREE bullets.

Unfortunately for the Commission, not more than three bullets could have been fired, for it was determined from the Zapruder film and the time needed to reload the Carcano bolt-action rifle, that Oswald could not have fired more than three shots in the 6 seconds from the first shot to the final headshot. For its conclusion, the Commission contended that three spent shell casings were found under the window of the sixth floor of the School Book Depository.

Again, it is surprisingly simple to demolish this conclusion, based on the Commission's own evidence, for the original FBI receipt of the shell casings showed only TWO spent casings and ONE live round. Hence, not more than two bullets could have been fired from that window.

These documents prove again that only TWO shell casings and ONE LIVE round were obtained. The Warren Commission changed the number of spent casings to three and left out the live round.

It is also important to note that Specter invented the single bullet theory ONLY AFTER the Warren Commission could no longer ignore the testimony of James Tague. Before that, they had three hits (Kennedy back, Kennedy head and Connally). Now, the logical and responsible investigative approach when you have to account for an extra miss and explain all those wounds with just two bullets, is to go and look for more shots and thus more gunmen. Instead they desperately clung to their "lone nut" and concocted the pristine magic bullet, accounting for all wounds of BOTH JFK and Connally. In addition, It can now be proven they LIED and TAMPERED to pull it off. See the interview with James Sibert (Realplayer required) Click here.

Reprint from http://jfkmurdersolved.com/warren.htm

The Headshots

Note that JFK's head moves forward first. This is just a fraction of a second from the impact of a bullet that hits JFK in the back of the head. Then the head moves violently back and to the left from the impact of another bullet from the front in the right temple.

From the confession of James Files: "When I got to the point where I thought it would be the last field of fire, I had zeroed in to the left side of the head there that I had because if I wait any longer then Jacqueline Kennedy would have been in the line of fire and I had been instructed for nothing to happen to her and at that moment I figured this is my last chance for a shot and he had still not been hit in the head. So, as I fired that round, Mr. Nicoletti and I fired approximately at the same time as the head started forward then it went backward. I would have to say that his shell struck approximately 1000th of a second ahead of mine maybe but that what's started pushing the head forward which caused me to miss from the left eye and I came in on the left side of the temple."

Shortly after the assassination press secretary for the White House Malcolm Kilduff points at his right temple to indicate the frontal headshot.

Houston Chronicle coverage,

Published Nov. 22, 1963:

Dr. Kemp Clark, neurosurgeon, said:

"I was called because the President had sustained a brain injury."

"It was apparent the President had sustained a lethal wound," Dr. Clark said.

"A missile had gone in and out of the back of his head, causing extensive lacerations and loss of brain tissue. Shortly after I arrived, the President's heart stopped. We attempted resuscitation, initiating closed chest heart massage, but to no avail.

"We were able to obtain a palpable pulse by this method but again to no avail.

President Kennedy died on the emergency table after 20 minutes.

To view more accounts of witnesses who saw the location of the headwound Click here.

The debris exiting from the back of JFK's head is traveling too fast to be captured in the 18 frame per second Zapruder film. But in a frame of the Nix film you can clearly see how the back of his head is blown out.

For those who wonder about the debris pattern at the right front of JFK's head, the pictures hereunder illustrate how the debris patterns behave at the impact of a bullet.

With thanks to Ian Kerr and Bill Miller for providing these pictures.

See also this video clip (Quicktime) of Lee Bowers Click here.

Mark Lane: Mr Bowers, how many shots did you hear?

Lee Bowers: There were three shots and these were spaced with one shot, then a pause and then two shots in very close order, such as perhaps (knocking on table) knock ..... knock-knock. Almost on top of each other, while there was some pause between the first and the second shots.

Lane: Did you tell that to the Dallas Police?

Bowers: Yes, I told this to the police and then also told it to the FBI, and also I had a discussion two or three days later with them concerning this, and they made no comment other than the fact that when stated that I felt like the third and the second and third shot could not have been fired from the same rifle, they reminded me that I was not an expert. And I had to agree (Bowers smiles sourly).

(Lee Bowers died in 1966 in a mysterious car crash without witnesses on a lone Texas country road)

See also this video clip (Quicktime) analyzing the headshots Click here.

See also this video clip (Windows media) of Dealey Plaza witness Bill Newman Click here.

Reprint of: http://jfkmurdersolved.com/headshot.htm

The Autopsy Pictures

How do the top two photographs match with the two at the bottom?

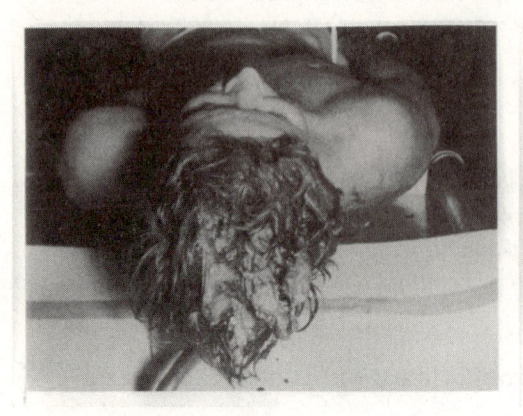

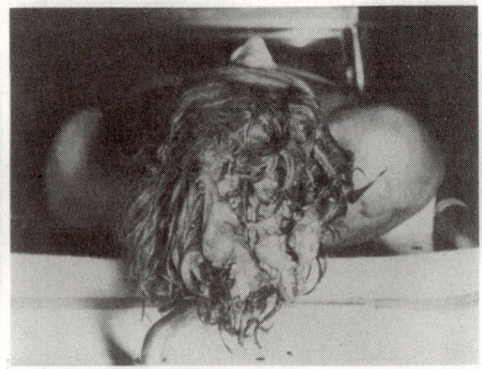

These two pictures are genuine. The damage to the top and back of Kennedy's head can clearly be seen. Blood and brainmatter are plainly visible. Even the curls that are so typical for the brains, are exposed in these pictures.

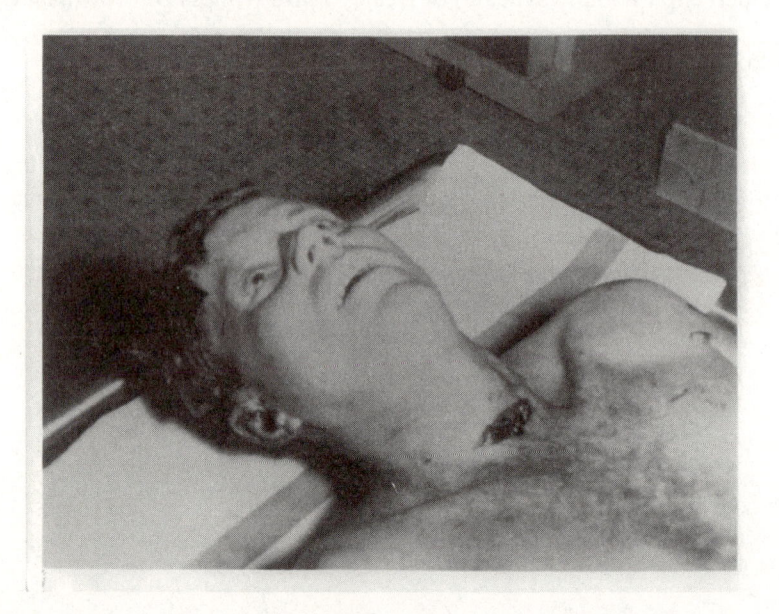

Virtually all the doctors at Parkland Hospital validated the throatwound as an entry wound from a bullet. It was described as a neat little hole of entrance. If the wound in this picture is - like the Warren Commission told us - the result of the tracheotomy, performed in Parkland Hospital by Dr. Malcolm Perry, who was an excellent doctor, then his "incision" would have done the job of killing JFK. Even your local butcher would have been ashamed of this. How could the American public ever accept this nonsense? The alternative explanation that someone tampered with this wound between Dallas and Bethesda, either to remove a bullet or give it the appearance of an exit wound, is therefore valid to consider.

Dr. Charles Crenshaw, surgeon at Parkland Hospital: *As I was cutting off his trousers around his waist, I was on the right side, there was a small entrance wound, about 4 to 8 millimeters in size. Clearly an entrance wound in the lower third of the neck, below the adam's apple in the throat. Dr. Carrico had put in the tracheotomy tube to try to assist him with breathing.*

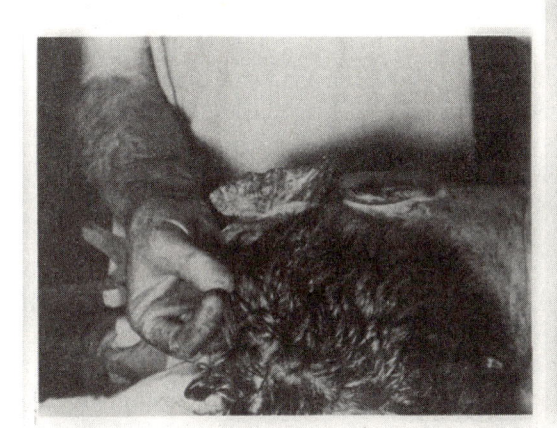

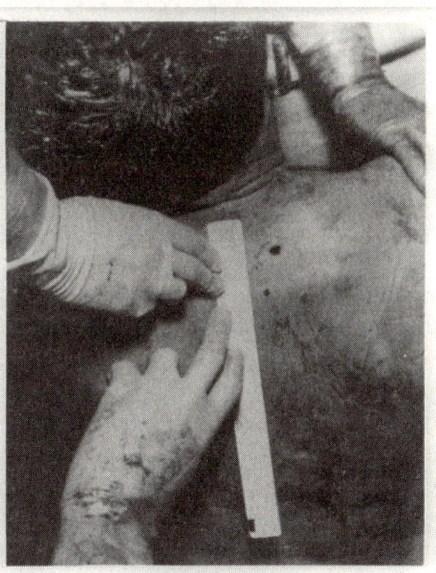

These pictures were the ones "fit" for publication if necessary. How do these pictures match the pictures at the top of the page? What happened to the length of Kennedy's hair? What happened to the damage? Where has all the mess gone? Where is the blood and brain?

Dr. Charles Crenshaw, surgeon at Parkland Hospital: *The headwound was difficult to see when he was laying on the back of his head. However, afterwards when they moved his face towards the left, one could see the large, right rear parietal, occipital, blasted out hole, the size of my fist, which is 2 and a half inches in diameter. The brain, cerebreal portion had been flurred out and also there was the cerebrellum hanging out from that wound. It was clearly an exit wound from the right rear, behind the ear. A right occipital area hole, the size of my fist.*

Doris Nelson, emergency room nurse at Parkland Hospital: *We wrapped him up .... and I saw his whole head ... There was no hair back there ... It was blown away. Some of his head was blown away and his brains were fallen down on the stretcher.*

To view more accounts of witnesses who saw the location of the headwound Click here.

If someone has a better explanation, other than that the pictures of an in-tact head have been faked by the conspirators, please share it with us at info@jfkmurdersolved.com.

See also this video clip (Windows media) of Dealey Plaza witness Bill Newman Click here.

To read an interesting article about the autopsy photographs Click here

Reprint from: http://jfkmurdersolved.com/autopsy.htm

Gerald Ford's motto: Attack is Best Defense

Interview with James W. Sibert

To see it (Realplayer required) Click here.

Special announcement for immediate and unrestricted release:

Gerald Ford, former President and last surviving member of the Warren Commission, has demonstrated his strategy again: Disguise your crimes by attacking the attacker. I am increasingly flabbergasted about what is possible in America. Why is the world and the History Channel swallowing his attack on the documentary "The guilty men"? For those who missed this headline news, it is the last episode of "The men who killed Kennedy" series, aired last November and originally scheduled for re-runs over the next nine years, which makes a case for Lyndon Johnson as a main conspirator in JFK's murder. Ford's coordinated protest with former Johnson cronies like Bill Moyers, Jack Valenti and Johnson's widow, has now even resulted in complete cancellation of all three new episodes, including those which were not attacked, like "The Love Affair" with Judyth Vary Baker, who makes a credible case for having been Lee Harvey Oswald's girlfriend, exonerating him from the Government's THEORY that he was the lone assassin. To my knowledge, this is an unprecedented form of censorship in the United States.

In all the heated discussions and controversy about the History Channel's documentary, whether LBJ had a role in the JFK assassination or not, it seems that one thing is overlooked : In this case, Lyndon Baines Johnson and his next door neighbour and close buddy J. Edgar Hoover are guilty of the assassination of President John F. Kennedy, not because we can prove they ordered it or because we can prove they had any direct connection to the killing, but because we can prove beyond any reasonable doubt that those two men took steps and took actions that covered up the truth of the crime. Washing out and refurbishing the President's limousine is just one of many examples of destroying crucial evidence. This makes them AT LEAST accessories after the fact. And was it not to Bill Moyers that Deputy Attorney General Nicholas Katzenbach sent the infamous memo: "The public should be satisfied that Oswald was the lone assassin"?

But what's more, Ford himself is guilty! Not only was it learned that he was secretly reporting on the Commission to FBI Director Hoover, but also, forced by declassified files, he has admitted that he instructed the Warren Commission to move Kennedy's backwound up by several inches !!! *The significance of this cannot be overstated! For with a wound in the original location, there cannot be a single bullet theory and without a single bullet theory there cannot be a lone gunman.* Last time I looked, this was called "tampering with evidence", which is a federal crime and in such an important case as the death of a president, it is also TREASON. Raised with my naive and Dutch set of values on freedom and democracy, I believe the man should be in jail, despite his rehearsed repetitions that the Commission "found no evidence of a conspiracy, foreign or domestic". Instead, he is allowed to bury essentially good documentaries. What is happening to America?

All three men, Johnson, Hoover AND Ford, took steps that altered, destroyed and hid evidence, ... and this, by the way, is what changes what otherwise would have been a Texas homicide, to a national coup d'etat!

In order to provide a contra-weight to these outrageous proceedings of the on-going cover-up, I have made available for the public the first ever camera-interview with former special FBI agent James W. Sibert. This interview will be part of an upcoming film/documentary "Second Look, FBI agents re-examine the JFK assassination" (wanted: uncontrolled broadcasters). James Sibert, 84 years young, a former World War II hero and B-52 pilot, 21 year career FBI agent and American patriot, was present at Kennedy's autopsy in Bethesda. Like every other retired FBI agent featured in Second Look, he is also PISSED with his government for covering up such a major crime.

See and hear what he has to say about Gerald Ford and senator Arlen Specter, architect of the notorious single bullet theory that was (and still is) pushed down our throat.

Right here: http://www.jfkmurdersolved.com/sibert.htm

This is age of the Internet, the new revolutionary and independent medium that can spread the truth. Recent studies show that the web has surpassed conventional media as a news source. If you share my amazement, SPREAD THIS! Email to friends and/or your favorite news-outlets. This message is also posted there, thus forwarding the link is enough. The videoclip may be downloaded and used for any website.

Signed,

Wim Dankbaar (Netherlands)

"During times of universal deceit, telling the truth becomes a revolutionary act."

George Orwell

Mr. Ford said today that the change was intended to clarify meaning, not alter history. "My changes were only an attempt to be more precise."

How dumb does he take us for?

Image: Note bullet hole lower down on back. That hole is nowhere near where JFK's neck was. It was in his back.

Image: Photo of JFK's suit coat, showing that the bullet hole in the shirt and suit coat line up, discrediting the Warren Commmsion claim that the shirt had "bunched up" around JFK's neck when the bullet hit.

By MIKE FEINSILBER

The Associated Press

WASHINGTON (July 2) - Thirty-three years ago, Gerald R. Ford took pen in hand and changed - ever so slightly - the Warren Commission's key sentence on the place where a bullet entered John F. Kennedy's body when he was killed in Dallas.

The effect of Ford's change was to strengthen the commission's conclusion that a single bullet passed through Kennedy and severely wounded Texas Gov. John Connally - a crucial element in its finding that Lee Harvey Oswald was the sole gunman.

A small change, said Ford on Wednesday when it came to light, one intended to clarify meaning, not alter history.

"My changes had nothing to do with a conspiracy theory," he said in a telephone interview from Beaver Creek, Colo. "My changes were only an attempt to be more precise."

But still, his editing was seized upon by members of the conspiracy community, which rejects the commission's conclusion that Oswald acted alone.

"This is the most significant lie in the whole Warren Commission report," said Robert D. Morningstar, a computer systems specialist in New York City who said he has studied the assassination since it occurred and written an Internet book about it.

The effect of Ford's editing, Morningstar said, was to suggest that a bullet struck Kennedy in the neck, "raising the wound two or three inches. Without that alteration, they could never have hoodwinked the public as to the true number of assassins."

If the bullet had hit Kennedy in the back, it could not have struck Connolly in the way the commission said it did, he said.

The Warren Commission concluded in 1964 that a single bullet - fired by a "discontented" Oswald - passed through Kennedy's body and wounded his fellow motorcade passenger, Connally, and that a second, fatal bullet, fired from the same place, tore through Kennedy's head.

The assassination of the president occurred Nov. 22, 1963, in Dallas; Oswald was arrested that day but was shot and killed two days later as he was being transferred from the city jail to the county jail.

Conspiracy theorists reject the idea that a single bullet could have hit both Kennedy and Connally and done such damage. Thus they argue that a second gunman must have been involved.

Ford's changes tend to support the single-bullet theory by making a specific point that the bullet entered Kennedy's body "at the back of his neck" rather than in his uppermost back, as the commission staff originally wrote.

Ford's handwritten notes were contained in 40,000 pages of records kept by J. Lee Rankin, chief counsel of the Warren Commission.

They were made public Wednesday by the Assassination Record Review Board, an agency created by Congress to amass all relevant evidence in the case. The documents will be available to the public in the National Archives.

The staff of the commission had written: "A bullet had entered his back at a point slightly above the shoulder and to the right of the spine."

Ford suggested changing that to read: "A bullet had entered the back of his neck at a point slightly to the right of the spine."

The final report said: "A bullet had entered the base of the back of his neck slightly to the right of the spine."

Ford, then House Republican leader and later elevated to the presidency with the 1974 resignation of Richard Nixon, is the sole surviving member of the seven-member commission chaired by Chief Justice Earl Warren.

****

Memo from Nicholas Katzenbach, Deputy Attorney General to LBJ aide Bill Moyers

November 25, 1963

MEMORANDUM FOR MR. MOYERS

It is important that all of the facts surrounding President Kennedy's Assassination be made public in a way which will satisfy people in the United States and abroad that all the facts have been told and that a statement to this effect be made now.

1. The public must be satisfied that Oswald was the assassin; that he did not have confederates who are still at large; and that the evidence was such that he would have been convicted at trial.

2. Speculation about Oswald's motivation ought to be cut off, and we should have some basis for rebutting thought that this was a Communist conspiracy or (as the Iron Curtain press is saying) a right-wing conspiracy to blame it on the Communists. Unfortunately the facts on Oswald seem about too pat-- too obvious (Marxist, Cuba, Russian wife, etc.). The Dallas police have put out statements on the Communist conspiracy theory, and it was they who were in charge when he was shot and thus silenced.

3. The matter has been handled thus far with neither dignity nor conviction. Facts have been mixed with rumour and speculation. We can scarcely let the world see us totally in the image of the Dallas police when our President is murdered.

I think this objective may be satisfied by making public as soon as possible a complete and thorough FBI report on Oswald and the assassination. This may run into the difficulty of pointing to in- consistencies between this report and statements by Dallas police officials. But the reputation of the Bureau is such that it may do the whole job. The only other step would be the appointment of a Presidential Commission of unimpeachable personnel to review and examine the evidence and announce its conclusions. This has both advantages and disadvantages. It think it can await publication of the FBI report and public reaction to it here and abroad.

I think, however, that a statement that all the facts will be made public property in an orderly and responsible way should be made now. *We need something to head off public speculation or Congressional hearings of the wrong sort.*

Nicholas deB. Katzenbach

Deputy Attorney General

Read Barr McClellan's opinion: http://amarillonet.com/stories/031304/opi_guest.shtml

Learn why the Warren Report is a hoax: click here.

Reprint from http://jfkmurdersolved.com/sibert.htm

Did the Bushes help to kill JFK?

The question cannot be answered with absolute certainty, but the thesis is not without circumstantial evidence. If nothing else, these pages will show the reader the following:

- Although he does not recall when asked, George (Herbert Walker) Bush was in Dallas the day JFK was assassinated.

- Bush lies about the fact that he was a high-ranking CIA official at the time of JFK's death.

- Bush allowed the escape of a convicted terrorist from prison to go to work for him as an undercover CIA asset in Iran-Contra.

- Bush has released another convicted terrorist.

- Both these terrorists were present on Dealey Plaza on 11/22/1963.

- Both these terrorists were convicted for killing 73 people by blowing up an airliner.

- Bush is personal friends with a close associate of these convicted terrorists, who was also a participant in Iran Contra.

- Bush has taken a leading role as CIA official in structuring/organizing these terrorists in effective organizations.

Shall we say: "Only in America, the land of unlimited opportunities"?

==

+ All three generations Bush are members of a most powerful and most secret society. It's called The order of Skull and Bones. Those who want to learn more about Skull and Bones can do so by clicking here. Or read this book click here.

Image: Three generations

And those who argue that Skull and Bones is just a harmless fraternity or boy scout's club, may ask themselves whether it is okay for leaders of open and democratic societies, to be members of secret organizations whose agendas are not to be disclosed to the public.

"My senior year, I joined Skull & Bones, a secret

society, so secret, I can't say anything more."

George W. Bush, President of the United States

See George W. Bush admitting his membership of Skull and Bones by clicking here

The unauthorized biography of George H.W. Bush can be read here

Some more of many links on Bush connections to the JFK assassination:

http://www.ciajfk.com/home4.html

http://www.davidicke.net/tellthetruth/coverups/bronfmanbush.html

http://www.angelfire.com/ky/ohwhy/Bush.html

http://www.hereinreality.com/familyvalues.html

http://www.lizmichael.com/bushykno.htm

http://forums.alternet.org/guest/motet?show+-ugYR2t+-chjz+Currents+908+1

http://www.jrryan.cc/poetry/what_know.htm

http://www.sumeria.net/politics/kennedy.html

Image: Where were you, George?

+ Prescott Bush (father of George) made his fortune by financing the war effort of Adolph Hitler together with his banking partners and fellow "bonesmen" Averell and Roland Harriman. Prescott was stripped of his holdings in the Union Banking Corporation in 1942 under the "Trading with the Enemy Act".

"On March 19, 1934, Prescott Bush handed Averell Harriman a copy of that day's New York Times. The Polish government was applying to take over Consolidated Silesian Steel Corporation and Upper Silesian Coal and Steel Company from "German and American interests" because of rampant "mismanagement, excessive borrowing, fictitious bookkeeping and gambling in securities." The Polish government required the owners of the company, which accounted for over 45% of Poland's steel production, to pay at least its full share of back taxes. Bush and Harriman would eventually hire attorney *John Foster Dulles* to help cover up any improprieties that might arise under investigative scrutiny." Source: "Heir to the Holocaust" by Toby Rogers: http://www.clamormagazine.org/issues/14/feature3.shtml

John Foster Dulles was the brother of Allen Dulles, the later CIA director, who was the architect - together with Vice President Richard Nixon and George Bush - of the Bay of Pigs invasion to overthrow Fidel Castro's Cuba. Allen Dulles was fired by President Kennedy because of the fiasco of the Bay of Pigs. Yet Allen Dulles was appointed by Lyndon Johnson to serve on the Warren Commission to "investigate" JFK's death.

+ A vice-president of Empire Trust in Dallas was *Jack Crichton* (also president of Nafco Oil & Gas, Inc.) who was connected with Army Reserve Intelligence. In a 1995 book written by Fabian Escalante, the chief of a Cuban counterintelligence unit during the late 1950s and early 1960s, he describes that as soon as intelligence was received from agents in Cuba that Fidel Castro had "converted to communism," a plan called *"Operation 40"* was put into effect by the National Security Council, presided over by Vice-President Richard Nixon. Escalante indicates that *Nixon* was the Cuban "case officer" who had assembled an important group of businessmen headed by *George Bush and Jack Crichton*, both Texas oilmen, to gather the necessary funds for the operation. Source: http://www.davidicke.net/tellthetruth/coverups/bronfmanbush.html

In Dick Russell's book, The Man Who Knew Too Much (New York: Carroll & Graf Publishers/Richard Gallen, 1992), at pp. 614-615, under a section called "Origins of the Cover-up" there is a description of a group of Dallas men who surrounded Marina Oswald as soon as her husband had been arrested, but before he was killed by Jack Ruby. These were intelligence operatives seeking out Russian speakers. Ilya Mamantov knew George Bush and spoke Russian. A geologist with Sun Oil, he received a call five hours after the assassination from *Jack Crichton*, who was at that time the president of Nafco Oil and Gas, Inc. and a former Military Intelligence officer then attached to Army Reserve Intelligence. Crichton was also director of Dorchester Gas Producing Co. with D.H. Byrd, who owned the Texas School Book Depository building and was a close friend of Lyndon Johnson. Source: http://www.newsmakingnews.com/lm4,4,02,harvardtoenronpt2.htm

+ In 1968, six months after the assassination of Robert Kennedy, Prescott writes this letter (click here) to Clover Dulles, wife of Allen Dulles. Note that he blames the Kennedy's for the failure of the Bay of Pigs.

+ In the 1950's Prescott and the Harrimans are the founding fathers of CBS. In 1963, CBS reporter Dan Rather makes his career break with the Kennedy Assassination by lying to the American public that he sees JFK's head move violently FORWARD on the Zapruder film. To hear Dan Rather lying click here.

The lie is possible, because the Zapruder film was bought by Time Life and kept lock and barrel from the public for 14 years. Time Life is founded and owned by Henry Luce, also a member of Skull and Bones. Luce had many friends, among them general Edward Lansdale, a known covert operative for the CIA. Henry's wife, Clare Booth Luce, Congresswoman, is a radical supporter of the Anti-Castro movement and personal friends with another high-ranking covert operative for the CIA and a resident from Fort Worth: *David Atlee Phillips*. Edward Lansdale and David Phillips are widely accepted as key planners of the JFK assassination. They are also exact matches for the "covert operations specialist" (Phillips) and the "top brass in military intelligence from Asia" (Lansdale) as described in Sam Giancana's biography "Double Cross" (to read the page click here).

Image: David Atlee Phillips and Edward Lansdale

+ David Atlee Phillips was the mastermind for the CIA staged coup by Pinochet in 1973, as well as the overthrow in 1954 of the Guatemala regime headed by Jacobo Arbenz. He is working closely with CIA officer E. Howard Hunt, another suspect in the plot to kill JFK and the leader of the infamous Watergate burglar team. In the 1950's and 1960's, Phillips is the CIA case officer for the anti Castro Cubans in Havana and Mexico City. He is also the CIA controller for Lee Harvey Oswald and James Files. James Files has confessed that he fired the shot into JFK's head from behind the picket fence on the grassy knoll in Dealey Plaza. This story is completely ignored by the mainstream media, which seems strange, because even if he were lying, one would expect some exposure. The star of David Atlee Phillips rises to CIA director of Covert Operations for the Western Hemisphere. According to his nephew Shawn Phillips, who is quite a famous musician, David Atlee Phillips confirmed to his brother James Atlee Phillips that he was in Dallas the day Kennedy died. To read Shawn's email: click here.

+ Prescott Bush advised Eisenhower to run for President and then launched Richard Nixon into the Vice Presidency. Subsequently he was a major financer of Nixon's presidential campaign against Kennedy. Prescott Bush was an avid JFK opponent and Nixon has always been a puppet for the interests of the Bush family. To read the details click here.

Image: Prescott Bush with President Dwight Eisenhower

Image: Prescott with his protégé Dick Nixon

Image: Prescott and Ike

+ George Herbert Walker Bush is one of the very few Americans who does not recall where he was when JFK was killed. Yet, the following document, recently declassified, places him very close to Dallas within 2 hours of JFK's assassination:

But who says the Bush telephone call really came from Tyler, Texas? To his own admission, this document places Bush IN Dallas for the remainder of the day and night of November 22, 1963. He is implicating a political activist (James Parrott) in the process. Why did Bush want to keep his telephone call confidential? And why does he not remember it? Why did he give his warning AFTER the assassination, if he thought Parrott was a serious threat for Kennedy in Houston? Kennedy had just visited Houston the day before ! And why are the sources of this hearsay information unknown? Who told him this, if anyone? Or is this just a document to furnish Bush with an alibi and plausible denial? Thirty years later the same James Parrott that Bush was accusing is working on Bush's presidential campaign against Bill Clinton.

"Figure that one out; if someone had tried to finger me for killing President Kennedy, that person would have been my worst enemy. See volume one and ten for damning evidence. The FBI agent that took Bush's call was Graham Kitchel, whose brother George Kitchel knew both de Mohrenschildt (Oswald's best friend in Dallas) and Bush. (NOTE: Graham was a favourite of FBI Director, J. E. Hoover who was briefing Bush of the CIA on November 23, 1963). On October 13, 1999, Adamson called Kenneth B. Jackson the FBI agent who investigated Parrott and received Bush's complaint. Mr. Jackson, refused to return Adamson's phone call. why? " Source: Bruce Adamson http://www.ciajfk.com/home4.html

"The greater our knowledge increases the more our ignorance unfolds."

John F. Kennedy

+ Nixon admitted he was in Dallas, but gave conflicting accounts. To read about those conflicting accounts click here or click here.

Is there other evidence to tie Nixon to key players in the JFK assassination? Yes, there is! Look at this bombshell document that states Jack Ruby worked for Nixon: Click here. And Ruby was just a punk with no connections to anyone?

+ One of the most tantalizing nuggets about Nixon's possible inside knowledge of JFK assassination secrets was buried on a White House tape until 2002. On the tape, recorded in May of 1972, the president confided to two top aides that the Warren Commission pulled off "the greatest hoax that has ever been perpetuated." Unfortunately, he did not elaborate. But the context in which Nixon raised the matter shows just how low he could stoop in efforts to assassinate the character of his political adversaries.

The Republican president made the "hoax" observation in the immediate aftermath of the assassination attempt against White House hopeful George Wallace, a long-time Democratic governor of Alabama. The attempt left Wallace paralyzed below the waist. Nixon blurted out his comments about the falsity of the Warren findings in the middle of a conversation in which he repeatedly directed two of his most ruthless aides, Bob Haldeman and Chuck Colson, to carry out a monumental dirty trick. He urged them to plant a false news story linking the would-be Wallace assassin — Arthur Bremer — to two other Democrats, *Sen. Edward Kennedy* and Sen. George McGovern —possible Nixon opponents in that year's fall elections. "Screw the record," the president orders on at one point. "Just say he was a supporter of that nut (it isn't clear which of the two senators he is referring to). And put it out. Just say we have an authenticated report."

As well as helping to perpetuate the Kennedy assassination "hoax" by turning down Haldeman's proposal for a new JFK probe, Nixon had a major hand in perpetrating it. In November of 1964, on the eve of the official release of the Warren Report, private citizen Nixon went public in support of the panel's coming findings. In a piece for Reader's Digest, he portrayed Oswald as the sole assassin. And Nixon implied that Castro — "a hero in the warped mind of Oswald" — was the real culprit.

He claimed that Robert Kennedy, as attorney general, had authorized a larger number of wiretaps than his own administration. "But I don't criticize it," he declared, adding, "if he had ten more and — as a result of wiretaps — had been able to discover the Oswald Plan, it would have been worth it."

Whoops! The president apparently didn't realize his reference to "the Oswald Plan" didn't square with the government's official lone-killer finding. For if Lee Harvey Oswald had been solely responsible for the assassination, then there would not have been anyone for Oswald to conspire with about his "plan" — on a bugged telephone, or otherwise. Was Nixon inadvertently revealing his knowledge that Mob leaders (Robert Kennedy's main wiretap targets) had a role in President Kennedy's slaying? Was such a belief based on information acquired as a result of Nixon's own solid ties to organized crime and the Mafia-infested Teamsters union? Source: click here.

+ A photograph exists of the Texas School Book Depository while the Dallas Police is sealing off the building. Among the bystanders is a civilian that could be a twin brother of George H.W. Bush.

Image: George on one of his Zapata oil platforms

+ George H.W. Bush is provably lying about his CIA career. He claims that his CIA directorship in 1976 was his first job for the CIA. Difficult to believe? Page 3 will show the proof for this lie. The truth is that he was actively involved in the preparation and financing of the ill faithed Bay of Pigs invasion, as a high ranking CIA official, at which time he made acquaintance with the now notorious *CIA agent and Iran Contra operative Felix Rodriguez,* a veteran of the Bay of Pigs and Operation 40.

Image: Felix Rodriguez and Luis Posada Carriles:

Veterans of the Bay of Pigs, members of Operation 40, friends, anti-Castro Cuban exiles,

CIA assets, trained assassins and operatives for Iran Contra.

Jim Marrs : During that time, during the time of the Bay of Pigs, while you were training and moving around in the Caribbean, No Name Key and all that, did you ever hear the name George Herbert Walker Bush?

James Files: Oh Yeah!

Jim Marrs: What was his role?

James Files: George Herbert Walker Bush. I don't know if, I think a lot of people are not going to believe this, but he worked for the CIA back as early as 1961 that I know of.

Jim Marrs : How did he work? What did he do?

James Files : I don't know all he did, but he did a lot of recruiting work. I know he was there at the beginning for what we called Group 40, a special operations group, Group 40. If you wonder what Group 40 was, an assassination group.

Operation 40 was a top secret CIA project to train selected Cuban exiles in guerrilla warfare and assassinations, aimed against the Castro regime. Apart from Felix Rodriguez, other members were now infamous CIA agents and Anti Castro terrorists like Luis Posada Carriles, Orlando Bosch, Guillermo and Ignacio Novo Sampoll and later Watergate plumbers Frank Sturgis, Eugenio Martinez, Virgilio Gonzalez and E. Howard Hunt. Most of the operation 40 members were recruited from JM/Wave, a much larger clandestine operation to train a Cuban exile army for the Bay of Pigs invasion. JM/Wave is headed by CIA official *Theodore Shackley*. James Files, the confessed gunman on the grassy knoll, was recruited for the CIA by David Atlee Phillips on a recommendation of Ted Shackley. Shackley becomes George Bush's deputy director for Covert Operations in 1976. The CIA controller of JFK's assassin is provably close to Shackley, Shackley is provably close to Bush. Not significant?

Image: Ted Shackley

Shackley's second man in command of JM/Wave is David Sanchez Morales, who is also working close with David Atlee Phillips and develops a reputation as "best CIA assassin for Latin America". Cuban State security officials speculate that Morales was the "dark complected man" as seen by several witnesses in the 6th floor window of the Texas School Book Depository. Just after telling friends he was afraid of his "own people", and just before he was scheduled to testify for the House Select Committee of Assassinations, Morales died in 1977 a sudden heart attack under mysterious circumstances. Under influence of alcohol, he had hinted to close friends that he had been involved in the Kennedy assassination (We took care of that bastard, didn't we?"). Morales was a big muscular man of very dark complexion, nicknamed "el Indio". Several witnesses on Dealey Plaza, most of whom were not called to testify before the Warren Commission, described a man fitting Morales. These witnesses saw such a man in the windows of the sixth floor of the Texas School Book depository shortly before Kennedy's motorcade passed by, as well as minutes after the shooting, fleeing from the back of the building with two other men in a station wagon.

Image: David Sanchez Morales

Image: George and Felix chilling in the VP's office.

+ Bush and Rodriguez are still close personal friends today, as can be well documented. In 1967 Rodriguez is heading the CIA team that tracks down Che Guevara in Bolivia, ending with his murder.

Above is a picture of Felix Rodriguez with a captured Che Guevara. Rodriguez still shows Guevara's Rolex watch and the transcripts of the interrogations to intimate friends in his Miami home, which is decorated with photos of him and his old friend George. Below a 1988 Christmas note from George to Felix referring to Iran-Contra hearings.

Image: George and Felix

"The great enemy of the truth is very often not the lie, deliberate, contrived and dishonest, but the myth, persistent, persuasive and unrealistic."

John F. Kennedy

+ The architects for the Bay of Pigs were Vice President Richard Nixon and CIA director Allen Dulles. JFK inherited the plan from the Eisenhower administration. Nixon lost the race for the presidency to JFK and Dulles was fired by JFK for the failure of the Bay of Pigs. Yet Dulles is appointed by president Johnson as a Warren Commission member to "investigate" JFK's murder. The proof for Bush's lie about his CIA past can be found in a document, declassified in 1988.

It's a memorandum of FBI director J Edgar Hoover to the State department, dated 29 November 1963. It describes a meeting, one day after JFK's murder, between FBI and CIA officials talking about the reaction of the Cuban exile community to the Kennedy Assassination. The last paragraph states that the "the substance of the foregoing information was orally furnished to us and *George Bush of the Central Intelligence agency*". Here we have the name of George Bush mentioned as a CIA official in direct connection to the Kennedy assassination. When asked by journalists, he initially stated "It's not me, must be another Bush!" This was checked and found to be NOT true. When asked again, a spokesperson for Bush declined to comment any further. The obvious question is: Why does Bush need to lie about it?

+ Let's see how the Assassinations Records Review Board dealt with this information in their final report, chapter 6 :

4. George Bush

A November 29, 1963, memorandum from FBI Director J. Edgar Hoover to the Director of the Bureau of Intelligence and Research at the Department of State refers to the fact that information on the assassination of President Kennedy was "orally furnished to Mr. George Bush of the Central Intelligence Agency." At the request of the Review Board, the CIA made a thorough search of its records in an attempt to determine if the "George Bush" referred to in the memorandum might be identical to President and former Director of Central Intelligence George Herbert Walker Bush. That search determined that the CIA had no association with George Herbert Walker Bush during the time frame referenced in the document.

The records that the Review Board examined showed that the only other "George Bush" serving in the CIA in 1963 was a junior analyst who has repeatedly denied being the "George

Bush" referenced in the memorandum. The Review Board staff found one reference to an Army Major General George Bush in the calendars of Director of Central Intelligence Allen Dulles. There was no indication if this General Bush could be the referenced George Bush. The Review Board marked the calendar page as an assassination record.

So the George Bush mentioned in this memorandum could not be found by the CIA? Neither the Major General George Bush mentioned in the calendar of CIA director Allen Dulles? Even though Dulles, as we have seen, was on a first name basis with Prescott Bush? Was the Assassinations Records Review Board not advised that it is practically standard procedure for the CIA to purge the files of sensitive covert intelligence operatives? Why did the ARRB ask the fox to investigate who ate the chickens, and was then satisfied with the answer? Why are there no records on James Files, the man who claims to be the gunman on the grassy knoll? Why does his birth certificate state "deceased at birth"? How can this man be alive and well in prison, if he was deceased at birth? Did Hoover and Dulles make up a fictional George Bush?

+ It can now be conclusively shown that both Gerald Ford and Arlen Specter (now a senator for Pennsylvania) tampered with the medical evidence of JFK's autopsy and put these lies in the Warren Report.

+ Hale Boggs sat on the Warren Commission, which concluded that President Kennedy was slain by a lone assassin. Later, in 1971 and '72, Boggs said that the Warren Report was false and that J. Edgar Hoover's FBI not only helped cover up the JFK murder but blackmailed Congress with massive wire-tapping and spying. He named Warren Commission staff member Arlen Specter as a major cover-up artist. Congressman Boggs' plane disappeared on a flight to Alaska in 1972. The press, the military, and the CIA publicly proclaimed the plane could not be located. Investigators later said that was a lie, that the plane had been found. On the plane were Nick Begich, a very popular Democratic Congressman, and Don Jonz, an aide to Mr. Boggs. All were killed.

+ In 1976, George H.W. Bush was appointed CIA director by president and former Warren Commission member Gerald Ford at the exact time that newly erected investigative committees were probing the possible role of the CIA into the assassination plots to kill Fidel Castro, Martin Luther King and John F. Kennedy. Bush appoints his old friend from JM/Wave and the Bay of Pigs, Theodore Shackley, as his deputy director for Special Operations, the CIA's most important division. The above-mentioned investigations are heavily stonewalled by the CIA, holding back crucial documents and witnesses. Nevertheless, the House Select Committee on Assassinations concludes its investigation with a 95% probability that at least 4 shots were fired and Kennedy was killed as a result of a conspiracy, along with the recommendation to the Justice Department to follow up with a further investigation. This recommendation was never honored.

+ During the preparations of the House Select Committee on Assassinations, pressure is applied to Texan Bill Lord not to testify for the committee. Bill Lord was a fellow marine and roommate of Lee Harvey Oswald on a ship voyage to France. Lord expresses his concern in a letter to president Carter. He writes that Oswald was connected to the FBI and CIA and concludes that the CIA and the FBI are complicit in JFK's death and the coup d'etat that occurred on 11/22/1963. He also states that one of the Midland, TX politicians applying pressure to him, was *Mr. George W. Bush junior*. This letter to President Carter was declassified some years ago. Here's a fragment:

One of the parties which has blitzed me with telephone calls trying to persuade me to tell them what I know about Oswald, is engaged in a very costly project which allows them to locate, interview, monitor, and influence every single available person who ever knew Lee Oswald--and this, just in advance of the new governmental investigation by the house select committee on Assassinations. I finally consented, not to grant an interview, but to allow the publication's representative to explain their project to me in person. After a lunch interview with this researcher, I was told that if I had refused even to meet with him, pressure was in the offing from two Midland men: Mr. Jim Allison, publisher of the ultra-conservative Reporter-Telegram, my employer (out of necessity, and for the moment!), and *Mr. George Bush, Jr.*

... Shortly thereafter, my mother discovered that her telephone had been tampered with. The casing around the dialing apparatus had been pulled out about one-half inch... we cannot doubt that someone entered the house at a time when I was at work and my mother was away; she returned to the house, however, at an unaccustomed time... I have been in anguish for weeks, Mr. President, trying my best to laugh at my apprehensions and to see these events as fortuitous ones... Speaking as the man who spent more than two weeks in the same ship's cabin with Lee Oswald at the time of his 1959 "defection", and speaking as a man who has been the subject of the above.

See the original letter here (page 1) here (page 2) and here (page 3)

+ There are numerous indications and allegations that Nixon's Watergate scandal had a direct connection with the Kennedy assassination and that every time that Nixon is talking about the danger that the "Bay of Pigs thing" might be exposed because of Watergate, he was actually covertly referring to the Kennedy assassination. None of these rumours could solidify, because shortly before his resignation, Nixon replaced Spiro Agnew by Gerald Ford as his vice president, who promptly pardoned him from further prosecution. The allegations of a direct connection with Dallas are certainly not unfounded, considering the incomplete official story and the preponderance of Watergate individuals connected to the Bay of Pigs and the Kennedy assassination. When it became clear that Watergate may not be kept under the lid, Nixon fires and replaces his entire administration with the exception of George H.W. Bush, because "he will do anything for our cause".

From a radio interview with investigative journalist Jim Marrs:

J – Yes, and let me say this: I don't want everybody to think that just Lyndon Johnson was involved in this, or that it was just the democrats or whatever. I'm looking here at a book written by H.R Haldeman, who was ...

G – He was one of Nixon's men!

J – Yes, one of Nixon's boys, and here he writes, he says, if you all remember during Watergate the Nixon Tapes and all the focus over that: Nixon went to pay 2 million dollars to E. Howard Hunt, a CIA officer, who was leading and training the anti-Castro Cubans, he (Nixon) said: "Pay him the 2 million dollars! This could open up the whole Bay of Pigs thing! This could look bad for us, this could look bad for the CIA!" And in Haldeman's book, he says that it seems that in all these Nixon references to the Bay of Pigs, he was actually referring to the Kennedy assassination! More information here

+ George H.W. Bush failed to disclose his friendship with George De Mohrenschildt, a renowned oil geologist and Lee Harvey Oswald's best friend in Dallas. They knew each other since 1942, probably even longer, because in 1939 he went to work for Humble Oil, a company founded by Prescott Bush. In 1977, when De Mohrenschildt is located by investigators of the House Select Committee on Assassinations, who want to interview him, he allegedly commits suicide the following day. The last person to interview him on the day he died, is Jay Edward Epstein, a writer/historian and a known apologist for the Warren Report since day one. Epstein married a CIA agent and is the biographer of former CIA-director James Jesus Angleton, presumably in charge of Oswald's "defection" to Russia. Interestingly, Epstein is also the "consultant" that was suddenly hired by NBC in 1995, when NBC was making a program for national TV on the confession of James E. Files. The program was promptly cancelled.

Image: George De Mohrenschildt

In De Mohrenschildt's address book a telephone number is found for Bush's oil company Zapata Petroleum, with a further entry for "George Poppy Bush". It is well known that "Poppy" is a nickname for George H.W. Bush to his friends and family. Shortly before, De Mohrenschildt had sent his old friend George, now CIA director, a letter, asking if something could be done about the surveillance and harassment he was lately exposed to. Why would De Mohrenschildt suspect the harassment originated from the CIA? This letter is public domain now, but does not show up in the collections of correspondence that Bush put together in a book as a way of publishing his memoirs.

"And we shall vote for you when you run for President.

Your old friend G. De Mohrenschildt." See De Mohrenschildt's letter here (1) and here (2)

+ David Atlee Phillips was one of the planning CIA officials in the plot to kill JFK. He was a member of the Dallas Petroleum club, as was George Demohrenschildt and George Bush. All three were CIA, and knew each other. Yet time and again, during the Warren Commission, during the HSCA as a CIA director, and during the Assassinations Records Review Board as President, George Bush keeps his mouth shut about these liaisons, who were both CIA supervisors for Lee Harvey Oswald. Who wants to maintain that George's silence is insignificant?

More information here.

+ During the years after the Bay of Pigs, George H.W. Bush was calling for escalation in Vietnam and challenging Kennedy to "muster the courage" to try a second invasion of Cuba.

+ George H.W. Bush was not only actively involved in financing and planning the Bay of Pigs, he is a central man in organizing Anti-Castro groups and raids against Cuba in the years to follow. In 1976, while director of the CIA, he instructs the Anti Castro groups to organize themselves in one coherent group: CORU or Coordination of United Revolutionary Organizations. Most of the operation 40 members already mentioned, become members of CORU.

+ Later that year, Orlando Letelier, a former minister in the Chilean government of Salvador Allende, is assassinated in the streets of Washington. CORU members Ignacio and Guillermo

Novo Sampoll are charged with the assassination of Orlando Letelier. Guillermo Novo's initial conviction is overturned on his appeal.

+ Both the Novo brothers, Orlando Bosch and Watergate burglars E Howard Hunt and Frank Sturgis are also implicated in JFK's murder by the testimony under oath of female CIA agent Marita Lorenz in 1985. She was the former mistress of Fidel Castro and girl friend of Frank Sturgis. Her testimony in a libel suit against H. Howard Hunt, places all these men in Dallas on 11/22/1963. To read her testimony click here

+ James Files, the confessed assassin of JFK, also says that Sturgis and Bosch were in Dealey Plaza on November 22, 1963. Some researchers believe that Orlando Bosch was the unidentified dark complected man on the curb of Dealey Plaza. To read the analysis click here.

+Also in 1976, CORU masterminds the bombing of a Cuban airline jet, exploding in mid air, killing all 73 passengers. Orlando Bosch (nickname Dr. Death) and Luis Posada Carriles are charged and convicted for this crime by Venezuelan authorities with lifetime sentences.

Image: Luis Posada Carriles

"The difference between a patriot and a terrorist

is whose side of the fence you are on."

James Files, gunman on the grassy knoll

+ Posada Carriles was rescued by the Cuban-American National Foundation, a CIA sponsored organization that sent 50,000 dollars via Panama to finance his escape from his Caracas prison, which was successfully carried out on August 18, 1985. In a matter of hours, he turned up in El Salvador. He was visited there, having barely arrived, by the top leaders of the Foundation. He is given a new identity "Ramon Medina" and is placed under command of his former operation 40 classmate Felix Rodriguez, now working under the alias "Max Gomez". Those were the days of the dirty war in Nicaragua. He immediately began to execute important tasks under direct orders of the White House, in the air supply of weapons and explosives to the Contras in Nicaragua. These operations became known as the Iran Contra scandal and were directed from the Vice Presidency headed by George H.W. Bush.

"The very word 'secrecy' is repugnant in a free and open society; and we are as a people inherently and historically opposed to secret societies, to secret oaths, and to secret proceedings."

John F. Kennedy

+ Orlando Bosch is released in 1987 under diplomatic pressure of the then US ambassador for Venezuela Otto Reich. Otto Reich is from Cuban descent and an avid anti Castro Cuban exile. He was recently appointed assistant Secretary of State under Colin Powell in the current Bush administration. Back in Miami, Orlando Bosch is released from house arrest by presidential order as soon as Bush is president. No outcry was reported by the mainstream press.

While incarcerated in Caracas, both Luis Posada Carriles and Orlando Bosch were visited and interviewed by HSCA investigator Gaeton Fonzi. Not surprisingly they denied being in Dallas on November 22, 1963. However, neither of them could give a verifiable alibi. For a more in depth story by Geaton Fonzi documenting these intimate connections: http://cuban-exile.com/doc_051-075/doc0063.html or read his excellent book "The last investigation" online: http://cuban-exile.com/menu2/2fonzi.html

+ George H.W. Bush becomes the first President in American history to effectively grant himself a pardon in order to avoid prosecution for Iran Contra, by pardoning his numerous accomplices in that operation. Some of them are now holding posts in his son's administration.

+ George H.W. Bush has always been and still is vehemently opposed to declassifying files on the Kennedy Assassination. His son George W. Bush has just overturned a decision of the Clinton administration to declassify files about past presidents. The bogus excuse is always "national security". If JFK was killed by just one lone nut, as we are asked to believe, then where is the issue of national security? Declassification of the files would only confirm that theory, right? One might wonder whose security is really at risk here. But it is not the nation's!

Image: Guillermo Novo Sampol

+ The testimony of Chauncey Holt, one of the infamous "three tramps" arrested in Dealey Plaza after the assassination, reveals that Luis Posada Carriles was also present on Dealey Plaza on 11/22/1963. Whether Posada was there to pull a trigger is unknown, but he makes a perfect match for the Cuban Exile "friend", sent to Dallas by Santo Trafficante, who was "a former Havana vice cop, turned mobster", as described by Sam Giancana in his biography (to read the page click here). To learn more about Luis Posada Carriles click here.

Image: Still frame of Lee Harvey Oswald handing out pamphlets on Canal Street. Handwriting is of Chauncey Holt. Chauncey is the man with sunglasses on the far right. To read Holt's story click here.

Posada Carriles is currently in jail in Panama with 3 Cuban accomplices for the most recent plot to kill Fidel Castro, who visited a Latin American summit there in November 2000. One of Posada's jailed accomplices is a friend whose name is already familiar to the reader: *Guillermo Novo Sampol.* Remember that this man is also placed in Dallas on 11/22/1963 by the testimony under oath of Marita Lorenz. Washington is stonewalling their extradition to Cuba with a vengeance. Of further relevance is the almost complete blackout of American mass media reporting about this affair.

Update: Luis Posada Carriles and Guillermo Novo were pardoned and released by Panama in August 2004. Although Panama is like a province of the United States, pressure from the Bush administration is denied.

Image: CUBAN PRESIDENT CASTRO HOLDS UP PHOTO OF MAN HE ACCUSED OF PLANNING ASSASSINATION ATTEMPT Original caption: Cuban President Fidel Castro shows a photo of a Cuban exile living in the United States, Luis Posada, who Castro accused of masterminding a plot to assassinate him during his visit to Panama City, November 17, 2000. Leaders of Latin America, Spain and Portugal are set to meet in Panama over the weekend for the 10th Ibero American summit where they will discuss ways of combating child poverty and abuse in the region.

© Reuters/CORBIS

+ So we have at least four known CIA trained assassins that we know were present on Dealey Plaza: *Luis Posada Carriles, Frank Sturgis, Guillermo Novo Sampol and Orlando Bosch*. All these terrorists were members of Operation 40, an assassinations group Bush personally recruited for, and during which time he gets acquainted with his life-long pal Felix Rodriguez. Operation 40 and JM/Wave are supervised by two of Bush's CIA cohorts:

1) David Atlee Phillips, who is the CIA controller for both Lee Harvey Oswald and confessed grassy knoll gunman James Files.

2) Ted Shackley, who later becomes Bush's deputy director for Covert Operations.

All these terrorists have later been clearly protected by George Bush and his CIA. Yet Bush has officially no knowledge about JFK's assassination? And yet officially his son fights a War against Terror? I guess Prescott has thought his son Hitler's motto: "The bigger the lie, the easier it is accepted by the public, especially when it is repeated over and over again".

Image: Marita Lorenz and Frank Sturgis

+ And then there's this little piece of information from the book "Defrauding America":

Much has been written about the role of the CIA factions in the assassination of President John F. Kennedy. It isn't the purpose of this book to go into that subject. However, the statements of relatively high- ranking former or present ONI and Navy officers relating to the JFK assassination are given within these pages for the reader to ponder.

The Role of deep-cover CIA officer, Trenton Parker, has been described in earlier pages, and his function in the CIA's counter-intelligence unit, Pegasus. Parker had stated to me earlier that a CIA faction was responsible for the murder of JFK, and that Kennedy was advised three weeks before the assassination of a plan to assassinate him in one of three cities that Kennedy would be visiting.

During an August 21, 1993, conversation, in response to my questions, Parker said that his Pegasus group had tape recordings of plans to assassinate Kennedy. I asked him, "What group were these tapes identifying?" Parker replied: *"Rockefeller, Allen Dulles, Johnson of Texas, George Bush, and J. Edgar Hoover."* I asked, "What was the nature of the conversation on these tapes?"

I don't have the tapes now, because all the tape recordings were turned over to [Congressman] Larry McDonald. But I listened to the tape recordings and there were conversations between Rockefeller, [J. Edgar] Hoover, where [Nelson] Rockefeller asks, "Are we going to have any problems?" And he said, "No, we aren't going to have any problems. I checked with Dulles. If they do their job we'll do our job." There are a whole bunch of tapes, because Hoover didn't realize that his phone has been tapped.

Parker had earlier mentioned to me that he had turned over a full box of files and tapes, documentation, and micro-fiche for the Pegasus operation in the Caribbean to Congressman Larry McDonald shortly before the Congressman boarded the ill-fated Korean Airlines Flight 007 that was shot down by the Russians.

THE PROBLEM IS NO LONGER MINE. For 30 years I attacked these problems without success. At my age, it is no longer my problem to solve. I will be gone before the American public pays for what reaped. Good luck, you will need it!

Defrauding America, Rodney Stich, 3rd edition 1998 p. 638-639

Image: "Behind every success there is a crime"

Lyndon Baines Johnson

+ Other ties between Nelson Rockefeller and the principals in the JFK assassination can be found in this excellent article on Freeport Sulphur, connecting David Atlee Philips with Guy Banister and Sergio Arcacha Smith, as well as with Clay Shaw and David Ferrie, who were both prosecuted in Jim Garrison's JFK trial:
http://www.realhistoryarchives.com/collections/hidden/freeport-cuba.htm

It ends like this:

Which brings us to a crucial point. Freeport Sulphur is a company Wall Street considers a "Rockefeller" company. There are numerous Rockefeller ties to the board of directors (see the sidebar at right). There is a significant tie that led to the stockpiling investigation. And Adolph Berle and J. C. King, as well as John Hay Whitney, were all very closely tied to Nelson Rockefeller himself. So the revelation that J. C. King and Adolph Berle were conversing about the fate of a Rockefeller-controlled company is significant, credible, and highlights the ties between these players and the CIA, where J. C. King-and in later years David Atlee Phillips-presided as Chiefs of the Western Hemisphere Division. In a strange twist of fate, Rockefeller's good friend King was the authenticating officer on a cable giving authority to kill Castro's brother Raul. Interestingly, Whitney's cousin and friend Tracy Barnes sent the cable rescinding the original order a couple of hours later.

Image: Guy Banister, former FBI agent from Chicago, worked in New Orleans for Sam Giancana, Carlos Marcello and the CIA (David Atlee Phillips) with David Ferrie and Sergio Arcacha Smith.

Image: Picture of Lee Harvey Oswald and David Ferrie during a Civil Air Patrol picknick. David Ferrie died a mysterious death, which was ruled a suicide, only two days before he was scheduled to testify in the famous trial of District Attorney Jim Garrison, who accused him of being part of a conspiracy in the murder of JFK. David Ferrie had denied knowing Oswald. Jim Garrison later said he would have loved to have this picture at the time of his trial. David Ferrie died of a brain heamorrhage. James Files says the brain heamorrhage was inflicted with a nail file through the roof of the mouth, but he refuses to reveal his source. Note: Jim Garrison, David Ferrie and Guy Banister are played by Kevin Costner, Joe Pesci and Loe Asner in Oliver Stone's movie "JFK".

Image: Sam Giancana (second from right), mob boss of Chicago, with the Mcguire sisters, also a target of the Kennedy's after first being helped by him to win the elections in Illinois, felt betrayed by the Kennedy's. He sent his hitmen to Dealey Plaza, among others Charles Nicoletti and Johnny Roselli. All three were murdered in the 1970's shortly before they were called to testify before government committees investigating the murders of JFK and Martin Luther King. Charles Nicoletti was James Files' boss.

CONCLUSIONS:

The plot to kill JFK originates from the very same forces that were working together on the Bay of Pigs and the plots to assassinate Fidel Castro: All these forces had their own reasons to recapture Cuba and to hate Kennedy, whom they also blamed for the failure of the Bay of Pigs.

These groups were 1) The CIA with the approval of some of the highest government officials (like Johnson, Hoover, Ford and Nixon) 2) The anti Castro Cuban exiles 3) Mafiabosses Sam Giancana , Carlos Marcello and Santos Trafficante and 4) wealthy industrialists and Texan oilmen like H.L. Hunt, Syd Richardson and Clint Murchison. George H.W. Bush has documented connections to all four groups.

Sam Giancana states in his biography that he knew Lyndon Johnson and Richard Nixon personally (to read the page click here), as well as the aforementioned oil millionaires and George Demohrenshildt (to read the page click here), , and that they planned the JFK assassination together. James Files, the confessed grassy knoll assassin who fired the fatal shot into JFK's head, did not only work for Sam Giancana, but was recruited in the CIA to train Cuban exiles for the Bay of Pigs, by none other than David Atlee Phillips. He claims that one of his later senior supervisors in covert operations was George H.W. Bush. Lyndon Johnson told his mistress Madeline Brown: "It was the CIA and the Oilboys". Bush was both ! In addition he was up to his neck in the Bay of Pigs and the anti Castro movement. What is the chance he could not have known about the plot?

David Atlee Phillips was also the CIA supervisor for Lee Harvey Oswald, a heroic man that was unwittingly chosen to take the blame as the patsy, while led to believe he was to penetrate the group of assassins in order to sabotage the plot and prevent JFK's assassination.

On November 22, 1963 a criminal power elite seized control through a coup d'etat and a subsequent cover up of the truth that lasts until today. This is because they strengthened their position ever since. The key to unlocking the truth lies in one of their most powerful assets: the mainstream media. That is why you were not aware of most of the above !

It is clear that Bush protected the cover-up, as well as individuals and CIA elements that were involved in the JFK assassination. Although the above may not be conclusive evidence for Bush's involvement or knowledge about JFK's murder, all together a bigger and more criminal picture than many of us dare to imagine, emerges, with a direct connection to the political situation of today.

"And so, my fellow Americans, ask not what your country can do for you; ask what you can do for your country."

"A nation which has forgotten the quality of courage which in the past has been brought to public life is not as likely to insist upon or regard that quality in its chosen leaders today - and in fact we have forgotten."

"Do not pray for easy lives. Pray to be stronger men."

"A man does what he must-in spite of personal consequences, in spite of obstacles and dangers and pressures-and that is the basis of all human morality."

"A man may die, nations may rise and fall, but an idea lives on. "

John F. Kennedy

Reprint from http://jfkmurdersolved.com/bush.htm

Masters of Terror

The Bush family has a track record on terror you won't believe. The only problem: It is hardly known! Not that they place the bombs or pull the triggers themselves. The underlings will do that. It starts with granddaddy Prescott Bush, who was a great admirer of Adolf Hitler and got rich from financing his war effort. You weren't aware of this? Type in your favorite search engine: +Prescott +Hitler. Do the search click here.

An apple does not fall far from its tree. In the early sixties George H.W. Bush is personally involved in the formation of Operation 40, a supersecret CIA-team of assassins to eliminate unsympathetic political leaders. Initial target: Fidel Castro. But, as history will show, Operation 40 won't be confined to foreign leaders only. Try googling for: +"Operation 40" +Bush. Do the search click here.

Operation 40 is mainly assembled from Cuban exiles. A few names are: Felix Rodriguez, Luis Posada Carriles, Orlando Bosch, Guillermo Novo Sampol, Ignacio Novo Sampol, but also later Watergate burglars Frank Sturgis, Virgilio Gonzalez, Eugenio Martinez and E. Howard Hunt. Just type a few of these names with "Operation 40", like for example: +"Operation 40" +Hunt +Bosch. Do the search click here.

Father Bush is still friends with Orlando Bosch and Felix Rodriguez, the latter was in 1967 the head of the CIA team that tracked down and murdered Che Guevara in Bolivia. Felix is also a key figure in Iran-Contra, alongside Luis Posada Carriles. He reports directly to George. Get the facts: +"Felix Rodriguez" +Bush. Do the search click here.

Orlando Bosch and Luis Posada Carriles have a history of give or take five bombs a year. Have a look at their track record: click here

Not for nothing is Bosch nicknamed "Dr. Death." All supervised by George's CIA, the agency he finally heads in 1976. George immediately instructs Bosch to unite all anti-Castro groups into one effective organization: CORU, or Commanders of United Revolutionary Organizations. However, in 1976 Luis and Orlando are finally caught. For blowing up a Cuban airliner, killing all 73 passengers. What if it was your child ? Don't take my word for it. Enter: +"Cuban airline" +"Orlando Bosch". Do the search click here.

That same year, their Operation 40-classmate and fellow CORU-member Guillermo Novo Sampol is convicted for the murder of Chilean diplomat Orlando Letelier. His car explodes in the streets of Washington DC. With some pressure and tampering with evidence, orchestrated by the CIA, Novo is acquitted on his appeal. But you want the facts, right? Enter: +Letelier +Novo. Do the search click here.

Bosch and Posada Carriles are tried and convicted with lifetime sentences by Venezuelan authorities. However, in 1985 Luis Posada Carriles escapes with help of the CIA. In a matter of days, he pops up in El Salvador at the side of his mate Felix Rodriguez, to assist him with an operation, now known as Iran-Contra. For convenience they are now Ramon Medina and Max Gomez. At the Llopango airstrip, they are unloading planes with weapons, sending them back to the States with cocaine. That way the taxpayer isn't bothered with it. These operations are also directed by George, now Vice President. Orlando has to wait a little longer, but he too is released in 1987 as a result of diplomatic pressure of son Jeb Bush and ambassador for Venezuela Otto Reich, now assistant Secretary of State under Colin Powell. Back in Miami,

Bosch receives a Presidential pardon, shortly after George climbed to the highest office. Am I hallucinating? Enter: +Orlando Bosch +pardon. Do the search click here.

Bosch is reasonably quiet since then, but Luis Posada and Guillermo Novo are true die-hards. Since three years they are in a Panamese jail for their latest foiled murder attempt on Castro. Before Fidel could speak there on a Latin American summit, they were caught with bags full of explosives. However, Washington is working hard on their release. And why not? George W. publicly advocates the need for Castro's "removal". But why then is the Panama trial not reported in the mainstream press? See for yourself: +Posada +Novo +Panama. Do the search click here.

Ready for the kicker? On November 22, 1963, Luis Posada Carriles, Guillermo Novo, Orlando Bosch en Frank Sturgis, were all present in Dealey Plaza, the Dallas square were John F. Kennedy was assassinated. You don't believe it? Here's the proof .... Oh well, you know how to search now! And this is only the tip of the iceberg. For more detail: click here.

"During times of universal deceit, telling the truth becomes a revolutionary act."

George Orwell

Update: Luis Posada Carriles and Guillermo Novo were pardoned and released by Panama in August 2004. Although Panama is like a province of the United States, pressure from the Bush administration is denied.

Reprint from: http://jfkmurdersolved.com/moteng.htm

Luis Posada Carriles

THE MAN THAT PLACED LUIS POSADA CARRILES IN DEALEY PLAZA ON 11/22/63

Image: Chauncey Marvin Holt

Image: Luis Posada Carriles

The testimony of Chauncey Marvin Holt (deceased in 1997) is currently of extreme interest, now that anti-Castro terrorist Luis Posada Carriles has asked for asylum in the United States.

Posada Carriles is making bigger headlines by the day. And rightfully so. He is a convicted and escaped terrorist, trained by the CIA, obviously enjoying protection from the Bush administration.

He has a long record of terrorist atrocities and was convicted and jailed in Caracas for blowing up a Cuban airliner, killing all 73 passengers. He escaped from that prison in 1985, to become a key figure in the Iran-Contra scandal. Venezuela is asking for his extradition. Fidel Castro is voicing his outrage in daily TV speeches. US Congressmen are calling for a federal investigation into how Posada, a known terrorist, could have entered the country and slip through the mazes of Homeland Security in this era of the "War against terror". Established newsmedia are asking how the White House policies are rhymed with the statements that whoever harbors a terrorist, is an enemy of the United States. Meanwhile, President Bush remains silent on all fronts.

For the latest news on Posada just click here.

Our information can only add to the controversy: In a never shown documentary, titled "Spooks, Hoods and the hidden Elite", taped only eight days before his death, Chauncey Holt mentioned several of the characters he saw in Dealey Plaza november 11/22/1963. *One of them is Luis Posada Carriles.*

****

The following article comes from Newsweek magazine, December 23, 1991. Someone recently requested a copy of this article, which we provided; we present it here for anyone who might have missed it in its original form.

This article is in error when it states that Oliver Stone "doesn't tell the end of [Rose Cheramie's] story." He does --- in a snippet of dialogue too fast, apparently, for Newsweek ears.

Source: click here.

* * *

Of particular interest is the fact that Newsweek did not dare to print the names of several people Chauncey mentioned in the paragraph below: We have inserted the names in *italics*.

Illegal Chores: But Chauncey Holt is glad to talk--and the more publicly the better. Holt says he was once an accountant for mob financier Meyer Lansky, but spent most of his career forging documents and doing other illegal chores for the CIA. He says he was ordered to Dallas before the assassination--of which he had no foreknowledge-- to deliver fake Secret Service credentials. (Several people in Dealey Plaza said they'd encountered men claiming to be Secret Service agents of whom the Secret Service had no knowledge.) He says the men he traveled to Dallas with *(Charles Nicoletti and Leo Moceri)* were both contacted by the HSCA in the '70s: one was killed *(Nicoletti)* before he could testify, another disappeared *(Moceri)*. He readily names them; he also names the man he says gave him his orders, *(George Reynolds)* the man who gave the man his orders *(Philip Twombly)*, the gangster whose ranch he flew to *(Pete Licavoli)* when the Dallas police turned him loose and the pilot *(Joe Canty)* who flew him. Who, he says, later died in a plane crash. He knew his picture had been taken; he says the law partner *(Frank Belcher)* of a Warren Commission attorney *(Joseph Ball)* told him not to worry.

Newsweek magazine, December 23, 1991

Bottom Line: How Crazy Is It?

Unequivocol answer: it all depends. Welcome to the world of conspiracy.

In the opening minutes of Oliver Stone's "JFK" a man collapses, twitching, on a city sidewalk; a woman mumbles about the president's murder from a hospital bed. Moviegoers will see these simply as surrealistic omens. But a few people will instantly see that Stone did his homework. A man named Jerry Belknap really did have a seizure in Dealey Plaza minutes before President Kennedy's motorcade arrived. He was rushed to Parkland Memorial Hospital by the same drivers who were later to load the president's body into their ambulance for the trip from Parkland to the airport. It was probably not a staged distraction as plotters moved into place. Why didn't the hospital have a record? Belknap said he'd wandered out during the confusion when Kennedy was brought in.

The mumbling woman is something else again. Rose Cheramie, a prostitute and junkie, warned a doctor and a Louisiana state cop about the assassination in Dallas two days before it happened. She claimed she had been abandoned on the road by two men driving from Florida to Dallas who said they were going to shoot the president. She said she worked for a Dallas strip-joint owner named Jack Ruby. Stone doesn't tell the end of her story. ("JFK" is only a three-hour movie, after all, and Rose Cheramie is only a footnote to a footnote in the byzantine annals of the assassination.) In September 1965, a motorist outside Big Sandy, Texas, found her lying dead in the highway.

People who carry such information around are usually dismissed as assassination buffs. True, some are hobbyists, like rotisserie leaguers who buy Bill James's books of baseball stats. Others are careerists, like Mark Lane, whose 1966 "Rush to Judgment" was a best-selling attack on the official version of the assassination. But there's also a network of serious free-lance researchers who think the government dropped the ball on the Kennedy assassination; they have become citizen investigators, with overstuffed Rolodexes and overdue phone bills.

They're the people for whom Stone's improbably virtuous Jim Garrison is the paradigm: ordinary folks fighting the Power.

Last month in Dallas, the Assassination Symposium on John F. Kennedy drew specimens of all these types--plus a few hardcore zanies. (First Prize: the theory that Kennedy was shot by LBJ himself, who concealed his Six-guns under a cape.) As lower-profile researchers socialized and swapped leads, Lane threatened from the dais to sue researcher Jim Moore for libel. Moore, a onetime believer in a conspiracy, has become a maverick among mavericks: he now believes, as the Warren Commission said in 1964, that Lee Harvey Oswald was a lone nut who killed Kennedy and Jack Ruby was a lone nut who killed Oswald. He even defends the much-ridiculed "single bullet" hypothesis, made necessary by Abraham Zapruder's famous home movie, which serves as a clock for the assassination. Oswald had time to fire only three shots. One missed, one hit the president in the head. Ergo, one passed through Kennedy, broke Texas Gov. John Connally's wrist and one of his ribs. (This bullet is surprisingly little the worse for wear.) Critics say there's no "ergo" about it, and that the conclusion that Oswald was the lone assassin forced the commission into a scenario out of Rube Goldberg.

Folks at the symposium admired Moore's pluck, but they were more ready to listen to David Lifton reprising his grisly conclusions--that Kennedy's body was spirited away and tampered with to make it appear he was shot from behind. The symposium's real zinger, though, was a presentation by a Houston police artist named Lois Gibson in which she provided names and rap sheets for each of the famous three "tramps," mystery men photographed in police custody on Nov. 22.

Exactly how crazy is this stuff? Not especially, compared with what we've already found out to be true, like the loony Mafia-CIA schemes against Fidel Castro back in the early '60s-- which ranged from outright assassination to giving Castro a scuba suit permeated with LSD. Lyndon Johnson, who appointed the Warren Commission, said in 1973 that he had never believed its report. His candidate for Mr. Big: Castro. This has never been a popular theory: Castro himself said it would have been suicidally stupid.

Most dissenters from the Warren Commission would agree to something like the following: (1) Kennedy was killed by a conspiracy involving figures from the murky underground in which anti-Castro exiles, the Mafia and the CIA made common cause; (2) Lee Harvey Oswald was, as he claimed, a "patsy," and (3) the mob-contacted Jack Ruby was sent to silence him.

In a note to his lawyer, Ruby claimed another attorney put him up to saying he'd merely wanted to spare Mrs. Kennedy the ordeal of a trial. Larry Houston, the CIA's general counsel for more than 20 years, says that after the Warren Report, "I went through every one of these stories in detail and knocked them all out." Robert Tannenbaum doesn't buy it. "I'm not saying the CIA was involved," says Tannenbaum, deputy chief counsel of the Kennedy investigation for the 1976 House Select Committee on Assassinations (HSCA). "But there's no doubt in my mind that the CIA knows exactly what happened."

If conspiracy theorists seem paranoid about the CIA, the agency is partly to blame. In the late '60s, for instance, the CIA sent its agents a detailed memo explaining how to counter skepticism about the Warren Commission. It was accompanied by a New Yorker article highly critical of New Orleans D.A. Jim Garrison's investigation of the Kennedy case and suggested agents "employ propaganda assets [that is, friendly journalists] to answer and refute the tacks of the critics. Book reviews and feature articles are particularly appropriate for this purpose." In 1978, the CIA agent assigned as liaison to the HSCA was reportedly fired from the agency after rifling the safe containing the Kennedy autopsy photos and X-rays. The agent claimed he had an innocent explanation but would not give it to the press. "There's other things that are involved," he told The Washington Post's George Lardner, "that are detrimental to other things."

Despite its chronic suspicion of disinformation, the self-styled "research community" seems almost upbeat these days. "The case will break in one of three ways," says Dr. Cyril Wecht, distinguished forensic pathologist and colorfully intemperate Warren Commission critic. "Somebody will spill the beans, the technical analytical studies will be confirmed by appropriate experts, or we'll get into an appropriate legal forum." In fact, all these avenues have been tried over the years. Spilling the beans--assuming there are beans--seems to bring bad luck. John Roselli, who helped hatch CIA- Mafia assassination plots, was found, dismembered, in an oil drum after telling the HSCA he would testify that mob-connected Cubans were behind JFK's murder. And high-tech microanalyses of everything from Dealey Plaza photographs to police radio recordings from a motorcycle in the motorcade have led only to experts duking it out with other experts.

Dropped Dead: Jim Garrison provided the "appropriate legal forum," such as it was, in his disastrous 1967 prosecution of New Orleans businessman Clay Shaw. Shaw was acquitted of conspiring to kill Kennedy because Garrison (as he himself acknowledged) had no case--especially after Shaw's alleged coconspirator, David Ferrie, suddenly dropped dead. Garrison ran roughshod over fairness and common sense. He may also have been on to something, though God knows what. Shaw, it turns out, despite his denials, was a CIA "domestic contact"; Ferrie, a former airline pilot, spent the two weekends before the assassination conferring with Kennedy-hating Carlos Marcello, reputed New Orleans Mafia boss. The third supposed conspirator (also dead), ex-FBI agent Guy Banister, was an anti-Castro right-winger; why did the pro-Castro leaflets Oswald handed out in New Orleans bear the address of the small building that housed Banister's office?

Since Garrison, the research community has been burned time after time. Comedian-activist Dick Gregory once claimed Watergate spook E. Howard Hunt Jr. was one of the three "tramps." (Bottom line: he wasn't.) Last year Ricky White, son of a Dallas cop, said he'd produce a diary his late father kept of his role in an assassination plot. (Bottom line: no way.) Hunt turns up again this year as the villain of Mark Lane's "Plausible Denial." In 1985, Lane successfully defended the far-right Liberty Lobby in a libel suit over an article implicating Hunt in the assassination. Lane humiliated Hunt on the witness stand; according to forewoman Leslie Armstrong, Lane convinced a Florida jury the CIA "was directly involved in the assassination." Another juror, Suzanne Reach, told The Miami Herald that wasn't the reason for the verdict. Armstrong says Reach is "in total denial."

Lane's star witness, Marita Lorenz, testified she had been with Hunt plus his future Watergate colleague Frank Sturgis plus the actual gunmen in Dallas the day before the assassination--a story the HSCA had doubted. "I've met Marita many times," says well-respected researcher Gus Russo of Baltimore. "She's a nice person, but her stories are wacky, totally unverifiable." Other researchers are less printable; some suggest Marita is part of a disinformation scheme. Lane himself says the CIA has long attempted to discredit him.

Nobody at last month's symposium came right out and accused Lois Gibson of spreading disinformation, but someone will probably get around to it. She says she's helped solve the old mystery of the three "tramps" police found in a boxcar in the railroad yards near Dealey Plaza after the assassination. We know about them only because of news photos; the police kept no record. Gibson has helped solve scores of cases. She says she'd "bet the farm" on her identifications: Charles V. Harrelson, a hit man (and, incidentally, the father of actor Woody Harrelson) convicted of assassinating federal Judge John Wood with a high-powered rifle in 1982; Charles Rogers, chief suspect in the unsolved 1965 murder and dismemberment of his parents, and one Chauncey Holt, a self-described forger and career criminal. If it could be proved, the presence of someone like Harrelson--not to mention the other two--would be, to say the least, suspicious.

Gibson's photo comparisons looked persuasive, though no rigorous scientific analysis has been done. At the symposium Jerry Rose, publisher of a researchers' newsletter, stood up and urged Dallas's JFK Assassination Information Center, which cosponsored the event, not to endorse Gibson's work. Mark Lane's associate Steve Jaffe called the identification of Harrelson--which researchers have made before-- "the most irresponsible and inaccurate in my experience." Harrelson reportedly once told police he had shot Kennedy, then claimed he'd been skyrocketing on cocaine when he said it. He's now in a federal penitentiary in Illinois and couldn't be reached for comment. Rogers has been missing for years.

Illegal Chores: But Chauncey Holt is glad to talk--and the more publicly the better. Holt says he was once an accountant for mob financier Meyer Lansky, but spent most of his career forging documents and doing other illegal chores for the CIA. He says he was ordered to Dallas before the assassination--of which he had no foreknowledge-- to deliver fake Secret Service credentials. (Several people in Dealey Plaza said they'd encountered men claiming to be Secret Service agents of whom the Secret Service had no knowledge.) He says the men he traveled to Dallas with were both contacted by the HSCA in the '70s: one was killed before he could testify, another disappeared. He readily names them; he also names the man he says gave him his orders, the man who gave the man his orders, the gangster whose ranch he flew to when the Dallas police turned him loose and the pilot who flew him. Who, he says, later died in a plane crash. He knew his picture had been taken; he says the law partner of a Warren Commission attorney told him not to worry.

Holt says he met Lee Harvey Oswald in New Orleans ("he wasn't any dummy"), as well as David Ferrie ("the weirdest guy you would ever want to meet") and Guy Banister ("an extreme right-wing type of individual, into just about everything"). It says something for Holt's credibility that he doesn't claim to have known Jack Ruby too. "I never even heard the name," says Holt. "What he said was asinine. Someone might sympathize with Jacqueline Kennedy. but you can't tell me a guy who's running a strip joint and beating up women is worried that she'll have to come back to Texas for a trial. I think he was just a gofer for the syndicate down there."

Why would conspirators order Holt so unnecessarily to the scene of the crime? "Dallas that day was flooded with all kinds of people who ended up there for some reason," says Holt. "It's always been my theory that whoever was the architect of this thing--and no one will ever know who was behind it, manipulating all these people--I believe that they flooded this area with so many characters with nefarious reputations because they thought, 'Well, if all these people get scooped up it'll muddy the waters so much that they'll never straighten it out'." Whether Chauncey Holt is the real thing or not, that's something like what happened. The police did scoop up and release several mysterious people in Dallas that day: a man with a leather jacket and black gloves, a Latin man, a crew-cut blond man in a hooded sweat shirt. A man named Jim Braden, with a long criminal record; Holt says Braden was with him on the plane out of Dallas.

If Holt's story could be verified, it would be pretty scary: the mob and the agency, cover-ups and rubouts. It could also be the product of a runaway imagination, or yarn-spinning for the sake of a little attention. What Holt says fits well with what researchers have long suspected. That's what makes his story at once persuasive and open to question. Should Holt be checked out? Certainly. Will that settle the question of conspiracy? Probably not.

Random event: The best argument against conspiracy theories is that if any moment in history were to be scrutinized with the obsessiveness focused on 12:30 p.m., Nov. 22, 1963, you could come up with weird coincidences, hidden connections, terrifying portents. People who believe the official version of the assassination--that Kennedy was shot by a lunatic whose motives were probably beyond even his own understanding--say that conspiracy theorists need to grow up, to come to terms with the fact that this was a random event, the moral equivalent of a bolt of lightning. Those who find a pattern here, it's said, are indulging in wishful thinking: to them, even sinister meaning is more comforting than no meaning at all.

"I have chosen to offer a way out of the madness," writes Jim Moore at the end of "Conspiracy Of One." "To believe that President Kennedy was killed by a conspiracy is not always to believe in zombie CIA assassins and Watergate burglars on the grassy knoll or in a Secret Service-FBI cover-up, but it is a path to personal doubt and disaster. Only when you and I come to grips with the fact that this mammoth tragedy can, in fact, be blamed on one man, can the personal growth and the healing process begin." In other words, get a life. It's a powerful altar call (assuming he's got his facts straight). What we'd give to be able to run it by Rose Cheramie.

A PDF version of the original article can be viewed by clicking here.

More sources on Chauncey Holt click here or click here.

Reprint from: http://jfkmurdersolved.com/newsweek.htm

Posada Carriles' US asylum application connects to JFK assassination

THE MAN THAT PLACED LUIS POSADA CARRILES IN DEALEY PLAZA ON 11/22/63

Image: Chauncey Marvin Holt

Image: Luis Posada Carriles

An expert on the Kennedy assassination asks:

Does Posada have incriminating evidence against Bush senior?

By Jean Guy Allard - Special for Granma International

• "I am beginning to suspect that Posada has some very incriminating evidence against Bush senior to be released if he dies a suspicious death. Otherwise I can't imagine how he can get away with it, or why the Bush administration exposes itself to so such an embarrassment."

In an interview with Granma International, Wim Dankbaar is not hiding his astonishment over the request for asylum by international terrorist Luis Posada Carriles in Miami.

"It's just astounding. The apathy of the media even more so. Why does no media source write that the man is not pardoned from his sentence for killing 73 people, but that he ESCAPED and is still a convicted terrorist on the loose?"

Dankbaar, a Dutch businessman who has financed new investigations into the Kennedy shooting - with the collaboration of retired FBI agents - and who is assembling a documentary on the subject, has shown how one of the three individuals arrested by Dallas police shortly after the crime, placed Luis Posada Carriles in Dealey Plaza in Dallas when the assassination was carried out.

He affirms that Chauncey Holt, one of three alleged vagrants - in truth, they were Mafia hitmen in disguise - who were detained, testified on the facts in a 2-hour video recording made shortly before his death that was never transmitted. "In this recording," said Dankbaar, "Holt names a few Cuban-Americans, and among them is Luis Posada Carriles. "He identifies the other two tramps as Charles Rogers and Charles Harrelson. Harrelson is a convicted hitman serving life for another murder, and also the father of Hollywood actor Woody Harrelson."

Newsweek was the first to report on this story in 1991. (A reprint of that article can be found by clicking here.)

Meanwhile Dankbaar adds a lot more information: Chauncey Holt was working under the orders of Meyer Lansky, notorious chief of the Havana mafia during the 1950s, and Pete Licavoli, another U.S. mafia leader.

But Holt was also an operative for the CIA. His instructions for Dallas came from his undercover CIA supervisor Philip Twombly of the Bank of Fullerton, California. Those instructions were specifically to make and deliver secret service credentials to a rabid anti Castro militant named Homer Echevarria, who was a close associate of Cuban exile leader Paulino Sierra . Holt further relates that he made id cards in the names of Lee Harvey Oswald, Lee Henry Oswald, Leon Oswald, Leon Osborne and Alek Hidell. Furthermore he drove to Dallas from Licavoli's Arizona ranch in the company of Leo Moceri and Charles Nicoletti, both hitmen for mafia moguls Giancana and Licavoli. Holt's testimony on the Kennedy plot is therefore clear evidence of the collaboration between the CIA, Organized Crime and the Cuban exile community, with the consent of the highest elements in the US Government. His story even points out that Joseph Ball, counsel for the Warren Commission, was a CIA asset, who harboured several of the participants in a safe house in Acapulco, to keep them out of reach of the Commission.

According to Dankbaar, Holt came forward because all the principals are dead and he felt the American public was entitled to know the truth about the death of their President. He expressed particularly strong reservations on the CIA's use of Lee Harvey Oswald as a sacrificial lamb. Holt has left a number of documents to support his story, up to written instructions and private correspondence from his mafia and CIA superiors. 1

Dankbaar pointed out that mafia boss Sam Giancana's biography - edited by his brother - discloses the role played by two buddies of former Havana chief Santos Trafficante, one of which could perfectly be Posada, according to the description given.

The research financed by Dankbaar was led by retired detective Zack Shelton, who worked for the FBI for 28 years, principally in Chicago and Kansas City. The film entitled Second Look presents the results of his search for new information on the controversial subject.

According to Dankbaar, the presence in Dallas of several small groups of individuals linked both to the Cuban-American leadership of the Batista faction and the Italian mafia could be explained by the CIA's compartmentalization of its operations.

As well as Posada, the film shows that other known Cuban-American CIA operatives, such as Frank Sturgis and Orlando Bosch, were also present in Dealey Plaza. It further presents the story of another CIA operative and sidekick of Charles Nicoletti from the Chicago crime family, James E. Files, who has confessed to being the man who fired the headshot at JFK from the infamous grassy knoll.

A fragment of this videotaped confession is presented here.

"Some JFK researchers tell me that they have never heard of James Files. I then remind them they are not supposed to hear of covert CIA operatives. He did not achieve the notoriety of people like Bosch, Novo and Posada, who are implicated in the Cuban airline bombing and the assassination of Orlando Letelier. He just managed to keep a lower profile. But rest assured that he was active in the same circles".

Dankbaar refers to these documents:

Document 1

Document 2

Dankbaar does not discount the possibility that Posada could have been another triggermen firing at Kennedy. He points out that in his special address at the Havana Convention Centre on April 11, Fidel Castro stressed that a document declassified by US authorities talks about Carriles as belonging to a CIA group, with the code name of Cazador (Hunter). Although ironically, the Cuban President noted, Carriles was a hunter who blew up passenger airplanes. Fidel Castro indicated that the document revealed that the terrorist had received military training, graduating with the rank of lieutenant, boasted a certificate as an expert sharpshooter and gave courses on explosives and demolition.

"Posada was almost killed in Guatemala in 1990, which he publicly blamed on Castro agents. 2

But that may be a cover story, it may as well have been the CIA. This guy knows too much, and I don't think it is too far out to assume he has communicated some type of "insurance".

Remember how CIA drug smuggler and Iran-Contra operative Barry Seal was gunned down? If you believe his lawyer, Seal was in direct contact with George Bush. And the personal telephone number of George H. W. Bush was found in the trunk of Seal's car. They blamed his murder on the Medellin cartel, but he was scheduled to testify and there were a lot of rumors he had a video tape featuring Jeb and George W. Bush." 3

Dankbaar also cites the case of David Morales: "David Sanchez Morales is another CIA assassin involved in the JFK assassination who died under suspicious circumstances. He had secured his house with double alarm systems, but not against burglars. He confessed to a friend: "It's my own guys I am worried about. I know too damned much." 4

It's possible that Posada can blackmail the Bush Administration. Therefore I would not be surprised if he gets his asylum. James Files has been a target for discreditation as the CIA purged his files, even his birth certificate says "deceased at birth", but denying Posada's past is not so easy". 5

And does the fact that ex operative Porter Goss, who admits to having participated in terrorist acts against Cuba, is the new CIA director, facilitate the return of Posada?

"Of course. The man that Bush selected, has been part of the CIA efforts to overthrow the Castro regime and assassinate its leader", Dankbaar confirms. "Goss is an ideal man to keep possible scandals under the carpet for Bush and particularly, his father. They are both participants in the same history. " 6

I am sure it will come as a surprise if I say that Bush has his fingerprints all over this case, but that is purely because of ignorance of the public. And the public is being kept ignorant because the mainstream press does not report on it. But there is ample documentary and testimonial evidence to tie Bush senior to the Bay of Pigs, the anti-Castro cause and the Kennedy assassination. It's beyond the scope of this interview to list that evidence here, but you have to understand that the Kennedy assassination stems from the same forces that were trying to oust Fidel Castro, which were basically Organized Crime, Cuban exiles, CIA and Big Oil in Texas. Bush connects to all four. They all wanted Cuba back and saw the Kennedy's standing in their way.

Their collaboration is now a matter of public record, from the Bay of Pigs, but also in the CIA/Mafia plots to kill Castro. Organized crime was under an unprecedented attack from Robert Kennedy, JFK wanted to abolish the oil depletion allowance and splinter the autonomy of the CIA, and the hawks in the Pentagon found him soft on communism and war. On top of that they blamed him for the failure of the Bay of Pigs, to make it worse he fired the top three men of the CIA. They openly called him a traitor. He was threathening their existence. So he had to go. It is as simple as that. They got rid of him in a coup d' état, displaying an arrogance of power by shooting him from opposite directions in broad daylight, and then lying to the American public in a cover-up that should insult the intelligence of every American who has only remotely looked at the evidence. Even despite the fact that most of that evidence was kept away. Imagine you film the murder of a President today. You could sell it for millions of dollars and it would go over every TV screen in the world. But not in Kennedy's case.

Kennedy wouldn't be President in the first place if he had not made a deal with Giancana to rig his election in Illinois. 7

Nixon lost just barely and he was put forward by Prescott Bush, few people know that. Neither do they know that Allen Dulles, the CIA director fired by Kennedy and later member of the Warren Commission, was a close friend. 8

Even less that Nixon, Dulles and Bush had been the architects for the Bay of Pigs under Eisenhower. This can all be documented. Just like his friendship with George Demohrenschildt, who was Lee Harvey Oswald's closest friend in Dallas. 9

Why did Bush never disclose that? Withholding information about a crime, is also a crime. Why does he not recall his whereabouts on 11/22/63? When and where did he befriend the Cuban CIA agent Felix Rodriguez, who by the way is Posada's buddy, all the way from the Bay of Pigs to Iran Contra. All those kids with T-shirts of Che Guevara don't know that Rodriguez was his captor and probably his killer. 10

Why does he deny that he is the "George Bush of the CIA" in an FBI memo from Hoover about the Kennedy assassination? 11

Does he really expect us to swallow that his directorship was his first job for the Agency? Why did he pardon Orlando Bosch, Posada's accomplice in the airline bombing, who was also in Dealey Plaza that day? 12

Not to mention Guillermo Novo, also just pardoned and released by Panama and returned to Miami. I could go on and on. Most journalists don't ask these questions, because they are not even aware of the information. 13

And the Bushes themselves hardly make a secret of their symphaties. Look at what George W. is doing now, he is still calling for the removal of Castro, and he is still carressing the guys who have been trying to accomplish that for over 40 years. That's why Florida is "his" state. Don't get me wrong, I have no affiliation with Castro or his regime, my orientation is towards freedom and democracy, but the double standards of the Bush administration are just so insulting they are almost laughable.

Actually, what I find the most intriguing phenomenon in this case, is that no one believes the government version of JFK anymore, instead everyone believes it was a conspiracy, but if you say that Bush was involved they look at you as if you're crazy. What is so difficult in grasping that the ones who seized power from a coup d'etat, are still in charge today? Is it because it's too mindboggling?

Allen Dulles summarized his opinion about the American public at a Congressional meeting: *"But nobody reads. Don't believe people read in this country. There will be a few professors that will read the record... the public will read very little".*

I guess I am one of those "few professors" and thus more in support of this qoute:

"There is no doubt now that there was a conspiracy, yet most of us are not very angry about it. The conspiracy to kill the president of the United States was also a conspiracy against the democratic system --and thus a conspiracy against you. I think you should get very angry about that."

- Gaeton Fonzi, Investigator for the House Select Committee on Assassinations

I say the story is a little bigger than Castro's indignation about Bush harbouring and protecting terrorists. He is harbouring the killers of JFK.

Sources: see webpage

****

More details http://jfkmurdersolved.com

For the latest news on Posada just click here.

"Treason does never prosper. What's the reason? When it prospers, None dare call it treason."

- Sir John Harrington

"If you shut up the truth and bury it under the ground, it will but grow, and gather to itself such explosive power that the day it bursts through it will blow up everything in its way."

- French author Emile Zola

Reprint from http://jfkmurdersolved.com/truthout.htm

Background on Posada Carriles

Wim Dankbaar on Luis Posada Carriles, reflections from a foreigner.

Why does this terrorist get such protection from Bush? Here is the story!

"Without the support from higher powers, Posada Carriles would just be a pawn. A pawn who would not have been able to bribe his escape from prison, to plan and execute terrorist attacks, and to slip through the mazes of Homeland Security. In other words, Posada and his friends need finance, backing and guidance", says Wim Dankbaar, the Dutch specialist on Kennedy's assassination. "So let's have a look at where his support comes from."

We must go back in time. Where did it all begin? Well, we need a history lesson that Americans did not get in school. We must go back to the first major effort to overthrow Castro's Cuba in a CIA sponsored invasion. An invasion that failed and is now known as the infamous Bay of Pigs. An invasion that failed because Kennedy did not back it all the way. That is at least the resentment that still lives on in the anti-Castro community. The operational base in Florida to train this army, was only outmatched in size by the US Navy. It was codenamed the JM/Wave station. The commanding officer of this station was Theodore Shackley, who later became the deputy director of the CIA under George Bush senior. One of the men who worked under Shackley at JM/Wave is your present CIA director Porter Goss.

Washington Post, interview with Porter Goss: click here

The architects for this clandestine invasion were CIA director Allen Dulles and then vice president and later president Nixon. Luis Posada Carriles was recruited for that invasion. He was trained in Fort Benning as an assassin and an expert in explosives. But what many Americans do not know, is that from that army, a number of men were selected to form a secret group of assassins. This group was called Operation 40, and the CIA code name was ZR/Rifle. This is the stuff that American media do not report. The mission of Operation 40 was to assassinate Fidel Castro. It may be no surprise that Luis Posada Carriles was selected for Operation 40. I will give you the names of some more members of this assassination group. And it is important to remember these names, because they will get back in the story later on. One of those members was Felix Rodriguez. He was also trained in Fort Benning, along with Posada.

Image: Felix Rodriguez and Luis Posada Carriles:

Veterans of the Bay of Pigs, members of Operation 40, friends, anti-Castro Cuban exiles,

CIA assets, trained assassins and operatives for Iran Contra.

Another member was Frank Sturgis, who later gained notoriety in the Watergate scandal. He was one of the Watergate burglars. There were also the brothers Ignacio and Guillermo Novo Sampol. There was Pedro Diaz Lanz, Castro's former Air Force Chief. And another was a Cuban physician named Orlando Bosch. He later earned the nick name "Dr. Death" for his record of terrorist acts. Members of Organized Crime were tossed into the mix. John Roselli from the Chicago mafia is just one example. They also recruited Castro's former mistress Marita Lorenz.

One of the supervisors for Operation 40 was E. Howard Hunt, another CIA agent whose name became headline news when the Watergate scandal broke. He was the boss of the so called Watergate plumbers. Another supervisor was David Atlee Phillips. Mr. Phillips was, as declassified files of Cuban State Security have shown, along with declarations of anti-Castro operatives, the direct superior of Lee Harvey Oswald, the accused assassin of president Kennedy. Phillips eventually became the CIA chief for operations in the Western Hemisphere.

It is now part of the public record that both Phillips and Hunt worked in tandem to orchestrate the CIA coup of 1954 in Guatemala that ended the government of Jacobo Arbenz. Let me emphasize that this was a democratically elected government.

But back to the Bay of Pigs and Operation 40. Who financed that? Well, it was financed by a group of Texan businessmen, headed by Mr. George Bush senior, the former president. What they did not tell you in school, is that Mr. Bush was closely associated with Dulles and Nixon. In fact, Nixon was the protegé of his father, senator Prescott Bush. Prescott Bush was responsible for Nixon's political career, and he also contributed to his campaign against Kennedy. And contrary to what Bush Sr. may want to tell you, he worked for the CIA as far as back as the Bay of Pigs. This is why his name appears in a declassified FBI document of J. Edgar Hoover about the reaction of the Cuban exiles to the Kennedy assassination.

FBI Memorandum "George Bush of the Central Intelligence Agency"
http://jfkmurdersolved.com/images/bushmemo.jpg

We are talking about the period that Bush's friendship with the Cuban exile community in Miami began. It is the period wherein he befriended Felix Rodriguez. Felix Rodriguez is a close associate of Luis Posada Carriles. They ended up working side by side in el Salvador in an operation that eventually became known as the Iran-Contra scandal. This operation was also directed from the White House, when Bush was vice president. Felix reported directly to him. But their history goes much farther back. Remember that Felix Rodriguez was also recruited for Operation 40, some sources say by Bush personally. Whatever the case, and despite the fact that your media don't write about it, Bush hardly makes a secret of his friendship with Felix Rodriguez. They appear together in numerous photographs and there is also correspondence to testify to their warm relation. And just last year, Felix openly campaigned for the election of George W.

Source: click here

Ernesto "Che" Guevara has become an icon in the world, right or wrong. A symbol of the fight for freedom. But what is less known is that Felix Rodriguez was part of the CIA team that tracked him down in Bolivia, which ended with his murder. There is even a photograph of Rodriguez with a captured Che. These are all hard historical facts. If you weren't aware of them, you can find them on my website.

Image: George and Felix chilling in the VP's office.

Above is a picture of Felix Rodriguez with a captured Che Guevara. Rodriguez still shows Guevara 's Rolex watch and the transcripts of the interrogations to intimate friends in his Miami home, which is decorated with photos of him and his old friend George. Below a 1988 Christmas note from George to Felix referring to Iran-Contra hearings.

Image: George and Felix

So, your former president is not ashamed to support and protect known assassins and terrorists. You will start to see a pattern here. Let us have a look at Orlando Bosch. As we have seen, Bosch was also a member of Operation 40. In 1976, the year that Bush was appointed director of the CIA, Orlando Bosch unites the anti-Castro groups into one organisation. This group was called CORU, or Commanders of United Revolutionary Organizations. They planned terrorist attacks against Cuba and other targets. Of course, Felix Rodriguez and Luis Posada also joined this group, as well as their fellow Operation 40 classmates Ignacio and Guillermo Novo Sampol.

Orlando Bosch and Luis Posada were then caught and imprisoned in Venezuela for their part in the bombing of a Cuban civilian airplane. On October 6 of 1976, 73 people were killed in that mid-air explosion. Also, just a few weeks earlier on September 21 of that year, the former minister of Salvador Allende, Orlando Letelier was assassinated in the streets of Washington DC. His car was blown up in broad daylight. The explosion killed him and his young secretary, Ronni Moffit. Her husband Michael, also an American citizen, was severely injured, but he survived. All the evidence points out that both these jobs were masterminded by CORU. One can only guess what information Mr. Letelier did possess to assassinate him. But it is now clear that the CIA had a heavy hand in the coup that brought down the democratic government of Salvador Allende, and installed dictator Augusto Pinochet. If your Government would open all its files on "Operation Condor", we would get more insight than we already have. But I guess they don't want to highlight this at a time that you are asked for support to remove brutal dictators, not install them.

Both CORU terrorists Ignacio and Guillermo Novo Sampol were indicted, convicted and sent to prison for their part in the assassination of Orlando Letelier, but eventually their CIA sponsored lawyers came to their rescue and managed to overturn their conviction on appeal. The strategy that every covert CIA agent learns: "Deny, deny, deny, we'll get you off the hook later", clearly worked. It doesn't always work. Especially if you didn't do it to begin with. It didn't work for Lee Harvey Oswald.

For their part in the Cuban airline bombing, Bosch and Posada spent years in jail. But in 1985, again trough his CIA sponsored contacts, Posada was able to bribe his way out of his Caracas prison. He was then given another identity to join Felix Rodriguez for Iran Contra in Llopango, El Salvador. Posada was using the name of Ramon Medina and Rodriguez called himself Max Gomez.

And what happened to Orlando Bosch? Well, he was released in 1987 and he returned to Miami as a result of diplomatic pressure from Otto Reich and Jeb Bush. Reich was then the US ambassador for Venezuela and we all know who Jeb Bush is. Mr. Reich is now U.S. Special envoy to the Western Hemisphere, appointed by your current government. Mr. Bosch was subsequently pardoned in 1990 by then President Bush. Dr. Death walks the streets of Miami as a free man. As of this moment there is much indignation and publicity about the case of Luis Posada Carriles, but we must not forget that Orlando Bosch is just as much a terrorist, guilty of the same crimes. The airline bombing is just one in a row. Posada and Bosch blew up give or take 5 targets a year.

See: http://cuban-exile.com/doc_051-075/doc0057.html

To illustrate further the US protection that these characters enjoy, we must make a jump in time to the year 2000. In november of that year, Castro was scheduled to speak in Panama on a summit. The Panamese authorities detected just in time a plot to assassinate him with explosives. If the plot had been carried out successfully, then not only Castro, but hundreds of innocent people would have been blown to pieces. Who were arrested and convicted for this plot? They are familiar names by now: Luis Posada Carriles, Guillermo Novo Sampol and two more of their Cuban exile friends, Pedro Remón and Gaspar Jiménez Escobedo. Guillermo Novo, remember him? He was the Operation 40 and CORU member, convicted for the killing of Orlando Letelier, until he got off the hook by his Cuban American attorneys, only to be allowed to continue his terrorist career. The same is of course true for Luis Posada Carriles. And what happens then? Well, last year, the Bush administration intervened and bribed the outgoing President of Panama, Mireyas Moscoso, to release and pardon all these guys. Did you hear about this on CNN? Did you hear that Novo, Remón and Escobedo where escorted back to Miami? Did you hear how they were welcomed, how they were heralded as freedom fighters? Maybe you did hear about it recently, now that the asylum case of Luis Posada has made the headlines as a result of the international public opinion.

So let us ask ourselves why President Bush exposes himself to the public embarrassment of protecting this criminal? Despite the media brainwash and apathy, it is now recognized that indeed Posada is a terrorist by all standards. Including the standards of the American people and even the most right-wing newspapers. Even the Cuban American National Foundation is shy to openly voice their support for Posada Carriles. It just cannot be sold. Fighting Castro is okay, but not with terror. Not in this age, where we condemn Al Qaeda.

Well, I say the answer to the question can be found in another crime of 42 years ago, the assassination of one of your most popular Presidents, John F. Kennedy. He had just initiated diplomatic contacts for a co-existence with Castro's Cuba. I have told you about Operation 40 that was designed to assassinate the Cuban leader. It was a CIA group that was secretly assembled from elements of organized crime, Cuban exiles and other figures willing to operate outside the Constitution. We all know about the CIA/Mafia plots to kill Castro. They tried to kill him with the most outrageous methods, from poison pills to exploding cigars, to outright assassination by rifle shots. They even tried to kill him with a cancer causing agent, a method that Lee Harvey Oswald's assassin Jack Ruby claimed was eventually used on him.

Of course your schools still teach that Lee Harvey Oswald was the lone assassin. And right after the assassination, the CIA disinformation machine even cranked out stories that he was one of Castro's agents, in order to put the blame on Cuba. But as the evidence mounted that Lee Harvey Oswald had in fact been an agent for the CIA, that he was actually fiercely against the Cuban revolution, it was realized that this lie could not be pushed anymore. Thus he became a lone nut.

Could it be that these plans that were put in place to assassinate Castro, along with the opposing forces to Kennedy, backfired and were then used to assassinate him? Well, one of those opposing forces, who is still hostile towards Cuba, was certainly George Bush and his associates. It is actually kind of strange that the vast majority of the Americans now believes that Kennedy's murder was a conspiracy involving elements of the CIA or mafia or both, yet the official position of your government is still that Lee Harvey Oswald was the lone assassin. "We know better than you". Not a great example of democratic principle, is it? Now I understand where the saying comes from: "I love my country, but I don't trust my government."

Let us have a look at some of the evidence that is now known, but not well known. The evidence that they never teach your children in school. The evidence that your mainstream media don't tell. Let us have a look at the testimony under oath of Castro's mistress Marita Lorenz, who after that short romance, was recruited by the CIA to kill him. This is under no dispute whatsoever.

You may recall E. Howard Hunt, the supervisor for Operation 40 and the chief of the Watergate burglar team. Well, in 1985 Hunt has fought a libel suit against a magazine that had printed allegations that he was involved in the conspiracy to kill President Kennedy. Hunt lost this suit and he was unable to convince the jury that he had not been in Dallas. During that trial Marita Lorenz gave testimony that she had worked for the CIA and that she had been part of Operation 40. She further testified that in the week prior to Kennedy's assassination, she had travelled from Miami to Dallas with a group of fellow members of Operation 40. This group travelled in two cars with weapons in the trunks. She claimed that she was not told about the mission of this journey, other than that it was confidential. She was told so by Frank Sturgis, who was now her boy friend. Whether her taste had improved or not, is not for me to judge, but there is apparently room for romance even in covert operations:

Image: Marita and Frank

To see Marita on film with Frank Sturgis and other members of Operation 40: click here

She identified her other travel companions as characters that may now sound familiar to you: Pedro Diaz Lanz, and the brothers Ignacio and Guillermo Novo Sampol. She also mentioned that the group was operating under guidance from none other than Orlando Bosch. In fact, she said that a few weeks before, she had been present at a meeting of this group in a Miami safe house, where Orlando Bosch and Lee Harvey Oswald were also present. Lorenz was reluctant to mention these names, but was induced to do so under questioning by Hunt's lawyers. Her story then went on to say that the group took refuge in a Dallas motel, where they were visited first by Hunt and then by Jack Ruby. When she started to question the involvement of the mobster, she was then sent back by Frank Sturgis, who said that he had made a mistake in bringing her along. She took a plane back to Miami the day before Kennedy was killed.

Whether her story is true or not, the fact is that her testimony was given under oath. Thus at the risk of being prosecuted for perjury. It is also fact that her testimony is not widely known to the American public. It is a further fact that Hunt lost the lawsuit and that all the persons she mentioned, had proven connections with the CIA and covert operations, some of which are pure terror. Her testimony has been largely ignored by American mainstream media, and the coverage that was there, have mainly been attempts to discredit it. But another fact, one that that is never emphasized, is that none of these dangerous characters who were mentioned by Lorenz, have ever taken steps to prosecute her for perjury, libel or defamation. This is strange, as none of us would take it lightly to be implicated in the murder of a President. It may well be that publicity opens a can of worms that they rather keep closed. I bet they neither like the publicity that we now see about Posada Carriles.

What about Howard Hunt himself? Well, Mr. Hunt is still around and was recently interviewed for Slate Magazine by Ann Louise Bardach. She asked him for his thoughts on the accusation that his partner David Phillips had been involved in the Kennedy assassination. You know what he said? I'll give you the exact quotes:

Slate: I know there is a conspiracy theory saying that David Atlee Phillips-the Miami CIA station chief-was involved with the assassination of JFK.

Hunt: [Visibly uncomfortable] I have no comment.

From: http://slate.msn.com/id/2107718/

Except for Watergate, the government has never shown interest to question Mr. Hunt.

And Marita? Marita has emailed me that she stands firm behind her story as ever.

Testimony of Marita Lorenz: http://jfkmurdersolved.com/pdf/lorenz.doc

If the story is true, it is all the more evidence that Lee Harvey Oswald was one of their own ranks, selected to be "a patsy". Just like he said on television. It is also evidence that Jack Ruby, who silenced him before he could say more, was part of the conspiracy.

What is at least undisputed, is that the accused assassin was friends with one George DeMohrenschildt, who was an oil geologist in Dallas with proven CIA connections. That much we know. But what the public in general does not know, is that Mr. Demohrenschildt was also a personal friend of George Bush senior. It is a friendship that Bush himself has never disclosed. Mr. Demohrenschildt's address book and correspondence have disclosed it. Is it just a coincidence that he reportedly killed himself in 1977, just one day after he was located by investigator Gaeton Fonzi from the House Select Committee that re-examined the assassination of Kennedy?

Then there is another piece of unknown testimony that we have recently been hearing about. It is the story of former CIA operative and mafia associate, Chauncey Holt, who was recorded on video just before he died. He was a man who claims to be one of the three "tramps" that were apprehended and photographed in Dealey Plaza. He says the tall one was Charles Harrelson, Woody's dad, who is now in jail for another crime. This man, Chauncey Holt, tells on video that one of the Cuban characters he saw there, was none other than Luis Posada Carriles. It would be worthwhile to investigate the veracity of this man's claims. Likewise, it is an interesting question why the American public has never seen this video recording. You know why? Well, let me give it a try: Because in this videorecording he tells in great detail how the conspiracy and the cover-up went into work, who was involved and from whom he received his orders. He gives names of people, some of which are still alive. Names that Newsweek did not dare to print after they interviewed him. They just asked the reader if Chauncey's story would settle the question of conspiracy? And they filled in the answer for you: "Probably not". He gives dates and documents. Up to the written instructions from his superiors. That's right, written instructions that he was ordered to destroy. Instead he saved them. However, no investigative journalist seems overly eager to contact his family to view them. And take it from me that I have contacted a few of those journalists.

Contrary to the average American, it seems that your Government is not interested in solving this case, other than re-iterating its official lone assassin position, which is now perceived as a lie by so many. And correctly so. The polls show that 90% of Americans do not buy the lone assassin theory. They are right! But their government keeps saying: No, you are not! There is that democratic paradox again. I use the term lone assassin THEORY intentionally, as

opposed to "consiracy theory", which should actually be conspiracy FACT, despite what Peter Jennings may tell you on ABC.

Additionally, there is a man alive and well in a Chicago prison, a man who has been claiming for over a decade that he is one of the real assassins of President Kennedy. This man, his name is James Files, has been proven to be an associate of Charles Nicoletti, a notorious hitman from the crime family of Sam Giancana. It is the same man that Chauncey Holt said he drove to Dallas. James Files has identified this Nicoletti and John Roselli as other shooters in Dealey Plaza. Is it a coincidence that all these men were also recruited in the CIA/Mafia plots to assassinate Fidel Castro? Is it again a coincidence that all these men were murdered shortly before they were scheduled to testify? Why do we see the same pattern here? The pattern that the American authorities are not interested to investigate this man? The pattern that the American public has never heard about this man? This man says he knows George Bush from the Bay of Pigs, that George Bush did recruiting for Operation 40. This man also says that Orlando Bosch was right there on Dealey Plaza. Not an outrageous claim at all, since we know that Bosch and Posada worked together in other operations. The Cuban airline bombing is just one example.

The scarce media coverage on James Files was predictably lambasting his story, claiming he is just a convict trying to get attention. But the lead on James Files came from the FBI, they never mention that. And on my website I show FBI documents that prove beyond a shadow of a doubt that he was exactly what he says he was: A career criminal and a covert CIA operative. In fact, these documents show that he was involved in the exact same operations as Bosch, Novo and Posada, namely the assassination of Orlando Letelier and the Cuban airline bombing. They show that the explosives for both these acts, or Covert Operations as the CIA calls them, were picked up by James Files and came from the Falcondo Mining Company in Bonao in the Dominican Republic. Isn't that where former US attorney Lawrence Barcella just said that Posada had been present at a planning meeting?

http://www.miami.com/mld/miamiherald/news/11705857.htm

Let's see if reporters will bombard me with emails for copies of these documents.

Document 1 (Reprinted at the end of this article)

Document 2 (Reprinted at the end of this article)

Why was James Files not killed?, is what many researchers ask me. Well, he was never called to testify. Neither were Bosch, Novo and Posada. Besides, you can't keep killing them all, or it may become too obvious. Ignoring or discrediting them, is just as effective. And Chauncey tells he was warned that they were looking for him. By Regis Blahut, the CIA liaison on the House Select Committee on Assassinations. He was appointed to "assist" them in their investigation.

Finally, there is another man alive and well, a former CIA contract pilot, who declares to have flown John Roselli to Dallas on a CIA supported flight. This man has given testimony before on government commissions, like the Church Committee, some of it is still classified. There are many documents that testify to his past and credibility. Again, the US Government has shown no interest in the information of this man.

This history may shed light on why anti-Cuba terrorists, like Posada, Novo and Bosch, enjoy so much protection from the US authorities. It may well explain the lies and the obvious farce of Posada's detention. Consider that the US Government intervened to get Posada and his three terrorist accomplices, pardoned and released from Panama. And now they want to have us believe that they did not follow Posada's movements after that? That they were not aware of his whereabouts? That he slipped into the country undetected? That he was not caught in the tight net of Homeland Security for which you pay millions of tax dollars? That they only became aware of him just recently? I am asking: How dumb do they think the American people are? It's very simple. Posada was picked up because of international pressure and publicity. They knew exactly where he was and they knew exactly how he entered the country. They helped him do it.

On May 20, Bush received a small delegation of the Cuban-American National Foundation, a known and proven backer of Posada Carriles, he even said that himself. But the subject of Luis Posada Carriles was not discussed. How many lies do they think you can take?

Posada's benefactors and protectors have got him off the hook for every crime he did. Whoever thinks that he will be extradited for crimes he did on their behalf, is naïve. This guy knows way too much to let him go outside their control.

The Government has declared that Posada is not wanted for any crime in the US. But that is just because they don't tell you about all his crimes. This includes crimes against your own system. The assassination of your elected president, is a crime against your freedom and your Constitution. Maybe that will get you mad. If a lone nut did not do it, as most of you believe, then it was coup d' etat. A coup d' état that changed history and destiny. A coup d' etat in what they say is the freest country in the world. The example for all democracies. It is a crime against the same freedom they make you fight wars for in far away countries, sacrificing your soldiers. Maybe the American democracy should first clean out its own closet?

It would be advisable, that as long as Posada is not extradited, to question him about the assassination of your President. To scrutinize his alibi for that date in November 1963. And that of Orlando Bosch, Guillermo Novo and others as well. Buying their stories that they were sound asleep or watching television at home, is just not good enough. As a matter of fact, it may be a better idea to NOT extradite Posada .... but try him right within your own borders. In Dallas, Texas, to be precise. That is, if you still care about your Constitutional laws. Laws that command that, contrary to what the Warren Commission did, an unsolved homicide should be handled under he jurisdiction of the state where it happened. You've got a new sheriff there. She is female, Mexican, democrat and lesbian. All the things that George loves. Circumstances have never been better.

Wim Dankbaar, May 25, 2005

" The individual is handicapped by coming face-to-face with a conspiracy so monstrous he cannot believe it exists."

--J. Edgar Hoover

This article may be reprinted without permission. It may be picked up by the newswires, the Chicago Tribune, the Washington Post, Newsweek, The New York Times, The Miami Herald , The LA Times and all other media.

For more in depth information click here

****

• The United States yesterday rejected Venezuela's initial efforts to extradite a Cuban exile wanted for a 1976 airliner bombing that killed 73 people. The Bush administration told Venezuela its request that Luis Posada Carriles be arrested with a view to extradition was "clearly inadequate" because it lacked supporting evidence, the State Department said.- Reuters

What a joke, the evidence is all here:

http://www.gwu.edu/~nsarchiv/NSAEBB/NSAEBB153/index.htm

State Dept. Daily Press Briefing May 23, 2005

Wednesday, 25 May 2005, 11:31 am

Press Release: US State Department

QUESTION: Can we hold Venezuela?

MR. BOUCHER: Ma'am.

QUESTION: He also said that if U.S. don't extradite Posada Carriles, he'll think about reviewing the diplomatic relations, even shut down the U.S. -- the Venezuelan Embassy here in the U.S. So would you -- do you have any comment? This is one more of --

MR. BOUCHER: The question of an extradition, the question of all the matters facing Mr. Posada Carriles, this is a legal matter. *It's not a political matter. It's not a question of diplomatic relations. It's a legal matter.* And that as we look at his status here or we look at the provisional request for arrest, we'll look at it based on the legal facts. Our judicial system will deal with it, our Justice Department will deal with it. Any future requests, anything that goes on in that matter, needs to be based on a legal case and the facts of the matter. It's not a issue of political pressure or diplomatic pressure or threats to do this, that or the other. We'll look at it based on a legal situation.

QUESTION: Well, what about the, they say, threat of reviewing diplomatic relations with --

MR. BOUCHER: It has nothing to do with legal case. The legal case will be the legal case and that's how we'll look at it.

QUESTION: But this is one more, they say, one more of Mr. Chavez's, they say, statements against the United States or trying to push the United States to come up with -- is one more Mr. Chavez's statements.

MR. BOUCHER: So?

QUESTION: So? What do you have to say about that? Is it --

MR. BOUCHER: Nothing particular. It's one more of his statements. It's not relevant to the matter at hand so I don't think I need to deal with it.

QUESTION: Is there any way Mr. Chavez's public statements can sway the U.S. Government in the case?

MR. BOUCHER: As I said, it's a legal matter. What happens here in terms of our own situation with regard to status or any other matters before the U.S. courts will be made on the legal case. If the Venezuelan Government presents such a case, we'll look at it completely and fairly. But what we decide to do will be based on the legal -- on a legal basis, not on threats, not on diplomatic arguments, not on statements, not on outbursts or whatever you call them. It's going to be a legal matter.

Reprint from http://jfkmurdersolved.com/posada.htm

1 – 179 – 4328

FEDERAL GOVERNMENT

Associate Director

Sept. 16, 1983

Office of Enforcement Operations

Director, FBI

JAMES E. FILES.

Attached is a copy of a communication which furnishes information concerning a current investigation.

Subject: Sutton, James E. aka Files, James E. aka Castillo, Sergio A.

25 SEPT. 1976. During an interview with Aldo Vera he stated he had been expelled from accion Cuba in June of 1976 because of his informant activity. But in early July he had been at a meeting in Bonao in the Dominican Republic at the executive lodge of the Falcondo Mining Company to help plan an assassination and a bombing. The assassination was Orlando Letelier, and the bombing was a Cuban airliner.

Aldo Vera did not know everyone at the meeting but gave the names of: Michael Townley, Sergio Castillo, Sacha Volman, Frank Castro, and Jose Suarez. Three unknown subjects were also present. Aldo Vera stated he had never seen those three subjects before.

OCT. 6, 1976. A Cuban airliner was blown up killing (73) seventy-three people aboard.

AUG. 1978. Jose Suarez was released after serving (11) eleven months on contempt of court charges for refusing to answer questions ask by the Grand Jury.

Upon his release he disappeared. Presumed; deceased.

NOTE: x x x x x x x x x x x x x x x x x x x x x x x x x x x x x x x x x x x x x x x x x x x x x x x x x x x x x x x x Washington D.C. Supervisor x x x x x x x x x x x x x x x x x was advised by FBIHQ Supervisor x x x x x x x x x x x x x x x x.

Agent : A J Stokely

1 – 646 – 1072

FEDERAL GOVERNMENT

Associate Director

FEB. 23, 1984

Office of Enforcement Operation

Director, FBI

JAMES E. FILES:

Attached is a copy of a communication which furnishes information concerning a current investigation.

Jan. 16, 19, 23, 27, 1984: During this time (4) four subjects have been interviewed in Bonao, Paraguay. The (4) four subjects have all identified the picture of Sergio Castillo as that of Sutton, James E. aka Files, James E. And state that they remember him being in Bonao, Paraguay in July of 1976 with Sacha Volman. Sacha Volman was a forman employed by Falcondo Mining Company which is a part of Gulf and Western. The subjects all stated they remembered him because they were in the store room where the explosives were kept when Sacha Volman and a stranger (Sutton aka Files aka Castillo) walked in and Sacha Volman requisitioned two (2) cases of explosives and six (6) detonators. They thought this was strange but they were afraid to question Sacha Volman as they were afraid they would loose their jobs.

All four (4) subjects have volunteered to appear before a Grand Jury Hearing, and to answer questions and to identify subject Files aka Sutton aka Castillo.

x x x x x x x x x x x x x x x x x x x x x x x x x x x x x x x x x x x x x x x x x x x x x x.
x x x x x x x x x x x x x x x x x x x x x x x x x x x x x x x x x x x x x x x x x x x x x x x
x x x x x x x x x x x x x x x x x x x x x x x x x x x x x x x x x x x x x x x x x x x x x x x

Agent: AJ Stokely

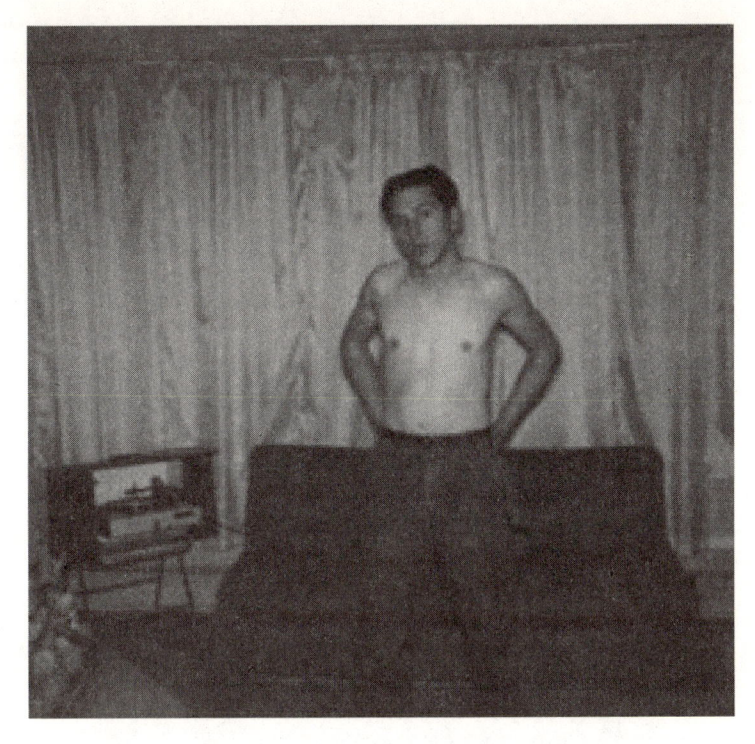

Picture of James Files taken in November 1963 by
Lee Harvey Oswald in the Lamplighter motel in Dallas.

Picture of James Files (left) age 20 with the man who killed officer J.D. Tippit

James Files and Joe West at their only meeting in the Stateville prison in Joliet, Illinois.

The Texas Schoolbook Depository as it looks today

The grassy knoll as it looks today

The Bothun picture was taken approximately 30 to 40 seconds after the assassination. The figure in background (top right) is probably James Files making his exit from Dealey Plaza. It is the only person walking away from the grassy knoll.

John Rademacher found the shell casing in 1987

This .222. Remington shell casing was found in Dealey Plaza 6 years before Files was located and made his confession. No one knew the cause of the indentations in it, until they were confirmed to be teethmarks by dental experts, after Files had said he had bitten down on his shell and left it there.

Bob Bennett

In my quest to piece together the puzzle of the Kennedy Assassination, I work a lot with the Google search engine. A few weeks ago I was trying to find information on some of the names that CIA contract pilot Tosh Plumlee had mentioned as his instructors who sent him and others on an abort mission to Dallas in order to prevent the pending assassination attempt of president Kennedy.

One of those names is Bob Bennett. When I typed that name in Google, I quickly found references to the US senator for Utah, Robert F. Bennett. Could this be the same man as Tosh's CIA instructor of 42 years ago? Well, I was immediately drawn to dig further when I saw that Bennett had been a candidate for Deep Throat, of Watergate fame. For those not familiar with the subject: Deep Throat was the secret source for Washington Post reporters Bob Woodward and Carl Bernstein, who broke the Watergate scandal, which eventually forced president Nixon to resign.

Image: Senator Bob Bennett

Let me first say that Tosh has not made the connection with senator Bennett of Utah. That was my "eureka".

Tosh just recalls his CIA instructor of 42 years ago as one Bob Bennett. So a few weeks ago I type this name in Google and I find links to the senator, and also that he had been a candidate for deep throat. Whether he is or not, upon some further digging I saw he was running "the Mullen Company", a CIA front for Howard Hughes.

We should also know that Robert Maheu, who worked for Howard Hughes, introduced the CIA to Johnny Roselli to enlist the help of the mafia in the now declassified CIA/Mafia plots to kill Fidel Castro. And of course we now know that Roselli was part of the abort team and one of the key players in Dealey Plaza.

Furthermore the Watergate burglary is widely rumored to have a connection with the Kennedy assassination, to which I wholeheartedly subscribe. I have good sources for the thesis that the break-in was done to seize hard evidence for the conspiracy to kill JFK, more specifically a film reel of CIA operatives with Lee Harvey Oswald. And the burglars themselves were of course all CIA operatives with direct links to the Bay of Pigs and the Kennedy assassination, like James McCord, Frank Sturgis, E. Howard Hunt and the anti-Castro Cubans. It is clear that Watergate is connected to the Kennedy assassination. Nixon himself gave his chief of staff H.R. Haldeman a hint to this connection, describing it as "hanky panky" in the infamous "smoking gun" tape:

Nixon: Of course, this is a, this is Hunt, you will-that will uncover a lot of things. You open that scab there's a hell of a lot of things and that we just feel that it would be very detrimental to have this thing go any further. This involves these Cubans, Hunt, and a lot of hanky-panky that we have nothing to do with ourselves. Well what the hell, did Mitchell know about this thing to any much of a degree?

****

Nixon: When you get in these people when you...get these people in, say: "Look, the problem is that this will open the whole, the whole Bay of Pigs thing, and the President just feels that" ah, without going into the details... don't, don't lie to them to the extent to say there is no involvement, but just say this is sort of a comedy of errors, bizarre, without getting into it, "the President believes that it is going to open the whole Bay of Pigs thing up again. And, ah because these people are plugging for, for keeps and that they should call the FBI in and say that we wish for the country, don't go any further into this case", period!

Source: http://www.watergate.info/tapes/72-06-23_smoking-gun.shtml

In his book, The Ends of Power, Haldeman cites several conversations where Nixon expressed concern about the Watergate affair becoming public knowledge and where this exposure might lead. Haldeman writes:

"In fact, I was puzzled when he [Nixon] told me, 'Tell Ehrlichman this whole group of Cubans [Watergate burglars] is tied to the Bay of Pigs.' After a pause I said, 'The Bay of Pigs? What does that have to do with this [the Watergate burglary]?' But Nixon merely said, 'Ehrlichman will know what I mean,' and dropped the subject."

Later in his book, Haldeman appears to answer his own question when he says, "It seems that in all of those Nixon references to the Bay of Pigs, he was actually referring to the Kennedy assassination."

If Haldeman's interpretation is correct, then Nixon's instructions for him to, "Tell Ehrlichman this whole group of [anti-Castro] Cubans is tied to the Bay of Pigs," was Nixon's way of telling him to inform Ehrlichman that the Watergate burglars were tied to Kennedy's murder. (It should be noted that many Cuban exiles blamed Kennedy for the failure to overthrow Castro at the Bay of Pigs, pointing to Kennedy's refusal to provide U.S. military support for the invasion.)

Source: http://mtracy9.tripod.com/kennedy.html

In the link below to an article by Don Fulsom, we can learn how Nixon orchestrated his own pardon from prosecution by replacing his vice president Spiro Agnew with Warren Commission member Gerald Ford. The reason is obvious: No one could afford further escalation of the Watergate scandal, because if it was properly investigated it would have led to Dallas 1963. And Mr. Ford had already proven his cover-up skills in the Warren Commission. To learn more about that click here.

http://crimemagazine.com/04/richardnixon,0830.htm

Image: Robert "Tosh" Plumlee

The final clincher came from Tosh himself when I confronted him with my discoveries. He said that indeed his CIA instructor was a tall distinguished looking gentleman. He estimated his age around thirty (Bennett is now 72). He also said that at that time he had joined the Mormon church for three years and the man who encouraged him to join, was none other than Bob Bennett.

As we can see in the link below, Bob Bennett is a mormon, and Utah is the capital state of the Mormons.

http://www.nndb.com/people/191/000032095/

Before the distractors - who will always pop up in anything credible, relevant to the JFK assassination - start to shout that Tosh is a flimsy source, let me give them some homework here.

This collection of CIA, DEA and FBI documents will not only show that Tosh is exactly who he says he is, but also the obstruction of justice and his story. Note especially the many redactions in these files.

I can only guess why Mr. Bennett never opened up about the Kennedy assassination, but then again, talking about that is not your best health insurance. I hope he will change his mind before he leaves the stage.

I have always maintained that it is a myth that all who know about the Kennedy conspiracy, are dead. Senator Bennett is just another example. What could he tell us about Dallas 11/22/1963?

Wim Dankbaar

May 17, 2005

Below are the relevant excerpts of the declarations of Tosh Plumlee:

Q: The general "they" that we've been talking about, can you be specific as to who gave you your instructions for November 22, 1963?

A: Yes, my handler at that point was a person by the name of *Bob Bennett*. The people that would be CIA direct liaison aliases names, Bill Rogers, Rex Beardsley, *Bob Bennett*, and Larry Allen. And a guy by the name of Johnny Smith, which was actually John Roselli, those are found in the 105 files.

Q: You said Roselli was one of the people you got your instructions from, correct?

A: Not on that particular day, not Roselli. That particular day my instructions came through Locksahatchie through *Robert Bennett* and also Rex Beardsley, I believe it was.

Q: But Roselli was a key figure and someone you did get instructions from?

A: Well, Roselli's name was mentioned that day that he would be picked up at Tampa airport and he was staying at the Congress Inn so I guess as far as that particular mission the first time I heard Roselli's name was through *Bob Bennett* who instructed me and Sergio and Rojas. Rojas came from Miami to Lantana and we came from Locksahatchie to Lantana but I was already instructed through *Bennett* that we were to pick up John Roselli, and he was referred to as the Colonel, and I knew who that was because I had already had previous contact on many, many occasions with Johnny Roselli.

I learned that it had been discussed by the abort team where to go, how to abort, and what to look for. I had not at first paid much attention to any of these details as bits and pieces unfolded. I was told that the abort team, for whom I was only the pilot at that time, would probably be looking for a minimum of 19 or 20 people that would be in the Plaza. Most of the team members felt that this was another false alarm, there had been many during the past few weeks. The detailed instructions to the team had come from *Robert Bennett* and Rex Beardsley, as well as another case officer whose name I can not recall.

The post-mission debriefing was held on November 25th, my birthday, in West Palm Beach by Rex Beardsley, *Bob Bennett* and, I believe, Tracy Barnes. There was some discomfort or unhappiness about my having been present in the Plaza without authorization. Sergio was reprimanded for taking me along as a 'spotter'. The report was transmitted to field headquarters Miami to JM/WAVE Headquarters, and the CIA's Miami Cuban Desk.

Source: http://jfkmurdersolved.com/toshfiles.htm

Update: On May 31, 2005, Mark Felt, former FBI Deputy director, came forward in an interview with Vanity Fair, revealing that he had been Deep Throat. This was then confirmed by The Washington Post and Bob Woodward. Thus Senator Bennett was not Deep Throat, but it looks like he is one of the men who sent a CIA abort team to Dallas.

Now that Deep Throat has come forward, it would be interesting to ask him some questions that nobody asks:

What did Nixon mean with "the whole Bay of Pigs thing"?

What did he mean with "hanky panky"?

How does Mr. Felt feel about the cover-up and Nixon's pardon by Ford? What were the true reasons for that?

Reprint from http://jfkmurdersolved.com/bennett.htm

Why is James Files in prison?

Well, the official account is "attempted murder of a police officer". However, as with the official version of the JFK assassination, a closer look reveals something different. On these pages we are giving you two sides of the story of the conviction of James Files and his partner David Morley.

To wrap up the official story: Morley and Files were car-chased by two police officers. When the officers forced them to stop, Files and Morley opened fire. Morley shot David Ostertag, one of the cops. That one shot was not fatal, he recovered from his wounds. Case closed: Attempted 1st degree murder of a police officer. Sentence: two consecutive prison terms of 15 years each.

But Files and Morley say something else, namely that the two police officers tried to kill them and it was the officers who opened fire. Let's investigate both sides of the story.

To see David Morley's mugshot and sentence information click here

To see James Files' mugshot and sentence information click here

To view the official account of the story click here

Let's see what James Files has to say:

J - Why don't you briefly tell why you are in prison right now?

JF - I am in prison for a specific reason. When I came out of the federal prison, I did a federal stretch and I was out for a little while and people started trying to kill me. When they started trying to kill me, the first time I was at Quentin road and Rilings, at Rilings Lake Beach, shortly past midnight, driving a little Chevy Chevette. And the cops had been harrassing me , they knew who I was. Every time they see me, they handcuffed me, get me out of the car, my papers, blew out my stuff all down the street. Well, in this particular night, I had pulled up the stoplight there, I am on Quentin road, fixed to make a right hand turn on Rilings road. I'm staying on my end (inaudible) this time about two blocks down from there.

I looked up in the rearview mirror and I see this car pulling up behind me with no lights, next lane. And I thought: Shit, cops again! You know, I 'm going to get hassled again. It's not a squad car, but I figured it's just detectives, you know. As it pulls up alongside of me, I'm looking in the mirror sitting by the door, the little door there on my side, and I see an SMG coming up. For anybody who doesn't know what that is, it's a small machine gun, an automatic weapon, and as I see it coming out of the window, I roll across the seat, hit the door , hit the ground, roll back up against the (inaudible) of the car. They put 30 holes in my car! Four clips they put into it. As they were pulling away, I come up off the ground on my feet , so I got off about four rounds. I'm on federal parole at that point, I'm not supposed to be carrying a weapon, but you never find me without a weapon. I got off four rounds, took the back window out, they kept going. I jumped back in my car, took a right onto Rilings road, went down to Grove Avenue, pulled into the house at (inaudible) 1620 Grove, went in there and got the tarp from my uncle out of the garage and put it over the car, so they couldn't see the bullet holes. That was the first attempt on my life.

J - When was that?

JF - Aah, I got out of federal prison in '88. This year was late '89 or early 90 I guess.

J - Has there been any attempt on your life in prison?

JF - Not in prison. I had a lot of fights, but that's not attempts on my life. I mean the things that happen here is just day-to-day living . I got a few scars from knives here and there, but that's irrelevant there.

J - You don't think it was people trying to take you out?

JF - Oh no, definitely not.

J - Well then, it doesn't have anything to do with the JFK job?

JF - No, definitely not. And when they started trying to kill me on the street, after the first attempt on my life in the free world, as I call it: Next day I went to see somebody down in the city and I wanted to ask him a specific question: If we had a problem? I said I did my federal time. I got busted on the chop shops. I didn't take nobody down with me. I said I went and kept my mouth shut, I didn't testify, I didn't give nobody up. I took the conviction, I have done my time. What is the problem? We got a problem? Let me know! And he told me: Jimmy - he always called me Jimmy - Jimmy boy, he says: Calm down, calm down! He says: Listen to me, he said: You got no problem with us! You did your things. He says: Hey, you didn't have no problems when you got down, you got money, we looked after certain people for you, took care of your family, you had no problems! When you came out , you went to the restaurant, everybody parked, everybody came by to see you. We dropped a lot of envelopes. He said: You have money when you come out. Everybody looked after you when you came out! That's respect! Don't think we are after you! Whatever you 've done, that's with your previous employers, not us! That's only the other side of the fence with people you worked for before. He said: No, not us, Jimmy, I'll give you my word on that!

The second attempt I was on my motorcycle and it's a long story and I won't go with you all through that ...

J - Hold a minute, so you are saying that attempt was not the mob, that was the Agency?

JF - That was the Agency, that was the government, somebody in the government!

J - So the government has tried to take you out ?

JF - That's what I honestly believe!

J - Okay, make a statement.

JF - Now then, the second time on my attempt, ... or are you talking about making a statement on the government?

J - Yeah

JF - After I talked to a certain party in Chicago down there in the city, about them trying to kill me, he was telling me that was my previous employers. What we're talking about here, is we're talking about a government agency. I won't say which agency it was trying to take me out, but at the time I had people with the DOD on me, because I had taken certain material off the computer at Oxford, from the arsenals that I worked, I had an access to classified materials there for building new tanks, new helicopters, everything (inaudible) with black hawk helicopters. I had the keys for everything, I had the range of firing, everything was classified because we made a lot of the stuff there. We made the nitrene? cable to fire the sidewinder missile, inside the federal prison.

Anyway, the second attempt, was .. - now I realize this is not the crime family that is after me, it has to be a government agency, the second attempt on my life was late at night, they ran me over on my motorcycle. They hit me so hard, they bent the frame on it. They towed the motorcycle out. That's all on record.

Next time that comes around, the third time, were these two off-duty officers. One of them is David Ostertag. *They will never admit they had a contract on my life* and I want to state here: I have no hard feelings against either one of these officers, even though they tried to kill me. I don't take this as anything personal. I think that they were doing a job. They were doing what they were paid to do. They just blew it! But the thing is this: I'm here because somebody opened up on my partner and me, they tried to kill us in broad daylight on May 7th, 1991, 3:15 PM, maybe 3:30, at the middle of route 12 in a little place called Buffalo Grove. We were between Quentin road and Long Grove road on route 12. They forced us off the road, when they forced us off the road - they say it was a high speed chase, it really wasn't a high speed chase, they spotted me at a gas station, I didn't even see them, I paid for the gas, got in the car with my partner David Morley, he was driving.

And we pulled out from there, they got in behind us. As they got up alongside, he started hitting the gas to go and I told him: No hold on! Pull over, we don't run from nobody! My exact words were: Fuck 'm, we don't run! Pull it over! We'll deal with it! As they cut us off, it's like he pulled into what was part of a driveway, it was gravel, a little fast, he hit the brakes and he littered a low tree. The tree we hit, wasn't any bigger than my arm. I threw the door open on my right hand side, to exit the car, this was a leased car, and after I opened the door to exit, they drove their car, which is a white unmarked car, into the side of our car. While I see the front of their car coming at the door, I jerked my leg back above the ground so I wouldn't get it cut off there and broken, and duck my head. And then they hit the door, the door hit me and knocked me back into the car and I bounced off the dash. And at that point, they opened fire. My partner David Morley, very good man, he saved my life on several occasions in the free world, his left hand is paralyzed, he has been shot a couple of times in shootouts. He can't use his left hand. At this point he's leaning down, fumbling under the seat of the car looking for his gun. Looking for a 9 mm. And I'm yelling: Get out! Get out! Get out!

And to me it seems like it's taking forever. When he got the 9, he put it up under his arm, he's gotta close that arm, he reached across, to open the door to exit. Well, this is only a few seconds, but it seems like a lifetime to me. And we come out of the car and when he comes out, he took the first shot: David Ostertag went down. At this point I come out, there's no need for me to even shoot. The other officer, Bitler - and I didn't know they were cops at that time, neither did my partner, we had no idea they were police officers - he crawled up under the car. And he was screaming I guess: They're gonna kill us both! They're gonna kill us both! David

Ostertag was already down. I grabbed the AK-47 out of the car, had it in the backseat. I had one picked out from the storage shed for a simple reason: I had a meeting prior to those people and somebody had poked me in the chest, and I just knocked him down and stumped on him a couple of times, and told him: Don't ever threaten me to tell me you're gonna trunk me! If you do, do it first and then come and tell me that you've done it! I went to tell David: We've got problems, I want to get the AK-47 out, got the ammo-can out., I had a 30-round clip in the AK-47, this is all in the logbooks, the ammo-can had 500 rounds of ammo in it. David Ostertag can tell you how many rounds we had for the 9 mm, the clips and all the loose rounds.

I went into a little swamp, it took them several hours to get me out. The AK-47, the tracker spring broke, it wouldn't fire. *(Note: Actually when the police found James Files in the swamp, he was under water, breathing through a cane stick, which is indicative of CIA training)*

W - Any witnesses to all this?

JF - A lot of people around. A lot of people. We had traffic backed up from the shooting incident there all the way to Wisconsin and all the way to the city of Chicago.

J - So who opened fire first?

JF - They opened fire first!

J - And they were in an unmarked car?

JF - Unmarked car!

J - Plain clothes?

JF - Plain clothes. They had a windbreaker on, they were wearing a badge under their gunbelt underneath the windbreaker jackets, sitting in the car. They were shooting from inside the car. David Ostertag had exited and was coming around and shooting when David Morley dropped him.

W - Did they ever say you were under arrest or..?

JF - No.

J - Did they identify themselves, did they yell: Police officer ?

JF- Nobody identified nothing. I mean: The shooting started.

W- How many shots were fired before your partner took the shot?

JF - Well I'm gonna say they got off probably the first 14 shots. They say they fired 3 and 11 out of 52. They said we fired the rest of them. But there's not that many shell casings on hand. And if the only weapons that were fired, were 9 mm's that day, and my weapon hadn't been fired, that leaves 3 clips. It's only 45 rounds. There's 15 rounds to a 9 mm in a staggered clip.

And they didn't fire that many, they still had rounds in theirs. So there's no way that 52 rounds were fired that day.

W - Are there witness reports on record?

JF - Oh, there's all kinds witnesses that have seen what went down. There's witnesses that plainly state as to who got out, who shot who, and who shot first. That's all in the court documents.

J - So how did they get a conviction if there are witnesses to say they fired first?

JF - That was very simple: We were tried in Lake County, Illinois. It didn't take them long to convict us. Everybody on the jury was related to a cop. You don't shoot a cop and walk away. If you shoot a cop, it don't matter whether it was self-defense or not.

W - Were these witness reports allowed? As evidence?

JF - Some of those were denied. I had witnesses that had come here to testify on my behalf and that was irrelevant and they were not permitted to testify. My own aunt was not permitted to testify at my trial.

W - So this was a frame-up?

JF - As far as I'm concerned, it was a frame-up. It was self-defense. Over and out. And I didn't even shoot nobody.

To view some of the signed witness reports click here

We also received an email from a close friend of James Files:

Mr. Ostertag and I spoke on January 3, 2003 when he returned my call placed at the States Attorney's Office when I tried to contact him there. Ostertag is a retired police detective for Round Lake Beach and also a retired detective for the Lake County States Attorney's Office.

As of January 2003, in addition to working for Discover Card, he also gives new police recruits talks about being shot in the line of duty. This shoot out incident with Dave Morley and James Files was the only time he was ever shot. Ostertag and his partner never identified themselves as police officers and did not say "you're under arrest". Ostertag and Gary Bitler started the shooting May 7, 1991 and Dave Morley returned fire when Ostertag was hit. James Files did not shoot a weapon that day. Dave Morley and James Files are in their 12th going on 13th year of prison for this case of self-defense.

Don't expect cooperation with Dave Ostertag. He has his story and Jimmy, Dave Morley, and two sworn eyewitnesses have their version. He told me that he hopes James Files stays in prison the rest of his life and never wants to see him get out. When I brought up the subject, Ostertag also thinks there needs to be a debriefing and counseling program for Special Forces men returning to civilian life. *He wishes that he was warned what he was up against to take out James Files. He feels betrayed by the government agencies who could have provided him that information. (FBI and CIA).* When I asked him if he was paid to kill James Files he just laughed it off and did not answer me. We spoke for about 45 minutes to an hour. I tried to explain that Jimmy is now a Christian and poses no harm to him or his family. He didn't care.

Pam

This picture was emailed to us by Mrs. Ray with the following information: "If you want, you can post this picture on the website with this information from me.

Pam"

Image: This picture was taken shortly before Jimmy went to Stateville. The shoot out incident May 7, 1991, with Ostertag and Bitler was the third unsuccessful attempt at killing James Files for what he believes is a "clean-up" operation to eliminate anyone, like Jimmy, who has first hand knowledge of the Mena -Bush -Clinton Cartel drug operations. He does not believe the attempts on his life were for his involvement with the JFK assassination. Files also believes this sensitive area of CIA/DEA US GOVERNMENT Drug operations is why Clinton and Reno classified James Files as a threat to National Security. That and James Files also wrote terrorist manuals called "CBW's" for George Bush's CIA in the 1970's.

Conclusion

James Files has killed many many persons. No sane person will resent a penalty for that. Part of his killings were on the battlefields of Laos, another part were contract murders for organized crime, but many were executions on orders of a part of the government, that seems accountable to no one. According to Files, the FBI and the CIA have known about his participation in JFK's assassination since 1964, as well as many more government-sanctioned "black operations" since then. He also killed people on orders of the CIA just because they knew something or witnessed the "wrong" things.

Like we see so often in this milieu, the soldiers that know too much or become otherwise a liability, are silenced by "executive action", as they label it so nicely. James Files tells us that he survived at least three such attempts, before it was decided to go for the next best option: Lock him away for the remainder of his life. No tears should be shed about his incarceration, but if James Files and two sworn eye-witnesses are telling the truth, the real injustice is this:

The people that exploited men like Files, and actually ordered many of his murders, have not been brought to justice. They knew or know about numerous murders he did. Yet they put him away for one he did not even attempt. Can the American system be that corrupt? We believe it can. Just like the overwhelming majority of the American people who believe that JFK's assassination was a conspiracy up to the highest levels of the government, subsequently covered up by that same government. This is also why, as long as these people are in charge, the JFK Assassination will never be brought to justice. However, this does not stop us from learning the true events.

Reprint from : http://jfkmurdersolved.com/jail.htm

Dave Ostertag on the alt.assassination.jfk message board, 24 sep 2001:

Hello to all. I'm the Police Officer that James is in prison for. I was shot in the chest with an exit wound on the right butt cheek. Personally I think he is full of dung. His story changes to fit the facts. I think he is entertaining though. I'm glad that he and Dave Morley will probably be spending the rest of their life in prison. Some interesting things happened with File's military record and his criminal history during the sentencing part of his trial. The military refused to honor the subpoena for his records. In regards to his Criminal History. I had arrested Files in 1984 or 1985 for a bond forfeiture warrant for possession of explosives out of Texas. I remember looking at his criminal history at that time and saying, this is a guy I'm going to run into again. He had a hommicide and other arrests and convictions on the record that showed he was a true professional criminal as compared to the street thugs you normally come across. I saved the Criminal History knowing that I would see him again. At the time of my gunfight with Files and Morley his rap sheet was clean. Both Files and Morley had active Federal Parole warrants at that time. Neither warrant appeared in the NCIC computer queries. Morley had begun his criminal carreer in 1975. He and his Step Father broke Morley's Step Brother out of a prison in Florida. Morley shot twqo Prison Guards in the escape and was shot three times himself. He was dropped off at a Hospital in Atlanta where he was arrested. The Step Brother was killed by the FBI a year later in Mobile, Alabama. Morley was sentenced to prison for the breakout and for shooting the Guards. He escaped in 1982 and was later caought and sentenced for the 1982 escaped. He had done time for that and for three subsequent Federal convictions and prison sentences with Files for Bank robberies. The Federal Parole violation warrants outstanding at the time of my gunfight with them were for the last Bank Robbery convictions. When my department arrested Morley one week prior to our gunfight, he had no arrests or convictions or the warrant on his criminal history. Files also had a clean criminal history. The Probation Officer that prepared their pre-sentence investigations used the 1985 criminal history that I had saved for Files and, had to contact local Law Enforcement and the Florida Department of Corrections to rebuild Morley's. I'm sure that there is an explanation but, it does raise questions. I'm just glad the two of them will be spending the rest of their life in prison. Just wanted to check in and say hello.

Letter #812 James Files to Pamela Ray, October 25, 2004

As for what Ostertag put on the Internet, I already have a copy of it and I really don't care what the cop says. But he is wrong on one thing. He did not arrest me in 1984, or 1985 and he has never arrested me at anytime. I was in the federal prison in that time period and that can be checked out. Yes, I was indicted on a bombing and was at the MCC in Chicago, Illinois for trial, as that was a federal case. At that time Ostertag was not a federal agent that I know of. When we had the shoot-out and I caught this case, it was not Ostertag that arrested me. He was in the hospital with them digging the bullet out of his you know what. Anyway, I went to trial for that charge in 1982 & 1983…Now, there was the time when I was indicted in 1979, or it could have been 1978, when I gave Billy Dauber the explosives and a year later I was indicted for that. That is when I went to the Ol' Man and told him that Billy Dauber was a blank-blank stool pigeon. There was only the two of us and I did not go tell on myself. When I got out of the federal prison in 1988 I was arrested an old warrant and I do not remember the name of who come and got me that time. But I used a lawyer for that one and I never went to trial. He got it tossed out of court. So, I was not convicted on that charge. But I was arrested so many times, I can't remember all of them. But I know that Ostertag did not arrest me in 1984, or 1985…As far as I know, I had never met him before we had that run-in, back in 1991.

Interview with Fabian Escalante

FABIÁN ESCALANTE ON POSADA AND OPERATION 40

By Jean-Guy Allard in Havana

May 22, 2005, 15:28

Editor's Note: It has recently been our pleasure to meet **Jean-Guy Allard**, well known journalist and writer who lives in Havana, Cuba. As with so many of our friends and colleagues, we met Jean-Guy through correspondence, drawn to him by our mutual interests and a shared world view. We thank him for contributing this exclusive interview with Fabian Escalante to Axis of Logic. You can read more about the author, Jean-Guy Allard, at the bottom of the page. - *Les Blough, Editor*

"Who had the means and motives to kill Kennedy in 1963?"

"WHO in 1963 had the resources to assassinate Kennedy? Who had the means and who had the motives to kill the U.S. president?", asks General Fabian Escalante in an exclusive interview in his Havana office. And he gives the answer: "CIA agents from Operation 40 who were rabidly anti-Kennedy. And among them were Orlando Bosch, Luis Posada Carriles, Antonio Veciana and Felix Rodriguez Mendigutia."

"Who were the ones who had the training to murder Kennedy? The ones who had all of the capabilities to carry it out? Who were the expert marksmen?" continues Escalante, pointing out that the case of international terrorist Luis Posada Carriles has to be seen within the historical context of what he calls "the machinery of the Cuban American mafia."

And in the heart of that machinery is Operation 40, created by the CIA on the eve of the failed Bay of Pigs invasion, says the ex-chief of Cuban intelligence, author of **The Plot** (Ocean Press), about the assassination of the U.S. leader.

FIRST TESTIMONY: JOSE RAUL DE VARONA

"The first news that we have of Operation 40 is a statement made by a mercenary of the Bay of Pigs who was the chief of military intelligence of the invading brigade and whose name was Jose Raul de Varona Gonzalez," says Escalante.

"In his statement this man said the following: in the month of March, 1961, around the seventh, Mr. Vicente Leon arrived at the base in Guatemala at the head of some 53 men saying that he had been sent by the office of Mr. Joaquin Sanjenis, Chief of Civilian Intelligence, with a mission he said was called Operation 40. It was a special group that didn't have anything to do with the brigade and which would go in the rearguard occupying towns and cities. His prime mission was to take over the files of intelligence agencies, public buildings, banks, industries, and capture the heads and leaders in all of the cities and interrogate them. Interrogate them in his own way".

The individuals who comprised Operation 40 had been selected by Sangenis in Miami and taken to a nearby farm "where they took some courses and were subjected to a lie detector."

Joaquin Sangenis was Chief of Police in the time of President Carlos Prio, recalls Escalante. "I don't know if he was Chief of the Palace Secret Service but he was very close to Carlos Prio. And in 1973 he dies under very strange circumstances. He disappears. In Miami, people learn to their surprise -- without any prior illness and without any homicidal act -- that Sangenis, who wasn't that old in '73, had died unexpectedly. There was no wake. He was buried in a hurry."

Operation 40 had "in the year '61, 86 employees, of which 37 had been trained as case officers...while in Cuba we probably didn't have one single case officer trained. I didn't finish the course until July of '61 and I was in the first training group."

A unique photo of Barry & the Boys - meeting in Mexico.

After the failure of the Bay of Pigs invasion, the CIA organizes a Domestic Affairs Division. "For the first time, the CIA is going to work inside of the U.S. because until that moment, it wasn't doing it. It was prohibited.

"And at the head of this division they put Tracy Barnes, who was chief of the CIA operations group which operated against Jacobo Arbenz in Guatemala, and he brought to the same group of officers David Atlee Phillips, David Sanchez Morales and Howard Hunt, and two or three other Americans who just as surely worked on the Guatemala project."

The first CIA project against the Cuban revolution wasn't a landing and assault brigade, remarks the general. "The first CIA project was to create a civil war inside of Cuba. They were thinking of creating political leaders overseas, organizing a series of military cadres overseas who are the ones who will infiltrate Cuba and who will place themselves at the head of this civil war they are planning to carry out. And furthermore parallel to that, to make an intelligence network. All of this falls apart almost as soon as it is born.

"In October 1960, they realize that this project has failed, and that is when Brigade 2506 is formed, when due to the uprising of a group of patriotic military officers in Puerto Barrios in Guatemala and, this was in November, they send the Cuban mercenaries in Brigade 2506 to put down this operation."

DAVID MORALES AND DAVID PHILLIPS

Escalante remembers that in 1959 a "very strong" CIA center existed in Cuba with several case officers based in Havana. Among them two very important figures: David Sanchez Morales, registered as a diplomat with the U.S. embassy, and David Atlee Phillips who was doing business in Cuba since 1957.

"Phillips had a press agency, David Phillips Associates, which had offices on Humbolt St., behind the Rampa theater. We had information from a person who was his personal secretary at the time and he was using the Berlitz Academy, where he would meet with people he wanted to recruit. The Berlitz Academy was not his business, but he had recruited its director and that's why he was using it to train his agents.

"And at that time he recruits Antonio Veciana, Juan Manuel Salvat, Ricardo Morales Navarrete, Isidro Borjas, a person of Mexican origin, to carry out the internal counterrevolution."

Phillips will train illegal cadres while Morales, on his part, directs a group of North Americans who are infiltrated in the Rebel Army: Frank Sturgis, Gerry Hemming, William Morgan.

"When the revolution triumphs these people are officers in the Rebel Army, many of them in the air force because the chief there is Pedro Luis Diaz Lanz, who was the first chief of the rebel air force and who later leaves the country when an assassination attempt against Fidel fails. He will also direct **Howard Hunt**, who is visiting Cuba in '59 and '60 and who will write a far-fetched chronicle about Havana which is a series of lies. Hunt is a professional liar.

"There was information that at the end of '58, when CIA Inspector General **Lyman Kirkpatrick** came to tell Batista to leave power, he has an interview with a group of figures. And since this Phillips was passing himself off as a respectable North American businessman, Kirkpatrick has an interview with him. And Phillips explains to him that the situation is very difficult."

In this context, now in the middle of '58, the CIA plans an assassination attempt on Fidel with a North American citizen, Alan Robert Nye, and ex-marine recruited in Fort Lauderdale by agents of the FBI and by the Cuban military intelligence service.

"He was received here in Havana, they put him up at the Comodoro hotel, fortunately they paid his bill and that was how he was later discovered. They sent him to a zone near Bayamo where Fidel was, in a zone called Santa Rita and he was arrested there by the Rebel Army. He had instructions to introduce himself to Fidel as a sympathizer of the Cuban cause and to assassinate him at the first opportunity," recalls Escalante.

The man is arrested on December 12, 1958, by rebel forces and remains in custody until the beginning of 1959. "An officer of the Rebel Army is in charge of the investigation. **Knight** says that he was lodged at the Comodoro hotel and it turns out that the ones who had paid this gentleman's expenses were none other than Col. Orlando Piedra, the chief of the investigation bureau of the police, and Col. Tabernilla II, the son of the head of the army."

"THE PRINCIPAL ARTISTS"

"These are the principal artists," says the ex-chief of Cuban intelligence. "David Phillips; David Morales; Howard Hunt; a figure who disappeared later and who was head of the CIA until diplomatic relations were broken, James Noel; and several more who were working actively."

When the Domestic Affairs Division is created, the large CIA operations base in Miami was subordinate to the central division of the CIA; "that is to say that the JM/WAVE station, which had 400 officers plus 4,000 Cuban agents, was directed by the main center in Langley.

Photo caption **Fabian Escalante in Havana**

Fabian Escalante was chief of Cuban Security and the Cuban counterespionage services for many years. He loves baseball, painting and is a voracious reader. He retired in the mid 1990s and has authored 4 books.

"Whom are they going to use? Operation 40. That is to say all of the specialists who are already trained, have gone through the school, have already participated in operations against Cuba...I refer to the group of Felix Rodriguez Mendigutia, Luis Posada Carriles, Orlando Bosch, Virgilio Paz, Alvin Ross, Jose Dionisio Suarez, Antonio Veciana, Ricardo Morales Navarrete, Felipe Rivero, who recently died, the Novo Sampoll brothers, Gaspar "Gasparito" Jimenez Escobedo, Juan Manuel Salvat, Nazario Sargen, Carlos Bringuier, Antonio Cuesta, Eladio del Valle, Herminio Diaz, Pedro Luis Diaz Lanz, Rafael "Chichi" Quintero, Jose Basulto, Paulino Sierra, Bernard Baker, who was a Cuban with a North American name -- he was a guard at the U.S. embassy -- and Eugenio Martinez, alias 'Musculito.'

"And there was the team that brought together all of the North Americans: David Morales; David Phillips; Howard Hunt; William Harvey; Frank Sturgis; Gerry Hemming; John Rosselli, who was second head of the Chicago mafia and at that time in '62; Porter Goss, the current head of the CIA, who is in the JM/WAVE as a subordinate of Phillips and Morales."

THE "GRANDMOTHER" OF ALL OPERATIONS

"Operation 40 is the grandmother and great-grandmother of all of the operations that are formed later," continues Escalante.

"The Domestic Affairs Division will have its missions...You have to remember the scandal of the Pentagon papers; a long time later, the Watergate scandal...which are the things that were found out. These people were the plumbers of the division, the men that carried it out."

In 1966 and '67, Felix Rodriguez is in charge of the task force the CIA sends to Bolivia against Ernesto 'Che' Guevara. "He used several names. He is there and he ends up participating directly in the murder of Che. Also there, in another position, is Antonio Veciana. He is there as a bank consultant in La Paz but he runs the center which is coordinating intelligence gathering in the rear guard, working with the Bolivian intelligence services.

"This is very interesting because we are then going to see this whole group in the second large operation they organize, which is advising the secret police of Latin America. We are going to see Felix Rodriguez in 1980 in Argentina, we are going to see Posada in Venezuela..."

POSADA, TORTURER IN CARACAS

Luis Posada Carriles next appears in Venezuela.

"Posada says he arrived in Caracas in 1969, which is not true, he arrived in '67. What is happening is that he is a CIA advisor and it doesn't suit him in his book to talk about that; he says he was recruited in Miami by a chief of DIGEPOL. He's a tremendous storyteller. In reality, Posada is already there in '67 helping DIGEPOL as a CIA advisor.

"After that we are going to see Orlando Bosch's group: Virgilio Paz, Alvin Ross, Dionisio Suarez in Chile after '73. We are going to find 'Mono' Morales Navarrete in Venezuela and Felipe Rivero in Chile...That is to say that this group is going to be spread out in Latin America with actions everywhere."

All of them have devoted themselves, besides the subversive activities, "to drug smuggling, which began when they were training for the Bay of Pigs," says the general.

"The planes came from Miami to Guatemala loaded with weapons, ammunition, personnel, and they returned...even with blood plasma. They were even smuggling blood plasma which Manuel Artime commercialized with the dictatorship of Anastasio Somoza. Drugs started to be included, cocaine."

Phillips was head of Operation 40 from 1960 to 1973..."It is assumed that in '73 Operation 40 was 'discontinued,' as the North Americans say, but that is absolutely not true.

"You have to remember that in '73, the Watergate scandal broke out. Who were the ones who broke into the offices of the Democratic Party? This same group. We are talking about Bernard Baker, Eugenio Martinez, Frank Sturgis, Ferry Hemming, and we learned this from the documents from the Church Commission.

"And after he got out of prison, Eugenio Martinez came to Cuba. Martinez, alias 'Musculito,' was penalized for the Watergate scandal and is in prison for a time. And after he gets out of prison -- it's the Carter period, the period of dialogue, in '78, there is a different international climate -- Eugenio Martinez asks for a contract and one fine day he appears on a boat here...and of course he didn't make any big statements, he didn't say much that we didn't know but he talked about those things, about this Operation 40 group, about what they had done at the Democratic Party headquarters..."

And who are directing the operation against Allende, asks Escalante. "In the first and second part, David Phillips, first as chief of the operations group, and afterwards he moved up to Western Hemisphere division chief of the CIA until 1975. He participates in that and participates in the formation of Operation Condor, which was formed in 1974 when the first meeting of intelligence chiefs of the Southern Cone is held in Santiago, Chile." The veterans of Operation 40 will also participate in Operation Hoja de Parra, which Argentinian intelligence organizes to spy on political emigres throughout Latin America.

Then they appear in Operation Calypso, part of the Nicaraguan contras: "That is to say, when the Argentinian army sends Col. Osvaldo Rivero, first to Miami and then to Honduras, with a group of Argentinian specialists, they fail and the Cubans from Operation 40 have to come; Felix Rodriguez and Luis Posada who in '85 replace the Argentinians and transfer the general headquarters from Tegucigalpa to San Salvador. And the El Aguacate air base which belonged to the Hondurans stops being the main base of air supplies..."

All of the operations carried out, after a certain time, by members of Operation 40 are operations called "autonomous" where the CIA officer who directs the terrorist group -- we're talking about terrorist "action" groups, as they call them -- discusses the objectives of that group, approves it, facilitates all necessary resources "and afterwards reads about the results in the newspaper."

A SOURCE IDENTIFIES POSADA AND OSWALD

About the Kennedy case, Escalante recalls how Cuban intelligence services would receive in the '60s much information from North Americans, from Cubans outside of the country and from Central Americans, about subversive activities.

"By correspondence...Letters would arrive that many times, of course, they would come without a return address or with a fake address. And we started to have information from these figures through this means.

"There is a source who participates in a meeting in Miami in the year '63 in a CIA safe house and who, from what I remember, was related to Veciana, very close to Veciana. This source identifies Luis Posada Carriles, Pedro Luis Diaz Lanz and, I believe, the Novo Sampol brothers...and that same source later recognizes Lee Harvey Oswald as one of the participants.

"The last time we heard about this source was in the '70s when he refers to a meeting with Antonio Veciana and Phillips in Puerto Rico," says Escalante.

"I'm convinced that they wanted to kill Kennedy in different places. Probably that Dallas had better conditions. But I'm under the impression from some very fragmented information I had access to one time, that they wanted to assassinate him in Miami. And I can't exclude, without confirming it, because this information is very relative, that these people had been gathered there for that reason...

"There is another source, who is Maria Lorentz, who relates something similar to this, that is to say that she was in a meeting in Miami, that she saw these people, that she went with them to Dallas, around November 20."

Escalante underlines how a Cuban, Manuel "Manolito" Rodriguez Orcarberro, arrives in Dallas two months before the Kennedy assassination "and he leaves afterwards at full speed."

There he opens an office of Alpha 66, where Oswald will enter at one time, according to the testimony of the assistant police chief of Dallas.

"This Cuban sought asylum in 1960 in the Brazilian embassy together with two known CIA agents. Who were they? Ricardo 'El Mono' Morales Navarrete and Isidro Borgas, a figure of Mexican origin who looks a lot like one of the figures who is with Oswald handing out proclamations supposedly in favor of Cuba in New Orleans -- all of that which was a show put on where Carlos Bringuier goes to challenge them, a fight erupts, and the police arrest all of them..."

And who is the boss of Rodriguez and of Alpha 66? "Antonio Veciana, from Operation 40. That same Veciana whose testimony would lead Gaeton Fonzi to interview Luis Posada in Caracas when he was in prison, due to the similarity between the plan he prepared to assassinate Fidel in Chile and the Kennedy assassination."

Even more: the name that one of the "cameramen" used in Chile is Ramon Medina "which is a pseudonym Posada later used in Ilopango."

There are several sources who place Luis Posada Carriles in Dallas on November 20, 1963, says Escalante.

The ex-chief of Cuban security points to a recent investigation by the <u>Dutchman Wim Dankbaar</u>: "There are elements which even say that Posada was one of the shooters, which cannot be ruled out because Posada is an expert marksman.

[See Posada Carriles' U.S. asylum application re-opens JFK unsolved assassination case]

"Posada who is an expert marksman who graduated from a North American military school. Posada who afterwards becomes, together with Orlando Bosch and all of that gang, one of the leaders of the terrorist groups. Within the mechanism of Operation 40. Posada who since then has always been protected by U.S. authorities, protected by the Cuban American National Foundation, protected by Jorge Mas Canosa."

The assassination of Kennedy could not have been an improvised action in any manner, says Escalante. "If they detoured Kennedy from the avenue where he was traveling to drive around a park, it wasn't for any other reason than to slow down the car to be able to fire at him. Because this famous detour to Dealey Plaza makes no sense. Evidently this makes the vehicle travel at 20 kilometers per hour. And there the fatal shots are fired, from behind and from ahead.

"It had to be a complex operation in which a large group of people participated, because if they shot at him from three shooters' nests which had to have an element of communication as well, to have the means to get out of that place and afterwards to get out of Dallas. We are talking about between 10 and 15 people in the least of cases."

IN CARACAS, THE FBI WAS AWARE OF EVERYTHING

Returning to the subject of the explosion of the Cuban airplane in 1976, Escalante underlines that, in the weeks preceding the attack, Orlando Bosch is in the Dominican Republic, goes to Nicaragua, and then to Caracas with a fake Dominican passport.

"Allegedly invited by Orlando Garcia who if he wasn't head of DISIP at that time was chief of personal security for Carlos Andres Perez. This at the same time that Mono Morales Navarrete had become head of division 54 of DISIP.

"Navarrete arrived when Posada left DISIP, in '74, to organize that front of the Industrial and Commercial Investigations Office. A CIA front which was probably connected with Operation Condor...Why does Posada go over to DISIP? Why does he have disagreements? If he is operations chief of DISIP, he has contact with the U.S. embassy, he's supported by the CIA. Why is he tired of torturing, which is what he did there at DISIP?"

According to reports from the time, at the office of Posada's detectives agency in Caracas they also found plans for the assassination of Orlando **Letelier**, which occured in Washington on September 21, barely two weeks prior. "Bosch had coordinated the operation in Santiago where he met with General Manuel Contreras, head of DINA." [Chilean secret police -- tr.]

"In '74, Bosch had already gone to Chile with Virgilio Paz, Alvin Ross, Jose Dionisio Suarez to offer himself to Contreras and Pinochet as hit men for Condor...The same Bosch who in 1976 returns to the Dominican Republic, then goes to Nicaragua, meets with the Somoza dictatorship, and then to Venezuela for this operation...Bosch arrives in Venezuela in September and the blowing up of the Cubana airplane was on October 6.

"Where do instructions come from? Where is the plan drawn up? It is drawn up in Caracas. Who are in Caracas? Bosch, Posada and Morales Navarrete. Those are the three figures who are there. This is perfectly documented. As if that weren't enough, Morales Navarrete is an

FBI informant, they passed him the bill themselves in '82 for that reason. The FBI was aware of everything they were doing. Probably the CIA gave them the objectives with that cover of autonomous operations. Who was head of the CIA in '76? George Bush Sr. And so...as clear as day! Was Posada still with the CIA?

"In a declassified document from July 1976, the CIA says it broke off with Posada because it had suspicions that he was involved in drug smuggling. That's what it says, that's what it says...when David Phillips gave Veciana a quarter million dollars so he could go to prison for 18 months for a drug trafficking charge," answers the general.

Copyright 2005 by AxisofLogic.com ©

***Jean-Guy Allard** is a Canadian journalist, born in Shawinigan (Quebec) in 1948. He was successively a reporter and news editor for *Le Journal de Montréal* and *Le Journal de Québec*, the two main french-language dailies of both cities, from 1971 to 2000. He then retired in Cuba and has never been so active since, working with **Granma International**, the weekly edition of the main Cuban newspaper, published in seven languages.

Allard also regularly publishes on *cubadebate.cu*. He has two sons, one 18 years old and the other one... 13 months. He appreciates living in the big island, far from the snow, the publicity, the Canadian media and the Canadian income tax system. No bills in the door every morning, plenty of rumba y cha-cha, a good cigar from time to time on the beach under a palm tree, and the Cuban Revolution that gives him the opportunity to live a page of history. He doesn't really care if George and Jeb Bush nor Otto Reich do not agree.

Read more about the related, ongoing investigation by JFK Assassination Expert, Wim Dankbaar (Netherlands).

Reprint from: http://www.axisoflogic.com/artman/publish/article_17881.shtml

Internet Discussions

Wim,

Do you have a clue about who the man is that picked up Oswald at TSBD?

Mark

Yeah sure, David Sanchez Morales. I also believe he was the dark complected shooter in the TSBD.

Wim

Then there are others who believe it may have been Malcolm "Mac" Wallace.

Dawn Meredith

Malcolm Wallace could have been in the TSBD too, although I favour Richard Cain as a better candidate for the man with the horn rimmed glasses, as seen by Richard Randolph Carr. Whatever the case, that man (with the glasses) was definitely not the very dark complexed man, either Spanish or Cuban, as described by Carr.

Remember that a total of FOUR men was seen fleeing from the back of the TSBD.

Deputy Sheriff Roger Craig: Back to November 22, 1963. As I have earlier stated, the time was approximately 12:40 p.m. when I ran into Buddy Walthers. The traffic was very heavy as Patrolman Baker (assigned to Elm and Houston Streets) had left his post, allowing the traffic to travel west on Elm Street. As we were scanning the curb I heard a shrill whistle coming from the north side of Elm Street. I turned and saw a white male in his twenties running down the grassy knoll from the direction of the Texas School Book Depository Building. A light green Rambler station wagon was coming slowly west on Elm Street. **The driver of the station wagon was a husky looking Latin, with dark wavy hair, wearing a tan wind breaker type jacket.** He was looking up at the man running toward him. He pulled over to the north curb and picked up the man coming down the hill. I tried to cross Elm Street to stop them and find out who they were. The traffic was too heavy and I was unable to reach them. They drove away going west on Elm Street.

Source:

http://www.ratical.org/ratville/JFK/WTKaP.html

Q: Did you have occasion to observe the individual or individuals in the station wagon?

A: Yes, sir, I did. I saw the upper portion of the body and the entire head.

Q: How many persons were in the station wagon?

A: One.

Q: Could you give us a description of that individual?

A: **Very dark complected, Latin-looking with black hair. He was very muscular, had a bull neck and very strong face.**

Source: http://www.jfk-online.com/craigshaw.html

As you will see here, the dark Latin was the man behind the wheel, driving the Rambler away from the crimescene. You don't have to be a statistician to conclude that the same man was the driver of the Rambler, that picked up Lee Oswald some 10 minutes later. The more so since Roger Craig's description matched.

I made the interesting text **bold**

Source: http://www.jfk-online.com/carrshaw.html

CRIMINAL DISTRICT COURT
PARISH OF ORLEANS
STATE OF LOUISIANA

STATE OF LOUISIANA vs. CLAY L. SHAW

198-059
1426 (30)
SECTION "C"

EXCERPT OF THE TESTIMONY TAKEN IN OPEN COURT
February 19, 1969

B E F O R E: THE HONORABLE EDWARD A. HAGGERTY, JR., JUDGE, SECTION "C"

THE COURT: Call your next witness.

MR. GARRISON: Your Honor, Mr. Carr is unable to walk because of a recent accident, and we understand the Defense has no objection, if the Court will permit, to have Mr. Carr wheeled right in front of the State Counsel table.

THE COURT: That's all right. He can testify from there.

RICHARD RANDOLPH CARR, having been first duly sworn by the Minute Clerk, was examined and testified as follows:

DIRECT EXAMINATION BY MR. GARRISON:

Q: Mr. Carr, we can hear you if you speak into the microphone, sir, and it is important that the Jury be able to hear you and Defense Counsel over here (indicating) and the Court Reporter. What is your full name?

A: Richard Randolph Carr.

Q: And in what City do you live?

A: Dallas, Texas.

Q: And what city were you living in during the month of November, 1963?

A: Dallas, Texas, 322 North Canden, Oak Cliff.

Q: Can you recall the day of November 22, 1963?

A: Yes.

Q: Can you recall what part of the City you were in around the middle of the day on November 22?

A: Yes, I was on the Seventh Floor of the New Courthouse Building that was under construction at that time, located on Houston and Commerce, facing Dealey Plaza.

Q: Approximately what time were you on the Seventh Floor of that building facing Dealey Plaza?

A: Sir, I can't recall the exact time, but it was at the time that the parade was coming down towards Dealey Plaza. I did not have a watch at the time.

Q: Were you in a position where you could see the parade?

A: Yes, sir.

Q: Do you recall seeing anything unusual happening?

A: Yes, I do.

Q: Would you tell us what happened.

A: At the time the parade came down towards -- going to the School Book Depository, Dealey Plaza would have been to my left where I was standing, and at the Fifth Floor of the School Book Depository I noticed a man at the third window, this man was dressed -- he had on a light hat, and I saw this man later going down Houston Street, to the corner of Commerce, and then turned toward town on Commerce, and at that time before this happened I heard a single shot which sounded like a small arms, maybe a pistol, and I immediately, immediately there was a slight pause and immediately after that I heard three rifle shots in succession, they seemed to be fired from an automatic rifle and they came --

MR. DYMOND: We object to the witness giving his conclusions on this.

THE COURT: Mr. Carr, do not give your conclusions on this point.

BY MR. GARRISON:
Q: Go ahead and tell us what you heard.

A: I heard three rifle shots fired from a high-powered rifle --

MR. DYMOND: We object to that unless the man is qualified as an expert. I ask the Jury be instructed to disregard that.

THE COURT: It is a question whether or not an ordinary human being, whether he would know a rifle shot or not. I do not know --

MR. DYMOND: We don't know this man had rifles since he was a child, we don't know that he ever had been a hunter, and this man --

MR. GARRISON: We can clarify that very easily.

Q: Mr. Carr, have you ever heard rifle fire before?

A: I have.

Q: Where?

A: I was a member of the Fifth Ranger Battalion in World War II. I qualified as an expert with a bolt-action rifle which is called a thirty aught six, in the Army it is a 30-caliber rifle, since that time I was -- I used a 225 Winchester, I hunted with a 70 millimeter Remington, I have also loaded my own ammunition, which I do until this day.

Q: Were you ever wounded in action?

A: Yes.

Q: How many times?

MR. DYMOND: I object to that as irrelevant.

THE COURT: That is irrelevant. Why don't you tender Mr. Carr over to the Defense as an expert, at least in the field that he knows a rifle shot when he hears it?

MR. GARRISON: One other question.

BY MR. GARRISON:
Q: Have you ever heard rifle fire in combat?

A: Yes, I have heard rifle fire in combat.

Q: On how many occasions?

A: I was in -- I landed in Casablanca, I went through North Africa, I was in two major offensives in Africa, and from there I went to Anzio beachhead and my battalion was annihilated, 13 men left in the Fifth Ranger Battalion.

Q: How many of these places did you hear rifle fire?

A: In all of them I heard rifle fire, sir.

MR. GARRISON: We tender the witness.

CROSS-EXAMINATION BY MR. DYMOND:
Q: Mr. Carr, when you were qualified in the Army as an expert with a rifle, did that, was that pertaining to marksmanship or the identification of the type of rifle being fired from the noise made?

A: Sir, clarify that.

Q: Your qualification as an expert rifleman in the Army, was that in marksmanship and the breaking down of rifles or the identification of rifle sounds?

A: I became an expert on the range in the act of firing a rifle.

Q: In other words, that would be marksmanship, would it not, sir?

A: Yes.

Q: Now, these various actions in which your battalion took place, do you know what type of rifles were being fired at you?

A: No, sir, I do not.

Q: Do you know whether there was more than one type of rifle being fired at me.

A: Yes, I do know there was more than one type of rifle being fired at me.

Q: But you can't name the different types. Is that correct?

A: Well, I did not see them, and without seeing, I could not name them.

MR. DYMOND: That's all.

THE COURT: Is the matter submitted?

MR. GARRISON: Yes, the State would add that Mr. Carr is about as expert in the sounds of gunfire as you could be and still be walking around.

MR. DYMOND: If the Court please, this gentleman may have been fired at many times, but he does not know what type of rifles were being fired, he was never called upon to distinguish as between sounds of various different rifles, and if you hold this man out as an expert, every many including myself who was in combat during World War II would be an expert. I certainly don't hold myself out as one.

THE COURT: I rule that Mr. Carr is qualified as an expert and can give his opinion on whether a shot or a noise he heard is from a rifle or not, but not what type rifle.

MR. DYMOND: To which ruling Counsel objects and reserves a bill of exception, making all the testimony up until this point, the Defense objection, the Court's ruling, and the entire record parts of the bill.

MR. GARRISON: The Judge has ruled that you can tell us whether or not the noise you heard was from a rifle but not what type rifle.

THE WITNESS: No, sir, I would not say what type of a rifle, I would not say it was a thirty aught six --

MR. DYMOND:
Objection, there was no question asked.

BY MR. GARRISON:
Q: Let's go back to where we were and can you tell us what you heard?

A: Yes, a pipefitter and myself were standing on the Seventh Floor of the -- on the outside of the structure of this courthouse, we were looking, as I told before in my statement the FBI and everyone else --

MR. DYMOND: I object to his previous statements to the FBI, Your Honor.

THE COURT: Answer the question.

BY MR. GARRISON:
Q: You can go on and tell us what you observed, tell us what you observed and what you heard.

A: All right. As I stated before, I noticed this fellow in the window, and this gentleman, the pipefitter and myself, he made the statement to --

MR. DYMOND: I object to what the man made a statement concerning.

**BY MR. GARRISON:
Q: You can say what you said.**

A: I thought he was a Secret Agent man or an FBI man.

Q: What did the man in the window look like?

A: He had on a hat, a felt hat, a light hat, he had on heavy-rimmed glasses, dark, the glasses were heavy-rimmed, and heavy ear pieces on his glasses.

Q: Go ahead.

A: He had on a tie, he had on a light shirt, a tan sport coat.

Q: Now, you say you heard gunfire. Will you tell us again what you heard.

A: Yes, sir. The first I heard, I made the statement before the objection, I say it was small arms, a pistol --

MR. DYMOND: He has not been qualified --

THE COURT: Just say what kind of noise you heard.

BY MR. GARRISON:
Q: What kind of noise did you hear?

A: I heard a shot. There was a pause and immediately after that there were three shots in succession.

Q: Were you able to tell from where the first shot was coming?

A: No, sir, not the first one I could not tell the direction it come from.

Q: Were you able to tell from where the three shots came from which followed?

A: Yes, I was.

Q: Where did they come from?

A: They came from the -- from where I was standing at the new courthouse, they came from in this direction here, behind this picket fence, and one knocked a bunch of grass up along in this area here (indicating), this area here is flat, looking at it from here, but the actual way it is, it is on a slope up this way and you could tell from the way it knocked it up that the bullet came from this direction (indicating).

Q: Now, when you just touched the ruler to this mockup, what was the area which you were describing as the source of the three shots, can you describe it a little more precisely?

A: Yes, there was a picket fence along in this area here, it does not show it in here, and it seems the shots came from this direction, and underneath that slope there were people.

Q: And what happened?

A: The shots came from this direction, from behind this picket fence that I do not see here, and there is a slope here, there is a grassy slope down here and there were a lot of people, spectators down here, below on this grassy slope, but when those shots were fired the motorcycle policemen, the Secret Service and what-have-you, all came in this direction, the way the shots came from, some of the people that were sitting there or standing fell to the ground as if the shots were coming off of those --

MR. DYMOND: I object to his conclusion, Your Honor.

THE WITNESS: It is not a conclusion, Your Honor, I saw it.

MR. DYMOND: I ask the witness be instructed to wait for the Court's ruling.

THE COURT: I overrule the objection.

MR. DYMOND: To which ruling Counsel objects and reserves a bill of exception on the conclusions of the witness. I will make the Defense objection, all the questions propounded to this witness, the entire record and the Court's ruling, parts of the bill.

BY MR. GARRISON:
Q: Now, of those shots, which of the three shots did you hear coming from that area you have just pointed out by the picket fence on the knoll?

A: The three shots, the last three shots came from this area.

Q: Did the three shots seem break apart in time or very close in time?

A: No, sir, they were fired from a semi-automatic or either --

MR. DYMOND: I object to this.

THE COURT: Just tell us the sequence, Mr. Carr.

BY MR. GARRISON:
Q: You can tell us whether they sounded close or separate.

A: Yes, they were very close together.

Q: If you were to say with your voice "BOOM" three times, could you give us the approximate separation as you recall it?

A: Well, BOOM-BOOM-BOOM, just in that order.

Q: All right. Now, I am not going into the whole thing there, but just so that we can see where the spot was on the photomap, now, "S-34," Mr. Carr, that you are looking at now, an aerial photograph of the scene --

A: Yes.

Q: -- could you orient yourself, can you identify everything by looking at the area photograph?

A: Yes.

Q: Can you show us the are from which you heard the three shots coming on the area photograph?

A: The three shots came from in this direction right here (indicating).

Q: Can you recognize the cement arcade in the area photograph?

A: Yes.

Q: Now, are you able to recall from which ends of the cement arcade the three shots came from, was it from the end towards the Depository or the end towards the overpass?

A: At the end towards the overpass, right here.

MR. GARRISON: Let the record show that Mr. Carr just indicated, would you point your ruler up there -- let the record show Mr. Carr is indicating an area on the grassy knoll in the vicinity of the picket fence.

THE COURT: Let it be noted on the record.

BY MR. GARRISON:
Q: Now, after the shots, did you notice any movement of any kind --

A: Yes, I did.

Q: -- as unusual, that was unusual?

A: Yes, I did.

Q: Would you tell us what you observed.

A: Should I point it out, sir?

Q: Yes.

A: At this point right here, at this School Book Depository there was a Rambler Station Wagon there with a rack on the back, built on the top of this.

Q: Which way was the station wagon facing?

A: It was parked on the wrong side of the street, next to the School Book Depository heading north.

Q: North being the top of the photomap, north is the top as you have indicated?

A: North is the top, and it was headed in this direction towards the railroad tracks, and immediately after the shooting there was three men that emerged from behind the School Book Depository, there was a Latin, I can't say whether he was Spanish, Cuban, but he was real dark-complected, stepped out and opened the door, there was two men entered that station wagon, and the Latin drove it north on Houston. The car was in motion before the rear door was closed, and this one man got in the front, and then he slid in from the -- from the driver's side over, and the Latin got back and they proceeded north and it was moving before the rear door was closed, and the other man that I described to you being in this window which would have been one, two, the third

window over here came across the street, he came down, coming towards the construction site on Houston Street, to Commerce, in a very big hurry, he came to Commerce Street and he turned toward town on Commerce Street and every once in a while he would look over his shoulder as if he was being followed.

Q: Now, Mr. Carr, did you have occasion to give this information to any law enforcement agencies?

A: Yes, I did.

Q: Did anyone tell you not to say anything about this?

A: Yes.

MR. DYMOND: I object to what anyone told him, Your Honor, on the grounds it's hearsay.

THE COURT: A moment ago you asked Mrs. Parker if anybody threatened her. Is it your question, Mr. Garrison, whether or not Mr. Carr was threatened by someone? Is your question to the witness a question of whether or not anyone threatened Mr. Carr?

MR. GARRISON: I will rephrase it.

BY MR. GARRISON:
Q: Did anyone threaten you?

MR. DYMOND: At this time we object to the Court's suggesting questions to Counsel for the State. The suggested question is completely different from the question previously propounded by the State. This is not the function of a Trial Judge in any trail.

MR. GARRISON: May it please the Court, I will phrase my own questions on this.

BY MR. GARRISON:
Q: Mr. Carr, did you talk to any FBI agents about this incident?

A: Yes, I did.

Q: Did they tell you to forget about it?

MR. DYMOND: I object to that as hearsay.

BY MR. GARRISON:
Q: Were you threatened in any way --

THE COURT: I sustain the objection. You cannot tell us the words used by someone who spoke to you because of hearsay; however, you can state that you had conversations with them and what did you do as a result of the conversation, I will permit that.

BY MR. GARRISON:

Q: As the result of the conversations with the Federal Bureau of Investigation, what did you do?

A: I done as I was instructed, I shut my mouth.

Q: Were you called to testify before the Warren Commission?

A: No, sir.

MR. GARRISON: I tender the witness.

RECROSS EXAMINATION BY MR. DYMOND:
Q: When did you first notice that President Kennedy had been shot?

A: About an hour and 15 minutes after it happened, sir.

Q: Is it your testimony that you did not realize that anything had gone wrong in the Presidential motorcade?

A: I realized something had gone wrong but I did not know what.

Q: Did you realize that anyone had been shot?

A: No, sir, I did not.

Q: Until an hour and 15 minutes after it happened, is that your testimony?

A: Yes.

Q: I see. Now, wasn't it your testimony that you heard what you thought were gunshot --

A: Yes.

Q: -- noises?

A: Yes, I did not think it was gunshots, I knew it was gunshots.

Q: I see. Didn't you also testify that you saw people running up to the grassy knoll area?

A: I did.

Q: Did you draw any conclusions from that?

A: Your Honor, you asked me not to have any conclusions a while ago, did you not?

THE COURT: You can answer this question.

THE WITNESS: I have conclusions, yes, I did.

BY MR. DYMOND:

Q: Did you conclude that anybody had been shot?

A: I concluded someone had been shot or shot at, yes.

Q: Did you detect any commotion or unusual activities in the vicinity of the Presidential vehicle?

A: I detected the vehicles gathering speed and moving on, yes, I did.

Q: Did you attach any importance to that or think it was unusual?

A: I thought it was very unusual, yes.

Q: Now, when did you see the Presidential vehicle gathering speed in relation to the gunshots?

A: It was shortly after.

Q: Would I be fair in saying it was immediately after the gunshots?

A: I would say there was a pause and it looked like, it looked like somebody trying to get home from where I was at.

Q: By clapping your hands, first indicating the last gunshot, and then the time that you saw the unusual activity around the Presidential vehicle, clapping them again, so as to show us the space of time, would you please do that, sir.

A: That has been five years ago, and it seemed like minutes, which it was only seconds.

Q: In other words, it's your testimony now that it was only seconds between the last shot and your seeing commotion and unusual activity around the Presidential vehicle. Is that correct?

A: Well, now, I ain't said nothing about seeing commotion around the Presidential vehicle, what type of commotion I noticed mostly was people running to the area that I described, this area right here, sir.

Q: That happened right after the shots were fired?

A: Yes, that happened immediately.

Q: Would you say that happened before or after you saw the Presidential vehicle accelerate and start to go faster?

A: That happened before.

Q: All right. After seeing the people run up the grassy knoll, which happened right after you heard the shots, right after that you saw --

MR. ALCOCK: That is not what he said, that is not his testimony.

(Whereupon, the testimony pertinent to this point was ready by the Reporter.)

BY MR. DYMOND:
Q: Right after that you saw the Presidential vehicle accelerate. Is that correct?

A: Yes.

Q: All right. Now, when you saw the Presidential vehicle accelerate, did that attract your attention?

A: No, sir, not so much as I turned and looked back, as I told you before, I saw these people come out from behind the School Book Depository and I am going to try to make this clear to you so where you can understand it, from where I was at I could not tell whether they came out this side entrance here, there is a side entrance to the School Book Depository, or whether they came from behind it, but they came either from the side entrance or they came from behind it, and got into this station wagon.

Q: Now, how about the rest of the motorcade, did it accelerate along with the Presidential --

A: The crowd crowded in so fast until I could not tell anything about the rest of the motorcade or nothing else, there was a lot of commotion there from then on.

Q: Was there a great deal of traffic on Stemmons Freeway at that time?

A: Stemmons Freeway is on up here.

Q: I am talking about Elm Street going ...

A: You said Stemmons Freeway, Elm Street is here, sir. No, sir, there was not much traffic on Elm Street.

Q: Not much traffic?

A: Elm Street had been blocked off for the motorcade.

Q: About how many automobiles were in the motorcade?

A: I don't know.

Q: Would you say plenty or just one or two?

A: Well, at the time this happened, I saw three.

Q: You only saw three vehicles, three automobiles in the Presidential motorcade. Is that correct?

A: At the time it happened I had only seen three, part of them were on back, had not got to that point yet.

Q: Did you ever see any more than these three?

A: Sir, I saw no more because I explained to you that the commotion was so great that everybody stopped there, there were a lot of people on the streets, on both sides, there were people up here, spectators, there were people lined everywhere along that route, all over there.

Q: Mr. Carr, weren't you interested in looking at this commotion and trying to see what was causing it?

A: Was I interested in knowing what was causing it?

Q: That is correct.

A: I would like to have known, but I could not have got through the crowd to find out it I had to.

Q: You had a pretty good spot from which to look, didn't you?

A: Yes.

Q: Were you looking to try to see what caused it?

A: I say were you looking to try to see what went on, what caused it?

A: To see what caused the commotion?

Q: That's right.

A: No, sir, not to see what caused it, I was looking to see what was going on.

Q: You were looking where, to see what was going on?

A: I was looking to see why all of the commotion down here and why these people were running.

Q: And at the same time you were looking up towards the Texas Book Depository seeing three men come out from behind it. Is that right?

A: Do you see these dots on this --

Q: Would you answer my question and then explain, please, sir. I say would you answer the question and then explain.

A: Yes, I will answer your question, repeat it, please.

THE COURT: Mr. Carr, when a question is put to you, you can answer it yes or no, but you have a right to explain your answer so you cannot be cut off, so if you wish to explain the answer, you are permitted by law to do so.

(Whereupon, the question was read back by the Reporter.)

A: Yes, that's right.

BY MR. DYMOND:
Q: And also at the same time you were watching the man whom you say you had seen on the Fifth Floor of the Book Depository walk on Houston Street towards Main. Is that right?

A: Yes, and I have -- may I explain that?

Q: Yes.

THE COURT: You may explain.

A: The same man that I saw here in this window was with the three men that I told you a minute ago, they came out from behind the School Book Depository, got in the station wagon, one man crossed the street and then came down this side of Houston Street and turned onto Commerce Street.

BY MR. DYMOND:
Q: And you were watching that procedure at the same time that you were watching what was going on in the grassy knoll area?

A: No, sir.

Q: And what was going on around the Presidential vehicle and in the motorcade, right?

A: No, sir, I was watching that man at that time, and I watched him until I could see him no longer, but that man acted as if he was in a hurry and someone was following him, and I would know that man if I ever saw him again.

Q: And right before the three successive shots you saw a bullet hit in the middle of Dealey Plaza, is that correct?

A: Repeat that, please.

Q: Right before hearing the three successive shots you saw a bullet hit in the middle of Dealey Plaza, right?

A: No, sir, upon hearing the three successive shots, sir, I saw one, one of those three hit in Dealey Plaza in the grass.

Q: I see. Did you ever go and look for the hole where it hit?

A: No, sir, I have not.

Q: Did you ever try to recover the pellet?

A: No, sir, I have not.

Q: Now, is it your testimony that the three, that is, the group of these three shots were equally spaced, that is, the space of time between the first and second was just about the same as that between the second and third?

A: The three shots were consecutively.

Q: I take it then that you would deny that there was one shot and then a relatively long period and then two fast shots. Is that correct?

A: Yes, I sure would.

Q: I take it -- go ahead, sir.

A: I am sorry, sir, go ahead. I said I heard one shot, there was a pause and then I heard three consecutive shots.

Q: I take it then that you would also deny that of those three successive shots, there were two rapid ones and then a relatively long period and then a third one. Is that right?

A: Yes, I would.

MR. DYMOND: That's all, sir.

FURTHER REDIRECT EXAMINATION BY MR. GARRISON:
Q: Just one more question, Mr. Carr. Would you just take your -- would you just take your time and in your own words describe with reference to the photomap the direction of that shot which you observed furrowing on through the grass, from what area to what area, could you describe that, from what point to what point?

A: The shot was fired from somewhere in here.

Q: Just a minute, sir. This is going to be written down, what do you mean by "in here," from somewhere to where?

A: From this direction in here that shot was fired.

Q: You are indicating, to begin with, the grassy knoll area by the picket fence. Is that right?

A: Yes, sir, this is the first thing that attracted by attention as I explained to you before.

Q: But the direction would have been from there to where?

A: To in this vicinity right here (indicating).

Q: Well, if you carry the line down, would you identify some building or something on the map so that we will know precisely what you mean?

A: Yes, I will say the Criminal Courts Building right here (indicating).

Q: If the shot would have continued, you mean to say --

MR. DYMOND: I object to leading the witness, Your Honor.

BY MR. GARRISON:
Q: I will rephrase the question. If the shot had continued --

A: If the shot had not hit the grass, it would have hit the Criminal Courts Building, sir.

MR. GARRISON: That's all I have.

FURTHER RECROSS EXAMINATION BY MR. DYMOND:
Q: Just a couple of questions. Mr. Carr, is it your testimony that you saw this bullet furrowing through the grass?

A: I saw the grass come up.

Q: You saw the grass come up?

A: Yes.

Q: And from that you are telling us from what direction the shot came and where it would have gone if it would have kept on going. Is that right?

A: Yes.

MR. DYMOND: That's all.

THE COURT: Is Mr. Carr released from the obligations of his subpoena?

MR. ALCOCK: Yes, Your Honor.

THE COURT: You are excused as a witness.

THE WITNESS: Thank you, Judge.

THE COURT: Let everybody have a seat, Sheriff. Now, you see, it is about one minute to 12:00. We are going to recess for lunch. Let everybody have a seat. Gentlemen of the Jury, as I have so many times, I must admonish you and instruct you not to discuss the case with one another or anyone else. It is very, very important that you adhere to my instructions. With those instructions, I will turn you over to the Sheriffs, and we will be in recess for lunch. You are released under your same bond, Mr. Shaw.

(Whereupon, a luncheon recess was taken.)

C E R T I F I C A T E

I, the undersigned, a Deputy Official Court Reporter, in and for the State of Louisiana, authorized and empowered by law to administer oaths and to take the depositions of witnesses under L.R.S. 13:961.1, as amended, do hereby certify that the above and foregoing deposition is true and correct as taken by me in the above-entitled and numbered cause(s). I further certify that I am not of counsel nor related to any of the parties to this cause or in anywise interested in the event thereof.

NEW ORLEANS, LOUISIANA, on the 26th day of May, 1969.

/s/ Paul W. Williams

DEPUTY OFFICIAL COURT REPORTER
STATE OF LOUISIANA

But why did Morales pick up Oswald at the TSBD? It means that Oswald was part of it somehow. Lee must have known that Morales was at the sixth floor. Or maybe Lee tried to sabotage it.

Mark

That is the intriguing question that I cannot answer completely. It is obvious that Lee "was part of it somehow". The fact that he spent the week with James Files already tells you that. And Judyth's account is that he infiltrated the plot in order to sabotage it. The fact that Morales, James Files and Lee all shared the same CIA supervisor (David Phillips) indicates to me that Lee was duped in a big way. According to Judyth he started to grasp that in the end. In their last telephone call on the night of Wednesday 11/20, he told her never to forget the name "David Atlee Phillips", because he was a "traitor".

He also did not listen to Judyth's pleadings to get out of it. To report sick for work or something. He said: **If I stay it will be one less bullet aimed at Kennedy.**

And this is the man that went down in history as the killer of JFK.

This is also why I believe Morales was the Mexican looking visitor to Silvia Odio. There is no doubt in my mind that this was staged by Phillips.

You also have to keep in mind that Morales was the Chief of Operations at JM/Wave (the station for the preparation of the Bay of Pigs) reporting directly to Ted Shackley, who ended up as deputy director for special operations under George Bush. Get the big picture?

Wim

Yup, I get it now.....

You said that there were 4 shooters at the TSBD. Is there any witness who saw all of them running out from the TSBD. Or did they leave thru a backdoor?

Mark

No, I said that FOUR MEN were seen making their exit from the TSBD. Which of those were shooters I cannot say. But given Morales' reputation as "the Agency's top assassin for Latin America", I think it is rather safe to say he was a shooter.

And yes, they left thru a backdoor. Another witness who saw this is James Worrell.

There are witnesses who saw one and two men with rifles in the windows of the TSBD. A few of those described one as dark or dark complexed.

Wim

http://www.geocities.com/metsman_2001/6thfloor.html

Fifteen minutes before the assassination, a bystander called Arnold Rowland asked his wife if she would like to see a Secret Service agent. He pointed to a window on the sixth floor where he noticed "a man back from the window- he was standing and holding a rifle... we thought momentarily that maybe we should tell someone, but then the thought came to us that it is a security agent." Rowland testified that he had seen the rifle clearly enough to make out the telescopic sight and realize it was a high-powered weapon. The man he saw was not in the famous window, at the right-hand end of the sixth floor, but in the far left-hand window. Rowland also said that, at the same time, he spotted a second figure, at the famous right-hand window. The second man was dark complexioned, and Rowland thought he was a Negro. (Summers, Anthony. "Conspiracy", pg.42)

Shortly before the assassination a female bystander, Mrs. Ruby Henderson, saw two men standing back from a window on one of the upper floors of the Book Depository. Like Rowland, she noticed that one of the men "had dark hair... a darker complexion than the other." (Summers. "Conspiracy", pgs. 42-43)

Wim

Tim,

I saw you wrote an article on Ted Shackley (he died a few months ago by the way). I hereby give you my thoughts on David Sanchez Morales, which I think Fabian Escalante will find interesting too. I have read that he also has speculated that Morales was the driver of the Rambler stationwagon (owned by the Paines?). You have to keep in mind that Morales died mysteriously in hospital after a sudden "heart attack" in 1977 in his hometown Wilson, Arizona, and that Morales was the chief of operations for JM/Wave, directly under Shackley, and that he also was the sidekick of David Atlee Phillips. David Atlee Phillips was the CIA handler for both James Files AND Lee Harvey Oswald. Morales later developed a reputation as "best CIA assassin for Latin America" and under influence of booze, has made a hint to his being involved in the Kennedy assassination (We took care of that bastard didn't we?)

Shackley took Morales, Rodriguez and Posada to Vietnam, where they were heavily involved in operation Phoenix.

However, I do not have absolute conclusive evidence, other then eyewitness accounts and their absolute perfect positions to have been selected as gunmen for the hit.

By the way, Richard Cain was also "Giancana's man" in the sheriff's office of Cook county Chicago. On the afternoon after the murder, the Dallas police received a tip on Oswald's "mail order" for the rifle from ...., yes: the sheriff's office of Cook county Chicago

So besides the actual gunmen we have uncovered (Files, grassy knoll, Nicoletti, Daltex building, Roselli as his back up, Marshall Caifano, behind pergola?), my candidates for other shooters are: Richard Cain, Luis Posada, Cesar Diosdado, Charles Harrelson.

By the way, I now believe, that the dark complexed guy, fleeing the TSBD and entering the station wagon, and later picking up Oswald on Elm, was David Morales. Fabian Escalante, the Cuban general, has already speculated to this effect.

Have you seen photos of him? I can send you two:

This is the description Roger Craig gave of him:

http://mcadams.posc.mu.edu/craig.htm

As we were scanning the curb I heard a shrill whistle coming from the north side of Elm Street. I turned and saw a white male in his twenties running down the grassy knoll from the direction of the Texas School Book Depository Building. A light green Rambler station wagon was coming slowly west on Elm Street. The driver of the station wagon was a husky looking Latin, with dark wavy hair, wearing a tan wind-breaker type jacket. He was looking up at the man running toward him. He pulled over to the north curb and picked up the man coming down the hill. I tried to cross Elm Street to stop them and find out who they were. The traffic was too heavy and I was unable to reach them. They drove away going west on Elm Street.

http://www.jfk-online.com/craigshaw.html

Q: Could you give us a description of that individual?
A: Very dark complected, Latin-looking with black hair. He was very muscular, had a bull neck and very strong face.
Q: Can you describe the individual running down the slope and the individual that got in the station wagon?
A: Yes, he looked to me oh, approximately 5 foot 9, 150 pounds, sandy hair, Caucasian.
MR. ALCOCK: You want to take the stand again. Mr. Craig?

It's a perfect perfect match with Morales. Oswald did not do that cab and busdrive at all. Griffith did some nice work on this:

http://ourworld.cs.com/mikegriffith1/id95.htm

He was picked up (by Morales) and dropped off at his apartment, probably for Tippit to kill him (or help him escape to Redbird airport, I'm not sure on that).

****

(CAPITAL emphasis mine)
(34) Richard Randolph Carr stated to the FBI on January 4, 1964, that he saw a man looking out of a window on the top floor of the depository a few minutes before Carr heard shots.(99) He described the man as white, wearing a hat, tan sport coat and **GLASSES**.(100) He said

that at the time of the motorcade, he was standing on about the sixth floor of the new courthouse which was under construction at Houston and Commerce Streets.(101)

Carr said that from that spot he could only see the top floor and roof of the depository building.(102) It was from that location that he observed the man in the depository window.(103) Carr said that after the shots he was going toward the direction of the triple underpass; when he got to the intersection of Houston and Commerce Streets, he saw a man whom he believed to be the same individual he had seen in the window of the depository.(104)

(35) Carr was not called to testify before the Warren Commission. He did testify on February 19, 1969 in the Parish County Criminal District Court in New Orleans in State of Louisiana v. Clay L. Shaw, a case involving charges of conspiring to assassinate President Kennedy. According to the transcript of his testimony, Carr stated that he saw the man in the fifth floor window of the Texas School Book Depository.(105) He said he later saw the man going down Houston Street; turning at Commerce Street.(106) Carr also described the hat worn by the man as felt and said his glasses were **HEAVY - RIMMED** with heavy ear pieces.(107) He had on a tie and a tan sport coat.(108) As the man ran, he was continually looking over his shoulder as though he was being followed.(109)

(36) During his testimony at the Clay Shaw trial, Carr also reported seeing men in Dealey Plaza at the time of the assassination who were not mentioned in the report of his FBI interview in January 1964. Carr was asked during the Shaw trial if he noticed any movement after the shots which seemed "unusual."(110) Carr then said that he saw a Rambler station wagon with a rack on top parked on the wrong side of the street, heading north and facing in the direction of the railroad tracks, next to the depository.(111)
(37) Carr said that immediately after the shots he saw three men emerge from behind the depository and enter the station wagon.(112) He gave a description of one of them: he was "real dark-complected" and appeared to be Spanish or Cuban; he drove the car away, going north on Houston Street.(113)

(38) During the Shaw trial testimony, Carr said he had reported this information to law enforcement officers and that someone had told him not to repeat this information.(114) At that point, defense counsel objected to hearsay by Carr, and no further details were elicited about the reported coercion of Carr, other than his statement that he did what the FBI told him to do, "I shut my mouth."(115)
(39) Committee investigators did not locate Richard Carr to discuss this information with him.

****

Now compare this with Giancana in Double Cross (page 466):

From Chicago, Mooney brought in Richard Cain, Chuckie Nicoletti, and Milwaukee Phil, all having worked previously on "the Bay of Pigs deal". Mooney said that both Cain and Nicoletti were actual gunmen for the hit, being placed at opposite ends of the Dallas Book Depository, In fact, he asserted it was Cain, not Oswald who'd actually fired from the infamous sixth story window.

(Giancana does not have the details strait on placing Nicoletti, but after all, he was not there)

James Files being asked about people who were on Dealey Plaza November 22 1963:

Richard Cain?

"Yes."

Milwaukee Phil Alderisio?

"Some of these people are still alive....yes, he was there."

Have a look at Richard Cain (attachment). Richard Cain had the *heavy horn rimmed glasses*.

Wim

Post by Bruce P. Brychek (one of James Files' best friends, who visits James regularly)

As of 03.26.2005, Jimmy states as follows, concerning Veck's neck wound
query:
1. Before the JFK Assassination,
2. During the JFK Assassination,
3. After the JFK Assassination, and
4. As of 03.26.2005, Jimmy was/is unaware of any second team of
shooters. Though this is possible, but not probable, it would have been
on a "Need to Know" basis, assuming arguendo, that there was a
Second Team of Shooters, and further assuming that they were
deployed by the "Same Source," capable of even sharing the knowledge.
Jimmy's thought on the neck would are, that he was shooting Mercury loads, because they purposely explode upon impact. He thinks that
pieces from his Mercury load came through Kennedy's neck, and also
hit the windshield from the inside.

Answer from Wim:

Jimmy should stay away from speculation. Although his need to know knowledge actually enhances his credibility, and also proves that he is not "well read" on the assassination, there is no way that the throat wound was inflicted by a fragment from his bullet. The throat wound was caused by another bullet from the front (it could only have been from the south knoll in my opinion). It was a neat little round hole, recognised by all the Parkland doctors as an entry wound from a small caliber bullet.

As far as Jimmy is concerned, he believes that he and Nicoletti were the only two shooters, an assumption that can be ruled out beyond any doubt. Jimmy fired only one shot, and Nicoletti could not possibly have caused the rest of the misses and wounds of Connally and JFK. He could at best have fired off three rounds (more likely two), one of which hit Kennedy in the back of the head, causing the forward headsnap. That leaves a maximum of two more rounds. Two rounds only could not have caused:

1) the throat wound,
2) the miss that stretched the curb, wounding James Tague,
3) the bullet that hit the grass south of Elm
4) piercing Connally's torso,
5) shattering Connally's wrist
6) the shallow wound in JFK's back.
7) The nick in the windshield chrome
8) The stretch on the pavement of Elm street.

Moreover, there is no doubt that more gunmen were on the 6th floor of the TSBD.

More than SIX (6) witnesses saw one or two men with rifles in the windows, none of them fitting the description of Oswald. Arnold Rowland, Ruby Henderson, Richard Randolph Carr, James Worrell and Johnny Powell, are just some of those witnesses.

Wim (Note from Wim 2007: I have since come to the understanding that Jimmy's speculation was correct: He was the only shooter from the front and the throat wound was caused by an exiting fragment or a mercury drop from his explosive bullet.)

Approximately the same time Mrs. Ruby Henderson saw two men with a rifle on the sixth floor, one with a dark complexion. [119] Seconds before the motorcade entered the plaza, Mrs. Carolyn Walther, standing on the east side of Houston Street, about 50 or 60 feet south of the south curb of Elm Street, noticed two men on an upper floor of the Depository, one of the men was holding a rifle in his hands. She described the rifle as having a short barrel. Neither Mrs. Henderson or Walther were called to testify before the Warren Commission. [120] Both Walters and Richard Carr said they saw a man in a brown or tan coat in one of the upper floors of the Depository just seconds before the shooting. A man matching this description was seen by two witnesses quickly walking out the back door of the Depository just after the shooting. Witnesses with another view of the sixth floor were inmates of the county jail. John Powell saw two men on the sixth floor "fooling with a scope" on a rifle. He noticed that one of the men on the sixth floor had a darker complexion than the other, and said that other inmates saw the same thing and believed that the men were security agents. Powell's story was not known in 1963; he was not interviewed by the Warren Commission. [121] Posner discredits this incident by citing a December 15, 1964 FBI memo that declared Powell unreliable, since he had been arrested on several occasions on lunacy charges. The memo reported that the only area of the jail that had a clear view of the Depository's sixth floor was a corner of the jail that had an iron-mesh grid with windows so dirty that any view would be distorted and almost impossible to see. [122]

Answer from Bruce:

Mr. Wim Dankbaar's analysis, understanding, and points are very well
taken. He is highly knowledgeable, articulate, well read, well versed,
and immensely intelligent.

I think we should all be grateful for his efforts.

I will take a copy of his reply to Jimmy this week.

Respectfully,
Bruce Patrick Brychek.

Answer from Wim:

Credits are due for Joe West , James, Zack Shelton, Holt, Plumlee and others in the past and future (even Bob Vernon to a certain extent and until a certain point in time)

Wim

A little Novel writing

The following pages I wrote with a fellow author who is writing a book about the Kennedys and Marilyn Monroe. As his book will be in the style of a novel, we came to the result below.

Chauncey Holt had arrived in Dallas at daybreak on November 22nd. He had driven all the way from the Grace Ranch in Arizona. Located just outside of Tucson, the Grace Ranch was owned by Cleveland mob boss Pete Licavoli. Being a remote mansion with a landing strip, it served as a base for drug smuggling and CIA covert operations. Chauncey was not alone. With him in the car were Charles Nicoletti from Chicago and Leo Moceri. The fourth passenger was Joe Canty, a CIA contract pilot who was to fly Chauncey Holt back from Red Bird airport.

Leo Moceri was Licavoli's underboss and Charles Nicoletti was Sam Giancana's most trusted hit man. Holt was told they were underway to New Orleans to meet with crime boss Carlos Marcello. Originally, Holt was to fly to Dallas with his own plane, but Licavoli had sent him a note to stop by the ranch to pick up Nicoletti and Moceri. They wanted to make the hop to Dallas together with Holt. However, Chauncey Holt had not counted on their extremely heavy luggage. The Cessna was too underpowered to carry the four men including their bags.

So it was decided to make the drive in one of Licavoli's cars, an Oldsmobile station wagon. It was a fourteen hour trip if they drove without stops, except for gas, so they would took turns driving. As always with the Mob, they drove the speed limit at all times to avoid attention from highway patrols along their route. It was standard operating procedure for the Mafia.

They had planned to arrive at the Dallas Cabana Hotel the afternoon of Thursday, November, 21st. But car trouble and a severe sand storm had delayed them. The storm was so strong, the sand had blasted paint off the car, and visibility on the highway was poor. They had no choice but to stop. This delayed their arrival in Dallas, and they finally pulled into the Cabana Hotel in Dallas at sunrise on November 22nd.

Chauncey Holt's instructions were to deliver a set of forged Secret Service lapel pins to Homer Echevarria, an extreme Cuban exile who was vigorously anti-Castro. Holt was supposed to meet with Charles Harrelson and Carlos Montoya in the parking lot near the railroad yard, behind the Texas School Book Depository. Holt gave Harrelson a set of forged identification badges from the ATF (Alcohol, Tobacco, and Firearms division of the Justice Department). If things went sour, they would be covered as ATF agents, and they could explain their presence in the railroad yard as undercover agents seizing a train with hot goods.

Chauncey Holt's instructions came from his CIA contact, named Philip Twombly. Twombly had been a vice president for Coca Cola. Together with Donald Kendall of Pepsi Cola, he was considered the eyes and ears for the CIA in the Caribbean and South America. But he had changed his cover for the Bank of Fullerton in California, a full proprietary CIA asset, in which he owned a majority interest. Twombly had instructed Holt to take part in an anti-Castro demonstration, to create a protest diversion for Kennedy's visit. This turned out to be a lie.

Holt was instructed to dress casually to blend in with the railroad workers. In case of problems, he was to seek refuge in boxcar number 22 of the Rock Island train. As it turned out, after the assassination Holt was joined in the boxcar by Charles Harrelson and Carlos Montoya. The boxcar would look sealed from the outside. The train would then be driven out of the train yard. The plan didn't work exactly as planned. Later that day, Chauncey would be detained by the Dallas Police, together with Harrelson and Montoya. The photos of Holt, Harrelson and Montoya being escorted by two officers holding their shotguns through Dealey Plaza to the police department would be known in history as "the three tramps."

Johnny Roselli had just flown into Dallas on a CIA supported flight. According to James Files, Roselli, (aka Colonel Ralston), was the liaison between the CIA and the Mob. Emanuel Rojas and Tosh Plumlee, CIA pilots, flew the military air transport plane that brought Roselli from Miami to Dallas. Plumlee would later state that their mission was to abort the assassination, on orders from the CIA.

Nicoletti had ordered his driver and protégé, 21 year old James E. Files, to pick up Roselli at the Cabana Hotel at 7:00 AM.

Files was also an experienced hit man who had begun his career with the CIA after he killed two of his own men with headshots in the US Army 82nd Airborne Division, as they were running away from him. He did this to earn favor with his allies in Laos. Files had been recruited to the CIA by David Atlee Phillips, who was his controller on the day of the JFK assassination.

David Atlee Phillips (aka Maurice Bishop) had sent Lee Harvey Oswald to show Files around Dallas the week before, making sure Files knew all the getaway routes, ensuring that he would not be chased into any dead ends. If so, Files was well armed with a Colt 45 pistol and a grenade in case he would have to shoot his way out. But that should be a last resort.

As Files drove up, Roselli was already standing outside speaking with another man. Roselli gestured to Files, indicating that he needed to wait for a few minutes.

"Hey Johnny!" said Files as Roselli hopped in, *"Who was that?"*

"That's Jim Braden, one of our guys in California", Roselli replied. *"Now, take me to Fort Worth. I need to pick up something from Jack Ruby. Do you know him?"*

"No I don't," Files said decisively, as he stepped on the gas.

"He runs the Carousel Club for us here in Dallas. It's a strip joint. You should have gone there for some fun!"

"Mr. Nicoletti doesn't want me to have fun while I'm on a job," Files explained. *"Why all the way to Fort Worth, if he's from Dallas"?*

"Because I don't wanna be seen with him. Everyone knows this guy. He acts like a fucking celebrity. By the way, are you packing?"

"Have you ever known me to be without a weapon?" Files asked with a smile.

"Good! We're going to the pancake house in Fort Worth. I want you to cover my ass in case anything happens. Just think like I'm Chuck, okay?"

"Don't worry, Johnny, I'll cover you like I do Mr. Nicoletti. He told me to take good care of you."

"I am going to be sitting at that table in the back, Jimmy," Roselli whispered to Files with a nod as they walked through the door of the pancake house, *"Station yourself where you can see us and the door, and be ready for anything."*

Files sat at the coffee bar, nursing a cup of strong coffee when Jack Ruby entered the restaurant, wearing dark glasses and one of the ubiquitous dark hats, worn by most businessmen in Texas. Files had a 45 caliber pistol tucked into his belt. Ruby was carrying a manila 8 by 12 inch envelope, which he quietly passed to Roselli. Files watched carefully as Roselli and Ruby spoke for less than five minutes. After Ruby walked out, Files followed him to make certain the parking lot was clear. Roselli took his time exiting the restaurant, while Files pulled the car up to the front door.

On the way back to Dallas, Roselli pulled the contents out of the envelope. As he was driving, Files glanced over and easily recognized the Secret Service badges, and a map of the final route the presidential motorcade would take through downtown Dallas. Files kept his mouth shut, although proof of involvement on the part of another agency of the federal Government raised many questions in his mind.

"Good. They only made one change in the route," Roselli commented, *"They are going to slow down to make this turn into Dealey Plaza from Main Street onto Houston, and*

then left onto Elm before getting onto the Stemmons Freeway. It's perfect. Kennedy will be a sitting duck!"

As the men arrived back at the Cabana Hotel, Roselli stepped out and told Files to wait outside for Charles Nicoletti. It took several minutes for Nicoletti to come down. Nicoletti ordered Files to drive to Dealey Plaza where they parked the car in front of the Dal-Tex building. As the men walked around the plaza on that damp, grey morning, the sun broke through the clouds.

"It's going to be fucking beautiful," Files remarked.

"Jimmy, you can wash my cars, but you can't wash your mouth!" Nicoletti rejected his driver's profanity.

The rebuke from his boss resulted in a pause in their conversation, as Files and Nicoletti stood in the center of Dealey Plaza, scoping it out for the best lines of fire.

"Jimmy," Nicoletti said carefully, "How would you feel about backing me up on this?"

Files was caught by the question. "What happened to Johnny?" he asked. "I thought he was going to be your backup!"

"Johnny is a little paranoid on this one. Johnny will be with me, but he doesn't want to be a shooter. He will be my spotter. Some of the wrong guys in the CIA got wind of the plan and want the hit stopped. Johnny just flew in and gave that information to Mr. Giancana."

"And what do you say?" inquired Files.

"Fuck' em! It's a go anyway! Only Sam can stop this now. I talked to him this morning, and we are going!"

"Jesus, Mr. Nicoletti, I would be honored to back you up! That bastard Kennedy had all my Cuban friends that I trained slaughtered at the Bay of Pigs!"

"Okay, Jimmy, what do you think would be the best spot for you?"

"I would put myself behind that fence on the knoll there. With my jacket I could pass for a railroad worker and that large tree gives me good cover. I will stand just to the left of it where that branch is hanging over."

"Good, that's exactly the spot I had in mind for you. Now remember, Jimmy, we want everything from behind and we're going for a headshot. So you must only shoot if I miss, or if I don't hit him in the head. Kennedy cannot leave Dealey Plaza alive. You're just my insurance in case I blow it. Got that?"

"Don't worry Mr. Nicolleti! Headshots are my trade, as you know. That's why the Agency recruited me."

"What weapon do you go with?"

"I'll go with the Fireball."

"The Fireball? Why's that? That's a single shot weapon!"

"If you miss, Mr. Nicoletti, a single shot is all I'm gonna get. I have been practicing all week with the Fireball. It's my favorite gun and from that fence as he approaches, Kennedy will be a fish in a barrel. I'll use one of the mercury rounds Wolfman made for me. That should split his treacherous head open like a melon."

"Okay Jimmy, it's your call. I trust it won't be necessary. What would you say is the best spot for me?"

"I think in that building where we parked the car."

"Good! That's the place we had picked."

"But how do you get in there?"

"Don't worry, we have someone to get us in. He's one of our people in California that you don't know."

"Is that the guy I saw with Johnny this morning? Braden or something?"

"Yes, that was him. I need you to park the car where we are parked now - with the trunk to the building, so I have quick access and can put the Marlin in without being seen. And one more thing, Jimmy, when you walk out of there, head for the car, and just walk relaxed, no running. We've got this thing covered. There will be people covering you. You won't know who they are, and that's the best way."

"Okay, Mr. Nicoletti. I'd like to say one more thing. You've got to aim a little higher, because Kennedy's car will be moving away from you. This is not like a normal job when we pop a guy between the eyes."

"I know, Jimmy, you explained that to me before with moving targets. I haven't forgotten. Your military background and your marksmanship is why I am asking you to do this."

"I won't let you down, Mr. Nicoletti. But there is one thing that bothers me."

"What's that, Jimmy?"

"It's Lee Oswald?"

"Lee Oswald? Who is Lee Oswald?"

"He's with the Agency, one of Phillips' guys. Phillips sent him over to my motel to help me out here. I've spent the whole week with him. I'm a little nervous about him, because he's a tie back to me. And I am a tie back to you and Sam, if you catch my drift."

"Don't worry about it, Jimmy, I will talk to Mr. Giancana, and he will fix it with Phillips."

Eugene Hale Brading (aka Jim Braden) had a contact in the Dal-Tex Building, located across Houston Street from the book depository, who gave the assassins access to the second floor window that Nicoletti needed for a clear shot at Kennedy from behind, unlike from the sixth floor depository window which was partially obstructed by a Texas Live Oak tree.

The CIA had given Files a brand new weapon that had just passed the prototype stage of development. Files had spent several days with Oswald near a landfill outside of Dallas, training with the weapon, and perfecting his aim with the scope. Remington had developed a miniature rifle that looked and operated like a handgun. The Remington XP-100 Fireball was a bolt action, single shot weapon with a 3X scope, that fired a reinforced .222 round. Files had a friend nicknamed Wolfman, who was an expert at making ammunition and modifying guns for Giancana's men. Wolfman had drilled into the tip of the bullets, filled the cavities with liquid mercury, and sealed the bullet nose with wax. When this fragmentary round strikes a man's head, the heavier mercury rushes forward forcefully, like water inside a fast moving balloon, causing the bullet to explode. This would send metal fragments and a spray of mercury throughout the target's brain, resulting in instant death.

Correspondence between Joe West and James Files

Note from Wim: James Files has the habit of sending a card with almost every letter. He draws them himself. They are pencil or ink drawings in full color, they can be serious or a funny cartoon, and they are accompanied by a text, which often puts a smile on your face. Due to space and technical limits, we cannot print the cards, but we have transcribed the texts on them. Some of the cards and drawings are on the website.

July 24, 1992

Dear :

I am Joe West, a retired Private Investigator. I have spent the last
three years researching and investigating the assassination of John F. Kennedy for Truth, Inc. a Non Profit, Educational Foundation, of which I am the President.

The purpose of my letter is to ask you for the privilege of talking with you by phone and then visiting with you personally to discuss with you anything that you might know that could contribute to this research and investigation.

If you would allow me this privilege, then please call me collect anytime day or night at (713) 787-5111. Thanking you for your consideration in this matter, I am,

Sincerely,

Joe H. West, CLI
President, Truth, Inc.

Thursday, 30 July 1992

Joe West
1231 Campbell
Houston, TX 77055

Dear Mr. West:

In regards to your letter of 24 July, I sincerely wish that I could be of some help to you. But that is not possible. Please forgive me for not calling, but at the present time we are in total lock-down status. One shower, one phone call per week. I use that call, to call home, sorry.

I realize investigations cost money, and my knowledge of your investigation is not worth the cost of your coming to see me.

The two items that I know, outside the movies and the books are:
1. David Phillips perjured himself while giving testimony during the "House of Assassinations Committee". And I'm sure you already know that.
2. The grassy knoll, the man in the beat up fedora type hat wearing the old brown leather bomber jacket. I AM NOT saying it was Frank Sturgis, but it sure looked a lot like him. The last I heard, he's alive and doing well. That's all I know.

But I am rather curious as how my name surfaced for your investigation. At that time, I was under a different name; that man deceased in 1964. Sorry that I cannot be of more help.

Sincerely

James Files

August 5, 1992

Dear :

It was a pleasure to receive your letter today. I feel like I already know you because of all the information about you I have in my files. The direction of my research and investigation has been about others that you are personally acquainted with and your name has come up only because of your relationship with them.

This may sound strange for me to tell you that I already know most of the answers to the questions that I would like to ask you. However, I need to corroborate them by as many sources as possible. Hopefully, you will have some of the answers that I don't have yet.

Some of the questions that I would like to talk with you about concern Chuck Nicoletti and Filippo Sacco alias Johnny Rosselli and their whereabouts in November of 1963. There are other important things also that you can help me with.

It would be a pleasure to talk with you by phone and to meet you personally. Would you call me (collect) as soon as possible at (713) 787-5111. I will be in your area in a few days and would like to visit with you if you would put me on your visitors list.

Please write as often as you can. Let me give you an address that will reach me faster: 7611 Olympia, Houston, Texas 77063. I'm looking forward to hearing from you as soon as possible.

Sincerely,

Joe H. West

August 20, 1992

Dear:

It was a pleasure to meet you finally. I'm looking forward to getting some of your art work and music. Before I left, I talked with the Asst. Warden and ask for the thing we talked about.

Yesterday, I contacted the police station, but they did not have the brief case or its contents. However, they are going to check with another station next door to see if it might be there.

Take a close look at the enclosed pictures and see if you recognize any of them. If you do, write me all the information that you know about them. What about the name Bruce Carlin ? Also, Did Johnny give an envelop or receive one ? Could that red chevy have been in Big Sandy (East Texas) in September 1965.

I have also started the wheels rolling with the Federal Attorney. Thanks again for all your help and I'll be looking forward to hearing from you. As eve,

Your Friend,

Joe H. West

Sunday, 22 August 1992

Joe West
1231 Campbell
Houston, TX 77055

Hello Joe,

Just a few lines to say hello and to say I hope that you made it home safe and sound. It was a pleasure meeting you and I really enjoyed our visit. As for me I'm doing fine. I'm still after the Warden for a single cell. But that will take some time.

We were talking about David Atlee Phillips and old memories come alive. David plus some other people and I remember he loved scotch and was one hell of a writer. Especially when it came to propaganda. We worked in the White, Gray, and Black area. White, truth! Gray, half and half! Black, all lies! And he was really good with the Gray and Black. (smile) Like the piece he did for the news when Chianos Bay came apart. What a disaster. He wrote the article about the tanks and planes cutting the Cubans down. He made it sound like a fight and it was just a slaughter. The Cubans never had a chance, we let them down. All my life I've blamed Kennedy for that, right or wrong I don't know.

Anyway I just wanted to say hello and from first impression, you're "A Number One" in my book. Take care and may God keep you safe.

Friends always

Jim Files

Thursday, 27 August 1992

TRUTH INC.
Joe West
1231 Campbell
Houston, TX

Dear Joe,

I received your letter last night and was happy to hear from you. But it sure gave me a big headache.☺ Those copy's of people are very deceiving. They give impressions and it's been so long for me, it's truly hard to remember. I'm afraid I'm not going to be a very good wittnes (sic) for you. I'm sorry if I disapoint (sic) you. I met so many people, some I was never even told their names. Some of these people lead into other areas that I dare not enter. I want to help you, not hurt you. But I don't want to put anyone in jail. O.K. I will go along on the bottom end of the Kennedy thing. I only wish you could find someone else.

A very close friend of mine just died last week. He use (sic) to supply arms and ammo for Chuck and me. His name was George Collura. We called him the "Wolfman". I had him on my visiting list to come see me. I wanted to talk to him about this thing and the "Fireball". I wanted to ask him to come forward and meet you. He died like 4 days after I ask (sic) him. I hope it wasn't me that gave him the heart attack. Back to your letter.

It was also a pleasure to meet you and I'm looking forward to our next meeting. But I hope that it's in the free world. Also, thank you for talking with the Asst. Warden for me.

The police station only has the piece it's self (sic). When the kid took it from the house, he put a brick back inside the briefcase, so if someone picked up the briefcase, there'd still be some weight to it. I had either 5 or 6 "Special Rounds" in the briefcase with a loading press for that piece. The kid was shooting birds and got picked up, by the police. He told them it belong (sic) to someone in the family that was doing time. That someone was me.

My Aunt's house burned down shortly after that. I don't know if the briefcase burned up or not. Tonight, I used my one phone call to call Aunt Kay, she was out, so I couldn't talk to her. If you can, call her and ask her. Phone 2_____. Please explain to my Aunt Kay, what your (sic) trying to do and that you will protect me. I told her what's going on, I trust her with my life. But she thinks I'm crazy. I don't think she believes a word I told her. But she can keep a secret. I love her and trust her with all my heart. She also knew Chuck, he use (sic) to come to our restaurant in Melrose Park. Anyway, I'm sure that it has not been destroyed. Some cop has it. Bet on it.

I looked at all the copy's (sic), I hope my answers will be of some help. I hope I got some of them right.☺

Bruce Carlin does not ring a bell. That I'm very sure of.

Lee was a little shorter than me. Maybe 5' 9" or 5' 10", 160 or 170 lbs. Wore t. shirts most of the time. Big ears, unusual hairline, and to me his eyes were kind. I remember he had a small scar by his mouth, like the edge of cheek. But I don't remember what side.

Chuck Nicoletti was very hansome(sic), very suave, like fluid motion. I'm telling you, he was beautiful, he walked on water. There was no one else like him, and his eyes were very gentle. He was unlike Johnny Roselli, Johnny was very flamboyant. He like to flash.

Remember, I told you I picked Johnny Roselli up at a hotel in Dallas. I'm sure the hotel was Dallas something Hotel. When I pulled up out front, Johnny was talking to some one. Looking at those copy's (sic), I'm sure it was Braden. When Johnny got in the car, he said, "I ran into a guy I know, he's staying here also." But I never ask him who the man was. We went on to Fortworth (sic), there Johnny <u>received</u> an envelope. I do not know what was in it. Size was standard 4 ¼ x 9 ½, brown, looked kinda like your envelope. ☺

Big Sandy, could have been I guess. I remember Chuck traded it for a 1965 Chevy Caprice. He didn't tell me he was trading the 1963 in. Broke my heart, the 1965 wasn't near as quick.

I made a map. I think I got it right, but I sure wouldn't bet my life on it. I couldn't remember all the streets. You made me remember Elm. Main Street I can remember. The street running north and south, I think was wider than Main St. I know the maps (sic) not important. I'm trying to get my memory back. I've spent my life forgetting things, now I'm trying to wake up sleeping dogs. Not easy. I wish I could remember names and dates for you, but it's just been too long. Like I told you, I never ask questions.

Take care of yourself and may God keep you safe. I'll send some of my songs in the next letter. I've got enough here for two envelopes, I hope they're not over weight, if they are, they'll return them to me.

Oh yes, I'm working on that picture of me from 1963. There is one or two available, but she wants to have copy's(sic) made for they're the only ones she has. She says she still loves me, so she won't give up the only ones. She dosen't (sic) have me, but she's got my daughter, and what a beautiful daughter she gave me. Our daughter is now 26 years old.

Joe, I best close. Again, take care and may God keep you safe.

Friends,

Jimmy

P.S. if you can, send me another set of those copy's(sic), so I can keep looking at them and thinking. O.K.

TRUTH, INC.
1231 Campbell
Houston, Texas 77055
713-932-6075

September 5, 1992

James Files N14006
P.O. Box 112
Joliet, IL 60434-0112

Dear Jimmy:

It's always exciting to get your letters. I'm sorry about Wolfman! It would have been a pleasure to have met him and talked with him. How is your appeal doing? I hope it goes well and your [sic] out real soon.

I have talked with six different Police Departments in the Round Lake area. Each have said they do not have in their possession a Remington 221, nor do they have any arrest records for a Chris Van Vorus in December of 84 or January of 85. I just hung up from talking with Kay and she said that it was definetly [sic] the Round Lake Hights [sic] Police Department. I will zero in on them tomorrow since it's about 9:00 p.m. now. What kind of ammo does the "Fireball" shoot?... is it 221 or 222? What are the "Special Rounds" you mentioned in your last letter?

By the way, Bruce Carlin was the husband of "Little Lynn" that worked for Jack Ruby and they lived in the area of Fort Worth where the restaurant was. Did you ever meet Marina? Was James Braden involved? You are right on his picture. You are also right on David Phillips picture. Tell me about when you first met him and your working relation with him and also anything you can remember about Braden.

Your map is very accurate. Try to remember everything you can about who was there and exactly what happened. This is your moment in history and it's very important for you to remember. I can't wait to get that picture. When I get your songs, I'm going to show them to a friend of mine who is a Music Producer and see if there is anything he can do with them. He was Fats Domino's manager for over ten year's [sic].

I'm enclosing the pictures and adding a couple more to jog your memory. I've been ask [sic] to do a Documentary for Television. I would like for you to be in it. We can put a blue dot over your face if you want to. I will ask the Warden for permission to bring a camera inside if your agree and I will make all of the camera crew sign a "confidentiality agreement" about your identity and that way no one will ever now but me who you are. However, we won't need this if we get the immunity first. I'm working on the immunity as my first priority.

I am looking forward to visiting with you again soon. In the meantime, write as often as you can and take care of yourself… and may the Grace of our Lord and Savior Jesus Christ be with you now and ever more.

Your Friend,

Joe H. West

Tuesday, 15 September 1992

Joe West
7611 Olympia
Houston, TX 77063

Dear Joe,

I received your letter the other day and was delighted to hear from you. I look forward to your letter, but gee, you sure know how to give a guy a head-ach. ☺ And a very big one at that. As a matter of fact, I've had a head-ach since I got your very first letter. And that my friend, is the truth.☺ You've made me remember things that I've tried to forget for ever.

You know Joe, I don't really know where to begin answering this letter. I know so little about what you want to know and too damn much about everything else. If you wasn't such a likeable guy, I could learn to hate you real easy. But I like you too damn much, hell, you could be my brother.

Well let's answer your letter by the questions you ask in order. O.K.

About my appeal, it's going slow, I'm having trouble getting the trial transcripts out of Lake County, Ill. They've filed for extra time on getting the transcripts ready.

I'm sorry the Police Dept. are giving you the run-a-round on the Fireball. But one of those cops has the gun. There is no way they would destroy a gun like that. And this kid Chris Van Vorus was arrested.

As far as the ammo, the Special Rounds were Mercury. I'm positive that I used 221 and 222 rounds in it. Wolfman had shown me a couple of things on loading the rounds. I also had rounds for an AR 15 which fired 2.23 rounds. That one had a folding stock that folded to the side of the magazine and could be fired with a pistol grip. At that time we, (Chuck and me) had over 40 weapons put away for various types of work. Small arms to big game rifles.

No I never met Bruce Carlin, little Lynn, or anyone named Marina as far as I know. I may have seen them, but never introduced. So, I really have no way of knowing. So I'm sure the answer is no.

I have no way of knowing if James Braden was involved. But I believe if he was involved, Johnny R. would have known he was staying at the hotel. Therefore, he would not have been talking in front of the hotel when I pulled up. I think if Johnny had known he was there, they'd have met inside in one of the rooms. Everyone was so concerned about keeping a low profile and staying out of sight.

David Phillips as far as I know wasn't involved in the Kennedy assassination. My work with him went in a different direction and was related strictly with the Central Intelligence Agency. I prefer to leave those areas alone as long as there's no connection to your investigation. There we get into deep water.

There's not much to remember about James Braden. He was a crook, a wanna be gangster. He was tied in with Jimmy the Weasel. Jimmy's last name was Franitianno. I'm not sure of the spelling but that's close I think, Jimmy was out of Cleveland or Youngstown, Ohio. At one time he worked for James Licavoli, nick name "Blackie". James Licavoli I knew very well. We did time together in Oxford. He had the cell across from me. I was with him when he died.

As far as for me being remembered in history, hell, I want to be forgotten.☺ And you're right. The F.B.I. would love to sit and listen to me clear my conscience, (or however you spell it). I'm remembering things that I forgot ever happened.

I'm still waiting for the lady to send me the picture from 1963. It should be here any time. As soon as I get it, I'll send it to you.

This extra picture you enclosed, jars my mind again. But not on the Kennedy assassination, off in another direction. The 9-F: older version, profile picture looks like Jimmy the Weasel. But I believe it's "Civello" from Dallas. He was hooked up with some guy named "Campisa" or something like that. I don't believe he was involved in the Kennedy thing. Chuck N. knew him and told me he (meaning Civello) had dirty money. Chuck didn't believe in drugs and often told me, "Don't ever let me catch you with any drugs." And to this day, I've never used drugs or smoked a pot cigarette. Any way from what I understand Civello's thing was "Heroin". That was number one, plus a piece of everything that went on in Dallas. He had another guy, partners with him in a warehouse or something, but I don't remember his name. In 1979, I'm sure he was still alive and well. Either he had a car wash or his kid had it. I believe it was just off the 635 interchange just north of either 30 or 40, I don't remember which it is that runs East-West thru Texas. But anyway, you got my files from Tarrent (?) County, so you know about my case, a little of it anyway.

I was moving a very large number of stolen cars and trucks into Texas. From there, most of them went south of the border. We were printing our own titles, Wisconsin Titles. Plus we were making our own vent(?) tags and federal door stickers. I was dealing mostly with a multi-millionaire. His name is in my case. He carried his weight and did not try to hurt me during my trial. Anyway, he introduced me to this ol' man, who had the car wash. I use to unload my transport trailer there and get all the cars detailed, for this "we'll call him L.B." Ok. Anyway the man at the car wash told me, (he didn't work there), that he still looked after things in that area. He'd help me if I could give him a "Special Deal" on cars and trucks. So these two men, L.B., my partner and me all went to lunch. Then the ol' man ordered 122 cars and trucks, knowing they were stolen, and that I was using Wisconsin Titles. Once I got the cars to Texas I took the Wis. Titles to the Tarrent County court house and got what they call in Texas a "Quick Title". Then we had a legal title and could sell them to dealers who then shipped them out of the country. Plus I was shipping auto parts into Texas from our chop shops. On my first load of cars, to the ol' man, (which was two carriers loaded) 14 cars, he met us at the car wash and gave me $77,000 cash. A very good deal for him, he could more than double his money. But I had cars and trucks going all over the state of Texas. The F.B.I. said it was one of the best operations they had run across. The agent in charge was James? I don't remember the last name. But we got along good. I refused to talk about my operation and he respected that. I respected him because he didn't badger me. We talked about everything but crime. ☺

I started a trial, but after a few days, I went ahead and pled guilty. The _____ buried me with his testimony.

Oh yes, Jimmy the Weasel, left Ohio in the 60's and moved to Calif. Became big time out there, then turned rat.

I wish I could remember these people a little better. I'm afraid I'm not going to make you a very good witness. About the camera crew, that's a lot of money to hear me talk for 60 seconds, for you to come that far. I can only answer a couple of questions. It'd be cheaper for you to hook up by phone or something, or read a statement and show my picture and say I'm in _____ and they wouldn't let me come to Texas. ☺ But honest, before I say something that could get me charged, I have to have immunity first. Also, I'd like to have my appeal over with. They find out about me and this Kennedy deal, they might just decide to leave me in prison. Anything is possible.

I'm sending a separate envelope with some of my songs. I know they're not great, but I write, play the guitar and sing because I enjoy it. It's all for me. Also, I can't sing, but I try. But if some one can use them, hey that's great. You and me, we split, if there's any money to be made.

I hope this letter doesn't bore you to death, I feel like it's part of my life. And yes, that's very boring. So I'll close for now. You take care of yourself and may God keep you safe.

And if you get this way again, please stop in, I'll enjoy seeing you again.

Your friend,

Jimmy

September 29, 1992

Dear :

The day I received your last letter was the first day of the most awful case of the flu I have ever had. Today, is one week later, and I'm
just starting to come back to the land of the living. I still have not gotten anywhere on finding the "Fireball", but, I'm still working on it.

I'm enclosing two more pictures. Nine F (9-F) is another picture of the same person that I sent you in the last letter. I am adding one more to the others I have already sent you, (10-F).

I still would like to bring a Video Camera up the next time and record, for the sake of HISTORY, the things you know and can tell. We can put a blue dot over your face and obscure your voice, then on one would know who you are until we can get Immunity. We could be there Oct. 8th or 9th if your willing.

I filed my lawsuit in Dallas against the Medical Examiner
(92-10500-H) to Exhume and Autopsy the body of John F. Kennedy. The District Attorney's office has answered the lawsuit and now DISCOVERY has begun. This is taking a lot of my time.

Write as soon as you can and let me know if you recognize these two dudes. I'll be watching the mailbox for your next letter. By the way… I have a Major Music Producer who wants to hear your music. Who knows, You may end up in Nashville, rather than _____!!!

Your Friend,

Joe H. West

Thursday, 08 Oct. 1992

Joe West
7611 Olympia
Houston, TX 77063

Dear Joe,

I will at this time try to answer your letter that I received this past Saturday evening. Sorry it has taken me this long to respond to it, but I've had a rough week here. But nothing I can't deal with.

It was really nice talking with you on Sunday, I enjoyed our little chat. I'm sorry that you have been sick, but I sure hope that your (sic) better and up and around by now.

The "Fireball" is real and exists. But I believe that you know that, just from talking with Aunt Kay.

Also, I want to say congratulations on your investigations on Kennedy and also for getting it back into court. I know that you must be pleased and I'm very happy for you. I'm sorry about not wanting to do the video right now. But if we film and make a tape and all, without the immunity, I'd be forced to dance around the questions that you would ask. I'm sure that is not what your (sic) looking for. Also I don't want to appear as a fool on camera. I want to be able to give direct answers not dance around your questions. Also, I don't know how far beyond Kennedy I can go without hanging myself. Do you know what I'm saying? I lied to you about the spot I was standing in.

Joe, believe me, if you and Chuck could have met, you guys would have got along great. I know you would not have approved of his way of life, but as a person, you would have liked him.

Joe, I don't know if you have the assassination on film or not, the part where Kennedy was shot. If you do, look at it real close, in slow motion, and see if you can tell what Jackie was trying to do. I've seen the film clip on T.V. but I can't slow it down. But I don't have to, I know what she was trying to do. But the thing is this, I'm not sure if the camera caught it, or if it was edditted. (Please excuse my spelling.) When I see you again, I'll tell you what my <u>mind</u> saw. Then someday, I'll tell you my thoughts to her reaction.
Joe, I'm afraid to say too much, so I don't want to hurt someone that may still be alive. I could never put another man in prison. I'd rather die first. Yea, I know, I'm crazy. I wasn't even a member, but I always believed in "Omerta". Now Chuck was a member, but I guess he tarnished it in the end. That's the part that's hard for me to believe.

I've even considder (sic) giving you a double murder to give to the F.B.I. to work on. The man that was hit, was a contract killing. The woman that was killed, was one of the hit man's wife. She learned too much. They said she committed sucide (sic), but it was murder in the first degree. No! It was not Chuck and me! A couple of people I did not care for. I only wish I was rotten enough to give the feds their names. You know why I hated those guys, they burned up some horses at the race track for insurance. Me, I love all animals, except for man. I am not to (sic) fond of the human race. Animals have never hurt me or caused me pain. People have!!! No, I'm not mixed up or confused, just set in my ways.

I saw a cartoon that I thought was cute. So I sketched it out for you. At times I bet even you get the feeling.

I'm also enclosing another song, one I wrote last year in the County jail. It's another slow-mad(?) type. But I've only played it in my mind.

I'm going to send you something I wrote called "Soldier Past", it's not a song, more of a poem in lymeric (sic) form. Nothing fancy, just plain, it's for all the "grunts", the backbone of the service, for those who served in the "Nam". All the vets that have read it have ask (sic) for copys (sic), they believe it's them. And I've seen some mighty big men cry. But worst of all, I've seen too many good men die. What was it Rudyard Kipling said: "And the measure of our torment is the measure of our youth. God help us, for we knew the worst too young!" That was from "Gentlemen-Rankers".

Well Joe, I'll close for now. Please take care and may God keep you safe.

Your Friend,

Jimmy

Soldier Past
****

The night is warm and the air so very still.
With-in my soul, an emptiness I feel.
My mind it races oh so fast,
my thoughts are carried to the past.
When just a lad they asked what I wish to be.
A soldier I said, to do a great and just deed.
At early age I ran and signed you see.
A brave soldier I couldn't wait to be.
I shook my father's hand and said goodbye.
Hugged and kissed my mother, told her not to cry.
With bag in hand I caught my train.
How heavy the heart when filled with pain.

With destination reached at last,
my heart it beats oh so fast.
Many days of marching in the sun,
and then we had the midnight run.
They wore us down and made us new,
but we were proud for we were few.
They made us believe we were the best,
we never feared we couldn't pass the test.
We were honored at the graduations,
and Generals read the presentations.
With shoulder patches earned,
in war we find there is much to learn.

With training done we sit and wait,
for orders to be cut with a date.
Then at last the orders come,
now we must hurry, pack and run.
We scramble for the six-by and the jeep.
The Sargent yells I don't want to hear a peep.
After traveling most of the night,
we boarded C-130's with just a little fright.
The pilot laughs and calls, it's just the local flight.
We're exhausted from the order of the day,
with little time left, we bow our heads to pray.

With flight so fast,
we have arrived at last.
With forty men and cargo to a plane,
we pray no holes in our landing lane.
I'd read of hero's and I want the same.
Yes, let me take part in this deadly game.
We form our columns, two by two,
now we must go, see and do.
We have walked and searched the terrain,
we have been soaked by the monsoon rain.
As we march down the Purple Heart Trail,
we're all shouting, we'll give the V.C. hell.

We have fought and took the Di La Pass,
there we kicked the V.C. in the ass.
Now take these hills without a name,
we must hold them to achieve our fame.
In the darkness I can sense the enemy is near.
It's much too quiet, never have I felt such fear.
Generals call to ask, how many and how near.
Forgive me Sir, I cannot count, I've too much fear.
Oh God what a dreadful place for me to die.
Oh God give me courage,--don't let me cry.
Oh God give me strength and take this fear,
don't desert me now, please stay near.

I can feel the presence of the enemy.
I hear a voice, I feel they're calling me.
Trembling fingers, my heart is beating fast.
Sweat begins to run, how long will the battle last?
LISTEN! I hear a noise in the darkness of the night.
We're told let them get close, we must hold tight.
Then blinding flashes and exploding shells.
I see tracers soaring through the sky,
Such deadly things still hold beauty to the eye.
The chatter of rifles and lead comes like rain.
I hear the cries of agony of men in pain.

Through the night the battle rages on.
How many shall perish before the dawn?
Yes! We have craved and longed for combat.
Now we've tasted blood, who wants that!
As I look across the M.L.R. I see death's hand.
Yes, for we are men of deaths gray land.
I've never seen so many slain,
as I sit and watch the corpses in the rain.
My mind races back, I know I've not seen this before.
Oh forgive me Sir, I can't count them anymore.
No longer am I a child that wants to play,
for I have gained manhood in less than a day.

While stopping to catch my breath,
I watch young hero's rush to their death.
Yes, death is absurd and life absurder.
Do we not feel sickness, or remorse of murder?
No! We have been taught that killing is our game.
Proud soldiers we are, that is our fame.
See the dead, see the maimed, have you forgotten yet?
Swear by the slain of war, that you'll never forget.
Then I hear the order, fix bayonet,
no, the battles not over yet.
As we make the charge, we bellow out our name.
We scream to the V.C. that killing is our game.

As soon as we leave our cover, I watch brave soldiers fall.
Oh God, give them mercy, hear their call.
Yes, we're in a hurry to flight and win our fame.
But when the battles over, we'll find that war is just a bloody game.

Yes, it was bloody and very deadly there,
for power was on us as we slashed bones bare.
The V.C. began to run,
excited, we gave chase and yelled what fun.
We have tasted battle and the blood we fed upon.
Can I give all this up, just to be sent home?

Oh God, forgive me for what I feel.
But while in battle I love to kill.
The power of killing rushes through my bones.
Oh God, let me stay, please don't send me home.
Am I the only one that feels this way?
Do I only live to kill another day?
How many soldiers feel as I?
How many nights shall we cry?
Some will cry for love, some will cry for death.
Some will go to sleep, while others fight for their last breath.
I stand and watch the medic running all around,
for so many soldiers lie upon the ground.

Many are the soldiers that are maimed,
I wonder what made the enemy miss his aim.
These men are wounded, some will die.
Letters will be sent and the mothers, they will cry.
A soldier cries for arm and leg are gone,
let me die, a burden I wish not to be at home.
A broken man I am, yes, I'm maimed for life,
don't send me back like this, for it would hurt my wife.
No longer can I get up and run,
Nor can I play ball with my son.
So don't send me home to make loved ones lie.
Oh God give me mercy and let me die.

Yes, there was much to see and oh so much to tell,
I know not what to say, but believe me it was hell.
So stand up soldier, like me you never want to be.
 Look me up and down tell me what you see.
You start to wonder,
then you ask my name at last.
What! You still don't know?
Why! I'm Soldier Past!

James E. Files
82nd Airborne Rangers
10/04/1982

Joe West
7611 Olympia
Houston, TX 77063

Dear Joe,

Just a few lines to say hello and to get these two pictures on their way to you. I just got them, like 10 minutes ago. Please have some copies made and return these two, so that I can return them. She didn't really want to let these go.☺ I feel like she doesn't trust me.

No, she's not my mother, my mother was killed in 1964. A car accident in Adolphus, Kentucky. My father left my mother before I was born. My sister was killed by her husband in 1959 in St. Louis, MO. I think I told you about my brother, he was killed in Mexico city. Who's left? Just little ol' me. ☺ This woman is a "Special Friend". I would never involve her in anything. She's good people, but knows I'm crazy. ☺ But by now you know that.

I'm enclosing another song that I wrote. A long time ago, when I was doing federal time. It's a very slow song. I only wish that I could sing. I mailed you two songs last night, maybe this one will catch up with them. For now I'll close, take care and God Bless.

Friends always,

Jimmy

P. S. These photos are in 1963, a little before…

October 14, 1992

Dear,

It almost felt like Christmas when the postman brought me three letters at one time. As I get to know you better, it's almost like you being several people rather than just one because of your poetry, music, art, comic characterizations and other abilities. The poem "Soldier Past" is a classic and certainly should be published. The song "Eight By Ten" should be Number One on the charts in Nashville. The cartoon represents every one's secret desire and especially mine!!! The only change I would make is to make the list longer to take care of some of the bad days I have.

I guess the pictures caught my attention as much as the other interesting things in the letter. Who is the other person in the picture with you? I am going to take them and have copies made today. I will send them back as soon as they are finished along with a copy for you.

The Round Lake Heights Police Department is no longer cooperating in the search for the "Fireball". They are not taking my calls anymore. They are making me write letters in any communication that I have with them. I will not let up until I find that weapon. I'm working hard on the Immunity. As you know, it's like a miracle to get it. I spend most of my time on the Lawsuit to exhume the body of JFK. If I prevail in court, and the body can be autopsied by Forensic Pathologists, then the world will know whether the shots came from above and behind or from other directions. The Immunity will make it possible for you to come to Dallas and help solve these details.

I really appreciate you being truthful about your location that day. Your letter also indicates that you were with "10-F" a little before noon as the sun was coming out. Please help as much as you can by telling me all that you can about the details of that day. I have watched every film taken that day and have also watched them in slow motion. Tell me what you think about Jackie and then I can tell you exactly what's in the films. I did not get to make the last trip in your direction, but I hope to be coming that way soon because I'm looking forward to seeing you again…I can't wait to hear you sing some of your song's and to talk about things that are needed to be recorded in history. It would be VERY HELPFUL if you would give the information about the man and woman in exchange for Immunity. Write me all the details you can and this will be very helpful in encouraging the Federal Attorney to give Immunity.

Please write and call as often as you can. Take good care of yourself and stay well and save. I can never thank you enough for helping me and being my friend. Your letters, homes, songs, cartoons and information are making life very interesting. I am looking forward to the future as you take a special place in HISTORY for helping the world to know the truth about November 22, 1963.

Your Friend,

_____
Joe H. West

Monday, 19 Oct. 1992

Joe West
7611 Olympia
Houston, TX 77063

Dear Joe,

I just received your letter and as always, I was delighted in hearing from you. Your letters never fail to excite me, and the compliments make me feel sooooooo gooood. ☺ You know that you are giving me a big head. One so big that not even Texas will have a hat that will fit me.

But I am glad that you liked "Soldier Past". That is my favorite piece of work. When I wrote that, my heart was really in it. I'm also glad that you liked the song Eight by Ten. It's also one of my favorites. And believe me, I've got plenty of bad songs. I keep saying that some day I'll rewrite them. But I know that I should just trash them.

Let me say that I'm glad that you are over the flu and up and around. I'm sure that the flu really had you worn down to a frazzle. So welcome back to the real world.

So the pictures caught your eye? Well I hope the same will be of some help to you. Are you surprised at what I looked like back then? ☺ For the life of me, I can't remember ever being that young. I feel like I was born as an adult. It's hard for me to remember my child's life. My friend in the picture, forget him, he's still alive. Besides, he's not important.

I'm sorry that the Round Lake Heights Police Department is giving you a rough time. Try to get hold of this "Chris" kid and see if he can remember which cop took it from him. With a little luck, this kid could be doing time, which could make it easy to find him. Too bad he's not here with me. I could choke it out of him.

Yes, I know that immunity is hard to get for someone. If you need help with it, let me know. Help will be available after the 1st of the year. But I'll tell you in person about that Joe, I have to be very careful about what I write in letters, or say on a phone. Especially, about the man and woman. Plus, what I say about a lot of things. All my mail is read, going out and coming in and all phones are recorded. Sometimes I'm afraid that I've already said too much.
Yes, I was with "10-F" till the sun came out. We were talking about the weather and other things in general. Do you remember which building I said I was pretty sure I put the car behind? But not the book building, where they said Oswald was. The one across the street from it. Did you ever figure out why I put it there? Also, Jackie crawled out on the trunk, or rear of the Lincoln to get a piece of skull with hair and

tissue still attached to it. I would say about the size of a half dollar. It looked as if I could reach out and touch her. The car was almost at a standstill, a large man, (Secret Service I figure) ran up and jumped on the left side of the bumper. But he never tried to help Jackie, just stood there, hands on the deck lid and watched her pick it up and try to put his head back together. I admire her, she never panicked, oh she was crying, but not for her self, but for John. I don't know, maybe I'm wrong, but that's the way I remember it. Also, I believe that he died in the car when his head opened up. I will never believe he lived to reach the hospital, not with at least 30 to 50 percent of his brain missing. Later on, I'll have more to say about that.

And for God-sakes, you don't ever want to hear me sing, I only write them. I have a terrible voice and that is the truth so help me God. ☺ Yep, that is a fact.

When you get this way again, stop in and say hello. In my book you are A-number one. I enjoy talking with you. But please, no cameras or tapes. O.K. ☺ Don't worry, we won't loose history.

Please take care of your self and may God keep you and your family safe.

Your Friend,

Jimmy

October 23, 1992

Dear,

I just got back from getting your pictures from the photo shop and your letter was waiting for me. It's almost like when I was a kid and I couldn't wait for Saturday to come around to see the next series of Gene Autry or "Batman" at the movies. However, this is not fiction, and that makes your letters many times more interesting. I'm still looking forward to the next one.

Is there any way for you to get a recorder and record these songs so I can hear what the tune sounds like? My curiosity is killing me. Also, it would make it possible for me to try to get them Published for you. I can already hear "Willie" singing the "OUTLAW BLUES". This song is by for one of your best.

The building you talked about in your last letter really has my attention. Who all was in there and what did each one do? Did any thing else happen that caused you to park there? Please tell me as much as you can. Also it's very important to know where the "X" really belongs on the map. It's like I'm down on one knee as I ask where "10-F" was? The strange thing is that I know most of the above answers, but I need you to document your answers by telling me first.

You were exactly right about Jackie. She later handed the piece of brain to Dr. Pepper Jenkins at Parkland Hospital. The Lawsuit in Dallas is progressing rapidly. I'm working hard on the Immunity so that you can come to Dallas and testify freely. Your information will be very important, along with the other witnesses, to write the record of history straight. It was sad to hear of Jim Garrison's death this week. The case I filled is only the second time in history that a case has been filed on the JFK Assassination. The Difference is that I have avoided as much publicity as possible and I am not going into court EMPTY HANDED like Jim Garrison did. By the way, his son is assisting in research on the legal team.

I am enclosing the two original photos and a copy for you. Again, thanks for the photos. I'm looking forward to coming to see you as soon as I can. I've been delayed from traveling your way because of HEALTH reasons. I won't bore you with the details. All of us end up with some aches and pains when you get to my age. Keep me on your visitors list and call every change you get. Keep yourself safe and may the Lord be with you until I see you again.

Sincerely,

_____
Joe H. West

Tuesday, 27 Oct. 1992

Joe West
7611 Olympia
Houston, TX 77063

Dear Joe,

I just received your welcome letter and the four pictures. Thank you very much. I just put the large ones in my photo album. ☺ I'll send the other two back to the lady tonight. That was very kind of you to get these enlarged for me.

What is the matter with your health? I thought you were over the flu. I pray that it's not something serious wrong with you. Please let me know. I think of you as a friend, so that gives me the right to worry about you.

As for me, I'm feeling pretty good. But, the entire prison is back on lock-down. For how long I don't know. I don't even know what happened. I heard a rumor a guard got hurt, another that a guard was killed. I really don't know. But there's no showers or phones. ☹

They won't let a recorder in here, they're banned. So there's no way that I can make a recording for you. But thanks for the compliment on "Outlaw Blues". I too would love to hear "Willie" sing that one. Just him singing it would make it a hit.

You are so right, this is not fiction, but I sure wish it was. I'll be honest, I'm nervous about things I write and say. I don't want to get myself any new cases. What I say and write can be used against me in a court of law. The phones here are recorded, my mail is checked and read before it is sent out. For all I know they may even XEROX it!!! Joe I trust you, but I don't trust these people or the F.B.I. or the Secret Service or the A.T.F. Or the D.E.A., or D.O.D. Plus the N.S.A. or the N.S.C. I'm stupid I guess, but I still trust the C.I.A. and for damn sure I don't trust the O.C. people (mob). ☺ The only one of those I ever trusted was (10 F).

Yes, it was a shame about Jim Garrison. My question is, was it really natural? I wish you complete success on this investigation. Just watch your self and take care. O.K.

But back to the above, I can't move the X on the map just yet, I don't have the immunity and also, I still have a chance on my appeal. I'm afraid that all this is going to kill any chance for me winning my appeal. And I have a good chance at winning it. I hope you understand, I'm caught in between.

Before I forget, next time you write or talk to your friend in Nashville, to please ask him for the address where I can subscribe for the music book, "Country Song Roundup". If you can get me the address I would really appreciate it very much. Nashville is the only place that I can get it from.

Now, back to Business…Once upon a time…there was this little city called Las Vegas. They owned casinos and hotels. When you have a bunch of hotels, you need your own laundry service. So you buy one of those. Then you need detergent for your laundry service. So they bought one down in New Mexico. Financed by Teamsters money like everything else. Then one day a man from Melrose Park, Ill. Went to New Mexico and the plant went booooooooooom, all gone. The star witness was a guy named Dan or Dave Siefert or Seifert, I'm not sure on the spelling. Anyway, he was a government witness and there were some people worried, from Chicago to Las Vegas. In Las Vegas, Tony Spilotra, (or however you spell it), was worried and several people in Chicago was worried. Anyway, the F.B.I. escorted this man to work one late fall day in 1974, I believe. That was in Elmhurst or Bensenville, Ill. long time ago. Anyway, they failed to escort him inside. He was chased by gunmen through the factory, to the parking lot and there killed. Leaving the scene, the 3 hitmen hit a car pulling into the parking lot. Two cars were used that morning, a green ford and a dodge I believe. I don't remember which was used for which, but any way, they switched cars at a car dealer ship close by on Grand Ave. But they were spotted and a pursuit took place. Cops chased them back to Melrose Park, Ill. But the cops lost them on 25th Ave., just north of Lake St. They drove the green dodge (I believe) into this private garage and closed the door. There was a lot of heat on so they couldn't get the car out of his garage. Big write up in the news papers. Then his wife goes out to the garage and sees this car. She is terrified. She is deathly afraid of her husband. She ran into me at the Harlo Grill on 24th and North Ave., and ask (sic) me if I knew what her husband had been involved in and tells me about the car in the garage. I tell her to forget you ever seen it and not to ask questions. She don't listen, she goes to Tony Accardo who lives in River Forest and ask (sic) him to help her husband get out of trouble. She has not yet told her husband that she suspects anything. Tony A. huggs (sic) her, kiss's (sic) her, pats her on the head and says, don't worry, Uncle Tony will fix everything. On New Years Eve, she got all dressed up like she was going out. Went out in the garage got in her car, started it up and committed sucied (sic), so the police report reads. Her husband druged (sic) her and put her in the car in a closed garage and went out to party. She was found the next day. NO! 10F and I were not envolved (sic) in any of it. The job was way too sloppy for 10F an (sic) me to have done it. Two of the three lived in Melrose Park, Ill., the third man I don't know. If you wish have the F.B.I. check out these facts, please do, as I don't want you to think your (sic) dealing with a nut case. Also, maybe it will help towards the immunity.

If I get sick and go to die, I'll have you come with pen and paper and I'll give you a "Best Seller" to write after they put me in the ground and cover me with concrete. ☺ Even 10F and me had a few cowboy jobs. He preferred the quiet ones, me, I liked a lot of noise.

Wow, I'm on page five. I best shut up and close this out. I don't mean to bore you to death. Oh yes, when you call the F.B.I. just read this to them, don't give them the letter it's (sic) self, o.k.

Well my friend, I'll close for now, you take care and get well. May God keep you and your family safe and in good health.

P.S. When you were here to see me, did I give you my other name, back then, when I was young?

November 8, 1992

Dear,

I'm late answering your last letter for several good reasons. One is that I had hoped that I would have some answers on Immunity, but they are a little slow getting here. I will write the minute they get here. I hated to hear that you are in lock-down again. I hope its not for long because I would like to come up and see you again. Let me know when its over.

How are things going on your appeal? I know you must be doing a lot of hard work in that direction. I'm hoping for the best and that you will be successful. I've looked everywhere for the music book "Country Song Roundup". I finally found out it is no longer in publication. It was published in Poughkeepsie, New York. I wasn't even able to find a second hand copy....Sorry!

Is there any chance that the "little fire" did not occur and those things are still around? It really scared me when I read the last page where you talked about getting sick and dying....first, because you're my friend and next because I would like to preserve for history a true record of the important information you have.

My case in Dallas is going well at this point, however, the big battles are still ahead. I have worked hard to keep it out of the Media. That was Jim Garrison's big mistake because he couldn't resist sticking his face in front of every camera he could find. I'm enclosing a copy of the Original Petition. I will be filling an Amended Petition in about two weeks that will have more specifics in it. Also enclosed is an article from AP that went out all over the world. AP seems to know everything even when your trying to keep it quite. I spend a lot of my time staying away from reporters and also saying "NO COMMENT" when they call. I hope you can do the same if anything leaks out about you and they start calling you.

Please try to answer all the questions you can and tell me all that you can in a way that you and I will understand. I understand your concern about the eyes and ears all around, but try the best you can to send me a few smoke signals or something.

Thanks again for keeping some excitement in my life when I receive your letters. I hope you stay well with winter coming on. Thanks again for being my friend and helping me in this Investigation. I am sincerely.

Your Friend,

_____
Joe H. West

Wednesday, 19 Nov. 1992

Joe West
7611 Olympia
Houston, TX 77063

Dear Joe,

I received your letter this past Saturday, the 14th. Usually I answer right away, but this time I've been lazy, feeling down, think I got a cold coming on. But as always, I was delighted to receive your letter and other very interesting articles. Especially the Petition! Very, very interesting. Also, the case law behind it.

Now to try to answer some of your questions. Even when we're on lock-down, I can still get visitors. But we're off lock-down. ☺ For a while anyway.

My appeal won't even be filed until May of 1993. Due to the courts being over crowded.

Thank you for checking on "Country Song Roundup" for me. I really appreciate it. Thank you.

The little fire? Yes it did take place and the ashes scattered and broke up. Sorry! As for me getting sick and dying, don't worry. Only the good die young! I'll live for ever. ☺

I'm happy to hear that your case is going well. Yes, A.P. always did seem to find out a lot. I learned about them in Nam! And, I don't give interviews, especially to the media. I'm still trying to figure out why I talked to you. You My Friend are a first! On the case I'm on now the media tried to get an interview with me, no way. Then some reporter wanted to do my side of the story on the cop shooting and write about my past. I told him I wasn't that stupid. The less people find out about me the better. But I still couldn't get a fair trial. So please ease your mind about me and the press.

Right now my mind is a blank, so I'm not sending any smoke signals this time. But I was curious, did you pass the last to the F.B.I.?

I made up a little card for you. I finally got some colored pencils. So now I can get back to my cartoons. ☺ It helps to pass the time.

On my end there's not much news. I'm in a slump I guess. I wish there was some more I could tell you but there's not. In the mean time you take care of your self and I'll see you the next time your (sic) up this way. May God keep you and your family safe.

Your Friend,

Jimmy

Tuesday, 01 Dec. 1992

Joe West
7611 Olympia
Houston, TX 77063

Dear Joe,

Just a few lines to say hello and to thank you for the very cute card. It really put a smile on my face. I hope the one I made puts a smile on your face. I wish you and Earlene a very Merry Christmas and may the Holidays be Joyous.

Today the entire prison went on lock-down again. But I'm glad. ☺ I broke my right foot on the 21st and it hurt like crazy trying to hobble back and forth to the mess hall. This way I get room service. ☺

Not much news on my end. I got my daughters visiting rights re-instated, so she was here the other day to see me. She is one very Beautiful girl. Someday I hope you get to meet her. When she was small, she was never around me. We didn't get to know each other till she was eighteen. But we have a wonderful relationship now.

You and your wife take care and may God keep you safe. Merry Christmas.

Your Friend,

Jimmy

Sunday, 06 Dec. 1992

Joe West
7611 Olympia
Houston, TX 77063

Dear Joe,

What a shock it was to hear about you having a heart attack. I am very happy to hear that you are back up and around, on your feet feeling pretty good. Let's thank the Good Lord for that. Since I've got your letter, I've been saying a prayer for you every night. Just take extra good care of your self.

What happens if they don't grant me immunity? ☺ Also, can you send me the case citing # for Murphy vs. Waterfront. I'd like to try and look it up in the law library the next time I get over there, when ever that will be. When we're on lock-down, there is no law library. Right now I'm working on trying to get me an electric typewriter sent in from the street. They sell manuel (sic) ones in the Commissary, but they're cheap and not very good and they're not worth the $100.00 they ask for them. They're more like a $29.95 job from K. Mart! ☺

I've got a lot of law work ahead of me, and with all the lock-downs, I need one very bad. I just started a law suite (sic) against Lake County, Ill. for $100,000.00, 100,000 and 150,000. Every one said I should go for two and a half million, but I want the case accepted in the Federal Courts in Chicago, not rejected. Know what I mean. Then I want to have my appeal filed in May. So I've got a long road ahead of me.

I hope I don't come to Texas, till after the first of the year. I'd rather be here for Christmas, so I can see my daughter over the holidays. But what ever has to be will be. ☺

Just remember, I'm not sure how much I can help you. For instance I was not in the building with #10F. I know that's where he was supposed to be, and afterwards, he said he was, in so many words that is. Also, I only seen #4F that morning in front of the Hotel talking to Johnny. No, I'm not chickening out, ☺ I'm just wondering how much I can say without hanging my self. In that respect, I am worried. Please try to let me know a little in advance when I'm being subpoena (sic) if possible. That way I can get my personal property secured here where maybe it won't be stolen while I'm gone.

Where will they keep me at in Dallas, the County jail or the federal lock-up? And what are the (sic) like? If it's better than here, maybe when I come down, they can just keep me till it's all over with.

I appreciate the kind thought of your wanting to make me more comfortable. But that's not possible. Even if it were, I couldn't accept it. I want to take the stand and when asked I can honestly say no, I've received nothing and I've been promised nothing. It has to be that way. I don't want anyone to think I'm selling out for a few dollars. And as for the news media, no problem, I don't talk to them. If I say nothing, then nothing can be twisted. But let me ask you for your honest opinion. How <u>BAD</u> can this hurt my appeal? It's bad enough I'm in for allegedly shooting a police officer. Your trial is going to happen ahead of my appeal. There's no way my testimony is going to be kept out of the news media. People back here are going to hear it. That will really make the appeals court think before ruling on my case. See what I mean. Yes, I am concerned. ☺ Can you blame me. I have given this <u>much, much</u> thought!!!

I hope that your gathering with the attorneys went rather well. I wish you the best all the way around. Please keep me posted and take care of your self. I hope you like your get well card. May God keep you and your family safe.

Your Friend,

Jimmy

Joe H. West, CLI
7611 Olympia
Houston, Texas 77063
(713)787-5111

December 11, 1992

Dear,

I sure wish I were an artist so I could send you cards that cheered you up as much as your cards do to me. You are certainly a <u>CREATIVE GENIUS.</u> You could make a million dollars with your art when you are out. I'm going to frame these and hang them on my office wall along with any others you send me.

What happened to your foot!!! I guess your walking around like "Chester" on <u>GUNSMOKE.</u> It sounds like you might have been the reason for the Lockdown. I'm glad your daughter was able to visit you. From what you say, she must have the best of your charm and personality. I would like to meet her someday.

Even though I don't have the Immunity yet, I feel positive that it is coming. The only reason for the delay is that it's taking some time to do some things that I said I would do first. I would think that they would transfer you to the County Facility which is on Dealey Plaza. If all goes well, it will be after the first of the year and then it will only be for a deposition then. The trial is at least a year off. The deposition will probably be kept from the media, however, I'm sure the trial will have a lot of media attention. So, it shouldn't have nay affect on your Appeal. I would not do anything intentionally that would hurt your chances for Appeal.

Let me know if your typewriter deal works out. I know that's important to help in your legal work. If you don't get one, be sure to let me know. The reference number is Murphy vs. Waterfront Commission of New York Harbor, 378 U.S. 52, 84 S.Ct. 1594 (1964). Was 4F doing the same thing as 10F, or was he just helping 10F in any way…or was it that 4F just happened to be there like he told the deputies that questioned him? What floor did each of them <u>stop</u> on?

Thanks again for the wonderful cards….and LETTERS. I am, Sincerely,

Your Friend,

Joe H. West

Sunday 20 Dec. 1992

Joe West
7611 Olympia
Houston, TX 77603

Dear Joe,

Merry Christmas and Happy New Year and may the coming year bring you and your family "Good Health" and the Best of all.

I'm sorry I've been so long in answering your last letter. I always try to answer within forty eight hours, so this time I'm way beyond the time limit. But I've had a couple of problems here and I've also had the flu. My foot is much better and I've also got my dentures back from the dentist. I had to have two teeth put back in. December has been a bad month for me. But nothing I can't deal with.

Thank you for all the kind compliments on my work. You are very kind. I don't remember if I did Donald Duck in trouble or not. But anyway, I'm sending you one of my favorites. And the verse inside is my own, and like some of my music it speaks the truth, such as my songs "Soldiers of Fortune" and, "Bring Me Some Flowers While I'm Living". Yes, sometimes I feel that both of us are on thin ice and may fall in over our heads. Hell Joe, I'll go down with the best. But after I open up and say what I kept hidden in the shadows of my mind. What kind of shadows will I leave cast over my two daughter's lives? They're age 17 and 26. What I did is not something they can be proud of. How will this affect them? Is there a chance some one might try to hurt them? I feel that you all ready know where the X on the map belongs. I figure you've known that all along. But we'll worry about these things after the immunity. Then we can talk more open and you can give me your best advice. O.K. ☺

My oldest daughter, Kathy, was here to see me today. We had a really great visit. She is a wonderful girl and very, very Beautiful (sic). In a lot of ways, she's like me, hard headed, and very independent, also a very hard worker and wants things out of life.

Yesterday, I went to the law library and looked up "Murphy vs. Waterfront" and read it. Very interesting. Also, who will transport me to Dallas? I have a very hard time trusting government people. But that's another story. 4F and 10F we'll talk more about after the immunity. But there's not much I can tell you about 4F. No, I haven't had a change of heart, just sharing some of my thoughts with you. That's all. I'm ready for Dallas when ever they come. ☺

There's not much news on my end. They just put us back in lock-down. Someone broke into the commissary store and robbed it. Some body's always doing something dumb. We'll be off lock-down in a day or two. No big deal.

I do hope that your (sic) back in good health and that your (sic) taking care of your self. After I win my appeal and I'm free, I'm looking forward to you and me taking a nice little trip cross country on bikes and maybe getting in a little fishing. Who knows, maybe we can even find me a job in Houston. I'm good at painting houses, doing drywall, driving tractor and trailer. Manual labor, making just enough to live on. No more work, like with 10F ☺ I'm retired.

After all this is over with, about my life story. No! That can never be told. Besides, the only ones who would believe it would be the F.B.I. and they would love my story with all the names they have in the files. ☺ The A.T.F. would also go crazy, and maybe a few others. But I don't need those problems. I just want to live a quiet life and enjoy it. That's all I want for the few years I have left. I want to enjoy my children and they're kids if they have any. ☺ I'll close for now. Take care and may God keep you safe.

Friends,

Jimmy

Sunday 27 Dec 1992

Joe H. West
7611 Olympia
Houston, TX 77063

Dear Joe,

Just a few lines to say hello and Happy New Year. Also that I hope that your (sic) back in good health. As for me, I am feeling much better and walking pretty good.

My Daughter was here today to see me and we really had a terrific visit. She is the only one that I look forward to seeing. I don't encourage visits; I try to not think about the free world. I don't ever let my girlfriend come to visit.

Could you please check and see what a small electric typewriter, self correcting would cost, and let me know. Maybe, we could get one delivered to me at the county jail, placed into my personal property with paper work. That way, I could bring it back with me and get it in. Some guys come from a medium security prison and they bring electric typewriters with them that they had purchased there. I can have the money sent to you. Do you think they would accept it at the county jail? Let me know what you think, O.K. ☺

I hope that this little card I made puts a smile on your face. It cracked up a few people around here. I'm also sending you a song I wrote back when I was up in Oxford Federal Prison.

After I get back here I may be able to get my guitar in. I signed up to join a band. I had one of the best bands in the federal system when I was at Oxford. I only wish I could sing. But I got a terrible voice. I can only do crazy type songs where you don't have to be a good singer, just make people laugh. ☺

Well we finally got off lock-down this morning. So we're getting showers once again. This place just ain't no real fun. They say this is the toughest joint in Ill., some say in the Midwest. Me, I don't know, I never did state time before. But I know that this is the most max. I'm still trying to get my security lowered.

Oh yea, remind me to tell you about the F.B.I. getting run over when they had 10F under surveillance one night in Melrose Park. I'm sure it's in their files on him. ☺ It happened in front of my restaurant, the_____. Boy were they pissed off that night. It's no big deal, just a funny story, but they wasn't laughing. But then it's been said that I got a morbid sense of humor. Well my friend I'll close for now. Please take care and may God keep you and your family safe. Happy New Year.

Your Friend,

Jimmy

Joe H. West, CLI
7611 Olympia
Houston, Texas 77063
(713)787-5111

January 1, 1993

Dear,

Happy New Year!!! Your letter came on Christmas Eve, but…we had a NICE and long Christmas that seem to go right up through New Year's Eve. It's interesting that my dentist told me a couple of months ago that I had to get my remaining teeth pulled and get a set of Dentures Immediately. So, that's going to be on my schedule soon.

I really like my card on "Thin Ice". I have been there so many times. However, I think from here on… You and I will be standing on a "Rock" more than we ever have in all of our lives. It's really tough to make some HARD DECISIONS like you made last year when you began to open up your life, but in the end it will cause you to be stronger mentally and emotionally. It will make you feel and experience a <u>FREEDOM</u> far greater than any that you have ever felt before. I think your two wonderful daughters would be very proud of you for having the COURAGE to step forward and tell the "truth, the whole truth and nothing but the truth". If I can be of any help by writing them or talking with them, it would an honor and a privilege to help in any way.

I am scheduled to be in Dallas to complete the arrangements for Immunity toward the end of the month. After that, I am planning on coming to see you and having a log talk. Then, I would like to Subpoena you to Dallas. The Dallas Court would have a Deputy bring you to Dallas for the Deposition. At that time we could arrange for you to take us on a "scene tour" of some interesting places in Dallas.

It would be a pleasure for you to come to Houston when your out. I would be glad to have a "fishing buddy" and also help in any way to find you work in this area. I hope the Appeal works out soon so we can get started. My "Bike" is collecting dust and is ready to go. God bless you for being a friend,

Sincerely,

Joe H. West

Wednesday 06 Jan 1993

Joe H. West
7611 Olympia
Houston, TX 77063

Dear Joe,

Last night I received your letter and as always, enjoyed hearing from you. I will try to answer it today. I have a very bad cold and my thinking is not to plain today. But I did do another card. One that speaks the truth. You have drove me crazy. ☺ But now you can show your wife what I really look like. I call it my self portrait. ☺ Some of the guys here say I really captured myself with this card.

I'm very glad to know that your (sic) much better and up and around. But I'm sorry to hear about your teeth. But after you get use (sic) to the dentures, they're great. I love mine. But it took a while to get use (sic) to them.

I'm glad you liked the card "thin ice", yes, I'm sure you have been there more than a few times. I've spent better than 90 percent of my life on thin ice. I still don't know what possessed me to talk to you last year. Really, only 6 months ago. For all my life I have believed that silence is golden. And since talking to you, (please don't be mad at me, o.k.), but I have not experienced a freedom, nor have I been released mental or emotional freedom. I have only felt something eating at my insides and my nerves stretching. I'm not the least bit proud about talking. I felt a lot better keeping the secret locked deep inside. Now I feel like I peeped inside "Pandora's Box" and let Hell itself escape. I can live with the dead, it's the people alive that I worry about.

Thank you for volunteering to talk to my daughter. I really do appreciate it. But I must keep them out of this. I don't want to wreck their lives.

Yes, I'm looking forward to seeing you again soon. I do enjoy talking with you. And I would love for us to go fishing when I get out. I like Houston, as I've been all over Texas. I like "Corpus Christi" the best. But Houston offers more work. I don't need a lot to get by on. My only bad habbits (sic) are guns, fast money and pretty women. And I'm giving up everything but the pretty women. ☺

And if I ever start talking about anything that is unsolved, other that this Kennedy thing, stick a plug in my mouth and kick me in the ass, o.k.

Like this nut today on "Inside Edition". He says he shot Hoffa. ☺ I laughed myself silly over that one. And no, I didn't shoot him either. And Hoffa wasn't carried to anybody's house with hit men waiting. This guys got an imagination like, "The Doc", that testified against me in Texas. When he told them I was the one that snatched "Butch Petrocelli" and killed him in my chop-shop. I stabbed him in the hands, face, legs, and tortured him, like using a torch to burn his eyes out, before I finally killed him. He had his lawyer trying to find out who the secret witness were against. He didn't know that his girlfriend was the secret witness. She went to the F.B.I. because she feared me. He almost got his Chicago lawyer indicted in Texas for conspiracy to committ (sic) murder. Texas ran his lawyer out of Texas and back to Chicago. In Texas "Fortworth"(sic) when I went for a bond hearing, the F.B.I. introduced what they called a "torture murder kit" that they took out of one of my chop shops. I'll tell you the story when I see you. I've been to trial on all that, so its public knowledge. Sad, but still funny. For this violent world that I lived in, a lot of funny things sure did happen.

Please try to let me know when your (sic) coming to see me and I'll advise my people here not to come visit me that week. Unless, your (sic) only going to be here one day. Maybe I'll even let you meet my oldest Daughter if you promise not to pump her about me. We only got together a few years ago. And I don't want to do anything to hurt our relationship. She's such a wonderful girl. I love her more than life its self. And I'm really scared about the news media fishing all this up. I've already talked with my daughter about this thing. But don't worry about me and the news media. At the trial, I hope they don't let cameras into the court room. I don't want the media to get my picture. Let them take yours. ☺ I just want to be forgotten when all this is over with. That's why I don't want my picture made. People will forget much faster if they don't see my face in papers or on T.V. If they know who I am, I'll never be able to get a job. I can change me name easy, but not my face. Hey, I better close before I bore you to tears. I'm on page 4 already. When you come, don't forget to ask me about the F.B.I. getting run over. No one got hurt, just their pride. ☺ I have pulled a few pranks on them in my time. But only because they tried to get snitches next to me.

Oh yea, one more question. That gallery where you got 10F's picture, do they have a picture of me? Just curious, as I've always tried to keep a very low profile. But being a long time friend of 10F, I just wonder if they tied me to him?

Well I'll close for now. May God keep you safe. Please take care.

Your Friend,

Jimmy

P.S. We've been back on lock-down for the last week. Crazy place.

Joe H. West, CLI
7611 Olympia
Houston, Texas 77063-1920
(713)787-5111

January 8, 1993

Dear,

You'll never know how special the "Happy New Year" card made my family feel. My wife and three children are crazy in love with cats. Thanks for including them in your wonderful world of ART. I'm glad your daughter is bringing a lot of sunshine into your life by visiting you. I know a daughter can be so close to a daddy's heart.

I would be glad to get you a typewriter. Enclosed are some for you to consider. If you like one of these, let me know which one it is, or if there is another brand you like, let me know and I'll find it for you. I'll also inquire and request them to let me bring it to you in Dallas.

I talked with the D.A.'s office yesterday. It's important at this time for me to know where the "X" was during that SIX SECONDS in Dallas and who was standing or sitting close by. This is necessary for a final decision on Immunity. Did you have on a cap or hat, umbrella, radio or anything visible in your hand, etc. that can verify you in any of the photos that were taken that day. I need this information for "Proof" and would withhold it until the Immunity is signed and then exchange it for the final document.

This is a great opportunity in life for you to take your rightful place in history by helping to solve the greatest crime of this century. I'm trusting that God will watch over you and your family and keep you safe.

Your Friend,

_____
Joe H. West

Tuesday 19 Jan. 1993

Joe West
7611 Olympia
Houston, TX 77063

Dear Joe,

Just a few lines to say hello and to let you know that I received your letter this past Friday, the 15th. As always, I was delighted to hear from (you). But this time I took a few days to answer. I had to think this letter over. Very carefull (sic)!!!

First, let me say thank you for sending information on the typewriter. I'll see my daughter this Friday and talk it over with her. And make sure she has the money on hand to send(?) to you for it.

Yes, "Run Outlaw Run" is a good song. But you ever hear me sing, you get up and run, and never come back. ☺ That is a fact!

I'm glad you liked the last card. Thought I'd (do) another cat for you and the family. But the "Yeeeaaaaaahhhhhhh", put it to the voice of "Edward G. Robbinson" (sic) back when he played "Al Capone". I'm sure you saw that movie.

About the "SIX SECONDS" I cannot give you that at this time. I'm sorry! But all my mail is checked, and I've been told coppied, (sic) Xeroxed, or whatever. And I'm not making a signed confession at this time. I trust you Joe, but I don't trust these people, mail or phone. And also, what if I don't get the immunity and the government ordered you to turn over all your information pertaining to me. Also, you never answered if we'll be able to get me in and out of court at the trial without getting my kisser all over the T.V. screen. My name is one thing, I can change easy enough. But the 24th of this month, I'll be 51 and I've kind a grown to love this ol' face of mine, its (sic) took a long time for me to get use (sic) to . Each day I pray for you to find a way to get the job done without me. I <u>do</u> <u>not</u> want to take my place in history. I do not want to be famous. I had enough publicity off this case to last a life time. This 50 years I got is not for what I did, but for who I am. Those two cops did not try to arrest me. They tried to kill me. It was an out and out ambush on Route 12 that day. A lot of people seen it go down. But I'm still in prison. Well enough of that. ☺

Joe, I pray that all goes well for you. But please try to understand, I can not make a signed statement at this time. I must know that I have the immunity. I have to protect myself. I don't want any more time. I hope your (sic) not upset with me for not sending you this information t this time. For now, please take care and may God keep you and your family safe.

Your Friend,

Jimmy

Wednesday 17 Feb 1993

Joe H. West
7611 Olympia
Houston, TX 77063

Dear Joe,

Just a few lines to say hello and to say that I hope your (sic) in good health and your (sic) just mad at me. ☺ That I can live with.

I'm sorry about not sending you what you ask for, but it just wasn't feasible for me to comply. Yes, I can understand your (sic) being upset. But please forgive me and try to see it from my side of the fence. If I had already lost my appeal, then it wouldn't make any difference to me, as 50 years is a life sentence for me. I believe that I'll win my appeal and be free in a couple of years.

As for me, I'm about the same, nothing changes around here.

I hope my little card puts a smile on your face and I will continue to pray each night for your good health and your family.

I wish you the "Best God Bless" and take care.

Your Friend,

Jimmy

7611 Olympia
Houston, Texas   77063
March 10, 1993

Thank you for calling me on Monday night. It would have been very hard to tell you in a letter about Joe's going home to be with the Lord. We are a very close family and this loss has been devastating to ALL of us. Each of us is dealing with the loss in a different way. That's normal I'm told.

I appreciate you understanding that I will go on with Joe's Documentary. I know in my heart that it's the way he would have wanted it.

I am enclosing a letter from Robert (Bob) Vernon - an introduction to him. Joe had worked with him for over a year and was excited about the outcome. I hope you will decide to correspond with Bob Vernon. He's a good honest man and you can trust him. Also, a couple, who have been very close, longtime friends of Joe's and mine, are helping me sort through papers and necessary things in life at this time.

Let me hear from you whenever you can and you'll be hearing from me.

God Bless You,

Your friend,

Earlene West

Letters from James Files to Bob Vernon

These letters were transcribed by Cher Johnson. When she was about halfway I was curious what she thought. Her views do not necessarily represent mine, but below is her answer.

----- Original Message -----
From: Wim Dankbaar
To: Cher Johnson
Sent: Tuesday, February 22, 2005 12:59 PM
Subject: Re: James E. Files letter 12

Thanks very much. What do you think now about James Files? You are one of the first people to read these letters.

Wim

You know, I am very torn about my feelings toward James Files. I can't help it...I like the guy. What he did was terrible in so many ways, but I also feel that he looked at it as just another job. If he didn't do it, somebody else would. I know that Kennedy wasn't the only person he killed, but he has this other side to him that is kind and loving--very humble and unassuming. He has other good qualities as well. He is extremely loyal and trustworthy, and would do anything for a friend or loved one; even if it means sacrificing himself. AND, this is a big one toward winning me over...he loves animals. I also find animals to be superior to humans in most every respect.

I found him to be compassionate and admiring of Jackie while at the same time devastating her, her children, the American people, and perhaps the world.

I believe him when he says he did it. I believe he was, to a certain degree, a victim of his own circumstances. Especially when you consider that he was under the influence of these people (mobsters), from the time he was an impressionable child, and then was put into a similar situation upon entering the service, and then exploited by C.I.A.; all before the tender age of 21.

James Files is a very complicated, simple man.

Cher

Monday 15 March 1993

Dear Bob,

I received your letter with "Earlene's" this past Saturday evening. Thank you for writing to me.

Yes, all of us lost a great deal when God called Joe home. To me, Joe was very Special. When we first met, I felt as if I had known him all my life. It was like magic, I can't explain it. But I felt right off that I could trust Joe. I still don't know why I opened up to him. Joe West is the only person I ever opened up to. I gave him what little I did know, which is not all that much. But I never did tell him where the X on the map went. I was waiting for the immunity. I don't know how much you know of what I told Joe, but maybe by now you have read the reports.

For me, phone calls are hard to get. So I won't promise to call soon. I'm in the most secure prison in Ill. and I hate it here. But it's just one more step in life that I have to endure. No, I'm not crying about it. I'm use to carrying a big load.

Thank you for wanting to help with my music. It would be really nice to hear some of my songs over the radio. I've never really tried getting them published. I wrote them because it's what I enjoy. Also, I <u>can not sing.</u> I've got no voice at all for singing, but I sit and yell a lot. ☺ Right now I really miss my guitar. If I should loose [sic] my appeal, then I'll try to get it in.

I just got a letter from my lawyer the other day and he filed for a time extension on my appeal for Sept. 1993.

Please feel free to write me at any time. But all my mail is checked, coming and going. So I won't write anything about that "Six Seconds" until I have the immunity.

I'd like to figure out a way to get you the melody for my songs. That would make it easier to get them published. Oh well, in time we'll work on it.

I'll close for now. You take care and again, thanks for writing. God Bless You.

Respectfully

James Files.

Monday 05 April 1993

Dear Bob,

I just received your letter with the reading material. The prison held it up for about a week for the Review Board to examine it and approve it. Next time mark the envelope "Confidential Investigative Report" then they won't keep it tied up. They'll speed up the process.

I enjoyed your letter and also the reading material. Very interesting! But some of the facts are wrong. Roselli, Ruby and I did not have breakfast together that morning. There was no Sam Giancana gang. I was not hired by a member for the assassination. The .222 was not C. Nicoletti's favorite gun. That was my favorite gun. All these facts are close, but they've been changed just a little. I picked up Johnny at the Dallas Cabana and we drove to Fort Worth. I sit [sic] at the counter and had coffee, with two guns so I could cover J. R. while he had coffee with a man who was to suppose to be Jack Ruby. I never met him! I was there in case something went wrong. I was to cover John. If I had been sitting in the booth and something had jumped off, I'd have been dead meat before I could reach for my guns. I watched from the counter while John received an envelope from a man.

Next, I was not hired. Chuck told me who we was [sic] going to do. We never talked about money at any time for any job. Chuck always gave me money and took care of me. He gave me money every week and after [a] job I received bonus's [sic]. If we ever get to talk, I'll try to explain this to you. Only two people could give me orders that were involved in the crime family. Chuck, he was one, the other is still alive, so I can't name him. Out side the crime family, only David Atlee Phillips could give me orders. Also, I was never a member of organized crime. The F.B.I. may think I was a member, but I never was. The F.B.I. had talked with Joe. Joe ask [sic] me if I would talk with them. They want me to tell them about 12 murders in the Chicago area. They too offered immunity. But to them I said <u>NO!</u> If you ever come this way, stop and see me. My mail is read and all phone calls are recorded.

I've thought about writing a song on Six Seconds, that is since I've received your letter. I never though of it before. I had put Dallas out of my mind after the day. Gee, I wonder why. ☺ No really, Chuck and me never talked about things that we had done. When a job was over, we never talked about it again.

Also, we can have no tape recorder in here. I can't even get in Country tapes to play on my radio cassette player. But I will try to get something worked out for you to hear the melodies.

But for now, let me wish you a Happy Easter. I hope you like the card I made. I'm no artist, but I like to doodle.

I hope you can read my writing. I'm writing fast to get it ready before they pick up the mail. I had about 20 Easter cards I made to get ready to send out. ☺

Please take care and God Bless You.

Respectfully,

Jim Files

Happy Easter

*May Your
Easter
be Blessed
with much
Love
&
Happiness…*

Respectfully

Jim Files

Wednesday 07 April 1993

Dear Bob

Just a few lines to say hello and to let you know that I received your April 3rd letter last night. As always, I was delighted to hear from you.

Thanks for letting me know about the immunity as that is a necessity for me. Sometimes I feel as if I've already said too much. I wanted to tell Joe where the X went on the map and the details he wanted to know so bad. I believe that Joe already knew the answers but wanted more than anything to hear me say it. And now I feel bad because Joe's gone and I can't tell him. Bob, believe me, if I could have givin [sic] Joe my remaining years so that he may live on, I would have. I'd have taken his place on that list. Hell, I've already lived too long. In my business we're suppose to die young and leave a beautiful body for all to come and see at the wake. ☺ Yea, I know I got a morbid sense of humor. But to me, life and death is all the same. Both are an adventure.

I can only receive tapes that come direct from the store or from a company in Houston called: R.G.V. Productions, Audio, Video, Film & Music. I think they would let them in from that company. My radio has a tape player and I would love to hear the tunes.

The other night we had our first band meeting about getting our instruments sent in. So I just wrote a letter to my daughter and told her what to ship to me. I really miss my guitar. I love to sit and play and yell a lot as I can't sing. But I sure do enjoy trying to make music.

This morning on T.V. I heard "Willie" sing his new song during an interview. It's called "Valentine" and I love it. I wrote one in Feb. for my girlfriend call Valentine, but it's not near as good as Willie's. ☺

Hope you like the card, it's my baby, "G.I. Joe". I guess I just like doing cartoons.

Well I'll close for now, take care and tell Mrs. West I said hello, and may God keep you all safe.

Respectfully,

Jimmy

Even for

My "3" year

Old G.I.

Joe.
☺

*Hope this one
puts a smile
on your face.*

Respectfully

Jimmy

Dear Bob,

I just received your most welcome letter with the most extraordinary stationary. What a nice surprise, thank you very much.

Mr. Ervin may speak to me at anytime. I hope that he can get the immunity for me. And if he comes here with [sic], the two of you can come in as an attorney visit. That would be the easy way. Visiting hours are 7 days a week, 8:00 A.M. to 3:00 P.M. Monday thru Fri., two hour visits. Sat. & Sun. only a one hour visit.

But!!! You may not want to come and visit me. Like I had told Joe from the beginning, get me the immunity and I will testify for you at the trial. But no T.V. or news interviews. I don't want the publicity and I hope they can keep the cameras out of the court room.

Joe is the <u>only</u> person I ever opened up to. And I never told him everything as I didn't have the immunity. Joe knew I was holding back, like he knew the X on the map had to be moved. I explained all this to Joe at the very start. Joe wanted to put me on film in case something happened to me. I told him no! I said, "What if something happens to you, this tape could fall into the wrong hands." I was afraid the government might wind up with it. I'm sure Joe knew exactly where I was on the map. But him knowing it and me saying it, is two different things. Also, it would not be smart for me to put my face on national T.V. ☺ I might get a few more cases. But enough of that.

I'm working on a song about, "Six Seconds". But it's coming very slow. And as for me singing and putting a song on tape, "Honest Injun," I can't sing a lick. That is the truth.

Yes, I will keep in touch with Earlene. I too, enjoy her letters very much. I explained to her about not writing earlier. I knew she had a million things to do and that I didn't want to be a burden. I do enjoy writing her and making cards.

I hope you like my D.D. card. He's one of my favorites. I've [sic] trying to do cartoon people. But once I get my guitar, I know the art work will fall by the way side. ☺

Oh yes, I would love the lyrics to "My Old Mule". I bet it's cute. Also, any lyrics to old time country from the 50's & 60's I'd enjoy. If you have any lying around. Bob, I'll close for now. Take care and I thank you, and may God keep you safe.

Your Friend,

Jimmy

The

Personalized

Stationary

is just

Great...

I really

Appreciate

it...

Thank You,
Your Friend
Jimmy

Sunday 25 April 1993

Dear Bob,

I received your letter last night and as always, delighted to hear from you. And I'm looking forward to the tape. But the tape must be sent seald [sic] in plastic from the studio with a price on it. O.K.

I'm looking forward to seeing you and Mr. Ervin. When you get here, sign in as an attorney and investigator client visit. You should have no problem. Just don't let them turn you away.

About talking to the F.B.I., I talked to no agent. Joe was talking to them in Dallas about the Siefert killing. The only F.B.I. agent I've ever talked to was in Fort Worth when I went to trial there, and that was only about sports and weather. They ask Joe to ask me if I would talk with them, I said, NO! They'd said they give me blanket immunity on every crime I've ever done, if I'd solve 12 murders in the Chicago area. That I will not do. Chuck may be dead but there are other people still alive. I will put no man in prison. I will talk to you more when I see you, as all mail and phones are checked. In prison there are no secrets.

Well Bob, I'll close for now and hope to see you soon. And I hope that you won't be disappointed when we talk. And please, re-reading letters to Joe again. O.K. God Bless You.

Your Friend

Jimmy

Dear Bob,

I just received your letter of April 21. As always, delighted to hear from you.

I'm also excited about seeing you and Mr. Ervin this coming week.

Thought I'd do a shadow cartoon for you this time. This is the first one I've ever done. It's not my own idea, I saw it in my art book, thought it was cute. I did it and gave it a tittle [sic]. Give my love to Earlene. I think she's great.

Friends,

Jimmy

The following pages are Bob Vernon's recollections from his first meeting with James Files:

I MEET THE ASSASSIN

The West family gave me total access to Joe's files on the JFK assassination. Joe's lifelong friend, Charles Barksdale, spent several days with me sorting out the important files from the "junk". When we finished I was able to sit down and take a hard serious look at the overall Kennedy case from Joe's personal and private perspective.

The night I read the prisoner's letters to Joe was one of the most memorable nights of my life. I know my mouth must have hung open as I was reading. In the letters he had confessed amazing things to Joe. The entire JFK conspiracy plot began to form right in front of my eyes. There was a picture of him and Joe taken at the prison. At least I now know how he looked. Joe West had, indeed, brought home the bacon. Now all we needed were the eggs and grits and we could eat.

I asked Mrs. West to introduce me to the prisoner so she wrote a nice letter to him. I enclosed my first letter to him with hers. A few days later, I got my first collect call from a prison.

I'll call the man "F" from here on. F told me how sorry he was that Joe had died. He seemed extremely sincere. We talked about the JFK investigation and I told him that I wanted to come visit him in the near future. He agreed.

By the time that I got to the prison on May 3, 1993, the hospital and doctor bills were at $177,000 according to Mrs. West. There would be more to come. I arrived at the prison on a rainy morning. My friend Barry Adelman was with me. He flew in from Los Angeles and I flew in from Houston. We checked in at the gate and we were sent to the waiting room. It seemed like forever just sitting there. Barry and I traded jokes about wondering if they would let us out now that they had us locked inside. We smiled but we didn't laugh.

Our number was called and we walked up a flight of stairs until we came to the first gate. We were searched. I couldn't even carry in cigarettes or a pencil or a pen. I did manage to sneak in a release for the prisoner to sign to give us the right to use his letters in our TV program and in the book.
After being led through a second gate (this was maximum security), we were directed through the main visitor area to a "family visiting area" across the hall. I spotted F immediately. It's hard to miss a man with long, white hair. He shook my hand and I introduced him to Barry.

I explained who Barry was (Barry works for a major LA television company), and F got permission from the room guard to let us carry a table and three chairs into the far corner of the room so we could talk "privately", at least without being overheard by other prisoners.
We started off very casually, just getting to know each other I guess you'd say. I explained to him how I met Joe and how much I missed Joe. F missed Joe, too. I got the feeling that Joe had been one of his only friends. We explained the huge bills that Mrs. West had to pay because Joe did not have any medical insurance. F expressed his concern for Mrs. West although he had never met her.

After thirty minutes or so, I asked F to tell me about November 22, 1963. I wasn't ready for what was about to happen. This is what he told me:

"Mr. F" participated in his first murder at the age of 16. He killed the man who had killed his sister. He started working with mobster/hitman Charles Nicoletti at the age of 19. "Mr. F" later ran the mafia "chop shop" car operation. "Mr. F" said he transported thousands of cars for the "mob" and that he was arrested for same. Charles Nicoletti and Sam Giancana went to a party at mob boss Tony Accardo's house in Chicago in 1963. Nicoletti then came to "Mr. F" and told him that they were "going to hit his buddy". "Mr. F" thought that Nicoletti meant someone around the neighborhood. Nicoletti (often referred to as Chuckie by "Mr. F") then told "Mr. F" that the hit was to be on President Kennedy. "Mr. F" said it was "just another hit to him" for "Mr. F" and Chuckie had killed lots of people "all in a days work". "Mr. F" stated that the CIA had once flown him and others into South America where they had "wiped out" 40-50 people at once, including "men, women and children. "Mr. F" stated he had "no remorse" for anyone he killed and that he had "never killed anyone that didn't deserve to be killed". "Mr. F" said that he had not cared for Kennedy at all. "Mr. F" made a statement pertaining to the fact that Kennedy was trying to "do away with the CIA and that he had always blamed Kennedy for the Bay of Pigs fiasco". "Mr. F" said that Chuckie had ordered him to bring guns, ammunition and hand grenades to Dallas in 1963. They had planned a hit on Kennedy for Chicago but that was "too close to home" "Mr. F" drove to Dallas in Chuckie's car, a 1963 burgundy Chevy, that "Mr. F" said "everyone talks about". Mr. F" said that he had a Remington Fireball, a .222 high velocity pistol with a scope, that had a bullet velocity of over 3,000 feet per second.

"Mr. F" said that he and "Wolfman" (a friend who is now dead) had made special "Mercury rounds for the .222." He also stated there was a "30-06 rifle" in the trunk of the Chevy. I informed "Mr. F" that two .222 shell casings had been found in Dealey Plaza. "Mr. F" said there was only "one" from his gun and that I would know it by his teeth marks. I asked him why he bit it and he said that he "likes to put the warm bullet in his mouth and taste the gunpowder." He further said he "left it on the wall" and that he "knew someone would find it." He told me that it did not have any fingerprints on it because he "isn't that stupid."

"Mr. F" said that the end where you put the powder was "oval, not round." He said he parked the car near Dealey Plaza by the Dal-Tex building for Chuckie wanted to be able to leave his spot in the Dal-Tex building and "jump into the car." "Mr. F" that since he "was younger than Chuckie" that he could "run the hundred yards to the car easy."

"Mr. F" said that on the morning of November 22, 1963 that he picked up "John Roselli at the Dallas Cabana Hotel." Roselli was talking to "Eugene Hale Brading alias Jim Braden" when he first pulled up to pick up Roselli. "Mr. F" said that Roselli had "flown into Dallas on a military intelligence flight." He said Nicoletti had flown in on a "commercial flight." "Mr. F" did not know for sure when Roselli flew in but thinks it "was the day before." "Mr. F" said that his job was to "cover Roselli in case something broke out." "Mr. F" sat at a counter while Roselli met with "Jack Ruby." "Mr. F" explained that he had been at the counter for if he had "sat at the table" he wouldn't have been able to pull his guns if there had been trouble.

Ruby "handed Roselli an envelope" which contained "the last minute change in the parade route." "Mr. F" said that they had toured the entire parade route looking for the best spot to "hit Kennedy." "Mr. F" said he "arrived at Dealey Plaza before noon" and stood around in the pergola (knoll) area. "Mr. F" said he saw "Frank Sturgis of the CIA" standing behind him. "Mr. F" said he saw lots of faces he knew. "Mr. F" said it "looked like old home week." "Mr. F" said he did not know where Nicoletti and Roselli were during the shooting but that Chuckie was "supposed to be in the Dal-Tex building."

"Mr. F" showed me an accurate hand drawn map of Dealey Plaza with a "x" on the spot where he was standing. "Mr. F" said that the "x" was not in the right spot but that he would put it in "the right spot" after he receives the immunity. "Mr. F" said that he thinks "five or six shots were fired." "Mr. F" said that "two shots were fired almost at once."

He said that "the shooter behind the fence" fired a shot at approximately the same time as Nicoletti fired a shot and that both shots hit Kennedy's head within a "split second" of each other.

"Mr. F." used my head to show me where the "head shots hit Kennedy." He pointed and placed his finger on my right front temple between my right eye and my right ear. He touched the rear of my head to show where the front shot exited and touched the top left side of my bald spot to show where Nicoletti's almost simultaneous shot hit Kennedy. He said the "shooter behind the fence had Kennedy in his sights for some time."

"Mr. F" said that Chuckie hit Kennedy in the back and in the top left rear head and that they "discussed it later." "Mr. F" also said that one of Nicoletti's shots "hit Connally." "Mr. F" did not know anything about the wound to James Teague down by the triple overpass but said that he probably was hit by "concrete" or a piece of "shrapnel." Mr. Adelman asked "Mr. F" if the guns they were using displayed smoke when fired and "Mr. F" said "yes." "Mr. F" said that after the shooting, he placed his gun into a case, took off his jacket and reversed it and put it back on, pulled a cap out from under his arm and put it on and went to the car.

"Mr. F" said that he, Nicoletti and Roselli drove out of the Plaza area in the Chevy. "Mr. F" said he let Nicoletti and Roselli out of the car at a restaurant just north of Highway 66. "Mr. F" said he then went back to his motel in Mesquite, took a shower and shaved and put "hot wax" on his "hand, forearm and face" to remove any sign of firing a gun (via a paraffin test). He said that when he crossed the "Texas state line," headed north back to Chicago, that he knew he "had it made." Toward the end of the meeting, "Mr. F" specifically stated that "<u>Chuck Nicoletti and I killed John F. Kennedy</u>."

Barry and I drove silently away from the prison. F had signed the release and we were in a hurry to get as far away from that prison as we could. I was in a big hurry to get back to Texas so I could call the man that dug up the .222 shell casings in Dealey Plaza in 1987. I had read about him in Joe West's files.

May 4, 1993

MEMO

TO: DICK CLARK
           AVIVA BERGMAN

FROM: BOB VERNON

RE: 5/3/93 MEETING WITH PRISONER

As per Barry Adelman's request, the following is an attempt to provide you with a written report between Barry Adelman, Bob Vernon and inmate James E. Files held on May 3, 1993 at the Illinois State Prison in Joliet, Illinois.

Due to the extreme mass of information and topics discussed during that meeting, please understand that this reconstruction is based entirely from my memory and is presented to you by the individual topics discussed although not necessarily in the order in which these topics were discussed. It is virtually impossible to provide you with a 100% accurate reconstructure due to the length of the meeting (almost 4 hours) and the vast topics covered. Any and all of the verbatim statements of the prisoner will be enclosed by quotation marks (" "). I will now attempt to provide you with a factual reconstruction to the best of my ability.

Barry Adelman and I arrived at the prison at approximately 9:00 a.m. on Monday, May 3, 1993. After over an hour of clearance procedures and waiting, we were allowed to enter the maximum security prison and led to the area where we talked with Mr. Files. The meeting room was hot and humid and we were allowed to sit in a far corner with the prisoner for as much privacy as possible.

Mr. Files appeared calm and mannerly. He has long silver-white hair and he resembles Willie Nelson, particularly when he smiles. He is around 52 years old. He was dressed in standard prison dress and he had on a Western blue jean jacket.

TOPIC: DON ERVIN

I explained to Files that Houston attorney Don Ervin, who was previously scheduled to be present, had been unable to come due to a conflict in his schedule due to the fact that he represents many of the David Koresh – Waco – members which have recently made international news. I further explained that I had faxed Mr. Ervin answers to some of his initial questions concerning Files' meeting with FBI agents and that Mr. Ervin would be continuing his quest for immunity for Files. I further stated that Files would be meeting with Mr. Ervin in the very near future, hopefully in the next 10 – 14 days. I explained that Mr. Ervin would be coming to meet privately with Files in the form of an attorney visit.

TOPIC: JOE AND EARLENE WEST

Files expressed his fondness for the late Joe West and his widow, Earlene. Files stated that he couldn't explain how he and West had hit it off right from their first meeting, but that it was "magic" of some sort. Files expressed care and sentiment for Earlene due to the loss of Joe West in February of 1993. I explained to Files how Joe West died and reassured him that the death was due to medical complications following open heart surgery. I further informed the prisoner that Joe's medical bills had left Earlene with $177,000 in debt. I further explained that the only way Earlene could hope to pay these huge bills was to license the right to the investigative legacy of Joe West, which legacy is West's investigative findings into the murder of John F. Kennedy. I explained that West and I had completed a television and book presentation of which Files himself was the last chapter in both. Files agreed to help Earlene in any way possible and stated his concern for her well being and comfort. Files said that he would not be able to go on television and be interviewed without immunity for he could be indicted for what he knows. Again, I stressed the fact that attorney Ervin is working on his immunity and that I believed it would come forth very quickly. I further explained that Mr. Ervin had been involved in gaining immunity for other persons and that the immunity process takes around 2 months or so.

TOPIC: dick clark productions

I introduced Barry Adelman to Files. I asked Barry to please give Files a business card. Files seemed very impressed with card and asked to keep it for his scrap book. Barry explained that because of Dick Clark's great respect for the late Joe West, that Dick was willing to attempt to get a broadcast deal for Joe's television program on the 30th anniversary program if successful. Barry then explained that he understood from talking with the late Joe West, Earlene, and Bob Vernon, that Files may have some additional information that could be added to the program content. Files again stated that he must have immunity before allowing himself to be video taped. Barry and I expressed our understanding of the immunity request.

TOPIC: THE MURDER OF JFK

NOTE: Dick, the following information was provided by Files over the course of almost 4 hours. What follows is a complete summary of his testimony and verbal confessions to the best of my memory and my ability, so help me God:

Files participated in his first murder at the age of 16. He started working with mobster/hitman Charles Nicoletti at the age of 19. Files later ran the mafia "chop shop" car operation. Files said he transported thousands of cars for the "mob" and that he was arrested for same. Charles Nicoletti and Sam Giancana went to a party at mob boss Tony Accardo's house in Chicago in 1963. Nicoletti then came to Files and told him they were going to hit his buddy. Files thought that Nicoletti meant someone from around the neighborhood. Nicoletti (often referred to as Chuckie by Files) then told Files that the hit was to be on President Kennedy. Files said it was "just another hit to him" for Files and Chuckie had killed lots of people "all in a day's work." Files expressed concern over so much interest in the death of "one man" since he had been directly involved in the deaths of many people at once. Files stated that the CIA had once flown him and others into South America where they had "wiped out 40 – 50 people at once, including men, women and children."

Files stated that he had no remorse for anyone he had ever killed and that he had "never killed anyone that hadn't deserved to be killed." Files said that he had not cared for Kennedy at all.

(NOTE: Dick, perhaps Barry can elaborate on how Files stated his hate for Kennedy for I simply cannot remember everything due to the mass of statements made by Files.)

Files made a statement pertaining to the fact that Kennedy was trying to "do away with the CIA." Files said that Chuckie had ordered him to bring the guns, ammunition and hand grenades to Dallas in 1963. They had planned a hit on Kennedy for Chicago but that was "too close to home." Files drove to Dallas in Chuckie's car, a 1963 burgundy Chevy, that Files said "everyone talks about." Files said that he had a Remington Fireball, a .222 high velocity pistol with a scope, that had a bullet velocity of over 3,000 feet per second. Files said that he and "Wolfman" (a friend who is now dead) had made special "Mercury rounds for the .222." He also stated there was a "30-06 rifle" in the trunk of the Chevy. He said he parked the car near Dealey Plaza by the Dal-Tex building for Chuckie wanted to be able to leave his spot in the Dal-Tex building and "jump into the car." Files said that since he was younger than Chuckie "that he could run the hundred yards to the car easy." Files said that on the morning of November 22, 1963 that he picked up "John Roselli at the Dallas Cabana Hotel." Roselli was talking to "Eugene Hale Brading alias Jim Braden" when he first pulled up to pick up Roselli. Files said that Roselli had "flown in on a 'commercial' flight." Files did not know for sure when Roselli flew in but "thinks it was the day before." Files said that he drove "Roselli to breakfast in Fort Worth." Files said that his job was to "cover Roselli in case something broke out." Files sat at a counter while Roselli met with "Jack Ruby." Files explained that he had been at the counter for if he had "sat at the table," he wouldn't have been able to pull his guns if there had been trouble. Ruby "handed Roselli an envelope "which contained "the last minute change in the parade route." Files said that they had toured the entire parade route looking for the best spot to "hit Kennedy." Files said he "arrived at Dealey Plaza before noon" and stood around in the pergola (knoll) area. Files said he saw "Frank Sturgis of the CIA" standing behind him. Files said that he saw lots of faces he knew. Files said it "looked like old home week."

Files said he did not know where Nicoletti and Roselli were during the shooting but that "Chuckie was supposed to be in the Dal-Tex building." Files showed Barry and I an accurate hand drawn map of Dealey Plaza with a "X" on the spot where he was standing. Files said that the "X" was not in the right spot but that he would put it in the "right spot" after he receives the immunity." Files said that he thinks that "five or six shots were fired." Files said that "two shots were fired almost at once." He said that the "shooter behind the fence" fired a shot at approximately the same time as Nicoletti fired a shot and that both shots hit Kennedy's head within a "split second of each other." Files used my head to show Barry and I where the "head shots hit Kennedy." He pointed and placed his finger on my right front temple between my right eye and my right ear. He touched the rear of my head to show where the front shot exited and touched the top left side of my bald spot to show where Nicoletti's almost simultaneous shot hit Kennedy. He said the "shooter behind the fence had Kennedy in his sights for some time." Files said that Chuckie hit Kennedy in the back and in the top left rear head and that they "discussed it later." Files also said that one of Nicoletti's shots "hit Connally." Files did not know anything about the wound to James Teague down by the triple overpass, but said he was probably hit by "concrete or a piece of 'shrapnel'." Barry asked Files if the guns they were using displayed smoke when fired and Files said "yes." Files said that after the shooting, he placed his gun into a case, took off his jacket and reversed it and put it back on, pulled a cap out from under his arm and put it on and went to the car. Files said that he, Nicoletti and Roselli drove out of the Plaza area in the chevy. I do not recall where he said he let Nicoletti and Roselli out of the car. Files said he then went back to his motel in Mesquite, took a shower and shaved and put "hot wax on his hand and forearm and face" to remove any sign of firing a gun (via a paraffin test.) He said that when he crossed the "Texas state line," headed north back to Chicago, that he knew he "had it made." **SPECIAL NOTE:** Dick, please understand that throughout the lengthy meeting with Files, he was very careful not to say exactly where he was standing. He stated over and over that he could not do that until he received immunity. Toward the end of the meeting, James E. Files (real name: Sutton) specifically stated to Barry and I that "Chuck Nicoletti and I killed John F. Kennedy." Barry and I both heard him confess to this and I will never forget it. Barry and I feel that he let this slip and Barry and I discussed the fact that we do not believe it was intentional. Barry will provide you with further details.

TOPIC: OTHER

Files told Barry and I a lot more about his life and many other gruesome murders and crimes he has committed. Since these other crimes are not important to us at this time. I do not feel it is necessary to elaborate on them.

Also, please understand that the room and conditions to which Barry and I were subjected were less than human. As crude as this may seem to you, we were actually in a room where visiting wives and girlfriends were masturbating their inmate husbands and boyfriends. At one point, we were interrupted by a black prisoner who passed behind Files to get a mop bucket and mop so that the black prisoner could clean up sexual fluids on the floor. The temperature was over 100 degrees in the room and the mixture of heat and sexual stench was extremely disgusting and uncomfortable. At one point, I actually felt faint from heat exhaustion. I assure you that I will never be able to forget our meeting with Mr. Files.

In closing, I'm sure Barry can fill in the blank spots and tie up the loose ends for you. In the event that I am able to recall any further details of our meeting with Files, I will fax them to you.

I am totally convinced that James E. Files was involved in the murder of John F. Kennedy and that he was an actual gunman and participant in the murder. According to his blatant and unashamed confession to Barry and I, please understand that I am even further convinced that James E. Files fired the fatal frontal head shot that is morbidly displayed in the film of Abraham Zapruder.

God bless Joe West. May his soul rest in peace for eternity.

cc: Suzanne Phillips
    Earlene West

Tuesday 04 May 1993

Dear Bob

Just a few lines to say hello and to tell you it was a pleasure and also an Honor to meet you. Thank you for coming. But I'm sorry I talked so much and kept you so long. I couldn't believe it was four hours we visited. The time sure did fly.

It was also an Honor and pleasure to meet Barry. He seems really nice. I like both of you and I know that Joe thought the world of you.

The book on Kennedy I couldn't remember was called "High Treason by Robert J. Groden and Harrison Edward Livingstone" [sic] printing, March 1989. Cost $6.99. Not worth the price. ☺

I hope my card puts a smile on your face. Just something different.

Bob, I'll do all I can for Earlene, let's bail her out. If you can think of other ways we can help her, please let me know. O.K.

I'll go for now, take care and may God keep you safe.

Friends,

Jimmy

P.S. I just got the package of paper. Thank you very much.

***Who Shot
J.F.K.?***

*was it
O. C.
or the
C.I.A.?..*

***That could make a
Catchy little tune.***

***Friends,
Jimmy***

Wednesday 19 May 1993

Dear Bob,

I'll answer your welcome letter of May 8th. I enjoyed your letter very much and thank you for all the compliments. Now my head is so big my hat don't fit no more. ☺

I hope every one on your end is doing fine. As for me, I'm O.K. I'm sorry I didn't answer sooner, but I've been busy re-writing over and over the two songs I'm enclosing. "The Shots of Dallas" is the one I did for six seconds. I hope it's not too corny. The other song, "I remember Jackie" is something I was kicking around. Both songs are true to the facts. But I don't feel they're the kind you publish for the public. I've been messing around with one about Oswald, and one about the people in general that were there. I must tell you Bob, our Dear Friend Joe, really took me back in time. I feel like I'm remembering too much and that I'm now living in the past. In my heart I wish it were all still forgotten and lost in time.

I want to thank you very much for being kind to Greg. He's a very nice person, but his music is…well not my kind of music. But then I'm all Country. And Willie's #1 to me, he's my God. When I was in the band before, I wore my black t-shirt and red bandana. Every one called me Willie Jim. It was great. I wish I had some of the pictures to send to you. It was really great.

I would love to get one of my songs published, but I've never felt they were that good. I wrote just for me, it's what I enjoy. Just your faith in me alone, makes me feel wonderful. Thank you, your much too kind.

Your new toy really sounds great. I'd love to be there with you, to help you play with it. ☺ From you I could learn a very good deal. And you know all about the things I love and enjoy. I'm now learning how to read music and I'm just fascinated with it. To me, it's something new and exciting. Oh yea, this Saturday night, the 22nd, I'll be watching Willie's Birthday party on T.V. I know it's going to be a fantastic show. I'm really looking forward to it.

By chance, if you have acess [sic] to sheet music and could make me a copy, I'd love the sheet music to, "Blue Eyes Crying in the Rain", "Always on my mind" and "Folsom Prison" by Johnny Cash. I know the lyrics, and the melody, but I'd love to learn to play the lead. I love those 3 songs. I got maybe 200 favorites, ☺ most of them in my head. Like George Straits early music, "Fifteen Years Together". That's a beautiful song. And if you have the lyrics for "Together Again" I'd love to get them. I can sit for hours by my-self just playing and singing. I'm not good at either one, but I enjoy it so much. The only thing I've ever been good at, was guns. But on the street, I only carried a gun sometimes, but my guitar, it went everywhere with me.

Yes, I did get my writing paper from up front. Every one is crazy about it. Especially me.

Yes Bob, I too feel that we will be friends for a long time. And when they get the copy machine fixed, I'm going to send you some copy of news paper clippings about my case and signed statement by eye witness. Hey, I best close for now. Give Earlene my love and you take care. God Bless You.

Friends always

Jimmy

The Shots of Dallas

The word went out in early sixty-three
That they must stop this crazy Kennedy
Three men who specialized in death would meet
To share a closely guarded secret they would keep.

From back east they called Big Sam in Chicago
Sam's team was waiting for the word to go.
He said he had a team the G could never stop.
For a special job like this he had the cream of the crop.

It was early morning,
The rain was slowly falling
Nicoletti told his driver,
I hear destiny a calling.
Just past noon the sun broke thru, Kennedy in sight
Shots were fired behind and one fired from the right.

For word went out in early sixty-three
That we must stop this crazy Kennedy.
Nicoletti and Roselli's dead and now I'm old
After thirty years of lies, the truth can now be told.

TAG: Yes, the truth can now be told.

Written by James Files (08 May 1993)

I Remember Jackie
"Kennedy"

I remember back in sixty-three
How Jackie looked that day.
I saw her heart break into, (in two)
Watched her wipe the tears away.
Jackie showed no fear that day
Her anger was too strong
For in her heart she knew,
Her man would not last long.

From my hiding place I watched her
I saw this heartbreaking scene.
She reached for a piece of Kennedy
And she held it in her hand
On her lips the words I read,
"Oh God try to help me understand."

With-in six seconds John was hit four times
and into her arms he fell
She held him close, she cursed us all
Said may we rot in hell.
Some one yelled, the car shot forward,
Away from there it sped.
And in my heart I knew for sure
That John Kennedy was dead.

Written by James Files
May 7th 1993

945 Hours: Thursday 27 May 1993

Dear Bob,

I sure did enjoy our little talk today. Thank you for taking my calls.

This song is the first song I've ever been excited over. Oh I know it's no hit. But I'm excited just because I wrote it about Willie. To me, Willie can walk on water. I murder his songs when I sing them, but I still love him. ☺

I'm very thankful for getting the chance to meet Joe, you and Barry. I think the world of all 3 of you. Joe may be gone, but in my heart, his memory lives on. The 3 of you are the most exciting things to ever happen in my life. Should something happen to me, I just want you to know, I think your [sic] all great. Thank you, for being my friend.

Oh yea, right after I talked with you, we went on lock-down again. I still don't know what happened? Hey, I hope this song makes you smile. Take care and God Bless You.

Friends,

Jimmy

Willie Your My Hero

1) Willie I saw you on T.V.
Just the other night
Watched all your friends wish you Happy Birthday
And hug you tight.
But let me tell you Willie
All your friends wasn't there
Willie you're my hero
And I sure was wishin'
I was there.

2) I was here at the big Stateville,
A pickin' my guitar
I was a pickin' and a grinnin'
With all them stars.
Yea Willie you're a livin' legend
And in my heart I know
That your the very best there is
Willie your my hero

CHORUS:

Willie when they're talkin' 'bout Texas
They're talkin' 'bout you
And when they talk about you
They're talkin' 'bout Texas
It's you and wide open spaces
That's the combination for Texas
Willie your my hero
And without you
There ain't no Texas

3) Willie sing me another song
Make it sweet and make it long
Cause I can sit for hours,
Just a listenin' to your songs
I love to hear about them outlaws
Broken hearts and loves gone wrong
Willie your my hero
Won't you sing me another song?

REPEAT CHORUS:

TAG: Willie you're my hero
And I love you and Texas

Fade: I love you and Texas
Fade out: I love you and Texas

26 May 1993
James Files

To Willie Nelson I dedicate this song
My Hero
The very best there is.

God Bless You Willie
I Love You.

Best of Luck,

Jimmy

Happy Birthday
Willie

Happy
Birthday

Big
6-0

Happy Birthday
Mr. Nelson,
One of your many fans,

James Files

And You are My Hero.

Monday 14 June 1993

Dear Bob,

Just a few lines to say hello and a card to say thank you for the personalized stationary. Thank you, you are very kind.

I hope you received my last letter with Willie's Birthday Card. Sometimes, I have trouble here with my mail. Like with my guitar, it's been here over two months and I still don't have it. My last two money orders have been lost. That makes for 8 money orders lost in the past year. Two of those were cashed by someone named "Davis". At least my people got their money back. ☺

Mr. Ervin was here to visit me on the 11th. He was here 6 hours, it seemed like only minutes. He's really a nice guy. After ten minutes I knew he was a #1! I enjoyed our visit and he made me laugh a lot.

I'm enclosing a song, on the gospel side. A guy in our band wrote it. I told him I'd like to send a copy to you for your opinion. I gave Greg your address and I'm not giving it to anyone else. If you like the song, his name and number is on the bottom of it. If you don't like it, let me know and I'll tell him. Me, I like it and if it's any good, maybe you can work with it. I figure your [sic] in the business to make money. To me, money is second nature. Money is not my great love. Oh don't get me wrong, I like money. But I don't care about living high on the hog. I'll be happy being free, a little job and a small apt., and a hundred dollar beater. But a nice bike! Hell, I ain't never growin' up! ☺ When I'm 90, I'll still be a kid.

Well Bob, I hope this letter finds you and your family in good health. I also hope that Earlene is doing fine. God Bless you all and take care.

Your Friend,

Jimmy

Monday 21 June 1993

Dear Bob,

Received your welcome letter the other day and I called you. What a surprise that was, about my life story, that is. If we did my life story, we would make a lot of people tremble, some might even have a heart-a-tac! [sic] ☺

Joe and me spoke of that in the beginning. Like I told Joe at that time, I just wanted to crawl back into the wood work and be forgotten. But you did bring out a very good point. My daughters' futures. I will talk to my oldest daughter about it before I decide, O.K. I also think that she should talk with you, for she will ask me questions that I cannot give her an honest answer on because I won't know the answer, about book rights and things like that.

The picture of the casing is hard to answer truthfully on, but yes, it could be.

I'm glad that Don likes me. I like him a great deal. He put me at ease right away. He's very easy to communicate with. I believe that he is a "First Class Lawyer". I just hope he can perform miracles. That's what I need to get out of prison. ☺ Gee, I wonder, can Don walk on water?

I was very happy to hear that Earlene is doing just fine. Having a car so she can get around will help her a-lot.

You better believe it! You can't live with them and you can't live with-out them. But I'm sure going to try and live with-out them. No more getting married for me. My last wife broke me from the habbit [sic] of getting married. ☺ But I'm sure that your wife is a very wonderful woman. The girl I love with all my heart, I can never have. And I doubt if I'll ever love again. But that's O.K. too. It leaves me free to move around.

Well Bob, I'll close for now. Please take care and God Bless You and Your Family. [sic]

Friends,

Jimmy

P.S. They just put a letter in my door slot, from "Barry". He just got back from Florida and he's fine, and Thank You, for the paper.

Take care. I hope the card makes you smile…

My daughter: Kathy Files. Work phone # (708) 931-8853. She works in Collections. Takes after me in my line of work.☺ I use to collect juice money, ☺ high interest.

(cartoon bubble)

HELLO!

**You have
Reached Death
Row! We're busy
with a send-off!**

**At the sound
of the beep,
Please
Leave
Name,
Number,
Ect,
Ect,
Ect.
[sic]**

And…

We Do

Hope that

Your call

was not one

of importance…

Thank You for Calling!

**Your Crazy Friend,
Jimmy**

Wednesday 23 June 1993

Earlene West
7611 Olympia
Houston, TX 77063

Dear Earlene,

I received your Beautiful [sic] card and letter and as always, I was delighted to hear from you, and very happy to hear your [sic] alright. But very sorry to hear about Mr. Barksdale, having a heart-attack. Glad to hear he's coming along just fine.

Thank you for the lovely card. That's very thoughtful of you and I appreciate it. But <u>please</u> save your money. Those dollars can add up. But a small scrap of paper with just a few words from you will be cherished just as much as any card. ☺ Your [sic] like Joe I'm sure, the "Best".

I'm glad you've got a car and your [sic] able to get out and around. That will be good for you. Each night you and your family are in my prayers and I ask God to let Joe be residing in "His" home.

I met Mr. Ervin and I really like him. I think he's great. I hope everything works out the way you and Bob want it to. I'll be real happy when it's all over. ☺

As for me, I'm doing alright, getting over a bad cold, trying to stay out of trouble. But here that can be hard to do.

Well I'll close for now. You and the family take care and I wish you the Best [sic].
God Bless You and your Family [sic].

Friends,

Jimmy

Do You,

***ever get the
feeling that Someone
is thinking about***

You???

I

sure hope so!

For all your

Friends,

are thinking

of

You!!!

***One of Your many
Friends,***

Jimmy

Friday 02 July 1993

Dear Bob,

Just a few lines to say hello and to tell you it was really great talking with you on the phone today. I sure did enjoy our little chat. Thanks for making my day that much brighter.

When you come back to visit me, I definitely want to hear more about Joe's death. To me, it came off(oops!) awful fast.

Before I forget, I best you [sic] give you the name and address for the art room deal. Contact: Nic Howell, Public Info. Concordia Court, Springfield, Ill. My art teacher is Jeff Whitfield, in charge of L.S.T. Activities.

I'm enclosing "Soldier Past". I'm not really sure what can be done with it. Guess we could make a short version of it. ☺

Also is a copy of "Eight By Ten", that's a very slow song. It's one of my favorites. And the other song, "Outlaw Blues" is just a ballad, mod. speed, something like "Branded Man" by Merle Haggard. Please excuse all my mistakes. But today I'm running in brain-lock. I'm not thinking too clear.

I hope you like the card, thought I'd give you some flowers for a change. I'm working on a large picture of a flower for when you go through the art room. This will be my first large drawing, that is if I complete it. It's just like the card I'm sending but much bigger, 17 x 23. I just hope it comes out O.K. In time I hope to get much better. I have to develope [sic] my stroke, the flow, the style ect [sic]. But I enjoy what I do now and I like to think up new cartoons. ☺

We just had one heck of a thunderstorm, it knocked out the power and the T.V. cable. But that's O.K. I got my guitar, so I'll just pick and grin awhile and yell some.

I'd give anything if I could just sing a little. But I got a terrible voice. But just maybe, we might record a couple of my songs while your [sic] here. I'll work on them. O.K. <u>But I am not promising</u>!!! Besides, I'd hate for you to have a heart a-tack [sic] from laughing too hard. Hey, is Barry going to be with you? And when Don comes with "Justice" this will be the first time I ever sit [sic] and talked civilized to them. ☺

Well my Friend, I'll close for now, take care and God Bless You and your family.

Friends,

Jimmy

J. Files
1982 or 83

"Eight by Ten"

You had to leave and went away
But I prayed you wouldn't stay.
Your picture is all that remains.

When I awake and gaze through tears,
I whisper softly I Love You Dear
But in absence you don't hear me.

I hold the frame and kiss the glass
That holds you in _____.
And say I love you to a world of Eight by Ten.

I saw some friends the other day
And they said you had gone away
I said no, you must be wrong, must be her twin

Then I hurried home to see,
If you were still there with me.
And there you sit with that special candid grin.

I hurried home and through the door.
Knew you were there, but must be sure.
And found you safe locked in your world of 8 x 10.

I held the frame and kissed the glass
That holds you in _____.
And said I Love You to a world of eight by ten.

TAG:
Then said good-night to my world of eight by ten.

Outlaw Blues

Too many long nights left out in the storm.
With no one to hold me, or keep me from harm.
They call me an outlaw and I guess that it's true.
Sure I get them low down outlaw blues.

Now I've tried livin' straight, like good citizens do
But I can't settle down, I've just got to move

The far away places, keep calling you see
Calling the outlaw, that lives inside me.

So like the blind fool, that we all sometimes are
I loaded my pistol and stole me a car.
Sat out on that long road, with these thoughts in mind
Good whisky, good drugs, wild women so fine.

Now it's life in the fast lane, with no turning back
Too late I realize, this deck has been stacked.
With the law close behind me, I'll soon have to pay
I may die tomorrow, but I'll do it my way.

Should you visit my grave, on some cold stormy day
You'll remember I lived, I loved and I paid
You may read on my tombstone, some win and some lose
And some just get them low down outlaw blues.

TAG:
Lord I gottem' the low down outlaw blues.

James Files.
1986

A

Real

Quacker!

Quack

Quack

☺

Bob, have a
Nice Day.

Friends,
Jimmy

Wednesday 07 July 1993

Dear Bob,

I received your welcome letter last night and as always, I was delighted to hear from you. And what a good laugh I got. I really love the "Business Card". Does this mean we're opening shop once I'm free? ☺ Just teasing, we're both pretty nice guys.

I'm glad you enjoyed talking with my daughter. She is a wonderful girl and wait till [sic] you see how Beautiful [sic] she is.

Tell Earlene I said hello and I hope that this all works out O.K. I'm just sorry that she owes so much money. Maybe we could do a movie, a true story, to help her out. About a killing of a government wittness [sic] that's to testify against Organized Crime. Just a thought. That's better than my life story and no ones [sic] made a movie about this wittness [sic].

I'm glad that Barry likes me, I like him too. He reminds me of some one I once knew a long time ago.

This time of year Willie's away, busy. But I hope you catch up with hi soon. I've never met him, but I Love [sic] him too. I think he's the Greatest! [sic] You told me you did some work with him and the boys, but you didn't say it was his first two "Outlaw Festivals". And yes, I bet you guys did have a great time.

I just got a letter from Don and he says things look pretty good. So maybe soon we can get busy. As for me talking to someone, don't worry about it.

I did you another flower this time. A rose, one of my favorites. The purple flower I sent you last time, I'm doing a large drawing like it, 17 x 23 for the art show. If it don't sell, I'll be broken hearted. ☹ That's why I've never entered anything before. A couple months back, we had a big showing at a gallery in Chicago. Some of the guys here sold a lot of their work. Me, I've never taken my drawing serious. To me it's a way to pass many boring hours here at the Ville. I tell you, I wish I was doing federal time. ☺

Well Bob, take care and may God keep you and your family safe. God Bless You all.

Friends,

Jimmy

Thank

You...

for Your

Help,

Concern,

And

Understanding.

Believe Me,

All is

Appreciated.

Bob, Thank You
Very much.

Friends,
Jimmy

Monday 16 Aug 1993

Dear Bob,

Just a few lines to bring you up to date on things and to say "Thank You" very much for the card and the magazine. The magazine is just great. That's the one I've been looking for, for the past year. I thought it came out of Nashville, but it comes out of Derby, Ct. When I was doing Federal Time [sic], I use to get it monthly. So it was a real surprise when I opened the envelope and found a C.S.R. "Country Song Round". Thank you very, very, much.

Oliver and Rick both were fine. I liked both of them. They said they'd be in touch later.

I was going to give you the drawing of me (that was done by David Lee), when you got here. I wanted you to see it first, to make sure you wanted it. But I don't know when you'll get this way. So, I'm going to try to get it mailed out in the next day or two. I'm sending the art order with this letter. Call the 1-800 number and see which is easier for you to place the order. The order has to come from the Galesburg, Ill. store.

If you don't like the drawing, after you see it, I'll have my daughter Kathy re-imburse [sic] you for it. She has seen it and she thinks it's real good. It was drawn from one of her wedding pictures, which was 4 years ago.

Next, I've had all kinds of people here to see me. I'm not going to be able to give an interview. I tried to reach you and Don last week, and I could not. So, I went ahead and seen these people. I won't get into details at this time. But for now we have to put a lid on things. I signed an agreement with you saying that you could use the letters, but you had to protect my identity. Things have been made very clear to me about the "3 Appellate Judges".

I must do my appeal first. Once I'm free, I'll give you some documents to see. I'll bring them to you in Texas. We'll cut off any corner of the paper you choose, you can have the paper tested, to prove its age. I'll let you make Xerox copys [sic] so you can have the handwriting analized. [sic] Dates and signatures are on the papers. They will blow your mind and prove that I levelled [sic] with you on all things except for one; "Government involvement". When the time is right, I'll tell you why I had to do all in my power to protect certain people. I'm truly sorry about not being able to give the interview, but Organized Crime is kid stuff compared to the Government. But hell, you already know that! You've been around the block a few times yourself.

I hope that we will still be friends. Bob, I don't use anyone, or take advantage of anyone. I play by the rules and I value friendship. Bob, even if Don gets the immunity, I still cannot talk. My letters are read, the phones are monitored, so someday I'll explain it all to you. O.K.

I hope you like the card, I think it's cute. And right about now, it's the way I feel. ☺

Tell Don and Earlene I said hello and send best wish's. [sic] You and the family take care and God Bless You all. I'll call when I can.

Friends always,

Jimmy

P.S. You said you had the songs about Kennedy worked out. If you can put them on a cassette, could you please send a tape to: James Files N14006 c/o Ken Brown. H. House Band. P.O. Box 112 Joliet, Ill. 60434-0112. (I would love to hear them) ☺ Thank you.

I PLANNED TO WRITE WHEN MY SEX LIFE IMPROVED…

But Hell Bob, I may not Live that Long!!!
☺

God Bless and Take Care,

**Friends,
Jimmy**

"I PLANNED to WRITE WHEN MY SEX LIFE IMPROVED..."

But Hell Bob, U may not Live that Long!!! ☺

God Bless and take Care,
Friends,
Jimmy

Friday 27 Aug. 1993

Barry Adelman
3003 W. Olive
Burbank, CA 91510

Dear Barry,

Just a few lines to say hello and to thank you for sending the model. But they wouldn't let it in, so I asked them to ship it back to you. But thank you very much for thinking of me.

I can only receive magazines and paper-back books. That's why I was asking for a listing of a couple of coustom (sic) car shops. I'm trying to locate the address for a company in England that builds full size kit cars. They're the ones that came up with the wild-cat model. It comes closest to my partner's and my drawing of our own design. We were fixing to build it when we caught this case. We wanted the drawing for the specs. We wanted ours widder (sic) like the Vette, but another 5 inches.

Bob told me he saw you and that you (sic) fine. I was happy to hear _____ _____ wouldn't be able to do the interviews.

The government was here to see me and came down pretty hard. If I open my mouth, they'll talk to the "3" appellate judges and my appeal won't even be heard. They're going to discredit me and I won't let out a whisper.

Once I win my appeal, and I'm free, I'm going to show Bob something that will blow his mind on this thing. I will also let you see it too. We just can't go public with it. Barry, I'm **NOT CRAZY** and I have proof to back my story. Someday you'll see it. Dates, (the paper can be tested for age) and the signatures can be verified. But that's all down the road.

When Joe first talked to me, I was worried about my appeal, but Joe, said **NO PROBLEM!** But there is a very big problem. My only chance out is to win my appeal, and that's what I'm working on.

Please excuse all my mistakes, but it's very hot and humid in my cell, and I'm writing fast. Please take care of yourself and I hope that someday, with in a few years that we'll meet again. God Bless.

Friends, Jimmy

Monday 30 Aug 1993

R. Vernon
1707 Roan Wood Ct
Houston, TX 77090

Dear Bob,

Just a few lines to say hello and to let you know that I received your welcome letter the other day. As always, I was delighted to hear from you.

I'm glad you got the picture, I was worried about it getting out of here. I have mail that gets lost all the time. Even money orders get lost that are sent to me. Two money orders were cashed, one in Joliet, the other just down the road in Lamont. Anyway, I'm real happy you like the picture. I wrote my daughter a letter and told her to call you. I didn't see her this past week, and I can't call her, we're on a major lock down; the entire prison. Please excuse my mistakes. I'm under a lot of pressure. I've been working out with the weights to relax myself. But now that we're on lock-down, I can't even do that.

I think I'm going to start going to the "Shrink", "Head Doctor", or what ever. I've got to get all this behind me. I'm starting to get very short tempered. For me, that can mean another case. And that I don't need.

As for people trying to reach me, I sent a message, loud and clear. No Book, No Movie, No interview, and no visits. That I know nothing and that I've got nothing to say. I haven't heard from anyone for two weeks, so maybe they went away.

For those "3" Appellate judges, the I do have to worry about.

I do sincerely hope that we can help Earlene. But with-out me going on T.V. But if that's the only way, I'll give it my best shot and take the chance. I have lately, received an offer of help and I'm considering it. I'll let you know about that later.

I'm down to about 4 letterheads, if you don't mind, I'd appreciate it. These letter heads are real nice and everyone likes them.

I think this card will tell you how I feel. I was going to do some flowers, but I just couldn't get in the mood, so I did the cartoon. I've been picking and singing the blues. Hey, I'm even starting to carry a tune ☺. My music class teacher says I'm starting to sound pretty good. ☺

Well Bob, take care and give my Best [sic] to Earlene. God Bless you all.

Friends,

Jimmy

***FEEL CONFUSED?
LIKE YOUR IN A
MINEFIELD!***

***DAMN
RIGHT
I DO!***

SEE HOW

CONFUSED

I AM...

*Friends,
Jimmy*

*And Thank You for
being a Friend.*

James E. Files
P.O. Box 112
Joliet, Illinois
60434-0112

Sept. 26, 1993

R. Vernon
1707 Roan Wood Crt.
Houston, TX 77090

Dear Bob,

Just a few lines to say hello and to thank you for the new letter heads. They're really great. But you mentioned a [sic] another package on the phone, and in this letter. Those, I never received.

I was happy, as always, to hear from you. But sorry to hear about the wolve's [sic] at Earlene's door. This whole thing has gotten into such a mess. I've made a lot of people very nervous, including my own people. I have received word to lie down and stop talking. I have been reminded, how wonderful silence can be. For the time being, I'm going to take that advice. Some people think I'm giving people up in order to get out of prison.

As for the "proffer agreement" on immunity. I don't want it. That might very well hurt other people that I know.

I've never heard of "Charles Carver", and please don't hire him since I'm not able to make the interview at this time.

The best thing to do, is to go ahead with what you have. I signed for you to use the letters. This I have explained to certain people. They just want me to let this blow over, keep my ugly face off the T.V. ☺ and try to win my appeal. They're afraid I may hurt some one very dear to the family. They want to help me but they want me to shut up. I'm sure you can understand their concern.

Please don't blame Don for what the F.B.I. did. I told everyone in the beginning what the government would do. Going around Don was routine for them. They would not want a wittness, [sic] when they put their point across to me. Even Don did not think they would go around him. I even ask [sic] him about it when he first told me. He said "No way" would they do that. I told him they, (the G.) could not be trusted. Hell, the G's the ones that kiddnapped [sic] me after "Chuck" was killed. Call Aunt Kay and ask her about my kiddnapping [sic]. Anyway, it is not "Don's" fault.

Well Bob, I'll close for now. I hope you're not too upset. God Bless You and the family. I'll call soon. Take care & God Bless.

Friends,
Jimmy

> I'm Glad we're so much alike!

I'd Hate to Be this Weird all By My-Self! :)

Friends,
Jimmy

*I'm Glad
we're so
much alike!*

*I'd
Hate to
Be
this
Weird
All
By
Myself!* ☺

*Friends,
Jimmy*

James E. Files
P.O. BOX 112
JOLIET, ILLINOIS

Wednesday 29 Sept 1993

R. Vernon
1707 Roan Wood Ct
Houston, TX 77090

Dear Bob,

Just a note to say hello and to tell you to stop wasting money on that over night mail. That's a waste. They still open it and copy it. ☺ Save your money!

I just mailed you a letter the other day. So this one is a follow up, to let you know that I received your letter today. ☺

I would call you, but we're back on lock-down, the entire prison. I've been waiting for my Daughter [sic] to come see me so I could have her call you for me. For I don't know when we'll be off lock down.

I'm sorry about the interview, but you will have to go with the letters that I signed for you to use. I do hope that you and Earlene will understand. But right now you might say I have a "gag order" on me.

If I give an interview, the government wants me to agree that Oswald acted alone. The Family says, "Don't say nuttin."

In all respect, I am to carry my secrets to the grave. After all, "Silence is Golden" and I never should have broken that silence by talking with Joe. That fact has been pointed out to me several times the past few months.

Anyway, you have the letters to use, maybe, you'll make enough to cover your expensives [sic] and to help Earlene some, maybe buy her more time. I hope to be free with-in the year.

In prison, I'm trapped in a cage and there is no place to run. I've seen things in prison you would not believe. But murder is very cheap in prison. There is always some one waiting for a mission. Me, I'm waiting for my Freedom!!!

You and the family take care and God Bless.

Friends,

Jimmy

Hi Bob,
I'm here at
the "Ville",
Thinking About
What a…

Charming

Witty

Good Looking

Intelligent

Understanding

Person
You
Are!

You
Certainly
Do
Check
Out

Yea!
You're A-O-K!

Friends
Jimmy

6:00 Sunday 16 Oct 1993

Dear Bob,

I'm sorry I've waited for so long to answer your letter. Please forgive me. I've so much to say and I don't know how to say it. But we'll get to that part later. ☺

As always, I was delighted to hear from you. And on this past Friday 15 Oct. I finally received your letter of Sept 6th that was mailed on Sept 11th. It was held up here for 30 days before they gave it to me. That is strickly [sic] <u>Bull</u> <u>Shit!</u>

But anyway thank you for the letter, the stationary, it was just great and the M. Jackson material was just fantastic. The Billing and the Pee Wee letter, just fantastic. I've had a lot of fun with that. ☺ Thank you. As for the stationary, I love it all! You do some great work.

I'm going to start by first answering your letter of Sept. 6th. O.K. So just bear with me.

This marker style print is very different, but cute, I like it.

I didn't go see them, but "Sixty Minutes" wanted to see me. They went to the F.B.I. about all this. At least that's what the official told me, some guy named "Lou" from "Sixty Minutes". I don't remember they're [sic] last name. Then a couple of lawyers wanted to come see me and I sent word back. <u>NO!</u> So for now things seem peaceful. But I am expecting a visit this morning from a friend that is a representive [sic] of the Chicago Section. Has some news he will only discuss in person.

We were on lock-down, got off for a day then went back on lock-down. We just got off Friday morning the 15th. My Daughter [sic] was here to visit me, the reason she didn't call you was some one took her rolex [sic] off her desk at work and she didn't have your number wrote [sic] down any where else. But I gave it to her again. I can't call her as I'm in an 815 area code and so is she, so I can't call her from the prison. I know that sounds crazy, but other guys here have the same problem.

I called Don the other day from the yard, a guy gave me 5 minutes of his phone time. I used 3 minutes for Don, he wasn't in, but I left a message with his secretary and called home and yelled "Money Honey" that took two minutes. I'll try to call you this coming week if we don't get back down on lock-down. They're already talking about hitting some one else. This place is crazy, wild, unreal and I hate it. But I get bye [sic]. I can handle the bull-shit.

Anyway, I'm glad to hear that your [sic] fine and the [sic] Earlene is O.K. I'll try to write her this coming week. I've mostly just been playing my guitar and yelling in my cell. I've was

[sic] working on a "Jungle Picture" for the art show that's coming up, but it's so damp in my cell the paper is too wet to work with, colored pencils don't take well on damp paper.

As of this past week, the art supplies still haven't gotten here. They may be in the mail-room, the mail-room is way behind. We're checking on that now.

If possible could you send a copy of that picture to a very "Special Lady" for me. She is "One" of the "Two" women that I love. I've got two women out there and I do love them both, have for many years. Yea, I know that's crazy. Anyway, the One's name is, Henriette Del Pierre, P.O. Box 51 Lake Villa, Ill. 60046-0051. She is really a great lady, she's from France, Blonde and Beautiful and I love her accent.

My Daughter's mailing address is, Kathy Files, 561 Darlington Lane #8 Crystal Lake, Ill. 60014.

I love the story about the shrink. That was great! But I'll never believe your [sic] crazy, unless it's crazy like a fox. ☺

About the model of the Jaguar that Barry sent me, that was sent back to him. I signed a money voucher for the postage. <u>Please</u> let me know if he got it back? If not, I'll get to checking on it.

You know, I still think about the time you and Barry come to visit me. Remember, we was talking about Kennedy and you ask [sic] me if there was anything I could tell you that hadn't been wrote [sic] about or anyone else knew? I'll never forget the @#$% (excuse) looks on yours and Barry's face when I told you about the casing of the 222 round, especially when I told you to go check it in Dallas. Remember, I told you, "You'll know its mine by the teeth marks on it". Remember I said the marks were on the ridge by the orifice. You and Barry looked at me like it was crazy for me to bite it, then leave it for them. But there were others I left certain things with. Sometime remind me to tell you about the coins, I've left. But that's something else.

Even when I use to go hunting and I would fire, I'd catch the spent casing and stick it in my mouth; I loved the taste and smell of burnt gun powder. Hell, that was better than coffee.

Yes, it was unethical for the F.B.I. to go around Mr. Ervin. But they wanted to see me alone. They got the point across to me about Kennedy on their Oswald theory. The Family Friends also made their point. That's why I can't sign the forms you sent me. I ask [sic] Don's secretary to type up some new forms and send them to me. Just for this upcoming T.V. show and for that only. I have to put all this to bed, let it go to sleep, be burried [sic] with me. Hell, no one cares about History anyway. Especially me!

This whole thing got started when Joe West come to see me. He wanted to take this case to trial. If it went to trial, I needed immunity. That's the only reason I ask for immunity. I told Joe, No T.V., books, movie, or interviews. I had even ask [sic] for no cameras in the Court Room. Hell, publicity is the last thing I need. I'm doing time now for shooting a cop. I don't need to add a president to my list of shootings. I'm sure that you understand that.

The G. has been talking to several of my friends about me. Stiring [sic] the pot a little as you might say. ☺

I'm still waiting for the picture of Willie that will be my most prized possession. Thank you very much. I sure hope it gets here this coming week. I also hope that you got your car fixed. Some of these mechanics don't know beans.

Hey, this is 5 pages, I best close, hope I didn't bore you to tears with this letter. Take care & God Bless.

Friends,

Jimmy

Thinking of You...

...and Wishing You

Bright Sunny Days!

Friends,
Jimmy

Hi Bob,
I'm here at the "Ville", Thinking about WHAT A...

☑ Charming
☑ Witty
☑ Good Looking
☑ Intelligent
☑ <u>Understanding</u>

Person You Are!

You Certainly Do **Check Out** ☑

Yea! Your A-O-K!

Friends
Jimmy

Thinking of you...

...and Wishing you Bright Sunny Days!

*Friends,
Jimmy*

Sunday 06 Dec 1993

Dear Bob,

I'll try to answer your welcome letter that I received the other day. As always, I was happy to hear from you. Glad to know that you're alright. As for me, I'm still kicking. Sorry I haven't been able to call, but we've was [sic] on lock-down. We get day room for 1 hour on Mon. Wed. & Fri. from 11:30 to 12:30. If I can get on the phone, I'll call. O.K.

I'll try to answer your questions in the letter in the order you ask them. But first, I had a visit today from a friend. He told me that Frank S. died yesterday in Miami. I'm very sorry to hear that. The list keeps getting shorter and shorter!

Yes, it sounds like you've been very busy getting around and seeing this wonderful country.

Yes, I received the release from Don, signed it and sent it back to him. Please let me know when you finish the program and go to air it.

No, I did not get the picture of Willie. No, Lee never got the art supplies. I had my daughter "Kathy" call "Dick Blick Art Supplies" in Galesburgh, Ill. and they said they never received the order. No big deal! I had my daughter buy a $40.00 money order and send it to Lee. So that's taken care of. So you best stop payment on your check. Also, no and no! My girlfriend and my daughter never received the pictures that you sent them.

I'm sorry that you've been getting some disturbing phone calls. I don't know who would be calling, but if I was to guess, I'd say the boy's from back East. Such as D.O.D./ D.I.A./C.I.A./ N.S.A. or F.B.I. Your guess is as good as mine. They wanted to see me a week or 10 days ago, but I wouldn't see them. I was called down to the Supt. (?) Office, but I refused to go up front. When I get a visit now, I make them tell me who it is before I go up front.

I wish I knew what the boys were asking you? Was it about me? They tell everyone I'm crazy. Maybe I am. I think I'm going to see a shrink. Maybe he'll tell me it's all a bad dream, I'll wake up, then I can go home. ☺

I told you why they went around Don, they had a special message for me. They want me to see things their way. After they gave me the rules of the game, they made a tape. They ask me if I shot Kennedy, with out the immunity I was not going to make a confession for them on tape, so I said <u>NO!</u> End of story. Hey, I seen it on T.V. Oswald done it, all by him little ol' self. ☺ God Bless Oswald if that be the case. May he be resting in Heaven, for God truly needs some good soldiers.

Gee Bob, why wouldn't they tell you the truth, the Government don't lie. Sorry, I'm just trying to be funny, trying to make myself smile. I guess tonight I have a poor since [sic] of Humor. I guess I'm just on the down side tonight.

Well before I close, I want to wish you and the family a Merry Christmas and a Happy New Year and may 1994 be a wonderful year for all of you. You and the Family take care and God Bless.

Friends,

Jimmy

*It's
Beginning
to look a lot like
Christmas…*

**The cat just barfed
up some
Tinsel!!!**

Merry Christmas

Friends, Jimmy

Friday 17 Dec 1993

Dear Bob,

Just a few lines to say hello and to bring you up to date. Also, an extra Christmas Card to put a smile on your face. I believe both of us can use a good laugh. ☺

About the Fireball, I'm sending you a letter from Joe. It explaines [sic] it's self [sic]. O.K. This is why I told you about the marks. Remember? Enough of that. But, if they have it now, why didn't they have it before. I believe it's a switch! Why? I'll get to that now.

I've been ask [sic], to ask you, to drop the investigation. O.K. Your [sic] asked! Now, they're going to discredit me, but we knew that a long time ago. I've been ask [sic] to stop helping you and telling you things. Hell, there's nothing left to tell. You and me knew that 6 months ago. You just watch your self and take care. Don't take any chances, watch your rearview mirror when your [sic] out. Don't park in dark areas, hell, you know the ropes, both of us has been a round the block a few times. ☺

Merry Christmas and Happy New Year.

Your Friend,

Jimmy

The Stockings
Were hung by
The Chimney
With Care…

I'd worn
Them for
Weeks and
They needed
The Air!!!

P U!!!
☺
Merry
Christmas

Friends,
Jimmy

Wednesday 05 Jan 1994

Dear Bob,

I just received your second letter yesterday and as always, I was happy to hear from you. Sorry I haven't answered sooner, but Dec. 23rd, I tore up my left shoulder working out. Then I tried to work out the next day doing squats. I put 220 lbs. on my shoulder to squat, and I felt it tear all the way down my back arm. Then for Christmas we went on lock-down, and just got off, Jan. 3rd. I've been so damn sore, I couldn't sit long enough to write or draw.

I do hope that things are fine with you and your family. I am happy to know that you're safe and doing well. Now to your letter!!!

I received a visit from the G. and I would guess they are unhappy. Again they refused to show me their I.D. Said they were from the Chicago office, just like last time when they went around Don, anyway, I refused to say anything. It only lasted about 2 minutes. The family ask(ed) me to keep quiet and not talk. But I told you that when they ask(ed) me. But they ever ask(ed) me to tell you to drop it.

I understand where you're coming from and I respect you for it. If I had no children I wouldn't worry at all. I've looked at death and spit in his face too many times. I've got the scars on my body to wear like medals. The scars inside of me only show during my dreams. I hate to leave you alone at this time, but I truly love my two daughters. So all I can say is, "Give'm Hell", and every night I pray for your safety. If you can, let me know when it's going to be aired. O.K. And I wish you all the luck with the show.

Now, why would I use a Mercury Load? ☺ Very simple! I like to be sure of things. Here's the story: The 222 would not explode on contact, it would fragmetate [sic], there is a difference. Also, if you hit your target on an angle shot, 4 times out of 10 it would (ricochette) in other words, deflect from the target. We had the same problem in Nam with the M-16's. Therefore, when working an assignment, you like to be sure. The Wolfman could do miracles for us. He was the first in our area to come up with "Rent-a-gun."☺ I'll explain that to you some time. This man was a real treasure and knew his work. He was an expert's expert. When ever I used explosives I always used two detonators to insure the job. But then I've had my superior's accuse me of over-kill. I've just never liked to fail at anything I guess.

The name Pepper sticks in the back of my mind. But nothing outstanding, so I'm not sure. It's been a long, long time. I would have to check my list I have put away for dates and times of operations to remember his face. I don't want to say, if I'm not sure. I only tell you what I'm sure of, so that way you find the true facts. I WILL NOT send you on a wild goose chase. I respect you too much.

I hope this card makes you smile. Please excuse my writing and my spelling. But my shoulder is killing me and I'm rushing and my mind is not all that clear.

Tell Earlene I said hello and Barry and Don. And you and your family take care, keep a close watch and may God keep you safe and out of harms-way.

Your Friend,

Jimmy

I hope soon we'll get to go fishing and talk about the ol' days. Then you'll realize I am crazy. ☺

Take-care.

P.S. Again:

One important fact on the 222 mercury load. At approx. 100 F.P.S. you had entry before expulsion, (removing internal parts with exit.) The standard rounds, would not do that. I found that out from experience, or trial by error. Know what I mean. Please, take care.

Hey Bob!
Your
Number One
And I'm Still…

Hangin'
On!!!
☺

Friends,
Jimmy

Dear Bob,

I received your letter and the brief this past Friday. As always, it was a pleasure to hear from you. Happy to hear that you and Earlene are alright. As for me, I'm fine and my left shoulder is much better. I'm back to working out again.

Things here have been pretty wild, beatings, stabbings and so forth, with lots of lock downs. You know, same ol' crap. ☺ just different people.

Yes, I would love to see the V.C.R. tape. I talked to the Superintendent Nelson and he said yes, it would be possible to see the tape. But you have to have Don Ervin or Julius Echeles call the prison, talk to Asst. Warden Springborn and let him know about the tape and that Superintendent Nelson and I have talked about the tape all ready. Julius Echeles phone # is 312-782-0711. You know Bob, you could call I guess and get it set up, then mail the tape to : Assist Warden Springborn, for Super. Nelson, Stateville Prison, Joliet, Ill. 60434-0112. After I view it, I can ship it back to you, or if you don't want it back, I'll send it to my daughter to keep for me. I hope to be free soon. Julius is doing an excellent job for me. My partner already has his case re-versed [sic]. So I've got high hopes.

Thanks for the letter heads, they're really great, I like them. And, I wish you luck with the show. And I'll drop a few lines to Earlene and fix her a card. Yes, I'm sure that she miss's [sic] Joe.

The F.B.I. is desperate in more ways than one. You know how I feel about them. I never have liked the boys upstairs.

Too bad you didn't have more time in Miami. I hope that A.V. is fine and doing well. If I get out soon, I'll stop by the Marina and say hello. I wonder if he'll recognize me. ☺

Gee! I also wonder who has the power to find out who works for who and who those people are that can get unlisted phone numbers? Are they trying to tell you that they're keeping an eye on you? Are you still sleeping with the shotgun beside your bed?

Don't worry about the pictures or the money, its not that important. O.K.

No! I haven't been in contact with Don Ervin lately. I know he's very busy, always on the go like you. But I'll drop him a line later this week.

Bob, all my notes are not here in prison with me. I've only told what I could remember acurately (please excuse my spelling, sometimes I get brain lock) ☺

All my notes are in storage, but I have listings for people in all the groups that I told you about. When we met, I told you that I was working on a book; I was calling it, "To Kill a Country". Not about Kennedy, not my life story, but about black operations, distrust, betrayal and assassinations. I would never have that kind of information in prison with me. Just like I have good friends that I won't write or call on the phone.

That's why, when I'm free, I'll be able to prove something to you. What I show you will blow your mind, but we can't go public. I just want you to know I'm not crazy. Also, I'm not after publicity or that 15 minutes of fame that everyone talks about. I know who I am and I'm not of [sic] ashamed of me. I can hold my head up and I'm proud of who I am. If it wasn't' for endangering my daughters, we'd really do a story, with pictures with time and date marked. Remember how the old photos used to be marked on the edge, like Feb. 63 and Nov. 1963. ☺ These photos are locked away safe, and they don't involve O.C. people.

Hey, I hope you like the card. ☺ I think it's cute. I'll close for now, take care. Every night you, your family and Earlene are in my prayers. Oh by the way, did Earlene sell Joe's Harley?

Well God Bless you all and take care.

Friends,

Jimmy

Hey Bob,

Is the Water

Getting Hot?

Naaaahhh...

It never

Gets to Hot

For

You!!!
☺

Your Friend

Jimmy

JAMES E. FILES
TOP SECRET

N14006   P.O. Box 112   Joliet, Illinois   60434-0112

Bob Vernon, 1707 Roan Wood Crt.   Houston, TX   77090

Monday 07 March 1994

Dear Bob,

I just received your welcome letter and all the letter heads, wow! What a nice surprise. Thank you very, very much. And it's always a pleasure to hear from you.

I'm looking forward to seeing you, Don and your friend. But I'm not telling anyone your [sic] coming to see me. It might make them nervous. Know what I mean. But it will be nice to see you again. Have Don try to get the cassette in as legal materials, which it is, as it pertains to the Kennedy thing. I can't wait to hear it, what name or tittle [sic] is the song? Also, did you send the demo tape for me to see?

It's very hard to believe that Joe's been gone for a year already. Time sure flies. I know it must have been rough on Earlene.

I like all the letter heads, but I chose this one. But please add my number to it. ☺ My number has to be on everything coming and going. Or I don't get it, or it don't get out of here without my number.

I've got guitar strings, but thanks for thinking of me. What I would like is a Hank Williams Sr. music book with songs like, "Cold, Cold Heart, Your Cheatin' Heart, Lost Highway, I could never be ashamed of you, my lips could tell the lies but my heart would know." Ect ect! [sic] Those kind of songs. I love Willie, but there'll never be another Hank Williams Sr. ☺

This afternoon we just went back on lock-down. This one may last awhile. There's been lots of trouble here. Beatings and stabbings almost every day. Nothing but animals here.

When you get here, I'll bring you up to date on my end. Right now, things are looking pretty good.

Hey, I hope you like the card, I'm going to close for now and get this in the mail, they just yelled 10 min. till pick up time. I'm going to start entering my flowers in the art show. My art teacher says they'll sell. I don't know about that but I'm going to find out. ☺

Tell everyone hello and god Bless you all. Looking forward to seeing you. Take care.

Friends,

Jimmy

> I can be a Real ass !!! :)
>
> Friends,
> Jimmy

> Sometimes Bob...

Sometimes

Bob…

I

Can be

a

Real

Ass!!!
☺

Friends,

Jimmy

Happy

Easter

to a

Special

Family…

May this

Easter

be filled

with much

Love

And

Happiness…

Friends,
Jimmy

JAMES E. FILES
N14006
P.O. Box 112
Joliet, Illinois
60434-0112

Thursday 07 April 1994

R. Vernon
1707 Roan Wood Crt.
Houston, TX 77090

Dear Bob,

I just received your welcome letter and the Greatest Book of all time. Thank you very, very much. That means a great deal to me. Much more than you can ever guess. Right now I'm in Hillbilly Heaven. ☺

Yes, it was also great to see you again and I do hope we'll be able to do some fishing pretty soon.

I'm looking forward to seeing my daughter this Sunday 10th April. I have no idea what she is going to say to me as she was against me giving an interview. She worries too much about me. ☺

I've already did [sic] about a dozen Hank Williams songs. I bet my singing makes him roll over in his grave. ☺ If he was alive, I bet he'd pay me not to sing his songs.

I haven't heard from our friends in the Chicago office, but I did hear from the "Company" back east. ☺ How ever, "I'm not stupid, therefore, I should realize that Oswald acted a lone, as a lone assassin, with no help what so ever!" So Bob, I guess I've got everyone upset over nothing. Gee, I'm so sorry for upsetting everyone. ☺ Do you think they'll get over it? ☺ Hey, please don't air this part!!! 'Cause I think I've pissed on them enough. ☺

Tell Barry I said hello and I'm glad you're happy with the interview. But I've a funny story to tell you when I see you.

Also, I didn't take the name Files till Sept. or Oct. of 1963. When I applied for a marriage license.

I got my art supplies today. Now, I have to improve on my art. In our next art show, I'm going to enter a half dozen pictures. I hope I sell some of them, but I don't believe my work is that good. I need a lot of improvement.

Well I'll close for now; you take care, keep a close watch, and God Bless! And again, thanks a million for the H.W. Book; it's Great.

Your Friend

Jimmy

*Thank
You…*

for being

You,

for being a

friend,

for the many

Things

You have done

for me.

I truly

Appreciate it.

Friends, Jimmy

Tuesday 12 April 1994

Dear Bob,

Just a few lines to say hello and to thank you for the wonderful Hank Williams song book. Is it ever Great! Thank you so very much.

It was really nice seeing you for 2 days. I always enjoy your company. You're a Great Guy, and that proves I'm a very good judge of character. ☺

You look a lot better than my cartoon, but I was trying to capture you at work, doing your thing. ☺

The warden gave me the book and had a nice little talk with me. Gave me some good advice also.

Well let's hop for the best. You and the family take care and God Bless.

Friends,

Jimmy

Life

Sure is

a

Bitch!!!

***Friends,
Jimmy***

1900 hrs: Monday 02 May 1994

R. Vernon
3003 Olive
Burbank, Calif. 91510-784

Dear Bob,

Just a few lines to say hello and to say I'm sorry about the little thing I put you through. But I'm under pressure to stop the show. But what's done is done. I'm very sorry. But I like you and respect you. So I do hope that you will forgive me.

Thanks a million for the Willie Nelson Music Book. It's just Great. But if Willie could hear me murdering his songs, trying to sing them, he would shoot me. ☺ And that's a fact. When you get back to Texas I've got a new song for you. One you just might make money with.

I' sorry we got cut off this morning, but they never give us a warning. They just turn the phones (off), when yard time is over. But at 7:30 A.M. here, I was pumping iron, you were still sleeping I bet. ☺ Hey, take care and I hope this card makes you smile. Good Luck on your project. If it don't air, I won't cry.

Friends,

Jimmy

P.S. Sometime, I'll tell you a funny story about this and the people that send messages. ☺

2nd P.S. You'll have to give Warden Godinez written permission to release the tape to my daughter or let him keep that one and send her another for me. Also, please send the Warden the cassette with the song on it at the end of the show. O.K. ☺

Happy
Mother's Day
to a...

Real
Muther!
☺

You're alright Pal.

Friends,
Jimmy

TRANSCRIPT
JAMES E. FILES/BARRY ADELMAN TELEPHONE CALL
MAY 4, 1994

Files: I'm going to tell you what I told Bob earlier today.
Barry: O. K.
Files: I don't want the show to air.
Barry: I know… you told me that too.
Files: I told you that too… I didn't know if I did or not… I wrote you a card and sent you a letter apologizing for the way I acted on the phone last time… for being testy.
Barry: Yeah… he…
Files: But they had just turned me down on my appeal and you got me about an hour later.
Barry: No, he told me all that… he did convey that to me. The last time we spoke on the phone you told me you wished this show would go away…
Files: Yeah… and so does a lot of other people here.
Barry: Yeah. Do you mind if I ask you… first of all… let me ask you…would you repeat for me what you told Bob this morning just so I know I've got it accurate.
Files: Well, like I told Bob, you know, I threw that curve in there trying to stop the show because I had people come here and they wanted the show stopped, they don't want it to air, even my daughter don't want it to air…
Barry: And, let me ask… I'm sorry I missed you, Jimmy…
Files: About the brother, that's why I wrote the note so she would talk to you guys Otherwise she would have never said a word… all I wanted to do was stop the show.
Barry: Why did you think that story would stop the show?
Files: I just wanted to discredit myself some.
Barry: Ah-huh…
Files: Somebody had talked to my daughter and my daughter has already talked to me and my daughter asked me last Sunday, she said, Dad why don't you just call a news press conference and tell the newspapers that you made it all up and you lied. I told her, I said, I've got push and pull, I've got people that I've committed myself to, to help, and I said I haven't hurt anybody. I didn't give nobody up in in the government and I gave nobody up in organized crime… that's why I made the interview so I could stipulate that on the tape and they could see that. But I hurt nobody on either side of the fence… that's what it's all about…
Barry: I see… well let me ask you this… if you don't mind… at one time you told Bob that Eleanor was gonna visit you this week… and you said to Bob at that time, I'm asking her to come here for the last time…
Files: Yeah…
Barry: What did you mean by that?
Files: What I meant by that was I don't want to cause her any problems and one of the main reasons that I don't want to have anything to do with her is that my daughter doesn't want me to have anything to do with her… it's just personal family stuff…
Barry: Yeah… O.K.
Files: It has no bearing on this whole deal whatsoever…
Barry: O.K.
Files: I just wanted to talk to her and explain things to her, tell her… that this is it, you know I brought the letters down… the warden… he even seen the letter that that she sent me with the love and all this other bullshit on it you know… and … her and I've got a close relationship over the years and… we still have you know stopped her from coming because I waned to keep everybody away from it… wanted to keep my family

out of it... my kids out of it. My daughter don't even want this to air... like I say... you know...
Barry: Um-mmm... Bob just handed me a note saying that you told him this morning. That there were a couple of... factions... trying to stop this show...
Files: Right... I don't' know what they'll do but like I say, they don't want it to air...
Barry: And who are those people?
Files: Well, I'm not going to give you no names of those people... O.K.?
Barry: O.K.... well, you assume that this call is being recorded...?
Files: I know it is.
Barry: Let me ask you this... when did you first tell Eleanor the twin story?
Files: I'm not going to get into all that Barry, because like I say... I promised some people I would not help this story go any further... and if they can kill it... kill it... and that's where we're at pal, I hate to do that to you guys but... we're at the end you know... when it comes to the family and everything else.. I gave you guys everything... the casing... down the line... to everything else... play by play... my family had no part of it... they are not involved... my kids wasn't even born then... the main players... they're dead... this is where we're at...
Barry: We came across a letter, Jimmy, this morning... ah, that was back in '92 that you had written to Joe West...
Files: Um-mmm...
Barry: And in that letter you talk about your family and how they are all gone and unfortunately they all went through tragedy...
Files: Right...
Barry: But at that time... you talk about a brother who was killed in Mexico City...
Files: Yeah...
Barry: What was that?
Files: We're not getting into that...
Barry: O.K.
Files: Like I say... my family has nothing to do with it...
Barry: Alright...
Files: At that time... I never thought somebody would have cameras on the grassy Knoll and that they would make my picture.... It would have made my life a whole lot easier if I had of... maybe... but you know... we just don't do things like that... Most people that know me... even in Melrose Park... when you go talk to them... they're not going to tell you anything that I shot anybody or I did this or I did that...
Barry: How are you feeling right now as far as helping us as far as nailing down the truth on this because we've got some major loose ends here... we've got Eleanor saying one story... we got you saying another story... we got you now wishing that the show would go away...
Files: Right, and that's what I want now more than anything...
Barry: But you're still sticking to the story that you told us on tape?
Files: Yes, that's the truth... that's all I can tell you.
Barry: O.K.
Files: That's the truth, that's all I can tell you. What I told you people was the truth... wish I had never given the interview... I made a mistake by doing it... I realize that... and the people in the family... they realize that... that's all I can say... when I say I ain't got no family... I ain't got no family except for my daughters.
Barry: I understand. And you mentioned to Bob this morning about the grand jury as well...
Files: Um-mmmm...
Barry: Do you have any idea when that's coming down?

Files: I don't think it's gonna be too far away… I'm hoping that I get my co-defendant back to trial before this comes down because I'm gonna testify in his behalf… but I'd like to see him get off this case…
Barry: But they didn't give you any indication of any date where that might happen?
Files: Not yet… no.
Barry: And Bob told me that you really don't want to go through that whole grand jury thing if you can help it…
Files: Right… All I can do is go ahead and tell 'em… I've got nothing to say… I can tell 'em you know… talk to everybody else… talk to the people you've called…talk to those people… you've got everything else… the whole thing is this… once my face is shown on TV, me getting a trial on this other case is going to be very hard… my lawyer pointed out several indications to me… also after the show he said that if I wanted to talk to someone he had someone at the Tribune that could kind of smooth it over maybe… take some of the heat off…
Barry: Smooth it over in what way… do you know?
Files: In what way… you know… try to play it down a little bit… you know… Let me ask you something… what is the chance of this show being scratched?
Barry: I think that right now it's in about a 50/50 position…
Files: Well, I've got a chance then…
Barry: Yeah, I think you do… I mean we want the show to go forward for all the reasons we told you in the beginning…
Files: I want to help Earlene, too but like I say at this point, you know, I've just got too much pressure coming…
Barry: Well, if you were trying to derail it, if you haven't knocked it off track, you certainly knocked it on its ass a bit…
Files: O.K.
Barry: So we're trying to pick ourselves up ad dust ourselves off and get back up. But you did a good job of that…
Files: Well, that is what I was… you know… I don't want to get into that because I know that this is all being recorded…
Barry: Right…
Files: So, listen, I'm gonna let you guys go for now and all I can say is good luck…but like I say…I'm not bringing my family, I'm not giving nobody up…O.K.?
Files: What you guys got… if you go with it…if you can… if you can't, I'll be one happy person… O.K.…
Files: Thank you guys very much and I'll talk to you later… O.K.?
Barry: Bye.

Monday 30 May 1994

R. Vernon
1707 Roan Wood Crt.
Houston, TX 77090

Dear Bob,

Just a few lines to say hello and I sure hope that your [sic] feeling much better. It was real nice talking with you yesterday. But you sure sounded bad. <u>Please</u> take care of your self. I don't want anything to happen to you.

I hope you like the card. I did this one in water color. I've just started using water colors. I like working with them. As soon as I can order some water color paper, I'll do you a @#$% (oops.) regular picture in water color. The paper I'm trying to use is much too thin. It's alright for cards, but a large sheet, when wet, curls up all over. ☺

My Daughter came today to see me, she's doing fine. We had a very nice visit. I'm looking forward to seeing you again soon. Not much news on my end. Take care and tell Earlene I said hello and get well soon.

Friends,

Jimmy

P.S. I won't be able to call you. We're back on lock-down. ☹

Get
Well
Soon...

*So Sorry
to Hear,
that You've
been ill.*

*But Prayers
Are said, for
You to Soon
be Well.*

*So warm wish's
And Prayers, I send
to My Good Friend.*

Hey Pal, Get Well Soon.
Friends,
Jimmy

Thursday 09 June 1994

R. Vernon
1707 Roan Wood Crt
Houston, TX 77090

Dear Bob,

Just a few lines to say hello and to say I do hope your [sic] feeling much better. Also, to say thank you for the package. I just got it, a little over an hour ago. Thank you very much.

Thank you for sending my G.E.D. Diploma. When I got here, I told these people I already had 3 G.E.D.'s but they didn't believe me. So I had to take the test over again. ☺

Gee, you seen [sic] some of my mad ravings from when I first started trying to learn to write. Terrible, and I haven't learned much since.

Thank you very much for the sheets to write music on. Now I just have to come up with something good.

Hey, that one song, "I'll Remember Jackie" you think we could do anything with that. Just wondering, with her passing away and all.

We're still on lock-down and I have no idea yet as to when we'll get off it. No one seems to know anything.

By chance, do you have any close friends that are Jewish and still have close ties to Israel? If so, please let me know.

Listen, no one knows about that one deal except, you, my daughter and me, also, D. C. I think I would like to keep it that way whether the film airs or not. So if you talk with my Chicago lawyer, please don't say anything. But, I am going to mention to him that if this film aires,[sic] I'll be able to finish paying him as people wanted to do something for my daughter. After, we filmed this interview, all my financial help was pulled. That's how mad everyone got. Anyway, we just got my appeal filed in the Supreme Court. I'll talk to you more about that when I see you. I can't believe that everyone got so upset over the interview. I mean life long friends are not even talking to me. Gee, if I had said something really important, what would they have done, kill me? ☺

Well Bob I will close for now. I do hope that you have a speedy recovery and will soon be feeling in tip top shape. So please take care and God Bless.

Friends,

Jimmy

P.S. Hope you like my Snuffy Smith.
You do remember him? Right. ☺

1800 HR. Thursday 21 July 1994

R. Vernon
1707 Roan Wood Crt.
Houston, TX 77090

Dear Bob,

I received your welcome letter the other day and as always, I was delighted to hear from you.

I hope this letter finds you well and in good spirits. Just be sure to keep a close watch over your shoulder. As for me, I'm fine, just trying to keep out of trouble. This place is about ready to blow. They just locked F house down. Some Superintendent got the side of his head caved in this morning. Then yesterday, in my unit, the blacks and whites almost got into it. This is one crazy place. I just hope things work out with Julius and my appeal.

Tell Earlene I said hello and I send best wish's [sic] her way. I hope that pretty soon you'll be able to get the wolves away from her door.

What is the name of the book and what are you calling the interview? I have several people asking me that question. I feel kind of dumb not having an answer. ☺

I can't wait to get the George Jones books. I love all his music and I'm forever trying to do his songs. I've been a George Jones fan since 1958. "The Window Up Above." I'm sure you remember that one.

When you stop in Nashville, give my Aunt Christine my love. Just don't let her kidnap you like in that movie, "Misery." ☺ Aunt Christine is (a) wonderful lady. And then I'll start looking for you right after Nashville. And don't forget to bring the cassette tape with you.

I gave you Kathy's address over the phone, but I'm sending it again in this letter so you'll have it on record. ☺ 2 Wheaton Center #1603, Wheaton, Ill. 60187 phone #708-260-8046.

Yes, I hope that very soon, we'll be able to go fishing. I'm really looking forward to spending some time with you. I bet we'll have lots of laughs. Maybe even do another book about crimes and chop shopes [sic].☺ Or would that make people nervous. The book would be hard core in a world of violence, but also a lot of laughs too, because there were so many crazy things that happened. This would be an easy book to do, cause a lot of my people are still alive and they'd be willing to talk because the statute of limitations is over with. Plus, there's lots of court records to prove it all happened, even cops. Oh well, it's something to think about. Bet we could have a lot of laughs working on it. Also, some great pictures of the areas we worked in and did all those crazy things.

I hope the card I made, puts a smile on your face. ☺ I'm waiting to get some water color paper, (which I've already waited two months on), but when I do get it, I'll do you a nice water color picture and send it to you. I've also been thinking about having Kathy order me some acrylic paints and canvas and do a painting, looking down from the grassy knoll on-to Kennedy in the limo, with the cross hairs focused on his right eye, or the back of his head being expelled. Then after the book and the movie, put the picture on loan to an art gallery or a museum. That's one picture, I wouldn't sell. But I best wait and see if I get indicted before I do anything else. Right!!! ☺

Hey, I don't mean to rattle on so much. I hope you didn't fall asleep reading this. You and the family take care and give my love to Earlene, and you My Friend, <u>Please</u> keep a watch over your shoulder. I <u>don't</u> <u>want</u> <u>to</u> <u>loose</u> [sic] <u>you.</u> O.K.! Take care & God Bless.

Friends,

Jimmy

P.S. Someday, maybe I'll tell you the rest of the story. Keep the faith!!!

***Mornings
at the
Ville
are Terrible…***

***Till I
Have
My Coffee
and Start
Thinking
of the
Can of Snakes
You & Me
Opened!*** ☺

*Then I laugh like Hell!
Watch yourself and take care.*

*Friends,
Jimmy*

Till I Have My Coffee and Start Thinking of the Can of Snakes You & Me Opens L! :)

Then I laugh like Hell!
Watch yourself and take care,
    Friends, Jimmy

Mornings at the Ville are Terrible...

Monday 10 Oct. 1994

Robert Vernon
1224 Cambronne
New Orleans, LA 70118

Dear Bob,

Just a note with the card to say hello and to say I hope that all is well with you. I only wish that I was there to help you chase all those young girls. ☺

Warden Godinez, sent officers for me and brought me straight back to the Ville. I'm sure glad I didn't have to go by way of Joliet Prison.

Anyway, it sure is nice to back in my cell. T.V., my guitar and music and all my art material. Now I can keep myself busy, cook decent food and not go to bed hungry. And if I want coffee, I can have it. At that County jail, they don't give me anything, except a hard time. ☺

Hey Pal, you're a producer, and I've got one hell of an idea for a T.V. show. When you see me, remind me to tell you about it. I can rough write some of the stories, then you could do it right. I've got some other ideas, some that will make you a multi-millionaire. ☺ All facts, all true, all can be checked out.☺ Well, I'll close for now, you take care & please let me know about Texas.

Your Friend,

Jimmy

(enlosed newspaper article)

Two men were indicted on federal explosive and mail fraud Charges in the March, 1980, bombing of a Near North Side Auto dealership owned by one of them. James F. Gaudio, 59, of 1671 E. Mission Hill, Northbrook was arrested. James E. Files, 41, is in the Metropolitan Correctional Center. Gaudio and Files were charged with illegal use of explosives in the bombing of Austin Motors, a used-car dealership owned by Gaudio. FBI Special Agent Ed Hagarty and U.S. Attorney Dan K. Webb said. The two also face mail charges of trying to defraud insurance companies by filing claims on the destroyed business.

*Hi
Bob!*

*Just
Wanted
to Say
Hello
and let You
Know
Where I'm at!*
☺

*Friends,
Jimmy*

Sunday 23 Oct 1994

Dear Bob,

Just a few lines to say hello and to let you know that I received your welcome letter. Also, I want to wish you a Happy Halloween. I wish to hell I was there with you. We'd go out for Halloween and trick all the young girls and get lots of treats. ☺ Yea, if I was there, I could be your Gopher, do most of your running for you. We'd have a laugh a minute.

Good luck at the Kennedy Review Board. I know you'll give them hell, but I hope they don't call me. You caught a bad break on this story with the O. J. Simpson case catching the media hype. I hope to hell you get your money back and make a profit.

By now, maybe your [sic] un-packed and getting your life on track. I'm truly sorrow [sic] about your divorce. I know that had to be a hell of a shock to you. But I want to wish you all the Luck in the World, you deserve the Best!

Nope, Lake County was not better to me this time. With them it's always the same ol' shit. But it's sure nice to be back here, if I have to do time that is. I hope to be able to get my art work in this next art show as I missed the last one. I hope to sell some of my work this time, it sure would be nice to move some of it.

I'm enclosing a news article that was ran [sic] some time back. I just now got hold of a copy of it, well I got it two weeks ago, but we went on lock-down and it took a while for me to get a copy made. It was written by the girl that wants to come and visit me. I told her no cameras, no recorders, or pen and paper. But I won't say anything of importance. If she wasn't a Friend, of "Our Friend" I wouldn't even see her.

We lost "Oral Arguments" on my case. I was hoping to be free soon as I wanted to go dig up some very important papers to show you. They would knock your socks off. ☺ But I guess all that will have to wait a little longer. But that's O.K., as their [sic] safe. They can't burn and they'll be dry.

I hope we get to sit and talk for a while pretty soon. Got some ideas I want to run by you. You may be interested. Please excuse my sloppy writting [sic], but I'm watching football while I'm writting [sic] to you. ☺

Well I'll close for now, you take care and keep a close watch over your shoulder, and stay safe. I don't want to loose [sic] a good friend as I've a shortage on friends.

Your Friend,

Jimmy

Stateville inmate says he killed JFK

By Stewart Warren
COPLEY NEWS SERVICE

Crest Hill—Movie director Oliver Stone missed a big scoop last year when he filmed *Natural Born Killers* at Stateville Correctional Center here.
A Stateville inmate claims to have murdered President John F. Kennedy.

He's James Files, a long-haired 52-year-old, who says he fired the fatal shot Nov. 22, 1963, from the grassy knoll in Dallas, Texas. In September 1964, the Warren Commission announced that Lee Harvey Oswald had shot Kennedy from a sixth-floor window at the Texas School Book Depository Building. Oswald was killed by Jack Ruby on Nov. 24, 1963. Files says Oswald was innocent, though he planted misleading evidence to confuse police. Files has been serving a 50-year sentence for the 1991 attempted murders of two Round Lake Beach police officers. Currently, Files is jailed at the Lake County lockup. He's there because the Illinois Appellate Court ordered a new trial in the case.

One man says he has Files' videotaped confession—Bob Vernon, 47, a Houston-based television producer who also says he is responsible for exposing Jimmy Swaggart. The colorful Texan interviewed Files on March 22 and April 22 this year at Stateville.
"Some of the things that he has to say would tell the entire truth about what happened in Dealey Plaza. He has told me enough already to fry him in the electric chair, in Texas, of course," said Vernon who says he rarely leaves his home these days because he has received death threats as a result of his work with Files. An FBI agent exposed Files, Vernon's former partner Joe West, a Texas private investigator who died last year of natural causes, got the tip and started the project.

Files told Vernon that he was 21 when he shot Kennedy. The inmate said he was a driver for Charles Nicoletti, a mob figure who, according to Files, masterminded the assassination and also fired one of the shots that killed the president, Vernon said.
Another mystery surrounds Files. Chicago lawyer Julius Echeles, who represents Files in the new Lake County trial, says he doesn't know who hired him to do the work. He says he received a cashier's check inside an anonymous letter asking him to represent Files. The missive was signed "Friends of James Files."

Echeles said this week he is unconcerned about Files' claim to infamy. He said he was hired simply to represent the man in the Lake County case.

Lake County prosecutors have asked Vernon for a copy of Files' taped confession. They want to use it in the new attempted murder trial to discredit Files. So far, Vernon has refused to give them the tape. Steven McCollum, Lake County's chief deputy state's attorney, called Files a braggart. "I just don't believe there was a conspiracy to kill John Kennedy," McCollum said, "If there was one, James Files wasn't a part of it."

Hi Bob!
Happy
Halloween

Hey Pal,

I Hope

You Get

lots of

Treats

Out of those

Young Girls +

No Tricks!
☺
Your Friend
Jimmy

Sunday 11 Dec. 1994

Dear Bob,

I' very sorry for taking so long to write you. But I'm one sick puppy with the flu. I mean it's kicking my ass royal. I just hope that you're in good health, and that you're taking care of yourself.

But First: Merry Christmas, Happy New Year, and May the New Year bring you all that you want.

That list of names you sent me went missing for over a week. Then one morning I woke up and it was on my floor by the cell door. Anyway, there were a couple of ol' time mobsters on here that were friends of that stool Pigeon Lenny Patrick. I guess maybe their [sic] dead by now. And of course you know about the white ships (?) that belonged to the company. But none of them had a direct link to Nov. 22 that I know about. Remember, at that time I was just a gopher, go for this, go for that. Just a driver, no one of really any importance. After learning or I should say really thinking about it a lot, I honestly believe that the reason J. R. decided not to fire that morning was because of the attempt to stop it. I now think he was afraid he would piss off the wrong people. That's why [sic] maybe why my friend ask(ed) me to be his support that morning. But I guess I'll never know for sure. Besides, to me it doesn't really matter. My friend had the faith in me to ask me, and I said yes, and I know in my heart that I did not fail him, and that is what matters most to me. "He" believed in me, and I proved myself worthy of that belief. To me, C. N. was the Greatest, the Best, he was "Number One" in many ways. Like I told you "He" walked on water.

I'm going to have to lay back down. I'm feeling very woogy. I hope the card puts a smile on your face and again I wish you a Merry Christmas. Also, I think of you as a very close friend and I still hope to give you a bigger and better story than ever, bigger than this other one. Oh well, that's later. You take good care and watch your back. I don't want to loose [sic] a good friend. Oh yea, please send me the manuscript of my book, "To Kill a Country," O.K. Thanks a lot. Again, take care and I'll write more later.

Merry Christmas,
Friends Always,

Jimmy
P.S. Tell Earlene I said hello and Merry Christmas. I couldn't send her a card as I don't have her address. But tell her I'm thinking of her and by the way, you never did send me a copy of what was said at the hearings. I read the copy our friend had, but would like one for my records. Thank you. Merry X. ☺

Merry Christmas

*May Your Home
be filled with
The Magic of Christmas*

*Your Friend,
Jimmy*

Tuesday 21 Feb. 1995

Dear Bob,

Just a few lines to say hello and that I hope you're in good health and high spirits. As for me, I'm alright, got a slight cold and we been on lock-down since the 5th. We still don't know when we're getting off.

From what I hear there's a contract on the new warden. He don't make deals with the gangs, he calls the shots. I admire him for that. I still haven't met him; I guess he's got his hands full.

This past Sunday night (19th Feb) I was watching "Sixty Minutes" on T.V. and low and behold, who shows up on T.V.? "Ol' Robert Tosh Plumlee." ☺ He was talking about airplanes and the C.I.A., but thank God, not about Dallas. Did he ever tell you about flying weapons to the "Ranch in _____ ☺ Central America. I best not give the location, in case he hasn't told anyone. Yes, I trust you, but not the people who reads my mail before it leaves here. ☺

And besides all that, they took the phone out of my unit and we can no longer make phone calls. They're so nice to us! ☺

But what piss's [sic] me off the most is all these people on T.V. talking about how nice we got in prison. Those ass-holes just haven't done any time here at the Ville.

That song I wrote, "I Remember Jackie," is it O.K. if I send that out to someone, or should we sit on it a little longer?

Also, the papers you have about my friend here with me. Next time you talk to Leo, please ask him to keep that party here with me to watch my back-side. O.K. With our friend gone, I don't look for any favors. Know what I mean. There's only two people here doing time with me I trust to watch my back and I think both of them may be shipped, so I'll be alone, and then I'll become an easy target. Through the Ol' Grapevine, I hear your show won't air and your book won't get anywhere. Just watch yourself out there, don't take chances. O.K. Your [sic] One Friend I don't want to lose over all this B.S. I'd rather have you safe and sound.

Well, I'll close for now, you and the new family take (care), and may God keep all of you safe.

Your Friend always,

Jimmy

*Thinking
of
You…*

…and

Thought I'd

Send a

Friendly

Hello

Your

Way…

*Your Friend,
Jimmy*

Ya Know
I like Easter
much better than
Christmas...

Nice talking with you yesterday. I was happy to know your [sic] alright. I wish you and the family a Happy Easter and hope that things go well for you. Wishing You the Best.

Friends always,
Jimmy

...us Bunny's
don't make
Moral
Judgments
like
Santa!

Happy Easter!

Your Friend,
Jimmy

Sunday 23 April 1995

Dear Bob,

Just a few lines to say hello and to wish you and the family good health and high spirits. As for me, I'm fine, but we're still on lock-down.

Yesterday morning, some guy killed his cell partner. And with us being on lock-down, that don't help matters any, know what I mean.

Hey, I hope this card makes you smile. If I had you for a cellie, we'd pass the day playing gin and casino and some pinochle.

Hey, I got a big favor to ask. We can-not [sic] drag my friends name into this mess. (Nick) You know who I mean. Him and the other one (Steve). When I see you, I'll try to explain it. But <u>please</u> keep those two names covered.

Also, let me know how our friend is doing over in Lansing. I've sent him a couple of letters, trying to keep him up to date.

Also, what do you think about Jesse's story. Please let me know on that. Also, how do things look with our friends in Ca.?

The way things are going back here, I'm about to run out of financial backing and Julius is looking for more money. I'm going to have to do something pretty soon. Either shit or get off the pot. I just got a letter from Julius and he says things look real good for me. But hell, I'd like an early Christmas. I'm tired of this place!

There's not a whole lot of news on my end. Oh yea, I still haven't received the papers on Bradley A. I'm really curious as to what he said at the hearings.

Well you and the family take care and keep a close watch over your shoulder. I don't want to lose a good friend.

                                              God Bless,
                                              Friends,
                                              Jimmy

Nice talking with you yesterday. I was happy to know your alright. I wish you and the family a Happy Easter and hope that things go well for you. Wishing You the Best.

       Friends always,
       Jimmy

Ya Know, I like Easter much better than Christmas...

B. Bunny
Carrot-Patch
Route one
U.S.A.

...Us Bunny's don't make Moral Judgments like Santa!

Happy Easter!

  Your Friend,
  Jimmy

... are we having Fun or What? :)

Your Friend
Jimmy

Keep on Smiling!

O.K. Bob, Name what Else you Want to Do?

O.K. Bob,

Name what
Else you
Want to Do?

...are we
having
Fun or
What?
☺

Your Friend,
Jimmy

Keep on Smiling!
☺

Friday 02 June 1995

R. Vernon
2206 Foxhill Dr.
Martinez, Ca

Dear Bob,

Just a note to say hello, and I hope this finds you and your family in the best of health. As for me, I'm fine.

The last time I talked with you, you said that you had mailed me a letter. So far, I have not received it and that was over 2 weeks ago.

We finally got off lock-down, but not for long. We're back on again. They hit a Captain, stabbed him in the back several times and he's in the hospital in pretty bad shape. So I expect we'll be on lock-down for some time.

I have no idea when they'll decide to let us have a phone call, but if you need to talk to me, call SuperI. Nelson and get me, as I still haven't talked to the warden. I've never even said hello to him. ☺

Well, that's all for now drop me a line and bring me up to date on things. By the way, I did talk to our Friend Mr. G. Please ask him, if I'm to send his letters to the address on the card he gave me and please let me know A.S.A.P. O.K. ☺

                                                  Your Friend,

                                                  Jimmy

Panel 1: "Ya know Bob, When God Made You, He Threw Away the Mold..."

Panel 2: "He Knew Trouble When He Saw it!"

Your Friend Jimmy

Ya Know Bob,
When God
Made You,
He Threw Away
the Mold...

He Knew
Trouble
When He
Saw it!

Your Friend
Jimmy

Sunday 18 June 1995

Dear Bob,

Just a few lines to say hello and to wish you a Happy Father's Day. I hope this finds you in the best of health and high spirits. As for me, I'm doing fine. We're still of (off) lock-down ☺ and I'm getting to the yard to work-out. I'm beat red and sore all over. I got in an excellent work-out this morning on the bench. Plus I did inclines and declines. But I'm feeling good.

I still haven't received anything from you, mail or Fax! Whenever I hear from you, I always answer right back.

I'm playing my guitar and doing some art pictures for the next art show. I hope I sell some at this show. I missed the last 2 art shows because of lock-downs.

Well, not much news on my end. You take care and watch your back. Not everybody out there loves us. ☺

Take care.

Your Friend,

Jimmy

*You've Got
That Certain
Something…*

*…but
What it is,
I
Really
Don't
Know!*
☺

*Friends,
Jimmy*

*It's That
Time
Again,
got the
Urge…*

*…to
Wish
You
A
Merry
Christmas!*

*Your Crazy Friend,
Jimmy*

Monday 26 Aug. 1996

Dear Bob,

I just received the package two hours ago. I've read it only once, but I'll read it a few more times. Something keeps nagging at the back of my brain. Thank you very much for sending it.

As soon as I finished reading it, I made a card for you, had to rush it, as it's almost mail-time, (pick up to go out), and I wanted to write you a few lines.

I've a couple of things, I'd like for you to check if possible. See if this "Pete Licavoli," had a brother named "Jack" that died in a Federal Prison, "OXFORD" that's in Wis., where I was at. I was with Jack when he died at Oxford. His cell was right across from mine. That morning, me and a friend help(ed) him go to the Med, line, on the compound. He told the P.A. "I feel bad, I think I had a heart-a-tac [sic] earlier." They told him go lay down and take an asprin [sic]. At noon, we did the same thing over again. Later that afternoon, the Ol' man was in very bad shape. We kept yelling for a Med-Tec(h), but he never came till Jack was dead. "Jack Licavoli" was out of the Cleveland and Youngstown Ohio area. He was the "Man" for that area. You know what I mean.

This Guy Holt, and Twombly, I swear I cannot remember either one of them. But by some of the things Holt says, our paths should have crossed way before the assassination. They should have crossed in Southern FL., Atlanta or Savannah.

Also, if you know what Federal Prison O. Bosch is in, and if you write him and he will write you, please send him a photo of me and see if he remembers me, especially from the 70's. But he may be leery about talking about me, but I'd just like to know if he remembers me.

If you can't find out any of these items, please don't worry about it. O.K.

I hope this finds you and the family in good health and tell your wife I said hello and send best wish's [sic].

Mail pick up 5 min, got to run. Take care, watch yourself and God Bless.

Friends,

Jimmy

Thank You for the Reading Material, I really enjoyed it.

*Friends,
Jimmy*

Tuesday, 01 Oct. 1996

Dear Bob,

Just a few lines to say hello and to let you know that I received your letter last night and as always, I was delighted to hear from you.

But first let me say, "I AM NOT MAD AT YOU." It is entirely my fault, for saying too much. I should never have opened my big mouth. I broke my own rule! But that's now history, no sense dwelling on it. Right!

Now on to the future. Yes, I know there is a big drive on to discreadit [sic] me. If there wasn't then I'd really be worried.

But the people trying to help me are not F.B.I. They're mostly trying to keep me from being indicted. I will not make a deal with the F.B.I.! That is out of the Question. The people from the Dirksen Building (Feds) in Chicago are wasting their time if they come back out here. So we can forget all about that. But be sure to tell Don that I appreciate his concern very much. Oh yea, I can never accept a "Proffer Agreement" on any terms not even for my freedom.

I do not expect you to go to jail for obstructing justice. Therefore, I will not endanger you, by saying anything to put you on the spot.

I am very thankful that I never let you go pick up the paper work that is put away. For had you turned that over to the judge, I would have several friends in prison at this time. And you can-not [sic] believe how close you was to me giving that up to you. I shudder even to think about it.

I am not going to hurt this second video. I am going to stall the people back East till well after the first of the year. I am going to try and help push this second video. I want you and Ms. West to receive your share of the money from the interview, therefore, if I can help push this second one from M.P.I., I will.

I know I said I was going to kill it, but I'm not. I only wish you had told me before, how tight your money was, then I would not have called so often. Hell, anything I had to say, I could say by letter. I do not want to be an added burden to you.

I'm going to drop a line to M.P.I. and ask if there's anyway that I can help promote the video. I got a couple of ideas, but I best check before I do it. I'd hate to cost you money at this stage.

I'm thinking about answering the letter from "Kreiter" at "U.P.I." This person hates me so bad, I should be able to get some real controversy free advertising out of them. ☺ They sent me a list of questions maybe I can get their goat!

I always enjoy your visits, but if it cost <u>you</u> money to come here, stay home and write me.

Hey, I couldn't pass up doing this card for you. ☺ I'm sure you remember "Marvin the Martian", and I just had to toss in the 12 Group for the hell of it.

Oh yea, they showed on T.V. why Ruby killed Oswald, he had an Alien inside him that made him do it. This series Dark Skies is really cracking me up. If anyone believes any of that shit, they really have to be dumb. Yet, I guess there will be some that do believe it.

Please excuse my sloppy writing, but I'm writing too fast. Tell your wife I said hello, take care and watch yourself.

Friends,

Jimmy

Thursday 03 Oct 1996

Dear Bob,

Just a few lines to bring you up to date. I wanted to write you last night but I was too sick. I barely made it through the C.M.A. awards.

I hope this finds you feeling better and up and about. As for me, I'm not sure which end is up.

Yesterday, "Ali" from "M.P.I." came to see me. When I got back, my lunch tray was on my chuck-hole door. I ate it, then about 15 minutes later, I got dizzy, my stomach was rolling, I was getting cramps, then I started barfing everything up. I got most of it out of me. Then I drank some warm salt water to put some thing in my stomach, so I'd have something else I could barf, to wash out my stomach. So anyway, 3 hours later I've still got pain in all my joints, but it's fading. Anyway, I'm able to sit up and write. I think the meal on my tray was bad. The funny thing is, no one else on my wing was sick.

Anyway, I wanted to write you last night and tell you about the visit. I was willing to help on the second video, like I told you I would. Anyway before I got to that part, he ask(ed) me some questions and I didn't feel like answering them. As time progressed, I had a change of heart. Besides, I started to read between things that were not being said.

"Ali" has his own pipe-line I guess. He seemed concerned about some one punching a couple holes and me saying nothing. Besides, he doesn't seem too, what do you call it, "enthusiasm" [sic] I guess. Anyway, I get the feeling he wants to drop it. I think maybe he's afraid of investing a lot of money, then losing his ass. Now I'm not saying that's what's happening, it's just my feeling. Him and I will have to talk again at a later date after things calm down. Don't get me wrong, he was very nice. I think most of it was me. Maybe I was being too tight, too much on guard. After all, I'm very leery about saying, about talking, to people anymore, or trusting anyone. Hell I don't know what will be turned over to the F.B.I.

I told him I was thinking of getting us some free publicity. I was going to start some shit by talking to that "Kreitier" reporter from "U.P.I.", here in Chicago. But he dosen't [sic] want me to talk to any news people at all.

I promised you, I wouldn't talk to anyone. I kept my word on that. But a couple of months ago, you said our agreement was finished and I could now talk to anyone I wanted to. Well, I still haven't talked to anyone. But now, I feel like having a little fun, and, I have <u>NO</u> agreements with anyone else. So if I want to stir up a pot of shit, then I don't see why I can't. ☺

Oh yea, those songs about Kennedy? Am I free to send them to a publishing Co., or do you hold the rights on them. I think they would make a good lead story to the Star or Globe, or I can send them to someone I think that might be interested in them, and they might even get published, just because of the video that's out. Please let me know. As I don't want to do anything to hurt you.

I'm going to speak point blank to you. And I'm not referring to "Ali" in what I have to say. This took place before you got involved with him. But it's people around you, were trying to use you to make a buck, which is O.K., as every one looks out for themselves, but you didn't know that some people were trying to sell you out one hundred and one percent. Someday, I'll tell you about it. When I tell you, you will know I'm not lying to you, as I've had no contact with any of your people other than "Ervin" and this never came from him.

I wish I could have kept the notes to show you, but that would have been much too risky. After our phone conversation from the yard, that Friday morning when the phone kept being cut off. Well, when I go back to my cell, it had been thoroughly searched. I mean turned upside down. Anyway, the only one around you, that's been working with you, is Ms. West, that you can trust. You better be very dam(n) careful about anyone else. You see, no, I don't know how to say this on paper. Read between the lines. One little pig went to the farm so that he could steal the corn. But was caught by the farmer then tried to make a deal. But the farmer thought, if this greedy little pig doesn't want to share with the other little pigs, then how can I trust him to be honest with me?

Someday, I'll tell you the whole story and it will make more sense to you. But for now, just please be careful in who you trust and what you say to other people.

You and me gave away the biggest story of the century. Hell, I never believed it was that big or that, that many people cared. You and me, we're a day late and a bundle short. Oh well, that's life.

Sorry there's no card this time, but I'm too sick to draw anything and I've wrote [sic] 4 pages more than I was going to. I was just going to send a note to bring you up to date on things.

Tell Kathy hello and I'll keep you posted, be careful, take care and God Bless.

Friends,

Jimmy

P.S. Hope you can read this!!!

Sunday 06 Oct 1996

Dear Bob,

Just a few lines to say hello and to say it was really nice to see you yesterday. Sorry the time was so short. Also, I got your letter last night and when they opened it to inspect it, they cut the picture in two. But I was able to tape it together and it looks alright. Thank you very much.

When I saw that picture, I thought I might break right down and cry. It sure brought back some wonderful memory's [sic].

First of all, I got one thing to say! You and I have a friendship, Waleed and I do not. I have very few friends. A lot of associates, but very few friends. SO I AM NOT TAKING FRIEND-SHIP-OVER-FRIEND-SHIP.

If not for you and Ms. West, this thing would never have happened. I'm trying to help you and Ms. West with the second video that M.P.I. was suspose [sic] to do. I've kept my word with every-one. And with the second video, I've nothing coming from that, but I was willing to help get it promoted. But now it's up to you, Waleed Ali and the lawyers.

About Judge Carver, true, the confidential letters you sent him may well be in his safe all locked up and secure. But, THAT DOES NOT MEAN HE DID NOT MAKE COPY'S AND SEND THEM TO THE F.B.I.!!!

Next, it dosen't [sic] matter how long he met with Zack Shelton. Anything he gave to the F.B.I. would have been sent to his main office in that area.

Next, I have had NO-CONTAC [sic] with D. Clark or Barry, so I got nothing from them! As for Waleed, he hasn't givin' me anything, encluding [sic] the time of day. SO-NO-HE-WAS NOT THE SOURCE!

Next, all my information comes from the Dirksen Build. (Federal) out of Chicago, Back East, New York, Langley and down South, Florida. And I've told them nothing, they've told me. Most of them I can-not call or write direct.

I'm truly sorry that you got envolved [sic] with Dick Clark and all the other people. But what's done is done. There's nothing we can do about that. And yes, I see your point!

The Book Jim Marrs is writting [sic]. Who gets the money from that? You and Ms. West, or Dick Clark and M.P.I.?

Did you read the contract that you signed with "Dick Clark" and "M.P.I."? Also, do you have a copy of it and by chance can I get a copy of it? I would like to see it and see if there is some way I can help with-out over stepping any bounds and also by not doing another video.

You know, I still find it hard to believe that you just signed everything over to someone else and lost control. I know I signed all rights over to you and Ms. West. But I just wanted to help you guys and you know I wasn't happy about encluding [sic] the book deal with the video interview.

One more thing, I do not have a deal cooking with anyone, except for my friends back East who have ask(ed) me to sit on my tongue for a while and let them work, while I keep a low profile.

I have turned down several offers, some for big money. I don't go up front any more to see them, as you found out and I don't even answer their letters anymore and I've refused to take their messages from the main control center. I had those thrown away with-out even looking at them. Really I'm tired of all this stuff. At first I got a kick out of all of it. Now I'm just tired of it all.

One other question, if and when I get out, who gets the page from the diary? Do you get it or does Dick Clark and Ali get it due to the contract that you signed?

Also, please let me know who has what to do with the words to the song I wrote, "I Remember Jackie"? I would like to send that to someone if possible, just to see what they think of it.

Hey, I hope this card brings a smile to your face. I bet you haven't seen her for awhile. I really use to get a kick out of her cartoons. Every now and then I see a cartoon of her on channel 11, late at night. It makes me think of when I was a kid.

Listen, tell your wife I said hello and both of you take care and I pray that things will work out. And, <u>you</u> are <u>one</u> of the very few friends that I have.

God Bless,
Friends,

Jimmy

Tuesday 22 Oct 1996

Dear Bob,

I just 2 hrs. ago received your most welcome letter. As always, I'm delighted in hearing from you. But I'm so sorry to hear about your heart attack. Thank God you're alright and at home with your wife.

I'm so happy to hear that you're much better. Just listen to Kathy and try to re-lax [sic] and get plenty rest. I have very few friends and I sure don't want to lose you. So please, take it easy.

Forget about coming here to do another interview. Right now, for me everything is at a <u>FULL-STOP!!!</u> I'm <u>NOT</u> saying another word till I get answers that can only come from back East!

For right now; M.P.I. has two taped interviews of me that you did. There's over 2 ½ hrs. (of) tape. They used the one interview for the first video. Right! So they still got the 2nd interview tape. Right! This is the one they were suppose to go ahead and market. I made an offer to help out. But some where there's a failure to communicate! I don't know who's at fault, but I'll say maybe me.

Anyway, there's a lot of shit going on back East. I'm not sure what it is, but I hope to learn some-thing [sic] with-in [sic] the next 2-or 3 weeks. Someone , really put some shit in at the Company, <u>NOT</u> Family. You get the meaning. ☺

But the thing is this, <u>IF</u>, I plan or decide to go forward with anything, it will be maybe early Spring of 1997!

If M.P.I. decides to go ahead with the second video, it's fine with me. I will try not to hurt or hinder that in anyway.

But it's been a little over 4 years since all this shit started. So I feel that another 6 months won't make that much difference.

There's so much I want to say, but I'm out of time as they'll pick up the mail in about 10 min. And I want this in the mail tonight. I hope you like the card.

I haven't answered Don's letter yet and I'm not signing the contract he sent. But I'll answer his letter in the next day or so. I've been trying to get out for a phone call but I'm not having any luck, it's hard to reach some people in the A.M. hours. I'll write more later. Please take care, and give your wife my love. You're Both Terrific.

Friends,

Jimmy

P.S. They just stabbed a guard in I-House, so there won't be any phone calls for a while.

Get Well Soon...

*Dear Friend,
I sure hope
that you're feeling
much better
and that You're
up and around.
Please take care
And get well soon!*

*Friends,
Jimmy*

Tuesday 05 Nov 1996

Dear Bob,

Just a few lines to say hello and I hope that you're feeling much better.

I tried to call you this past Saturday morning and again this morning, as I wanted to know if you're alright. But I guess you've had a block put on your phone line as the recording says, "Phone calls are not being accepted at this number."

Even if you're mad at me, at least drop a line and let me know that your [sic] alright as I still think of you as a friend, and I am worried about your health.

When I said in my other letter, "don't come to the prison," I ment [sic] while your [sic] in bad health and need your rest. You will always be on my visiting list and I always enjoy seeing you. But when your [sic] in bad health, I just don't think you should be traveling and get your self all upset.

As for interviews, I'm not doing any and I still don't know what M.P.I. is going to do. I've got several people wanting to see me, but I'm seeing no one except my daughter. Waleed came to see me a while back, but like I told you back then, we didn't accomplish anything. So I guess the second video is still up in the air.

I told Don in my last letter to him that maybe down the road we can try to do something so that you and Ms. West can regain some of your money. Right now I'm waiting to see what is ahead for me as far as freedom is concerned.

So on my end there is really nothing new. So I'll close for now. Tell your wife I said hello and you my friend, slow down and take it easy. Take care of your health, O.K. And if your [sic] back this way, please drop by for a visit, like I say, you will always be on list.

      Take Care & God Bless,

      Your Friend, Jimmy

Friday 25 Dec 1998

Dear Bob,

Just a few lines to say hello and Merry Christmas. It's Christmas Day here at the "Ville" and all through the cells, the convicts are locked-up and madder than hell. ☺

Yep, last night we went on lock-down and this will be a long one. Last night coming out of the chow, some one jumped on a couple of cops, beat them up and stabbed them. How bad, I don't know. But we are down for a while, no phone calls, no showers, nothing.

Oh well, that's life here at the "Ville."

But on to business. Please don't send Don. Don't waste the money. We can't do anything. Truly, I'm sorry. But I have to travel the road I started. Tell Zack I said hello and I really did enjoy our visit. Hey, next time you talk to Zack, ask him if he remembers the night the Feds were tailing Chuckie and when he left the Restaurant, on 13th & Lake St. in Melrose Park, and they pulled out to follow him, they hit the kid in the van when he made the U-turn in front of them? The feds were driving a blue buick skylark and they wanted to take the kid to jail. He ran in my resturant [sic] yelling for help. I had the Melrose Park Cops take the kid to the West Lake hosp. So they couldn't arrest him. ☺ They were really pissed that night. Also, the last load of Swing(?) beef I was going to sell them, I never did. Because when we stole the same tractor twice I got nervous. So I sold the load to someone else. But every time I think of Zack sitting next to me playing the pinball machines, I get a big smile on my face. Hey, the man was just doing his job. You know, I do like him, but I don't trust the feds and I think maybe he's still working for them. I'm really surprised he hasn't went [sic] digging for the box I burried [sic]. Believe me, if what he said was true, and I believe him, cause he knew some very small details that other people didn't know, then he was really sitting all over me.☺ Small world my Friend, small world.

Well Pal, I'll close for now. You and the Family take care and Happy New Year.

                                                              Friends,

                                                              Jimmy

Season's

Greetings

To wish you

all the joys

of this very

special season.

Happy New Year

Friends,
Jimmy

----- Original Message -----
From: Cher Johnson
To: Wim Dankbaar
Sent: Tuesday, March 22, 2005 7:06 AM
Subject: Re: last 4

Hey Wim,

Here's the last 4 and I have to say I'm sad there aren't any more. I feel like I'm losing a friend.

I have greatly enjoyed transcribing Jimmy's letters and I'm tempted to write to him myself!

I don't know if there were other letters written between Jimmy and Bob that you don't have possession of, but if there aren't any more, it seems that Bob either became afraid that "they" were trying to kill him too, or that once he couldn't get any more information from Jimmy, he no longer wanted to be bothered with him.

I get the feeling that Jimmy was used and abused all of his life and I feel sorry for him, especially if Bob was just another user as well. I guess this is why I give any thought to writing Jimmy myself--to show him that there are people who are not interested only in what they can get from him. but I would never do this without permission from you. I would not ever interfere with what you're doing.

I have no bad feelings toward Jimmy, even knowing some of the things he did. He was only doing a job. Who ever ordered the hit on Kennedy is to blame. I'm sure turning a job down, whether a "Company" job or a "Family" job doesn't assure you a very long life. I think of Jimmy to a certain extent as a victim himself. A victim of a ruined family life, a victim of the military, the C.I.A., the government, and the "Mob," and perhaps by so-called friends. He was so young when he got involved in all of this.

Anyway, thank you for the opportunity to do this for you and for the opportunity to get to know Jimmy. If you ever need my help again, please don't hesitate to ask.

Cher

Correspondence with Pamela Ray

Preface

Forty years ago, on November 22, 1963, there was a conspiracy for a sudden and violent overthrow of the Constitutional government in United States of America. It happened one day in Dallas, Texas at a place called Dealey Plaza. America experienced a COUP D'ETAT - A SUDDEN OVERTHROW OF A GOVERNMENT BY A GROUP OF PERSONS IN OR PREVIOUSLY IN POSITIONS OF AUTHORITY IN DELIBERATE VIOLATION OF CONSTITUTIONAL FORMS.

A rare and unique opportunity has presented itself to get the inside story from one of the participants involved in the actual shooting of President John F. Kennedy. The "open door" into history, which the reader will pass through, will be more like entering the proverbial Pandora's box. The shocking true account James Files reveals about the dual Mafia/ CIA role in the overthrow of America's government is very disturbing to say the least.

Mr. Files has a very interesting background and history. He has worked for the United States Military, the CIA and the "Family" out of Chicago. His duties included working in Laos in 1959 as an "advisor", a driver for Organized Crime Chicago hit man Charles Nicoletti, a hired contract assassin for the government of the United States of America –The CIA.

James E. Files was the gunman who fired the infamous headshot to President John F. Kennedy from behind the picket fence on the grassy knoll in Dealey Plaza November 22, 1963.

His CIA-controller, David Atlee Phillips, was the one who provided the XP-100 Remington "Fireball" pistol/rifle to James Files. Phillips was also the one who told Lee Harvey Oswald where Files was staying the week prior to the assassination.

James Files' mafia- mentor Charles Nicoletti, along with Johnny Roselli, was in the Dal-Tex Building. Charles Nicoletti did the shooting from the back. Just for the record, not to mention the HELL Marina Oswald Porter and her family have suffered over the years, Lee Harvey Oswald didn't fire a single shot that day. Like he said during his brief custody, he DID NOT kill President John F. Kennedy or Officer J. D. Tippit. (See Oswald's last words included in this book.) Lee H. Oswald was, is, and ever will be the "official" government patsy.

James Files was merely a pawn in the "game of princes." He was a contract government employee and has provided many first hand accounts of some of the most famous CIA events in recent history; including but not limited to the assassination of President John F. Kennedy, the CIA's "secret wars" in Southeast Asia, CIA international drug smuggling better known as the "War on Drugs", and the CIA overthrow of Chile, as well as the 1976 assassination of Orlando Letelier in "the only daylight assassination carried out on Washington D.C.'s Embassy Row".

Files recalls seeing the President of Chile, Salvador Allende, being shot for good measure in a stairway as each soldier passed by his lifeless body. Allende did not commit suicide.

The question of "Why was President Kennedy assassinated?" has been covered in Jim Garrison's *On the Trail of the Assassins*, L. Fletcher Prouty's 1992 book *JFK: The CIA, Vietnam, and the Plot to Assassinate John F. Kennedy*, Jim Marrs' 1989 *CROSSFIRE: The Plot that Killed Kennedy*, to name just a few works published. With this book, we will start answering the questions "Who assassinated President Kennedy? Who were the co-conspirators? "Who has the power and means to cover it up?" What are the obvious implications AND most importantly, "What, as citizen's of a free country, are we going to do about it?"

The definition of **"conspiracy"** from The American Heritage Dictionary, 1976 Second College Edition, is as follows:

1. An agreement to perform together an illegal, treacherous, or evil act.

2. A group of conspirators.

3. A combining or acting together, as if by evil design: *a conspiracy of natural forces*.

4. *Law* An agreement between two or more persons to commit a crime or to accomplish a legal purpose through illegal action. **Synonyms**: *conspiracy, plot, machination, collusion, intrigue, cabal*. These nouns denote secret plans or schemes. *Conspiracy* refers to such a plan by a group intent usually on a bold purpose, such as overthrowing a government. *Plot* stresses sinister means and motives but may be small or large in number of participants and scope. *Machination*, usually in the plural, strongly implies crafty, underhand dealing by one or more persons, but is generally less forceful that the preceding terms. *Collusion* refers to secret agreement between persons, usually with intent to defraud others. *Intrigue* denotes a complex, clandestine scheme; usually it implies selfish, petty actions rather than criminal ends. *Cabal* refers to a conspiratorial group or to its actions, which usually are directed against a government or political leader.

Before leaving the technical and legal definitions of conspiracy, here is what former navy pilot in WWII, airline captain with domestic and international flights, inspector-investigator for the FAA, member of Association of Former Intelligence Agents, member of International Society of Air Safety Investigators, member of the Lawyer-Pilots Bar Association, among other prestigious groups not listed, author and crusader Rodney Stich has to say about CONSPIRACY from his book Defrauding America 3rd Edition 1998, p. 712-713:

Conspiracy is an agreement between two or more persons to accomplish an unlawful act. Conspiracy is a separate offense over and above whatever other acts the parties conspired to accomplish. The existence of a conspiracy is usually determined from *circumstantial evidence*, looked at collectively. This is usually the only means of determining a conspiracy, (United States v. Calaway 9th Cir. 524 F.2d 609.) and is generally established by *a number of indefinite acts, each of which, standing alone, might have little weight. But taken collectively, they point unerringly to the existence of a conspiracy*. (State v. Horton, 275 NC 651, 170 SE2d 466.) The existence of a conspiracy may be proven by *inference from conduct, statements, documents and facts and circumstances* which disclose a common design on the part of the accused persons and others to act together in pursuance of a common criminal purpose. This offense is rampant throughout these pages. It is a common tactic to ridicule anyone claiming a conspiracy exists, even though conspiracies are possibly the most common offense committed, being a simply an agreement between two or more people to commit some act.

****

We hold these truths to be self- evident: that all men are created equal; that they are endowed by their Creator with certain inalienable rights; that among these are life, liberty, and the pursuit of happiness. That to secure these rights, governments are instituted among men, deriving their just powers from the consent of the governed; that whenever any form of government becomes destructive of these ends it is the right of the people to alter or to abolish it, and to institute a new government, laying its foundation on such principles, and organizing its powers in safety and happiness. Prudence, indeed, will dictate, that governments long established should not be changed for light and transient causes; and accordingly all experience hath shown, that mankind are more disposed to suffer, while evils are sufferable, than to right themselves by abolishing the forms to which they are accustomed. BUT when <u>a long train of abuses and usurpations</u>, pursuing invariably the same object, evinces design to reduce them under absolute despotism, <u>it is their right, IT IS THEIR DUTY, TO THROW OFF SUCH GOVERNMENT, AND TO PROVIDE NEW GUARDS FOR THEIR FUTURE SECURITY."</u>

Declaration of Independence in Congress July 4th, 1776

"The President, Vice-President, and all civil officers of the United States shall be removed from office on impeachment for, and conviction of treason, bribery, or other high crimes and misdemeanors."

- United States of America Constitution, Article 2 Section 4.

In the journeys during the course of my research I came across a film at Blockbuster Video filmed in 1994 and released in 1996 called <u>*THE MURDER OF JFK: CONFESSION OF AN ASSASSIN.*</u> This is how I originally found out about James Files in late 1998. I was very impressed that he was endangering himself and showed courage to tell the truth about the events surrounding the assassination of President John F. Kennedy. On February 22, 1999 I wrote him a simple letter thanking him for telling the truth. We developed a friendship and on September 6-7, 2000 I visited James Files at Stateville Prison. It was then he asked me to do this book. I said, "Yes, with God's help." It hasn't been easy to communicate with James Files being a political prisoner of the FBI and CIA, incarcerated at a maximum-security prison. Letters usually take a minimum of two to three weeks to get to him, sensitive information usually a month or longer. HIGHLY MONITORED, taped phone calls, give or take all the lock-downs, have only been since April 2000.

Little did I know when starting this project I would witness the most horrific terrorist attack on the American people by its own government September 11, 2001. Knowing full well how the U.S. Government really operates, Files has a lot to say on this terrible event and many other "Black-Ops" sanctioned by the leaders of our country, starting with his involvement in Southeast Asia, and Central and South America.

James Files - Brief Background

P.J.: For the record, please state your full name and any other names you have gone by, starting with your birth name.

James: My full name is James Earl Sutton. I was born at home in Oakman, Alabama on the 24th day of January 1942. Since that time I have used too many different names to remember all of them. But some are recorded and on record through criminal investigations concerning my past history. Some of them are; Henry Sanders, John Felter, Sergio Castillo, which were all real living people, and the name that I am now currently incarcerated under is James Earl Files. (Files has used this last name since 1963- authorized by the U.S. government. SSN: 323-34-9241. FBI No. 2703-0579-1514 L. Government copy of Birth Certificate says "Death at birth." The man who doesn't exist. His first arrest was 07-03-59.)

P: What brought you to Melrose Park, Illinois? When was this?

J: J. D. Files was run out of Alabama by the law for bootlegging, gambling, fighting and making all kinds of trouble for the law. He went to St. Louis, Missouri and my mother went to Mobile, Alabama looking for work in order to take care of my sister and me. While she was in Mobile, Alabama, she met a navy captain by the name of Les Sutton. What I learned many years later, they had an affair. Les Sutton is my father. Les Sutton resigned from the Navy in San Diego, California. Upon his discharge, he sent for my mother and she went to California to marry him. My mother had left my sister and me with our grandparents while she went to California to marry him. They returned to Alabama and got my sister and me and took us back to California with them so we could be a family. Life was good, but all of a sudden, bad luck. Les Sutton was injured at Boulder Dam when a large pipe fell on him causing a serious injury. Shortly thereafter, my mother took my sister and me and relocated to the Chicago area. We first settled in Northlake, Illinois, just next door to Melrose Park, Illinois. There I attended a school by the name of Sunnyside in Berkley, Illinois. Later we moved into Melrose Park, Illinois so my mother would be closer to her work within walking distance, as we had no car. There I attended the Melrose Park Public School under the name James Sutton and graduated under that name. I started high school at Proviso East, also under the name James Sutton but I never finished the first year. I believe that was 1958. At that time I got into some serious trouble.

P: At what age did Charles Nicoletti approached you to be his driver?

J: That would have been 1962. I would have been 20 years of age.

Nicoletti, Charles
AKA: Chuck, Chuckie, Charles Nicoletta
DESCRIPTION: Born December 3, 1916; 5'10", 180 pounds, brown eyes, dark but graying hair, dark complexion, gold front tooth; Edu: 8th grade; RO: Italian: FH: brother Carl; stepfather, Paul Tergo, deported following prison term in ISPJ (Illinois State Penitentiary, Joliet). FREQUENTS: Caravelle Motel, Blackie's Pizzeria, Italian-American National Union No. 9. Resides at 1638 N. 19th Ave., Melrose Park.
RECORD: FBI No. 1426506. (Chicago Identification Record) CIR No. 1634. (United States Penitentiary, Milan, Michigan) USPM No. 10113. Record dates back to 1934, more than 12 arrests: furnishing equipment to handbook operators, conspiracy, gambling, possession of auto rigged as "hit car," murder – questioned in most of the gang killings involving top

hoods and politicians in the past 30 years (shot and killed his father in 1929 during an assault on subject and mother – ruled justifiable homicide). Convictions: burglary, 1 year probation and $5,000 fine; narcotics, 18 months in USPM.
BUSINESS: Several auto and insurance agencies, taverns, restaurants, variety stores.
MODUS OPERANDI: Gambling boss of Monroe Police District on West Side. A Syndicate enforcer in charge of planning and executing gangland murders; active in narcotics.
Demaris, Ovid, <u>CAPTIVE CITY: CHICAGO IN CHAINS</u>, New York, NY, Lyle Stuart, Inc., 1969, p-347-348

P: Have you ever served in the United States Military? In what capacity, where, and for how long?

J: Yes, I served in the U.S. Army in the 82nd Airborne. I took my airborne training at Fort Bragg in North Carolina. In July of 1959 I was shipped out to Laos. I was with Special Operations and we were heavily involved in "Operation White Star." I worked in the capacity of an "Advisor." I specialized in small arms and explosives. Most of our work was training Laos's soldiers to hit and run and set up M.A.'s (mechanical ambush) and how to disrupt communications and supply lines. I was in Laos for about 14 months.

P: After returning from Laos back to the United States, please explain what happened and who approached you from the CIA, and for what reason?

J: Upon my return from Laos, I was at Fort Mead and from there to the Veteran's Hospital in Maywood, Illinois. I was there for evaluation. Some people wanted to see if I was crazy or not. Just before my return to the States, there was a problem and I handled it my way. My way of handling the problem was in question, so I was sent for evaluation. Just prior to my release from the hospital, David Atlee Phillips came to see me and introduced himself to me. Said he had a job I might be interested in. At that time he never said he worked for the CIA, but I knew he was from the government without him telling me that. It's just one of those things you know without being told. He recruited me to train some people in guerrilla warfare. At that time I did not realize I was being recruited for the "Bay of Pigs."

P: When you were assisting Mr. Nicoletti what type of work were you involved in? What group or Family did he work for? Who was the Boss at that time?

J: With Mr. Nicoletti I drove the car for him when he went out to attend to business. Mostly contract murder. He worked for Mr. Giancana. But at that time Mr. Giancana was taking his orders from Mr. Tony Accardo. Better known as "Big Tuna."

Mr. Accardo was calling all the shots. He told Mr. Giancana what was to be done and everyone got their orders from Mr. Giancana. The last time I saw and spoke with Mr. Accardo was around September 1963 when I was standing guard at his new home. I was on the outer parameter.

P: Who was handing down orders in 1963?

J: Mr. Tony Accardo.

("Bittersweet it will be in Chicago when Tony Accardo leaves the O.C. scene one way or another, because he is the only living link between the LCN today and the Capone era.

Accardo was a soldier under Capone in the 1920's, a capo under Nitti in the 1930's, the underboss under Ricca in the 1940's, the boss himself from the mid 1940's until 1957, the consiglieri to Giancana, Battaglia, Alderisio and Cerone in the 1960's, a member of the trumvirate which led the Chicago mob in the 1970's and since then the consiglieri again to the present time. [1984] A most important Chicago functionary, the most important, for parts of seven decades.

Accardo is undoubtedly the most important O.C. leader in the world today. I have been doing, as you know, extensive work on O.C. in New York, for instance, since I retired and there is no one there today with anywhere near the stature of Accardo." p-430 William F. Roemer Jr., ACCARDO: THE GENUINE GOODFATHER, 1995. Mr. Roemer is a former FBI agent, thirty years as the senior agent on the organized-crime squad in Chicago.)

Accardo, Anthony Joseph

AKA: (nee Antonio Leonardo Accardo) Tony Accardo, Arcado, Joe Batters, Big Tuna, Joe Batty.

DESCRIPTION: Born April 28, 1906, Chicago; 5 feet 9 ½ inches, 190 pounds, brown eyes, black hair, dark complexion, tattoo of "Dove" base of right thumb outer, several irregular scars back of left hand; Edu: 6th grade; MS; rejected; RO: Sicilian; FH: son, Anthony Ross; brother Martin Leonardo; sisters, Martha (Mrs. Dominick Senese), Maria (Mrs. Tarquin Simonelli).

FREQUENTS: Singapore Steak and Chop House, Armory Lounge, Mike's Fish and Fritzes's restaurants, and other favorite hoodlum hangouts in the Loop, Near North Side and western suburbs. Resides at 1407 Ashland Ave., River Forest.

RECORD: FBI No. 1410106. CPD No. D-83436. FPC NO. 31-WMO/4-W-OI. Record dates back to 1922, more than 27 arrests: carrying concealed weapons, gambling, extortion, kidnapping, murder. Convicted of income tax evasion, sentenced to 6 years in prison, fined $15,000 – reversed on appeal, acquitted in second trial. Prime suspect in several murders. Cited as on of 28 Public Enemies by Chicago Crime Commission in 1931, where he was listed as a suspect in the murders of Joe Aiello, Jack Zuta and "Mike de Pike" Heitler, and suspected gunman in the St. Valentine's Day Massacre. Never spent a night in jail. Cited for contempt of Congress in Kefauver hearings; took Fifth 144 times before McClellan Committee.

BUSINESS: In everything from baking to trucking, from coal and lumber to hotels and restaurants, from currency exchanges to travel agencies. Has substantial investments in Florida, Arizona, Nevada, California, and South America.

MODUS OPERANDI: Former bodyguard of Al Capone, he came to power following the suicide of Frank Nitti in 1943. Ruled Syndicate until 1956, when Giancana became chief enforcer. Presently chairman of the Syndicate's board of directors, and one of the top Mafiosi in the nation.

Demaris, Ovid, CAPTIVE CITY: CHICAGO IN CHAINS, New York, NY, Lyle Stuart, Inc., 1969, p-322-323.

Tony Accardo died May 27, 1992 in St. Mary's of Nazareth Hospital on the west side of Chicago at the age of 86. The cause of death was congestive heart failure, acute respiratory failure, pneumonia and chronic obstructive pulmonary disease. <u>ACCARDO</u>, p-429.

Giancana, Sam

AKA: (born Gilormo Giangono, baptized Momo Salvatore Giangono), Momo, Moe, The Cigar, Sam Mooney, Sam Moonie, J. Moonie, Sam Gincani, Giancaco, Gianenna, Gianeana, Giancona, Albert Masusco, Albert Manusco, Michael Mancuso, G. Stanley, P. Rosie, Sam Flood, Sam Volpe.

DESCRIPTION: Born May 24, 1908 (baptismal record says June 15, 1908), Chicago; 5 feet 9 inches, 165 pounds, brown eyes, black hair (balding), fair complexion, oblique scar 2 centimeters right front of nose; Edu: 6th grade; MS: rejected, classified as psychopath; RO: Sicilian; FH: daughters, Antoinette (Mrs. Carmen Manno), Bonita Lucille (Mrs. Anthony Tisci), Francine Marie (Mrs. James Perno); brothers, Joseph and Charles; nephew-in-law, State Senator Anthony DeTolve.

FREQUENTS: Fresh Meadows Golf Club, Armory Lounge, Airliner Lounge, Mike's Restaurant, Central Envelope & Lithographic Co., Maggio's Steak House, clubs along Mannheim Road, Fontainebleau Hotel (Miami), visits Mexico, Europe, Hawaii, and Las Vegas. Resides at 1147 S. Wenonah Ave., Oak Park now in Cuernavaca, Mexico.

RECORD: FBI No. 58437. (Chicago Police Department) CPD No. E-27465. (Illinois State Penitentiary, Joliet) ISPJ No. 2807. (United States Penitentiary, Terre Haute, Indiana) USPTH No. 104. (Fingerprinting code classification) FPC No.25-10-15/4-00. Record dates back to 1925, more than 70 arrests: contributing to delinquency, vagrancy, burglary, assault and battery, larceny, fugitive, assault to kill, damage by violence, conspiracy to operate a "book," possession of burglar tools and concealed weapons, bombing suspect, gambling, fictitious driver's license, murder; prime suspect in countless murder investigations, three before the age of twenty: indicted on one at 18, released on bail, charge stricken following the murder of key witnesses. Convictions: auto theft, 30 days; burglary, 1 to 5 years in ISPJ; operating a still, 4 years in USPTH. Served 1 year for contempt of federal grand jury, released June 1, 1966. Took Fifth 35 times before McClellan Committee.

BUSINESS: Nationwide investments in legitimate enterprises through fronts. Substantial interests in Florida, Nevada and West Indies.

MODUS OPERANDI: Boss of all bosses in the Chicago Syndicate and member of the Mafia's National Commission. <u>Captive City: Chicago in Chains</u>, 1969, p-341-342.

Sam Giancana was murdered in his home June 18, 1975. The FBI agent in charge of Chicago's O.C. squad, William Roemer, speculates Tony Accardo ordered his death and used Butch Blasi. (p-321-322 <u>ACCARDO</u>)

James Files speculates it was the government that ordered the hit and they used someone who crossed the lines between the government (CIA) and O.C. - perhaps Johnny Roselli. He did see him driving towards Sam's house that night and heard about the murder before it was announced in the morning news.

P: Who approached Mr. Giancana for work to be done? Were you aware of Sam Giancana's association with Johnny Roselli at this point in time? Do you know if David Atlee Phillips ever had direct contact with Sam Giancana?

J: I have no idea who would approach Mr. Giancana for work to be done. But anything major would have to be cleared with Mr. Accardo. Yes, I was aware of Sam Giancana's association with Johnny Roselli. I do not know if David Atlee Phillips ever had direct contact with Sam Giancana.

P: Jimmy where were you on November 22, 1963?

J: I was in Dallas, Texas in Dealey Plaza.

P: Why did you come to Dallas, Texas?

J: To transport weapons for the assassination of John F. Kennedy.

P: Please take me back to the first conversations that were had concerning the assassination of JFK?

J: It was early 1963. I was at the Harlo Grill in Melrose Park, Illinois playing the pinball machines. Mr. Nicoletti came in and told me "Let's go for a ride we need to talk. I said "Yeah, in a few minutes as soon as I finish this game." Mr. Nicoletti tilted the machine on me and said, "You're finished. Let's go." I never said a word; I just got up and followed him out. Mr. Nicoletti didn't like me throwing my money away. I used to blow all my money playing pinball machines and betting on horses at the track. I'd bet my last dollar and go hungry. He could never understand that part of me. But, neither could I. Anyway, he told me that we were going to do my friend. I thought at first that he was referring to one of my good friends that I was going to the track with. My friend had been robbing the vending machines and the people were not happy with him. (At a later date this friend of mine was killed for robbing the vending machines.)

Letter 516 December 21, 2002 James Files to author

Now, before I get off on to something else, let me go back to the printed material in 445, with 26 pages total. Most of it I have already commented on. What I still have to comment on is the JFK stuff. I'm sitting here looking at the black and white picture of Kennedy and I have to say, the printer did a good job on that picture.

On the 7 pages that you ask me to comment on:

Page one "Is the map Charles Nicoletti and you received from Jack Ruby like this one?"

(*Dallas Times Herald* November 21, 1963 evening edition showing the zigzag off main to Houston and Elm on the front page. The other map I sent to him was from *The Dallas Morning News* November 22, 1963 where the Presidential Motorcade Route was published showing the arrival at Love Field and no change off Main Street going straight onto Stemmons Freeway to end at the Trade Mart. Somebody at the *Dallas Times Herald* "knew" of the last minute changes of the motorcade route. Maps from Dallas Public Library – History & Archives Division. May 2, 2001.)

No, it had been hand drawn in pencil I believe. It's been a long time, but yes it was hand drawn. And I'm almost one hundred percent sure it was done in pencil. As for page two, the hand drawn map was only of the Plaza, not all the routes that they are showing in this paper. We had all of that like a month before I ever went down there, maybe even longer, as we had - Chuck and me - already figured that there would be changes made before the date ever arrived. We had also been told that the other routes had been considered. But when you took the map of Dallas, there wasn't that many different routes that you use. And, we knew that he had to travel slow in order for the people to see him. I mean, this didn't need Einstein to figure this one out. All we really needed was a place of arrival and destination. Then get a little last minute information like we did in order to make it all a success. But Chuck would have never planned something like this from just a newspaper.

And as for page three, there's not much I can say about that.

(*The Dallas Morning News* November 23, 1963 Section 1 page 3

Pictures: Close up of the window and boxes, view from the Texas School Book Depository - Caption: "This is the sixth-floor window where the killer lay in wait. He watched through a telescope sight as President John F. Kennedy's motorcade moved along Elm Street."

Picture of the front of the TSBD's looking from Main Street. Caption: "Bullets come from the sixth floor of Texas School Book Depository."

Headline: "Witness From The News Describes Assassination"

By Mary E. Woodward

Four of us from Women's News, Maggie Brown, Aurella Alonzo, my roommate Ann Donaldson, and myself had decided to spend our lunch hour by going to see the President.

We took our lunch along – some crackers and apples – and started walking down Houston Street. **We decided to cross Elm and wait there on the grassy slope just east of the Triple Underpass**, since there weren't many people there and we could get a better view.

We had been waiting about half an hour when the first motorcycle escorts came by, followed shortly by the President's car. The President was looking straight ahead and we were afraid we would not get to see his face. But we started clapping and cheering and both he and Mrs. Kennedy turned and smiled and waved directly at us, it seemed. Jackie was wearing a beautiful pink suit with beret to match. Two of us, who had seen the President last during the final weeks of the 1960 campaign, remarked almost simultaneously how relaxed and robust he looked.

As it turned out, we were almost certainly the last faces he noticed in the crowd.

After acknowledging our cheers, he faced forward again and suddenly there was a horrible ear-shattering noise coming from behind us and a little to the right.

My first reaction, and also my friends, was that as a joke, someone had backfired their car. Apparently the driver and occupants of the President's car had the same impression, because of instead of speeding up, the car came almost to a halt.

Things are a little hazy from this point. I don't believe anyone was hit with the first bullet. The President and Mrs. Kennedy turned and looked around, as if they, too, didn't believe the noise was really coming from a gun.

Then after a moment's pause there was another shot and I saw the President start slumping in the car.

This was followed rapidly by another shot. Mrs. Kennedy stood up in the car, turned halfway around, then fell on top of her husband's body. Not until this minute did it sink in what actually was happening. We had witnessed the assassination of the President.

The cars behind stopped and several men – Secret Service men I suppose – got out and started rushing forward, obstructing our view of the President's car.

Then I started looking around at the stunned crowd. About 10 feet from where we were standing, a man and woman had thrown their small child to the ground and covered his body with theirs. Apparently the bullets had whizzed directly over their heads. Next to us were two Negro women. One collapsed in the other's arms, weeping and uttering what everyone else was thinking: "They've shot him." It still seems like a horrible nightmare.

It will be a real-life nightmare to haunt us all for a long time to come.

Headline: SEVEN HAVE DIED IN OFFICE, FOUR BY ASSASSIN'S HAND

Headline: OTHER ATTEMPTS Assassins' Bullets Killed 4 Presidents

Headline: Most Dallas Firms, Offices Shut Doors

Headline: Hoover Voices Shock and Grief

Headline: Military Bases Will Fire Guns Each Half Hour

Headline: STORAGE FLOOR Kennedy Killer Hid In Area Used Little

Headline: Speech Cancelled By Goldwater

Headline: FLOOR PLANS OF ASSASSIN'S HIDEOUT

Page five is a very good picture of the funeral and **yes, it was a COUP D'ETAT**. Did we change history that day? There is no way that anyone can ever know the answer to that one. In my own mind I like to think that we did make things a little better for the country. But at that time I wasn't even thinking along those lines. I was just ask to do a job and that's what I did that day. I make no excuses.

(View is looking across a grieving, crowd-lined Arlington Memorial Bridge with the military funeral procession heading into the cemetery. The empty flag draped coffin is rounding the corner by horse drawn carriage guarded by military officers on every side. The picture is from *There was a President Seventy hours and thirty minutes: the weekend no on will ever forget*, National Broadcasting Company, Inc., 1966. The book was taken out of the Carter Library

Schofield Barracks Property of U.S. Army and given away to the ten cents bookstore where I found it.)

As for page six, Hoover himself. What can I say? I think maybe that he would have looked better had he been wearing his pink chiffon and black pumps. Ha-ha…just me being funny.

(Photo of FBI Director J. Edgar Hoover on same page as former CIA contract agent Richard C. Nagell's sworn affidavit - 21 November 1975- concerning his warning letter to J. Edgar Hoover in September 1963. *The Man Who Knew Too Much: Hired To Kill Oswald and Prevent the Assassination of JFK Richard Case Nagell is,* by Dick Russell, 1992.)

As for page seven, all the ol' time play-mates from years gone by. Someday I can tell you more about these people.

(Cover photo from Daniel Hopsicker's book *Barry and 'the boys'*. The book is about DEA/CIA pilot-drug runner Barry Seal who knew Lee Oswald and David Ferrie in the Civil Air patrol. When Seal was gunned down in "supposed federal protection," he had George H.W. Bush's private phone number in his wallet.)

But right now, that information is not, how do I say it, nothing to do with Kennedy. Yes, they were more than likely involved in some way or the other. But I'm speaking of the other things. (CIA drugs/arms business) The only one in the picture on page seven that were involved I believe was David Phillips. These other people had their own agenda. Antonio Veciana, I do not for one minute believe he had any part of JFK that day. I believe that he knew what was coming down, like many others. Had it happened on his turf, then I would say yes, he was involved. If you have anything on the death of John Paisley, please let me know what it says. If this is the right Paisley, then I read the police report of his death, when he went out on his boat to meet someone that night. But for now I'm going to sign off.

Feb. 5, 2001 cont.

CIA/Bay of Pigs "5412"

P: Did the Bay of Pigs failed CIA invasion of Cuba have anything to do with the CIA's hatred for JFK?

J: I don't believe that the Bay of Pigs had anything to do with the assassination of John F. Kennedy. The hatred was already there due to previous experiences they had with his administration. Then there was the fiasco in Europe when the CIA had to ask to help out with an assassination over there on an American citizen. The CIA was told "NO!" They could not be involved in any way what so ever. They could not supply the technology, the weapons, manpower, or anything at all. The CIA was told to keep their hands off. Well, the CIA did what they always did. They went ahead and instead of helping, they did the assassination themselves. That's when John F. Kennedy gave his big speech and pounded his fist on the podium and said he was going to smash the CIA into either a thousand or a million pieces. I know he said he was going to smash them. But he never got the chance. In reality, I think the only ones; that hated Kennedy for the failed Bay of Pigs was the Cubans. I didn't like Kennedy and I was ticked off at him big time for screwing us over with it, but I can't say I hated him for it. Hate is a very strong word. I've never killed anyone just because I hated them. Hate is not a reason to kill. At least to me it's not. For me, it's just following orders. Nothing personal.

P: Was John Kennedy a real threat to their existence (CIA) as a "legitimate agency" of the United States Government? Were you aware of the order that took all the power of the CIA away from them and gave it to the Joints Chief's of Staff?

J: Yes, Kennedy was a threat to the CIA, but not to destroy them, only to tie their hands and control them. But there was no way that he could just up and do away with it. The "5412 Committee" would never have held still for that. No way. The CIA at that time was their "Dogs of War." And the "5412" used them a lot in other countries. As for the Joints Chief's of Staff getting the power from the CIA, that wasn't about to happen, no matter what Kennedy wanted. The only thing the Joints Chief's of Staff ever worried about was their careers. All their decisions would have been based on whether or not it was good for their careers. They would have never gotten anything done.

P: Please explain your involvement with the Bay of Pigs.

J: I was recruited by David Atlee Phillips to train me with assault weapons, explosives and hand to hand combat.

P: Where was this training done?

J: This training took place at several locations. The Florida Keys, Louisiana, Mexico, Guatemala and even right here in Chicago. I was mostly in the Florida Keys, on occasion in Louisiana, and a week in downtown Chicago. The CIA had a top floor in Chicago where they had a class for explosives. Some far out stuff in the bomb-making field.

CIA/Above the Law

P: Were the American advisors and trainers aware it was illegal to perform covert CIA activities on U.S. soil? What was their attitude towards this policy and law?

J: All of us knew the law about covert activities on U.S. soil. But there were no covert activities being carried out. Training yes, but there was no aggression being carried out on U.S. soil. So as far as we were concerned, it was all legal as well as sanctioned. None of us were worried about that.

Dallas 1963

P: Let's go back to November 1963. Were you alone driving down from Chicago to Dallas, Texas?

J: Yes, I was alone.

P: Where did you go when you first arrived in the Dallas area?

J: I stopped at Mesquite and rented a room. I didn't go on to Dallas till the next day. I knew Mesquite was close to Dallas, and I didn't want to be in Dallas all the time I was there. This was more like a hide-away for me from Dallas. It was a nice quiet little place and I could park right in front of my room and keep an eye on my car and everything else. Also, there was a little restaurant, Truck Stop style; about two miles back east of the motel. I had past it and it was convenient for me for eating and getting coffee to go. Plus, the area was pretty open, you know barren, and I could see what was going on around me.

James Files and Lee Harvey Oswald

P: Were you aware when Lee Oswald showed up to assist you at The Lamplighter Motel in Mesquite, Texas that he was being set up as the "patsy"?

J: No, I wasn't aware of that and I'm not really sure that was the case. If he was being set up as the patsy, I had no idea of it at that time. I think he became the patsy after I had second thoughts. When I got to the Mesquite motel and got a room, I went back to the restaurant to use the phone there. I called two people and only two people. I called and told Mr. Nicoletti where I was, and then I called a number back east, that would put me in touch with David Atlee Phillips, no matter where he was. With the Company (CIA) that was a big thing. You never knew where anyone was, you called the assigned number and you got through to who ever your controller was. Anyway, I told Phillips where I was at, he said "Fine." that was it. Now I'm sure that Oswald had never met Mr. Nicoletti, so when Oswald showed up the next morning and told me he had been contacted and told to meet me there, I was surprised. I knew who told him to come there. It could only have been David Atlee Phillips. I was surprised, as I had asked for no help and didn't really want anyone to know where I was, except for Mr. Nicoletti and David Phillips. I knew what my job was and I knew how to do it. But with Oswald there, I was doing a lot of thinking. This wasn't a government deal; you know, a sanctioned assassination. This was the crime family, so why was Oswald all of a sudden here with me. I didn't like it. I figure that is when the other man was called in to do Oswald. But I think Oswald got nervous after the assassination and went to meet Phillips at the theatre and that's why the man missed Oswald at his place and he wound up shooting the cop J. D. Tippit. Then my friend showed up at my place, the motel, and tells me what happened. Once I had got my point across to the people, you know, the Family, they sent this guy to see me and to have him tidy things up when it was over. I figure with Oswald at his place afterwards, there'd be no problem. But, as you know, there was. So, if anyone had any ideas about setting Oswald up before he showed up to help, I have no idea about it. I always figured that I was the one responsible for his death. You have to understand, I was the guy Oswald would lead them back to if he got picked up by the cops or FBI or whoever. Anyway, I was the one who needed Oswald out of the picture. Then when he got himself arrested, yeah, I was nervous. But I think you can understand why.

P: Did you have any conversations with Lee Oswald that week in Texas about why you needed to test fire weapons?

J: The only thing I told Oswald was that I had to get them calibrated for someone. I never told him who and we never discussed anything about the Kennedy assassination. We talked mostly about Clinton, Louisiana and some of the things that we did there and about Phillips. But like I said, we never discussed anything about why I was there, or what was in the air. With the training we had, neither of us would ever ask the other that question.

P: Did Lee Oswald shoot any weapons around you? Ever? In your professional opinion was he a marksman or sharp shooter?

J: I never saw Lee Harvey Oswald fire a weapon in my lifetime. When I was calibrating my scopes and firing my weapons, he never asked to fire any of them. The only time he touched anything was when he was picking up my shell casings that had been expended. That's when he got the nitrates on his right hand that showed up on the paraffin test that they gave him. Believe me, Lee Harvey Oswald never fired a weapon that day. Lee Harvey Oswald killed no one that day.

P: When Lee Oswald was at your motel in Mesquite, did he take any pictures of you? What happened to that roll of film?

J: Back then I never went anywhere without my camera. I was always taking pictures of everything. I had Lee Oswald take several pictures of me there at the motel, plus several pictures of me there in Dallas. I guess there were maybe 8 pictures of me, some with weapons, others without. Me in the room, sitting on the trunk of the car, there at the motel. Just casual stuff. Anyway, later on I dropped that roll of film off in Nashville, Tennessee to my Uncle Jim. He had his own dark room and I used to take special film to develop for me. Pictures of things that I didn't want anyone at the drug store to see. Some were pictures of guys in a trunk that had the s—t shot out of them. So, things like that had to go to my uncle. After I had the pictures made, the ones taken by Lee Oswald, I got to thinking that these pictures of me in Dallas maybe wasn't such a good idea. So I just put them away and my next trip to Nashville, I gave them to my uncle to develop and hold onto for me.

P: When was the last time you saw Lee H. Oswald before the assassination?

J: The day before, about 3:00 P.M.

Phone conversation with James Files and author November 24, 2002

P: When you were hanging around Oswald, did you guys ever talk about him having a girlfriend?

J: No.

P: 'Cause there's this lady named Judyth Vary Baker who says she was… you know… his girlfriend. She's 59 now and she's aware of you and your situation, right? And she said a lot of what you say confirms what he told her. Like right before.. and he was trying to make it stop. He was trying to make the assassination stop.

J: When we got together we wouldn't talk personal like that; wives, girlfriends whatever, kids none of that. We wouldn't say "Oh how's little Mary or Johnny?" it was dangerous to pass information with a co-worker in the Agency. We talked about Clinton, Louisiana and David Phillips and things like that. It puts a man in a very difficult position if taken for questioning if you know too much. But they talk about two Oswalds. The Oswald I saw was real and the real Oswald had a scar above his lip from the marines firing range. People said he didn't drive and I know he did.

P: Do you remember what color his eyes were?

J: I don't look at guy's eyes! (Laugh)

P: I know (laugh) these are just a couple questions…and do you remember if he had like clean hands or dirty fingernails? Do you remember anything about his hands?

J: They were about average, they weren't super clean, and they weren't dirty. Just a workin' mans hands you know?

P: Yeah. And how tall would you say he is…was?

J: I think he was about 6' tall.

P: 'Bout 6'? He's just a little taller than you?

J: To me it was about the same size – only 1" difference.

P: You guys do back to back in the mirror? (Laugh)

J: We didn't do back to back in the mirror. I'm not sure why we're talking about how tall he was…

P: Oh, because I was asking you about Oswald and I was telling you about his girlfriend and she…

J: We never talked about his girlfriend, I never met anybody, uh… we were there that week before Kennedy together and he drove out to Mesquite. People said he didn't drive but he did.

P: Okay, and when you guys were driving around were you in your car or his car?

J: We was in mine.

P: Right. What kind of car was he driving?

J: DON'T BUMP THE CHORD! DON'T HIT THE CHORD! DON'T DRAG THE CHORD! DON'T DRAG THE CHORD…IT WILL CUT ME OFF! And uh… I had a Chevy, a burgundy Chevy down there. He had a blue Ford Falcon when he come out there and seen me at the hotel.

P: A blue Ford Falcon?

J: Yep.

P: Okay, anyway, do you remember any other conversations you had with him prior to the …

J: We drove out to that old place…

P: Was it a firing range or was it just a place you could shoot?

J: No, it was out in the middle of an open field.

P: Uh huh.

J: (Pause) I would never go to a firing range with a high power pistol to check on scopes and accuracy of firing.

P: Yeah. That would be a little obvious.

J: Huh?

P: That would be a little obvious.

J: He knew me but we didn't talk about the assassination. He never asked me about it. I had no reason to bring it up…(can't hear tape)

P: But you were saying you didn't know you were going to be one of the shooters until that day so…

J: I was there to transport and test fire the weapons.

P: Right. As far as Oswald knew at that point you were just somebody that…

J: Oswald never knew I was a shooter.

P: He never knew you pulled the trigger?

J: Never.

P: Did you ever say Charles Nicoletti's name to him?

J: No.

P: Or Johnny Roselli?

J: No.

P: So you guys didn't say anybody's name?

J: No names.

P: Not even David Phillips that day…

J: Oh yeah, David Phillips, "I talked to him a hour ago." Or "We talked last night." Things like that. He was the same controller for both of us. It wasn't too safe to know too much about the other guy. When we were driving around we'd say, "Do you want to stop and get a snack? Oh yeah, get me some pork rind chips and a soda." We never talked about important things or what was happening.

P: Did Oswald know Tosh Plumlee?

J: Pardon me?

P: Did Lee Oswald know Tosh Plumlee?

J: I couldn't tell you. I knew he and David Ferrie knew each other.

P: Was David Ferrie supposed to drive him out of…or not drive but fly him out of the Dallas area?

J: David Ferrie was involved but to what extent at that time I don't know. People ask me about how Charles Nicoletti and John Roselli left and all I know is how I left Dallas.

P: Because this lady that was the girlfriend of Oswald said he was supposed to meet David Ferrie and call him at a skating rink in Houston and that's why David Ferrie went to Houston and was at the skating rink.

J: You have to understand we both were trained in the trade...

P: And you guys had conversations accordingly.

J: Right.

P: Huh. Well, I thought I'd ask a couple more questions about that aspect…(can't hear and tape side one ends.)

Feb. 5, 2001 cont.

Charles Nicoletti/Johnny Roselli O.C. & CIA

P: Besides Charles Nicoletti, who else was part of the team to assassinate JFK?

J: Besides Mr. Nicoletti and myself, there was Johnny Roselli.

P: When and where did you meet Johnny Roselli? Who introduced the two of you?

J: Early 1962 in Miami, Florida was when Mr. Nicoletti introduced me to Johnny Roselli.

Roselli, Johnny

Roselli was a Las Vegas – based Mafia figure and link in the CIA-Mafia chain. He had close ties to three Mafia bosses associated with the Kennedy assassination: Sam Giancana of Chicago, Santos Trafficante of Florida, and Carlos Marcello of New Orleans. According to columnist Jack Anderson, Roselli told him that mob leaders had ordered Jack Ruby to kill Lee Harvey Oswald because they were afraid he might crack and reveal their part in the conspiracy to kill President Kennedy.

In July 1976, shortly before Roselli was to be questioned by the Senate Intelligence Committee, his body was discovered floating in Dumfoundling Bay in Miami. He had been strangled and stabbed; his legs had been sawed off and stuffed into an empty oil drum along with the rest of his body. It is believed that Roselli was killed by someone working for Trafficante because he was talking too much about the Kennedy assassination. The Assassination of John F. Kennedy: A Complete Book of Facts, 1992, p-109. Source CONSPIRACY, Anthony Summers, 1989.

James Files believes "the Cubans down there in Miami were more than likely the ones who killed Johnny Roselli on orders of the CIA."

P: Before going on to the events in Dealey Plaza, please explain why, if Johnny Roselli was flown in by a CIA pilot to abort the mission, did he go with you to the pancake house in Ft. Worth to pick up the package from Jack Ruby that had the map with the motorcade route change and fake Secret Service ID's?

J: That's easy to answer. Johnny Roselli may have been the liaison between the family and the CIA but he knew that he had better go along with what Sam Giancana wanted. Mr. Nicoletti could have insisted that Johnny Roselli follow through as the second shooter. But both of us felt that he might just miss if forced to shoot. But since I was there, it was best if I follow through with that part. But as far as going to meet Jack Ruby, he didn't have a choice. And it didn't matter what the CIA wanted, no one could stop what was about to happen. The only person that could call it off was Sam Giancana. He was in Dallas that day and if he had wanted it stopped, he would have sent Mr. Nicoletti instructions to that effect. As long as we had not been told differently, it was going to go down by the numbers, just like we planned.

P: Was this a CIA trick to deny culpability in the crime to shift the blame and focus on the Mafia involvement?

J: It very well could have been, but to be honest, I have no idea. I know David Phillips never tried to get a message to me and he knew where I was. But I don't think he knew or ever found out that I was the second shooter. He never asked me anything about what happened that day. It was like he didn't want to know anything at all. That alone is just a little strange. But I sort of figured he had a better pipeline than me to fill him in on the events of that day and anything else he wanted to know about. After all, Ed Lansdale was there for the Company and he never reached out to stop it.

November 21, 1963

P: Please give a brief overview of the day before the assassination November 21, 1963, leading into full details of November 22, 1963, on through to the evening of the same day.

J: On November 21, 1963 I got up early and went down to the truck stop for breakfast then drove into Dallas and looked the area over for a final time. At 10:00 A.M. I found a phone and made a call and was informed that Mr. Nicoletti I would be in as planned. I was told that there would be a message left for me at my motel and I should check for it at 6:00 A.M. on the morning of the 22nd. I didn't have a phone in my room and the message would be left in the office for me to pick up. Anyway, I met Lee Oswald in Dealey Plaza around noon and we went for a ride and stopped off at a little grocery store to buy something to eat, as neither one of us felt like going to a restaurant. I left him at about, a little before 3:00 P.M. and then I went back to my place and took a shower and listened to the radio. About 6:00, maybe it was even 7:00 P.M. I went back to the truck stop and had my dinner and got a coffee to go and went back to my room. I didn't know, but I thought Mr. Nicoletti would stop by there on his way in to give me a final message or something. But no one showed up that night. I had stopped by the office and picked up my message. I was to call Mr. Nicoletti at the Dallas Cabana and ask for Leo. I got another message at that point. I was told by someone to be in front of the Dallas Cabana at 7:00 A.M. …Sharp!

Cabana Motel

About midnight, the night before the Kennedy murder, Jack Ruby visited Lawrence Meyers, a guest at the Cabana Motel. Meyers was accompanied by a female companion named Jean West, who is believed to have had ties with Oswald associate David Ferrie, a New Orleans figure investigated by District Attorney Jim Garrison. Staying at the Cabana Motel at the same time was alleged Mafia courier Eugene Hale Brading, who was registered under the alias Jim Braden. The following day, Braden was detained briefly by police near Dealey Plaza shortly after the assassination, but was released.

THE ASSASSINATION OF JOHN F. KENNEDY: A Complete Book of Facts p –105.
Sources: Crossfire; High Treason.

November 22, 1963

I was there early, but cruised till 7:00 A.M. I did not want to be just sitting out there. Mr. Nicoletti did not show up, instead it was Johnny Roselli that met me. He came over, got in the car, and said, "Let's go. Head for Fort Worth and take a left on University and stop at the Pancake House." Joking around I said "That's a long way to go for breakfast when there's work to be done." Johnny Roselli looked over at me and smiled and said "Hey smart-a--, I gotta meet somebody. That OK with you?" We laughed and bantered words back and forth for a while and he ask me if I knew Jack. I said "Who? Jack S—t?" He cuffed me on the shoulder and said "Ruby, smart-a--. Jack Ruby. He owns the Carousel Club. I thought you went by there." I said "Nope. Never been there and don't know the man and don't want to know anyone from down here." Then Johnny told me that he had to meet this guy and get something from him. Johnny told me to let him go in first, for me to park the car where I could keep an eye on it and when I come in not to come by him, but sit where I could keep him covered should something go wrong. Then he goes "You are packin' aren't you?" I said, "I ain't ever naked." He laughed and said "Keep my a—covered." I said, "Are we expecting trouble?" He say's "You never know. Just be ready and take care of me like I was Chuckie." He knew I'd never let anything happen to Chuck.

Fort Worth, Texas

Anyway, we get there, I pull up along side the place where no one can see Johnny getting out of the car and he goes in. I park and then I go in. We got there early, as planned, so we could see who pulled up in the parking lot. Johnny was sitting in a booth and I took a seat at the counter and ordered coffee. I had a perfect spot in case I had to do any shooting. I could shoot on an angle and it would be hard for them to fire back at me and Johnny would be in no danger from my end. After about 20 minutes this stocky built guy comes in and walks over by Johnny and sits down in the booth with him. They shake hands and Jack orders coffee. Then a few minutes later Jack gives Johnny a brown envelope, I'd say 5x8. Then Jack gets up and leaves. I lay some money on the counter and go outside maybe 15 seconds behind Jack. I don't know him, don't trust him and I want to make sure he's leaving the area before Johnny come out and got in the car. We headed back to Dallas. Johnny pulled the brown envelope out of his pocket and opened it up. There were several sets of Secret Service Identification and a hand drawn map of the detour for the motorcade.

Anyway, I pulled up at the Dallas Cabana and Johnny told me to wait for Chuck to come down. Johnny went in and about five or six minutes later Mr. Nicoletti came out and got in the car with me. He said for me to drive over to the plaza. On the way we made small talk about how each other was and what we thought.

Dealey Plaza

Mr. Nicoletti told me to park the car and we walked the area of Dealey Plaza and talked about the terrain and where the best places were at for what we wanted to do. That's when I found out that Johnny wasn't going to be the second shooter. That's when Mr. Nicoletti ask me to back him up. For me that was an automatic yes. For me to be his back up was a great honor and one I knew I would full fill. And as everyone knows, the assassination did take place. After Mr. Nicoletti and me toured Dealey Plaza and talked things out. I took him back to the Dallas Cabana, and then took a drive for maybe an hour.

Eugene Brading was the key to getting Mr. Nicoletti and Johnny Roselli into the Dal-Tex Building. He went inside and was waiting for them and opened an exit door that could only be opened from the inside. As for his background, I don't know him very well. But I do know that James "Jim" Braden was in fact Eugene Hale Brading. He had a lot of friends within organized crime. He was mostly "West Coast" but had reaches all the way across the country. He was pretty well known in certain circles.

The Hunts and Eugene Hale Brading

"James Braden" was actually an alias for Eugene Hale Brading. Within minutes of the assassination, he had been among a dozen or so people rounded up for questioning, after the police found him having taken an elevator to the ground floor of the Dal-Tex Building, across the street from the book depository. He said he had gone inside to try to make a phone call on the third floor, and that he was in the oil business in Beverly Hills. The police soon released "Jim Braden," unaware that he had a long history of associates in the criminal underworld. Indeed, Los Angeles TV newsman Peter Noyes devoted a large portion of his 1973 book *Legacy of Doubt* to Brading. Besides Brading's sudden interest in oil speculation in Louisiana and Texas during the fall of 1963, Noyes discovered that Brading had worked a few feet away from David Ferrie's office that October in New Orleans' Pere Marquette Building. On November 21, 1963, Brading had checked in with a Dallas probation officer, provided his real name, and "advised that he planned to see Lamar Hunt and other oil speculators while here." Later, Brading would deny to the FBI having gone to the Hunt offices, saying that one of his California traveling companions went instead. But Rothermel (Paul Rothermel Jr.- the Hunt family's security chief) told author Noyes that he was sure Brading had indeed dropped in. The visitors' log for that day showed that three other men "and friend" visited both Lamar and Nelson Bunker Hunt. While staying in Dallas, Brading was staying at the Cabana Motel – where Jack Ruby also visited late on the night of November 21, 1963. Brading also told the FBI that he departed Dallas for Houston right after his brief time in custody on November 22. Records checked by the authorities, however, did not show him arriving in Houston until four days later. Hence the Hunt internal memo that Brading had come in "both prior to and after the assassination" appears to have validity.

The grassy knoll"

Then I took my briefcase and went back to the railroad and made like I was inspecting boxcars passing time till I should go by the stockade fence. I remained close to that area waiting to hear the crowd reaction and the I walked over to the fence, laid my briefcase on the ground, opened it up, removed the "Twenty-Two Two Remington Fireball" which I placed my special round in the chamber and held to my side till the motorcade made the left back onto Elm St. And then I raised my weapon and laid it on the fence and watched through the scope while the motorcade proceeded down Elm Street. When I heard the first shot I started counting not one but two, three. I counted each shot as a miss, miss, miss as I knew we wanted a head shot to make sure he was killed. At this point I had to make a decision as I was fixing to lose my field of fire. It had been made very plain that only JFK was to be hit, no one else. Well, I was at the place to either fire, or put it in the case and leave. I knew what I was there for and I pulled the trigger and I saw Kennedy's head explode. At that moment, I knew he was dead. I knew that no one could survive that hit. I removed the shell casing, placed it in my mouth bit the casing and placed it on the fence, laid the Fireball back in the case, closed it and walked away. As I walked away from the fence, I saw the cop drop the motorcycle on its side and run up the hill with another cop close by. They were stopped by two men wearing suites and showing some kind of ID's. I was preparing to pull my Colt .45 from under my jacket and shoot them when they were stopped. I just kept right on walking like I was going back to work from my lunch break.

Report: Grassy knoll shot correct
The Herald News
March 26, 2001 p. - A6
THE WASHINGTON POST
WASHINGTON-The House Assassinations Committee may have been right after all: there was a shot from the grassy knoll.
That was the finding of the congressional investigation that concluded 22 years ago that President John F. Kennedy's murder in Dallas in 1963 was "probably…the result of a conspiracy." A shot from the grassy knoll meant that two gunmen must have fired at the president within a split-second sequence. Lee Harvey Oswald, accused of firing three shots at Kennedy from a perch at the Texas School Book Depository, could not have been in two places at once.
A special panel of the National Academy of Sciences subsequently disputed the evidence of a forth shot contained on a police dictabelt of the sounds in Dealey Plaza that day, and insisted that it was simply random noise, perhaps static, recorded about a minute after the shooting while Kennedy's motorcade was enroute to Parkland Hospital.
A new peer-reviewed article in science and Justice, a quarterly publication of Britain's Forensic Science Society, says the NAS panel's study was seriously flawed, having failed to take into account the words of a Dallas patrolman that show the gunshot-like noises occurred "at the exact instant that John F. Kennedy was assassinated."
In fact, the author of the article, D.B. Thomas, a government scientist and JFK assassination researcher, said it was more than 96 percent certain that there was a shot from the grassy knoll t o the right of the president's limousine, in addition to the three shots from a book depository window above and behind the presidential limousine.
Former House Assassinations Committee chief counsel G. Robert Blakey said the NAS panel's study always bothered him because it dismissed all four putative shots as random noise even though the three soundbursts from the book depository matched up precisely with film of the assassination and other evidence such as the echo patterns in Dealey Plaza and the motorcade.
"This is an honest, careful scientific examination of everything we did, with all the appropriate statistical checks," Blakey said of Thomas's work. "It shows that we made mistakes too, but minor mistakes. The main thing is when push comes to shove, he increased the degree of confidence that the shot from the grassy knoll was real, not static. We thought

there was a 95 percent chance it was a shot. He puts it at 96.3 percent. Either way, that's 'beyond a reasonable doubt.'"
Physicist Norman Ramsey of Harvard, chairman of the NAS panel, said this weekend that he was "still fairly confident" of his group's work, but he said he wanted to study the Science and Justice article carefully before making any further comment.

Phone conversation January 1, 2003 James Files with author

PJ: In one of your letters you mentioned nobody asked you why you and Chuck knew the bubble top was off?
JF: Yeah.
P: Well, I guess I didn't dwell on it too much. How did you guys know?
J: Well, we'd been informed it was to be off. It was the only time it was ever off…they didn't have it off in Houston.
P: Who told who?
J: Sam told Chuck … it would be off.
P: It would be off so…
J: We had…once we had secured everything we had no way of knowing.
P: Did you have bullets that would have gone through the bubble top?
J: I wanted to use armor steel piercing on the hillside (Chicago expressway) but they wouldn't let me do that, but I'll explain all that to you later. But they said we couldn't hit a target moving at 60 miles an hour…they just didn't know me very well.
 (Jimmy told me when I visited him at Stateville that when he was a kid of six years old he used to shoot a gun and if they had meat at dinner it was because he had killed a squirrel or a rabbit. He asked me if I ever had red eye gravy and I said no. He said it is gravy made from that type of meat. He has been hitting moving targets since he was a boy.)
P: Oh.
J: But anyway, other than that when we got down there, we went down there with the assumption there would be no bubble on it. When we was planning it, if it was in place, we weren't prepared for that. The teams would have left.
P: How many teams were there?
J: There was only three that I know of.
P: Yeah.
J: Now there might have been somebody there to determine why it wouldn't be used because in Houston they followed operation procedures…(can't hear tape or Jimmy clearly)
P: So when did Chuck find out from Sam about that?
J: Chuck found out the previous night. He and Chauncey Holt got in that night – him and Chuck come in from Arizona together.
P: Right.
J: But by the time they got into Dallas they was meetin' Sam there that night. But Sam did not travel there that night – he was on his own but I figured Sam had one of his top lieutenants with him. Know what I mean? (Files told me earlier that Richard Cain was with him at the Adolphus Hotel in Dallas)
P: Did Sam drive to Dallas or did he fly?
J: I don't know. I never ask.
P: Oh.
J: You see, inside the Family, we don't ask questions like that.
P: Oh.
J: You make people nervous when you start askin' questions.
P: (Laugh)

J: You accept the orders and you carry them out.
P: Oh.
J: In the army you can ask a point man why he wants you to this or that but in the family you don't ask. It is a standing order and you carry it out.
P: Well anyway, I was just curious about that.
J: Yeah, I know. But like I say, that's 'cause that's how I was raised – to never question anyone about Dallas.
P: Well, it was going to rain that day and then it got nice.
J: Um hum. Well, like I say, at the last minute we still wasn't sure if we were in position but we were ready.
P: Did you have ammunition that would have pierced…
J: No.
P: the bubble top?
J: We would have took our…little play toys and would've went back home…just figure another day, another location.
P: (Silence) Well, what about all the explosives in the boxcars? What was that for? J: I have no idea. I had no part of that.
P: Oh.
J: That was to create a diversion for somebody else who might need it. But I knew nothing about that. That wasn't part of my operation to know about. You know, you can have one operation with six different teams in it and not know all them there. You know what you're supposed to do because that's the way you're trained. You know what you're supposed to do and that's what you do.
P: Is that typical in a coup situation?
J: Typical in what?
P: In a coup d'etat situation where you're taking over a country. You're having a bunch of different things going on so the propaganda machine can crank out a bunch of different stories?
J: Right. You do your thing, the rest of 'em are doin' their thing. There were thirty teams operating in Laos in Operation White Star at one time. And not ONE of us knew what the other team was doing or knew who the team's advisors was.
P: Hum.
J: That's strictly for intelligence. That's what we call intelligence. If you don't know you can't tell. You can't finger anybody as long as you don't know.
P: Yeah.
J: That's how you always keep the doors closed and when the door is shut they can't tell on nobody else.
P: And even if they give you some kind of drug to try and make you tell the truth, you just don't know.
J: You just don't know. Anyway, it was like Lee Oswald that day. Oswald…the only person that he could really tie anything to was me and David Phillips. Oswald didn't know about anybody else.
P: Was the guy that killed Tippit…was he um…dressed up as a cop?
J: No.
P: He was dressed up as a businessperson?
J: Let me put it to you this way. When the guy come by the motel to see me…uh…he was wearin' just a pair of slacks, a sports shirt and that's it.
P: And he didn't say that he'd been dressed up as a cop or anything?
J: No, I wouldn't even let him in. He stood at the door and I ask him, "What the HELL you doin' here?" He said, "I had a problem." He'd shot a cop and wanted me to carry his piece. I

said, "HELL NO! I don't want your piece! You get rid of it! That's yours and I don't want…I don't want that piece! You shot the cop, you get rid of it! I don't want it around me. Get the HELL OUT OF HERE! We ain't supposed to be together." He turned and walked away, got in his vehicle and left.

P: So, he never told you later what he did with that gun?
J: No. I never ask him and he don't ask me what I did with mine. Why should he?
P: When was the next time you saw him after he came by that day?
J: Oh… four or five weeks I guess.
P: Four or five weeks later you saw him?
J: Yeah.
P: And you guys just didn't even talk about it?
J: No! (Laugh) That was unheard of.
P: You just act like none of that happened?
J: It didn't happen.
P: NEXT!
J: That's it.
P: Oh God!
J: I got that from Chuck. We done something, Chuck did NOT want me to talk about it the next day. We didn't even talk about it with each other. The only time he ever criticized me was that day we were leavin' and he ask me says, "Jimmy, don't you think you fired a little too soon?" And I said, "Well, I was fixin' to loose my field of fire – it was either that or not at all." And he said, "Okay then." And that was all that was discussed about it.
P: And then the next time it was slightly brought up was when he paid you and that was it?
J: He gave me the money and I never ask him.
P: But you knew it was for part of that?
J: Let me put it this way; we had done something before Dallas, okay? (Operator cuts in and tells us we have 30 seconds left. Jimmy starts praying and I say amen - end of phone call.)

The getaway

I went back to the Chevy and Mr. Nicoletti was in the front seat and Johnny Roselli was in the back seat. I opened the drivers' door, placed my case on the rear floor of the car, got in, and started the car and drove away. I headed north on Houston for maybe 5 or 6 blocks to a major street and hung a left and went down by the expressway. There was a gas station there by the underpass and they had a car waiting for them. They got out of our car and walked across the parking lot and I pulled out and turned left. So I have no idea which way or where they went. Me, I went back to my place in Mesquite. I pulled in, parked my car, secured it then went to my room that I had rented for the past several days. I stripped, took a shower, and then used hot wax to remove any resin from my skin pores that the shower didn't remove. Then I waited till dusk, just after twilight when I felt it was dark enough for me to bring in the gun cases and clean the weapons. When it was after midnight and all the other lights were out, I took them back out and secured them in a special compartment behind the back seat hat had been made for that purpose. Then I went back in and went to sleep till daylight. The next day I drove back to the southern part of Illinois and stayed there overnight. The following day I drove on into Chicago. Before I left to go to Texas, Mr. Nicoletti had instructed me not to speed and not to travel at nighttime. He didn't want me taking any chances of getting pulled over by the police. We both felt that I should only travel during daylight hours. I did the same routine going and coming back.

David Atlee Phillips and Edward G. Lansdale / CIA & U.S. Military Present at Dealey Plaza

P: Looking back now, how large of a role would you say David A. Phillips had in the planning of the assassination of JFK? (David Atlee Phillips was in the CIA 1950-1975.)

J: I don't really know. But I would think he played a great part in overseeing it and planning it with Lansdale (Edward Geary- Major General United States Air Force). On the government side, Lansdale was in charge of the covert part and I know that Phillips was with him on some of it.

****

(See letter from Fletcher Prouty to Jim Garrison - When I contacted Len Osanic, the person who monitors Mr. Prouty's website since his death in 2001, he sent me this:

Hello Pamela,
You do not have permission as they are on the "The Collected Works Of Col. L. Fletcher Prouty CD-ROM"
which by agreement from Fletcher I have publishing rights to his material.
I wish the letters to only be available on the CD-ROM.

I think you will find serious research does not support Mr. Files claims
He may have been there. But he has lied about certain items, so it throws his credibility out the window. What he did or didn't do...
will be up to him to substantiate.

Good luck with your research,
Len Osanic
www.prouty.org)

To which I replied:

Aloha Len,
Thank you for your prompt reply. I'm wondering what, in your opinion, James Files is lying about?
*I was hoping to expose Col. Prouty's work (one letter) to the general public. Currently, it seems to me, only JFK researchers know of him. When I ask people if they have heard of Mr. Prouty they just look at me with a blank stare and say no. Most people my age, 44 (and younger), have never even heard of Jim Garrison. They **have** heard of the JFK assassination and don't believe that the Warren Commission told the truth and leave it at that.*
Good luck with your CD-ROM sales.
Pamela

****

P: Did David Phillips take his orders directly from Allen Dulles, or was there another link in the chain of command?

J: I have no way of knowing that. But I do not believe that Allen Dulles would put himself in such a position as that. At all times he had to remain sterile. They could let nothing get back to him.

P: Would you say David Phillips was the primary person in setting up Lee H. Oswald as the patsy for the assassination?

J: On that I'm not sure. But I am certain that David Phillips knew for a fact that I was very unhappy that Lee H. Oswald had been put in place to give me a helping hand. What had been planned for Lee H. Oswald before I got there, I'll never know.

P: Since David Phillips was your CIA controller, did he ever directly talk to you about the plans to assassinate JFK?

J: No. There's no way that we could talk about something like that. See, "the government was not involved" therefore we couldn't discuss it. Sort of like, if you're not there, it never happened.

P: Did his CIA jurisdiction include overseeing and controlling others such as David Ferrie and Clay Shaw? Frank Sturgis? Howard Hunt? Eugene/Jim Braden?

J: David Phillips had a far reach when it came to jurisdiction with the CIA. He had several operatives. He could give orders to Clay Shaw, David Ferrie and Frank Sturgis. But Howard Hunt and Eugene Braden were not his operatives. But they did work together at times. What I'm saying is that he had control over me, but not them. They danced to someone else's tune.

Lee Oswald, David Ferrie, and Clay Shaw

P: When and where had you met Lee Oswald, David Ferrie, and Clay Shaw before November 1963?

J: The first time I ever met Lee H. Oswald was in 1962 just outside of Clinton, Louisiana. He was with David A. Phillips and I had taken a load of guns down to them. And, as you know, people say that Lee couldn't drive, well, he could drive. He was in a pickup truck at that time and he drove it away alone. David Phillips stayed and talked with me for a while. As for David Ferrie and Clay Shaw, I met them, but only to say hello. It was 1963, maybe March or early April. It was long ago and I had nothing to do with them anyway. Years later, I would encounter David Ferrie, but at this time we won't discuss that meeting due to civil process.

P: In your opinion why do you think David Ferrie had to be silenced? Was he going to talk openly in the Clay Shaw trial about the Outfit/CIA role in the JFK assassination? Who was more concerned – the Agency or the Outfit? Which side ordered his hit?

J: WOW! A four-part question in one. O.K., why do I think David Ferrie had to be silenced? David Ferrie had been drinking heavy and when he'd drink, he'd talk out of school. He got to babbling about things that should not be talked about, like the JFK matter. Anyway, certain people began to think he was unreliable. When you get involved with the Agency in certain ways, you don't get fired, you get retired permanently. It was decided David Ferrie had to go, before the Clay Shaw trial. No one could afford to take that chance.

Who knew what he might say? So an insurance policy was taken out to guarantee secrecy and to protect all. In other words, the insurance was a contract.

As for who was more concerned, the Agency was. As for who ordered the hit, the Agency. They had more to lose than the Outfit. The Agency seen the Outfit was letting things go a little too far, so they made an executive decision. Someone was sent to dispatch David Ferrie. The autopsy report read cerebral brain hemorrhage cause of death. And yes, that is what he died of. But it was inflicted by man. A fingernail file had been inserted through the roof of his mouth to penetrate the brain. When using a fingernail file, the edges have the grooves that cross the flat part of the file. This is very important, as the rough sides penetrate the brain it gives the illusion of tissue tearing, therefore causing a verdict of natural causes. If you had used a knife, the cut would be detected right away. Results? Problem solved.

P: You've already mentioned you had the same CIA controller as Lee Oswald, David A. Phillips. Who else was in Dealey Plaza that day under his CIA jurisdiction?

J: Edward G. Lansdale was there that day, but I would have to say he was operating on his own, as he would have been higher up than David A. Phillips. I could be wrong about him having a higher GS number. I never thought about that until now. But Frank Sturgis was also there. Also, there were a few Cubans there that I knew but I didn't know if they were there for work or not. But they would have been under David Phillips jurisdiction.

P: Did you see Jack Ruby in Dealey Plaza, the same man you had seen earlier in the morning with Johnny Roselli?

J: I could swear that I saw Jack Ruby just minutes before the motorcade arrived standing on Elm Street, on the north side curb. Everyone else says he wasn't there. I could be wrong, but I will always believe that it was Jack Ruby that I saw.

Any Other Shooters?

P: To your knowledge, was there anyone else that might have been firing from the front of the motorcade?

J: To my knowledge, no, there was no one else there. I'm not saying there wasn't. I'm saying no, not to my knowledge.

The Umbrella System: Prelude to an Assassination

April 14, 2002 updated comments (see the article following these comments)

J: On the first page of one of five, "To my knowledge, no, there was no one else there. I'm not saying there wasn't. I'm saying no, not to my knowledge." As far as I know, there were no other "SHOOTERS" than Chuck and me. Yes, there was ground control, you know, the radio people and people to run interference. But I do not know who all those people were. That was not part of my operation. Chuck and me had our part and they had theirs. I know that's not much help, but it's the truth. And for this (dave "who can do? ratmandu!" ratcliffe) I've no idea who he is and I've never read the article, Prelude to an Assassination.

Sent to James Files for comment March 30, 2002 (#357)

THE UMBRELLA SYSTEM: PRELUDE TO AN ASSASSINATION

by Richard E. Sprague and Robert Cutler

Page two I've highlighted. If someone, (like whoever wrote that article) would have checked the weather, they would have found out it had been drizzling rain that morning in Dallas, Texas. The sun came out just prior to the arrival of the motorcade. What were the people with umbrellas supposed to do, just toss them in the trash? But, back to the umbrella and the world of intrigue. Yes, we do have weapons like that and more in similar style. There is a walking cane that shoots the same round. Some are solid-state fuel and others operate off compressed air, like the old Daisy B.B. gun. These things have been built into cameras, like when we were going to do "Castro" in Santiago that time. We had a gun mounted inside a camera. They even discussed using a lethal dart at that time, but Townley (*Michael*) and me preferred to use live ammo. Nothing like the real stuff to get the job done right. But there were plenty of people that could get the use of weapons like that, even back in sixty-three. The "Umbrella Weapon" was not something brand new. It had been around even during the OSS years, the prelude to the CIA.

Note from Wim: Files has stated that Michael Townley could confirm him. He also said that Townley's wife is named Mary Ann and they have two kids.

On page three I highlighted the part that you also sent me, and why would anyone want to take a chance on poison doing the job? And, as for the flechette round, someone else could have been killed and that was a BIG NO-NO in our operation. Sam (Giancana) made it plain to us that only JFK was to be hit. Had I had it my way, I would have obliterated the car and all of its occupants. But neither Sam nor Chuck liked that idea. That's what I wanted to do in Hillside, Illinois on the expressway when JFK came to Chicago.

Also, the umbrella was not a very accurate weapon when trying to hit something with it. You had to almost be touching the subject with it to hit what you wanted. It was invented and intended to be used at train stations and later on it was a big item for use at very crowded airports. Most people when killed by it are ruled "heart attack" victims. Now I'm not saying there was not that type of umbrella on hand. I'm saying if there was, I did not know about it and to me it would not make sense to even try to even try to use it there. Too big of a chance of failure.

On page five you ask who he was in contact with, **Hunt, Sturgis**? I really don't know, so I cannot give you an honest answer on that. I wish I could, but I have no idea and I don't feel I should give my opinion on that part of it. **But let's face it; both of them were there that day, plus other CIA people and their assets as well**. And that I know for a fact and it is also the truth. I knew a lot of the people there that day and I also know who they were with or should I say worked for. And no, I did not go by and chat with any of them. I walked by two people that I knew and never even acknowledged them. That would have been highly out of character for one to have done that.

Also, on page five I've highlighted the part **about it being a highly planned CIA intelligence operation. The fact is, it was a well-planned operation and everyone had their part to do**. But Chuck and me, we were just the shooters, the peons, of the higher rank and file. We were the nobody's, only tools of the trade, someone who could be discarded if need be. In that part of an operation, we were at the foot of the ladder, or bottom of the hill, where if the you know what rolls down, we're the ones that got it all over us. And in the end, it cost Chuck his life. And yes, they should have killed me back then also. But for some reason, "God" has watched over me and kept me alive for some very special reason. That I have to believe. Too many times I've been in the line of fire where I should have been killed. I've had cops put guns to my head and threaten to kill me. People in the Family even tried to kill me in a power struggle. A close friend of mine tried to kill me while I was driving one night and he was in the seat next to me. He pulled a gun on me and it jammed; it wouldn't fire. And there have been many other occasions where I knew I was going to die and I was given the insight to prevent it. Several times I saw the image of me being killed in one way or another, and that image saved my life. So, yes, "God" has kept me alive for a very special reason and in time I'm sure that I will learn what that reason is. And, I'm very thankful to "God" for all that "He" has done for me, especially for bringing you into my life. Also, for the two visits that "He" sent "His Son Jesus" on to make sure that I was a believer and to tell me to get my life in order. Yes, I can feel the time is near and soon I will know why "God" has been so good to me. I will know and understand things I never dreamed or thought of. But there was a reason and soon I shall know it, for I believe that with all my heart and soul.

On page six, there were pictures of the autopsy report with the neck wounds. I wasn't there at the morgue, so all I can do is tell you what I think. OK…

The small wound in the neck that everybody keeps talking about, I believe is an exit wound from the round that I used. I used a round that would explode on impact. This round was traveling at over 3,200 feet per second which would cause fragmentation on impact. And at that speed would penetrate, before exploding, which gives the effect that one wants for a guaranteed kill. That small wound they keep talking about, I believe is where a fragment exited from my round through his neck. But there is no way for me to prove that. Some will believe that he was shot from the front and hit in the neck, others will believe that the Umbrella Man shot him with a dart, and others, who knows what they believe.

Note from Wim: I believe the throat shot was inflicted by another shooter on the south knoll, a shooter that James Files was not aware of, nor was told about. That shot went through the windshield and caused a thru and thru bullet hole. Evidence for this and more shooters can be found on www.jfkmurdersolved.com.

I had informed Joe West that there had been mercury in the round that had been fired that day from the front and that if he could get the body exhumed, it could be tested for the trace of mercury. But Joe died before that could be done. That was more than likely the reason his medication was messed with. The government did not want anyone to know the true secret; that JFK's body was not there in Arlington. Had his grave been opened, what a shock that would have been for the people.

Letter 492 November 6, 2002 James Files to author

I was digging in my box the other day, seeing what all I could throw away, as I need more room in my property box, and I ran across some legal work that Joe West had in court trying to get JFK's body exhumed. Anyway, if you want I can copy the paperwork and send it to you, if you think it might be of some help. This way you can show a couple of things that are court exhibits to verify that what you are saying is true and Joe was trying very hard to get the body dug up. Let me know what you think. I can never think of everything that I want to ask you when we're talking on the phone and I hate to take up our time talking about all this, but I know it has to be done. (Put this paperwork on Joe West in appendix)

Feb. 5, 2001 cont.

P: Who gave you the orders to assassinate JFK?

J: The only person to ever tell me that we were going to assassinate John F. Kennedy was Mr. Nicoletti. I never ask him, but I knew that Sam Giancana had to be the man to hand out the contract to Mr. Nicoletti and I also knew that he would have gotten his orders from Mr. Tony Accardo. He was still the man calling the shots at that time. For the public and those who didn't know, it was Sam Giancana calling the shots. But for the ones on the inside, they knew that Tony "Big Tuna" Accardo was the man with the power.

P: When was the next time you saw Charles Nicoletti and Johnny Roselli after November 22, 1963?

J: I saw Mr. Nicoletti a week later in Melrose Park, Illinois. It was almost a year before I saw Johnny Roselli again and that was in Miami, Florida.

Money $

P: How much money were you paid for the job in Dallas?

J: I had done a job in Chicago with Mr. Nicoletti the week before I left to take the weapons to Dallas. At that point I had received no money, which was not unusual. When Mr. Nicoletti got the money, he would always pay me. Never did I go and ask him for money when we had done a job. Then we did the one in Dallas. After I returned to Chicago, within a few days, I received an envelope for $30,000. That was for both jobs. So you could say half of that was for Kennedy. Or it could have been 20 and 10. I never ask. I really wasn't interested. I trusted Mr. Nicoletti and I had no reason to ask about the money. Had I never received a dime, I would never have said a word and I would not have been upset by it. There were several times I did things and never got money for it. But when there were many times that I did nothing for weeks on end and every two weeks I still got my envelope with money in it for doing nothing. To me it always worked out. I never worried about those things. For me, it was an honor to just be around Mr. Nicoletti.

CIA/MOSSAD

P: In 1963 were you aware of the Mossad's (Israel's intelligence/terrorist agency) involvement in the JFK assassination plot? Did they have aerial photographs of Dealey Plaza from November 22, 1963? Have you ever seen them? Who has them today?

J: Yes, I was aware that Mossad was on station that day. I never ask why, but I saw someone that I knew and I knew who he was. And yes, they had aerial photographs of what happened that day. I told Robert Vernon that some years back when we were doing the video about the assassination. But no, I've never seen the photographs. There was no reason for me to ever see them, but I do know that they exist and I know that Langley has a set of them. Whether or not they got them from Mossad, or whether they made their own that day, I have no way of knowing. And as for who has them today, I would say the Mossad has theirs and the CIA has theirs.

P: Had the CIA and Mossad worked together before on any other projects that you were aware of?

J: Yes, on several. But I don't think they've ever been declassified. But I do believe that the two of them were working together that day in Dallas. I believe that Mossad was there only because they knew that it was going down. Don't forget, the NSA knew in advance that Kennedy was going to be assassinated. They had pulled that from the airwaves at their base in Scotland. I've got a copy of the letter of the guy that caught it. And if the NSA knew for sure, you better believe that Mossad knew. And with the CIA knowing, I figure they would have slipped the information to the Mossad themselves. They shared a lot of information that I do know.

P: James, why are you giving me this interview? Why are you telling the truth after all these years? Please include the part about Joe West and Mr. Vernon.

J: I'm giving you this interview because I believe in you and **I believe you want the truth to get out to the PEOPLE.** To be honest, I had always planned to take this secret with all the others I have to my grave. But a man by the name of Joe West heard about me through the FBI from one of its agents. Joe West came to visit me. But first he called and left his number with the warden. The warden called me to his office and asks me to call Joe West. Mr. West informed me that he wanted to talk to me about the Kennedy assassination. I ask him "Which one?" and he said "JFK." I ask him "why I should talk to you?" And he said, "I know a lot about you and that day. I want to come to the prison and see you." I told him, "You got 60 seconds to convince me why I should talk to you." He started sputtering off several very personal things and about 30 seconds later I said, "Hold on! You convinced me. Come and see me but I don't know if I will discuss the assassination with you or not. You might be wasting your time and money coming here to see me." He said he was willing to take that chance. Mr. West came to visit me. The first day we talked about football, auto racing, the weather, prison life, guns and many other subjects. He stayed for the whole day and the came back the next day. The second day we touched base on the JFK assassination. I liked Mr. West a great deal. He was one of those people who you could talk to for a while and know that they were very serious about what they were doing. He had court action going to have JFK's body dug up and to have a new autopsy done on it and check for the cause of death. He was interested in which shot killed him. I told him when he got the body dug up to be checked, have them check it for traces of mercury. But before Mr. West could get the court to rule in his favor, he passed away. (Letter #259 April 28, 2001 But back to our phone conversation about JFK's body. I think I mentioned this to you before, but I'm not sure if I did or not. Joe West was trying very hard and he had it in court, before a judge, to get JFK's body dug up and checked for traces of mercury. For a while things were looking pretty good. Then Joe had the severe heart problems and had to go in for heart surgery, He came through that part real good and it looked like a speedy recovery was in order. But all of a sudden there was problem and Joe died very fast. I cannot prove this, but a friend of mine from back East, in the intelligence community, informed me that someone had tampered with Joe's medicine and that was the reason for Joe's death. He said Joe's surgery was a success. He is the same man that informed me that we had been sold out by "Stockwell". And you know what? The man was right about "Stockwell" But at the time, when I told Vernon and some others, they said I was wrong. But they found out the hard way. Anyway, with Joe's death, the court case for getting JFK's body checked for traces of mercury died with him. When Joe was here to visit me we talked about this and I told Joe at that time that he was wasting his time in court and he couldn't win his case because Kennedy was not buried in Arlington. Then I ran it down for Joe. (Phone conversation between author and Files 2001- "Back in 1966 or early 1967 a group of us were sitting around having a few drinks, this was before I stopped drinking alcohol. The people were CIA and DOD. They didn't know I was one of the shooters in Dallas. The conversation turned to JFK and what happened to his body. Ted Shackley said 'we kicked the box out of the plane into the sea. That's what the family wanted'") Bob Vernon and me never got into this as he was not interested in getting Kennedy's body exhumed. Vernon was not interested in the truth like Joe was. I don't really blame Vernon in one sense as he had all his money tied up in this video thing and he wanted to recover his money and make a profit. He said he wanted to finish up Mr. West's work and he asked me to help him, which I agreed to. The one thing that I feel bad about is that Mr. West died, not ever knowing that I was one of the two shooters. I was waiting for the lawyer, Don Erwin, to get me immunity for the crime so that I could speak freely and not be charged for it. But Mr. West died before that ever happened. I did go ahead and help Mr. Robert Vernon do his story. I gave him a complete interview on the JFK assassination. He produced a video called "Confession of an Assassin" and please do not confuse the video with the movie "The Assassin". There is nothing to connect them, except the word "assassin".

Note from Wim: That is why I say to the critics: Wanna prove Files a hoax? Dig up JFK's body! If there is a body in Arlington, under that eternal flame, the Files story is in trouble.

The United States Government non-regard for the LAW

P: Has anyone from the U.S. Government or Organized Crime threatened you for talking about your role in the JFK assassination?

J: YES! The government put a lot of pressure on me. There were some outside threats made on my family. The government made those threats and tried to blame it on Organized Crime. Organized Crime has NEVER made any threats against my family or me. When the video was completed, Mr. Vernon called the CIA and told them that he had an unedited tape of my interview and they went straight to Houston, Texas and viewed the tape in the presence of Mr. Vernon. The CIA said they had no problem with what I had said. Mr. Vernon then contacted a lawyer in Chicago, Illinois and I instructed him that a tape of my confession was being mailed to him that was unedited. The lawyer came to visit me and told me that the people in Chicago had no problem with my interview. But however, before I gave the interview, a woman from the Department of Defense came here to Stateville prison and read me the riot act and threatened me with the OSA. "The Official Secrecy Act." Warden Godinez was there at the time and I said some things to her that made her leave in a hurry. Then two FBI agents came to visit me and made it clear, that if I gave an interview on the JFK assassination, that they would make sure that I lost my appeal and that they would have me taken back to court and get me some more time. I told them to do what they had to, but not in those words and I don't use those other words any more. Anyway, I gave the interview on the JFK assassination and sure enough, I lost my appeal.
("Cop-killer" James Files did not shoot a police officer. He was with someone who did fire his gun for self-protection. The police officer his associate shot was not killed. The police were out of uniform and out of jurisdiction when the incident happened. James Files thinks there was a contract out on him and they were trying to make some side money. They never

identified themselves as police or said they were under arrest. The out of uniform men fired off 14 rounds before Files' partner returned fire. I'm not trying to say James Files was an upstanding citizen but in this case, he was imprisoned for something he did not do. He's been incarcerated for attempted murder-kill injure since 1991 for this incident. February 3, 2003 I spoke with David Ostertag, the man James Files partner, Dave Morley, shot in self-defense. He is a former sergeant in the police force and later he was promoted as an investigator to the Illinois States Attorney's Office. He said Morley fired the first shot that hit him. Two notarized eyewitness accounts of the incident that were not allowed as defense evidence concur with Files and Morley's version of the story. The other men shot at Files and Morley FIRST. Morley returned fire in self defense. Ostertag was disturbed that he wasn't informed on the background of James Files and feels like it was a miracle that he and his associate lived through the incident. He was also disturbed that James Files criminal records and history have disappeared from FBI files. His police records still exist but not the FBI's. Mr. Ostertag is now retired from police work and holds a job at a credit card company.)

Not long afterwards, I was taken back to court in Lake County, Illinois and went before the judge and the reinstated counts either 4 & 5, 5 & 6, anyway the judge gave me the max on each count, which they had been dropped at my regular trial and were now brought back against me and I received 15 years on each count to run consecutive to each other. And this is a fact and it's in the court records. So that is easy to check. To this day, the only people to ever give me a problem about the JFK interview are in our own government. Never once have the people from Organized Crime section ever given me a problem. I have never testified against any of the people and I never will. In December of 1998, and it is on record that Robert Vernon and FBI agent Zack Shelton and one other man, can't remember his name, were here to visit me and to make me an offer to get me out of prison. They wanted the ledger or diary that Mr. Nicoletti kept of the things that we had done and who was buried where. I refused to give it to them for my freedom. I will never roll over on the people. I may not have much here in prison and I do not like it here, but I will never be a snitch for them. I prefer "Death to Dishonor." That is how I lived my life and I am too old to change now. Mr. Nicoletti always told me, "Jimmy, it don't matter how much money you make, if you don't have your word, then you've got nothing." I have always lived by those standards.

The FBI's knowledge of James Files since 1963

P: How early did the FBI know of your involvement in the assassination of JFK? What year did you learn of this?

J: The FBI knew of my involvement in the JFK assassination as early as either late 1963 or mid 1964. I never knew this until late 1996 or maybe early 1997. I was shocked to learn that one of the Cubans that was in one of our groups, was also an informant for the FBI. I never told any of them that I was involved. I figure that it was leaked through David Atlee Phillips, as it was one of his people that informed the FBI. He was one of our pilots and he was paid by the CIA out of one of our banks in Miami. So the FBI has known the truth all these years and have just let the sleeping dogs lie. Gee, I wonder why? One more point. The NSA sent me a copy of a letter that was declassified wanting to know if I wrote it. If I wasn't known in those circles, then why would they do this? And, the letter states that they knew in advance that John F. Kennedy was going to be assassinated.

Jim Garrison and the FBI

July 26, 2002 phone conversation

P: What do you know about Jim Garrison being involved with the FBI and that guy…

J: I know nothing about Jim Garrison.

P: Carlos Marcello…

J: Carlos I know, I know nothing about Jim Garrison.

P: Was he protecting anybody in New Orleans?

J: Who? Jim Garrison?

P: Jim Garrison.

J: I could not give you an honest answer to none of that.

P: And you don't have an opinion about him or anything?

J: No. None whatsoever.

P: OK. I just thought there was some talk in the background about him being…

J: I'm not sure who it was, but when Warden Godinez was still our warden here, and the prosecutor out of New Orleans called the prison. They called the prison, they had a Lear jet on stand by, and they wanted to come here and see me and sit down and talk to me about the murder of David Ferrie, OK?

P: What year was this?

J: (Files asks cell partner what year Warden Godinez was still at the prison) …it would have been in '95 because it was right before Godinez left here. And I told Godinez, when they was gonna put me on the speaker phone…you just tell 'em I don't want to talk to 'em…I says you tell 'em I don't want to see 'em …they got no business and I got nothin' to say to 'em.

P: There's nothin' to say.

J: And… I'm not sure who it was…who the prosecutor was at that time…because they wanted to talk to me about the death of David Ferrie…a lot of things weren't made public…and I told then not to waste their time.

P: Hum…

J: And that was when Warden Godinez was the warden here. He knows me very, very, very well. He's also a professor at a college, and he used to bring college students by here to ask me questions.

Silencing the lambs

P: After Sam Giancana (1975), Johnny Roselli (1976) and Charles Nicoletti (1977) were murdered; did you ever wonder why you weren't silenced as well?

J: After Lee Harvey Oswald was killed; all of us thought we had it made. The Warren committee said that Lee Harvey Oswald acted alone and that made it look like an open and shut case. None of us were worried until 1975 when they called Sam Giancana to appear before the new committee. With that, everyone was wondering what was going on. After Sam was executed in his home, then Johnny Roselli in Miami, and then Mr. Nicoletti, yeah, I figured I was next. Before that I was still a valuable asset to the CIA as a contract agent, as I was keeping busy in Central and South America. But all along I felt that no one knew that I was one of the shooters that day in Dallas. I felt that everyone thought it was Mr. Nicoletti and Johnny Roselli. Never in my life did I think or dream that the FBI knew about me from the very beginning. Had someone told me then I would have told them "No way!" I never really felt that I had a need to worry. Just goes to prove that you can't really trust anyone.

George Bush "Clear and Present Danger"

P: I was going to ask you, during the years between 1963-1980, how big of a part was George H. W. Bush in the cover-up of the assassination of John F. Kennedy?
J: That I have no idea.
P: You don't know, how big of a part he had? What year did you meet him? Our last phone conversation was all static-y and I couldn't even hear.
J: Uh, it was at mid '66, late '66, I believe it was. He was still with the CIA and he come down there to Little Havana and we was running some special ops out of there and we had the truck work going on taking control of it. You could probably still get clips in the newspaper about all the murders that took place there in Miami and we were killing people right and left – leaving shopping bags loaded with money laying in the supermarket. Us, we wanted everybody to know this was not robbery. This was POWER. This was CONTROL.
P: Right.
J: And this was in '66 and '67 and there were so many deaths down there it was incredible.
P: But that's when you first met him? (G.H.W. Bush)
J: He come down there and we were doing things that were getting ready for me (click on phone) to go to Mexico on a deal, and this is the part we talked about where Frank Sturgis had to come and get me out down there?
P: Um-hum
J: He bailed me out in Mexico and I said it wasn't jail?
P: Um-hum
J: Right before this was when George Bush was down there and he shook our hands and told us and all this…he told us "If you men need *anything* from *anywhere* in the world and it can be moved on an airplane, you'll have it in 72 hours".
P: Yeah.
J: George Bush, like I say, maybe he was a lousy President, whatever. I don't know, maybe he's Skull and Bones and everything else, but I gotta say one thing, when he was Director of the CIA he did support us. And he did back us and gave us everything we needed.
P: Well, if you're going to do that kind of work, you want to know somebody is backing you up instead of being all talk.
J: Well, if it wasn't for Frank Sturgis I would have died, I would have died in Mexico. Because they didn't want to send nobody, but Frank Sturgis took his people and chopper and

he says "I'm getting my people out! I'm going in after them!" And they didn't want the, ah, they didn't want any involvement because they gave us very, very bad intelligence, ok?
P: Oh.
J: And we went in, I took a handful of men and jumped into a thing, instead of hitting just a few, like we thought, we jumped into a whole company.
P: Uh-oh!
J: And I mean we were out numbered something between 50-20 to 1 and you can imagine the beatin' we was takin'. We fought our way back, right up to the Gulf of Mexico there, and we were in the rocks and when they come with the choppers, and we had a couple gun ships we were layin' down trying to pick up our dead and wounded and get them back to the choppers.
P: Wow.
J: So, ... but like I say, Frank Sturgis... I owe him my life.
P: Well, see? I need to know that.
J: Without Frank Sturgis ... did you ever see the movie "Clear and Present Danger"?
P: Yeah.
J: Remember how they pulled out and left the guys, abandoned them, down in Columbia?
P: Um-hum.
J: They made the movie, when they show that one scene, it was wrong. It was Mexico, ok?
P: Yeah.
J: And we went in there for...(can't hear)
P: You went in there for what?
J: To take out the Russian advisors training Cubans there in Mexico.
P: Uh-huh
J: We were training Cubans right there in Mexico, ok?
P: Uh-huh
J: They were flyin' a Russian flag and a Cuban flag, mixing the troops, and when we went into the shrubs of it we thought there was only a small group being trained there. We didn't think that we would endanger eight or ten advisors capacity, special groups, you know? The Russian Special Forces? Specnaz.
P: Um-hum
J: And, ah, we went in there shootin' and there were more than 30 and a whole company.
P: (sigh)
J: It was another detail - those people were going to Africa, they were supposed to disrupt so we didn't get any causalities
P: Right.
J: And so we were told to stop it. Well, what we were led to believe was one thing and we got there and found out it was a whole new thing and we just couldn't handle it. We did what we could, you know, we was just totally outnumbered.
P: Gosh.
J: But we didn't realize that until we already went in an' kicked, kicked the tin can over. You know what I mean?
P: Yeah. Do you think it was intentional that you weren't given all the intelligence information you needed?
J: I almost think... at times I almost think it was intentional. I think they thought if they could write us all off at that point, nobody would know the difference. They were tryin' to get rid of a lot of us who were in the "black operations."
P: Yeah. That's what I was wondering. If they sent you on missions to...
J: I almost at times, I used to think... at first I didn't... "Oh, just bad intelligence." But at times I felt "Well, I think these people want to get rid of us" when they felt we would all die there. (Mexico 1966)

P: Yeah. Then dead men tell no tales.

May 21, 2001 written interview continued – James Files sent back to P.J. in #291 July 18, 2001.

P.J.: To your knowledge did Sam Giancana or Tony Accardo have any associations or business with Aristotle Onassis or Howard Hughes?

James Files: To my knowledge, no. None that I ever heard of.

P: In your opinion why didn't Lee Oswald say he was CIA when he knew he was going down as the patsy and the cameras were rolling on November 22, 1963 at the Dallas Police Station? It was his only chance to survive. Why didn't he take it? Is this part of your training in the Agency?

J: Why didn't Lee Oswald say he was CIA when he realized that he was going down as the patsy? Well, one of the first things that you learn when you're at one of the Agency's academies is that you're ALWAYS to deny being involved with the Agency in any way. DENY, DENY, DENY!!! Never tell anyone that you are associated with the Agency. If you are arrested, keep your mouth shut, you always have a number to a lawyer's office that is sterile from the Agency, but that lawyer knows who to call. Once that call is made, then the problem goes away and you walk out of a police station without a report ever being written. There is no record of that arrest. At that time Lee Oswald may have told them that he was a contract agent for the CIA. He may have even told them that he was a spy for the CIA; no one knows for sure what he told the investigators as part of their report was lost or censored. And, had Lee Oswald started yelling, "Hey! I'm CIA and I'm being sacrificed" who in their right mind would have believed him? No one! They would have thought him a nut like he had been portrayed. You must remember; character assassination always precedes physical assassination. That part is in the CIA training manual.

Patsy versus. Immunity

P: So let me get this straight. Some guys go down as patsies – they are sacrificed – and some guys are protected and immune from prosecution or even questioning?

Example: Frank Sturgis in Russia. (I thought James Files said in a phone conversation that Frank Sturgis had gone to Russia.)

J: It happens all the time. Some go down as the patsy and when they claim they work for the CIA, they have no way of proving it. Look at me for example. My whole past history has been wiped out. My birth certificate reads, "Deceased at birth". There are no school records of me or anything. Look how many people think I'm crazy. But in my case, I didn't go down as a patsy. I got a case for shooting cops that were trying to kill me. But back in 1977, three men and me were taking care of business for the Agency when a pedestrian was hit during a firefight. When the cops arrived, I told my team to lay down their weapons. We went to the station and we kept our mouths shut. I made the phone call and within two and a half hours we walked out with our weapons and there was no trace of us ever having been arrested or even taken in for questioning. And yes, there are those who are not allowed to be questioned. And some are immune from prosecution due to "National Security" being put at risk. **There are many things that would shock the American people if they only knew the truth.** But as for Frank Sturgis, I never knew he went to Russia. I know that Frank Terpil wound up in Russia after our deal went bad in South America. We sold about 10,000 machine guns to the FBI instead of this guy who claimed to be working with this revolutionary group. Anyway, Frank Terpil wound up going to trial and the morning in New York when the judge was going to revoke his bond, Frank Terpil left the courthouse to get some cigarettes and he never came back. They had the trial without him being there and gave him 52 years I believe. He left the country, went to Uganda, then on to Beirut and finally wound up in Russia. But I know nothing of Frank Sturgis going to Russia.

(Frank Terpil is a former CIA agent hired, along with fellow former CIA man Edwin Wilson, by Muammar al-Quaddafi to train and equip Libyan military special forces during the 1970's. Terpil was dismissed from his CIA position in 1971. Among the former agents' most infamous dealings were sales to Libya of enormous quantities of the plastic explosive Semtex, portions of which have turned up in terrorist attacks by various groups around the world. It is believed that Terpil and Wilson sold as much as 20 tons of Semtex to the Libyans. Terpil has also been implicated in several assassinations in Africa and an unsuccessful coup attempt in Chad in 1978. He remains at large. *Almanac of Modern Terrorism*, 1991, p-237 Reference: Richard Lloyd, *Beyond the CIA: The Frank Terpil Story*, New York, Seaver Books, 1983.)

#783 Wednesday August 18, 2004, James Files letter to Pamela Ray

Back to the other point that I want to clear up. Bob Vernon had all of my papers, including the original manuscript and my notes for "To Kill A Country," and he gave them to at that time, "warden Godinez" who is now the D.D. for the D.O.C. And in writing, I had it plainly stated the Orlando Letelier was killed by a bomb, that had the explosives transported by me, to Buckley, and Michael Townley put the bomb in his car, a Chevy Nova, if my memory is correct and the car exploded in front of the Chilean Embassy on Sheridan Circle, better known as Embassy Row. The explosives came from the Falcondo Mining Co. and they were 60 per-cent strength dynamite, that is referred to as "engineering explosives." The man that I shot was sitting in the back seat of the limo when I pulled my .45 and shot the S.O.B. and yes, I ticked off a lot of people. But he was Russian, he was not a Chilean. Bob had all of the paperwork on all of this. Bob knows what I had down in writing and I even had the route that he, Orlando Letelier, took to work that morning. Ronnie Moffit and Michael Moffit were in the car with him. She was killed, but Michael survived it. Please tell them to get their facts straight. I know what I said.

Phone conversation August 16, 2002 James Files and author

P: What years were you a contract agent for the CIA? Starting in what year and ending in what year?
J: Starting in what year? 19 and 60…1960, when I met … it would have been December 1960 my hire date.
P: And when was the last time you did a contract for the CIA?
J: '77.
P: 1977.
J: Yeah.
P: Were you over in Iran?
J: No.
P: You never went over there?
J: No. Never went over there.

P: That's good.

J: But uh…some of my friends in my outfit went in…a lot of intelligence…they had a lot of things there…a lot of programs and stuff. I knew a lot of them.

P: Well, I was going to ask you if you were over there if you were part of that…um…SAVAK…because I guess a lot of American people went over there and trained them and…

J: No…

P: I'm glad to hear that.

J: The only part of that country I really had anything to do with was when I went into Libya three different times, and we were suppose to train people up in the bay of Sirt…and uh…it was all screwed up and uh…Bernstein committed suicide and his girlfriend and the shotgun (can't hear).

P: Who was that you were saying?

J: Bernstein. (Wim: He means Duberstein, as Ed Wilson emailed me)

P: Bernstein.

J: Bernstein whatever his name… he was Jewish…a little bitty guy. Here was a guy who was scared to death of guns. They said he killed himself, whatever you want to call it…he would have NEVER taken a gun and shot himself – but he went out and bought himself a brand new shotgun, went to his girlfriends apartment, where he was keeping her up and uh…he went down to the basement by the laundry room and shot himself.

P: Wow.

J: Somebody took and killed him when he went over to see her.

P: I know…a lot of these "suicides", so called suicides that are done with shotguns…that doesn't make sense. If you're going to kill yourself, most people would, if they really meant business, they would do it with a handgun wouldn't they?

J: Yeah but you have to understand something, if they use a handgun…ballistics. If they got a shotgun there's no ballistics.

P: Right…but I'm just saying if somebody seriously wants to kill himself or herself by shooting themselves, they wouldn't care about ballistics and all that.

J: Right.

P: They would use a handgun; they wouldn't use a shotgun…or a rifle.

J: Anyway, a lot of these guys who shot themselves, stabbed themselves, this one guy tied a weight around their boots and killed himself…they got the body back and he had a size 8 shoe and his friend said he wears a size 7. Anyway, long story forget about all that.

P: OK. I just had a couple questions about Iran…but...never mind. I don't want to waste our phone call on it.

Libya

Phone conversation August 16, 2002 James Files and author

P: When you were in Libya, did you ever sell explosives to the government over there? Is that what you guys were doing?

J: Did I ever sell explosives to the government?

P: In Libya.

J: No I didn't sell them we transported them, we gave them explosives.

P: Right. And you were working with that guy Frank Terpil and Edwin Wilson?

J: Yep.

P: OK. Because I'm quoting some of that stuff in one of the sections of the book and I wanted to make sure that was right. Anyway, change the subject quick.

J: Yeah that all got messed up.

Who gets to play God?

P: Who in the CIA, or anywhere else, decides who gets a retirement plan or RETIRED? Who gets to play God?

J: Who gets to make the big decisions on retirement plans and who gets to play God, I honestly don't have any idea. But I would guess that is decided in the covert department and on what the situation was. The thing would be who's who and how valuable of an asset that person was. They look at a lot of different things before they make the assessment.

P: I guess having "friends in high places" isn't a guarantee on safety. Remember Vince Foster and John F. Kennedy Jr.?

J: When you're in the game with any intelligence organization you're never safe from anyone. There are times when no one can protect you. As for Vince Foster and John F. Kennedy Jr., they both died for different reasons. Foster, because he knew too much and John Jr. because he was thinking about politics and had he run against Hillary Clinton, he would have won with a landslide. She would have had NO chance at all to win and everybody knows that. But that is how the real world works and murder or assassinations come cheap. Remember…no one is safe!!!

Files on Oswald

December 7, 2001 Letter #357 page 3, from James Files to author regarding Lee Harvey Oswald and the following article.

The material you sent me in letter # 310 on Oswald, I had never seen or read and I found it pretty interesting. But people should really stop and ask themselves why there was no statements or notes taken at that time. Anytime a suspect is questioned, there is supposed to be two officers and a record of everything that is said taken down. In the case of Oswald, there is nothing. Well, I believe that notes were taken as well as a statement was made. But I think the FBI took it all and disposed of it. Then there has always been the paraffin test that the Dallas Police Department gave Oswald and that alone proved he never fired a weapon, especially a rifle! They said that the residue on his right hand might have conformed as a pattern from firing a revolver. NOT TRUE! The residue was in the palm of his hand. The residue upon discharge would have blown backward, on top, by the valley between the thumb and first finger and across the wrist. Not in the palm of the hand. Lee Harvey Oswald got that residue in the palm of his hand when he was with me, picking up the shell casing that I was ejecting when I was calibrating the scope on Chucks weapons and mine. The residue they are speaking of was the shell casing that Oswald was holding in the palm of his hand for me and therefore he closed his hand on them and that is how he got it in the palm of his right hand. Anyway, I found it all very interesting. But as many times as I've been arrested, I do know police procedure.

They will never change the history books and a hundred years, even a thousand years from now the books will read that Lee Harvey Oswald did the act and that he acted alone. **All of our history is based on one lie after another. But after all, that's the AMERICAN WAY**. The handful of people that run this country, figures that the people need not know and that's how it is. They have to hide the truth from the people. But one day I hope the people will wake up before it's too late, and they find themselves inside a "FEMA" detainment center. Then that will be too late and they'll sit there with a stupid look on their face wondering how it all came about. Enough of that.

Barry Seal – Flying Guns and Drugs for CIA Blavk Ops

James Files knew Barry Seal as a DEA/CIA co-worker-pilot flying firearms and explosives to Central and South America in exchange for drugs on the return flight home to United States of America. Files made these comments from the preface and first chapter of *Barry and 'the Boys'* (B & B).

#435 20 Oct 2002 sent back to author 27 Nov. 2002

B & B: (from Preface) At another hanger, he said, "That hanger's owned by a guy who smuggled heroin through Laos back in the Seventies."

Files: What they was talking about here was "The China Trail."

B & B: This is the story of Barry Seal, the biggest drug smuggler in American history, who died in a hail of bullets with George Bush's private phone number in his wallet…p-3

He saw it coming, and covered his ears with his hands. Then, with his head settled onto the Cadillac's steering column, Barry Seal slipped into history in the soft Baton Rouge twilight of February 19, 1986, dead instantly. P-4

Files: The clean up and cover-up of Mena, Arkansas begins.

B & B: "It looked like they were getting rid of people who knew too much about Mena," stated one observer at the time. P-5

Files: This is why they wanted me out of the way when I first got out of federal prison.

B & B: The second event which made Barry Seal famous came seven months later. It became the milestone event of the Reagan '80's, the shooting down over Nicaragua of Seal's C-123 military cargo plane, with Eugene Hasenfuss on board. The crash cracked open the Iran Contra Scandal and inspired an ambitious burst of emergency damage control by Lt. Col. Oliver North, who embarked on a three-day shredding spree reportedly designed to remove any trace of the name "Barry Seal" from his files. P-7

Files: This guy Gene was out of Wisconsin. He was not supposed to have a chute on board.

B & B: Lt. Col. North's ties with Barry Seal are covered in this book. As former CIA pilot and lawyer Gary Eitel remarked about North, "Going to church doesn't make you a Christian, anymore that going to a carwash makes you a car." P-7

Files: This line is very true...

B & B: "The CIA rigged a hidden camera in the plane, enabling him to snap photos of several men, including Pablo Escobar and high ranking Sandinista official Federico Vaughn, loading cocaine aboard his C-123 military cargo plane. These pictures later resulted in the indictment on narcotics smuggling charges of the Medellin Cartel, Jorge Ochoa and Pablo Escobar." P-8

Files: They should get their facts straight. It was the DEA and not the CIA who put the cameras in the wings of the plane.

B & B: For well over a decade disturbing allegations have dribbled out about a clandestine operation in Mena involving arms sales, drug trafficking, two American Presidents, and all the elements of a fast-paced-thriller: daring drug smugglers, gunrunners, duffel bags filled with cash dropping from the sky, murder by ambush, revenge in the dead of night...p-9

Files: This all started in the '70's and more than likely, it's still going on today.

B & B: Seal's slaying was a crucial first strike in a successful operation that effectively neutralized a key ingredient in any functioning democracy: the truth. It was opening salvo in a clean-up operation designed to cover the tracks of what has been called the most massive covert operation in this nation's history, Operation Black Eagle. P-16

Files: I never knew of "Operation Black Eagle" at that time. When I got out of the federal prison, I thought they were trying to kill me for the JFK thing.

B & B: "I know that we took a load of equipment and a bag-full of money to buy drugs, and I set up all the communications for them (the Sandinistas) so they could talk back and forth, putting in high-frequency radios from E-Systems. We supplied the Sandinistas with communication equipment," Hall said, "and I don't think that's ever come out before." P-17

Files: Tosh is the one that flew most of this equipment down there.

B & B: Events in Baton Rouge the night of Seal's death have been whispered about by investigators for years. One enduring mystery swirls around the appearance of what local law enforcement officials on the scene nervously referred to as "The Men in Black."

Late the night of Seal's slaying a squad of FBI and other federal agents swooped down in force on the Baton Rouge headquarters of the Louisiana State Police, and confiscated, at virtual gunpoint, material evidence in the case from investigating homicide officers charged by law with preserving it uncompromised for the prosecution of the capital crime of murder.

"It was a 'clean-up' crew pure and simple," said one state lawman who was there. P-18

Files: Sure sounds like the same people who showed up at the bombed Murrah Building in Oklahoma City and collected all the files, (damaging to the Clinton's and George Bush and his black ops "crew") while stopping a rescue operation. After all, the files are more important than human lives.

B & B: Following the thread of Seal's life will lead us back to the very headwaters of this secret history…Miami, before the Bay of Pigs fiasco, the failed operation which introduced so many crucial players in our story: Brigade 2506, the Shooter Teams, Ted Shackley, Howard Hunt, Frank Sturgis, Felix Rodriguez…and George Bush.

Seal was initiated into covert operations in Miami in the early '60's, when guys paid to protect us – *CIA guys* – hobnobbed, schemed, wheeled and dealed with people most Americans assume they're being paid to protect us *against*… 'Made' guys. Mobsters. Organized Crime. Miami was the largest CIA station in the world, until the stink grew so bad in 1965 that the station was disbanded after its fleet of planes was shown to be engaged in drug smuggling.

Then these men, "Barry and 'the boys,'" all go to Southeast Asia. Laos was where they went; because Laos was where the *money* was. "Barry was not a soldier of fortune or a mercenary – he was a covert operative. It was the 70's when I saw Barry again," says friend 'Red' Hall, delivering a bombshell. "Right after he got caught flying drugs in a 747 out of the Orient during the Vietnam War. He had a lot of government connections; that's a fact." P-20

Files: Barry took off for South East Asia and got there for the tail end of "The China Trail."

B & B: Barry Seal, we will discover, was a contemporary of Lee Harvey Oswald's in the Louisiana Civil Air Patrol, where both young men came under the tutelage of CIA pilot David Ferrie, who was himself murdered, we will hear from cops working surveillance on Ferrie when he died, the night before he was to be called to testify before Jim Garrison's grand jury probe of the Kennedy assassination.

While still an impressionable teenager Barry Seal came under the tutelage of a man you wouldn't want your worst enemies' kid to know…David Ferrie, a pedophile, and worse. P-23

Files: I told you before about Ferrie's murder and I told Bob Vernon several years ago about how he died, but never said who did him.

B & B: This individual, with some obvious concerns, was with Seal when he played his role in the Watergate Scandal, when he was arrested less than two weeks after the bungled burglary by CIA Cubans like Frank Sturgis, with 13,500 pounds of plastic C4 explosives destine for anti-Castro Cubans in Mexico.

"Mena is very real," Hurston (Joe) concluded, before declining to talk further, at least on the record. "And what did happen back then is tied to that. And you mess with '72, and you're messing with Mena. And Mena is tied right in to current stuff. So there is a strong connection, and you should be aware of it." P-24

Files: The very beginning…

B & B: What possible connection could there be between Barry Seal and the massive drug smuggling in Mena, Arkansas in the 1980's and the swirling intrigue in Mexico City in 1963 that preceded the Kennedy assassination?

We couldn't have imagined that there was one - until we saw what we've come to refer to as *"the picture."* It was taken at a nightclub in Mexico City on January 22, 1963, ten months to the day that preceded the Kennedy assassination.

Files: I'm positive that this picture had nothing to do with the Dallas Party.

Note from Wim: I agree, the picture is much later than 1963. Tosh Plumlee says he is in that picture, he says it was not taken in 1963 and it had nothing to do with Dallas. I believe him.

Files #483 Nov.9, 2002:

And as for the last page in the letter, the picture of *Barry & 'the boys'*, they all look familiar in a way, after all, there all GOOMBAS! You know, like they came out of the same mold. I was hoping for some more of the updated pictures. I know I've changed a lot in all of those years. Those guys all start out looking like that and in the end, they all look alike; fat, big belly and smoke a cigar or they shrink in size and wind up a skinny ol' man all bent over with a cane smoking a cigar. Some time I'll have to take you into one of the old neighborhoods so you can see for your self. (No thanks Jimmy; I trust your opinion on this.)

Files in #496 Nov. 16, 2002: The picture of Barry and the boys' from letter 428, the second from the front on the right, in the material you sent me, they seem to think that this is Frank Sturgis with the coat pulled in front of his face. I'm saying that it's not Frank. I'm enclosing a copy of another photograph, where I cut it out, the head that is, for you to slide by that photo in the book to match it with. Notice the hair, the forehead and the ears. Then tell me if you think they are one and the same. If so, then the man with the coat pulled in front of him is not Frank!

Note from Wim: I agree. It is Tosh Plumlee, just as Tosh says

And 435 is the material on Barry Seal, which I have read and found very interesting. What do I think of it? WOW! I'm not really sure. There's so much that I don't really know. You see, in our school, we didn't sit around and tell our secrets. We all knew one another and we did favors for each other, but none of us were really friends or led a social life together. Yes, we knew each other, we knew we were doing wrong, knew the government was our master and we did our jobs and went on with life. We all heard rumors about each other and so forth. Anyway, Hopsicker, and I think I may have told you this in my last letter, anyway, it was the DEA and not the CIA that put the cameras in the wings of the 123, better known as "The Fat Lady" and I told you this back when you was here to visit me. Anyway, what Hopsicker wrote, I figure is pretty much the truth.

As for Barry Seal flying the get-a-way plane out of Dallas that day, I don't really know. Is it possible? Yes! I said in my interview, that I drove back to Chicago that I did not know how Chuck and Johnny got out of Dallas. Barry may have flown that plane and if he did, you can bet your last doughnut that Sam Giancana was on that plane leaving Dallas. Do I know for sure? No, I never ask and I was never told. Sometimes, in the world that I lived in, the less you knew the safer and smarter you were.

J.F. letter to P.J. May 28, 1999

Like I said in my other letter, I've read very little on the Kennedy assassination, as everyone was doing a lot of guessing. Besides, what I didn't say about the Kennedy assassination would fill a book. But you must understand, I was doing my best to protect a lot of people and also, not give them enough to hang me. As long as I was just talking, I knew I would never go to trial, as they would not want to make the Warren Commission look dumb. But, should I give them everything I've got put away, then I would force them to put me on trial and that my dear, is not in my best interest. I want to get out, not stay in the joint forever. Bob Vernon did everything in the world to get me indicted. He even sent confidential information to a federal judge in Texas. I think his name was Carver. I've got it with all my legal material. Anyway, Bob was sending him all these letters and he was sending it on to Washington D.C., and there a friend of mine ran across them and he made copies and sent them to Chicago. Then they were hand delivered to me late one night. They had been shrunk down in size, that I had to take them to work and put them under this big magnifying glass in order to read them. Let me tell you, I was shocked and very ticked off at Bob Vernon over how he had betrayed me. Kennedy was one thing, as I never worried about that. But there were other things I didn't want the Department of Justice to know about. It just got me really ticked off at how hard he tried to get me indicted. Oh well, my fault for trusting him. I don't know if I told you this before or not, but Joe West died not knowing that I was one of the shooters. He never knew that I was the one behind the fence. When Joe died, I was relieved; I thought it was all over with. But then I let Bob Vernon talk me into helping out Mrs. West so she would have the money to pay off the hospital bills that Joe left her with. She was broke and hurting, so I agreed. Bob also betrayed me on another deal, but that's another story, just between him and me. At least he didn't go to the cops on that one.

I'll try to send you something Bob wrote me and the background, all researched by the Dept. of Defense. It goes all the way back to the Bay of Pigs.

The Kroll Agency tried everything they could to discredit me. One story they put out was that I couldn't have been in Dallas that day, as my wife was giving birth to our daughter that day. When I was asked about it, I said yes, I was at the hospital that day. But that means Kennedy was not assassinated until September 26, 1966. I said that is the day my daughter was born go check the hospital records. That ended that.

A lot of people said I was too young to kill anyone at that time. I told them that I don't remember seeing old men out on the battlefield during combat. In Nam all I saw were a lot of young kids dying, ages between 17 and 21 years of age.

Also, I cannot for the life of me, see a man fire a weapon, a rifle, like the man Ed Hoffman said he saw, throw it to someone else, while he runs off. If they catch this other guy with the rifle, what's keeping him from telling on the one who pulled the trigger? I would never give a weapon to anyone that I had just used, to trust them to get rid of it. That is plain stupid.

Then we had another "expert" on organized crime killings say that when a mob-hit went down, there were usually 12 to 15 guys involved. That is really stupid. Most of the time it's a two man hit team. After Charles Nicoletti's death, I preferred to work alone. That way there is no chance that someone can later on turn against you. That's like the ol' man from here in Chicago, Lenny Patrick, who told stories about me whacking people. He never saw anything and I never told him anything. He was only repeating stories that had been told around town. All hearsay!!! Anyway, the Feds are talking about indicting me for something that happened in Pennsylvania back in the 70's, but they don't have a case. They have a federal retainer on me right now, which means, once I'm released from the state, they'll come and pick me up. But they can only hold me for 90 days, as I will file for a fast and speedy trial act. Besides, if I was a nobody, why did the Feds chase me for so long and spend so much money trying to put me away? Then when they did get me, for a minor crime, why was I hammered so hard, for so much time? My federal number is 892787-024 and my federal case # is 66945E and I was released from Oxford FCI in 1988.

J.F. letter to P.J. May 18, 1999

Now, on to your questions….

Do I know a Jimmy Fratianno? Yes!!! And I'm not him. James Fratianno was known as "Jimmy the Weasel." He was a big time snitch. At one time he was acting boss of the L.A. Family. The Feds finally caught up with him and he became a snitch for them to save his rotten skin. He testified at several trials and got approximately forty convictions for the Feds and that was before he testified for the "President's Commission on Organized Crime and Money Laundering" in 1984. There's a long story behind all that and yes, I know most of it. I've been asked to do a book on it and him giving up the husband and wife that worked for the FBI and gave the information to O.C. so the witnesses in the Federal Protection Program could be hit. Anyway, he died of a heart attack about two and a half years ago. There was a big price on his head.

No, I've never read the "Gemstone File." What is it about?

Yes, I knew Murray the Camel. A very nice man. He was known as "The Fixer." They claimed he could fix anything in Chicago, and I believe it. He was tied in with some very big politicians such as, "Libonati" a U.S. Congressman. Also, Tommy O'Brien, better known as "Blind Tommy." Then there was Pat Marcy, John D'Arco, etc. etc. etc…. And yes, Charles Nicoletti did have dealings with him. That I know for a fact.

"I went into the room [in 1952] and there were four gentlemen of the Outfit there with my father and another man. One of the gentlemen said to me: 'What do you think of Dwight D. Eisenhower?' I said I'd vote for him if I could, to be the next President of the United States. The man next to me said: 'Thank you very much young lady.' It was General Eisenhower. I felt very small but I hadn't recognized him without his uniform…Five men there in a room in Chicago decided who was going to be the next President of the United States."

-Llewella Humphreys, in conversation, 1983

<u>The Prince of Crime</u> Ch. 12, Vegas, the Senate, and Eisenhower p. 135

Within one week of Eisenhower's election he had appointed Nelson Rockefeller chairman of a Presidential Advisory Committee on Government Organization. Rockefeller was responsible for planning the reorganization of the government, something he had dreamed of for many years." - William Cooper

<u>BEHOLD A PALE HORSE</u> Ch. 12, The Secret Government, p. 201

Do I know Joe Alito? No!

Did Jim Garrison's office ever contact me? No!!!

Do I know Ed Hoffman? No, but I know who he is. I was the only one behind the fence. But there was another man in the railroad yard walking by some boxcars. I kept my eyes on him in case he should become a problem, that I might have to eliminate.

About Jackie Kennedy working for Allen Dulles and the CIA, I've never heard of anything like that.

Back to your answers to my questions. The thing about Jackie Kennedy I found in a book called <u>All Too Human</u> by Edward Klein p. 41, 51, 52.

p. 41 "Jackie was determined to break the mold, and thanks to her connections, she had an interesting job offer. A friend of her stepfather, Allen Dulles, the deputy director for plans for the CIA, had lined up an entry-level post for her at the CIA." [Her stepfather Hugh Dudley ("Hughdie") Auchincloss Jr.]

p. 51 "Mummy," Jackie said, "I'm going to ask Mr. Dulles to let me out of my commitment to the CIA job so I can accept the Prix de Paris."]

p. 52 "At the end of the summer, Lee would enter college at Sarah Lawrence in Bronxville, and Jackie would take Mr. Dulles nice little job at the CIA and live at home with her mother and stepfather. Everything had been settled."

What do you think about all that? I think because this book was published in 1996 and she died in 1994 might have something to do with it.

P.J. letter to J.F. May 30, 1999

In the early 60's yes, the CIA was working with the Mossad.

I have no idea who ordered the hit from the top. I was never inclined to ask a question like that as it would have made people nervous and would have gotten me a shorter life span.

I value our friendship and I thank you for taking the time to write to me. I feel you are one very nice lady and that is why I answered your letter and agreed to answer as many of your questions as I can, as I believe we are on the same wavelength. I had a large map of the "New World Order" that told who was who, with their rank and station. But during the shakedown, the cops took it. I wish we could sit down and talk face to face for several hours. There is so much I'd like to talk to you about.

J.F. letter to P.J. May 25, 1999

Please tell Debra Conway at JFK Lancer that I don't need a name in prison. Stateville Prison is located just outside of Chicago, only thirty minutes away, and that I already had a name before I got here. That everyone already knew who I was connected to. So I didn't need JFK s--- in any type or form and that if the federal agent "ZACK SHELTON" had never given my name to Joe West, I would have never have said a word. As it was, the JFK thing killed any chance I had for an appeal.

As for Ed Hoffman's statement, I think he got a little confused or tried to add a little extra, kind of dress it up. Then again, maybe he believes he saw it that way. I know there were other people in the railway yard that morning like the "tramps." Also, one of the boxcars was loaded with explosives. Did you know that? And that they could be detonated by radio or manual control? So who knows who he was really looking at. The only thing he got right was me kneeling down putting the weapon away.

The picture they show of someone behind the fence is so fuzzy; I can't tell if it's a man or a shadow. So I can't really say if it's a picture of me or not. And who believes me besides you? A lot of people. I've had several offers to do books, interviews, etc., etc., but I'm not really interested in any of that. I told them to keep their money.

You may find this very hard to believe but I've read very little about the assassination. I know those who have written about it don't know squat about what they're writing about. But they are only guessing and trying to put together a story that will sell so they can make a few bucks. I take it you have read a great deal about the assassination so maybe you can answer these questions for me. Ok…

Have you ever read in any of the books and ran across some of these names? And these are only a few, such as Twombly or Kendall? How about Chauncey Holt? How 'bout Pete Licavoli or his ranch in Arizona called "Grace Ranch?" Maybe you've heard of Leo Moceri, he was a friend of Nicoletti's and mine. There are many more questions that I could ask you, but I won't trouble you with them. Someday, maybe I'll finish telling the rest of the story. I just don't want to harm anyone and give them major problems. I think you can understand that.

I'm enclosing a few things you might find interesting. A photo of the shell casing that I spoke of and a copy of the agreement that Bob Vernon and Oliver Stone tried to get me to sign when Stone was here making the movie, "Natural Born Killers." I met with Stone at least four times; he kept trying to get me to sign to let him put me on film. I told him no way. With a few extra words added. Ha-ha…I just didn't like Stone. I'm also enclosing in a separate envelope a letter just declassified about a year ago from the NSA. You might find it interesting also. Certain people thought that I wrote it some years ago.

(Wim: The NSA letter can be viewed at http://jfkmurdersolved.com/NSA.htm)

****

The Warren Commission

On Wednesday morning, January 22, 1964, the commission was informed of a rumor that **Lee Harvey Oswald had been a $200-a-month FBI undercover agent from September 1962 until the assassination.** This information was telephoned to the flabbergasted Rankin by Texas Attorney General Carr, who revealed that he had heard it from Dallas District Attorney Henry Wade, a former FBI agent.

Chairman Warren, whose mind could have hardly been on Supreme Court matters the rest of that day, immediately called an emergency meeting of the seven commissioners at 5:30 p.m. that day. Congressman Ford was summoned out of a House Military Affairs Subcommittee meeting to attend. John J. McCloy flew down from New York. "I can never recall having attended a meeting more tense and hushed," Ford later said.

The shocked commissioners agreed to request both Carr and Wade to fly from Texas to Washington to confer with Warren and Rankin immediately. At 7:30 p.m., the meeting broke up with all the commissioners and Rankin determined not to discuss this rumor even with their wives. Warren skipped dinner. An hour later, he was the long-scheduled speaker at the dedication of the Smithsonian Institution's National Museum of History and Technology.

A day and a half later, on Friday morning, January 24, Carr and Wade arrived in Washington to confer secretly with Warren and Rankin. Although neither Texan could document the rumor's original source, both offered "information" about Oswald's alleged employment as FBI agent S. 179. They reported having heard this indirectly from two Texan newsmen and a Dallas assistant district attorney.

On Monday, January 27, a closed-door executive session was held. The seven commissioners, Rankin and a stenographer were present. The transcript was kept top secret and not declassified by the National Archives (under the Freedom of Information Act) until nearly nine years later on June 12, 1974 – less than a month before Earl Warren died.

"We have a dirty rumor that is very bad for the commission," began Rankin, "very damaging to the agencies that are involved and must be wiped out insofar as possible to do so by this commission."

Warren suggested going to the rumor's source to see if there was any substance to the claim.

A spirited discussion ended. Should FBI Director Hoover be asked directly about the truth of falsity of the rumor, or should it be investigated independently of him?

Former CIA Director Dulles offered some cynical seasoned counsel: If Oswald really *was* an FBI employee, the person who recruited him certainly wouldn't tell.

"Wouldn't tell it under oath?" asked Warren incredulously.

"No, I wouldn't think that he would tell it even under oath," repeated Dulles.

"Why?"

"Agencies do employ undercover men who are terribly bad characters," explained Dulles. Congressman Boggs urged that Hoover be given an opportunity to clear the FBI *before* the commission began to investigate.
"We must go at this thing from *both* ends, " interjected Warren, "from the end of the rumormongers and from the end of the FBI. If we come to a cul-de-sac—well, there we are. But we can report on it."
Rankin recommended that the commission inform Hoover of what they had heard and tell him that "We would like to go ahead and find out what we could about these –"

"Well, Lee," cut in Warren, "I wouldn't be in favor of going to *any* agency and saying 'We would like to do this,' I think we ought to know what we are going to do and do it-and then take our chances one way or another. The fair thing to do would be to try and find out if this is fact or fiction."

Some pro-FBI commissioners, including Ford, voiced concern that the supersensitive Hoover might think the commission was investigating *him*.

"We *are* investigating him, that's true," said Warren. "I don't believe we should apologize or make it look that we are in any way reticent about making any investigation that comes to the commission."

After this exchange had been leaked back to the FBI director by Ford, it festered the mutual hostility between Warren and Hoover which had been sparked by the Chief Justice's earlier civil libertarian rulings.

On February 6, 1964, FBI Director Hoover submitted an affidavit to the Warren Commission flatly denying that Oswald had ever been a paid employee or informant of the FBI. Fourteen years later, the release of the 80,000-word FBI "raw file" on the assassination seemed to confirm that Oswald never had been an FBI agent or informer. The CIA made a similar denial, presumably after searching its records.

Later, when Assistant FBI Director Alan H. Belmont testified before the Warren Commission on May 6, he offered to leave the bureau's "entire" Oswald file with it.

"I'm not going to look at it," ruled Chairman Warren.

Senator Russell asked to examine it.

"And *you* are not going to look at it either," added Warren before his amazed fellow commissioners and the staff. The chairman softened this decision, explaining, "Well, the same people who would deem that we see everything of this kind would also demand that they be entitled to see it. But if it is a security matter, we can't let them see it."

A week later, on May 14, Hoover personally testified before the commission. Again, he categorically denied that the unstable Oswald had ever had any FBI affiliation whatsoever, and insisted that the FBI had no reason to believe that this Marxist "loner" was capable of violence.

Warren has been widely criticized

Earl Warren: The Judge Who Changed America, 1979, p-236-239.

Marilyn Monroe *Killed* (not suicide) by Organized Crime & U.S. Government

August 4, 1962 Los Angeles, California

The following information relates to the events leading up to the JFK assassination. Marilyn Monroe was murdered to keep her extra-marital affair and pregnancy with JFK's baby a secret. She refused get an abortion and wanted to go public with everything relating to the Kennedys. By declaring these intentions, Marilyn signed her own murder contract. The Kennedys and their protectors put in a call to Chicago and Sam Giancana dispatched a team of assassins from Illinois to handle the dirty work that was ordered. At this time in history, Sam Giancana was still in communication with the White House. The "DOUBLE-CROSS" had not yet occurred. In addition to securing the Kennedy narrowly won 1960 presidential election with crucial votes from Chicago, Giancana held even more incriminating secrets about the Kennedys in regards to the fate of Monroe. Later, with Robert Kennedy acting as the Kennedy administration's Attorney General, the Kennedys ended up double-crossing Giancana by turning up the legal heat on Giancana and his associates with arrests, indictments, and prosecutions.

August 4, 1962, James Files took the team that included Charles Nicoletti to the small Palwaukie airport to catch a plane destined for Los Angeles. Files didn't think this information should go into the book because it would be hard to prove that she was pregnant. I think it would be easy to prove, providing her body is still buried in LA. It could be established if she was pregnant and the DNA from the baby could be analyzed. The FBI has very modern forensic abilities to solve old crimes, that is, if they want to.

On November 22, 1963, according to James Files, Sam Giancana was the only one who could call off the JFK assassination from his Dallas, Texas Adolphus Hotel room where Giancana was staying with Richard Cain. (In 1963, the Adolphus Hotel was located at 1312 ½ Commerce Street, across from the Carousel Club - owned by mafia-man, Oswald associate and murderer, Jack Ruby). Giancana never sent word to the assassins to call it off. James Files and Charles Nicoletti, with Johnny Roselli close by, did what they were ordered to do – shoot the president and make sure he died by aiming for a headshot. After firing the fatal headshot from behind the picket fence on the grassy knoll, James Files bit down on the shell casing when he removed it from the "fireball" rifle and put it up on the stockade fence. This shell casing was discovered in Dealey Plaza by John Rademacher in 1987 and had Files' teeth marks on it where he indicated he had bit down on it. The U.S. Army retains Files' dental records. "If anybody wants to discredit me, all's they have to do is match the indentations on the shell casing with the dental records. The FBI knows what time of day it is and won't release this evidence. After all, the FBI has known about my involvement in JFK since 1963, but I didn't learn of their knowledge of me being involved until 1996. I guess the intelligence community considered me a valuable mercenary asset and that is why I wasn't killed back when Sam, Chuck and Johnny were killed in the 1970's. The CIA had work for me to do in many countries."

July 20, 1999 James Files to author in letter

About the M.M. case, I'm sorry, but Jimmy Hoffa wasn't behind that one. Yes, she was going public about her and JFK, but everyone already knew that part. What they didn't know was that M.M. was carrying JFK's baby. They (the Kennedy's and The White House) wanted her to get an abortion like Judith (Campbell-Exner) did.
[Other reports of abortions necessitated by JFK's womanizing have circulated, most notable among them the claim by Judith Campbell Exner in the January 1997 issue of *Vanity Fair*. According to Exner's account, she was impregnated by JFK in December 1962, the last time they slept together. Upon discovering her condition some weeks later she telephoned the president, who told her she could keep the baby if she wanted to. "We can arrange it," he said. "That's an absolute impossibility because of who you are," Exner responded. "We'd never get away with it!" JFK then asked her to call Sam Giancana to set up the abortion, which she underwent at Chicago's Grant Hospital. *RFK: A Candid Biography of Robert F. Kennedy*, p-235.]
But M.M. said no blankin' way. She said she was going to have that baby. Don't forget, this is before JFK had a falling out with the Family. The call went out to Chicago and then a meeting was called and then someone drove three people to the little airport (Palwaukie) just north of Chicago and put them on a private plane west to take care of business. And this is not hearsay, OK? Anyway, the rest is history. Someday the truth will come out and some day maybe I'll be able to tell you more. But I have to be very careful on what I put on paper as all my mail is monitored. Oh yeah, the fifty thousand dollars everyone talks about, that's the money they tried to buy M.M. with and she told them where to put it. I can't tell you the

exact words that Sam G. said, as you're a lady and a Christian and I don't use those words with women. Sam was complaining about her refusing the money. I tried not to laugh, but I couldn't help it and I burst out and then I caught the devil from Sam about it. He said I was one sick you know what.

August 5, 1999, James Files to author in letter

Let's go on to M. M. Those things I know about. Yes M.M. was carrying JFK's baby. Everyone thought that M.M. and RFK (Robert F. Kennedy) were having an affair. But all those visits between M.M. and RFK were meetings where RFK was trying to buy her off. Trying to pay her to get the abortion. Sam G. had things set up for her here in Chicago, just like with Judith. But M.M. wasn't going for that. She was determined to have the baby. Right now let's come to the present. In the book by Seymour Hersh, *THE DARK SIDE OF CAMELOT*, Hersh had documents stating that M.M. was blackmailing the government. How do I know this? Because a good friend of mine in D.C., Don Fulsom, who works for the A.P. writes to me. He wrote and told me about the documents. I wrote back to him and told him to tell Hersh the documents he had were forgeries, not to use them, for him to have them checked out. He had already put those chapters in his book. But, had he checked them, yes they were false!

[In early 1996, a number of documents purportedly found in the files of the late Lawrence X. Cusack, a New York City-based attorney, indicated that JFK paid Marilyn Monroe in excess of $1 million in exchange for her silence over the affair, and her supposed knowledge of his ties to the mob. These documents found their way into the hands of Pulitzer Prize-winning journalist Seymour Hersh, who planned to use them in the *The Dark Side of Camelot*, his book on the Kennedys. Hersh also used the documents to convince ABC-TV to produce a two-hour documentary based on his book. ABC later discovered the documents to be forgeries, thus raising serious questions as to the validity of Hersh's research techniques. RFK p-321]

Now, back to the past. When M.M. told them to f--- off, (in those words) "I'm having my baby and no one is going to stop me from having it!" Well, there was only one thing left to do. Yes, they could have made her have a miscarriage, but then the media would have picked up on it. And then the secret would have been out. And speaking of the media, the White House has always had a full staff of "Media Manipulators." I'm sure you're familiar with them. They handle damage control for the scandals against the President and Vice-President. They twist the blame and put it on a scapegoat.

["Press manipulation was commonplace during the Kennedy years," commented Phillipe de Bausset, Washington bureau chief for *Paris Match*. "The JFK administration was one huge public relations show. I used to think how amazed the country would be to find out that Jacqueline Kennedy, supposedly the most desirable and exciting woman on earth, couldn't satisfy her husband. It wasn't entirely her fault. Kennedy was too intent on enjoying himself. This may or may not have hindered his ability to run the country, but it didn't help matters either. Had he lived, many of his indiscretions would have become public knowledge. He would not have been re-elected. As is, he didn't succeed in carrying out his political agenda. We were prisoners of a myth we helped to create. Professional image makers built an image; journalists bought into the propaganda and were later forced to go along with it." RFK, p-237-238.]

No, Jimmy Hoffa had nothing to do with the murder of M.M. and never knew what was going down. Everything came right out of my backyard, under orders of the Ol' Man, and I dropped the team off at "Palwaukie Airport" that morning. In another letter I'll try to explain as much of Jimmy Hoffa as I can. But as bad as my memory is getting, you may have to remind me.

About Anthony Summers, (Author of *Goddess: The Secret Lives of Marilyn Monroe* 1985) I know nothing about him. So there is nothing I can say on the subject.

July 27, 2001 James Files on phone with author

P: Do you remember what time you took Charles Nicoletti to the airport on August 4, 1962?

J: It was early morning.

P: Did Charles Nicoletti have any conversations about being in contact with people who had her (Marilyn Monroe) house bugged? So they knew the right time to go to her house?

J: No conversation about that.

P: How else would he have known when it was the right time to go in there? Unless he knew from the bug people when it was cool?

J: Sam Giancana told him.

P: Sam told him?

J: Yeah. Sam says "Do this. Do that." And then, boom! You know what I mean?

P: Well then, maybe Sam was in touch with the people that had the bugs in her house.

J: More than likely. Well, he was in touch with the people in Washington. This was before the falling out with the Kennedy family.
P: And do you think it would be taking it out too far to mention about… her being pregnant with JFK's baby?

J: I think so, because it would be hard to prove that.

P: Well, did they kick her body out to sea too? Or is she still buried in LA?

J: As far as I can tell. I don't know. I took them to the airport. I knew where they went and I knew what was happening. But that was about it.

P: Yeah, because if her body's still there, they could tell if she was pregnant or not.

J: But I knew she was pregnant before they went out there. Because they were talking about it… oh probably a week before Chuck got the word to go.

P: Um-hum

J: I won't say the things they were saying because I don't want to talk that way in front of you. You know what I mean?

P: Yeah. I don't understand how the Kennedy's …

J: I don't know about putting that in the book. You might let that pass right now.

P: Yeah.

J: Because we've got so much other stuff to go in. And that's really got nothing to do with the New World Order. You know what I mean?

P: Well, it just shows the connection between the Mafia and the government.

J: Organized Crime and the government. That's right.

(Silence)

P: It's a way people can understand that's what happened.

J: Right.

["Both Jack and Bobby had much to lose should Marilyn have gone public about her relationships with the two of them," declared Jeanne Carmen. (Friend and neighbor of Marilyn Monroe) "If they hadn't taken her out, she would have ruined both of them. I tried to warn her that these people didn't fool around, but she regarded it all as a big game. Even when we used to hang around with Johnny Roselli, the gangster, she used to say things to me like, 'Gosh, they actually *kill* people!" And I'd tell her, 'Yeah, like their friends, their mothers and anyone else who gets in their way.'

"But, you know, Marilyn was drinking a lot and taking pills, and I think her hold on reality was not so great. Marilyn never thought anything would happen to her. She was an innocent. She never believed she would get hurt." RFK, p-325.]

August 30, 1999, James Files to author in letter

Did you ever see the movie, "The Jimmy Hoffa Story?" I think that was the name of it. It was out two or three years ago. Anyway, it was pretty close to real life, except the ending. He was killed by a young gun, but the car was not loaded into a tractor-trailer. It was driven away from the area and to one of the sanitation yards and the body went into a furnace and the ashes went all over Detroit and the suburbs. That is a fact. Also, the "Mafia" did not kill Jimmy Hoffa!!! His death (1975) was ordered by the government. The government was terrified of Jimmy Hoffa. The man had too much power. The government was afraid that he might run for President and he would have won by a landslide. The workingman loved him more than any politician and they all believed in him. When he called for that one strike, he shut the country down and that really got the government's attention. That's when they said, "Hoffa has to go." The order came down from the top and my old "Company" was the ones that handled it.

Note from Wim: Compare the date of the above letter with the date of article below. See bold text .

Hoffa mystery gets deeper in new tale

A deathbed account is attributed to onetime associate in Teamsters

March 13, 2004

BY DAVID ASHENFELTER

FREE PRESS STAFF WRITER

The FBI plans to investigate the purported deathbed confession of a former Pennsylvania Teamsters official that says he helped dispose of the body of Teamsters boss Jimmy Hoffa.

The confession, said to have been written by Francis (Frank) Sheeran before he died Dec. 14 at age 83 in a nursing home near Philadelphia, says he flew to Pontiac in a small plane on the day Hoffa disappeared, picked up Hoffa's body from the killers and drove it to **a Hamtramck trash incinerator where it was burned.**

But the three-page document may turn out to be another false lead, like so many the FBI has tracked down since Hoffa vanished July 30, 1975. He was on his way to a reconciliation meeting with Anthony (Tony Pro) Provenzano, a New Jersey Teamsters boss, and Anthony (Tony Jack) Giacalone, a Detroit Mafia captain.

"It's definitely a forgery -- it's not his signature," Sheeran's daughter, Dolores Miller, of West Chester, Pa., said this week.

Miller said she thinks the document was created by Sheeran biographer John Zeitts of Omaha, Neb., to upstage a book to be published in June by another Sheeran biographer, Charles Brandt, a former Delaware chief deputy state attorney general.

Zeitts plans to bring his book out by late December.

Miller -- who is collaborating with Brandt -- said the purported confession's wording is strikingly similar to Brandt's earlier outlines, which Zeitts could have read during visits with Sheeran.

Zeitts, 59, said Friday that the confession is genuine and that Sheeran wrote it to clear his conscience about his role in Hoffa's disappearance. The FBI has said it believes Hoffa was killed to prevent him from regaining the Teamsters presidency and ending mob access to union pension funds.

Zeitts said Sheeran sent him the confession in November and he forwarded it last week to Hoffa's daughter, Barbara Crancer, a judge in St. Louis.

Crancer gave it to the FBI and the Free Press.

Sheeran, former president of Teamsters Local 326 in Wilmington, Del., was a longtime Hoffa loyalist and convicted racketeer who spent nine years in prison after Hoffa vanished.

In 1975, he took the Fifth Amendment before a federal grand jury in Detroit in the Hoffa case. Sheeran said in the 1990s that he knew who killed Hoffa, but denied personal involvement.

Sheeran told Philadelphia reporters that he'd tell all in a biography that he and Zeitts were writing. It was never published.

Zeitts said in a phone interview this week that he served time with Sheeran in a federal prison. He said he was there for sending pornography through the mail.

The confession doesn't contain a title, date or witness signatures.

It alleges:

Hoffa called Sheeran on July 27, 1975, to set up a meeting between Hoffa and Pennsylvania crime boss Russell Bufalino to resolve Hoffa's conflict with Provenzano. Hoffa called back the next day to say that he had set up a meeting with Provenzano for July 30 and that Hoffa wanted Sheeran there to "watch his back."

That night, Bufalino hinted to Sheeran that Hoffa would be killed so there was no reason for Sheeran to attend the meeting.

On July 30, Sheeran, Bufalino, their wives and Bufalino's sister-in-law headed to Detroit from Pennsylvania to attend a wedding.

Along the way, Sheeran left the group, went to an airstrip, flew to Pontiac and got into a car that had an address in the glove box.

Sheeran drove to the address and was met by Provenzano henchmen Salvatore Briguglio and brothers Thomas and Stephen Andretta, who were suspected but never charged in Hoffa's disappearance.

"The deed had already been done," the document said.

It said Sheeran drove Hoffa's body to **Central States Waste Management trash incinerator, located in Hamtramck, and the body was burned.**

Sheeran returned to Pontiac and flew back to the airstrip to rejoin his group.

"By having me in it, Russell was keeping me alive," the document said. "Important eyes were watching, and Russell was showing that my loyalty was to him first and that I would not be a 'loose end.' And being in it, there was no danger of me testifying."

Days later, the document said, Sheeran met at a New York City restaurant with incinerator owners Peter Vitale and Raffael Quasarano and others.

"After lunch, while walking to our cars, Pete Vitale told me that if I waited long enough, I could pay my respects to Hoffa in the soot surrounding his trash incinerator," the document said.

Miller said her father and Zeitts had talked for years about writing the book, but never did.

Several years ago, she said, Sheeran teamed up with Brandt, who had written a detective novel.

Brandt wouldn't discuss his book or how its details compare with the confession.

The FBI said it plans to look into the matter.

"The case is still open and we run down any leads we receive on it," FBI spokeswoman Dawn Clenney said Friday.

The entire document can be read at www.freep.com.

Contact DAVID ASHENFELTER at 313-223-4490 or ashenf@freepress.com.

To: Barr McClellan
         Zack Shelton
From:
Date: June 7, 2004
Re: Information Concerning Assassination/Subjects Involved
        Disclosed in New Non-Fiction Work Published This Week

The following information was obtained in reviewing this weekend the contents of a new book identified as follows:

Author: Brandt, Charles (note: former Chief Deputy Attorney General for the State of Delaware)

Title: "I Heard You Paint Houses," The Inside Story of the Mafia, The Teamsters, & the Last Ride of Jimmy Hoffa"

ISBN: 1-58642-077-1

Publisher: Steerforth Press L.C., 25 Lebanon Street, Hanover, New Hampshire 03755

The subject of the book is the late Francis Joseph Sheeran (died, natural causes, December 2003), an associate of the late Western Pennsylvania LCN "boss" Russell Bufalino, and a key lieutenant of the missing IBT leader James Riddle Hoffa.

Brandt's book describes Sheeran as alleging as follows, concerning our subject of investigation:

1. Jack Ruby, prior to the murder of Lee Harvey Oswald, worked in the past directly for Sam "Momo" Giancana, "boss" of the Chicago "Outfit." Further, that Ruby was sent by Giancana to Cuba to bribe officials there in order to obtain the release from jail of another LCN boss, Santos Trafficante. (p.19)

2. Sheeran met Ruby "a few times." Jimmy Hoffa's "kid" (presumably James P. Hoffa), met Ruby too, and the meetings took place at a place called the "Edgewater." "Ruby was with Giancana and he was with Red Dorfman. . . ." (p.119)

3. Sheeran met Carlos Marcello's pilot at Joe Sonken's Restaurant in Hollywood, Florida during the same period. Marcello's pilot was identified by Sheeran as David Ferrie. (p.128-129)

4. Sheeran alleged that he picked up rifles possibly used in the assassination from Genovese Family figures at Monte's Restaurant in South Brooklyn and delivered these to Marcello's pilot, David Ferrie, a short time before the assassination. (p. 162-163)

5. Sheeran said that in a conversation between his boss, Russell Bufalino and James Riddle Hoffa, shortly before Hoffa's disappearance, Bufalino intimated to Hoffa that he was "demonstrating a failure to show appreciation" for, what he whispered, "Dallas." (p.240)

6. Sheeran further alleged that in a subsequent conversation with Hoffa, Hoffa said that the "package" that Sheeran had delivered from Brooklyn to Baltimore (to Marcello's pilot, Ferrie) consisted of "high-powered rifles for the Kennedy hit in Dallas." He went on to reportedly state, "The stupid bastards lost their own rifles in the trunk of a Thunderbird that crashed when their driver got drunk. That pilot for Carlos was involved in delivering the replacements that you brought down. Those fuckers used both of us on that deal. We were patsies. What do you think of that? They had fake cops and real cops involved in it. Jack Ruby's cops were supposed to take care of Oswald but Ruby bungled it. That's why he had to go in and finish the job on Oswald. If he didn't take care of Oswald, what do you think they would have done to him – put Ruby on a meat hook. Don't kid yourself. Santo and Carlos and Giancana and some of their element, they were all in on Kennedy. Every single one of the same cast of characters that were in on the Bay of Pigs. They even had a plot to kill Castro with Momo and Roselli. I've got enough to hang everybody. And every last bit of it comes out if anything unnatural happens to me. They will all pay. All those who fucked me will pay." (p.242)

Note from Wim: The day before the video-interview, on November 18, 2003, I had a 4 hour talk with James Files and Pamela Ray. I brought the conversation to the murder of Jimmy Hoffa, and he said he did not want to discuss that. I then asked "But you do know who did that?" He said yes. I then confronted him with a book I had read, wherein a contract killer (Donald Frankos) had confessed that he had taken part in the murder and that Hoffa was killed in a home with a shot in the back of the head just after he sat down in a chair. Files commented that this was all "bullshit" and that "Hoffa was killed in a parking lot, in a wide open area". So then I asked Files if he knew what happened to the body, and he said yes. I asked him if there was any merit to the rumors that the body was put in the concrete of Yankee stadium. Files said no and added: "I'll give you this: There is no body, his ashes are all over Detroit, but I will deny I ever told you that." Again, this was well before the above article came out.

P: It is 2001 and a lot has happened in your life Jimmy. Do you believe in God? Please explain what has happened to you in the last couple years.

J: Yes a lot has happened to me in the past couple years. And yes I do believe in "God." That fact alone may shock a lot of people, but yes I believe in "God" with all my heart. I know that "God" is real. Now some one might say, "How do you know that or how can you make such a statement?" Now what I'm fixing to say next, a lot of people are going to say it was just a dream. Well, maybe it was. But for me it was very real and I believe that it was real and no one will ever convince me that this was not a real experience, But a couple of years ago, I woke up from a sound sleep to find Jesus kneeling beside my bed. I ask "Him" what he was doing here? He told me that the Father had sent "Him" to see me and I ask "Him" why? "Jesus " told me that the "Father told Him" that I was a non believer, and that "He" should come and see me and tell me that the only way to the "Father" was through "Him, Jesus Christ." Well, "Jesus and me talked about many things and "He" told me all about the hate and the poison inside that I had bottled up inside of me. That "He wanted to take all of this from me and that" He" wanted to carry my burden for me. Come morning when I woke up, I woke up with a smile on my face and a song in my heart. **I didn't hate anymore and for the first time in my life I had compassion for my fellow man**. Back when I first got here, this was a terrible place to try and survive. I've got several knife scars on me still today that have never gone away. Here, you'd get up in the morning and you'd tape a few magazines to your body for body armor. That made it harder for someone to stick a shank into you. Back then when you got up, you thought about making it through another day and that was as far as it went. But after my visit with "Jesus" I was a new man. **I had been born again.** I knew that I was different. I knew that my whole life had been changed. Now I was a man that could kill at any time without remorse. But all of a sudden, even though I'm in prison, I know I no longer have any worry, or any burdens to carry. "Jesus" is now caring all of my burdens.

I went to the chow hall and there were a bunch of us joking around and one of the guys said something to me. And I said, "Not me brother, I love you. "Jesus" has been to see me and "He" told me all about "God." I no longer believe in violence." They all laughed. I told him to go ahead and slap me that I would only turn the other cheek. He said, "Are you nuts? I slap you and you'll kill me!" I assured him that I wouldn't; yet he wouldn't slap me. Now just a few months ago, "Jesus" came to pay me a second visit. Yes, twice in my lifetime, "Jesus" has come to visit me. This last time when I woke up from a sound sleep in the middle of the night and found "Jesus" kneeling by my bed, I was again surprised. I ask "Him" why "He" was back again? "Jesus" replied, "The "Father" has sent "Me" to tell you to get your life in order, that "He" will soon call you home." I ask "Him" "How long is soon?" "He" replied, " The Father never said when, only soon. No one knows, just the "Father." But listen to what I'm saying, get your life in order." Well, when I woke up I just knew that I was going to die pretty soon. So I did a few things that I could do in prison and I got down on my knees and I had a talk with the "Father." I had made my peace and I had no fear of dying. As a matter of fact, I was pretty excited; happy you might say. How many people really know that they are going to heaven? I've been blessed twice. I mean to be with "Jesus" to talk with "Him" twice, that is unheard of. So yes, I was excited. When I was reading in my Bible and I turned to Matthew Chapter 24. As I read the passages I knew that I wasn't dying soon. What I realized was that the end of time is near for all of us and that "God" sent "Jesus" to tell me to get my life in order for the time when "He" would come to claim us all. (*Born-again- from-above believers in the finished work of Jesus Christ known as the Body of Christ- i.e. real Christians*) And for the many people that haven't read the Bible, please turn to Matthew chapter 24 and read it. Then you will know what I'm talking about. Now I never read this before. When I had just read that, it was the first time for me. As a matter of fact, the Bible that I'm reading is the Bible P.J. sent to me. P.J. is the one that sent me the word of "God." From her first letter on, I felt like I had been touched by an angel. Yes, a lot of you are going to say that it was only a dream. But to me it was real and I will always believe that. I will never change my mind about those two visits and I will never renounce "God." For I believe with all my heart that "God" is real. Why? Because both times "Jesus" told me that it was the "Father" that had sent "Him." How can I not believe? Am I ready to be called home? Yes, I am, more than ever, and I've never felt the peace or comfort or happiness that I now feel. This is not jailhouse religion, nor is it a trick to try and help me get out of here. I've asked for nothing from any of the administration. If "God" wants me free, then I will be set free. I ask "God" to watch over my loved ones and to keep me safe till it is time for me to come home. I no longer worry about anything, for I know that "God" will provide everything that I need. **For "God" has turned my heart from something that was very cold and uncaring, to something with feeling and filled with love for all mankind. God bless you all**....................Amen.

HEARTACHE IN HELL!!!

My home is one of heartache,

A place of steel and stone.

Just one cell, my place in hell

And here I sit alone.

For my crimes I pay with time,

Where no man wants to be.

I smell the fear and shed a tear,

And pray the Lord will look after me.

My body cramps from the cold and damp,

That chills me to the bone.

And though I'm forced to stay here now,

This will never be my home.

At times I rage and pace my cage,

And terror is my friend.

This is the place where no man wants,

To say that he has been.

I hear the ring, the metal swing,

Of keys in metal locks.

The scrape of feet upon concrete,

As guards patrol the blocks.

Convict's knives take human lives,

No place holds more danger.

The passing days behind the wall,

Each man remains a stranger.

James Files

Letter 490 November 2, 2002 James Files to author

Last night I received 431 with the printed material about "Operation Gladio."

(Removing Nazi criminals, approximately 30,000, from Europe through P2 Masonic/Vatican "ratlines" with the knowledge and blessings of highly placed US and British government officials, 1978 assassination of Prime Minister of Italy Aldo Moro, murder of Albino Luciani, Pope John Paul I, 1982 murder of Roberto Calvi, Vatican Bank scandals, greed, power, murder, Mafioso, mayhem and cover-up that literally stinks to high heaven!

"Secretly granted immunity these and thousands of other battle hardened Nazi soldiers were to form the fighting nucleus of a top secret Allied contingency group conceived by the first Director of the CIA, Allen Dulles. Loosely known as operation 'Stay Behind,' the idea was to build a Europe wide secret network of anti communist guerrillas who would fight behind the lines in the event of a Soviet invasion. The plan was later codified under the umbrella of the Clandestine Coordinating Committee of the Supreme Headquarters Allied Powers Europe (SHAPE), the military arm of NATO" http://www.deepblacklies.co.uk/operation_Gladio.htm by David Guyatt)

And I found all of that pretty interesting. I'll jump ahead of your other letters to that one, just for the simple reason I don't know anything about it. So, there is not much I can say about it. Ha-ha…You got me on that one. Most of the Nazi names I read about when I was in school. But as for "Operation Gladio" this is the first that I've heard of it. (A more compartmentalized version of Gladio was Operation Paperclip) If I ever read about it before, I don't remember it. But I have read about how the Nazi War Criminal Machine escaped going to trial and all of that. (Just like Henry Kissinger never goes to trial as a genocidal -crimes- against- humanity global thug!) And to be honest , you know more about that than I do. And as for knowing anything about the Vatican, I know nothing. At one time I ran through the doors of the Catholic Church for a few minutes and dropped a few dollars in the plate and followed the guys to the booths to say a few Hail Mary's so I could be forgiven of criminal activity for that week. Then I got fed up with that after about 3 times and then I'd just drive the car and let them run in and I'd wait and keep the motor running. So, that's about all that I know of that kind of life. But from the movie *The Godfather*, I seen how they try to buy their way to heaven, and that is not cool. I do wish that I could have been of some help to you with that subject.

And as for the other article, "Tearful 9/11 Families Ask For Investigation," is also interesting. But you know as well as I do that the truth will never be revealed as to what happened that day. Oh we'll hear rumors about who was behind it, who planned it, who all was involved, but there will never be any proof of any kind and you know why that is. For all of the EVIDENCE was DESTROYED! Everything was hauled away, most of it by outside contractors, from across the big pond. How handy all of that was. Like a beautiful piece of artwork. We blame the people from another country for attacking us, and then hire contractors from a foreign country to carry most of the damage away, to dispose of the evidence. Yes, a brilliant piece of artwork, by the Shadow Government that controls our lives daily. Enough of that.

Sometimes when I talk to Jessie (Files' cell partner) about "God" he'll say that he believes in "God" and all that. But Jessie is not ready to be reborn again. He is under a great deal of pressure and he has no faith most of the time. He has a lot of hate inside, and he has a very hard time dealing with it. He lets the smallest things upset him. Maybe I'm too dumb to let things bother me, I don't know. I guess that I had a lot more training than Jessie had. Maybe

I should say I was brainwashed to the first degree. I was trained to survive, to endure, to do without, that pain was only a figment of the imagination. I was trained to go into someplace and do a job, to do it at all cost, give your life if need be, for getting back was not an important issue. To succeed was all that mattered. I think that is why I'm able to handle this place I'm trapped in. I don't let the people play head games with me. I endure without complaining. I never whine about anything that happens here. If I whine any at all, it's because that I cannot be there with you. I miss you, I love you, and for me this is a first time in my life. And when I get sick, I endure that as well. I stay away from their doctors. For me this is like a long extended operation that I'm on, and in my heart, I know in the end I'll come home to you and then all of this will be forgotten and put behind me. As for Jessie, I can't say, for I believe that only "God" knows the answer to that question. I don't think this is the answer that you was looking for, but that is how I see things here. Sometimes we talk about "God" and other times…I guess we just talk. Most of our time is spent not really arguing, more like debating things of no importance from like 40 and 50 years ago.

Yes, I do know what you mean about Jesus giving you His love and support. Me, I believe that "God" knew that I had been damaged – in the brain –so to speak, and that what I needed to get over the hump was a visit. So, "God" sent Jesus to see me and tell me that the Father had sent Him to tell me that He was real, as "God" knew I was an unbeliever. Oh I'd look up and ask "God" to get me out of some mess when the smelly stuff would hit the fan and "God" always seen me through these times of trials. Then there was the second visit, but you already know all about that. Hey, I love "God" and I do believe. And when possible, I tell others that "God" is real.

As for the bad dreams, I've had them for many years and taking the trip down memory lane (I asked him to tell me about the CIA Death Squads) had nothing to do with my dreams. Like I said, they've always been there. I've always had them. That trip down memory lane just help me to realize how wonderful life can really be, when you find the right one to be with the rest of your life. Just to find your love, I'd do it all again. I only wish there was some way that I could tell you just how much I love you and how very much you mean to me.

As for the Death Squads, I'll get back to them and more about Chile after I get your letters caught up. I like to try and answer and comment and everything you ask me, and when I miss something, please ask me again. And if I'm kind a hazy in some of my answers, please ask them again. Sometimes I'll answer something and not explain. Like the one letter I sent you, I was talking about the "RRT's" and it dawned on me that I hadn't spelled them out; that I was only using initials and I wasn't sure if you remembered me telling you about them before or not. Heck, you might say that at one time I lived in an alphabet world; CIA, DEA, ATF, FBI, RRT's, NSA, NSC, and there's just no end to them all.

****

"How could I contradict the official story? All my witnesses kept dying on me." - **Jim Garrison**

Following the assassination of president Kennedy, many marginally related individuals died in suspicious circumstances. Starting with Lee Harvey Oswald's murder by Jack Ruby in a Dallas police station, many of those who witnessed the presidential killing, were somehow linked to the myraid of conspiracies surrounding it, or were mentioned in the Warren Report have conveniently met untimely ends. Are these deaths, coincidental, or are they yet another sign pointing at a vast conspiracy?

List of Kennedy-Related Deaths

11/63 - Karyn Kupicinet - Daughter of TV host who was overheard talking about JFK's death prior to the assassination - Murder

2/64 - Betty MacDonald - Former stripper at Ruby's Carousel Club. Provided an alibi for Darrell W. Garner after he was arrested for shooting Warren Reynolds in the head. Reynolds was the man who chased Patrolman J.D. Tippit's killer and later failed to identify him as Oswald. One week after Gardner's release, she was arrested by Dallas police for disturbing the peace. In jail, she was found hanged from her toreador pants - Suicide

2/64 - Eddy Benavides - Brother of Domingo Benavides, one of the witnesses in the shooting of patrolman J.D. Tippit. Domingo failed to identify Oswald as the shooter until his brother was shot in the head in a Dallas bar. Then he recognized Oswald. - Gunshot

3/64 - Bill Chesher - Had information linking Oswald and Ruby - Heart attack

3/64 - Hank Killam - A house painter who lived at Mrs. A.C. Johnson's rooming house at the same time as Lee Harvey Oswald. His wife, Wanda, was a former Ruby employee. Though Killam was hounded by federal investigators after the assassination, all references to him were extripated from the Warren Report - Murder

4/64 - Bill Hunter - One of the two reporters who met with George Senator and Dallas Attorney Tom Howard in Ruby's apartment the night Oswald was shot - Accidental shooting by policeman

5/64 - Gary Underhill - CIA agent who accused the Agency of being behind the assassination - Self-inflicted gunshot to the head

5/64 - Hugh Ward - Private investigator working with Guy Banister and David Ferrie - Plane crash

5/64 - DeLesseps Morrison - New Orleans Mayor. Linked to Banister and Ferrie - Plane crash

8/64 - Teresa Norton - Former Ruby employee - Gunshot

6/64 - Guy Banister - Ex-FBI agent in New Orleans who was linked to Ferrie, mobster Carlos Marcello, antu-Castro Cuban groups, the CIA and Oswald - Heart attack

9/64 - Jim Koethe - The second reporter who was in Ruby's apartment on the night after he killed Oswald. Killed by a karate chop to the throat as he emerged from a shower in his apartment. No one was charged with the killing - Murder

9/64 - C.D. Jackson - Life magazine senior Vicepresident who bought the Zapruder film and locked it away - Unknown

10/64 - Mary Pinchot - JFK's alleged lover whose diary was taken by CIA chief James Angleton after her death - Murder

3/65 - Tom Howard - Ruby's lawyer. Was observed acting strangely to his friends two days before his death. No autopsy was performed - Heart attack

5/65 - Maurice Gatlin - Pilot for Guy Banister - Fatal fall

8/65 - Mona B. Saenz - Texas Employment clerk who interviewed Oswald - Hit by a bus in Dallas

9/65 - Rose Cheramie - Had previous knowledge of the assassination. Claimed to have travelled to Dallas with Cubans - Hit and run victim

11/65 - Dorothy Kilgallen - Journalist who had private interview with Ruby. Said she was "going to break this case wide open." - Drug overdose

11/65 - Mrs. Earl Smith - Friend to Dorothy Kilgallen. Died two days after the columnist. May have kept Kilgallen's notes - Undetermined

12/65 - William Whaley - Cab driver who reportedly drove Oswald to the Oak Cliff section of Dallas where he murdered Patrolman J.D. Tippit - Car crash

1966 - Judge Joe Brown - Presided over Ruby's trial - Heart attack

1966 - Karen Carlin - A dancer at Ruby's club. She phoned Ruby the morning before he shot Oswald and asked him to wire her $25 that she needed for rent and groceries. Curiously, there is no clear evidence that Carlin is dead. Many believe she is still alive under an assumed name the witness protection program. - Gunshot

1/66 - Earlene Roberts - Oswald's landlady. Testified that while Oswald was in his room after the assassination, two uniformed cops pulled up in front of the rooming house and honked twice. After testifying, she was subjected to intensive police harassment and complained about of being "worried to death" by the police. - Heart attack

2/66 - Albert Bogard - Car salesman at a Dallas downtown Lincoln-Mercury dealership who said Oswald test drove a new car days before the assassination. Oswald, or someone impersonating him, allegedly told Bogard he was about to obtain a large sum of money. Shortly after Bogard testified to a Warren Commission attorney in Dallas, he was badly beaten and had to be hospitalized. Upon his release, he was fearful for his safety. He was found dead in his car Valentine's Day with a rubber hose was attached to the exhaust and the other end extending into the car. - Suicide

6/66 - Cpt. Frank Martin - Dallas policeman who witnessed the Oswald slaying. Martin told the Warren Commission, "there's a lot to be said but probably be better if I don't say it" - "Sudden" cancer

8/66 - Lee Bowers - A towerman for the Union Terminal Co. who told the Warren Commission he witnessed two strangers behind picket fence on Grassy Knoll and may have seen a flash of light or puff of smoke coming from them. - Car crash

9/66 - Delilah Walle - Another dancer who worked in Ruby's club. Shot by husband after 1 month their wedding. Was supposedly working on a book about the assassination. - Gunshot

10/66 - Lt. William Pitzer - JFK autopsy photographer who described his duty as "horrifying experience" - Gunshot rule suicided

11/66 - Jimmy Levens - Fort Worth nightclub owner who hired Ruby employees- Natural causes

11/66 - James Worrell Jr. - Saw man flee rear of Texas School Book Depository - Car crash

1966 - Clarence Oliver - District Attorney Investigator who worked on the Ruby case - Unknown

12/66 - Hank Suydam - Life magazine official in charge of JFK stories - Heart attack

1967 - Leonard Pullin - Civilian Navy employee who worked as an advisor on the Kennedy-assassination film, "Last Two Days" - Car crash

1/67 - Jack Ruby - He was taken into the hospital with pneumonia. Twenty-eight days later, he died of lung cancer. Told family members he was "injected with cancer cells" - "Sudden" cancer

2/67 - Harold Russell - Was with Warren Reynolds when the J.D. Tippit shooting took place. Russell identified the fleeing man was Oswald. He progressively became more paranoid and told friends that he was going to be killed and begged them to hide him. He apparently lost his mind at a party and the police were called. When they arrived, Russelle was knocked in the head with a gun. Several hours later he was pronounced dead. The cause of death was listed as heart failure. - "Heart failure"

2/67 - David Ferrie - A childhood friend of Oswald's in New Orleans. He was the only real link between Oswald and former FBI-agent Guy Banister. Died of a brain aneurysm, with indications that it was medically induced. - Brain aneurism

2/67 - Eladio Del Valle - Anti-Castro Cuban associate of David Ferrie - Gunshot and ax wound to the head

5/67 - William Waters - His mother said William tried to talk Oswald and Killam out of getting involved in the plot to assassinate JFK. Waters called FBI agents after the assassination. The FBI told him he knew too much and to keep his mouth shut. He was arrested and kept in Memphis in a county jail for eight months on a misdemeanor charge. - Drug overdose

3/67 - Dr. Mary Sherman - Ferrie associate working on cancer research - Died in a fire (and possibly shot)

1/68 - A. D. Bowie - Assistant Dallas District Attorney prosecuting Ruby - Cancer

4/68 - Hiram Ingram - Dallas Deputy Sheriff, close friend to Roger Craig - "Sudden" cancer

5/68 - Dr. Nicholas Chetta - New Orleans coroner who signed Ferrie's death certificate - Heart attack

8/68 - Philip Geraci - Friend of Perry Russo. Knew about a conversation between Oswald and Shaw conversation - Electrocution

1/69 - Henry Delaune - Brother-in-law to coroner Chetta - Murder

1/69 - E.R. Walthers - A Dallas Deputy Sheriff who was involved in the Book Depository search and claimed to have found .45-cal. slug from the bullet that killed President Kennedy - Shot by a felon

1969 - Charles Mentesana - Filmed rifle other than Mannlicher-Carcano being taken from Depository - Heart attack

4/69 - Mary Bledsoe - Oswald's neighbor, also knew David Ferrie - Natural causes

4/69 - John Crawford - Close friend of both Ruby and Buell Wesley Frazier, the man who gave Oswald a ride from Irving to Dallas on the day of the assassination - Crash of private plane

7/69 - Rev. Clyde Johnson - Scheduled to testify about Clay Shaw/Oswald connection - Gunshot

1970 - George McGann - Underworld figure connected to Ruby. His wife, Beverly Oliver, claimed to knew that Oswald and Ruby where acquainted, and that David Ferrie was a regular in Ruby's Carousel Club. She also claimed to be the so-called "Babushka Lady" in Dealey Plaza and allegedly filmed the motorcade with a super-8 camera - Murder

1/70 - Darrell W. Garner - Arrested for shooting Warren Reynolds two months after Reynolds failed to identify Oswald as Tippit's shooter. Garner was released after an alibi from Betty MacDonald, a dancer in Ruby's Carousel Club - Drug overdose

8/70 - Bill Decker - Dallas Sheriff who saw bullet hit street in front of JFK - Natural causes

8/70 - Abraham Zapruder - Made the famous film of the JFK assassination - Natural causes

12/70 - Salvatore Granello - Mobster linked to both Hoffa, Trafficante, and several mob-initiated Castro assassination plots - Murder

2/71 - James Plumeri - Mobster with ties to the CIA. Was rumored to have been writing a book about the CIA's use of the Mafia in an attempt to kill Castro - Murder

3/71 - Clayton Fowler - Ruby's chief defense attorney. Died while planning a posthumous appeal of Ruby's conviction - Unknown causes

4/71 - Gen. Charles Cabell - CIA deputy director connected to anti-Castro Cubans - Collapsed and died after a physical exam at Fort Myers

1972 - Hale Boggs - House Majority Leader, member of Warren Commission who began to publicly express doubts about findings - Disappeared on Alaskan plane flight

9/73 - Thomas E. Davis - Gunrunner connected to both Ruby and CIA - Electrocuted trying to steal wire

2/74 - J.A. Milteer - Miami right-winger who predicted JFK's assassination and the capture of a scapegoat - Heater explosion

1974 - Dave Yaras - Close friend to both Hoffa and Jack Ruby - Murder

7/74 - Earl Warren - Chief Justice who reluctantly chaired Warren Commission - Heart attack

8/74 - Clay Shaw - Prime suspect in Garrison case, reportedly a CIA contact with Ferrie and E. Howard Hunt - Possible cancer

6/75 - Sam Giancana - Chicago Mafia boss slated to tell about CIA-mob death plots to Senate Committee - Murdered

12/75 - Gen. Earle Wheeler - Contact between JFK and CIA - Unknown

1976 - Ralph Paul - Ruby's business partner connected with crime figures - Heart attack

4/76 - James Chaney - Dallas motorcycle officer riding to JFK's right rear who said JFK "struck in the face" with bullet - Heart attack

4/76 - Dr. Charles Gregory - Governor John Connally's physician - Heart attack

6/76 - William Harvey - CIA coordinator for CIA-mob assassination plans against Castro - Complications from heart surgery

7/76 - John Roselli - Mobster who testified to Senate Committee and was to appear again - Stabbed and stuffed in metal drum

This list was originally compiled by **Jim Marrs**.

Questions and comments from James Files

I thought I'd stop by and see what kind of fur is flying on JFK Lancer forum these days. I've been too busy writing and trying to earn a living to come here more often. Have fun with the following:

Questions and comments from James Files
#638 07 September 2003

Yes, I know the vultures are circling for when the book is released. I have a few questions for the propaganda specialists.

If anyone has put out a book on the JFK assassination, exactly how much did it earn for you?
What is it exactly that makes a person an expert on the JFK assassination?
How many books did you have to read before you were able to give your opinion?
What is the total number of books you must read about the assassination in order to receive a degree as a so-called "research specialist?"
What do you do to make a living, or were you born rich?
How old were you November 22, 1963?
Where were you at when the assassination took place?
Were you in Dealey Plaza November 22, 1963?
If so, why were you there?
When it comes to my background, just look at who we got on our side saying that I was a Bad Boy – the ol' FBI will be right there with all of their records. They can all check my rap sheet. And, if I was truly a nobody and trying to make a name for myself, then why did the FBI spend so much time and money on chasing me and trying me for a lot of things that they could never put me in jail for? Hey the FBI are the ones that said I was a bad guy and it was the FBI, Special Agent Zack Shelton, that fronted me off on the Kennedy Assassination. Had they never snitched me off, I would have never said a word and that would have truly been a sad thing. Then we would have never met.

Back to my property and paperwork that the FBI now has. We don't really need the maps from Central America and South East Asia. We're not writing about the Drug Cartel (oh yes we are Jimmy, in TO KILL A COUNTRY part 2) and how everything was brought into this country. I figure that part was beat to death in what's his name's book, Barry and the Boys. So the stuff on the drugs is not important and I never wanted to write that part of it anyway. I would never do anything that could bring harm to you. And like I told you in the very beginning, no one really cares about the Kennedy Assassination.

Even all the way back to the ex-warden here, Godinez, when I use to sit with him in his office and we would talk for hours and hours about things and we even talked to the big shot in Louisiana on a Sunday morning and he had a Lear jet on stand by to fly here to see me, if I would talk with him about David Ferrie, his murder and the man told me and the warden that morning that he had no intention of indicting me for anything what-so-ever. Also, we talked to this one prosecutor in Dallas, as I was supposed to go down there and warden Godinez was going to go along with me to make sure that they didn't try to kill me.

Anyway, that man told us that I would never stand trial in Texas for Kennedy and as far as he was concerned, they should build a monument there for me. He said they would never indict me, as they would never find a jury that would convict me. That is the number one reason that I decided to go ahead with the interview. No one was interested in charging anyone for that crime.

As for #559,
(When will Posada confess to complicity in Kennedy's assassination?
http:/www.granma.cu/ingles/2003/agosto03/mar19/33kenn.html sent to James Files Aug. 26, 2003 - 7 pages total)
I'm not sure if I commented on that one or not. I have been so sick that I can't remember. As for the stuff about Cuba, I cannot comment on, as I do not know about most of it. Yes, I do know some of the Cubans and they also knew me. I believe some of them would remember me. Were some of the Cubans there that day in Dallas? Yes. Did I talk to them? No. Did they see me? I think maybe one or two did. They looked right in my direction, but never waved or

nodded or made any kind of recognition. That was not a time to be waving or smiling, or nodding at each other. Know what I mean? So as far as what he has written about the Cubans, I cannot give a valid answer. For I do not know!

****

From: "Pam"
To: "wim dankbaar"
Subject: James Files - Bob Vernon

Dear Wim,

The following is from the letter #377 Friday February 8, 2002 page 2-3. It is in response to the conversation I had with Bob Vernon January 24, 2002. It is unedited so please bear with the romantic language.

"My sweet love, it is now Saturday evening and I just a few minutes ago received Number 337, the transcript from the call of you and Vernon. I really got a good laugh out of that and I love the part where you blew him clean out of the water on the part about JFK and what Shackley had told me. No my love, I never told any of that to Vernon. But my Sweet Love, please put all of what Vernon said out of your mind. He cannot sue us for anything. I only wish he really could. If he could sue us, we'd get at least a hundred million dollars worth of free publicity for the book and it would be an overnight best seller. People would buy it just to see what they might be missing out on. But my love, there is nothing they can do. They can only copyright what they ask me during the interview. Had I told him something that was not put down on paper or film, he could not get a copyright on it. Only on what I've said and had out down in writing or on film. We've got nothing to worry about. And I really think that you should call him and tell him to bring on the lawsuit, that you would welcome it, or just call up and say, "Hey Bob, I'll be seeing you in court!" My love, I just love you soooooooo much and you really do bring a smile to my face. Baby, You're the Greatest!
I'll comment more on that later. But right now I'm going to jump all the way back and try to catch up on your sweet, wonderful, loving letters and cards I have been receiving from you. But before I go there, one other thing. When Bob is talking about Texas, he's talking about that retired federal judge down there and he is also nothing to worry about. I thought I had sent you copy's of those letters that Vernon had sent to him trying to get him to get a grand jury to call me before it. "IF" the FBI wanted me for the assassination of JF Kennedy, then all they'd have to do is release my dental records and they'd have me cold turkey. But they do not want me for that. They will never change the history books. They want the world to really believe, without a doubt, that L.H.O. ACTED ALONE!!! Anyway, the judge's name is Charles R. Carver, Texas District Judge, P.O. Box 3707, Beaumont, Texas, 77704... Anyway, that's the one he's talking about and there's nothing ever going to happen in that department. So my sweet love, no need to worry."

****

Phone conversation with Bob Vernon January 24, 2002

Bob Vernon: Is Pam there? Bob Vernon here. How you doin'?
P.J.: Good how are you?

Vernon: So James is having a birthday.
P.J. Yeah, Jimmy's having his birthday today.
Vernon: Yep…
P.J.: (laughter)
Vernon: One twenty-four forty-two.
P.J.: Yep.
Vernon: Well I'll be darned. When you said that (in e-mail earlier in the day) I said, "That's right."
P.J.: But you didn't remember today?
Vernon: Nah, I did not remember today was today till you said it then I remembered 1-24-42.
P.J.: Yep. Well hopefully next birthday we won't be so far apart. (laugh)
Vernon: (laugh) Good. So he's workin' on that huh?
P.J.: Yeah, he's workin' on it big time. And I'm workin' on it however I can help him on this end…gosh, there's a lot we need to talk about. (laugh) How have you been? Your health?
Vernon: Ah... been goin' crazy…ah…
P.J.: How's your health been?
Vernon: It's fine.
P.J.: For a while there you were havin' some trouble. You eyes and…
Vernon: I don't have any teeth in my head anymore I have false teeth.
P.J.: Well, Jimmy had those knocked out along time ago…
Vernon: Yeah, oh I understand.
P.J.: Did he ever tell you about that?
Vernon: Yep. He let me know all about it.
P.J.: Gosh…some of those stories I'd like to forget, but I mean its part of the story. Right?
Vernon: Yeah. So how you doin'? What are y'all up to? You're tryin' to do a book on him? Huh?
P.J.: Well, it's not on him necessarily, but it's kind of a lot of his stuff in there, obviously because, you know he's helping me with it, but…um…I'm almost done. A lot of his materials from…um…from TO KILL A COUNTRY…
Vernon: Yeah.
P.J.: But he didn't really… he was kind of compartmentalizing it…and making it more just like one or two countries, and I'm doing more of an overview…The New World Order.
Vernon: Yep.
P.J.: Yep. (laugh)
Vernon: Good.
P.J.: So, yeah…it's almost done. But I'm still going to use the title TO KILL A COUNTRY because he's like "What do you want to call it?" I'm like, "Well, your title sounds fine with me."
Vernon: Yep. That's a good title.
P.J.: That's what's going on, so that's the title. And I'm excited about it.
Vernon: Did you go into depth about Kennedy?
P.J.: Oh yeah. I used a little tiny bit of your interview, just so I didn't have to ask him the same thing, and also to expose people to the fact that there was a previous interview and kind of put it out there so people could be aware of it. And it's just a part at the beginning when you're asking a little bit of background information…I used the answers he gave on the video vs. asking him the same exact questions again.
Vernon: That's all copyright material.
P.J.: That's what I'm saying. It was like two different times that I did it to bring attention to you, so that you would, you know, have more people know about you.

Vernon: Well it's copyright material and you can't use any of it. (can't hear)…lawsuits in Miami…

P.J.: Well I'll take it out because it's only two different parts, but I thought you would appreciate it.

Vernon: When James, when he talks about the Kennedy, or his life story, or anything of that nature, it's gonna cause you a problem…because he's already signed his rights away. So…

P.J.: Well…anyway...

Vernon: It's out of my hands…it's not me.

P.J.: Right. Well, I thought you would appreciate knowing I at least brought some attention to your work and give you credit for where it's due.

Vernon: Nah, I appreciate all that stuff you know, but it's like I said. It's out of my hands. Copyrighting laws…

P.J.: So I shouldn't make any reference to anything? They wouldn't appreciate that at all?

Vernon: Anything to do with James Files life story at all, any way shape or form, he signed away. We have the documents signed. I understand that…(can't hear)

P.J.: So, I'll just take the part out where I referred to…there's maybe like two different paragraphs where it's referring to exact transcript information, off of the transcripts, so I'll just take it out and that's it.(It's OUT!) Everything else is original material from what he told me.

Vernon: Anything to do with James Files life, the story of his life, is copyrighted. So it's already with a company…

P.J.: Well who…

Vernon: So you have to be real careful.

P.J.: Who is the person that thinks that they can do that?

Vernon: The people that hold the contract. That's what I'm saying. He signed it away. He signed it away. That's how it works. I mean, don't be upset about it or anything. He should have told you. Because he talked about doing books with other people, and he's already signed those rights away.

P.J.: Hum…well, I'll make no reference to it because if it's going to cause some trouble…

Vernon: I'm not sure you heard what I said. Anything to do with James Files' life, what he's involved in, or his life story, he has…

P.J.: I need to talk to those people because you can't just sign your life away.

Vernon: No, no. He didn't sign his life away, he signed the story…away. with his own signature.

P.J.: Well, it's not like a story about Jimmy; it's a story about our government. And he…

Vernon: That's fine.

P.J.: And he's somebody that worked for our government.

Vernon: That's fine.

P.J.: It's not like it's a bibliography, I mean biography of James Files. You know what I'm saying? It's not about his life. It's about his part of what he did in our government, to kill a country.

Vernon: Oh I understand. I understand.

P.J.: Who's the person that would be the main overseer?

Vernon: Dick Clark.

P.J.: Dick Clark himself? Instead of just Dick Clark Productions and then there's…

Vernon: Dick Clark Productions.

P.J.: And Dick Clark is in charge of Dick Clark Productions?

Vernon: Well yeah. (laugh)

P.J.: Well, what's in a name? Right?

Vernon: Well his name a lot. He owns 76% of the company.

P.J.: He owns that MPI company?
Vernon: He owns the rights that were licensed to the MPI company.
P.J.: Hum…ok.
Bob Vernon: There's a lot of things going on right now concerning James and the Federal Government.
P.J.: Like what?
Vernon: Well, there's judges, attorneys, FBI guys…there's a lot of credibility now beginning to take place. Radio interviews recently. But, all I know is down in Texas, some judges, Department of Justice people, a lot of things coming down…a lot of them…
P.J.: What are they trying to do?
Vernon: Well, they're trying to get a Grand Jury and there's a judge called…(can't hear)
P.J.: They want to indict him for something?
Vernon: The Grand Jury to hear the evidence on him…
P.J.: On Kennedy or what?
Vernon: Yeah. Absolutely.
P.J.: Did you know that the …Kennedy's body is not in Arlington?
Vernon: Ah…I probably wouldn't be surprised.
P.J.: Is that the first you've heard of that?
Vernon: Uhm…
P.J.: Is that the first you've heard of that?
Vernon: Uhm…
P.J.: Because he said Joe West ….was starting to go kind of where he shouldn't have gone and he HIGHLY suspects that his death wasn't just, like, "because of natural causes."
Vernon: Well, so do I.
P.J.: And uhm…
Vernon: So do I, but Joe's family ask me to leave it alone. So I left it alone.
P.J.: Yeah, but Jimmy said that his body isn't there. "They kicked it out to sea." They (CIA and DOD) were in an airplane and that's when that guy Ted Shackley said that they're gonna just kick it out to sea "because that's what the family wanted." Did he ever tell you that?
Vernon: No, he never told me that.
P.J.: Yeah, it's not there. So, if they try and dig it up, Surprise! Surprise! It ain't there.
Vernon: Well, that's one of the reasons why they fought so hard on Joe that morning…(can't hear)…because there wasn't anything to be dug up.
P.J.: Nothing there. Yeah. Oh, it's like the brains gone, the body's gone, I guess it's all gone. I guess everybody is supposed to forget about it. But…
Vernon: How's Jimmy doing?
P.J.: He's doing good. I haven't talked to him for a couple weeks because they've been on lock-down, and I guess they're moving a bunch of people out of there. And he got moved into a double cell, which wasn't good but, at least he knows the guy and they're not having any trouble because he works different hours and so it's not too bad.
Vernon: I'll be in Chicago real soon and uh… I was hoping to meet up…my cell phone is goin' off…let me call you back. Kiddo, this is an important call that I have to take.
P.J.: Ok.
Vernon: I'll call you back.
P.J.: Ok.
(He never called back.)

****

8 October 2000 Interview with Kenny Larry

Kenny has known James for over 40 years from the suburbs of Chicago, especially Melrose Park, Illinois.

K.L: Hello?
P.J. Hi K.... This is P...
K: P..., How are you?
P: Good. How are you?
K: I talked to Jim last night.
P: Yeah. He said to give you a call and a...and that you're a friendly guy to talk to. And he told me before how you got your nick-name (The King) and I said, "Well, I like him already."
K: (laughter)
P: If you stood up at church and said how it is – I mean...I like that.
K: Oh yeah.
P: (Laughter)
I was like, "Well, did you tell him that I was related to Martin Luther?" And he goes no...
K: (Laughter)
P: So I guess you've known Jimmy for about forty years.
K: Yeah, I've known him for about forty years.
P: So, what, he was like a kid?
K: He was just in his teens at that time I think.
P: Wow...and he...
K: I'm a little older than he is but not too much. But a little bit. And I remember we lived in town, the same town he was working at a gas station. My young girls were bike riders and used to go there and get their bikes fixed by him and he did everything for them. Fixed their bikes and patched them. And then when they got older, and they got cars, and then he fixed their cars (laughter) and he always took care of my car. But he worked at the gas station there.
P: Uh huh. That's when you met him? That was Melrose Park?
K: Yeah, right. Melrose Park there.
P: His friend Mike, his brother Mark...
K: Yeah I know him.
P: He drove me through all that area (on the way to the airport)... so I could see...
K: Yeah. I like Mike.
P: And I saw the Harlo Grill.
K: Oh yeah?
P: And Jimmy said a lot of stuff happened there. (Laughter)
K: Oh yeah, that was his favorite place.
P: Well he said that's where you got your nick-name too at the...
K: Oh yeah.
P: At the Harlo Grill. (Laughter)
K: And that place was built almost...when was it built? 1953.
P: It looks like it's an older one.
K: It's quite old you know. And he was always hangin' there and his ex-wife used to work there and it was good you know. Everybody liked it, to hang there. I go there everyday. That's the only place I go, you know. I'm sure he told you I got multiple sclerosis.
P: Yeah, he says you don't get out at night too much, other wise when I was there I was going to invite you guys out.
K: Oh yeah. He told me you were going to call. He says you're going to be writing a book about him...

P: Well, he wanted me to co-author a book with him. He kind of started one and I liked the title "TO KILL A COUNTRY".
K: (Laughter) Right.
P: And then my subtitle is "The Assassination of JFK, America, and the Conspiracy for the New World Order". I know that's a big mouthful but…
K: Oh boy it is!
P: I've got a lot of stuff documented and…
K: Well he does too.
P: So, I think if we keep it on certain subjects, he seems to think that there is one area that we can't go to, but most of it we can cover, but there's just some stuff that you can't talk about.
K: Oh yeah, he doesn't want to talk about it if anybody is still alive, you know?
P: Well that, and some of the secret military stuff that's going on.
K: Oh yeah.
P: Down south and all that kind. (Antarctica)
K: Well you can't…you know that he said you couldn't prove that before… but I guess he told you about the historian, like a head of a …not that but he said…
P: John Grady? Joh…
K: Yeah from that 101st wherever…
P: The 82nd Airborne?
K: The 82nd Airborne. And he documented that Jimmy was where he said he was.
P: Uh huh.
K: Which you know …
P: That is important.
K: It shows Jimmy is not tellin' a fib. I don't believe he ever lied anyway.
P: No.
K: As long as I've known him, I've never really known him to tell me a lie.
P: You mean…
K: Everything he ever told me was true.
P: Sometimes you didn't want to hear what he was telling you but…(laughter)…it was the true stuff. That's very true! (Laughter)
K: That's true! Oh yeah!
P: Well, that's what…see that's how we met. I don't know if he told you about it, but I just wrote a thank you letter because I thanked him for telling the truth, because hardly anybody does that anymore.
K: Oh, that's absolutely right.
P: So, I was shocked that he did and I was thankful.
K: Oh I tell you Jimmy is a straight man, you know, <u>when he wants to tell you what it is – it is</u>.

****

Later in conversation………………………………

P: I don't think he is going to get out right away but I think he'll get out.
K: A couple of years?
P: I think yeah, after he gets through some court maneuvers, I think…because I'm a strong believer in prayer…(laugh). I don't know if he told you about that part of it all. It's going to take a miracle for him to get out.
K: They don't want him out.
P: I know. But if he makes a deal…

K: All that about Kennedy.
P: You see, if he makes a deal, I don't see why they can't just leave him alone, because there's a lot of stuff that they need to have kept a secret too.
K: Oh yeah. They know that too, I think.
P: Yeah, but they got all the big guns behind 'em. (Laugh)
K: Them people, they don't want him to go against the Warren Commission, and things like that. They don't want to believe what he said he did.
P: Yeah.
K: And yet he's got proof almost like when he talked about the bullet shell.
P: Yeah.
K: And it being buried there for all these years, and they finally found it.
P: That's amazing.
K: Just what he said.
P: Yeah.
K: And then when they wouldn't release uh…you know his dental charts, to prove that it was his teeth that made the marks, that kind of stuff is really…
P: Yeah, the army's got them or something.
K: They just don't want anybody to know that, or know what he did.
P: Well…
K: I believe he did…when he says he did it, I believe him.
P: Yeah, why would they not believe him? I mean…what does he have to gain?
K: Jimmy's good, I believe him.
P: Well, what I saw in him when I watched the video and saw and heard him telling the truth, I could tell he had a good heart – it's just he's never been told the truth about who God really is.
K: Oh, he has a good heart.
P: He's a good guy.
K: He sure is.
P: Inside… he just needed a little push.
K: (Didn't hear)
P: He's what?
K: He's unlucky.
P: Yeah.
K: It was difficult for him to get real lucky you know. Sure we knew he was a burglar and this and that- you know he robbed stuff like that but that's the way it was in those days.
P: Ah hum.
K: Comin' up through the town Melrose Park was know as bein' a burglar town- an outfit town.
P: What kind of town?
K: Outfit.
P: I'm not understanding what you're saying.
K: Well, it's like the syndicate; people that hang there and live there.
P: Uh hum.
K: And that's the way it was, because that's the way it always has been. That goes back to the Capone days.
P: And it was from that neighborhood, more so?
K: Oh yeah. He was raised in that neighborhood. They called it the "West End."
P: The West End.
K: Oh yeah and …
P: He…

K: Nobody went in the West End; it was affiliated with the hoodlums.
P: He said sometimes you can learn things through watching movies, and he said in the movie *Casino* when they showed the scenes about when they were back in Chicago…
K: Yeah, oh yeah…
P: They made that look like that area or something about the guys sitting around doing their cards and all that kind of stuff…
K: Oh yeah. They had everything like that in the town ya know. And that's probably- well those people- the Spilotro's - they were hanging around there all the time.
P: Uh huh.
K: And they had the one, the one Spilotro brother, the one that…uh…I forget his name now, my mind isn't working as great as it should.
P: Oh that's ok.
K: Mike. That's what it was. Michael, and …
P: Michael?
K: He used to have a tavern there on North Avenue just in the next town from Melrose Park. And Tony, he used to hang around Melrose, in fact we had a bar in the motel he used to come into all the time.
P: So are you still in the neighborhood or do you live somewhere else?
K: Oh yeah, I live in Elmhurst but… uh I'm still part owner of that motel over there. You know, its been there for probably 45 years. And the motel is still there and Jimmy used to come and hang around there all the time too.
P: Is it still open or is it closed?
K: Oh yeah, sure it is.
P: Oh good.
K: It's still open. I think it was the first motel in Chicago.
P: Wow!
K: Modern motel, you know? When you come you will see it.
P: Yeah, you'll have to give me a tour of it but I'm sure I didn't see even half of it or hear a quarter of the stories.
K: Right!
P: (Laugh)
K: There's a million stories.
P: I bet.
K: Jimmy's part of most of them! Ha-ha!
P: Yeah, well, we will have to talk about those later. (Laugh)
K: Oh yeah.
P: But he said it would be ok if I asked you about Charles Nicoletti.
K: Oh yeah, what about him?
P: Just that you knew him.
K: Oh yeah.
P: And that you were about his age – that's about the same…
K: Oh yeah sure.
P: And there's this other guy Murray Humphreys that you guys knew too?
K: Oh yeah.
P: So you knew him?
K: Yeah. We all hung around Melrose Park.
P: He was older though, than you?
K: Oh yeah, he was older.
P: Yeah, and he was like the "New York/Washington Man" right?
K: Yeah, right. He was like a "Brain" you know? He was like a "Godfather" you know?

P: He was? Because his daughter I guess wrote a book and it's titled *The Prince of Crime* and um…
K: All of 'em wrote books!
P: Yeah well…(laugh) this was at my 10 cents bookstore, outside in the free pile and you know - all the books they don't want you to read about right?
K: Right.
P: So, yeah, I read that he was over there in Chicago and then I had asked Jimmy if Charles Nicoletti knew him and he said yes.
K: Oh yeah.
P: Because in my research I was trying to find the connection between Chicago and Washington, there's a lot of them, but you know he (Murray Humphreys) was one of them.
K: There were "go-betweens" for those places. He was one of the "go-betweens".
P: Right. He was kind of like both.
K: Right.
P: Both Washington and Chicago.
K: Oh yeah.
P: Yeah.
K: Like Chuckie, he was, you know, he was strictly a hit man.
P: Well and he was strictly Chicago area, right?
K: Oh yeah.
P: I mean he would do stuff…
K: Mainly, Melrose Park.
P: Uh hum.
K: He lived there, you know. He lived right on 19th there. He had a big apartment building there. That's where he lived and died. He died at Manheim and North. He was killed there.
P: He was killed where?
K: At Manheim and North. At the Golden Horns.
P: Oh yeah.
K: But that picture of him that uh…I'm sure Jimmy told you had to…
P: What?
K: Witness in, uh… in Texas, drew a picture of supposedly Jimmy according to them. And it wasn't Jimmy it was Chuckie.
P: It was behind the fence?
K: No, it was a picture that they had seen him there in town – Dallas.
P: Uh hum.
K: And they said it was Jimmy Files, well it wasn't Jimmy Files it was Chuckie Nicoletti.
P: Was it right in Dealey Plaza, or was it in Dallas?
K: No, it was in the motel they had seen them in the car and these witnesses had supposedly knew…but you know hand drew a picture of him through a composite.
P: And they drew a picture of Charles Nicoletti.
K: And it was supposed to be of Jimmy. They were trying to say… it looked exactly like Chuckie.
P: Yeah.
K: We knew Chuckie and we knew Jimmy. Jimmy didn't look like that.
P: He was younger then.
K: Oh yeah. He was just a young man then.
P: And that was what? The Dallas Cabana Hotel?
K: I think so, yeah.
P: I think that's where…
K: He was in that television, what was that TV outfit wrote…

P: I'm not familiar with that.
K: I wouldn't talk to them until Jimmy told me it was ok.
P: Yeah.
K: Because what they had on the TV on that TV commercial, back on that expose they wrote…I'm sure you've probably seen it.
P: Probably not. When was this?
K: Oh…
P: Recently? Or a year ago? Or two?
K: Several years ago. About 3 or 4 years ago.
P: What was it called?
K: You know, I can't think of the title.
P: Huh, well if you remember write it down and when I talk to you again just tell me what it is.
K: My wife…
P: It bugs you when you can't remember, I know.
K: It was what? (K. to his wife) Inside Edition, like you know…
P: Inside Edition.
K: Published it too.
P: Ok.
K: But it was written by the Southside that…they were not nice people either. I guess they were interested in making money.
P: Making a story, making money.
K: Right.
P: And all that.
K: Trying to give more to it.
P: And Jimmy said it was ok if you talked to them?
K: Yeah. He said, "Yeah, go ahead and talk to them". He says, "It doesn't make any difference".
P: He probably just didn't care at that point.
K: No, he didn't care. Well, it's like right now. I guess they're trying to make a movie of him.
P: Well, Bob Vernon, I need to talk to him because…
K: Is that the man that…
P: Bob Vernon?
K: Talked to Jimmy's daughter, the daughter that never goes to see Jimmy.
P: The one, Shawn?
K: Shawn yeah. Now she came up to him and told him that these people from California want to make this movie. And they're talking to her and her mother, and their getting information about Jimmy and supposedly the assassination of Kennedy. And there- he supposedly did time and the man that never was.
P: Uh huh.
K: And I haven't heard and he hasn't heard more from Shawn either.
P: Well, I'm going to talk to Vernon probably tomorrow and just find out what's going on and PLUS, Jimmy wants his stuff back!
K: Oh yeah.
P: (Laugh nervously) He, ah… he seems to think it would be a good idea for me to acquire it but I don't know about that yet… I'm just trying to figure out where I'm going to put it once I get it!
K: He-he-he.
P: (laugh)

K: I tell you, there's a ream of it. It's like; there are a lot of papers Jimmy has – that he's got everything documented.
P: Uh huh.
K: Subtitles you know.
P: I know. He sent me a copy of that. I've got it. (Original notes and comments for TO KILL A COUNTRY)
K: That thing is something else!
P: Well, see…
K: I've got a grandson that took that thing in college and wrote an essay. His essay paper – he got an A+.
P: Well good for him!
K: (laugh)
P: I like him already!
K: A couple of times…
P: What's his name?
K: (laugh) His name is Dominic D..
P: I like Dominic.
K: Dominic D.. His dad Rocky D.- he was a fighter.
P: A fighter?
K: Yeah, middle weight professional fighter.
P: I'm sorry. I'm kind of ignorant about that kind of stuff.
K: He was raised in that town. Jimmy knows. He remembers him, and he's still in town. And my grandson, he fought in the Golden Gloves too – he came in second – in the Golden Gloves 'cause his father taught him how to fight.
P: That's right.
K: But, uh…they got some good stuff…some A+'s. In fact one of his teachers told her husband "Gee, do you think I better give him an A?"
K&P: (laughter)
K: I know it's true because like, "Papa knows- which is a word for grandfather-knows him <u>real well</u> and he doesn't lie." So when I said, "He's a killer." naturally the teacher told her husband, "I think we better give him an A."
K&P: (laughter)
P: Put a plus on there just for good measure! (Laugh) That's funny.
K: It is funny, but it was good. It was interesting. The kid learned a little bit too. You see how the government really works.
P: Oh I know. That's how I found out about Jimmy, because I started studying. I don't know if he told you this part but, I was at the church library and I was just looking through the books you know, they got a whole bunch of books in there, and there's this one section, kind of like miscellaneous, they don't know what to do with the book? And it was <u>High Treason The Assassination of John F. Kennedy What Really Happened</u>? by Harrison Livingstone. I thought, "Oh that's an interesting question…WHAT DID REALLY HAPPEN!?" So, I got the book, I read it, I was looking at all this stuff saying to myself, "This is not good! These people are still in power. This <u>is</u> <u>not</u> good." You know, I started freaking out. Then I went to my pastor, one of the associate pastors, and told him about all this and he's just like, "Oh no. Now she knows." And then he gave me the other books; he gave me Gary Allen books, *None Dare Call it Conspiracy* and *The Rockefeller File*.
K: Oh yeah.
P: He gave me those and said, "Here. This is what's going on and just don't let this consume you because it's going to wreck your life if you let it."

K: Right, you know it really can. When you see what people can do in the government and in the law enforcement. There is nothing they can't do. They can do anything they want.
P: Yeah, and there's no justice system. All the judges are corrupt and the Supreme Court and the Attorney General and the whole thing. It's all corrupt.
K: They got Jimmy down as never being born.
P: Yeah.
K: And that's ridiculous right there! There he is you know – he was born.
P: Duh! (Laugh)
K: Death at birth. Died at birth.
P: Well, have you heard of the Illuminati or the Skull and Bones and all that kind of stuff?
K: No.
P: It's the anti-christ spirit. It's, you know, you believe in, you know about God and satan, right?
K: Oh yeah.
P: See, these people, at the very highest levels in the most inner circle of circles – they worship lucifer and they're getting all their inspiration and power and illumination and light for all these plans to run the world from satan. And it's like, it's a BIG STORY, but most people can't really grasp that part of it because, you know, their spirits are…
K: They're out of control, out of whack.
P: Yeah, their spirits are just out of touch with God so they can't comprehend that kind of stuff…that's like alien to them.
K: But there are those who that do. And that's what it is with Jimmy. Some of the things about him that they say aren't possible that _are_ possible.
P: Oh yeah.
K: He's proved it you know everything he said was proven. And he's got witnesses and people who have documented what he said was true.
P: Um hum.
K: Me, I just believe him by faith alone, 'cause the man, like I said, never lied to me.
P: Yeah, that's…
K: I never caught him in a lie.
P: Well, the only lie I ever heard him start to tell was the one on the video where he's telling how much he got for the …for the thing in Dallas. He was saying, "Well, I got 15" and then he says, "30" you know he had told him earlier 15 and then he just said that he didn't want to talk about that because it was something he wanted to talk to Joe West about.
K: Right.
P: So, that was the only thing I ever saw that…
K: Well, that's…
P: I can understand why he wouldn't want to talk about the money.
K: Well, that's right…well why not?
P: Well, at this point yeah, why not? But back then I can understand…
K: About that time he bought that fancy car right after that. So he probably did get the $30,000.
P: Oh sure. But I'm just saying that was the only thing I ever even slightly caught him not saying the whole truth and nothing but the truth. And that was just like even half the truth. So, yeah, I know he's telling the truth.
K: Oh yeah, I know he is.
P: We agree on that 100%.
K: Oh no, that's…I believe him 100%.
P: Well,… and the whole thing about me having feelings for him…you guys probably wonder, "How in the heck does that happen?"

K & P: (Laugh)
K: That's a possibility – why wouldn't we wonder about it?
P: (Laugh)
K: I did – anyway.
P: You didn't want to bring it up – but you were hoping I'd mention it, right?
K: No, not really.
P: No – well (laugh) I just want to explain it because it's unexplainable. I was at a point in my life where I just…I wasn't going to really have anymore…like marriage, or boyfriend kind of things. I just signed off! You know, I've been through enough hard times with guys that…and the way they use me and abuse me, I'm, you know…I just didn't want to do it anymore. And then when I was writing Jimmy it was just to be his friend. I sincerely…just…wanted…to be…his friend – and that's it! Because I figured, you know, here he is, he's telling the truth, he's spilling his guts, I'm just going to invite him to come to the kingdom of God, and if he comes with me – great! I'll disciple him and, you know, I'm going to pray for him and he's like a pen pal. A friend of mine, you know? That I care about.
K: That's right. That's right.
P: That's all! It started out…
K: That kind of stuff is true you know – it happens.
P: And you hear about people meeting on the stupid computer Internet thing, right?
K: Right.
P: Well, I mean…
K: I got a daughter who does that. She writes to people… she writes to a prisoner who used to be mayor of Melrose Park.
P: Uh huh.
K: She writes to him up at Oxford, (*Menard?*) Wisconsin. And he wrote her one time, several times too, but they're like pen pals. [Side note from James Files who typed all my chicken-scratch transcribed notes from taped phone conversation – *"Menard is a state prison in Illinois. Oxford FCI is in Wisconsin. The mayor was Auggie Taddeo."*]
P: Yeah, but…
K: He knew her from when she was born in town…
P: Uh huh.
K: Because she was born in town and like he told her in one letter she showed me, that he said, here he was mayor for like 15-16 years and he got caught at something he did and they put him in jail. But NOBODY that was in his group that worked for him writes to him. And he says, "Here you write to me Sue, and nobody else does." That's the way it is.
P: Yeah. She writes to him, but…they don't have romantic feelings for each other, right?
K: Oh no.
P: But see? That's what Jimmy and I were scratchin' our heads about. It's like, "Why are we both having these feelings for each other?" It's like we fell in <u>love!</u>
K: The man is good…I mean he can do that to ya.
P: I g.u..ess so!!!
K: Oh yeah.
P: Because I've NEVER been loved like this in my life!
K: (laugh)
P: And we've only held hands in the visiting room! (Laugh) Well, I won't tell you about his dreams and all that he tells me about…but…
K: Oh yeah.
P: He's a…he's a number one guy in my book.
K: He is. He really is. He's a good man. I wouldn't bother talking to him all these years if I really didn't think he was the greatest…

P: Yeah.

K: And a good guy and believable. He doesn't tell you stories you know, like a lot of guys from that town, you can talk to and you know they're full of crap…(tape ends and K. keeps talking)

K: …in the motel, because the man had forgot his keys in the car and didn't want to bother – he had a girlfriend and that's why he was at the motel, but his car was running, it was a brand new car. So I says, "I'll get a hold of somebody to open it, right?" He says, "Alright." So I called Jimmy. It's in the middle of wintertime. Must have been –20 below zero. So I figure, "well, Jimmy knows how to break into a car".

P: (Laugh)

K: He came over in that light jacket with his ex-wife and she sat in the office with me, he was out there trying to get a slim jim to work, you know? He was there for two hours. Now he couldn't break into that car. And I told him, "You know, for a car burglar…you're kind of stupid."

P: You're kind of slow on the slim jim there buddy! (Laugh)

K: He never did get it open! In fact, we had a little metal ruler in the office of the motel, and we took that out and I think I got it open. But…

P: See?

K: We had to get the lock open…

P: You had to show him how it's done.

K: but evidently, Jimmy was supposed to be a burglar; a car burglar – couldn't get it open. And I told him, "Well, you are a nit-wit! You're out here freezing to death…

P: (laugh)

K: …you can't get it open." And we always laughed about that.

P: Another thing that I laugh about, that I kid around with this other friend of mine that's over here, we say "I'm tellin' Jimmy." Because Jimmy wrote to me that you used to say when guys were giving you a hard time or something, you'd just go, "I'm tellin' Jimmy."

K: That's right.

P: (Laugh)

K: That's the truth.

P: (laugh) "I'm tellin' Jimmy."

K: Mike, Mike used to say that.

P: Mikey used to say that?

K: Yeah. "I'm tellin' Jimmy."

P: (Laugh)

K: Because everybody knew Jimmy – that's right.

P: They're like Jimmy will be fair but if he's not on your team, and then, you know… you don't want to be around.

(Pause)

P: Well…

K: The man's got no fear.

P: Well, he puts that to use in God's kingdom and that's going to do lots of good things.

K: Oh yeah.

P: So, God's got His hand in all of this. I don't know exactly what and when the timing of it all is, but He's definitely got His hand in it.

K: He sure does.

P: When Jimmy first told me about you, he was telling me about you saying stuff in the Catholic Church and then preachin' at the Harlo Grill…

K: Oh yeah.

P: And I was like, well…I mean it's not just for me to pick up the phone and call somebody that I don't know out of the blue…
K: Oh yeah.
P: but I felt like I knew you already because he talked so much about you.
K: Oh yeah, well, they used to call me the "Deacon" over at the Harlo.
P: The Deacon at the Harlo Grill?
K: In a teasing way…but sometimes you can teach somebody something in a teasing way better than you can…
P: Well, that's how Jesus did it.
K: It works.
P: Jesus told stories all the time. He wasn't just standing in some church…talking to people about what's going on. He was just out, sitting by the campfire, or fishing with them or you know, the local places to sit down and have a meal or…
K: That's exactly right.
P: That's how it works. I mean church is great and all that but…
K: Oh yeah.
P: It has its time and place.
K: Oh yeah, you can also teach people doing it that way. And that's the way He did it.
P: Yes, and He went to the synagogue and read and taught and, you know… all that. That was fine but…
K: The Pharisee's teachings weren't the same as His teachings necessarily.
P: No, He was calling them bad names because…
K: Oh yeah.
P: He didn't really…He had a lot of compassion for everybody but when it came to the religious rulers that were making a mockery of God's love and word, He was knarly with them. It's like "I'm tellin' Jimmy- I'm tellin' Jesus!"
K & P: (Laugh)
K: That's right!
P: That's right!
K: It's the same thing.
P: It's the same thing.
K: If you're telling the truth you can't go wrong.
P: Well…
K: Especially if it's something that can be proved.
P: That's right.
K: And that's Jimmy. It's being proven everyday. And everybody of course said, "You know that man is c.r.a..z.y!"
P: I talked to the lady down in, I guess she's in California, but she kind of heads the group that's called the JFK Lancer…
K: Yeah.
P: and her name is Debra Conway. And I talked with her, and she thinks Jimmy is just trying to get attention. I go, "Well, don't you think that's an extreme measure – to confess to killing the President of the United States to get a few pen pals?"
K: (laughter in background)
P: Hello?
K: That's right. That's exactly what it is. Especially when as time goes by, everything he said comes out to be true.
P: Yeah, and just any…
K: It's been on the TV. I don't know if you see those things out there over in Hawaii but we get all these like A&E.

P: Yeah. We get all those shows over here.
K: They had on there people that…that are "experts" – supposedly about the…the case with JFK's assassination.
P: Yeah right! (Sarcastically)
K: And there were things to show how it really couldn't happen the way the Warren Commission said. Like Ruby couldn't have done that.
P: You mean Oswald.
K: …believes that he could of
P: You mean Oswald.
K: Oswald I mean.
P: Yeah.
K: But then they had two girls that worked for Ruby as I guess they were dancers or topless dancers or something?
P: Um hum.
K: They were older women, they weren't really young but, and they were in Ruby's nightclub and saw Oswald at Ruby's table. Now right there tells ya something's wrong. And why would they have to lie? They're not lying!
P: They have nothing to gain.
K: Nothing to gain by it – a lot of things. And why would they want to get their boss in trouble? It's Ruby although he's dead we know. Still, at all, why was Oswald there? Well, there's reasons why he was there probably. 'Cause it's Jimmy – when Jimmy tells it, it is true.
P: Yeah.
K: Oswald was a patsy.
P: Yep. Jimmy knew about the …the lower level working of …you know…the actual
K: Oh!
P: execution part of it, but as far as the upper levels, he had no clue and I filled him in on all that…about…you know…
K: Well he wasn't supposed to be in that, in the actual assassination anyway. That wasn't supposed to be his job. He was just going out there with Chuckie to drive the weapons out there.
P: Well, he was backup too because Chuck asked him if he would back him up.
K: He wasn't really back up, supposed to be. I don't believe that.
P: Well, that part of the video is …Jimmy says that Charles Nicoletti asked him…if he could back him up and only fire if he needed to.
K: Oh no – that's true now. But that's only <u>maybe</u> if they needed him.
P: But they…
K: At that point he…(can't hear K. clearly) would never have brought that in anyway…
P: Yeah, well, at that point though, when Jimmy fired, he hadn't seen that he had been hit in the head yet and that's why he fired because he knew even though he was shooting from the front, and that wasn't going to be good, the job wasn't getting done when he had hit him in the head. And so, I guess they fired at the same time and…made a big mess and…
K: Well that's true but you know Jimmy was only there in with Chuckie to get the job done. Which it didn't look like it was going to get done…
P: Yeah, it looked like they were hitting him in the back…and you know…it wasn't getting…
K: They didn't hit him on one shot. They hit that governor.
P: Governor Connally.
K: Right. So anyway, Jimmy made the shot and so did Chuckie, probably at the same time, and that could be but Jimmy's was the deadly one.
P: Yeah. His was from the front.
K: Right and they had that with an expert…

P: They had that on the Zapruder film (K. talking in background) you know that guy that was taking the home video?
K: Oh yeah.
P: Abraham Zapruder. They got all that on the video.
K: Oh yeah.
P: So, it's like…there it is.
K: That's right. And again, there's money involved, you know? 'Cause they sold that…did we see the whole movie? You know? The whole shot?
P: Well that's where Dan Rather's (CBS) whole part of this comes in.
K: That's right. I think it was true.
P: Speaking of Dan Rather, did you know that on tonight's 60 Minutes there's an interview with Frank Sinatra's daughter – either Nancy or Tina or whatever her name is?
K: My wife and I saw that.
P: Did you see it?
K: Neither one of us believes that Frank Sinatra would talk to his young daughter – you go back that far.
P: Antoinette? (Don't ask me why that name popped out) or to Frank's daughter?
K: No, that was…that was Frank Sinatra's daughter…she was not Antoinette. Antoinette was…
K & P: Sam's daughter.
K: Sam's daughter.
P: Right, but you don't think that Frank was going to talk to his daughter about that stuff?
K: No! He'd never talk…Frank Sinatra would never talk to his daughter like that, I don't think. We don't think he would anyway.
P: Did you meet him?
K: Who?
P: Frank.
K: Sinatra?
P: Yeah.
K: I met him once out in Vegas.
P: Uh huh.
K: But uh…
P: Just "Hi. How are ya?" kind of thing?
K: Yeah, we were gamblers too…there was this older man with me, and he was invited to the table 'cause he was a high roller but…uh…we didn't like the way he talked.
P: He was just foul mouth, yeah?
K: Foul mouth – oh he treated women bad.
P: Just _real_ disrespectful.
K: Very disrespectful. All of them out there did. That was at the Stardust Hotel – the main people that we knew and uh they were not, none of them were any good. They were just foul mouthed and women-offenders and everything.
P: Well! I wouldn't, I wouldn't have gotten along very well with Frank Sinatra – HA!
K: We walked away from the table…they invited us to sit at the table. We said, "No we're just going to gamble"…'cause we didn't want to sit down and listen to that crap.
P: No.
K: That's no fun.
P: That's not fun to be around.
K; We're out there for joy, not for…not to listen to that. But anyway, he wouldn't tell his daughter a thing like that.

P: So did they cover the stuff about the election (1960 Presidential Election) and Judy? Or what did they cover?
K: Dan Rather?
P: Well, whoever did the interview with Sinatra's kid.
K: Oh I don't know …that had to be…we…I didn't see that they just had the part on there this wasn't uh…
P: This was just…
K: Yeah it was Dan Rather.
P: It was tonight?
K: It was last night, or the night before.
P: Ok well, over here they're showing 60 Minutes on Sunday…
K: Time but anyway, they said she's writing a book about it.
P: Is she?
K: And that's ridiculous. Just like Sam's daughter.
P: *Mafia Princess.*
K: *Mafia Princess*.
P: Yeah, I've got that.
K: She's called me a couple times and all she wants to know is if Jimmy killed her father.
P: Johnny killed Sam. Right?
K: (Laugh)
P: I mean nobody wants to say it but…
K: Nobody wants to say it.
P: But everybody knows it was Johnny.
K: Yeah.
P: Well, so, she should just forgive Jimmy already…
K: She's married to a guy that used to be a lawyer for the Outfit. He's much older than her.
P: Not that guy Julius?
K: No, his name was McDonald
P: That's who she's married to?
K: That's the man she's married to.
P: Are they still together?
K: He was a lawyer. I don't know if he still has a practice but he is quite a bit older. He's older than me and I'm over 70.
P: Oh Jimmy, Jimmy doesn't like her that much.
K: No, them people are crazy, but she just wants to know, and she wrote those crazy books, you know…that's just selling, she didn't know that much either.
P: Yeah.
K: But she pretends that she knew. I mean…you know?
P: Well, Sam didn't come home and tell her what was goin'on.
K: You don't think I discuss with my daughters what goes on?
P: No.
K: Neither did they.
P: I mean… I don't even do…anything that you need to not talk about with my son and I don't even tell him half of the stuff I do.
K: That's right!
P: Hello?
K: It never goes that way. But they talk you know. She called me a couple times wanting to know this and that. Wanting to know if I thought Jimmy would talk to her…she did go out to the prison to see him.
P: Yeah-yeah he said that.

K: Oh, he said that?
P: He mentioned she had come out there.
K: But he didn't tell her anything.
P: No.
K: He had nothing to tell her. He had nothing worthwhile.
P: It's like, "Here's the facts honey, you do your homework and you figure out who killed your dad – because it ain't me!"
K: That's right.
P: "I'm tellin' you basically what happened and if you can't listen to me then I don't want to talk to you."
K: That's right.
P: You know?
K: That's about what it should have been, and that's the way it should be.
P: Well, I understand her wanting to know, but I mean if Jimmy's willing to tell her the truth and she won't listen, that's her problem for not listening.
K: They wouldn't go see Jimmy if they didn't know that he was supposedly implicated in something. But not particularly that, you know?
P: Yeah.
K: But maybe he knew through Chuck. But I don't think Chuckie would really be one to talk about that kind of stuff anyway.
P: No, and it's a matter of everybody's survival when it comes down to those kind of orders.
K: Oh yeah! That's right! But that's exactly what it is. But it's crazy anyway.
P: Yeah, I just tried to understand it all and I couldn't, so I just quit trying to figure it out.
K: Very difficult to do.
P: 'Cause I asked Jimmy, I go, "Well, what if they ask you to do somebody that you really can't do because they're just too much of a …a loyal trusted friend of yours and they expect you to do it?" and he goes, "Well, you gotta do it."
K: That's right.
P: And I go, I go, "Well, you're…"he told me this story about him and Mike and Mark and all this stuff and I'm just like, "(Gasp!) Oh My God!!"
K: (Laugh)
P: So, yeah…I know that story.
K: Yeah.
P: And you know, I know how close Mike and Jimmy are because of that story.
K: Well there was a lot of stuff like that. You know, like Jimmy was hurting a lot of times too for not being…by the police and things like that, and he was resisting them because of something he didn't want to tell them. You know?
P: Yeah.
K: And he didn't do it but probably knew who did it.
P: If people are still alive, you know, he's not going to rat on people.
K: He will not talk. That's one thing about Jimmy. He says, "Death before dishonor."
P: Well, see, he's the last of a dying breed. He says, "I'm a dinosaur."
K: I hate it when he does that, and I tell him so too. I says, "What do you mean? 'Death before dishonor'- go ahead and beep." Everybody's beeping today.
P: Yeah.
K: Look at all them who turned snitch.
P: Well, what about that guy from what's his name? John Gotti the Sammy…
K: "The Bull."
P: Sammy "The Bull" Grav…Gravano or whatever…
K: Yeah, sure, and…he did it.

P: I know, but...that's no...no respect. Right?

K: I told Jimmy, I says, "You know Jimmy...as long as you're there for as long as they want to hold you...why don't you just go ahead and tell them what they want to know? But tell them you want some time off. Everybody's doing it! But he says, "No, I can't do that but 'Death before dishonor'". I say, "Well that's crazy talk. You think those people appreciate what you're doin'!?" Nobody...

P: Tell them to read the book and they'll find out everything! Ha-ha!

K: That's right.

P: Have you heard of this guy Rodney Stich?

K: Who?

P: Rodney Stich. He wrote a book called *Defrauding America*.

K: No.

P: He's a former FAA Investigator, and ah pilots, former intelligence service people, anyway, he wrote this book called *Defrauding America* and he's got all the stuff documented. Oh my God, it's like, "He's alive!"

K: Oh yeah?

P: I'm surprised he's alive. I call every once in awhile to make sure he's still there!

K: That's what Jimmy says. You know he says if they let him out he don't think they'll let him live. If he got out of jail, Jimmy's been CIA, now I don't believe that, but he does.

P: Well, he knows how underhanded and wicked they are.

K: Yeah, but that doesn't...

P: They're straight from satan. So, but...you know what? I'm not...

K: Jimmy says, "I'll never get out."

P: You can't say that.

K: "...if I get out tomorrow I'll be dead the next day."

P: See, I can't receive that. And see that this whole thing is that I can't accept that because of our whole inheritance, the whole thing about the blood of Jesus, and I'm sorry, but you can appreciate me going off about, you know, sermonizing about something...

K: Oh sure.

P: But the blood of Jesus is not only for our salvation from our sins, but it is for our deliverance, it's for our healing, it's for our prosperity, it's for our...you know, lack and being imprisoned – it's for everything!

K: That's right.

P: And so the blood of Jesus is enough. Are we going to say that the scripture that says, "Nothing is impossible for God" doesn't apply to Jimmy?

K: Sure it is.

P: So it does! So that's why I'm saying there's so much faith inside of me for this. I'm not trying to work up some kind of faith frenzy, and believe-believe-believe that he's going to get out. I just know in my heart that I know what God's word says, I know Jesus...I know what Jimmy has signed up for with Jesus and he's entitled to it. And plus he's served his time. There's no...he's changed. A lot of guys never change before they get out.

K: Sure he has.

P: So let's make a deal.

K: Let's make a deal – that's what I said.

P: (Laugh) Let's make a deal.

K: And I told him, "Well Jimmy if you can't do that, then go crazy so they'll put you in a mental institution."

P: No.

K: "At least you'll have it easier."

P: No.

K: "…than where you're at." And then he's, "No, no, no." but they think he is crazy anyway.
P: Yeah, we know he's not.
K: We know he's not – but let 'em think he is! If he can get an easier place to go to if he's gotta serve all this time.
P: (Heavy sigh) Well, I'm not gonna…that's plan "Z" somewhere down the list. I want plan "A" and that's get out and not get killed.
K: And that's right.
P: I mean…it's easy to get out, but not getting killed – that's a whole other story. That's why you've gotta make a deal.
K: …city hall
P: That's why you gotta make the deal.
K: Well…(can't tell what he said)
P: (Laugh)
K: You know – you make the deal!
P: I'll go make the deal!
K: (Laugh)
P: Just give me the plane ticket, help me pay the rent, and I'll go make the deal!
K: That's right. It's the only thing you can do. The only thing you can do.
P: Well, I'm…I don't take no for an answer when I know something is right. So…
K: Well that's good.
P: He's got me on his team and I'm a good person to have on your team! (Laugh)
K: Oh yeah, well that's great.
P: Well, I don't want to talk your ear off and I'll call again soon.
K: Oh yeah, it's costing you a lot of money.
P: Nah, its Sunday – that's why I waited till Sunday 'cause…
K: Yeah.
P: It's easier to call.
K: You take care of yourself and you behave with Jimmy and I'm glad to hear, to meet ya on the phone even. And when you get up here we'll meet ya sometime.
P: Yeah, you will and I'll talk to you before that.
K: Ok sweetheart.
P: And we'll be in touch.
K: Good enough.
P: And when Jimmy calls tell him that we've talked.
K: I sure will.
P: And that we had a good talk.
K: He asked me last night or the night before that, he thought you had called and I said, "No, not yet." He says, "Well she will be. I gave her your number." I said, "Ok Jim- whatever you say, so ok."
P: Aww...see? Which is true.
K: Which is true.
P: It's all true.
K: So I'll let you go so both our ears…
P: Yeah. We've got the cauliflower ear right now! (Laugh)
K: (Laugh)
P: And tell your wife I appreciate loaning her husband out for a few minutes.
K: Ok, she's good. She likes Jimmy too.
P: Oh yeah, Jimmy told me a story about when she first didn't like Jimmy. (Laugh)
K: No – it wasn't that. It was…
P: She was scared.

K: He was spooky.
P: Yeah, she was scared.
K: He can be spooky! (Laugh) He used to come sit by the motel and watch everybody that comes in and makes sure nobody got fresh with her – nasty – 'cause that's a rough place anyway.
P: Yeah.
K: And that (laugh) scared her. But…
P: Well, that was…he was showing her respect.
K: It was good – but they don't know that.
P: Yeah but she was getting respect shown to her.
K: Oh yeah.
P: We like respect. Respect works! (Laugh)
K: He was making the customers un…uneasy (laugh) 'cause he's got a look on him, when he looks at ya…
P: In a certain way…
K: You better be careful…
P: Oh no…
K: (Laughter)
P: I hope I never see that look. (Laugh)
K: Yeah, you don't want to see that look.
P: Unless it's for somebody that's tryin' to do us some harm.
K: (Laugh) Well that's what he was doin'. Sure – make sure.
P: Yeah.
K: But he could give you that look and boy he could give you the look.
P: (Laugh) He says sometimes that guys at the prison, they talk about him and say, "Yeah, he's somebody you want to avoid." And yeah, just when he gets that look on him, it's the look of death.
K: Oh yeah.
P: I guess his eyes go black or something and they just…
K: They do.
P: You know, not the white part of his eye but the whole eye turns black…
K: It's a bad system in prison, believe me. The only way you can make it there…
P: Is to show that tough side of yourself.
K: That's right.
P: Otherwise you're just…
K: Abused.
P: Somebody's dog meat.
K: And everything else.
P: Whew!
K: It's terrible you know. It's an awful place to be.
P: Yeah, well it wasn't that bad for the part I saw just because I know when I go in there I'm coming out. But I can only imagine…
K: Yeah, they don't come out.
P: They got that wall and the other guys that are full of satan.
K: Bars when that door slams – it's for good. I'm glad he's in single cell.
P: Yeah, me too.
K: That's good.
P: Yeah, and he's got that job so …Mike was saying that they just transferred 75 people to Pontiac and some other place.
K: They could put him in an easier place.

P: Can't the warden say something though? Like "we need Jimmy here?"
K: They keep changing wardens there.
P: I know. I noticed that.
K: I asked him about this warden. He says he get along with him.
P: What? Warden Walls.
K: Yeah. He works with him in the printing shop.
P: Uh huh.
K: But are they gonna give Jimmy anything good? And that's all done by the CIA and the FBI.
P: It is?
K: Sure it is. They won't let him have it any easier. Fact is, I'm surprised he's got the position he does which…
P: Well, it's God's favor. It's because he's got a buddy praying for him. (Laugh)
K: Well that's good! Now that helps.
P: He always says he watches "Touched by an Angel" and he thinks I'm his angel.
K: He-he-he.
P: (Laugh) Well that's good. That's God.
K: You know, it gives him some reason to believe.
P: Well, we both…I hate to sound depressing or anything but, I mean, I was just kind of tired of all the lies and all this lying going on in the government and all this stuff and all the plans they have for everything, and I really didn't have this big "zest" for doing anything or going on because I was kind of tired of it and both Jimmy and I have like…found in each other…
K: Right.
P: Like this totally awesome, wonderful thing about our love.
K: Right.
P: And we want to go on.
K: Well sure you do.
P: So…
K: And that's great! It is great.
P: And I think it is wonderful.
K: I do too.
P: I was…because we were both at that point where we just…didn't care. That's not healthy…
K: That's right. Well, we want him to get out.
P: …but I'm just being honest with you about it because it was…
K: Not easy…because he's in there and you're outside. You're in – he's out. Your out –and he's in. And that's not good you know.
P: I know. But I can work around that but it was just refreshing to find a guy that was sincere and honest and loving as Jimmy is to me. And I was like WOW!
K: Oh yeah, it can be.
P: Am I supposed to shut the door on this or am I supposed to open up my heart?
K: Well, it's good that you did.
P: I did.
K: And it will be rewarded.
P: And I'll make sure I see you guys when I come over there.
K: Yeah! Good!
P: Ok?
K: Ok sweetie.
P: All righty.
K: Oky doky.

P: Well, give your wife a hug for me.
K: I sure will.
P: And you guys have a great evening and I'll talk to ya real soon.
K: Ok hon.
P: Ok.
K: Bye bye.
P: Bye bye.

END OF INTERVIEW

Monday July 19, 1999 James Files to PJ

About the book *Mafia Princess*, you asked if I knew **Antoinette Giancana** and if I knew any of the people that she wrote about. The answer is yes!!!
Antoinette has been approved and placed on my visiting list and she has been here to see me, under the name Giancana. She married an ol' time Outfit lawyer by the name of McDonald, which I added to my list and they both came to visit me. So yes, I know her very well, sorry to say.

Tony Accardo: Yes I knew him and I stood guard over his new home when it was being built in 1963 in River Forrest.

Joseph Aiuppa: Yes I knew him for many years. I used to go and play poker with him and his crew when he had the parking lot on Roosevelt Road. Then we'd always go out for breakfast after the game. I used to make him crazy at times. He thought I was a real nut.

Felix Alderiso: Yes I knew him and seen him on occasion, but we never did anything together. Maybe had coffee once or twice when he was meeting Jackie C.

Gus Alex: Yes I knew him and dropped money off to him from the people for him to take care of things and I did a few errands for him.

Sam Battaglia: Yes I knew him and saw him often at the club, The Armory. He used to call me the "Barefoot Hillbilly" and all kinds of crazy names. He enjoyed kidding me.

Dominic Blasi: Yes I knew him and I even helped him wash Sam's car a few times and went shopping several times with him for Sam.

I also knew the **Bonanno Family** and several of their workers and attended a few of their get togethers.

Fiore Buccieri: Yes I knew him, but only on a casual basis. To say hello and maybe have a coffee at times. He had his own crew.

John Caifano, aka Marshall Caifano: I knew Marshal very, very, well!!! We did five years together at Oxford Federal Prison in Wisconsin. I knew Marshal many years before that. But while I was at Oxford, not only was Marshall and me very good friends, I was also his bodyguard and his pinochle partner and his gin rummy partner. Marshall worked in the kitchen, as everyone has to have a job in federal prison. So we hooked him up an easy one. He had to fill up the salt and peppershakers, the sugar and make sure the napkin holders were full before the meal. When they took me out in 1983 for a battery and mayhem that happened in the prison and also for a bombing in Chicago that I was indicted for, Marshall hugged my neck and told me not to worry, that things would be all right. Other people there that didn't really know tried to start a rumor that I'd made a deal with the Feds. Marshall went to them and told them to their face not to say a word against me, as I was a man's man and that I would never speak against anyone. That I was one of the few who truly believed in "OMERTA" and that silence was golden, and I had lived my whole life that way since I was a kid. And, that no man had better speak badly of me or they would have to answer for what they said. I loved Marshall like an older brother or a father. He was really a great guy. But at times he would drive me nuts, like in a card game. He'd give me a big meld bid, I'd jump off the deep end, then he'd sit there and scratch his head and say, "Gee Jimmy, I think I messed up and sent you meld I don't have." Our friends Jimmy I. and Harry A. would be sitting there with a big smile on their face. They kid me later and say, "Boy, has Marshall got your number." See, he'd always have the meld, but would tease me by holding it and making me wait before he'd lay it down. In the mean time, I'd turn red in the face and my neck muscles would pop out and I'd not say a word. All of them would be laughing at me because everyone of them knew I loved that old man and that I would never yell at an elder and show disrespect. But there is nothing that I wouldn't do for Marshall. A black threatened him one time and I beat that guy senseless. It took a dozen cops to drag me off that guy. I was gonna kill him and I made it plain to everyone that if the old man gets hurt, they have to deal with me and that no prison guard could save them.

Richard Cain: Yes I knew him and if you've read the book *Double Cross*, in the last part there's the death of Richard Cain and how he died. After my video, and when people read that book, they'd send me a copy and say they knew that I was one of the two men that killed Cain. I didn't even answer their letters. I didn't want to make a comment. If you read that part, then you'll understand why.

John "Jackie" Cerone: Yes I knew him and that's in the first part of my video about him.

William Daddano, **Paul DeLucia**: Yes I knew them.

Sam DeStefano: I knew him very well. He lived in Westchester, Illinois about five minutes from my house in Melrose Park. He had his own torture chamber set up in his basement. I know, as I was in his basement and I saw this for myself.

Joseph DiVarco: I knew him and saw him often when I was with Chuck Nicoletti.

Charles English: I knew him and there were usually several of the guys around at the same time by the Armory or at the Thunderbird Inn on River Road out by Rosemont, Illinois.

Murray Humphreys: You already know that I knew him.

John Roselli: From my video you know Johnny and me went back along ways.

Joseph Zerilli: Yes I knew him as I met him through Jimmy Hoffa and I did a few things for him in Detroit.
I've known many crime figures, some well and some only casual and for some I did favors. Many of the old timers are not mentioned in the books, as it was never proved they were connected.

I'm going to send out a second envelope with just printed material. It's an untold story and still classified to this day. But you will get my drift of what it is about and it's not about the "nuclear power plant" (in Antarctica).

****

Wim,
Here are more comments Jimmy made in his letters. I think some of it should get posted.
Pam

 # 703 13 FEB 2004 p. 2-3

"As for Wim, I gave him what he ask for, the interview. That is all that I agreed to. Out of all the questions that he ask, the only one that pertains to JFK is where did I call Chuck at? I will answer that one, as I have answered it many times before and even in the first interview, if it was not cut out that is. *(Jimmy has never seen the Confession of an Assassin video. He has only seen transcripts with notes from Bob)* I called him in Chicago. Even if I did answer all of these questions, he would just call back and ask you to ask me more and give you another list. The only thing that I have ever agreed to talk about was the JFK thing. Why don't I answer all questions ask of me and give out my life story? That is easy, one thing leads to another and the next thing that you know, I'm indicted for several contract murders in Chicago and other places as well. Gee, some of these people even want to know where everyone is buried.

Anyway, I want to come home to you, not get more time. The Feds cannot put me on trial for Kennedy, but they would love to burry me on some of these others. From day one, before I ever talked to anyone about Kennedy, even with Joe West, right here from prison we *(former Warden Tony Godinez and James Files)* called Texas and they assured me that they would never indict me for that crime. So I never had to worry about that one. But let's take the Penn State Matters. Now the Feds would score a real winner, if they could get me for that bombing. I don't know why they think it was me. I guess it's just their very small mind. If people don't believe me, too bad! Tell Wim to put it on video and let the people make up their own mind. If he doesn't want to do that, then throw it in the trash can.... just do a video and let it get on the market.......

As for the M.M. part, you already know who flew the plane. I don't really want to go there, as I never wanted to be hauled into court with the pilot, on trial and then have to do time for contempt of court and there is no way that I would ever testify against him. I still believe in Honor and all of that when it come to the heavy part of the family, "Omerta" as well.

Besides, there is no way we can ever convince everyone to believe us. Remember that Old Fable of the Man and Boy with the Donkey and how they tried to please everyone? Can't be done. Besides, why does Wim want to keep messing with the people on the forum? All of them have their own opinions and he is never going to change their mind. Anyway, I sure am getting tired of all this. I just this past week received another half-dozen letters from people I don't know asking me questions and I just filed all of them under T for TRASH!!! I've got to the point that when I get a letter from someone that I don't know, I just rip it in half and put it in the trash. I don't even want to know what they have to say. My Love, I'm going to sign off for now. Just know that I love you. OXOXOXO"

#815 JF to PR November 1, 2004 p. 1-2

For those people asking why am I still alive? This was the third attempt on my life after I was released from a federal prison, (Oxford) and I'm here now because the cops were trying to kill me. If Ostertag wasn't trying to kill me, then why was he upset because the government failed to tell him who and what he was up against???

Anyway, why hasn't someone here in prison killed me? I learned how to survive in prison while I was doing federal time. Also, should someone in here kill me, how would they get paid from the government? No one in here trusts the government. Besides, I made a name for myself in here and I get a lot of respect from inmates and officers. Besides, how many white guys got the heart to go down and shower with about 40 black guys in a big open shower? Me, I think nothing about it. I don't worry about anyone jumping me. Most people fear dying. Me, I have no fear, for as you know My Sweet Love, fear is the word of satan, I refuse to recognize satan. I have FAITH, the Word of God and therefore, there can be no fear in me about anything at all. How many of those who judge me, can say with an honest heart, they have no fear of dying? I bet none of them! And I bet they are all non-believers and when Jesus comes to take us home, oh how they'll all cry then and swear that they are true believers! My Sweet Love, you must understand, to me it matters not what people say, or think of me. I only have to worry about what God will say when I stand before Him for my judgment!!!

p. 4

As for Nancy Eldreth, she wrote me to tell me about finding her lost family, bla-bla-bla and that she had been to the archives and a lot of records are missing and the people came out to talk to her and said yes, they were there, but they have no idea what happened to them and she also wanted to help me fix Bob Vernon and Wim. I told her the JFK thing was now history with me and don't even ask me about anything and that I did not want to fix Wim or Bob that I had nothing against them. That I pray for both of them every night. That I have nothing to get even for. If you would like, I will make a copy of her letter and send it to you. But I will not be answering any more letters from her. I made it clear where I stand on that subject.

As far as the truth, we can give that to the people, but they will only believe what they want. All we can do is put the facts out there for them in truth and let them decide for themselves.

#817 JF to PR November 5, 2004 p. 2-3

Right now, I'm trying to find out if I have a legal recourse, for Vernon stealing my property and then copyrighting it as his own, then selling it to Wim. We can now prove that Vernon STOLE MY PROPERTY out of my storage shed. We have copies of the things that he said he took. From my original manuscript, To Kill A Country, to other documents that he posted and said they came out of my storage shed, like the one they say, "The Documents that the CIA do not want you to see." Right now I would say I have enough evidence to prove that Vernon took my property and did a copyright on it in his name, then sold it to Wim. Ask the lawyers that wrote up the contract for you for the interview and see what their opinion is on that subject. I've ask here on my end and I was told that Vernon was in violation of the copyright law. I'm waiting to find out more about it. I also want and value your opinion on this subject. What I really want to know how much would this affect Wim. I cannot say that Wim knew he was receiving stolen property, as Vernon kept denying that he had my property. Everyone thought I was lying about Bob Vernon. Just like with Zack, I never saw Zack at the scene when they were torturing me. I never did put Zack at the scene. He put himself there on Dec. 1, 1998, right here at "The Ville," when he made that statement. At that point, I only thought that it was the FBI that had me. And that was only because they messed up and failed to kill me. I know how the Family and the CIA end a torture session. They make sure the subject is deceased. Especially when H. Hunt ran it and loved to take part in them, but only as the one administering the pain. Enough of that My Love.

#818 JF to PR November 8, 2004 p. 3

Thank you for sending me the information on Bobby Kennedy. As far as what happened with Bobby that day, I'm not sure and I never did ask anyone about it. I'm the least curious person that you will ever meet. The less I know, the smarter I am. So there's not much that I can shed on that day. (RFK's assassination June 4, 1968) But if you have a list of the most notorious, that were there that day, send it to me, or match it up with all the players, from the Bay of Pigs thru Watergate. I'm sure you'll find a match, maybe even more than that. Take the names of the people that you have from "Group Forty" and you may find it easier that way. Bob Vernon has a list of names for every man in that Group. He got it out of my storage shed and there was very little about Group Forty until Bob started pulling a lot of that stuff out, from the Alpha 66, to the White Hand and my notes were made and dated, before anyone ever wrote a book about them. My notes were taken back in the '60's & '70's and there were dates on my papers and the paper from back then is much different than the paper that is used today.

Phone call January 16, 2004

P: I understand. I understand. So has it been pretty quiet in there? Everybody leaving you alone and not giving you a hard time? (A couple of guards at Stateville that don't like James Files retaliated for him doing the interview on November 19, 2003. They trashed all of his, and his cell mate Jessie Sumners' personal property and set them up on bogus charges and sent them to seg December 18, 2003. After some phone calls and extreme outside intervention, the situation was cleared up and they were released from seg on December 31, 2003. James Files called me that day and told me what really had happened.)

J: I'm okay, they got B-House on lockdown.

Later...

J: They just got a few people here that ah...you got to realize, they don't like me and they like Kennedy, and you know, they think Kennedy was the greatest thing that ever...that ever lived or breathed air. And I guess one time they said something about me, and I told them I know what I know what I know. I don't pull no punches.

P: Yeah.

J: I tell the man, I speak what I believe.

P: Like anybody, he had his good points and his bad points. The fact that he wanted to take us off the Federal Reserve Notes was, you know...REAL GOOD point in my book. But the way he treated women, and the way he had Marilyn killed, I mean, that's PRETTY BAD.

J: Yep.

P: So, I mean, yeah, you can be real good, and you can be real bad, especially if you're a politician. Oh, another thing, have I ever heard from you details that Charles Nicoletti ever gave you, about the assassination of Marilyn Monroe?

J: (Quickly) No.

P: He never said she got the enema with barbiturates, or he never said nothin'?

J: Did he say something to me?

P: Yeah, did he ever tell you, tell you how it happened?

J: Yeah we talked about that a little bit uh...but uh...like I say, I never brought it up because this really didn't have anything to do with the assassination of John F. Kennedy. We had already talked about that before. And we know who flew the plane out there.

P: Right.

J: You know that as well as I do.

P: Right. Right, but...uh...it was a curiosity point as far as if Charles Nicoletti divulged the information on how she actually died.(Silence) And if it is indeed...still everybody is holding to the story that she was pregnant at the time, rather than that she had just recently had an abortion?

J: She had not had an abortion. She wouldn't have an abortion. She wouldn't get one. That's why Sam said, "Go west young man, go west."

P: (Silence, heavy sigh) ...sick of this.

J: But like I say, let's get off that part, that's irrelevant there. You and me, we never got into that, before, you know, I told you a little about it, that was the end of it. I told you why she had to die..that was it. But I won't get into a lot of details on it...

P: Well it kind of relates in some way because Kennedy had her killed because it was his kid.

J: Yeah.

P: So, I mean, that kind of is important...it had something do with John F. Kennedy. Right?

J: Yes it does.

P: Okay, well, so that's the only reason that I'm even...

J: Let me put it this way,

P: talkin' about it.

J: They asked us - we did him a favor. He called and asked us for a favor. And at that time, they was still....uh...in good standings.

P: I know.

J: And Sam thought he was a great guy. Later on, Sam didn't think he was a great guy, and Sam said some also very nasty things about him, which I won't repeat.

P: About John or about Bobby?

J: About John, (laugh) about both of 'em! The whole Kennedy family. (laugh) He decided he didn't like them after all.

PJ Ray: Honey, I don't want to talk gangster talk our whole conversation.

J: I just want to take a few minutes and pray...(he does)

P: And also take good care of Jimmy in Jesus' name amen.

J: Like I said, the logistics of all of it.Because you know, you read different things in different books about it and that's why I don't get into them books...

P: I know, a lot of it is why I never even wanted to have TO KILL A COUNTRY focused on JFK so much. You didn't even want it to be in the book and it was about Chile, right?

J: Yes.

P: It was going to be a book about Chile...

J: Yes.

P: and Southeast Asia.

J: I know people find this hard to believe but I can't understand it...I find nothing fascinating about the assassination of John F. Kennedy and look at it this way...

P: Honey, the thing is, that it's when the clocks of time STOPPED for our country. It's when we had our coup d'etat, and it really screwed up our country. And I'm not sayin' I'm mad at you, personally, I'm just sayin' it really screwed things up, because he was on a course to not be so WAR oriented and to get our money supply back the way it should be...and that really screwed up our country.

J: Mmmhum.

P: And you were just following orders and being a good soldier boy and did what you thought was right, but, I mean, it really wasn't a good thing for our country and that's why so many people are upset about it. And it's a wound in our national psyche that has yet to be healed, that hopefully this book will bring some healing.

J: Right. Like I say, you know, I really can't say because I really don't know about that coming about, like I say, far as I'm concerned, I just thought all of them should have been done. Saved everybody a lot of trouble. At that time, all the things about the Kennedy's...I don't know...I just didn't understand what it means back then myself...I just thought,

"Well, they're bad" so...who knows...who cares? But even today, you know, it's just one of those things Honey, I just don't...it don't hold my interest. I'm sorry.

I care more about bumping off snitches, you know singing like canaries? And ah...I probably found it more interesting doing them than I did Kennedy.

P: Well, you just have to understand that most people in this country don't know about any of those things happening, and, having John F. Kennedy, our President killed, and then his brother killed not too many years after, uh...people can still remember that if they can remember anything, they still remember that.

J: I don't know anything about that one but I do know one thing. If you take all the documents and letters, you go back to the Bay of Pigs you're gonna find all the people, the players, the same all the way through the game, all the way to modern day. Only thing is a few of them died along the way.

P: Right.

J: But for each one of those things that happened, with Kennedy, Bay of Pigs, Kennedy, ah...King, the Watergate, and all that stuff...Arkansas...all the different things, all the players, all the names keep popping up.

P: Yep. Well, one guy that isn't going to pop up that's not alive is Ted Shackley and I know he passed on. I mean, God rest his soul, but I'm glad he's not around to be fussy.

J: You know what his nickname was don't 'cha? (Silence) They called him "The Butcher."

P: The Butcher?

J: Yeah, it was on the Phoenix Program.

P: (Sarcastically) Pacification? Is that what they called it? Did they call it pacification?

J: Yes, pacification.

P: Doesn't that sound like a nice name...

Operator cuts in: your time will expire in 30 seconds

J: We'll talk about that another time. Sweetheart I love you I miss you and pray all things will work out.

#816 JF to PR November 3, 2004

I asked James Files to make a statement for the introduction to the November 2003 interview. This is what he had to say:

Hello to the American people and also the people throughout the world. I hope that everyone gets to see the interview I completed last year. This is the true story of what happened November 22, 1963 in Dallas, Texas - the assassination of President John F. Kennedy.

Just prior to the interview, I walked out of the room and refused to do it. Why? Because it was my understanding for the past several months leading up to November 2003 that Ms. Pamela Ray would be part of the interview since she is the author of the book we did together, *To Kill a Country: The Murder of JFK and the Coup d'etat in America – Revelations from the confessed assassin.*

When I walked into the room, I was informed that Ms. Ray would not be a part of this interview and she wasn't let into the prison. At that moment I turned and walked out saying over my shoulder, "then there will be no interview." Jim Marrs, journalist and author of *Crossfire* was to ask me the questions with Ms. Ray present. Mrs. French, the warden's spokesperson, was there and she ran after me down the hall to explain why Ms. Ray could not be there. She said there are rules about media and family or close associates being present during filming in the prison. Ms. Ray and I were not told this ahead of time.

Ms. Ray wrote a letter back at the motel telling me what happened at the prison. Jim Marrs was searching through his pockets for the letter Ms. Ray had given him. In the letter it stated that she wanted me to go ahead with the interview because it would help us get the book out sooner than later. Knowing that it would help her finish the book project, I agreed to do the interview.

The November 2003 interview deals with the assassination of John F. Kennedy and my role in it. What you hear will be the truth. I'm not trying to convince you, just putting the facts out there for everyone to see. You, the people, have to make up your own mind and I wouldn't want it any other way. Just please look at all the facts, take the time to do some of your research afterwards and don't let the self appointed "experts" mislead you.

For me, my part started about six months before November 1963 when Charles Nicoletti met me at the Harlo Grill in Melrose Park, Illinois, a suburb of Chicago. He asked me to take a ride with him and he informed me he had been given a murder contract on John Kennedy. Mr. Nicoletti wanted me to handle a few minor details like driving and moving weapons around. My answer was yes and there was no hesitation to do my assignment. From Chicago to Dallas and the assassination is what this interview is about. Due to a change in plans at the last minute with Charles Nicoletti and Johnny Roselli, I was the second shooter from behind the fence on the knoll in Dealey Plaza.

Many people question my age; such as I was too young to shoot anyone. I was 21 years old and I had tasted battle in South East Asia, specifically Laos. I already had several confirmed kills. For those of you who think a 21 year old is too young to shoot someone, then I suggest you go visit the Vietnam Memorial Wall and read the names and dates. The majority of the men listed on the wall were less than 21 years of age. There are not many older soldiers leading the young into battle. They are too smart for that. They stay behind and send them out on patrols. When and if the patrol returns, then they take the WIA and KIA names and numbers and file them.

What you are about to hear in this interview is the truth as it happened. Tony Accardo was the one who gave the murder contract to Sam Giancana, who handed it out to Charles Nicoletti, who in turn called in Johnny Roselli. Roselli was one of Sam Giancana's top men. Charles Nicoletti was a known mafia hit man. I was his driver, gopher, chasing to do whatever he asked me to do. Believe me, I was no kid, I was a grown man and I gained my manhood in less than a day on the battlefields in Laos during Operation White Star in 1959 and 1960. Once you have tasted battle, taken another's life, you are no longer a child – your life has been changed forever.

I hope that you listen closely to this interview, think things over carefully before you make up your mind, one way or another. Thank you for hearing me out.

James (Jimmy) Files

Joliet, Illinois

Note from the producers:
This interview is virtually unedited. Out of the total duration of 3 hours, we took out 15 minutes. Mainly irrelevant conversing between the interviewers, changes of tape, loss of sound, and stuff like that. Our goal is to give you the original interview exactly as it happened, without breaking the "flow" of it. It was not the original intent to leave the questions of the interviewers in. The interview was done to use snippets of it for a more comprehensive program. The interviewers had no separate microphones. At times the questions can hardly be heard or they are repeated and this may not always leave a professional impression. We apologize for that in advance. However we think your appreciation for the completeness of this presentation will make up for it.